Irishpulp

IRISHPULP

The Holy Ground
Copyright © Patrick Kearney 2002

Second edition 2002

Patrick Kearney asserts the moral right to be
identified as the author of this work

All Rights Reserved

No part of this book may be reproduced in any form
by photocopying, electronic on mechanical means,
including information storage or retrieval systems
without permission in writing from both the copyright owner
and the publisher of this book.

ISBN 0-9538802-1-4

Edited by Spud Red
Co-edited by Patrick Kearney

Book cover design by Enlightenment

First Published 2000 by
Irishpulp
'The Book Capital'
PO Box 23
Hay-on-Wye
HR3 5YF

www.irishpulp.com   email: irishpulp@irishpulp.com

for peace, justice and equality

Book One

Prologue

On his knees since dawn, his back breaking from weeding a sloping field of potato drills, the angry young man made up his mind that July day, 1945, to do what he had long contemplated. Anthony Brennan, tall, lean and broad shouldered in his eighteenth year, his wavy black hair swept back from a handsome face, stood stiffly and wiped beads of sweat from his brow with the back of a heavily worked hand. Daring to steal a minute's rest from his labour, he stretched himself and looked out to sea with hungry blue eyes. He was relieved to see a deep red sunset on its distant horizon, a beautiful, wondrous scene, but which was no longer reason enough to have him stay.

The second eldest of four boys and two girls, Anthony had been hard driven to his decision by the poverty and hardship all about him, the brutality meted out casually by bullish priests and sadistic teachers, their fiery dogma and harsh, punitive regimes all in the cause of saving souls. But what had Anthony finally deciding to steal away, was the escalating violence between he and his elder brother Christy. They fought daily over nothing in particular, for there was nothing much to fight about in the remote parish of Toome, straggling Ireland's northwestern peninsula. This reality to Anthony's thinking, unveiled the true desperateness of his circumstance. The brothers' feuding had thankfully gone largely unchecked by their moody, swaggering father, whom they all feared. He ruled with a rod of iron. Seeing him reach for that rusting spoke from the wheel of an old potato scutcher had them scurrying for cover. And mother? She had enough on her hands keeping them all fed and clothed on a pittance while barely coping with father's unpredictable mood swings and insatiable appetite, and not only for the drink. A creaking bed on the other side of the paper-thin partitioned wall separating consenting adults from their offspring was the telltale that the twenty-odd years father had over mother, was no excuse to let up in his old age.

'You finished thon field sonny?' Anthony's father barked from the brow of the hill where he stood menacingly with fired-up eyes glaring and white-knuckle fists clenched by his side. A wave of fear shuddered through Anthony on being caught unawares. He knew better than to lie and in an instant was down on his knees among the healthy green potato tops; his sore hands busy once more. After a little while he chanced to look over his shoulder and sighed with relief to see father gone, back into town for more liquor no doubt. With the evening light fading fast, Anthony took a little comfort knowing that it would not be long until he could throw himself down to sleep a few but precious hours. But he'd soon be rising again, though not to attend to his early morning chores but rather to put into action the plan in his head, known by no other living soul.

He didn't sleep much that sticky summer's night. Lying partly clothed on the outside edge of the big straw bed and with his back turned to his brothers sleeping head to toe, his younger sisters likewise in the smaller bed in the faraway corner, Anthony's mind was a riot of recriminating thoughts. In the pale moonlight seeping through the little window into the musty smelling lower bedroom, his eyes were fixed upon the picture of the Virgin Mary adorning the wall at the foot of the bed, keeping vigil with eyes forever watchful. Looking back in anger and recalling hard times, he begged the question without speaking. What good has all the penny candles done for this family? As never before Anthony longed for the dawn and to escape his dire surroundings. Freedom beckoned and he could not resist it another day. He had decided that it would not be America or Australia to where he would venture or indeed London. He'd heard the streets there were not paved with gold, and that notices proclaiming: No Blacks! No Dogs! No Irish Wanted! were a predominant feature in landlords' windows and some places of work. It was reported that the English harboured a grudge over Ireland's neutrality during the war. The returned exile speaking of hard times across the water on market day weeks earlier, had revealed another ugly truth in saying, 'Having the key to a room in London is like having the key to the gates of Heaven.' Though being a light-hearted remark, it had carried a serious message, which remained fresh in Anthony's mind. He had even considered if there was any sense in leaving such hard times behind, only to end up with more of the same among strangers.

With the first shimmering light, Anthony made his move. He gently eased himself off the bed so not to wake the others, an untidy heap of entangled arms and legs, with heads at odd angles. Their obnoxious though familiar body odours rose in his nostrils as he donned a clean shirt. Once dressed, he paused for a last look at his brothers and sisters, all sleeping peacefully. He silently bade them farewell and good luck - even Christy. Anthony bore no grudges now. With his well-worn boots tucked under an arm and grandfather's weighty tool bag - retrieved quietly from under the bed – slipped onto a shoulder, he tiptoed out of the tumbledown thatched cottage, so still and silent. Stepping nervously over old Jack, the working Collie dog whimpering in his sleep on the doorstep, Anthony fastened his boots with eyes glued fearfully to the half door, then grabbed hold of his father's sturdy black bicycle propped against the byre wall. Without daring to stop or look over his shoulder, he pedalled for dear life the nine miles out from the sleeping parish and on toward the market town. Reaching Buncrana in a cold sweat despite the early heat, he roused the local pawnbroker and pawned his father's bicycle. With enough money raised, he caught the first bus across the border to Derry and the cattle-boat to Scotland. He only breathed easily when the boat was several miles out on Lough Foyle. The dread of father's hand upon his shoulder had left his nerves shattered. Glad and relieved though he was to be rid of the cursed place, he felt a lump rise in his throat on seeing the green hills of Donegal fade out of sight. The thought of mother, poor soul, realising he was gone and fraught with worry, lay heavily on his mind, together with the fact that he was leaving his homeland, with all its hardships. At that moment it was indeed a terrible beauty that Anthony was fleeing. He could not help but wonder when or if he might ever see Ireland again.

Chapter One

In keeping to his word written in the brief note he'd left for his mother, Anthony secured work in Glasgow and sent small but regular amounts of money to her, part of which would help her indulge in her only vice, to secretly smoke a few Woodbines while the 'oul boy' was busy elsewhere. In private moments of reflection amid his tenement surroundings, Anthony laughed quietly on recalling the scene of mother huddled over the turf fire and mischievously blowing the cigarette smoke up the wide chimney while he kept lookout at the half door for father. He would wager that father had never even suspected, let alone discovered his wife's indulgence in a habit he considered fit only for men. Not forgetting his father, Anthony had, on receipt of his first wage, forwarded home enough money and the ticket to salvage the black bicycle from the pawnshop. He prayed that doing so would help settle grievances, but did not hold too high a hope on this. He knew his father to be a man with a long memory, who did not forgive easily.

Just as he had been vague to where he was headed for in his departing note, Anthony did not say exactly where in Glasgow he was, only that he was well and busy with work. He hoped to give the impression that he was travelling Scotland, as his fear of father seeking him out, even after two years, was real enough. Anthony at last held a job in John Brown's shipyard, on Clydebank, as a carpenter's mate. The skills of the trade had been self-taught at home where, since the age of twelve Anthony had sawn, planed, carved and jointed whatever pieces of workable timber he had stumbled across. It had been mostly driftwood retrieved from the beach and once finishing his many chores, had experimented on this with his late grandfather's tools. He too had been a carpenter by trade.

Presenting himself as a chippy's mate, Anthony had bluffed his way onto various building sites during that first year. Despite the numerous blunders made, he had somehow duped the eye of suspicion and doubt. The skills and self-confidence had come on strong since and learning by trial and error had put him in good stead. Work was steady though physically demanding, the wage modest but adequate, and the rent on a room in a large tenement in the Gorbals, reasonably affordable. Comradeship was plentiful. There was the local Scots, the Welsh, and of course, the Irish. And it had been Con McStravick that he'd been and remained closest to. The County Fermanagh man was twenty-two years his senior, a good, clean-living, churchgoing bachelor with the face of a saint and a heart to match. The man from the six counties was soon to dramatically change his destiny.

A letter sent by Con's father back home in Irvinestown, County Fermanagh, in the first week of August 1947, brought about the dramatic change of events. A prominent businessman and landowner, Con's father had been approached by the recent new arrival to the area, an aristocratic former British Army colonel and Great War veteran going by the somewhat inconsonant name of Cartwell. He sought skilled hands to help in the restoration of the local landmark, the old Irish monastery, Edenderry Abbey, which the Englishman had acquired through an overseas bid. The local auctioneer had informed the colonel that McStravick senior was the best man to organise a gang of skilled workers in those parts - few as they were at the time.

With two to three years steady work available for those fortunate to be employed on the project, Con's father considered it a convenient opportunity for his son to come home to work, for a while at least.

Work on the new passenger liner at John Brown's was near ending. Glad to have the opportunity to lend his mastered skills to the restoration of the old monastery which had contributed so much to his happy childhood days, those blissful fact-finding walks around its ruins on long summer evenings with father, Con readily offered Anthony a partnership deal in the contract to restore the abbey. From the estimated earnings outlined in his father's letter, Con convinced Anthony that two years back in Ireland would enable them both to set-up as joint contractors, either there or on their return to Scotland, which both had taken a strong liking to. Never before befriended like such or presented with a gift opportunity to better himself Anthony readily accepted, though did not confess his unease at returning to any part of Ireland. The memories he held of the place still remained bleak and desperate.

A friend of the McStravicks was a friend to the vast majority of the people of Irvinestown. Only a handful of established and lay people held onto their deep-rooted fears and suspicions that no Catholic, least of all one from the 'republican county' of Donegal, just across the border, was to be trusted.

Still somewhat naive to the North's troubled past, Anthony at first took little notice of the indifference shown to him on occasion amidst the predominately Protestant farming community. However his gradual realisation of being apart, separate in many ways from those about him, manifested when confronted with the harsh legal reality of having to acquire a Northern Ireland State Resident and Work Permit. It was an unfriendly civil servant who stamped the official document with obvious reluctance before thrusting the essential piece of paper to him. Using his local influence to secure issue of the permit, Con's father smiled contentedly at the somewhat naive new citizen of Northern Ireland when exiting the Town Hall. 'Take no notice my lad. Little bigots like that exist everywhere.'

It was Con's mother, a devout Christian and former overseas missionary worker, who had influenced her husband and son's understanding of the grievances of minority communities. But there had been times when the middle road the family walked in practising their liberal Christian faith, had proved a difficult path to follow, not least among their own predominant Presbyterian churchgoing community. On occasion the willingness of the well-to-do McStravicks to employ local Catholic labourers on their large farming estate, left them targets for such bigots who could send a chill down one's spine with a mere murderous glare across a market square or indeed a chapel pew.

The eccentric mannerisms and begrudging utterances of the retired Englishman added to Anthony's awakening of being viewed by the outsider as an outsider himself. Old tales of English injustices prosecuted against the Irish by the likes of Cromwell and overheard as a child around a blazing turf fire, resurfaced consequently. But Anthony considered it to be in the interest of all to keep his recriminating thoughts to himself. The last thing he wanted to do was to stir trouble for the McStravick family.

Riding horseback in best Irish tweed and knee-length riding boots, and briskly swigging scotch from the solid silver flask chained to his hip holster, the old soldier would regularly inspect his prize. The old monks' holy house, its sacred stones long since razed by Scottish Protestants, was to be the Englishman's castle and the acre upon rolling acre of lush green land, his grand estate. The 'Colonel', which he insisted on being referred to at all times, had been in these parts before, albeit briefly back in 1914 to recruit men for the British Army. He had been billeted in Enniskillen, a former fortress market town. When not officially fulfilling his commission, he had spent long summer evenings fly-fishing the lakes of Fermanagh. Captivated by the beauty of the Ulster countryside, a far cry from the killing fields of Flanders to which he was sent soon afterwards, he had vowed to return one day and live out his later years in peaceful bliss. The colonel had been badly wounded at Ypres in 1918, in the closing days of the Great War, and had returned to convalesce in the North of England, where his prosperous father owned vast tracts of land, rich in coal and dotted with many pits, their villages stains on the landscape. Even the rugged green moors were in stark contrast to the green tapestry of Fermanagh.

The abbey's workforce, consisting of house staff and farm labourers, daughters and sons of struggling local farmers, and tradesmen from the nearby town busy in the restoration of the once sacred building, all laughed mockingly at the Englishman's strange antics when his back was turned. But there had been occasions when the other outsider among them had found it difficult to simply dismiss the Englishman as an old fool.

The truth of this dawned for Anthony one glorious sunny day, when taking a break from the hammer and chisel to look out from an abbey skylight and to listen to the silent tranquillity all about. He compared the lush sprawling fields beyond, colossal in size and enriched with such fertile black soil, with those cursed patches of rock-riddled ground back home. He heard Con's step beside him as he, also, stopped to gaze in wonderment at the verdant landscape.

'He,' Con said passionately, gesturing with his hammer to the colonel below, surrounded by ugly beasts of dogs in the enclosed courtyard, 'and my father's people, came here from England and Scotland as settlers. They remain but guests in this country. Irish monks used to work those fields with their own hands ... bare hands, mark you, and made this holy ground what it is today before being banished to more desperate corners. Those ruined walls over yonder, once their house of prayer, and this very place, where they ate and slept, were torched by my ancestral folk. I feel I am somehow righting an ancient wrong by my work here. As for the Englishman's shilling? Well, it's only a means to an end. Our work will soon be done and our lives will only be beginning.' Con winked encouragingly at Anthony as he finished.

The parade-ground screams, Sandhurst trained, rose from the courtyard and, echoing all about Con and Anthony, destroyed their quiet contemplation.

'You up there!' They both looked out and down. 'Yes, you two! Lunch was an hour ago! Get a move on, damn your eyes! Those windows had best be well sealed, I tell you! This Irish weather isn't going to hold! We're damn lucky to have had it this good for so long!'

Sat pompously on a horse and pointing his whip with recrimination at them, the Englishman continued under his breath as if addressing the dogs, an excited pack milling about his horse. 'Damn bog-trotting Irish! So bloody lazy at times! They don't deserve their pleasures!' The colonel's provocations were borne away by the gentle breeze as he reined the thoroughbred hunter around half-circle to gallop off, dogs in hot pursuit.

'And that man is supposed to be educated.' Con sighed, shaking his head. 'The sooner we are finished here, the better.' Returning to work, Con vented his anger by driving home a six-inch nail with three heavy blows.

Anthony was not to forget those words spoken by his good friend that day. Prone to blinding headaches most of his adult life, Con had taken ill suddenly that very night at his parents' home and by the time a close neighbour had come to fetch Anthony from the small farmer's cottage less than half a mile away, let to him by the McStravick's, Con had died from a massive brain haemorrhage. Devastated by the shocking news, Anthony had wept unashamedly by Con's deathbed.

Irvinestown came to a standstill on the day of the burial. Hundreds turned out to mourn. Having literally locked himself away for the previous two days while the corpse had lain in a local Chapel of Rest, Anthony barely got through the day. He just could not come to terms with Con's death at all. He felt so alone, lost, almost. It was McStravick senior who pulled him through as Anthony soon realised that his grief in no way compared to that of Con's mother and father. Despite their advanced years and the mother so frail herself, they were determined to live through it.

'It's the way Cornelius would want it,' his father said, fighting back tears when comforting Anthony by the graveside.

It was out of respect for Con and his aspiration to restore Edenderry Abbey to its former splendour, that Anthony resigned himself to tolerating the Englishman's harangue and set about completing the work with renewed vigour.

Almost two years to the very day when first commencing the restoration, the work on the abbey was at last complete. Colonel Cartwell carried out his final inspection with military flair and could only congratulate Anthony on a job well done.

His money made and with a list of contacts and addresses to be called on once reaching his next destination, Anthony prepared to take his leave of Irvinestown the very next day. First though, he bade farewell to the McStravicks, then paid a last visit to Con's grave, upon which he left a piece of Irish oak cut from the original main beam and central support in the roof of the small chapel at the heart of the abbey. Carved by him into the shape of a dove in flight, it was inscribed: *Thy Work Is Done. R.I.P.*

Chapter Two

It was the first day of September 1949. Tool bag in hand, Anthony stepped down cautiously from the Ulster bus at the Central Bus Station on arriving in Belfast. From a distance the industrial capital of Northern Ireland bustled with matchstick people darting to and fro between bright red trolley buses and in and out of doorways to large department stores and office blocks. Life in Glasgow better stand good to me here, Anthony thought, feeling a little nervous as he gingerly made his way along the main thoroughfare to his first recommended port of call.

It was Con who had once suggested that they visit Belfast someday to call on his old friends, his former apprentices from the shipyard. As on Clydebank the drop of a name would open doors to new opportunities that the city had to offer. This was what Anthony now sought. He had contemplated returning to Scotland but knowing the hurt he would incur on visiting their old haunts there, where both he and Con had had so much fun together, dissuaded him.

The list of names and places Con had proposed to call on and the money that Anthony had saved, were his greatest resources. Mr

McStravick had readily handed the book of names and places to him on establishing his intentions, reinforcing what Con had said on many occasions: 'Through those people listed, help and opportunity will be at hand'. In this belief Anthony had boldly gone.

Belfast City Hall, an imposing grey Portland-stone building, overtly Victorian by design and standing at the heart of the Protestant and unionist dominated city, was the landmark from which to find direction, and heading west through the busy cobblestone streets, Anthony soon found his mark. Formerly known as The Klondike (Est. 1821) the Gresham Bar was not unlike those to be found in Glasgow, jam-packed at any hour of the day. On entering the bar through its etched-glass door the potent smell of tobacco and porter and of piss wafting in from the backyard jakes, hung thick in the air. The razor-sharp Belfast accent was harder on the ear than the granite-like Glaswegian for those not yet accustomed to it. Darkly clothed men in flat caps, their brogue shoes gleaming, cigarettes seemingly glued to their bottom lips as they spoke, sat cumbersomely around drinks laden beer barrels sited across the sawdust-strewn floor. Opposite the bar was a row of snugs. They were busy, with more men sat in discreet conversation over their fisted jars of black porter while others buried their faces in the *Irish News* racing sheets to earnestly study form in the hope of picking a winner. One young couple sitting in a corner looked uncomfortable, as though they should not be seen together. Perhaps a secret lovers' rendezvous, was the newcomer's evaluation. Standing at the bar in small groups were more formally dressed men, possibly out from the office for a lunchtime drink.

It was the short, heavily-built man behind and at the far end of the finely-carved dark-oak counter, his fleshy, moon-shaped face wobbling slightly as he merrily laughed along with a couple of patrons, in whom Anthony was interested the most. This was the man who would 'see him right'. Anthony ordered a stout and retreated to a snug just inside the front entrance to sit inconspicuously, tool bag at his feet. He was content to sip his pint and wait for the lunchtime crowd to dwindle before approaching the publican, who had paid him little if any attention apart from a hearty 'Hello Sir' when serving him. Anthony was to recollect well the initial exchange between the barman and he. There was a lull, and Anthony made his move.

On introducing himself over the bar and giving a brief though informative background to his circumstances, Felix Gresham's face broke into a broad, genuine smile. Once drying his meaty hands on the beer-stained towel he wore around his thick waist, he spontaneously reached across the counter and clasped them around Anthony's extended hand to say sincerely, in a soft Liverpudlian accent, 'A friend of Con's is a friend of mine, lad. Welcome to Belfast.'

Felix had to almost throw the last punter out that afternoon when closing up earlier than usual, before retreating with his wife Bernadette and Anthony to the sanctuary of the little back room beyond the bar. There was much he wanted to know about his old pal, Con. He and 'the missus' had been away to Liverpool on a week's holiday when Con had died and been buried. Felix had been shocked to learn of Con's death through Bernadette reading out of nosy habit the death notices in a week old *Irish News*.

For Anthony it was as if he had known the scouser all his life as his hospitality and that of his down-to-earth wife was overwhelming. Life stories were freely exchanged over a generous helping of fried bacon and eggs and necked bottles of porter; Bernadette easily keeping up with the men by drinking mug after mug of sweet black tea.

Felix had come to Belfast by accident. While an apprentice joiner carrying out general maintenance on a Liverpool to Belfast ferry, he'd got drunk with some workmates and had fallen asleep on one of its lower decks. Awaking the next morning, he'd staggered off the ferry to go home and wandered the streets in a drunken stupor, looking in vain for familiar landmarks before finally asking for directions. All he'd got were odd looks from folk who didn't know what the hell he was on about. The smell of liquor had tempted him into a street-corner bar to find the cure to his ailment and had been served by 'a great-looking girl.' In the course of their easy and free conversation, Felix had found out, as he put it, 'I was lost. I was in Belfast!' They all laughed heartily, with Felix, not at all embarrassed, bringing a grand ending to the tale. 'I may have been lost,' he said, smiling lovingly at his wife, who was that great-looking girl, 'but I found something wonderful in turn.'

Bernadette had been the publican's daughter and many a man had fallen for her - sometimes literally. One too many drinks consumed resulted in their foolishly revealing their desires to her, only to end up being thrown out into the street by her father, a burly man who brooked no nonsense. Full of apologies they would return a few days later to sit at the bar once again drooling over their drink at her staggering good looks - the long, curly black hair that hung freely over her shoulders, the sparkling emerald green eyes and a constant radiant smile upon a face so perfect in shape, as was her body.

Apart from that bar, hard by the Belfast docks (which her brother presently managed) Bernadette's father had also owned the bar in which her husband, Anthony and she now sat and which she'd inherited with her father dying. Felix had fallen head over heels in love with Bernadette, had come to Belfast and served his apprenticeship in the Queen's Island, where he had become great friends with Con, the country lad who had also been serving his apprenticeship. They had served out their time alongside each other and had worked together in Belfast for some ten years after.

With Felix getting married and entering the bar trade on his wife's inheritance, Con had gone his own way, leaving Belfast shortly after for

Scotland. Felix had not seen his best man since, but had received a card from Con each Christmas thereafter.

'Con was a saint,' mused Felix. 'He never drank, smoked, swore or gambled. He hadn't a bad word to say about anyone. He would do any soul a good turn. A godly man, yes indeed.' That said, Felix, Bernadette and Anthony raised their bottles and mug and toasted a blessing to Con. Felix's words for the deceased that day had been the truth if ever it had been spoken.

It was as if their lost friendship with Con was being reborn and while nature's decay was evident all about them that autumn, a strong friendship blossomed between Anthony and Felix. They were soon to be found spending a great deal of their free time together. Sure enough Anthony was able to say, that Felix did indeed 'see me right.' Felix had put his new friend in contact with the appropriate people. Through them, Anthony secured a very pleasant furnished room in a large terraced house on the Antrim Road, in the north of the city and convenient to the city centre, and employment with a local builder. The builder employed a small team of highly skilled tradesmen to convert rundown properties throughout the city for a local businessman, an established Jew, who either rented out or sold the properties at a huge profit. All this good-fortune had been possible through Felix's contacts, those with whom he had daily dealings across the bar. The bar, Anthony soon discovered, was a place where favours were given and taken freely by both parties.

Still young and learning, Anthony was presently content to be of employee status. He was saving a little money each week and added to the tidy sum with which he had come to Belfast, someday, maybe, he would give the Jew a little competition.

With Christmas of that year fast approaching, Anthony's thoughts once again turned to his family, to whom he still wrote. When living in Fermanagh he had felt guilty at being so near to them but yet dreading what he may encounter if returning to Donegal even for a brief visit. He had taken a chance though and had sent a forwarding address, the post office in Irvinestown itself, from where he had collected the return letters - two in all, just before Christmas of each year spent there. It had been clear from mother's replies that father remained sore after all these years at his leaving as indeed she was. The two younger boys and the girls had been very upset and missed him so to that very day.

Through mother's last letter, Anthony had not been surprised to learn that Christy had also since fled the nest. He was believed to be in London. Little more had been said about him, but Anthony had been left feeling that he was being held to blame for his older brother's sudden departure. This did not trouble him though. He took heart in knowing that his mother at least had been spared the gory sight of one son killing the other. That was how bad the conflict between Christy and he had become, the ragged scars crisscrossing his muscular forearms, mute testimony to their senseless violence. He just hoped that Christy was not battering someone else in whatever corner he now found himself to be.

Mother's letters had closed in the same manner each time - a simple thank you extended for the money sent and best wishes for the future.

This year, he hesitated again to give an address - his own, this time. However, he did, and with a little extra money enclosed, Anthony posted his letter home and looked forward to hearing from his folk once again.

On Christmas Eve the Gresham Bar brimmed over with Christmas spirit. The packed-to-the-rafters afternoon revellers relaxed into a party mood. Sitting alone over a stout in the same snug where he had first sat that September day, Anthony looked across the bar with amused interest. He admired Felix's agility as he reached out at a precarious full-stretch on a bar stool - barely taking the weight - to pin a sprig of mistletoe to the crossbeam above the counter. The high-spirited Felix stepped down heavily from the stool and placed a simply made collection box on the counter. The card attached to the box declared: LADIES ... KISSES FOR THE BARMAN - FREE TIPPLE! DONATIONS FOR ORPHANED CHILDREN WELCOMED! The bar erupted in catcalls and laughter at this, renewed when Felix quipped after motioning for quiet, 'I've got to keep the missus jealous to keep her interested!'

In that moment, Anthony's eyes were instantly drawn to the tall, slender woman who had just entered the bar, a chilling wind blowing in intrusively behind her. Her back was turned to him as she paused before moving confidently to the bar. A parcel neatly wrapped in rich Christmas paper was tucked under an arm. A hush fell over the place but only momentarily as all, bar one patron, returned to their pints and half measures. Engrossed in the female in their midst, Anthony looked on as Felix, aware of her presence also, moved quickly to the quieter end of the bar to receive her there. With a warm smile, he accepted the parcel passed to him over the bar counter. A brief, seemingly amicable conversation ensued between the two. Eager for a hint as to the identity of the mystery lady bearing gifts, Anthony sat forward over his pint to eavesdrop the tail end of the two-way friendly chat as the woman prepared to take her leave.

'Can I offer you a little sherry before you go?' asked Felix with a hopeful face, then glancing the collection box, added quickly, flushed with embarrassment it seemed, 'Not that I'm trying to entice you into anything, you understand.'

'I'm sure you're not, Mister Gresham,' chuckled the woman, and with her mood returning to normal, added, 'Well, I must be on my way ... *lots to do.*'

His ears pricked, Anthony overheard Felix say, 'Happy Christmas Sarah.' Then, holding the parcel aloft in one hand and with a much louder voice, add with a purpose, 'My thanks again to all at the mill. I'm sure the youngsters up at the orphanage will enjoy the treat.' Holding up a dismissive hand, the young woman replied in kind, 'Not at all.' She merrily bid the publican a happy Christmas, and turned, blushing a little, to take her leave.

Anthony's heart raced on seeing her face below the emerald green Tam O'Shanter she wore. So angelic was it, finely chiselled, with its well-defined cheekbones, cornflower blue eyes, and full lips wearing a coat of cherry-red lipstick. He glimpsed a thick mane of yellow hair tucked tidily under the high collar of a winter coat. Her eyes met his briefly, before falling away shyly, her blush deepening. He felt his face burn, too. Anthony felt the urge to follow her, but he was mesmerised by her. She was half out of the door. He stood up, near-empty glass in hand, to go after her. 'Don't be so daft,' said a voice in his head. He sat down again, and she was gone. 'But you may never see her again,' said another voice in his head. He was on his feet again, stalled. But what do I say? What do I do? Anthony mused, at a loss. A real voice, a shout across the bustling bar jolted him out of his reverie. 'Are you going to fill up that jar or not?' Felix demanded. A few heads turned and bemused looks were cast Anthony's way. 'If I'm depending on the likes of you for a living, then God help me!' Laughter welled up again. In a dreamlike state, Anthony walked to the bar, still in two minds about pursuing the girl called Sarah.

The question 'What's up?' was the cue for Anthony to pick his friend's brain. Felix felt awkward answering Anthony's questions without seeming to be holding anything back, which he was doing. Out of his esteem for Anthony - and unknown to Anthony - Felix had immediate anxieties over his friend's enthusiasm for Sarah, whom he knew very well. Much more than he dare ever say. What he did reveal about the young woman however, he did so in whispers, out of earshot of all others.

Anthony was feeling on top of the world as he set out for home later that night, disturbing the just-fallen soft snow and moving through that still feathering down from the darkling Christmas Eve sky. He knew enough about the girl called Sarah McParland to ensure that he would see her again by 'coincidence' early in the New Year. He was planning it as he walked. He would take a stroll up the Falls Road to Clonard, where her father's cobbler shop stood, and he would be sure to see her, sooner or later.

'Now, what to say?'

He was pleasantly stopped in his mental tracks by angelic voices, singing in joyous harmony. He paused on the street corner to look on and listen.

'*Silent night, holy night, all is calm, all is bright ...*'

The group of young boys and girls, clad in snow-speckled winter coats and scarves, huddled under the flickering yellow glow of the gas street lamp to sing their praises; the chill evening air catching their breath. Beyond them, a side street had become a playful battlefield. Little matchstick figures of children dodged the barrage of snowballs being tossed back and forth in the friendly combat. The calls of a mother to her son to 'Come in for bed' went unheeded by her combatant offspring.

At arms reach away a door opened. An old woman, draped in a black plaid shawl, her ghost-white hair outstanding beneath it, placed a ring of holly around the polished doorknocker. She spied Anthony, her beady eyes dancing with excitement in her old age.

'A merry Christmas to you, son, and God bless you,' she twinkled. She tottered back into her wee house, cast in the dim red glow of the lamp that burned below the picture of the Sacred Heart above the mantelpiece. The door closed outwards gently. It was as if his own mother had spoken to him through the old woman. The affect on Anthony was such that, on looking around him once more, the drab and dreary Belfast streets and slum mill houses, lifted a little with their coating of snow glistening under the glowing light of the gas lamps, were transformed into a peaceful, picturesque scene. He could feel the building excitement of the night all about him. Carrying along on his way, he offered up a whispered prayer for family and friends past and gone, and was thankful to the Lord above for those who were part of his life that day.

Chapter Three

Anthony had determined what his New Year's resolutions were to be. On the morning of New Year's Eve, 1949, much excited at the plans he'd made, he was up and out early. He intended to pay a visit to the Clonard that evening in the hope of seeing Sarah. Meantime, he would familiarise himself more with the centre of the city itself, then over to east Belfast and the Harland and Wolff shipyard. He wanted to see where Con had served his time as an apprentice. In his brief exploration of the city centre, Anthony compared the browny-gold granite stone buildings of Glasgow with the grey Portland-stone architecture of Belfast. He judged the latter to be easier on the eye, with their elaborate embellishments. Heading east, Anthony marvelled at the brightly yellow-painted crane standing dominant, almost scary, over the rooftops of the small terraced houses, made to look dwarfish by the steel monster towering over them, and which served to make this shipyard one of the most talked-about by dockers and seamen everywhere.

The streets approaching the shipyard echoed to riveters' hammers and were not unlike those around the Antrim Road, apart from one notable difference. The kerbs and lampposts here had been daubed red, white and blue. Walking a little further on, Anthony paused to admire the beautifully painted gable-end mural of an elegantly dressed man seated in a victorious pose astride a magnificent white charger. Must be someone very important, he thought, and curiously read the inscription below:

GOD SAVE WILLIAM OF ORANGE
VICTORIOUS AT THE BATTLE OF THE BOYNE 1690
NO SURRENDER!

Continuing on toward the shipyard gates, Anthony began to feel apprehensive amid his new surroundings. He suddenly felt that he did not belong. The two hard-faced men in greasy dungarees eyeing him suspiciously raised his fears.

'Y'looking for something, mister?' demanded the older, meaner-looking one of the two dockers, stealing an unofficial mid-morning break. To Anthony it sounded more like a statement than an inquiry.

'I was hoping to have a quick look round,' Anthony replied. The two dockers looked at each other, seemingly surprised. The elder threw a murderous look at Anthony with his next demand. 'You're not from around here, *are ya*?' This was a warning signal to Anthony, who paused to take stock of the dilemma he faced. His accent had given him away.

'He's a fucking popehead!' snapped the youngest, snipey-faced one, whose eyes and movements signalled that he was eager to put the boot in. Anthony turned heel and ran for his life. He did not have to look back to know that the two men were hot on his tail. Their work boots scraped and clattered on the cobbled street. A heavy-duty riveter's bolt skimmed his left ear and sent sparks flying on hitting the pavement in front of him.

'Run, yeh yellow papist bastard!' called one of the Protestant men.
'We don't want your likes here!' called the other.

Lucky not to be trampled to death beneath a horse-drawn cart as he scrambled across a busy main road, Anthony did not stop until he'd gone halfway down a side street, where he collapsed in a heap on the steps of a Catholic church. His heart pounding and legs trembling, his throat sore and dry, Anthony thanked God he was safe.

Felix Gresham found it difficult to contain his anger on hearing the terrifying details, recounted by an exhausted Anthony who gulped down a large whiskey between erratic breaths.

'Sure, you knew better than to go venturing into those parts,' Felix retorted. 'Did Con not warn you?'

Con had said nothing about such bigots working in the shipyard, nor, for that matter, had Felix.

Felix soon put Anthony in the picture; his detail added to by the old man - the resident philosopher sat up one corner of the bar. This first punter of the day had eavesdropped on the all-too-familiar experience related by the young man, and contributed to what Felix told him by casually butting in. 'In my day, you needed to have eyes in the back of your head, working among that lot,' he said. 'If you were a Fenian, that was. They'd stick a chisel in your back as quick as look at you. Not to be trusted! No, sir! Don't get me wrong, they were not all bad, but the ones who weren't could be counted on one hand, and were not always around to put you on your guard.' The old, weary-looking man coughed hard. 'I was forever going home to the missus soaked to the skin, for they were always throwing us into the water. And if you couldn't swim, you would soon learn to, and at the same time, dodge the hammers and chisels chucked in after you. There were a few not so lucky, though. They are lying up in Milltown now. And so is my wife. Those Orange bastards put her there. She died through living a life of worrying about me. Yet here I am today, fifty-nine years old, going on eighty. The oul body's riddled with the damn rheumatism. Ah, true enough, us Fenians were persecuted.'

Anthony did not dispute one word spoken.

By the time Felix had finished his lecture - a brief, terse history on the past thirty-odd turbulent years in Northern Ireland - Anthony was soberly left a lot wiser to the ways of the world. At least in that small part of it.

Lying on his back on his bed and staring unseeing at the ceiling, Anthony deliberated over what Felix had said in earnest across his kitchen table earlier that day, while Bernadette manned the bar. Felix, himself a Protestant before becoming a convert in order to marry Bernadette who was Catholic and staunch in her faith, had served ominous warning of the dangers the city of Belfast presented to those ignorant of its troubled history.

As a Protestant in those early days in Belfast, Felix had been very disturbed by what he'd described as a 'manic hatred for Catholics' by a number of those Belfast Protestants he'd known. Aspects of their traditions and culture were, he'd concluded, 'almost tribal and embroiled in bigotry.'

As an English-born Protestant, his father a staunch socialist and trade unionist, his mother a teacher by occupation, he had learned the values of tolerance and understanding as a child. His father, 'a very just man,' had told him that religion did not matter. 'The issue is that of justice', he had said. 'And equality for all'. His father's influence on his son had been evident to Anthony on hearing Felix sum up. 'The same sectarian bigots can be found on both sides of the community in Liverpool to this very day. So caught up are they in the politics of religion, their common enemy, those who exploit the working class, go unchallenged. Capitalism and state injustice, that's what the workers should be fighting against ... united as one!'

It all sounded to Anthony as if the people of Belfast had a lot to learn, as indeed did those at home in Donegal who suffered in silence, afraid to speak out against the injustices they faced in the home as well as outside it.

He longed for evening to fall and the hope of seeing Sarah lifted his spirits.

Determined not to have a repeat of the morning's nightmarish encounter, Anthony kept strictly within the boundaries Felix had recommended as he cut through the city centre thoroughfare and up the Falls Road by way of the deserted market place at its mouth. With most folk heading home early in preparation to see in the New Year, the city centre held the air of a ghost town. Only the rush of starlings swooping across the night sky to roost in the nooks and crannies of the City Hall's grey facade, brought sound and movement to it. However there was no such lack of life up the Falls. As he strolled along frosted footpaths, Anthony was entertained by the comings and goings of folk along the main road. In his mind's eye, it was like an artery, its people its lifeblood. The talk was about celebrating the New and cursing out the last of the Old. For many in those parts it had been a hard year, from what he overheard. The people's minds evidently preoccupied, no one seemed to pay him, a stranger, too much attention. Once bypassing the maze of darkened side streets known locally as Divis, along which, back to back and crumbling two-up two-down slum mill houses stood, the light from a large neon sign further along, cut through the darkness like a beacon and soon attracted his attention. It was the local cinema's billboard. It was the first showing of a new Hollywood film and already a queue was forming. It was mostly young women who eagerly waited to see their fantasy man, who from his billposter picture appeared rather ordinary to Anthony. Like someone you'd see at the mart on a Friday afternoon, he thought, mockingly.

In all his time, Anthony had never been to the pictures, so he decided to have this film as his first experience. However, before joining the rapidly lengthening queue, he would walk the short distance to where, according to Felix, the McParland cobbler shop stood.

There it was, right enough, about fifty yards further along, on the corner of the Falls Road and a side street opposite. It was closed, with its window blind half-drawn. At least he knew where to come to again in the hope of seeing Sarah. Then it dawned on him that he might well spy her at any moment as girls were converging on the picture house in droves. Some were on their own and others in small groups, arms linked in female comradeship as they walked along. They emerged from the spectral shadows and entered the unnatural glare of the neon light. Yet other girls walked up with a man on their arm. Anthony prayed that he would not see her so. What he did see then were the two suspicious-looking men, dressed in trench coats and broad-brimmed hats, standing in the half-shadows of a doorway to the building adjoining the cobbler shop. Studying hard the assembled crowd of which he was now part, the men unnerved him slightly. Their posture brought memories flooding back of the two bastards from earlier that morning.

Following the crowd in and seated with the house lights dimmed, Anthony marvelled at how the smoky beam of white light, catching the cloud of cigarette smoke above their heads, brought to life those men and women moving so erratically fast on the wide screen in front of him. His neck ached from craning it to find the source of light, and could just make out the head of a man in the box-window.

In front of him a sea of heads were transfixed. All eyes were on the screen. Loud outbursts of spontaneous laughter greeted the antics of the wee queer fellow, silently running rings around his obese, evil-eyed adversary to the accompaniment of a frantically tinkling piano. Engrossed in it all, Anthony relaxed into his seat and joined in naturally.

The mingled smells of tobacco, popcorn, perfume and Brylcreem filled the air all about him. An irritating crunching, slurping, sucking noise originating from beside him made him wince. On glancing to his right, the inconsistent flashes of light revealed the grotesquely fat face of a man. The man's cheeks exploded as he chomped a large mouthful of apple, possibly a whole apple, Anthony mused, which he devoured noisily. The man seemed totally insensitive to those about him, shifting uncomfortably in their seats as he attacked another of the crispy fruit, grappled from a paper bag on his lap. On looking to his left, Anthony saw a stern-faced, middle-aged woman throw a contemptuous look across him. She rolled her eyes and spoke sharply. 'If he doesn't give over, I'll give him one in the gob!'

No sooner had she spoken the house lights came on, to be greeted by groans from the audience. However the groans were stilled as a real-life drama unfolded on the stage in front of the screen. Two men, who Anthony recognised immediately from their posture as the same two men from across the road earlier, took up position at the centre-front of the stage. The heavy red velvet curtains whispering closed, colliding behind them, heightened their dramatic appearance. Their broad black brimmers, and trench coats pulled tight at the waist by Sam Browne belts, complete with holsters and pistols, drew and held everyone's silent attention. The shorter, barrel-chested one of the two spoke, in a loud, authoritarian voice.

'May we have your attention please. We do not seek to spoil your evening's entertainment, but we wish to relay an important communiqué to you from the Irish Republican Army ...

You could have heard a pin drop.

'It has come to the attention of the IRA that young nationalists across Belfast are being drawn into the confidence of the RUC who, you need not be reminded, have prosecuted many atrocities on our people. Let it be understood that contrary to the belief of many, the unionist bigots at Stormont, their paymasters in London, and the quislings in the Free State, the IRA is very much alive ... its arm, ready to strike at the opportune moment ...

No one dared to move or speak.

'Those who dance to the enemy's tune - Beware! We know who you are. Severe action will be taken against you if you do not cease forthwith your collaboration with the enemy of the Irish people ...

'Hear! Hear!' shouted a lone voice.

'Finally, the IRA wish to extend New Year's greetings to all those who genuinely await the freedom of our nation. God save Ireland!'

Spontaneous applause, cheers and shouts of 'Up the I-R-A!' erupted and filled the hall. Not sure of what it all meant, Anthony felt compelled to rise to his feet with the others and clap likewise. The fat man beside him winded him just then, jabbing him in the side with his elbow. On turning with the intention of laying the fat man out cold, Anthony received a piece of apple in the eye, spat out by the fat man. Exalted by what he'd seen and heard, the fat man spoke without emptying his mouth, spraying Anthony with half-eaten apple in the process.

'Jesus! Doesn't it do the heart good?' he beamed. 'What craic, eh?'

When the two IRA men had slipped away, all were seated and order restored again before the house lights faded and the main feature rolled. However, the spell had been broken and even halfway through the film the murmured talk was of the real drama earlier.

The same continued as Anthony was carried along and out with the crowd as the last of the credits faded on screen. Once outside under the harsh neon lights, Anthony scanned the dispersing crowd, anxious to see her. The shrieks of laughter from a group of girls standing nearby drew his attention and he instinctively moved towards them. He was soon rewarded for doing so. In the flare of a match lighting a cigarette in a friend's mouth, he saw her face, as beautiful as before. She had not spied him then as he stood nearby, watching her every move.

The four girls huddled close in a circle with heads and shoulders bent forward as a barrier against the cold night wind as they dragged on the thrill and passed it around. As they smoked, they fantasised over the lead man on the big screen. Anthony could not help but feel a tinge of jealousy creep over him on hearing his dream girl chip in with a rhetorical question.

'Ah, wasn't he gorgeous?' she asked, dreamily, her frosted breath rising above their heads.

'Some chance of meeting a fella like that around these parts,' butted in another, before drawing hard on the cigarette as if her life depended on it, then declared, 'Aahhh! I was *gasping* for that, so I was.' With an orgasmic expression upon her thin, common face, the louder girl exhaled the cigarette smoke through her nostrils. There were a few more 'Oohs' and 'Aahs' from the girls as they continued to drool over the antics of their hero.

Anthony moved closer to them without really knowing what to do or say. The loudest-voiced of the four saw him first and alerted the others, who all turned for a nosy. Their looks were encouraging in that they were inviting. Anthony's eyes were drawn to Sarah's and became instantly fixed. A warm, tingling sensation stirred within him and he felt his cheeks flush. In the poor light, he saw a warm smile crack on Sarah's face. He smiled back, nervously. She remembered him. She broke away from the circle of friends and came towards him a little hesitantly.

'Who is he?' asked one of the three, enviously, in a stage whisper.

'Hello,' Sarah smiled. 'You're the man from the Gresham Bar, aren't you?'

Anthony was momentarily taken aback by the fact that she was actually speaking to him. He took a second to collect himself before marshalling his thoughts into a reply. 'Yes, that's right,' he replied with a trembling voice. 'Christmas Eve.'

Her sweet fragrance lingered about them as she continued, their eyes still daringly fixed on each other. 'You're not from around these parts, are you?' The question fell so much easier, gentler on his ear than when asked mere hours earlier.

'No,' he replied, a little confidence coming to him. 'I'm from the South ... Donegal. Have you ever been to it at all?'

She laughed silently, displaying her perfect white teeth.

'No. But I would like to some day.'

He wanted to steal her away there and then to that secluded cove back home. It would be the perfect place to continue the conversation, but he was just so happy to be talking to her now.

'By the way, my name is Sarah,' she said. 'Sarah McParland.'

'Anthony Brennan,' he replied, feeling a little silly on introducing himself to a girl for the first time. He extended his hand, not knowing if it was the done thing. Her smooth, delicate hand slid into his heavily worked hand. It felt so good. He closed his much bigger hand around Sarah's, gently, he hoped, but tight enough to communicate to her how he felt about her.

'Nice to know you, Anthony,' she said, her eyes melting into his heart.

'And you, Sarah,' he replied, still holding her hand.

'Come on, Sarah, we're *freeeeezing* here,' moaned the loud one then, doing a tap dance on the spot.

'Alright, I'm coming,' Sarah assured, over her shoulder, without looking away from him. 'I've got to go ... sorry.' She shrugged her shoulders slightly and her hand slowly slid from his.

Anthony began to hurt, and stuttered, 'C-can I see you again?'

The moment's silence was torture for him.

'Sure,' she replied. 'I'd be happy to. When?'

He answered immediately. 'Tomorrow.'

'Where?'

'Here. Say, eight o'clock.'

A pause.

'See you tomorrow, then.'

Sarah smiled broadly before turning reluctantly away from him. Anthony looked on, still trembling, but oh, so happy as she joined the others, who besieged her, throwing hushed questions. As they started out up the road, arm-in-arm, Sarah looked back and still smiling, said aloud, 'Happy New Year Anthony!'

Anthony smiled broadly and replied, 'And to you too, Sarah!' He continued to look on until the four women had merged with the shadows.

Over the moon, the happiest man in Belfast, there was no doubt about it in his mind. For Anthony, it had been his lucky night. Checking his wristwatch, he saw that there were only a few hours to go before the New Year. He was anxious to celebrate, and for him there was only one place to head for.

There was very little Anthony remembered about the last hours of 1949 or indeed the first hours of 1950, such had he indulged himself in pints of porter. Asking Felix, who lay prostrate beside him on the floor of the little back room and evidently feeling as rough as himself, 'What's gone on?' it sounded as though there was a wild bear in the room, such were the barman's protests. Felix's head felt as though it were about to explode.

It had been well after midday before both men had dared to stir to sober themselves by downing the cure. Praying that his date for that night was not a figment of his imagination, Anthony used the excuse of the impending date to hurry home to get cleaned up. He did not say with whom he had a date, just in case, leaving Felix alone to mop up the sea of spilt liquor, cigarette stubs and decorations swamping the barroom floor.

A handwritten note that had been slipped under the door of his flat caught Anthony's eye on entering and it puzzled him greatly. It read: *URGENT! Dear Mr. Brennan. Please call to St. Mary & St. John's presbytery and ask for Fr. Timothy.*

Once shaved and changed, and thankfully nearly sober, helped by the brisk walk home, Anthony, bewildered by the summons, made his way the short distance to the Catholic church at the end of the road, standing so quiet on this new day.

Chapter Four

What he learnt from the timid, softly spoken old priest, so concise yet so considerate in how he transmitted the message, numbed Anthony into silence. He could not think. His mind was completely empty of thought, such was the shock he was in. The thick crystal-cut glass containing a generous measure of best whiskey, handed to him by the saintly man, served its purpose in bringing Anthony back to the horror of it all - reality.

Downing the rich malt in one and swallowing hard, Anthony slowly and painfully let the terrible news just told sink in. It was a major tragedy that had befallen the Brennan family. Seamus and Owen, Anthony's younger brothers, were both dead. They had drowned only yards from where their father's and old JohnJoe's boat was moored when not out on the lough.

'Why the hell were they on the strand on New Year's Eve?' Anthony begged of himself, anger surfacing. But out of respect for the priest placing a comforting hand upon his shoulder, he bit his bottom lip and controlled himself. And it was so hard to.

'Is there anyone you wish to contact my son?' asked the concerned priest. There was only one whom Anthony possibly could, though there was another in whose arms he longed to be, to comfort him in his loss, but knew this not to be possible now.

Thanking the priest for passing on the telephone call received from the parish priest in Toome earlier that morning, Anthony, weighed down greatly by the occasion, climbed into the car sent to collect him by Felix on receiving Anthony's despairing phone call. The humble, innocent-faced man behind the wheel of the roomy black Ford, the smell of its red leather interior quite distinct, nodded and extended a hand toward Anthony once in and said quietly, meaningfully, 'Hello there. The name is McNab. Sorry to hear about your trouble.' Anthony acknowledged the stranger's sympathetic words by accepting his hand.

Within the hour and through a telephone call locally, Felix had arranged for Anthony to be driven over the border and home to Donegal. Before taking the road south, Anthony called on his friends as they'd requested. Felix and Bernadette struggled to extend adequate words of sympathy. Before taking his leave, Anthony was assured by Felix over arrangements made. 'McNab's a good lad. He'll get you home safely. When you're ready, just ring me. I'll arrange for him to collect you. No problem at all. And don't be worrying about things here. Just go in God's name and be with your folk.' Both men embraced each other before parting. The car set out on the long road as darkness fell.

In consideration for Sarah, knowing that their proposed date was indeed real on finding the half torn cinema ticket in his jacket pocket earlier, Anthony had requested if Felix would oblige him another favour by way of getting a message to her to say he was sorry he could not make the date, but would see her soon, if that was okay. Anthony prayed it would be.

His initial fears fired by the proposed date, though not showing it, Felix relaxed Anthony's fret. The message, he again assured, would be delivered.

Content in mind that Sarah would surely understand under the circumstances, Anthony's thoughts turned totally to his family as the car progressed out from the city and into the Ulster countryside.

Turning up the collar of his trench coat against the biting cold wind, it had been no easy weekend for the IRA man who walked briskly to pay a visit to the publican with whom he needed to have words urgently. This time the previous night he had held audience with several hundred, tonight though, it would be with just one man. Normally such a meeting would take place elsewhere, on safer ground, with little prospect of being seen together. But with no time to spare and with the bar closing early after the previous night's hectic celebrations, the man considered it safe enough to make contact this way. A lot greyer and heavier than he should be for his forty years, Frank Barratt knew what questions to ask. He had been briefed beforehand by his new recruit and was hopeful business would not take too long. He was yearning for the warmth of his bed after another long day spent in the company of that same recruit, Martin Stack, a lad half his age - so popular with the girls at the flax mill where he laboured – and who was being broken-in by Barratt.

The raw recruit had a lot to learn and Barratt had pondered when Stack had taken the oath a month before, if he could do six years banged up in the Crumlin Road Jail, as he had been during the war years '39 – '45, interned without trial on suspicion of being a republican subversive, a threat to King and Country in her darkest hour. A month on, Barratt was more confident the volunteer would indeed take the rough with the smooth. In Barratt's evaluation the lad was sound: sharp-eyed, intelligent and reliable, and got things done on time. Barratt knew that in the days ahead, Stack would be quick to learn even more from a dab hand.

The IRA man entered the emptied public house by the side-alley door. The publican had been expecting him on receiving a brief telephone call only minutes after Anthony had departed south. Unknown to Felix then, and now, on leading the way into the empty barroom, it was that very same friend whom Barratt wished to speak to him about. Seated comfortably on a high stool at the bar and with his choice of drink on the house in front of him, the man with the questions began with little pleasantries. His voice low, Barratt set the condition for conversation to follow. 'Is it okay to talk?' Felix sought to assure the man. 'We're alone. It was murder last night, so the missus hit the sack early.' Barratt took a slug of brandy from his glass and swallowed hard. He was demanding with his words now. 'I want to know the identity of the tall, dark-haired stranger spending a lot of time in here recently. He was in again last night. You were seen to be quite pally with him.'

Felix considered his fears over Anthony's interest in Sarah and their potential relationship to be well founded. With his own mouth suddenly parched, he proceeded to give Barratt an accurate account of who the 'stranger' was, how he had come to be in Belfast, the basis of their friendship, and what the Donegal man's circumstances were presently. Felix knew Barratt would settle for nothing less than the whole story. Indeed he wanted more from him. 'Do you know anything about his contact with a certain girl in Clonard last night?' Barratt probed.

Passing himself off as being somewhat naive on this - in wanting the full story of the previous night's events - Felix in turn sought more details. Knowing the calibre of the man he was speaking to, Barratt obliged.

Together with young Stack, Barratt had studied Anthony's movements outside the Clonard picture house the night before, both before and after 'events' there. They had been the suspicious men lurking in the shadows before appearing so dramatically on the picture house stage. Afterwards, they had observed the picture house from the upstairs window of the sympathiser's house on the corner of the street opposite. They had looked on to see what would unfold in the wake of their very own show - if the RUC arrived on the scene on being tipped-off. The RUC had not showed, at least not apparently. The watchful eyes of the two IRA men had come to fall on Anthony and had observed him approaching Sarah McParland who, for one reason or another, they both knew, and in whom they held a respective interest. Suspicions aroused, Barratt had instructed Stack to shadow the stranger, not suspecting for one moment that Stack would tail the man back to the Gresham Bar, wherein, the lad, in the dark then and now as to the bar owner's other, less public role, had discreetly inquired after the stranger from several known and trusted patrons. Confident there was nothing to hide, nothing for anyone to fear as far as his good friend Anthony was concerned, Felix proceeded to give a full explanation, even enlightening Barratt to the cancellation of that proposed date. Minutes before Barratt's arrival Felix had been on the telephone to a customer who ran a corner grocery up the Falls, to request they pass a message on to Sarah McParland at the family home, further along that same street. Barratt paused for a moment's thought, then commanded in a determined voice, 'Okay. What I want you to do now is make another phone call. Those people in Fermanagh, the McStravicks, they should be on the telephone, right? Give them a call. Check out this Brennan lad's story.'

Felix immediately, though diplomatically, voiced his reluctance about doing so, pointing out that he had not spoken with the couple for some years.

'Make the call!' came the firm reply.

Knowing how determined Barratt could be, Felix stalled no longer and shuffled to the telephone mounted on the wall behind him. On dialling the Fermanagh number reluctantly, Felix used the occasion, the day itself, as the basis for his call and wished the McStravicks 'Happy New Year.'

It was Mr McStravick who had answered, and who mentioned Anthony's name first, in asking if he had arrived safely in Belfast. Knowing the couple would most probably learn of Anthony's own family tragedy in the newspapers over the next few days, Felix gave foresight to it and in so doing Con's name was soon mentioned. It was painfully obvious to Felix that Con was still very much on the minds of the bereaved parents. Eventually, with goodbyes and blessings exchanged down the line, Felix hung up. Barratt had listened in and was satisfied by what he had heard and was glad he could put this business to one side now. The tiring IRA man checked his wristwatch before knocking back his short, then, leaning over the bar, whispered, 'With your role in things Felix, we have to be very careful of strangers ... know what I mean?'

'Sure,' Felix replied earnestly.

'By the way, you got the big man's instructions okay?' Felix gave a nod. Barratt continued: 'You'll be hearing from him soon again. Anyway, let's hope if that wee girl of his takes up with this friend of yours, it all goes well, eh?'

'I hope so,' Felix replied, and he truly meant it. Barratt took his leave then, bidding Felix a rather sombre 'Happy New Year.' Felix replied in kind. Just as the barman went to bolt the door shut, Barratt popped his head back into the barroom to say with a hint of menace, 'By the way, Felix, I was never here tonight.'

On becoming a convert and witnessing at first hand how the Catholic people in Northern Ireland were treated by the state, wherein, for him as someone relatively new to the place, it was obviously advantageous to be a Protestant, Felix had soon concluded that it would take more than just words of protest to bring about change in that corner of Ireland. By endeavouring to live his father's philosophy of being proactive when seeking to right an injustice, Felix's grievance did not solely rest with Orangism, but rather with the more deep-rooted problem of British imperialism in Ireland. He was convinced, knowing what he did - his own country's history - that only through force of arms would the British be driven out of the country which he had come to love. Only then, did he believe, would there be the opportunity for the Catholic and Protestant working class to coexist through expressed self-determination; that the ultimate defeat of imperialism in Ireland through armed struggle would stir the working class in his own country of birth into uniting and rising above the privileged few who dictated their lives. Unknown to anyone else about him, Felix had been keen to play an active part in bringing this ideal into being. By ensuring to be seen in the right places, to be heard among the right people, he had eventually been approached and recruited, unknown to his most trusted friend, Bernadette, even to that very day. As for the IRA, whose cause he considered to be morally just, in their eyes Felix Gresham was a major asset and something of a 'coup' - an established, respected Englishman in Ireland, who was uniquely placed geographically to know what was going on at the very heart of life in Belfast, and more importantly, seemingly free to travel and attend to his affairs beyond the suspicion and hindrance of the RUC Special Branch. Felix wearily climbed the stairs to his bed, troubled by the nagging questions fired in his head. Why has Barratt come to ask me questions about the 'stranger'? Why not go straight to Sarah McParland? And more worrying in his calculation, Why, when the IRA Commandant in the North had himself stressed that no such encounter ever take place, put my security at risk through such a visit? But as a man on the outside of a lot that went on inside the IRA, being an outsider himself in the eyes of the doubters within the ranks, he wasn't saying anything to anyone as advised. Felix only hoped that whatever others pondered on the matter of his friend Anthony making contact with Sarah, that it would not interfere with that business in the New Year ahead, which would hopefully see his, and the determined efforts of others to dramatically carry the republican cause forward, bear fruit.

Chapter Five

To Anthony it seemed as if - as mother would often say blessing herself on looking terrified out the wee window at home - all the angels and saints were shedding tears of sorrow on such a tragedy, for the heavens had opened. The silver sheet of rain caught in the car's headlights danced on the tarmac in front and fell hard and noisily against the car's roof and long rounded bonnet. The car's windscreen wipers worked at a frantic, hypnotic pace in keeping the view ahead clear; the driver, huddled over the steering wheel, not daring to blink in such hazardous conditions. The last roadside signpost informed the driver and front seat passenger that the border crossing lay two miles ahead.

Fighting back his own tears, knowing the wake house was less than an hour's drive from the border, Anthony struggled to console himself. He recalled to mind those better times at home in years past, few as they were, when he and the others had had themselves some really good laughs, usually at the expense of someone else's discomfort, harmless mischief though it had been. Reliving those better times in clear pictures cast against the road ahead, he remembered that Halloween night when he, Seamus and Owen, egged on by the others too afraid to take up the dare, climbed onto the low thatched roof of old Mick and Sis (Onion) Dohertys' house, wherein a ceilidh was in full swing. They had already tied the rope to the hind legs of the dead fox - snared by father the day before - and then, slowly lowering it down the wide chimney, received great delight from hearing the muffled music, singing and laughter below, suddenly turn to shrieks of horror on the fox making its sudden, ghastly appearance above the burning turfs. They'd had to be quick to slide and jump from the thatch roof, then scurry away over ditches and fields with the others in tow, their hearts in their mouths as the ceilidh house emptied. With the crowd in uproar, the night air was filled with screams of abuse and threats. Old Mick Onion, his watery eyes - thus his nickname - standing in his craggy face, bawling his head off. 'Bejasus, if I get me hands on youse wee scitters, I'll tear you limb from limb!' They had never doubted him. Not even his son, young Mick Onion, who had instigated the whole escapade in return for a good laugh; a little escape from a life of drudgery and penance.

It was hard to believe that the two lads much talked about in mother's letter received just a few days before, were now dead, lying side-by-side in their coffins at home. That same letter had been read time and time again by Anthony in the hours since and he reached to remove it from the inside breast pocket of his coat once again. In the dim light within the car he strained his eyes to read his address neatly printed on the envelope in mother's tidy handwriting, and thought to himself, his heart breaking, Did she ever think, when writing to me, that within days we would be meeting once again over the dead bodies of two of her sons? He would cherish the letter, for it told of their last days. All had been well and happy, with Owen celebrating his nineteenth birthday only days before Christmas, which they'd all enjoyed thoroughly. Mother, father, the two boys, and Ann-Marie and Colleen, had spent the holy day together, with father cooking the biggest goose they had seen in years. As with every Christmas the boys and girls had taken great delight in reading all the cards and letters received by Christmas Eve, including his own.

Tears welling in his eyes, Anthony carefully folded the letter closed and recalled when as children they had raced each other excitedly along the rodden to be the first to reach 'the postie', his bicycle bell signalling his approach along the road. He would stop at the top of the rodden and hold out the letter teasingly. It would be snatched from his hand by the fastest one on the day, and the others milling around would crane their necks to nosy at the stamp. This would tell whom the letter was from, most often one of father or mother's many brothers dispersed to all four corners of the globe. With mother and father reading silently in turn the content of the letter first, only then would it be read to the children in part by mother as they huddled together around the elders' feet in front of the blazing turfs.

Replacing mother's letter in his inside pocket again, Anthony sniffed back tears on remembering how it had been such an important and greatly anticipated occasion to learn of an uncle's adventures and achievements overseas; mother, careful to leave out those details less suited for young innocent minds. For mother, it had been a life and death task to remove in one piece the much-prized stamp, which would be, if intact, added to the children's stamp book. If unsuccessful, they would not speak to her for days unless spoken to.

Owen, mother had written, still kept the stamp book well stocked over the years since.

It was the car slowing then which brought Anthony back to the moment in time. Directly ahead of him in the middle of the wet road and picked out of the atrocious night by the car's main light beam, stood an authoritative figure in a peak cap and long black cape, shiny with the rain against it. Torch in hand, the man signalled the car to halt. A makeshift road sign to one side, now illuminated, read: STOP! POLICE CHECKPOINT.

'Keep your mouth closed unless spoken to! I'll do the talking.'

It was an order of sorts which McNab had given and Anthony was feeling very uneasy as the man in front moved to the driver's side window, being wound down. The light from the torch cut into McNab's eyes and he was forced to close them momentarily. A head was at the window.

'Switch your engine off!' To Anthony's ear the stern voice was Scotch-Irish. McNab responded immediately. The engine silenced and the pelt of the rain could be heard upon the car's roof and bonnet. Two other similarly dressed B Specials appeared from out of the darkness. Both carried torches, and more ominously, long rifles close to their sides, the snub-nose barrels pointed to the ground. One moved to the rear of the car, the third stood to the right side of the one speaking again, his voice sharp and direct. 'Driving licence.'

McNab reached into his inside pocket and produced his papers. They were handed to the one at the door who shone the torchlight on them. Suddenly, the B Special stepped back from the car and barked an order. 'Both of you ... get out and place your hands on the car roof!'

'Jesus watch over us,' whispered McNab, and Anthony heard him. Anthony's heart was thumping as he stepped from the car. The cocking of rifles sent a chill down his spine as he stood leaning over the car roof, water trickling down the neck of his shirt. The torrential rain saturated him in seconds. A darkly figure, his face also cast in shadow, shone his torch directly in Anthony's face on coming to loom menacingly by his side.

'Identity papers!'

The voice was as threatening as that of the other B Special, who give NcNab a hard time, but it was difficult for Anthony to hear over the roar of the rain. The third man set about searching the car with a purpose.

With one hand still on the car roof, Anthony reached for his papers in a side pocket and handed them to the second B Special who snatched them from him. Anthony looked on as the rain quickly soaked the papers through, making them go limp in the other's hand. He wanted to protest at his treatment but remembered what the driver had said a moment ago. Shouldering his rifle, this B Special moved hastily around the front of the car to join the patrol sergeant standing by McNab. There was urgency in the words exchanged by both men. The B Special fast approached Anthony again, but did not have the papers.

'Stand as you are! Don't move!'

Anthony felt weak with fear. The B Special's hands were frantically running all over him. The letter from his inside jacket pocket was removed.

He half turned to see the man finger the letter from the envelope to read it under torchlight. Soon the writing paper also was limp with the rain. A rush of feet drew Anthony's attention. McNab was frog-marched to the front of the car.

'Get you over here too ... Fenian cunt!'

The snarled command was aimed at Anthony. The B Special closest to him crumpled the mother's letter into a mushy ball, then threw it to the ground and trod over it on stepping up closer to Anthony. The barrel of a rifle was jabbed into the left side of Anthony's face.

'You heard ... fucking move yourself!'

At a half-run, a rifle pointed at the small of his back, Anthony joined McNab at the front of the car, their backs to the bonnet. The three B Specials closed in.

'Yer man here tells me you're going to a wake! Is that right?'

There had been a mocking tone in the sergeant's voice. He waited impatiently for Anthony's answer. 'That's right. Two of my family were drowned yesterday.'

'D'yeh hear that lads? They're off to a wake indeed. And what a great night for it!' All three B Specials laughed mockingly. Anthony could not believe what he was hearing. His fear was turning to anger. It was McNab's pleading grip on his right wrist that calmed him. The heartless sergeant took a worrying step forward to look Anthony in the eye. 'Listen you,' he hissed. 'I don't want to get fucking drown't standing out on a night like this, so be on your way, and be quick about it!' The man shoved Anthony's papers against his chest. Anthony took the mushy pulp into his hands.

'Let's Go!'

McNab's prompt had Anthony moving somewhat dazed to the car's passenger side and scrambling in. Doing so, he saw the remnants of his mother's letter washed away by the driving rain. Behind the driver's wheel once again, McNab reached across Anthony and pulled the car door shut, then fumbled in the dark to find the car's ignition key. Finding and turning the key, the car engine would not start first time. The three B Specials stood and looked on menacingly from one side of the road. Physically shaking, McNab cursed under his breath. 'Start yeh bastard! C'mon!' The engine fired second time and the car was moving again. 'Thank Christ!' cried McNab as the car picked-up speed.

They drove a quarter of a mile in angry silence, trying to gather their confused thoughts before seeing another signpost. Illuminated, it read, both in Irish Gaelic and English: STOP! CUSTOMS AHEAD. They were crossing the border into Donegal.

A bedraggled uniformed figure, his official peak cap sitting askew a large, grey head, made a reluctant appearance in the illuminated doorway of the roadside customs house and debated whether or not to fulfil his official duty in stopping the approaching car to check for smuggled goods - a rampant business in those parts.

'If that Free State bastard tries to stop me, I'll run right over him!' McNab threatened. 'I'm not stopping this car until we get to where we're going!'

Anthony silently approved what the driver had said. McNab put his foot to the floor. The Republic's customs man, noting the downpour, paid no attention and returned to his chair close beside the fired-up stove, such a dreadful New Year's night that it was.

As with his accent betraying him the day before, so had it been McNab's driving licence giving his Falls Road address that had exposed them both to such an ordeal. McNab explained to Anthony why the RUC and B Specials operated such border patrols and why they were so hostile. Politics and religion were the culprits once again, and the fact that they had been the only people travelling the road in that late hour, in such terrible weather, had encouraged it all.

For Anthony it all tallied with what Felix had counselled the day previous. Like McNab, Anthony was seething with anger at what had happened. Something very precious had been taken from him: that letter from mother that he'd planned to keep safe for a lifetime. Anthony quietly cursed the first day of the New Year as he carefully lay his sodden identity papers along the car's dashboard, where he hoped they would dry out intact. A chill was seizing his bones but Anthony was not sure if he trembled due to the wetting or the experience just. He never thought he would do it, but he willed the car onward, and homeward.

The rain had eased to a fine drizzle. McNab dizzily followed the twists and turns in the road to Anthony's instructions. The car lights were late to pick out the rain-filled potholes and when hitting a bad one, McNab quipped, 'Jesus, we're not the only ones to take a hammering tonight!' Anthony managed a smile.

Beyond the car's lights and to each side of the narrow winding roads, it was pitch black. Only the faint distant light escaping from isolated cottages dotted here and there in no particular pattern signalled that they were not alone amid the dark of night. Though the rain had eased an angry crosswind jolted the car violently as they negotiated the open mountain road, with the swell of the vast Atlantic Ocean slamming against its rocky base. Coming downhill into a valley, McNab was forced to brake hard and sudden as the whitewashed walls of a thatched cottage loomed up in front of them. The sharp bend in the road led the car away from a head on collision with it.

'What a place to build a bloody house!' protested the driver, highly stressed. 'The roof on thon place was so low, it must be where the little people live.'

It was Anthony who revealed a little local history then. 'You couldn't be more mistaken McNab. Twenty-one children came out of that house, all six feet tall or more. God knows where they are now.'

'Some foreign shore, no doubt,' added McNab dryly, before inquiring with some enthusiasm, 'Have we far to go?'

Suddenly realising that it was not far, Anthony replied sombrely, 'No. Not far now. Just follow the road.'

Chapter Six

Despite the chill in the air, Barratt was breaking out in an uncomfortable sweat under his heavy winter coat as he made his way briskly up the Falls Road and through the deserted side streets of Clonard, his bit almost done for the day. It was a visit to the brigade OC's house that was next on the agenda. Three gentle raps on the front room window signalled that it was a familiar visitor who called. But even then, a cautious Fergal McHugh, conscious that his humble terrace house stood exposed on the edge of the Catholic enclave and less than a hundred yards from the Protestant Shankill, checked this out from behind the heavy curtain. Several bolts were released before the front door opened. McHugh invited Barratt to enter the darkened hallway. With the front door close and bolted once more, McHugh, knowing his way in the dark, led the way into the front room. A coal fire burned fiercely in the hearth and both men sat either side of it in big comfortable armchairs. The low light from a small table lamp in one corner of the room made it very cosy. A welcomed change from the bitter cold out, thought Barratt, wiping the beads of sweat from his forehead with the back of a thick, club hand. McHugh, a formidable-looking man in build and facial characteristics, with narrow, distrusting eyes, awaited his adjutant's report with interest. Barrratt proceeded to give a full run down of events in connection with his public statement on behalf of the IRA leadership at the Clonard Picture House. With his earlier suspicions as to the 'stranger' who had made contact with the eldest daughter of their Northern Command Commandant since soothed by Gresham, Barratt did not report to McHugh that he had suspected a possible infiltrator on the scene at a time when there was much army business at risk. The senior rank listened intently and paused in calculating thought before delivering his considered evaluation.

'All would seem to have gone well then, Frankie.'

Barratt gave a nod. McHugh added, 'Let's just hope that the young people pay heed to the warning. Our enemies in the RUC and at Dublin Castle have never been more in cahoots to thwart our efforts.'

McHugh did not waste time with business. He was up on his feet and showing his visitor to the door. On entering the hallway, now cast in a little light escaping from the front room, Barratt met Mrs McHugh, who was about to climb the stairs with a child fast asleep in each arm. Studying her face briefly, the wife and mother appeared haggard and depressed. She portrayed a non-expression when he acknowledged her.

'Goodnight missus.'

The woman icily looked straight past Barratt toward her husband. If looks could kill, Barratt thought, scurrying for the front door and was relieved to be out into the night again, cold as it was. He was glad he had not married and heading quickly back along an eerily quiet Kashmir Road for the safety of Clonard, Barratt was retrospective in his thinking. For sure it's a tough life for the women being married to the likes of me, he concluded.

McHugh too, had been interned along with him and had become OC of the IRA prisoners through his notoriety for being such a tough bastard, though smart with it. In '39 McHugh had left his missus with four kiddies. In the five years he had been out, with the ending of internment in '45, she had three more. The last two being twin boys.

Fergal didn't hang about in making up lost time with her, mused Barratt, quickening his pace to get off home early to his bed. It had been a long day.

Long after all others in the household had retired to their beds, McHugh sat late into the night in the quiet, though uneasy comfort of the front room. This IRA man's brain worked overtime as he calculated how best to bring-to-a-head a showdown between the IRA's northern brigades and, what was in his view, the army's docile leadership in the Free State, whom he judged to be taking the struggle nowhere fast. But before such a fait accompli could be, he had to apply his mind to removing a little local difficulty - the leadership's key man in the North, who to his thinking, being the sole northerner on the Army Council, had let himself become a lackey of the Free Staters. They in turn were only too ready to use the same man to their own expedient ends. Working to his secret agenda, McHugh was determined to see his scheme through to a successful close. But he knew that he would first have to manipulate Barratt - unknowingly a key-player in his scheme - into working against the close friend and ally that he had in the Northern Command Commandant. By so doing, McHugh would have finally prepared the ground for his decisive move in seizing control of the IRA from the leadership in the South.

The salty sea air filled the car as Anthony wound down the passenger side window. He inhaled deeply, taking its goodness far into his lungs and let it escape slowly through his nostrils. The wind was bitter cold against his face and it revived him greatly as the car sped along. McNab did not appreciate it as much. He moaned under his breath at being 'foundered.' Straining his eyes against the pitch black, Anthony could just make out the white crest of waves breaking against the rocky shore below. The drag on the strand as the tide retreated, sent a shudder through him. Ever since a child the sound of sea stones being sucked in and spat out by the sea had haunted him. They were on the shore road, on the final approach home. Looking out still, he recalled happy scenes to mind once again. He and the others, when children, racing half-naked on bright summer days along that golden sandy beach, the hot wet sand compressed between their toes. The wee Collie pup running ahead of them and their mouths watering at the thought of a nice slice of freshly baked bread hot off the fire, the home-made butter and jam melting upon it, and all washed down by a cool jug of milk, fresh from the cow that morning. Someone would shout, Last one home is a dunce! and they would run flat out. It was hard to accept, indeed believe, that the very place where they had roamed so carefree as children, collecting dulse and shellfish to eat and seaweed to spread on the land, where they had played and laughed so happily together, was to one day claim the lives of two of them so cruelly. He cursed the sea then. The vulgar words spat, carried away by the gusty wind.

'Is this the one? Is this it?' McNab jabbed an elbow into Anthony's side to get his attention. Bringing his windswept face in from the window, Anthony saw the car's headlights pick out the whitewashed boulder to his right, which marked the entrance to the rodden leading to the wake house. He sighed heavily. 'I'm home.'

The car made the steady climb up the sodden track where along those same bare feet had often trodden. After a short drive, McNab brought the car to a gentle stop in the middle of the sand-pebbled yard, the 'street' at the back of the farmer's cottage, once Anthony's humble abode. The illuminated whitewashed stonewalls of the thatched house and the adjoining tin-roofed byres were lined with black bicycles. Jack, once that wee Collie pup but now an old dog, stirred reluctantly from the stone slab at the foot of the weather-beaten half door. The black satin mourning bow fixed centre of the door served a heart-wrenching message to all who called. The light of the car's headlamps caught the dog's plaintive eyes and they flickered and shone like distant stars in the night sky. The dog did not bark as it normally would, but walked toward the car with its head hanging low, its tail tucked submissively between its legs. Pitifully it came to sit a short distance from the passenger side door. It's as if the animal knows what has happened, Anthony thought, stepping out from the car. The sad-looking dog looked up at him. 'And who's to say old faithful doesn't know?' Anthony bent low to take the dog's head in his hands. 'Hello Jack! I'm home.' The dog knew Anthony instantly and stirred a little, its tail wagging slightly. On straightening himself, the blood in Anthony's veins ran cold when feeling a grappling hand grip his right shoulder. Looking up to see his father's tortured face twisted with anger, his huge right fist drawn back, Anthony braced himself to hear the man say, 'I swore to myself, that if ever the opportunity arose, and God was good enough to give me the strength, I would give you the hardest belting you've ever had or likely to have!'

Instead, there was a pause. Dan Brennan, suddenly losing the urge to smash his fist into his son's face, let his raised hand fall as a dead weight against his thigh. A pathetic, pitiful sight, he stood with shoulders slumped and hands limp by his side, his head hung seemingly in shame.

Breathing a little easier, Anthony looked closely at his father and hardly recognised him as the same man of five years ago. His father had aged dramatically. To Anthony's thinking, he appeared more like a man of eighty-seven, than his sixty-seven years. Raising his head slowly from his chest, his father was speaking to him again, his voice breaking. 'This family is going through enough pain just now. So let bygones be bygones, I say. What do you say, son?' Still trembling, Anthony walked forward, wanting to speak but couldn't, and threw his arms around his father's broad back. He felt his father's grappling hands heavy upon his shoulders, pulling him close.

His hair, once a distinguished brown now snow white, his face bruised and swollen, father bore the hallmarks of what had been an horrendous experience. Anthony heard the full horror story as they stood under a full moon emerging. Standing close by, McNab did not speak a word and listened intently too, to the terrible tragedy told.

All of Anthony's unspoken questions were answered as his father relived the nightmare. There were no tears evident, but looking searchingly into his father's deep blue eyes, so sad, eyelids heavy now, Anthony knew the man was torn apart inside with grief.

Father and the boys had travelled by horse and cart to town that morning to stock up with extra groceries for New Year's Day, and also as a precaution as very unsettled weather had been forecast for the week ahead. An angry wind had been stirring when leaving town, but by the time they'd set out on the return trip a full-blown storm had broken. Coming over the shore road the boys had spotted the boats, moored high up on the strand on the way into town, being carried out to sea on a high swell. The sea was turning very rough and visibility poor as the sky turned a hellish dark-blue, the water, almost black in colour. Before father knew it, the boys had leapt from the cart and had cleared the ditch to sprint across the rough green and down onto the strand. He had been hard on their heels, screaming at them to come back; the roar of the wind and the drag on the strand drowning his pleas. As he reached the strand, the boys had begun wading their way to the nearest boat that had broken away from the other three, and had somehow clambered in. Taking an oar each, they'd then rowed further out beyond the pier to where father and JohnJoe's boat bobbed freely in the water, though still tied to the other two smaller boats that were a little further out. They had miraculously reached the prized boat, and Owen had jumped from one into the other to secure the snapped rope thrown to him by Seamus, and had then begun to row for dear life. They were attempting to bring all four boats in by towing the last two.

    Father had stood knee deep in seawater frantically waving and willing the boys in. They had not been far out, the leading boat no more than sixty feet away when father had seen it, and blessed himself, fearing what was to come. A rolling swell from far out had become a huge, thick black mountainous wall of water, which came to tower over the boys. Father would never forget the terror etched upon the boys' faces on realising their fate. Seamus had blessed himself in that moment before the mountain of water came crashing down on top of them, smashing the boats to smithereens and catapulting both boys into the water. Father had been tossed twenty feet or more up the strand and into the rushes by the surging wave. Only by grabbing a tight hold on the long, coarse grass there had prevented him from being dragged out to sea on the retreating wave. On finding his feet and turning to look back out over the water, the last signs of the freak wave was subsiding. Among the frothy foam and pieces of driftwood, the broken shaft of an oar among it, two bobbing heads suddenly appeared. One of the boys with a hand raised waved and shouted something, the words so faint so far out. Father had run forward not believing his eyes. It was Seamus's pure white face he'd seen. He looked so helpless against the black murky mass. He was struggling to keep Owen afloat. The brothers rose on the crest of a wave rising again. Seamus waved once more as if in slow motion, then vanished. It was as if something sinister lurking in the murky depths had got hold of their legs and with one almighty pull, dragged them under. Father had waited expectantly but they never reappeared. They had gone. Father's almighty cry No! had been heard by no one.

    It had been the horse and empty cart arriving in the street at the back of the homestead that raised the alarm. Young Mick Onion, who had called to the house earlier, followed by the girls, had raced along the shore road to find father kneeling on the strand, still looking out expectantly. The girls had gone hysterical on realising what had happened. It was their manic behaviour in trying to enter the water themselves in search of their brothers that had moved father to face the horror ongoing around him. He and Mick Onion had to drag the girls home to where the greatest challenge awaited. Mother had collapsed on hearing the truth, sending the girls hysterical again.

    His wafer thin body arched in facing a ferocious whipping wind, Mick Onion had struggled to neighbouring farms to break the dreadful news that then spread like wildfire. Within minutes, grief-stricken men and women had flocked to the house offering sympathy and support.

    Knowing mother and the girls were being comforted, father had set about organising the search parties. His determination to find the boys' bodies kept him sane. Every man from miles around had seemed to join in the search. Darkness was falling when the tide had turned, and with a welcome lull in the storm the bonfires had been lit all along the shorefront, for two miles or more. Men with torches linked arms to form human chains and waded waist deep in among the slippery rock pools in a combined earnest effort to find the boys. They'd followed the tide out and as midnight approached it had become a haunting scene to observe, with a hundred or more moving lights flickering as men moved searchingly between rocks. With the tide on the turn again morale had been low, the thought of their efforts being in vain plaguing most minds, when a cry struck up. Over here! Over here! The torches had come to congregate at that spot. It had since been remarked by a mourner from afar that the gathered light had been clearly seen across Lough Swilly, three miles wide.

The boys' bloated, half-naked bodies, torn and battered, had been discovered wedged between rocks, a half-mile along the strand. They were locked together in the arms of each other. Knowing all was lost they had not let go. It was the firm belief of local folk that the brothers had perished together sharing the same prayer. Grown men wept as the boys' finger bones snapped on being forcibly prised open, such was their death grip. Their bodies were carried in blankets to dry land, where father came to identify his sons. He'd fallen to his knees beside them and cried as a child, unashamedly.

Their bodies at home at last, the wake was underway. Anthony felt the bone-crushing grip on him tighten as father urged him to be strong and brave, before turning to lead the way into the grieving house.

A pall of tobacco smoke billowed from the wake house as father opened the door ahead of Anthony, for whom the smell of tobacco intermingling with that of burning wax, Irish malt whiskey, and snuff, was all-too-familiar. Many a wake he'd attended as a child. Indeed, for him, they'd been a welcomed event as most often a bowl of toffee sweets and imperial mints would be passed around the mourners, a rare treat sure enough. As then, somberly dressed mourners were in no short supply and packed the modestly furnished three-roomed cottage. A great turf fire burned fiercely in the wide-open hearth and those inside appreciated it on this sad night, turning bitter cold. The older women sat shoulder to shoulder along the white distempered stonewalls of the large kitchen cum living room, their black crochet shawls shrouding their hardened faces. Thick black beaded Rosaries rolled between withered thumbs and fingers as they prayed silently, their lips moving frantically. On the opposite side of the room the men forming small groups sat with their heads locked together in speculative hushed talk, so deadly serious, the smoke from their clay pipes narrowing their eyes. In the middle of the rough flagstone floor, the long table that had accommodated seven young hungry mouths was stacked high with plates of thickly-cut cheese sandwiches, kept stockpiled by the younger kindly-faced women who, working in shifts, kept the mourners' bellies filled, their throats wet. A silver tray - someone's best on loan - displayed a range of tipped and plain cigarettes. A half dozen bottles of whiskey, a tray of short crystal-cut glasses and a large milk jug filled with hot water, took up the remaining space.

Anthony noted familiar faces of extended family members and friends, all grief-stricken. It was a small community and such a tragedy was a huge blow and a sense of enormous loss to everyone. Those who noticed his presence acknowledged him with a simple nod of the head and a look that spoke volumes.

It was old JohnJoe, father's close friend for as long as anyone could remember, who came forward to greet Anthony, to pass on his very personal and deepest sympathy. The old fisherman, who'd never married, his first love being for the sea with which no woman could compete, was clearly a broken man too. Out of all the Brennan children he had been particularly fond of Seamus and Owen, the sons he himself never had, and who in turn idolised the old boy. Over the years and particularly on long winter nights, he had given great entertainment to them all with his fisherman tales. This man, it was said, had fished the waters as far north as Alaska and as far south as Cape Horn. It was out of concern for he and father's livelihood made on the sea, that the boys had sacrificed their lives. The old boat had been at the heart of many a conversation and had, until that previous day, brought much good fortune. Now, parts lay strewn in pieces along the strand, the remainder driftwood upon the broad Atlantic swell, the people it served, in pieces also, emotionally; none more so than this old man; his weather-beaten face streaming tears

Like most Irish families reunited, it was often through tragedy. Mother, now half the woman Anthony had once known, and the girls, their angelic faces so pale, clung to Anthony for dear life and sobbed their hearts out. Looking over their heads as they all stood just inside the door to mother and father's bedroom, serving as a rest parlour, Anthony took in the heart-wrenching scene and fought hard to be brave and strong. Two pale-oak coffins lay side-by-side, their lids upright in opposite corners complete with gold-plated nameplates read respectively: Seamus Joseph Brennan. Died 31.12.1949 aged 20 years. R.I.P. Owen Patrick Brennan. Died 31.12.1949 aged 19 years. R.I.P. Six, thick white candles burned on a side table, draped in white lace. All other furniture, bar half a dozen ladder-back chairs lined around the other walls, had been removed from the room; a picture of the Sacred Heart hung upon the wall, the Lord's mournful, sad eyes looking down mercifully on the dead.

On stepping forward to stand between the foot of the coffins, Anthony barely recognised his brothers and was distressed by what he saw. Their faces, partly hidden by white satin and lace were blackened and grotesquely swollen. Faint scratches were evident across their foreheads and cheeks. Their veal-coloured lips were seemingly sealed together by transparent mucus goo. He was sure Owen's nose was broken. Their hands, fingers clasped together around pearly-white Rosary beads - those with which their sisters had made their first communion - were black with bruises. Anthony knew the boys' fingers to be broken and considered the undertaker to have done a good job with the use of the Rosary beads in disguising the fact somewhat. The bodies, dressed in white and black Cross and Passion robes appeared much heavier and thicker set than their normal build. Shaken to the core on imagining their horrific death, and with a slight oppressive odour lingering in the room, Anthony was moved to look away and his eyes came to rest on the compassionate face of Jesus Christ looking down. For a moment he doubted his being. But with a fear of the unknown gripping him in that dark hour, Anthony prayed silently and earnestly for the repose of the souls of the dear departed.

A steady stream of mourners had passed through the house that night and the next day. They came from near and far. Among the throng, fishermen from across Lough Swilly and beyond: Killybegs, the Downings, the Rosses and Gweedore. Their journey had been a long and tedious one overland in atrocious weather. The northwest coastline of Donegal was being savaged by gale force ten winds. It was the worst storm known for years. No one felt safe on the road or even indoors as the thatched cottages were pounded by the sweeping winds, of which all were reminded each time the door to the wake house opened and closed with a mourner arriving or leaving.

    More prayers were said for safe passage for all. The Rosary was recited on the hour, every hour, and final preparations were being made for the funeral at noon the next day. Even at this late stage no contact had been made with Christy. He was reported to be on the move around England. No one knew his exact whereabouts. But there was no way the family could hold off with the arrangements. The parish church grave in which the boys would both be buried, had been dug by close family and friends as was the tradition and had been covered over in the meantime as best as possible as no one wanted to see the coffins lowered into a watery hole. Sandwiches and a bottle of whiskey had been dispensed with the family's sincere thanks to the eight men who'd worked tirelessly in shifts in digging a deep hole, for though no one talked openly of it, the grave would one day be reopened to receive other Brennans.

No one slept long that second night either, but a few hours catnapping in a chair or on top of the beds in the lower bedroom, helped folk to pace themselves. A heavy curtain that partitioned the bedroom provided some privacy for the men and women sleeping separately at any one time either side of it.

McNab had sought to stay on to the end with Anthony's permission. Grateful for the Belfast man's help, Anthony was more than glad to have his company. Experiencing an occasion, of which memories, he knew, would stay with him for the rest of his life, McNab remained in the background. He did not wish to detract attention from the family's grief, but nonetheless was the source of speculative talk among some folk, not sure as to who the man from Belfast was.

It was as though the good Lord above had listened and responded to all their prayers. On the morning of the funeral and only hours before the sad event, the sun at last broke through the heavy sky that had cloaked the mournful parish of Toome for three whole days. Gradually the clouds lifted, the wind compromised, and there was almost a spring feeling to the day, a day that would be hardest on them all.

Experiencing wind and rain like it only since coming over the border - his first ever trip south - McNab stood mesmerised by the beauty all about him on stepping out of the wake house early to stretch himself. He had never imagined his surroundings to be as beautiful as he had negotiated the winding roads in the dark of night two days earlier. He marvelled at how the whitewashed walls of tiny houses dotted here and there over the rugged landscape shone pearly-white in the bright morning sun. With a cold, refreshing westward breeze blowing in gently from the Atlantic, he could taste the sea-salt on his lips and smell the homely burning turfs. Away to his right, he could see the sea, much calmer now, its infant waves lapping those golden-sanded coves set between the ragged black rocks along the shore. The sea looked so inviting, so romantic - so beguiling. Looking inland then, the golden thatch drying out, contrasted nicely against the green backdrop, he thought, as did the brightly coloured painted half doors, with reds, greens and blues being most popular. The city dweller continued to gaze in wonder as the gloomy shadows cast on the green hills by the clouds lifting overhead, rolled back magically as a strong sun persisted. Around the peaks of blue-black mountains in the far off distance, an icy mist hung suspended, motionless it seemed. Acre upon acre of green, as far as the eye could see, were cut up into oddly-sized squares and rectangles by miles and miles of hand-built stonewalls, broken here and there by a makeshift gate of sorts and the odd tree or bush. The few cows, horses and sheep roaming freely therein, were glad to be out to feed no doubt. The animals had been housed for the duration of the vile weather. It all appeared as one huge jigsaw, which to McNab's thinking, came together perfectly to form the beautiful picture that it was.

From that day on however, it would be a painful picture for the Brennan family to view, as it would bring sad memories to bear.

Martin Stack had had a crush on Sarah McParland since early childhood days. But as then, she continued to cold-shoulder his advances, however subtle they may be. Though he was a favourite at the flax mill where they both worked, his muscular, blond, blue-eyed good looks drooled over by most doffers, Sarah just did not find him at all interesting, nor for that matter, attractive. She preferred the tall, dark-featured type, and as yet no one except for her screen idol had won her heart. However the man she should have dated the day before had, that New Year's Eve, left her excited at the prospect of seeing him again. So saddened had she been on receiving Anthony's message via the proprietor of the corner shop. Under the circumstances though she understood why he had not been able to see her as planned. And yes, she would be happy to see him again on his return to the city. She planned to leave a discreet message for Anthony at the Gresham Bar, with Felix, whom she suspected to have made that phone call - fully understanding his reasons for not disclosing his identity to the shopkeeper.

Seeing Stack idle by the mill gates unsettled Sarah, for her thoughts were solely with Anthony. Before leaving home she had read in the morning newspaper of the tragedy that had devastated his family. Approaching the main gate, she hoped Stack would not intrude on her private thoughts with one of his silly ploys. Trying to catch up with some of her workmates, she deliberately lowered her head, pretending not to have seen him.

'Hi'a, Sarah! Enjoy the New Year?'

Not wanting to be ignorant, Sarah threw Stack a faked smile, though still carried on her way. 'Yes thanks.'

Stack followed Sarah through the main gates and into the grounds of the mill. With hungry eyes he studied admiringly her slim ankles and the sway of her petite hips under her winter coat as she went. Not giving up on the chance easily, Stack probed: 'Sarah, I was wondering if you've been to see the new film?'

It was as if he was breathing down her neck and Sarah felt extremely uncomfortable. She pretended not to have heard. He persisted. 'Would you fancy going one of the nights?'

Sarah considered it best she gave Stack a direct answer - a blunt refusal. But she had never been late clocking-on and was not about to be over this pain in the arse. Walking on, Sarah casually tossed over her shoulder, 'No thanks, I've already been.'

Stack pried further. 'Oh! So it was you I saw the other night. Was that your fella you were with?' She'd had enough. Sarah stopped in her bustling tracks and turned heel. Stack halted just inches away from her and scrutinised her fiery expression. He was enjoying the woman's full attention. Sarah thought that she'd put to rest Stack's desires on her once and for all. 'As a matter of fact, it was *my fella*. And what's more, he wouldn't take kindly knowing someone was watching me or indeed trying to chat me up. So if I were you, *I'd back off*!' She saw Stack's face flush. He shifted uneasily on his feet. He'd got the message. As the work's siren screamed, Sarah turned and walked on, quickening her pace.

Stack's fears were realised. He cursed Sarah's fancy man under his breath and despite Frank Barratt saying that the 'stranger' had checked out okay, Stack was determined to see the Free Stater back across the border soon enough, regretting the day he had set foot in Belfast.

Chapter Seven

The arrival of the hearse rolling quietly into the street and its accompaniment of pallbearers, permanently sombre-faced in scary black attire of top hat and tails marked the end of the death vigil. The last of hundreds who had filed past the coffins over the two days and nights paid their respects then left only the immediate bereaved family in the room with the corpses. Locked arm-in-arm they stood grey-faced and fighting back tears in sharing the final moments with lost sons and brothers.

Father O'Dwyer, the bullish parish priest with a whiskey nose and cropped hair as white as snow, joined the family and sought to give comfort through prayer as the pallbearers made ready to place the lids on the coffins.

A supportive arm around each of his distraught sisters, Anthony looked on as mother, a pitiful state, supported by father, who hadn't slept at all these past three days and nights, moved forward to kiss the forehead of each of the dead in turn. 'Dear God, why? Why?' she keened, almost collapsing between the coffins. The whites of her knuckles visible as she gripped each coffin, not wanting to ever let go, mother sobbed aloud, her sense of loss nevertheless immeasurable.

'Farewell to thee,' murmured father, looking down at the boys one last time before gently guiding a reluctant mother away from the coffins and out into the kitchen. They all feared mother would collapse if seeing the coffins sealed.

The girls moved forward hesitantly and said their last farewell, then Anthony. He could just see the boys' faces now. Mass cards left by the mourners covered the corpses like enlarged confetti. He bent forward to kiss, first Seamus, then Owen on the forehead and felt their stone-cold sovereign skin against his lips and smelt the decay of their bodies rise in his nostrils. Like a hammer blow to the chest, it hit Anthony then that his younger brothers were truly dead. No more, only memories to be.

'Goodbye, God bless you both,' he whispered, before blessing himself. He stood back to observe a lid placed first onto Seamus's coffin, then Owen's. It shook him to the core to see a shadow cast over the faces of the dead as the lids were lowered into place and screwed down tight by long brass screws. The priest recited final prayers from his holy book as the pallbearers carried the coffins in single file and with much consideration through the house and out into the street. Resting again on sturdy wooden trestles at the rear of the house, the coffins were the focus of attention for the swollen crowd of mourners who stood waiting for the hour and minute hand to strike noon.

The solemn toll of church bells rang out the Angelus over the sad parish of Toome. Men and women, boys and girls, blessed themselves and bowed their heads in union. Sad and serious faces all about him now, stirred Anthony's awareness that everyone was just passing through time, until their own hour came to pass. For some that hour had come sooner than expected.

Studying hard the silent crowd, mixed emotions simmered. There were those standing about Anthony whom he respected and in equal number those he detested for what they were, and condemned them as such under his breath. 'Bastard hypocrites!' The main figure, the priest, the biggest one of all. Most often he had used his position of privilege and power adversely against his flock, terrifying people into submissive acceptance of even the most obvious injustices all about them, perpetrated by those servants of the state in positions of legal, social and moral responsibility. This 'servant of God' had, Anthony recalled, struck terror into him, when as a child he had sat cowering in the chapel pew as the priest, frothing at the mouth, ranted and raved in the pulpit about burning in the eternal flames of Hell if one was not a 'good Catholic', one who refrained from touching one's own body when deluged by thoughts of perverted filth. Most often the descriptive words transmitted by the priest but meaningless to a six year old, had half of the younger congregation hungrily scanning the pages of the dictionary in school on a Monday morning. Thus a first lesson in committing such sin had in many ways been imparted by the priest and young innocent minds corrupted. Finding this somewhat comical now, Anthony managed to smile a little, the only one who dared to amid the misery.

Few if any of his generation had held any confidence in the priest, who through his bullying ways - a sly dig in the gob, a vicious tug on the ear for the simplest of things, had resulted in many tripping to Mass out of fear of him, and for that matter, a God of Compassion and Mercy. To that day, grown men with children of their own, quaked in their boots in the mere presence of the priest, but who as the sole church official in those parts, Anthony only tolerated now as he rambled on. And on that day at least, he appeared to be doing some good.

Directly across from Anthony, beyond the tops of the coffins, stood the National Schoolmaster in his starched collar and mohair suit, his round wire spectacles adding to his sleeket, sadistic features. Master O'Doherty had not changed at all over the years. This thug had heaped misery on top of misery for those scholars about. He had ridiculed the most impoverished who - in the dark of winter mornings with black frost treacherous on the roads - set out in bare feet to walk five miles or more to class, only to arrive perhaps a few minutes late, much to the man's fury. The cane wielded almost in a frenzy would be swift in lifting the frozen skin of numbed hands, thankfully numbed enough to stem the pain. Full-blown punches to the head had not been uncommon either. Rumour had it that one young lad was constantly late because he was forever jumping ditches into farmers' fields to warm his bare feet in the freshly dropped cow dung. The lad had never denied it. Nor for that matter had fair chance to. In his ninth year at school the boy had died suddenly at home from a blood clot on the brain. People had had their suspicions, but had been too terrified to voice them. Nothing was said; nothing was done. It had been the boy's father, a good man, who had been left appearing the guilty one.

One day ... Anthony thought, looking on with malicious intent.

Garda 'Bullroot' MacNamara, his gleaming baldhead bowed low, who stood alongside the master, wasn't much better in Anthony's book. The man, thick as a pig, had sent old JohnJoe flying over the handlebars of his bike one night years ago when returning home from a ceilidh. Lying mischievously in wait by the roadside for some poor soul, Bullroot had jabbed his sturdy blackthorn stick through the front wheel spokes of JohnJoe's bicycle. The crime committed? No lights! JohnJoe had pleaded to the petty magistrate - sadly to no avail - that there had not been need for any on such a bright moonlit night, so bright you could see your shadow cast. But, 'not bright enough to see the oul bastard garda lying out', had been the verdict that Anthony's father had never let his closest friend live down.

The garda had received his comeuppance soon enough though. On cycling out some five miles from the village barrack one day to harass a young lad for not possessing a dog licence, the lad, busy at that moment painting the corrugated roof of the family home, had grown weary of the garda's bullying and had thrown a five gallon tin of red lead paint over the head of the threatening sergeant looking up, open-mouthed.

The lad had fled to Scotland that very same day and had not been seen since. But many a free pint would be stood for him if ever he returned. The garda? He had not been seen for a long time after. The story being, the nursing staff up in Letterkenny had sweated buckets in scrubbing him clean and that the local hardware store had been cleaned out of turpentine to enable them to do so.

Then there were those among the throng of lay people who, within minutes of receiving the Blessed Sacrament on their knees, would stand beyond the chapel gates condemning their neighbours as they past by. Jealousy and backstabbing was rife in these parts, the mentality being, one man's gain was another man's loss. Giving someone, even the most decent and honest of people, the benefit of the doubt, was very slow in coming from among this breed of folk; so-called good Catholics.

The lead pallbearer appearing at his side to whisper instructions into his ear interrupted Anthony's recriminating thoughts.

Arrangements had been made earlier. Father, Ann-Marie, old JohnJoe and father's remaining brother at home, Michael, would take the first lift of Seamus. Anthony, Colleen, mother's youngest brother Peader, and Mick Onion, Owen's best friend, would take the first lift of Owen. The coffins were to be carried shoulder high along the winding road to the church standing a mile away. Groups of four would alternate in taking lifts of each coffin along the way.

Anthony felt the smooth polished oak wood slide against his face as Owen's coffin was lifted and lowered onto his shoulder, taking the dead weight. He felt his sister's arm rest across his upper back, her hand clasp his free shoulder for dear life. Mick Onion was in front of him, paired with Uncle Peader at the foot of the coffin. Ahead of them, Seamus had been shouldered behind the hearse, which set off at a crawl. Four pallbearers served as a guard of honour on the flanks, the lead one ensuring it all went smoothly. Mother, supported by her two sisters, stood at the rear. Behind her, five hundred or more mourners - six abreast - would file in to form the cortege. On the signal from the lead pallbearer they all set out on the last leg of the boys' journey with the unrelenting sea wind beating against grey faces. Hundreds more sorrowful-faced folk lined the route on both sides of the country road. Young and old, some on their knees and with caps in hand blessed themselves and whispered a prayer as the coffins past by. Only the low rev of the hearse engine and the slow-of-pace shuffling of feet upon the beaten track disturbed the otherwise sombre silence. Periodically the procession halted as eight more men stepped readily forward from the crowd to take their lift, so relieving the previous volunteers.

From by mother's side, Anthony saw the solitary steeple of the parish church loom near and could see that the sloping graveyard was a mass of black. Hundreds more had gathered among the headstones. Perched here and there along the not so high, thick stonewalls encompassing the graveyard, young mischievous types sat to get a bird's-eye view under the chastising glare of Father O'Dwyer. The priest had gone ahead to prepare for the receiving of the corpses into the church and the Requiem Mass.

The head of the cortege narrowed to a point as the coffins were negotiated through the church gates, with family in tow. On moving slowly, steadily along the concrete path toward the church, Anthony spied on the edge of the crowd to his right, that girl the boys had all drooled over at school. Even now she was a distraction, her thick, curling chestnut hair softly nestling around such a pretty face, brown eyes forever melting, an ample bosom teasingly rising and falling with every breath. She knew how to tease and flirt and revelled in it, playing sweet and innocent. Men's eyes wandered and some heads turned. And Anthony understood. Many a torturous night he'd spent with her on his mind, his hands on top of the bedclothes as the eyes of the Virgin kept vigil. He had even attempted to avoid the Virgin's gaze by moving to a blind spot in one corner of the lower bedroom or so he'd thought. But the eyes, forever watchful, followed him. For years as a child he had believed those eyes to be alive.

Deliberately diverting his eyes and rejecting Satan's ways once more, Anthony saw the priest and saintly-faced altar boys assembled in line at the entrance to the church, their bright coloured vestments flapping noisily in the swirling wind. The priest prayed loudly and showered holy water over the coffins and bearers alike as the coffins were carried through the church doors and down the central aisle, where they were lowered once again onto trestles at the foot of the altar, side-by-side. The bereaved family and close friends quickly filled the first four rows of pews either side of the aisle. The church was soon swamped and many hundreds more stood among the graves outside waiting for the Mass to begin. Overhead dark clouds threatened. A hush fell over those inside and out. Only the subdued sobs of mother could be heard. The occasional hard throaty cough from old JohnJoe went unnoticed. The priest began: 'In the name of the Father, Son and the Holy Ghost,' and was joined by five hundred voices, 'Amen.' A thousand knees bent to kneel on wooden boards. Five hundred right arms made the sign of the cross. The Holy Mass had begun.

The wailing factory siren signalled lunch break and was welcomed by all. A thousand machines fell silent. Staying at her machine that day, Sarah reached for that small purse in her apron pocket. Removing her Rosary from it, she offered a decade to our Blessed Lady for Anthony and his family, and for the souls of their dear departed. She knew from the newspaper report that the Requiem Mass was being offered at that very moment. In thought and prayer she was with that man she longed to see once more.

The Mass over, the priest stepped forward from the altar to bless the coffins once again. The priest's posthumous praises of the deceased boys during the Mass had angered Anthony, for the man had never known them. He had only come calling to the house over the years when seeking stook money, most often to keep himself in best whiskey.

Father had been stupid enough to hand over the money when we could have done with it ourselves, thought Anthony, bitterly lost in the past. Holy water hitting his face startled him. The priest was busy again with the blessed vessel. Then, taking charge of the thurible that an altar boy had carried painstakingly, he swung it slightly by its long heavy chain as he paraded between and around the coffins. The smell of sulphuric incense quickly filled the packed church and dense grey clouds of it billowed upward to linger among the high wooden crossbeams in the pitched roof space, which creaked loudly under the force of sudden gusts gaining momentum outside.

Anthony studied the droplets of holy water floating, like huge teardrops it seemed, on top of the varnished oak lids of the coffins. The nameplates of the dead were splashed also. The cold bony fingers of the lead pallbearer placed on top of his, drew him to attending to final arrangements. With the front pew emptying first, the coffins were hoisted shoulder high once more. Taking his lift of Seamus this time, Anthony followed the priest and altar boys in front. A large gold-plated crucifix carried standard-style by the more mature altar boy at the head of the party, led the way to the final resting place.

The family assembled at the graveside as the priest consecrated the open ground and continued with the prayers, the blustery wind drowning out his words at times. As the first spits of rain fell, there was a tension among the crowd. A crying child antagonized all, but served to remind folk that with the passing of life comes new life.

To one side, stone-riddled yellow clay was heaped high in readiness to refill the wide and deep hole. On checking that the girls had a firm hold of mother, for this would be her greatest ordeal, Anthony stepped forward with his father, JohnJoe, and Mick Onion, who had organised and led the digging of the grave. Each man, hearts thumping, took a firm grip of the thick, smooth ropes. On instruction from the lead pallbearer the four men, two at the head and foot of each coffin, took the slack and lifted. On slowly and carefully finding their place around the grave, they lowered the first coffin down gently. Without pausing, the procedure was repeated, with Owen's coffin laid in place beside Seamus. Anthony wiped cold beads of sweat from his forehead and noticed the others were sweating also. He checked over his shoulder to see if mother was bearing up to it all. She was fighting hard to keep her composure. The scene just witnessed by her, broke her heart all over again; the agony of it etched on her sorrowful face evident to all. The girls, bearing up well, proved a tower of strength for her to cling to. Anthony forced a smile to demonstrate his admiration of them all.

With the rain falling heavy, it was a race against time. Anthony, father, JohnJoe and Mick Onion got busy with the shovels. Following tradition they set about filling in the grave. Tears streamed down Anthony's face as the coffins gradually disappeared with each shovel of stony clay slung into the hole, the first shovel load landing with a dull thud on the coffin lids. With the rain pelting their backs they did not stop until the job was done. Exhausted and wet through they took shelter against the wall of the church, where mother and the girls had stood looking on with other family members and close friends, one of whom was McNab. He shook Anthony's hand in giving support and encouragement to stay strong. The majority of the crowd had since dispersed under the downpour. The priest and altar boys had retreated to the presbytery, their day's work done. After a short while the rain eased enough for the family and friends to set out on the walk home, each silent, lost in their own thoughts.

The conversation among those family members, close friends and town-folk gathered on returning to the house for tea and sandwiches was muted. All but a few reflected on the day's events. They were in agreement that despite the ugly change in the weather, the arrangements had gone well. Mother sat in the fireside chair totally drained, her eyes falling closed. The girls were busy fixing up her and father's bed once again in the upper bedroom. They hoped to coax their mother into it early. All knew the rest would do her the power of good. A rest was what they all needed but there was still much to be done. The visitors needed attending to. Bottles of whiskey were handed out between the pallbearers as a thank you from the Brennan family. One bottle had been left earlier at the presbytery for Father O'Dwyer, who had promised to return to the house later. Another bottle went to the local grocery storeowner and his good wife, who had both donated so much food for the wake at half price. This done, and leaving father to do the rounds in thanking all others for their support, Anthony sat by mother's side. He knew she was not really resting, and they found much comfort in the company of each other. It was the first time in three days that they had chance to talk. Mother took Anthony's hand into hers, just as she had done when talking with them as children. Their eyes meeting, mother's pained with sorrow, Anthony spoke in a low voice, 'What thoughts do you have mother?'

Mother's quiet voice trembled. 'I was calling to mind Seamus and Owen's first communion and how excited they had been, and they so good on the day. It seems like only yesterday. It does for you all. But look at youse. You're a man now. I remember your first communion too.' Mother smiled through the hurt. Anthony did too. She continued expressing pent-up feelings, though quietly, privately. 'I know you children had it hard at times. I know, for it was hard, if not harder in my day, and no doubt more so when your father was young. You know, all his faults to one side, he has a good heart.' Leaning a little closer to Anthony, the mother was about to reveal a truth. 'One night not so long ago, the boys and girls already in their bed, I saw such a sad look on your father's face as he sat across from me looking into the fire, his mind elsewhere. I asked, just as you asked me, What are your thoughts Dan? And do you know, I would swear a tear came into his eye when he answered: "I know it has been hell for you to be married to the likes of me", said he. "There was seventeen of us. The only time I got close to my mother, was when she'd grab me by the scruff of the neck and bury my head in her lap to scrape the lice from it with a sharp toothcomb".' Mother choked back tears to add, 'Can you imagine the courage it took for him to say that? To bare his soul after all these years?'

Anthony was lost for words. His mother continued. 'I've been married to him now for twenty-six. Up until the day Seamus and Owen died, he never told me in twenty years that he loved me, nor any of you, though I know he does in his own way. That is what saddens me today ... that the boys died out of love for him, which he now knows, but *he* knowing he had never said to them, to anyone of you, "*I love you*".'

Anthony saw his mother struggle to remain composed.

'That first night, before he left this house to go searching for their bodies, he took me in his arms in the upper room and said, "I love you. Pray for me".' The bereaved mother's face was so intense now. 'I do pray for him, and I do love him. He is not to be hated ... more so pitied.' The despairing mother clasped her son's hand tightly and with a little renewed hope, added, 'Anthony, I want you to live your own life. I want all of you to have your independence. I only hope and pray that Christy, wherever he is, is safe in God's keeping this day. I never want to lose another one of my children without them knowing that your father and I love each of you, so very much.' Though it was so revealing of the man to whom he had been so indifferent over the years, Anthony respected the truth of what he had heard. Anthony smiled and leaned forward to tenderly kiss his mother on the forehead.

Looking on from across the room, father felt his spirits lifted.

It had been with quiet relief that Anthony had seen the last of the visitors to the door that night as he was staggering on his feet such was his fatigue. It had been another long day, which could have become even longer if he had not acted swiftly to get O'Dwyer offside fast. Arriving back at the house later that day obviously the worst for the bottle he had been given earlier, the priest had started to pontificate on the subject of good and evil while slumped in father's fireside chair, whiskey dribbling from his chin onto his dog collar and tunic. Thankfully mother had been spared the pathetic scene. She had been in conversation with the girls and some women folk in the privacy of the lower bedroom.

Only for the drunkard being a man of the cloth, Anthony had been tempted to land an uppercut to his sanctimonious head but instead had turned away from temptation once more and had urged McNab, with the help of Uncle Peader, to get the priest into the car and away home, seething from behind clenched teeth, 'Get him t'fuck out of my sight!' Sensitive to Anthony's potential to do hurt, the two men had wasted no time in carrying the drunken priest out of the house.

With the house at last emptied, McNab, kindly accepting the offer of Uncle Peader's spare bed, Mary and Dan Brennan, their son Anthony and his sisters, for the first time in days, years for that matter, sat alone together around the open turf fire and spent the last few hours before midnight sharing the few but precious, pleasant memories of days gone by, spent with those snatched so cruelly from them. There was the sharing also, of other experiences of life most recent. Though the dead were constantly in their thoughts, all others listened intently as Anthony revealed his experiences since leaving home. And when talking of Belfast, all were reminded that the Catholic people in the North faced a hardship of their own. Anthony heard himself speak when declaring his intention to return to Belfast.

'Most Belfast people are decent folk. The city offers me a future, and hopefully a happy one.' It was the message to himself that he'd needed to hear - to know where life for him went from that moment. Now he had thoughts of seeing Sarah but did not mention her name. He just hoped and prayed that she would meet with him again.

All others encouraged Anthony to pursue his wishes, reassuring him they would manage just fine. There was not many jobs the girls could not, indeed did not do, on the farm present day. Father would also spend more time about the house. His days and nights at sea were over, as were the heavy drinking sessions in between time. Uncle Mick and Peader helped with the harvest as did young Mick Onion, God bless him. Yes, the family had been so unselfish with their words, which had touched Anthony deeply.

Nonetheless, it will be hard for me to say goodbye to them, Anthony thought, looking across the lower bedroom and through the narrow gap in the curtain. The tortured faces of his sisters were bathed in the pale moonlight falling into the bedroom as they slept side-by-side in their own bed. He stretched himself in that big bed, which felt strange. It was the first time he had lay down to sleep in it alone. He whispered a short prayer for those around him whom he loved, those absent, and those gone forever, while studying that picture of the Virgin Mary, looking down, forever keeping vigil. Then closed his eyes.

Saying goodbye to loved ones was never easy, and under such circumstances Anthony found it particularly hard. They gathered outside the house to see him off. The mourning bow now gone from the half door brought a ray of hope for the future to the wee house. The early morning sun shone bright. A fresh breeze blew gently. McNab waited with car engine ticking over. They had the cursed border yet to cross once again. The girls stepped forward and kissed Anthony upon each cheek. Ann-Marie, speaking for all when saying, 'Look after yourself now.' They all nodded and smiled, holding back the tears.

'You too mother,' Anthony added, stepping up close to her. With that new hope in her eyes, his mother threw her arms around him, hugged him close and whispered into his ear, 'I love you. Take care.' Anthony moved along to father, close by mother's side. It was father who extended his grappling hand. 'Good luck, son.'

Mother looked on, willing and waiting.

Anthony took his father's hand in his. 'Thanks Da,' He paused a little, and with his voice loaded with emotion, said, 'I ah, just want you to know, I love you just as Seamus and Owen did ... we all do!'

Anthony saw his father's eyes brim with tears. Looking to mother, her face was radiant. The girls so pleased too. Truly, he had spoken for them all. Turning to father again, the elder smiled broadly and nodded in acknowledgment, his grip gently tightening around Anthony's hand. They parted then, Anthony turning to walk to the car. Once in, the car pulled slowly away from the street. Anthony did not look back. He would remember his loved ones standing side-by-side smiling, bravely facing the new day.

As the car progressed along the shore road, Anthony looked to his right. The Atlantic waves kept rolling in over the rocky strand. 'The sea will still be, long after we're dead and gone,' he mused, as the car gained speed.

'Thank Christ!' McNab sighed on being waved through the second border customs post. There was no sign of the RUC or B Specials, only the solitary Northern Ireland customs officer who seemed little interested in the convoy consisting one open top truck, void of any cargo, a likewise horse-drawn cart, and McNab's car in the rear. Anthony had had his papers at the ready, just in case. They had dried out intact, a little creased but readable nonetheless. He placed them back in his coat pocket and relaxed now.

The conversation between Anthony and McNab throughout the remainder of the return journey was to be free and easy. The Falls Road man give a humorous though cynical account of his own life thus far, in which Anthony found himself taking a casual interest. He even laughed once or twice at the driver's bare-knuckle observations and conclusions as to life along the Falls Road.

'Y'know. I used to curse me Ma and Da for being born Catholic, because the other crowd seemed to have it all their own way, know what I mean? Jobs! Houses! But as a Catholic I should count myself lucky, I suppose. My father came into some money years ago, just as I was finishing primary school. A wee inheritance it was; not much but enough to get him started. He bought an oul van and loaded it up with fresh fish and toured the streets. He even ventured among the other crowd and slowly built up his custom, and made a fair wee living at it, so he did. But he was never a well man and when he was dying he handed me, at the age of sixteen, a list of names, of neighbours, some in our own bloody street. In total they all owed him a small fortune and still do to this very day.' McNab sighed loudly. 'He died from a burst ulcer y'know, and he only forty-two years of age. The twist in the tale being, it was the custom from Protestant folk that kept me with clothes on my back and shoes on my feet. *Can ya imagine that*? It was our own bloody sort who were nearly the ruin of us! So I've got the Billys and Lizzys of this world to thank for a lot of things.'

Anthony quietly admired the Belfast man's fortitude. McNab sighed heavily again. 'My Da wanted me to carry the business on, but I could never be as generous or as stupid - depending on which way you look at it - for there was one thing for sure, I wasn't going to put myself in an early grave for that shower of tight bastards! No sir! So with the bit of money left to me, I bought this car, and when I feel like it, I'll run someone here or there for a few bob. I enjoy getting out and about. And as for those neighbours? Well, I get great satisfaction when they drop their heads when passing me by in the street, and they supposedly good Catholics! Huh! Sure there's better Catholics on the other side ... if you get my meaning? Ack, but sure, life goes on!'

Life will have to go on for myself too, thought Anthony. And in many ways he looked forward to the future.

Away to his right, as the car descended the mountain road to negotiate the perilous Horse-Shoe-Bend, the city of Belfast lay stretched between the shadow of the Black Mountain and the grey choppy waters of Belfast Lough; the grey-white smoke billowing from the city's many industrial and terrace chimneys cast a hazy, dirty backdrop to the multitude of church steeples piercing the blue-black sky, so gloomy and threatening overhead.

Looking out, McNab was sardonic in proclaiming aloud, 'Sure, it's grand to be back among youse all!'

Anthony hoped better days lay ahead for them both.

Chapter Eight

A queue of some twenty irate patrons had gathered at the counter in the Gresham Bar, with the main concern of its owners being the welcoming and making comfort of the two returners in the privacy of that back room beyond it.

'Tis grand to be back among friends,' Anthony declared sincerely to Felix and Bernadette, fussing over he and McNab. The moans of complaint stirring in the adjoining barroom went largely unnoticed. Anthony gladly received into his hand the large whiskey offered by Felix, McNab, a pioneer, the mug of tea from Bernadette. Huddled together around that kitchen table, the husband and wife team were delighted to see both men sitting opposite back safe in view of their experience on the border four days earlier. Felix despaired in giving his verdict on events told.

'Christ, there's some heartless bastards about Anthony. What with it coming on top of your run in at the shipyard, you must be asking yourself, What the hell have I done in coming to this place?'

Anthony had indeed been asking himself that very question over the previous few days. In fact just that very morning before setting out on the return trip. But through living in hope of winning the heart of Sarah, had returned to Belfast to put his plans to the test. And she was on his mind again.

'We're dying of thirst out here!' shouted someone from the bar.

With Bernadette forced to attend to the protesting drinkers-in-waiting, Anthony wasted no time in picking Felix's brain. 'Did you get the message to Sarah?'

It was clear to Felix that Anthony had other things on his mind - *that* which had brought him to the attention of those who were wary of outsiders making contact with one of their number. But at least his fears had been laid to rest over this by Barratt and so felt a good deal more at ease at the prospect of any relationship blossoming between Anthony and Sarah.

'Aye, I did that Anthony.'

His hopes raised, Anthony persisted. 'And?'

Feeling a little humour would not go amiss at this juncture Felix deliberated for a moment and found it difficult to keep a straight face when answering half seriously. 'Well, she said she *might* see you, but that you'll have to wait your turn.'

McNab knew Felix's game and it was a welcome relief from the past four days of tears and sorrow. Quick also to recognise the mischief in the barman's eyes and in his words, Anthony harassed him more. 'Away with that! C'mon, what did she say?'

Felix realised Anthony's desperation and quickly sought to satisfy his hunger for good news. 'Aye, no problem! Sarah said to get a message to her. She will meet with you whenever.'

'Are you serious?' Anthony asked, not totally convinced.

'Yes, straight up,' Felix assured.

The slap of a thigh sounded like a crack of a horsewhip as Anthony shot out of his chair with a sudden new lease of life. He disclosed his thoughts on what to do next.

'Right, I'll be on my way. I'll get cleaned up first, then over to the Falls.' He had an idea then. 'McNab, you could get a message to her for me ... you live that way. How about it?'

'A message to who?' asked a bewildered McNab, rising to his feet too. Prising the barely tasted mug of tea from the other's hand and impatient to make a move, Anthony said with urgency, 'C'mon, I'll tell you all about it on the way out.'

McNab had ferried Anthony this far so thought it only proper to see the man directly home. On being driven across the city centre to the Antrim Road, Anthony revealed all to the driver as to how he had come to know Sarah McParland.

'Sarah McParland! *Sean Mor's daughter*?' McNab cried with disbelief. Sensitive to this, Anthony queried the man's apparent alarm. 'What is it McNab? Who's Sean Mor?'

McNab knew to be careful with his words. Loose talk could cost lives. 'Sean Mor ... Big Sean! He has the cobbler shop up in Clonard. He's a popular figure with folk, what with being in the GAA and all ... know what I mean?'

'Sounds like the same girl to me from what you say about her father being a cobbler,' Anthony confirmed. Then, thinking for a moment longer, added with an air of despair, 'Oh no! Don't tell me. They're not one of those families are they ... one of the crowd who owe you money?'

Not diverting his eyes from the main road ahead, McNab chuckled. 'Far from it! They're decent folk Anthony, one of the best. You'll be well in there. I'm just surprised that the big fella would let his daughter go out with a Free Stater. Well, y'know what I mean ... a lad from down south, such as yourself.' McNab felt uncomfortable about the way he had put the point over and was conscious of Anthony's inquisitive glare.

Not too sure of what exactly McNab had meant or how to take it, Anthony pursued the matter. 'McNab, what do you mean, *her father wouldn't want his daughter going out with the likes of me?'*

Knowing he had made a balls up, McNab felt it only right and proper to tell Anthony straight. 'Well, it's like this Anthony. A lot of folk ... Catholic folk here in the North, have never forgiven Mick Collins for signing thon Treaty. They still see the Free Staters as having sold them out. But I'm sure, knowing Sean Mor as we all do, that he'll judge you as a man in your own right. So don't be worrying yourself.' McNab suspected all that he had said to be of little comfort to Anthony. He was right.

Coming from a family in which, at father's strict ruling, the subject of domestic politics was taboo, Anthony knew little of the historical facts to which McNab inferred. Talk of such had been suppressed in Toome, where wounds from the Irish Civil War were slow to heal among families torn apart by the stroke of Collins' pen all those years ago. Nevertheless Anthony was undeterred from doing what his heart and mind told him was right. As the car negotiated the roundabout at the mouth of the Antrim Road and on toward his humble abode, Anthony had only one thought in his mind and revealed it to McNab. 'Will you get a message to her for me?'

Admiring the Free Stater's steely determination, McNab replied, 'I will Anthony. I will indeed.' McNab only hoped that he would not live to regret playing a hand in bringing the young couple together.

With arrangements made to meet soon again with McNab, Anthony collected the dated newspapers just inside the door to his flat. It felt odd to read one paper's front-page story about his family tragedy. The appointed reporter dispatched from Belfast had accurately described the Brennans as an ordinary, hard working family torn apart so cruelly by nature's hand. In an adjoining column, he read of another event to which, in part, he had also been a witness, and which began: *The public appearance at a Belfast picture house on New Year's Eve by subversive elements mouthing threats and rising fears among an uninterested public, are to be investigated by the police ...* Worn out by the traumatic events of the past four days, Anthony let the newspaper slip from his hands before he'd finished reading the second story and collapsed onto his bed exhausted, with only the heavenly image of Sarah's face in front of him.

With McNab fulfilling his promise, Anthony felt nervously awkward as he stood waiting outside the City Hall - the agreed meeting place – and pondered on what his line of conversation would be. He considered talk of the drowning to be too morbid a subject on such an occasion, but yet did not wish to be closed to it so soon after the event. To do so, he judged, would appear cold and unconcerned on his part, and this was the last impression he wished to give. His toes were freezing on this bitter January night and he shuffled from side to side as he scanned the early evening pedestrians streaming into the town for a good night out. He longed for his night to be the same. The strike of the city's Albert Clock on the hour had him checking his wristwatch once again. He was growing despondent, for there was no sign of his date. The happy-go-lucky couple brushing past him, with eyes only for each other, left him in envy. The sight of Sarah stepping from the double-decker bus as it slowed and running a little toward him smiling sent his heart into a flutter. Suddenly she was in front of him, so lovely and full of life. Her eyes danced with excitement, sending the blood surging through his veins.

 Anthony felt like a film star with the leading lady on his arm as they walked the short distance to a quaint public house, chosen by Sarah. And a good choice at that, thought Anthony, surveying closely the splendidly carved woodwork all about him, while ordering the drinks at the bar. This public house had more grandeur in its decor and its clients were so reserved in comparison to those of the Gresham Bar. He returned to a quiet corner of the not-so-busy lounge room where Sarah, sitting with her legs crossed, slid out of her fur in a manner which had several male heads turning and Anthony's thoughts racing. The emerald green dress she wore hugged her petite, shapely figure perfectly. Its colour complemented her magnificent hair, the colour of sun-kissed barley, which was tied back, though the odd ringlet fell teasingly around her natural face, so alive. Only a hint of cherry-red lipstick accentuated her cupid mouth; the tiny white pearl drop earrings and fine necklace nestling in that glimpse of her acute milk-white cleavage, the elegant finishing touch.

 Close by each other's side and in between nervous sips from their glasses, they entered into their first real conversation. Within a few minutes Anthony felt himself all at ease. The woman was so thoughtful, so caring with her words. He knew then that she was very special, that he was so lucky to be the one to be with her that night.

 At Sarah's gentle prompting, Anthony told of the tragic events of recent days. She truly listened and shared his sorrow. Sarah and her family, her mother, father, sisters Caithlin and Bridget, and Aunt Bella, had all prayed for him and his family. Hearing this, knowing strangers as such had had him and others in their thoughts and prayers, brought Anthony much comfort.

On a lighter note and at times jovial, they shared insights into their own circumstances, where they lived, their family, work, and interests and hobbies.

Sarah's life is greatly more interesting than my own, Anthony thought, feeling so privileged that she should share so much with him so willingly.

'I'm a mill girl,' she'd begun proudly in telling her life story, and he had listened intently to every word then parting from her lips, so inviting. Sarah was a couple of years younger than he. She was the eldest of three sisters who lived at home with mother Rosie and father Sean, a cobbler by trade and who had his own little shop. The two younger girls were still at school, but were hoping to get into the flax mill also. They all took it in turns to look after dear Aunt Bella, mother's old auntie, who lived a few streets away in Clonard, and who was very poorly on her legs. They all thought the world of her. They'd run to the great aunt for guidance when times were hard. In between helping out, Sarah and her sisters had varying interests outside of the home. They were all well versed in playing an array of musical instruments, Sarah's favourite being the piano accordion. Until recently she had held the title of Belfast Irish Dancing Champion and had come runner-up several times in the Ulster Championship, but had, in her own words, 'grown out of it' much to her father's disquiet.

'He's the driving force behind it all, and if he had his own way, would have me playing Gaelic Football,' laughed Sarah, leaving Anthony enjoying her humour. Her father, Sean, Sean Mor true enough, was indeed the driving force in the local Gaelic Athletic Association, and according to Sarah, he devoted every hour to promoting its aims and purposes when not 'hammering away at the shop.'

Although by comparison, his routine being so mundane, Anthony shared an insight into his own life presently and was both surprised and heartened to find that Sarah was seemingly interested, particularly in his work. By the end of his lecture of sorts, she knew the ins and outs of how all the barroom's intricate woodcarvings and architrave had been achieved, and was fascinated. She made an ordinary carpenter such as he feel so important. On telling her this, Sarah quipped, 'Sure there's no shame in that. Wasn't our Lord a carpenter!' The ice was broken, a bond between them made. It was Sarah again who took the initiative by proposing they move on to a different venue where, she promised, they'd have 'a night to remember.'

The surroundings they'd just left had been appropriate for the first sharing of information. Now, arm-in-arm, they part ran, part walked in cutting across the front of the City Hall and down that main thoroughfare, coming alive with the night's socialites, then left into and down a side-alley toward the old tavern, wherein a throng of men and women of all ages, together as one, crammed themselves under a cloud of tobacco smoke to listen to the traditional music striking up. A group of individual musicians had congregated in one corner to play in informal session. It would indeed be a night to remember.

The music lifted everyone's spirits and all sang along heartily. Some danced the jig between the long sturdy wooden tables laden with pint tumblers and necked bottles of porter. The timber boards creaked under the stomping of feet. The grand finale came with Sarah, urged on by the enthusiastic crowd who knew her, taking to that tight space among the throng. She sent the place into ecstatic mayhem when enthusiastically, though respectfully, kicking her stocking feet high in perfect timing to the pace of the frenzied reel, played in perfect harmony by the casual session players pooling their huge talents. The glimpse of her long lean muscular legs, clad in fine black stockings, sent male pulses racing, none more so than one keen admirer looking on from a shadowy alcove nearby.

Enthralled by it all, feeling the luckiest man there as all others enviously admired the girl - his girl, Anthony clapped the loudest when Sarah finished, her ample bosom rapidly rising and falling as she squeezed through the grateful crowd to join him again. It was natural for him to take her in his arms and kiss her tenderly on the cheek, to increased applause. Drawing back and looking into her eyes dancing a jig of their own, he hoped his eyes would tell her just what his thoughts were in that moment. Sarah read his mind well and felt herself all aglow.

They were just in time to catch the last bus about to pull away. Turning heel and in a flash, Sarah kissed Anthony quickly on the lips. 'Thanks for a great night.' Pleasantly surprised and still conscious of her warm, moist, sweet-tasting lipstick upon his lips, Anthony replied, 'It was you who made the night great. I will not forget it.' Pausing to find courage, he sounded a little sheepish now. 'Can I see you again?'

Smiling broadly, Sarah nodded.

'Soon?'

'Yes,' came the reply and it made him so happy. Sarah turned and leapt onto the bus as it pulled out and she waved to Anthony as it gathered speed. He stood and looked on until the bus turned the corner, out of sight.

Unknown to Anthony at that moment, someone stood in the shadows of a shop doorway across the main thoroughfare and observed him with a damning eye. This man had been one of the envious, admiring males in the tavern earlier. From under the cover of an alcove, he had studied hard the dancing girl's every move, had silently drooled over every glimpse of her milky white flesh. As Anthony set out for home, Stack, now possessing the name of his rival, cursed him under his breath. 'Soon enough, Brennan. Soon enough.'

Chapter Nine

Anthony and Sarah met soon again, and thereafter perhaps three times a week, most often at their first meeting place, from where they would move on to a local dance hall or the tavern. Being local, Sarah always led the way. Occasionally if they both had a Saturday free they would hop on a train and journey up the Antrim coast to Ballycastle, a popular seaside town, where they'd ride the fairground attractions and eat fish and chips and candyfloss.

By the spring of 1950 they both knew their relationship had become something special. They were in love. It was Sarah's commitment to Aunt Bella with whom she now lived, which prevented them both from seeing each other most nights - every night, if Anthony had his way. They kissed and embraced each other passionately at every opportunity.

Talking casually of love and marriage in the early weeks, Sarah had unashamedly proclaimed her virginity as sacred, only to be surrendered on her wedding night, though had, with a twinkle in her eye, added quickly, 'I won't be married for a few years yet.'

Embarrassed to declare his virginity, though Sarah had her suspicions, Anthony was prepared to wait for that special night, knowing his self-discipline would be tested to the full in the meantime. But the thought of Sarah surrendering herself to him, would be, he was sure, the prize worth waiting for. Anthony was also prepared to wait for the right moment to make his proposal. He was sure he would know when to get down on one knee, two knees if necessary. Meanwhile, he would do everything and anything to keep Sarah's love, her friendship, their being together for always.

An invitation to Anthony from Sarah to meet with her family that Easter Saturday, gave him new hope that the right moment to propose would not be too long in coming. Despite what McNab had said, he hoped that the other McParlands would consider him a favourable partner for Sarah. From all that Anthony had heard of them, he felt as though he knew the other family members already. He had painted a positive picture of them in his mind's eye. They were good people.

On leaving his home to meet with the entire McParland family that Easter Saturday night, he prayed *that* picture would prove true to real.

Arriving punctually at their home, Sarah, looking fantastic in a new navy blue dress, received Anthony at the front door with a sheepish kiss. Taking his hand she led Anthony along the hallway to a door slightly ajar. He composed himself before entering the front room. Sarah gave his hand a reassuring squeeze before leading the way.

The family had gathered in the cosier of two downstairs rooms to greet Anthony and went out of their way to make him welcome. Nervously excited by the occasion, Anthony was overwhelmed by their enthusiasm to get to know him, though was immediately aware that it was all females who encircled him. The absence of the man of the house had a somewhat unsettling affect on him and he recalled to mind McNab's words then, hinting that Sarah's father may not be keen on a Free Stater as a contender for his daughter's hand.

Mrs McParland was first to embrace Anthony. She was a short, plump woman with dark features and a warm motherly face, whom Anthony felt at ease with instantly, though was slightly embarrassed as she threw her arms around him in a spontaneous act of greeting. She stood on tiptoe to plant a wet kiss on his cheek, her voice as warm as her nature.

'Welcome Anthony! At long last! It wasn't for us not asking Sarah to have you around earlier y'know. We were all very keen to meet you. Sarah speaks so highly of you. And I must say, you're more handsome than she first made out.'

Anthony felt himself blush.

'Shhh! Ma. Don't get making Anthony embarrassed.'

Anthony was glad for Sarah's intercession. She came to stand protectively by his side, taking his arm. 'I'd better keep an eye on you lot!' Sarah quipped, meaning mother, and her sisters who stepped forward now to eye Anthony up and down provocatively. Sarah introduced them in turn. Caithlin, ballerina in face and build, so petite, so slender, a little shorter than Sarah with jet-black straight hair down to her spine, was first to shake his hand; her dark brown eyes so inviting just as her smile. 'Pleased to meet you Anthony.' Conscious of Caithlin's roving eyes, Anthony acknowledged her with a simple smile. Knowing well Caithlin's ways, Sarah quickly moved on to Bridget. Fair-haired, with skin very white and crystal clear blue eyes she appeared very delicate though intelligent; her voice, soft and meaningful when saying, 'Nice to know you.' Conscious still of all the female attention, Anthony replied shyly, 'It's very nice to be here.'

The demanding, raised voice of an impatient older woman sitting behind the three budding flowers of youth caught all their attention. 'Let me have a gander at him!'

With Mrs McParland and her three daughters parting, Anthony saw a stern-faced old woman, dressed entirely in black, her laced up ankle boots gleaming, eye him searchingly from where she sat by the fireside. A blackthorn stick hooked to the side of her armchair served ominous warning. 'Come on! Come a bit closer so I can get a good look at you!' insisted the elder. There is no refusing this oul girl, Anthony thought, having been made wise to Aunt Bella's testing ways by Sarah, who looked at him now as if to say, *I told you so!*

Anthony moved forward anxiously, hoping the old girl would not embarrass him too much. The old woman narrowed her eyes in studying him long and hard. Everyone held breath.

'Ay, he's handsome right enough. But I've yet to see a man more handsome than my Jamesy. God rest his poor soul.'

'Auntie, don't be so cruel.' Sarah's voice sounded only half serious as she went to kneel beside her great-aunt to place a friendly arm across her shoulders.

'Take no notice, Anthony. She's a crabbed old woman!' Mrs McParland quipped, coming to stand protectively by his side and to look down with a scolding eye at her aunt. With a determined chin the old woman was quick to retort, 'Ah daughter, you'd be crabbed too if you had these cursed oul legs of mine.'

'I know sweetheart. I know,' was her niece's sympathetic reply. 'A wee cup of tea will make you feel better.' The old woman nodded blankly.

Anthony was hoping that the old woman had not got it in for him. And there was still no sign of the man himself. A reassuring smile from Sarah eased Anthony's concern a little.

They had all transferred into the back kitchen of the simply furnished terrace, with Sarah and Anthony aiding the aunt to her chair at the table which had been laid out in best china and a splendid spread of cooked hams, mixed salad, a mountain of buttered home-made bread and scones, cakes, and expensive looking biscuits.

It was Mrs McParland's exclaiming voice that informed Anthony that someone else had just joined them in the room.

'Just in time love; I'm about to pour the tea.'

Turning to investigate, Anthony was met by a tall, distinguished-looking man with sand-coloured hair and smiling brown eyes. He extended his hand and confidently introduced himself in a relaxed and friendly manner. 'Hello! I'm Sarah's father, Sean. Pleased to meet you, Anthony.' Anthony felt his hand shook firmly by the man of the house. 'I'm sorry I'm late. It's been a busy day at the shop.' Anthony felt easy with this his first contact with the man whom he had been apprehensive of meeting. He was left feeling that his anxiety of sorts had been ill founded. More so, with the man beckoning him to take a seat at the kitchen table and to make himself at home.

The conversation around the table was easy and good-humoured with only a touch of sarcasm evident in the banter between the old aunt and Sean Mor. They waged a mutual campaign of gentle provocation at each other, much to their respective enjoyment. Busy making more tea in the scullery, Mrs McParland persisted in bantering her aunty also by pleading to her to 'Go easy' on her husband, much to Sean Mor's delight. 'That's right Rosie, you tell her. She comes round here and eats us out of house and home and doesn't give me a minute's peace!'

The aunt could give as good as she got. 'Run away on you, you big lump,' she scolded, reaching for her stick, 'before I take this to you!' Sean Mor blew the fiery one a kiss across the table. Everyone else laughed on being entertained. Humoured by the craic, Anthony wished it had been the same around that table at home, instead of the moody silence which had most often prevailed; the young ones terrified of speaking out of turn and receiving a dig in the gob from father consequently.

Pleased to see Anthony enjoy himself, Sarah used the opportunity of her father momentarily excusing himself from the table to lean toward her man to whisper teasingly into his ear, 'I love you.' Only for being in company, Anthony would have taken great pleasure in revealing his feelings for Sarah too then. She meant everything to him. And the look he served Sarah said it all.

The craic inside the McParland home continued long into the evening and reached a climax on Caithlin and Bridget taking to the cleared kitchen floor in their glittering green and gold traditional dance dresses. As Sean Mor played his heart out on the fiddle to the timely beat of Aunt Bella's blackthorn stick, the dancing, upright sisters, did their father proud.

It was just after midnight when Aunt Bella proclaimed she'd had enough and needed her bed. Anthony offered to help Sarah see the aunt safely to her home. Privately, he hoped to catch five minutes alone with his girl. He was hurting for her badly. On the doorstep of No72, Sean Mor shook Anthony's hand meaningfully and invited him to call again anytime, impressing on him that he would be made welcome. The man's wife and younger daughters reinforced this in their farewells.

With Aunt Bella safe in the middle, young and old made their way up the darkened side street arm-in-arm, to walk the short distance to the elder's house, across and further back along the Falls Road, all quiet on this Easter Sunday morning.

Feeling his way around the darkened front room of the old woman's house and eventually finding the wide arm of the sofa, Anthony sat down and was soon conscious of the chill in the room. He could hear Aunt Bella protest at the ordeal of climbing the stairs.

'I wish I could have a new pair of legs in my oul age,' she sighed heavily, taking one stair at a time. Close behind her on the stairs with one hand at the ready, the other carrying the aunt's blackthorn stick, Sarah wished the same for the elder.

'Don't forget to pass me my Rosary,' said the older woman with an air of quiet resignation to her predicament. After a few more stairs were successfully scaled and once catching her breath, she was speaking again. 'I want to pray for those poor souls of nineteen-sixteen. It's thirty-four years to this very day when they set out, and here we are, not a step nearer to auld Ireland being free.'

'Don't fear Auntie, our day will come!' Sarah assured. The old woman's voice, fading then as they turned the landing, added dejectedly, 'Not in my day daughter, not in my day.'

There was more muffled talk in the room above, footsteps on bare boards, a dull thud, then another as the aunt's heavy boots were gently slid off her aching feet; a creaking bed, and subdued moans and groans as the elder eased herself into it with Sarah's helping hands. After a moment,

Sarah's voice saying, 'Goodnight Aunt Bella.' Hearing Sarah's feet come daintily down the stairs, Anthony was quickly on his feet and facing the door opening to him. In the room's low light she came to him and without speaking they embraced each other, their hot wet lips finding each other's instantly to begin a long, passionate kiss. The four loud taps in quick succession on the floor above sent both their hearts into a flutter. The couple broke away from each other instantly as though they had been caught in some horrible act. It was Aunt Bella. Sarah rushed to the foot of the stairs.

'Yes Aunt Bella?' The terse commandment came swiftly down the stairs. 'Time you were coming to your bed, and Anthony getting off home to his!'

'Yes Aunt Bella.' With a frantic wave of an arm, Sarah beckoned Anthony into the hall and toward the front door. The aunt was speaking again, this time with a little concern evident in her voice.

'Tell Anthony to mind how he goes. On a night such as this those bad bastes on the other side may well be looking out for easy prey. Tell him to be careful when cutting through the town.'

'Yes Aunt Bella.' Sarah opened the front door and followed Anthony out. Sarah stood on the doorstep holding the door ajar with the heel of her shoe. In a low voice, she said, 'She's right, be careful going home. With it being Easter Sunday, the Orangemen will be looking to give some poor Catholic a good kicking, so watch out!' Not wanting to keep her out in the bitter cold any longer, Anthony sought to lay Sarah's fears to rest. 'Don't worry. Go on to your bed. I'll be okay.' He moved forward and kissed her slowly, but briefly, and reluctantly parted his lips from hers.

'Goodnight, Sarah.'

'Goodnight, Anthony.'

Sarah eased back into the darkened hallway and gave Anthony a little wave before closing the door out gently.

Anthony made his way onto and down the Falls toward the city centre. The road and dimly lit side streets on either side were deadly quiet. Only the whimpering of a dog in a backyard and the quickness of his heavy footsteps broke an uncomfortable silence. The freezing night air caught his every breath - becoming more erratic. Under his heavy overcoat, a discomforting frosty sweat clung to his back as he hastened his step. After a short distance he stopped, listened intently and concentrated his focus into the road ahead of him, which in the half moonlight was cast in long shadows. After a moment's intense concentration and searching, he heard it first then saw it. The low burr of its engine, a faint whistle of sorts as its axles rotated under its own bulky weight, then the two dimmed headlights visible at a hundred feet, confirmed his suspicions. Instinctively Anthony leapt into the doorway of a shop, wishing the shadows there would swallow him up. The noisy axles became clearer, nearer, as the Shorland armoured car approached and snaked by. Its Browning machinegun on mounted turret pointed menacingly straight ahead, its old battle-grey, steel-plated shell barely distinguishable against the blue-black of the night. After his terrifying ordeal on the border, he feared falling victim to the B Specials yet again. He'd heard it said that with their bellies plied with drink, they prowled the Catholic ghettos after dark for vulnerable locals to batter, for just being Catholic. Anthony waited with bated breath for the patrol to disappear out of sight before tentatively emerging from the shadows. With it gone, he set out at a half run, checking the shadows as he went with his heart thumping and his fists clenched at the ready. Danger lurked on each street corner he approached and he sighed with relief on passing each one safely in turn. Words of caution mouthed by Felix Gresham echoed in his head and dark oppressive images of events on the border that night, were still fresh in his mind.

He felt so much more relaxed on seeing the roundabout just ahead, the road leading off to the right - the mouth of the Antrim Road. It was not far now to his humble abode. *'Christ Almighty*!' Anthony recoiled, his legs buckling in terror. Suddenly from out of nowhere, loomed a biblical-looking character with long, straggly white hair and beard. Black beady eyes stared Anthony out. Craggy-faced and ill-fittingly dressed in a tatty overcoat secured around the waist by a length of rope, the Goliath of a man stood swaying from side to side yet unyielding in front of Anthony, still too shocked to make out exactly what he was looking at. It was the stench of cheap wine on the breath of the other man that served Anthony the final clue. 'Give us the price of a drink son.' Anthony didn't know whether to laugh or scream, but felt compelled to speak his mind bluntly.

'I know what I'd like to give you. You scared the shite out of me you oul ...' Oh what's the use? Anthony thought, considering the risk of a barrage of abuse and perhaps worse, if he persisted. Becoming dramatic with his arms the tramp slobbered, 'Sorry brother. No harm intended.'

Reaching into his trouser pocket, Anthony found and withdrew a shilling, which he held out to the tramp who snatched it from him with astute precision. The tramp critically examined the coin with one eye closed. Anthony was amazed.

'God bless you brother,' said the tramp, burying the prized coin deep in a coat pocket, which he patted contentedly. Turning then to cross the deserted main road, the tramp sighed with satisfaction, 'Aye ... roll on tomorrow.'

Anthony wasted no time in carrying on his way, though did not take his eyes completely off the tramp who to his surprise, disappeared into the grounds of the local Orange Lodge. Anthony could not help but laugh quietly to himself at this as he carried on home, longing for the warmth and safety of his bed.

In the relative safety of a bed in a safe house further up the Falls Road, Sean Mor settled down for the night at long last. It had been a good day for him, though exhausting. Plans were in place for the dawn commemoration at Milltown Cemetery - opposite the safe house - in memory of the Irish Republican Martyrs of the 1916 Easter Rising. It would be a dignified, quiet affair, which physically he would not attend. With the risk of the RUC disrupting the planned calendar of events by swooping in the small hours to arrest key republican figures, he, in their books, being one of them, Sean Mor was taking precautions.

It had been decided by all at the last Army Council meeting, that once active members known to the enemy should 'lie low' so to give those who watched, listened and informed, the impression that one had disconnected all links, had abandoned a lost cause. It was crucial they regroup, plan and prepare for their next move discreetly, patiently. It would take time. But through this time, and bit by bit, the preparation would all come together. And when the moment was right, when everything was in place and the people were ready to support them once again, they'd make their move. Meantime only the trusted few knew of things to come. That's the way it had to be and remain. There were informers everywhere, thus the public warnings New Year's Eve, which he had argued against, judging it best to keep things quiet, not to give the enemy any inkling to their presence or intentions. But he had been outvoted seven to one. The southerners had got their way once again. They had considered the public warnings worth the risk to scare-off enemy collaborators, which in turn, they'd concluded, would assist the groundwork to be undertaken without challenge or betrayal - the greatest threat posed to their aim and objectives. Also, it was hoped that such a public show of defiance would capture the imagination of the young local men and women, who may be moved to come forward to join up, their numbers greatly needed to swell the skeleton ranks, not least in Belfast. Sean Mor wondered now if that other southerner, Anthony, would win his way too and one day seek Sarah's hand. She could do a lot worse, and well, little better, thought her father, considering possible contenders round about.

Sean Mor had taken a liking to Anthony, considered him a decent sort, and also knew him to be *sound*. His interest in him had been aroused when overhearing the message delivered on the doorstep to his daughter that New Year's Day past. There had been talk of a tragedy being the reason to cancel the planned date. He had not pried, preferring Sarah to confide in him and mother when she was ready, and had noted her solemnity the remainder of that day. Then on the following day Sarah had mentioned his name over breakfast and had told all of her brief encounter with the man named Anthony Brennan, and the horror befalling his family in Donegal about which they had all read in the *Irish News* later that same morning.

Making a point of casually approaching McNab in the local pub on the night of Anthony's return from his brothers' funerals, with McNab calling earlier on Sarah to relay the message from Anthony, Sean Mor had McNab confirm the origins of the man who had designs on his daughter. Consequently, McNab was to prove to have been the concerned father's eyes and ears throughout that sad occasion past, for he give Sean Mor an accurate insight into Anthony's circumstances from the outset. Everything appeared safe. But the innocent mention of a certain person's name by McNab, on the same occasion, and who had evidently also been somewhat of a go-between, between Anthony and Sarah, had played on Sean Mor's mind ever since. There had been grounds to be concerned initially. Obviously, apart from wanting to know whom his daughter was seeing, there had been the added dimension. With plans afoot such as there was, the sudden appearance of a stranger so close to home at that time, had aroused Sean Mor's fears that an enemy mole was being planted within his very midst. He no longer held that suspicion, that doubt. But now, in view of his daughter's relationship with Anthony going from strength to strength, there was a matter of extreme urgency to oversee which, when done, would not only reduce by some degree the threat to his own freedom - indeed his life, but more so that of Sarah, and Anthony, an innocent party. Sean Mor would approach his most trusted friend soon, proposing that she attend to the matter for him. He could not run the risk of exposing the plot underway, by doing so himself.

Chapter Ten

As instructed, Felix Gresham arrived at the designated rendezvous on time. The route out from the city had been very quiet, so early this Easter Monday. He parked his car at the rear of the market town's old-world tearoom and entered by its rear door. He was feeling a little anxious for a meeting had not been due for some months yet. The velvety-voiced crooner on the wireless played low but high enough to drown out the cacophony from the kitchen out back, failed to relax him. Felix placed his order with the retiring lady behind the counter and sat himself in a strategic corner of the quaint tearoom, from where he could monitor everything going on around him. The old lady with a fixed smile brought the order on a silver tray to his table. He poured his own tea, added milk and two sugars and sat back in his chair to deliberate. From where he sat he could see that the main street beyond the tearoom's bow window was deserted bar a stray mongrel rummaging for scraps. Knowing who the contact was to be, left him unsure as to the reason for this hastily called meeting, and wondered if it had anything to do with the visit from Frank Barratt on New Year's Eve past. To that very day, he personally questioned the motives behind it, but would be saying nothing of it until he heard what the contact had to say.

Felix braced himself on spying the contact alight from that early morning bus from Belfast, which had come close to running down the stray on pulling up to the kerb across the road. He observed carefully if anyone got off behind the contact. No one did. They had to be very careful. Crossing the deserted road and entering the otherwise empty tearoom, the woman came straight to his table. Her pretty face was expressionless. He judged this a bad omen.

Having already ordered a pot of tea and two cups, Felix poured the second cup of tea a little nervously as the woman slid into her seat opposite him. The old lady behind the till paid them little if any attention. The tearoom was a common rendezvous for secret lovers slipping out of the city. Leaning across the table, their faces inches apart as if trying to steal a kiss, Sarah McParland was first to speak, secretively.

'How's everything?'

'Fine. Just fine,' replied Felix, suspecting everything wasn't.

'I suppose you're wondering what this is all about?'

Felix nodded.

'Well, I'll come straight to the point. It is felt by a higher authority that there is a major risk presented to the scheme of things through your friendship with Anthony. He could, for example, be tailed from my father's house to your place. Special Branch could then be on to you. All that is planned could be compromised. Innocents would suffer together with the schemers. I'm sure, like me, you wouldn't wish this to happen.'

Felix paused to think for a moment. It was apparent to him now that the 'higher authority', Sarah's father, Sean Mor, had since been briefed by Barratt as to Anthony frequenting the bar. And now, with plans for a major arms deal for the IRA underway, he had to conclude that such a risk to the scheme could indeed be presented consequently, if his contact with Anthony continued. His only dilemma being what others were expecting him to do about this, so he begged the question, 'What do you suggest I do?'

Sarah could offer little in the way of advice as to how Felix break the link with Anthony, but rather placed emphasis on the fact that he must.

'It's early days I know. The shipment is not due for sometime yet, but we are at a critical stage of planning, so it's best you end the friendship immediately.'

'But how?' Felix pleaded, lost for ideas.

'That's just it, Felix, it won't be easy. But it's down to you.'

Sarah saw Felix's face grow long, his sense of unease surface at the prospect of what he had to do. She sought to lend a little comfort. 'Listen Felix! I know you've been a good friend to Anthony. He thinks very highly of you and considers you a very dear friend, though you may not credit this due to not seeing him much lately, but that's down to me trying to steer him clear of possible danger. You understand ... don't you?' Felix answered with his eyes. Sarah delivered the final message, a personal one with real meaning and simple logic.

'But if you, and I, truly consider him a dear friend also, then we must do this to protect him. To protect us all.'

Felix thought for a moment longer and studying Sarah's sincere face, replied with a committed voice. 'I do understand. I know you've got his interests at heart. No doubt your father has too. And being truthful, Sarah, I had my concerns for Anthony right from the start, when he showed a clear interest in you. I knew it could become a little complicated for us all under the circumstances.' With a smile of sorts Sarah signalled that she understood the point made. Blind to the consequences of what he was about to reveal, Felix continued. 'I am pleased though, that Barratt was willing to accept that Anthony was sound when he came to visit me at the bar. I think he was hoping he would not be.'

Hearing this, Sarah had immediate anxieties. To learn that Barratt had been checking out Anthony was news to her. She knew now that to bend Felix's ear over this would do little to instill confidence in him as to what was going on at leadership level, knowing it would appear as if her own father - by having Barratt sound out Anthony behind her back - did not even trust her, his own daughter completely. And Sarah was left asking herself if this indeed was the case? Felix interrupted her troubled thoughts. 'Our war with the British demands many sacrifices by us. Although I'd rather not, for Anthony is indeed a dear friend to me, I am prepared to end my contact with him.' Sarah forced a smile, and careful not to expose her own dilemma, affirmed, 'It will be best for us all.'

They proceeded to drink their cooled tea; Felix, wondering how he was to cut Anthony adrift; Sarah, how she was to confront father over what Felix had disclosed.

Sean Mor was unable to provide an explanation to his suspecting daughter as she stood facing him in the privacy of the front room at the family home, her eyes frantically searching his for the truth or lies.

It was news to Sean Mor and quite concerning news that others had been interested in Anthony. But he was confident that once talking with Barratt the cause of the worrying development would be unearthed. Taking his daughter in his arms, Sean Mor endeavoured to reassure his eldest, his most trusted friend, 'Believe me, Sarah, it was not my doing. It's more likely that Barratt is being extra cautious about security. Normally it would be a good thing, but in this case, I'll have a quiet word, okay?'

Sarah looked deep into her father's eyes. 'Okay.' She accepted her father's rationalisation of the situation and would leave him to sort it out.

Sean Mor deliberated. 'With things moving forward as they are, we are all a little edgy at the moment. Everyone is watchful. No one is taking any chances. There's a lot at stake. So it's a good thing Felix is to do what has been instructed. Just make sure Anthony stays well out of harm's way. He's a good lad. With two sons tragically lost to his poor parents already, I wouldn't want him to get caught up in any of this.' Sean Mor smiled warmly. Sarah felt much easier now, having listened to her father's sympathetic and wise words. Holding his daughter close again, Sean Mor's smile hid those real concerns he privately held over what and whom may ultimately lay behind the business with Anthony. And already he was scheming up moves to get solid answers to solid questions.

Sitting up late after all others in the household had climbed the stairs for bed, Sean Mor, the IRA's Northern Command Commandant, put final detail to the plans in his head. Top-level meetings were to be held with brigade OCs across the North throughout the summer and into the winter months to assess how recruitment, rearming and organisation were taking shape. The first such meeting would be in Belfast at the end of the month. He would use the occasion to present some questions to one of the men attending as to his interest in Anthony Brennan, demonstrated in a manner which risked blowing the cover of the IRA's biggest asset in the six counties – namely, Felix Gresham, and what he stood to deliver to the IRA.

Felix asked Anthony to wait over after closing time. Noting a lack of conversation from Felix throughout the evening, Anthony knew something was up. He suspected Felix was sore at him for not being in lately. But he was confident that Felix would understand his obligations to Sarah, now that they were courting steadily. And only for Sarah having an early night, he most probably would not have been in the Gresham Bar that night either.

    Bolting shut the front door behind the last patron out, and with Bernadette retiring early to her bed, Felix wasted no time in setting about the unenviable task beckoning, but only after pouring himself a very large whiskey. He joined Anthony in his usual corner, that first snug over by the front door. Knowing there was no getting out of it, that what he was about to do, had to be, Felix sat down and gulped a large mouthful of whiskey. It was a little Dutch courage he drew on now. Looking Anthony straight in the face, Felix said, 'Anthony, what do you really think of me as a person?' Taken aback somewhat by the directness of the question, Anthony hesitated to gather his thoughts. Felix persisted, 'C'mon … I'm serious.'

    By the expression on his face, Anthony knew Felix was indeed serious. Without further thought, Anthony spoke his mind and heart. 'I consider you to be my best friend … a decent, generous man, who has helped me no end since I arrived in this town. I respect you for the person you are.'

    There was a momentary silence before Felix responded. 'I think all of that and more of you, Anthony.' Felix hesitated before delivering the final verbal punch. 'You must believe me when I say to you, that what I ask of you this night, I ask out of consideration for you and your future. And if you do respect me so, please do as I request without question, out of *that* respect ... will you?' Anthony knew he owed everything to this man. And uncanny as it was, even the friendship he'd had with Con. Without even pausing to think what might be asked of him, and prepared to do Felix's will, Anthony nodded in agreement. Felix lowered his voice. 'Anthony, what I have to say tonight is not to be repeated to anyone!'

'I understand,' replied Anthony, braced for whatever it was he was about to hear. Felix was careful not to reveal all.

'There are events about to unfold in this country ... *in this city*, which I will be party to. Those central to bringing about these events run the risk of lengthy terms of imprisonment, and even death, as do their associates, however innocent they may be. Do you follow me?' Anthony had a fair idea. 'Yes. I'm listening.' Felix was pleased at this, but it would not make what he was about to say any easier. 'I have to ask you then, to walk out of here tonight, never to return until the day is ours.' There was so much more which Felix wanted to say, but could not.

Anthony's mind was in turmoil. Felix, as good to him as any brother could be, was lost to him forever, he feared. Anthony knew he had better go, for both their sakes. He stood and extended his hand. Felix stood too then and shook Anthony's hand boldly. Words would not come for either one of them. Anthony turned and, without looking back, walked out of the bar through its side door.

For Felix it could not have been done any other way. There could be no false pretence behind it. He had to tell it the way it was. Sarah had agreed. They both respected Anthony too much. Felix's only hope now was that Anthony would never discover Sarah's hand in developments, nor indeed her involvement in that very same cause.

Chapter Eleven

The IRA's Belfast Brigade staff, consisting six men, all in their late thirties to early forties gathered around the kitchen table in a safe house in the upper Falls to deliver verbally their respective reports to their Northern Command Commandant, Sean Mor. Like them, he was gravely depressed by the sad state of the Belfast Battalions. The low number of republican activists in the city was demoralising. Opting on this occasion to keep his innermost thoughts on the matter and the wider implications to himself, he swiftly brought the meeting to a close. The brigade adjutant, Frank Barratt, issuing commands in Gaelic, brought the parade to attention and to salute the senior rank. The parade was then dismissed. Sean Mor was quick to advise Barratt and the brigade OC, Fergal McHugh, to remain with him after the others - leaving at intervals two at a time by the back door -

had gone. Alone, the three men sat again around the table, Sean Mor at the head, Barratt to his right, McHugh on his left. Both brigade staff officers appeared a little nervous as they awaited their senior rank's address.

His voice calm, Sean Mor inquired point-blank, 'When was the last time either of you had contact with Felix Gresham?' Sean Mor saw Barratt shuffle uneasily in his seat. Barratt knew McHugh would now also be annoyed to learn that he had said nothing to him on the matter of his recent visit to the barman, and while fully aware of the weight McHugh carried with his rank, he knew also that in comparison to that of Sean Mor, McHugh was a lightweight. Sean Mor was a leviathan in being ruthless in his determination to get to the truth of the matter, and in getting his way, while keeping a cool head. This is why Sean Mor held the rank he did and not McHugh, although McHugh had been in the running for it on the violent death of their predecessor. Knowing which of the two he would prefer not to be in disfavour with, Barratt delayed no further with his answer. He looked Sean Mor straight in the eye when speaking. 'I met with Felix New Year's Day.'

'Where and for what reason?' Sean Mor fired immediately.

Barratt had not anticipated Sean Mor discovering his brief visit to Felix Gresham and feared what may be on being as truthful as he could with his answer, both for his own sake and not least young Stack, who had simply followed orders.

'I called on him at the bar. I felt that I needed to know the identity of someone who had appeared on the scene suddenly.'

'Go on.' Sean Mor probed.

McHugh was much excited by this sudden and unexpected development and Barratt's apparent embarrassment in the face of being challenged so, and in front of him. He sensed that he might yet be presented with a gift opportunity to win Barratt over against Sean Mor, if Barratt was to be left feeling humiliated.

'I'd become suspicious of a stranger seen hanging around the picture house New Year's Eve, and later, talking to your daughter, Sarah. I'd suspected the man to be Special Branch seeking information from punters on events earlier in the cinema. So I had a volunteer follow him. The stranger was seen to go into Gresham's Bar. Our lad, not knowing of Felix Gresham's connection, followed, made a few discreet inquiries, then briefed me. I thought it best to check yer man out further, so I had a quiet word with Gresham the following night. As it turned out, I discovered the stranger to be an acquaintance of your daughter. Felix said everything was sound, so it ended there.'

Sean Mor had listened carefully to what Barratt had said and had also read his face closely. Knowing Barratt as he did, he knew the man to be telling the truth. But working to his ulterior agenda in asking Barratt to account for himself in front of McHugh, Sean Mor persisted in asking the question. 'Why not go straight to Sarah to learn the stranger's identity?'

Again Barratt shuffled uneasily in his seat. He was indeed embarrassed by the situation unfolding but more so surprised ... shocked, by Sean Mor's tactics. Knowing Sean Mor as he did, he had not expected to be slapped-down in front of another comrade, and McHugh of all people, whom Barratt had never held in high regard. Given past form, he would have expected Sean Mor to have had a quiet word with him on the matter, in private. Ruffled, Barratt somewhat blurted out his reply. 'I had not wanted to lose the stranger if Sarah had not known his identity. Nor had I wanted to affront Sarah in anyway.'

Sean Mor had already anticipated the answer almost word-for-word. Quietly pleased to have Barratt confirm that he had done what he had done simply because of his constant alertness to infiltration at such a high-risk time, Sean Mor was more relieved to discover that there had not been a more sinister motive behind Barratt's actions. He had suspected that McHugh, an adversary of sorts for as long as he could remember, was up to no good again. McHugh had challenged him for the command of republican prisoners during the war years, and for the rank he now held. More recently, McHugh had been at loggerheads with the Army Council's ruling that a renewed border campaign be launched once a fresh supply of arms was secured and the army itself rebuilt and organised. McHugh had argued bitterly for a 'province wide campaign' designed to provoke civil war. Sean Mor remained of the belief however that McHugh had an agenda of his own in pursuing his argument, but not by means of internal debate or diplomatic persuasion. He knew he would have to produce solid evidence that this was the case before the Army Council would sanction any adjudication of McHugh, for at the moment in time, they were sensitive to splitting the ranks and damaging morale further in the aftermath of a futile, counterproductive '30s campaign. And while acknowledging McHugh in the past as a 'bit of a hothead', Sean Mor knew the Army Council would otherwise be reluctant to get rid of someone who had such gusto and raw energy, and who was an established figurehead among the hard-line grassroots, not least in Belfast.

In considering all of this, Sean Mor had known he would have to play his hand very carefully indeed when dealing with McHugh. And he calculated that he had just played it, by deliberately giving McHugh cause to think that the potential existed to turn Barratt against him. Sean Mor knew that McHugh was aware that he, McHugh, could never have his own way in solely determining IRA action across the country without first wrestling control of the IRA in Belfast, and only with the support of Frank Barratt. Because of Barratt's sound republican principles and reputation as a firm but fair comrade, he was held in the highest regard by the IRA rank and file across the city, whereas McHugh was recognised as being more of a manipulator, a careerist. Sean Mor however, hoped that he, himself, was not so well-known. He purposely wished to remain low-key so to protect himself and the huge responsibility that came with his high-ranking status within the republican movement.

Sean Mor now moved to convince McHugh that such potential to turn Barratt did indeed exist, though he did not doubt one iota Barratt's steadfast loyalty to him. Sean Mor was about to put McHugh to the test when the continued existence of the IRA was itself soon to be put to the test. At a time when the IRA stood to come into ownership of the means to bring about major history-changing events that could at last see the republican movement realise its most cherished goal – a United Ireland, it was nevermore his responsibility to ensure that no possibility existed for dissidents to be at work within the army. If McHugh were to fail the test Sean Mor would personally see to it, that the name Fergal McHugh would be an abomination in the minds of republicans for all time.

Sean Mor donned the gravest of faces to reprimand Barratt in front of McHugh. 'Yes, we are all fully aware of the threat of infiltration. We cannot drop our guard for one moment, particularly now. But there are ways and means of ensuring security, and this is not through methods that, paradoxically, leave ourselves exposed. The fact is, the enemy's eyes and ears are everywhere. The risk of someone, somewhere, seeing or hearing something, no matter how minuscule, was too great a risk for you to take through approaching Gresham in the manner you did. No one can say otherwise.' Sean Mor paused deliberately, daring another to challenge him. McHugh's face was expressionless, Barratt's, sympathetic and understanding. Sean Mor continued to concentrate his eyes solely on Barratt. 'There is to be no further contact with Gresham without my expressed permission. As for the *stranger*, you now know him to be my daughter's boyfriend. He is not to be interfered with. He is, and will remain, a civilian.' And it was with more than a hint of dissatisfaction and resolve, with which Sean Mor closed. 'Finally, lines of communication between us must be open and clear. I will not tolerate ambiguous actions within this brigade or any other. I only hope that Felix Gresham's sense of trust and confidence in us has not been undermined through your stupidity, which must not be repeated!' Sean Mor looked searchingly into the harried face of Barratt, long and hard. Barratt felt his face burn red, and McHugh, careful not to show his glee, was lapping it up. While not enjoying Barratt's obvious discomfort, Sean Mor took quiet pleasure knowing that he could now sit back a while to await McHugh's move, for he doubted not that McHugh was scheming it, right at that very moment.

The meeting over, both Barratt and McHugh were on their feet and stood to attention as Sean Mor left the room and the house by its back door. With Sean Mor gone, McHugh leaned across the table to say meaningfully to Barratt, 'Sean Mor was out of fucking order talking to you like that in front of me. After all, you only did what you thought best.'

Barratt wasn't in the mood for McHugh's shit-stirring, which he knew the man to be good at. He just wanted to clear his head and quickly took his leave. McHugh grinned behind Barratt's back, knowing Barratt was proper fed-up.

Barratt felt his stomach churn on exiting the yard of the safe house into that back entry beyond, to find Sean Mor evidently awaiting him, and with a message at that.

'Meet me at eight tonight ... Falls Park.'

Looking on as the big man walked away confidently, a gravely worried Barratt was thinking to himself, The next six hours are gonna be fucking long ones!

Still quietly rejoicing at Sean Mor's lambasting of Barratt, McHugh sat down again at that table over which death, destruction and utter mayhem had been conspired and seen through in years past. Taking stock of the 'opportunity' presenting itself, he decided that firstly, he would string along meantime with the scheme of things planned by the Army Council - Sean Mor being one of their number. He would keep his head down and would let matters unfold regarding their planned arms shipment. If successful or not, then he would make his next move. Secondly, he was confident of the support from others when it came to the crunch, particularly that of former cellmates, now also of brigade staff rank in the border counties. They, like he, had grown increasingly impatient with the present day IRA leadership, their lethargy in mobilising a new campaign, which he so eagerly sought.

While the leadership in Dublin pontificated over a strategy for resuming the armed struggle, he had advocated an intensification of the armed campaign right across the six counties as opposed to the concentrated border campaign favoured by the leadership, one which was designed mainly at hitting the state's governmental and economic infrastructure. But it was McHugh's aspiration and that of comrades of similar thinking, to propel Northern Ireland into civil war through unleashing a rampant campaign of shooting and bombing, with not only government buildings, communications, police barracks, and military personnel targeted, but also industrial and commercial property, unionist politicians, judges and top civil servants, while carrying such a campaign to England was not ruled out. Through wreaking such bloody carnage with much ferocity would - McHugh believed firmly - ultimately force the British Government to relinquish their colonial stranglehold on his country. Not only did he seek to make Northern Ireland a heavy burden on the pockets of the British taxpayer, but a prize only to be had by the British at the expense of untold death and massive destruction. A price, he was sure, they were no longer willing to pay. To his thinking, such a campaign would see the British withdraw, the unionist veto smashed, and partition ended within five to ten years - just as his own children would be young men and women themselves, bearing him his first grandchildren, who would inherit the new thirty-two county Irish Republic. McHugh knew however, that before any of this would be possible, there remained the need to purge the ranks of the old blood in order for the more militant, radical breed to come forth. Through Sean Mor's shameless but much welcomed put-down of Barratt just, he was confident that the 'persuading' of Barratt to side with him had been made all the more easier. He also deduced that Gresham, left unsure perhaps as to who was in control of the IRA in light of the recent carry-on, would not interpret a change of leadership so dramatic. Thus would not recoil and withdraw his much sought after 'services'. McHugh was keen to keep Gresham and his contacts overseas in his back pocket.

McHugh's immediate interest however was with Barratt, whom he knew could make or break him - the whole scheme afoot. Knowing fully of his adjutant's popularity among the Belfast rank and file and that Barratt could deliver to him the whole brigade with a simple nod of the head, Barratt, in McHugh's calculation, was a key-player to have on-side. He knew that this would be far from easy, considering Barratt's steadfast loyalty to Sean Mor over the years. It was for this very reason that McHugh judged it crucial to the success of his plans that he persevere in gaining Barratt's confidence and support; and if Barratt were seen to be siding with him, then all others would fall in line. McHugh's dilemma now, was by what methods he could best achieve this. But he was confident in the knowledge that once presented with another opportunity to resume his undermining of Sean Mor and the gradual securing of Barratt's influence and control - greatly accelerated by Sean Mor's heavy-handedness that day - he would act swiftly, ruthlessly, to seize the leadership of the IRA in the North.

Chapter Twelve

Sean Mor had taken time to consider his own concerns over McHugh, who up to now had been an irritation more than anything else, but who he now suspected of planning a proactive campaign to agitate with possible dire effect for all. He was determined to nip this in the bud with the help of another. On spying that short, barrel-chested man and his dog come through the Falls Park main gate, Sean Mor stirred from the park bench a short distance away to join them.

The two IRA men, the smooth, white-haired Jack Russell waddling between them, walked briskly through the Falls Park, alive with folk on such a pleasant long summer evening - the eve of the cursed Twelfth of July. Courting couples, happy in loving embrace, sat on park benches with eyes only for each other. Carefree children played riotously in vast open spaces, and here and there elderly couples strolled arm-in-arm, enjoying the sweet scent rising from the assorted flower beds, the spectacular colour dazzling, the memories of blissful courting days spent here too, fondly recalled.

It's too nice a day to be plotting and scheming, thought Sean Mor. But the sudden intrusion of Orange flutes to the beat of a lambeg drum played enthusiastically by the 'Billy Boys' practising in the not-too-far distance, brought with it an air of tension descending gloomily on those only too aware of the rhetoric behind it as always at this time of the year - the marching season. On the green, a group of children, too young and innocent to know, marched mockingly in line to the stirring tune, like troops into battle. Looking on and feeling somewhat sad, Sean Mor thought, In time, you little souls will discover the brutal truth behind the drum beat. This only served to remind Sean Mor amid the splendour of his surroundings, that there remained the real need for such tensions to be removed from the society in which they all lived. This he believed to be only possible once the British withdrew and the conditions created for the people on both sides of the divide to pursue their own destiny, within a just and peaceful Ireland. So to matters in hand. Continuing, in the eyes of the unsuspecting observer, with their casual stroll through the park, the little dog straining at the leash, Sean Mor spoke to Barratt in a less authoritative tone in the hope that Barratt would sympathise with his predicament.

'Frank, while I meant what I said earlier about you meeting with Gresham in the circumstances you did, I was deliberately heavy-handed with you in front of McHugh.'

Barratt was mystified by Sean Mor's revelation. 'What's up, Sean?'

Sean Mor enlightened his friend. 'We both know that McHugh is too spontaneous at times. That while his heart may be in the right place, his head isn't. And as they say, patience is a virtue. He's lacking one or two virtues. And this concerns me, now that we are finalising details for the arms deal. So when the three of us met this afternoon, I laid the bait. I wanted McHugh to see a possible opening to winning you over to whatever it is he is scheming, for that I do not doubt. Consequently, Frank, I must ask you to keep a close eye on McHugh. I want to know immediately if he makes any moves that may, intentionally or not, jeopardize the whole show.'

Barratt's head was buzzing now. Sean Mor hadn't finished though. 'One other thing, what is the name of the volunteer who tailed Anthony that New Year's Eve?'

Still coming to terms with what had already been asked of him and knowing what he now did, Barratt volunteered the name without any fear for the safety of his raw recruit. 'Stack, Martin Stack.'

'What sort of character is he?' Sean Mor probed.

'He's a good lad.' Barratt affirmed.

'Good! Keep him pure. We may need him at a later date,' said Sean Mor. 'Meanwhile, if you need to contact me, call into the shop or to the house after dark. Goodnight Frankie.'

Feeling a little light-headed, Barratt sat on a vacant park bench nearby to collect his troubled thoughts. His old trusted four-legged friend threw its little muscly weight across its master's aching feet. Looking on to see Sean Mor cut a path home across the sprawling green in front, Barratt knew the man to be the smarter one, and he, for the time being, piggy in the middle. But there was no way he was going to disappoint the big man now. Bending forward to pat old faithful on the head, Barratt said, 'Ah, if only everyone was as loyal as you boy, we'd be all right.'

The glorious Twelfth had come to pass relatively peacefully for all. There had only been one reported skirmish at the end of the main parade from the city centre up through the Shankill. A few dozen Catholic boys had appeared in a side street just off the Lower Falls to taunt the Orangemen with an Irish Tricolour, waved antagonistically. The enraged mob of loyalists had broken away from the march to give pursuit. It was the elderly inhabitants of the street who'd paid the price, with bricks and bottles sent crashing through their windows by the vengeful mob.

Anthony was much surprised to hear Caithlin and Bridget reveal to Sarah in Aunt Bella's front room later that day, that they had been witness to the violence, having anonymously stood as spectators as the march had passed.

'Our Da would slaughter you if he knew you'd been on the Shankill today.' Sarah scolded, peeved at their stupidity. Caithlin sought to casually dismiss Sarah's fears.

'Ack sure, it was only a bit of a day out. Anyway, we were bored.'

The latter had Sarah jumping out of her seat and rolling up her sleeves to face her sisters, slouched on the sofa like spoilt children. Her voice restrained, but almost hysterical, she seethed, 'Bored you say! Well by Jesus we can soon cure that! Here's me exhausted, not a wink of sleep all night with Aunt Bella, and those bastards on their drums didn't help matters either, and this morning, pulling the gut out of myself washing soiled sheets and bandages. And what are you two doing? Standing, looking on at that shower causing a nuisance! Well, I'll tell you something, you can get that war paint off your faces and get your arses into that scullery! There's floors to be scrubbed and spuds peeled!'

Fearing that claws drawn were about to lash out, Anthony sought to calm the situation. 'Careful now girls, you'll wake the oul girl.'

'*Wake the oul girl*!' Sarah fumed. 'If Aunt Bella knew where these two so and so's have been today, she'd crawl out of that bed happily to scalp their arses. And if they don't shift themselves this instant, I might just shout her!' Sarah's threat was enough to make the younger two jump to it, their faces beetroot in colour on being put down so in front of

Anthony. He struggled to keep a straight face as they scurried out of the room.

'As for you, you great lump! Do your shirt up. We're going for a dander.' Sarah's wrath had Anthony promptly straightening himself in his chair.

As the courting couple walked out together they could hear the frantic scrubbing of potatoes behind them, and smell the carbolic soap begin to waft through from the scullery. Turning to Anthony then, Sarah said with a determined look, 'I only hope for their sake it was not my make-up they've used. If it is, I'll murder them!'

Anthony had never before seen this aggressive side of Sarah, the way she'd used her face and body so dramatically to get her message across. If he was ever to suffer a woman's tantrums in married life, he wanted it to be Sarah's. On jokingly revealing this to Sarah, stretched beside him on the park's grass, Sarah let a yelp of laughter escape and her body shook as she went into a fit of hysterics. With heads turning to investigate, Anthony was left a little embarrassed. Composing herself, and still on the flat of her back, Sarah turned her face toward Anthony. A laughter tear streamed from an eye. 'Whatever you do, don't get proposing to me today. Not on the Twelfth of July of all days. Aunt Bella would never forgive you.' Anthony smiled broadly; his heart was filled with joy. In that moment he knew she would indeed be that very woman. He raised himself on one elbow to lean over Sarah, and kiss her passionately.

The loss of Felix's companionship left Anthony feeling very low in spirit at times, which he tried to hide when in the company of Sarah. In slowly coming to terms with the tragic death of his brothers, and just that of Con's, Anthony was determined not to lose Sarah, not ever. He knew that if this were to happen, it would be the end of his world.

Towards the end of the summer he felt the time was right to ask Sarah to marry him. She had responded warmly to his hinting of it. He feared that if they could not be together soon as man and wife, then the strain of not being able to explore their feelings, emotions, and bodily urges for each other fully, would ultimately force them apart. He'd respected Sarah's wish to hold dear her virginity until married, not least due to the fact that when they were intimate with each other, it was most often in her great-aunt's home, and in his book, it would not be right to seduce each other under the old woman's roof, not least because the elder was so ill. And no matter how desperate his urges, Anthony had long been determined - even if opportunity arose - not to make love to a woman in some back alley or rat-infested air-raid shelter, despite the bragging by his workmates. He'd considered this to be demeaning to the act itself, and not least the participants.

It's damn bloody hard being a good Catholic boy, thought Anthony, hungrily eyeing his girl as she descended the stairs in Aunt Bella's as they prepared to go out on the town. Sarah looked as sensual as ever. The devil in him was stirring. But he was determined to do things right by Sarah. For Anthony now, it felt as though the little parcel he carried so excitedly was burning a hole in his jacket pocket. But the moment had not yet arrived.

Exiting the corner shop and lighting up his cigarette, Stack spied the courting couple turn and walk carefree along the opposite side of the Falls Road towards the city centre. His imagination stirred at the sight of Sarah in a new summer dress; his frustration over her heightened. He had been turning ideas over in his head as to how he could get the Free Stater offside, so to be in there with a chance. Looking on at the happy couple, Stack thought aloud. 'Someday ... just maybe.'

They had danced the night away beneath the mirror ball as the twelve-piece Big Time Show Band made it a night never to forget. Drenched in sweat, their feet aching, Anthony and Sarah now sat on the top deck of the bus admiring the deep red skyline over the Black Mountain as they journeyed up the Falls. Arriving back at Aunt Bella's - whom Caithlin had been sitting that night - Sarah and Anthony, on tiptoe, made it to the front room without disturbing those sleeping upstairs. The streetlight falling into the darkened room reflected on both their faces as they snuggled up on the sofa. Sarah slipped off her stilettos quietly. Without talking, they embraced and kissed passionately, their mouths wet and hot, their chests pressed hard against each other's. Sarah could feel Anthony's heart thump against hers, his hands nervous and clammy on the nape of her bare back, where her dress was cut in a 'V' shape. Breaking for breath, she commented jokingly on his condition. 'If I have this affect on you Anthony, I think your days are numbered.' They laughed quietly. Then Anthony seized the moment. 'The affect you have on me Sarah, results in this.' Anthony produced the small parcel from his jacket pocket and placed it in the palm of Sarah's right hand. He saw her face alive with curiosity as she carefully unwrapped the parcel turn to an expression of quiet amazement. The tasteful crystal diamond ring glinted in the light from the street lamp beyond the window.

'Oh, Anthony, it's so beautiful!' Sarah's voice trembled with emotion. So too did Anthony's now.

'Sarah.'

Sarah looked Anthony in the eye; her body shook in excited anticipation of what he was about to say.

'Will you marry me?'

The moment's silence was killing him slowly.

For Sarah, a dream had come true. There was only one answer she could possibly give.

'Yes. I'll be very happy to marry you, Anthony. I love you.'

Neither of them slept in their beds that night. In the single bed in the spare room at Aunt Bella's, Sarah counted the hours until dawn broke and for the first stirring of the others, so that she could share the wonderful news. On doing so, both Caithlin and Aunt Bella shed tears of joy with her on top of the big bed. Aunt Bell made the younger ones laugh heartily when saying, 'Well, I'd better get myself in shape for the big day. You never know, I might be lucky enough to catch the bride's bouquet.'

Anthony had tossed and turned all night, his mind reliving over and over again the moment Sarah had said 'Yes'. He tried to imagine how it would be on the wedding day, to actually become husband and wife.

It was just before dawn when he had eventually drifted to sleep, praying that he would not awake to discover it all to be a cruel dream.

Chapter Thirteen

Meeting with the County Fermanagh IRA brigade staff in an isolated thatched cottage to give and receive their respective briefings, Sean Mor had his work cut out keeping their grievances at bay. While the men from Tyrone - with whom he'd met two weeks previous - had him worried, it was the eagerness of the Fermanagh men to pursue the war 'here and now,' which unnerved him.

The O'Rourke brothers, small, wiry, impatient types, with eyes full of malice, were deemed to be stirring it to Sean Mor's thinking. It was evident to him that the two were itching to live up to their late father's fame among republican circles. Dan 'Mad' O'Rourke was reputed to have struck terror into the very souls of Black 'n' Tans and Free Staters alike, with his blazing Thompson machinegun. The brooding, unnerving brothers had given Sean Mor the roughest time to date. Their immediate OC, Liam Sexton, the expressionless, heavily-set man, had apparently fallen under their spell too. He demanded also that the leadership bring forward the armed struggle as, in his own ominous words, 'patience among the rank and file is waning.'

The argument, *the fact*, that there was insufficient resources by way of weaponry and indeed manpower at their disposal collectively as a movement - nowhere more so than in the very same county - had saved the day. The voice of the other three more moderate brigade staff lending albeit half-hearted acceptance to this reality, had assisted Sean Mor to rest his case. Sean Mor's guarantee however that the Army Council were presently actively exploring 'ways and means' of overcoming the disadvantages highlighted, had the Fermanagh men sitting on the edge of their seats. But playing his cards deliberately close to his chest for security reasons, Sean Mor did not and would not elaborate. He had called for 'cool heads' and 'patience' before taking his leave. The heated meeting had closed with lukewarm farewells.

Throughout the return journey to Belfast later that day, Sean Mor, a back seat passenger in a trustee's car, contemplated what may transpire from his meeting with Felix Gresham, due back from England the following day. Everything that he had guaranteed that night and to others over the summer months, hung in the balance, dependant on Gresham's negotiation skills.

Two days later, in the shadow of the picturesque Mourne Mountains, Sean Mor felt the cold cutting wind blowing in off the Irish sea scrape the back of his throat and fill his congested lungs as he walked briskly along the seaside town's golden beach. The sea wind revived him greatly and was much needed. The past months had been heavy going with meetings on top of meetings, loaded with terse conversation, in which every word he uttered had to be carefully considered and delivered. He'd had to calm, reassure and pacify others, while at times applying on those more extreme elements the full weight of authority his position within the movement afforded him. All that he had said to carry those brooding elements and the mainstream with him over this time was rooted in the anticipated outcome of the crucial meeting now. If proving fruitful, it could also quite possibly save his neck and, not least, allow him to relax with his wife and family - if only for a little while. It was with hopes raised that Sean Mor approached that other solitary figure on the beach walking towards him.

The Belfast republican and the Liverpudlian sympathiser boldly shook hands at the water's edge in self-congratulation. The planning and scheming, the secret rendezvous and slipped messages between the two over the last eighteen months had paid off. Felix Gresham had successfully made contact and secured a deal with those Left Wing sources in central Europe through trusted intermediaries - associates of his late father - who, for a substantial financial return, would deliver all but a few of the arsenal of weapons and munitions determined by the Quartermaster General. The arms list had been concealed beneath the lid to the shoebox presented to Felix, together with the donated bars of chocolate, by the Belfast man's daughter on Christmas Eve past. The huge shipment, some fifty tons of Eastern Bloc manufactured rifles, machineguns, pistols, revolvers, mortars and shells, landmines, grenades, plastic explosives and detonators, together with enough ammunition to refill every magazine clip a hundred times or more, could be shipped to and landed in Ireland in less than twelve months. It was down to the IRA to make ready final logistic arrangements to receive, transport and conceal the consignment once landed. It would be a major task, demanding a massive effort from the many planning, coordinating and executing such an operation. The greatest challenge presented being that of maintaining secrecy and security. So much so, that the 'Go-between', Felix Gresham, had never, would never, disclose to anyone, the name of his contacts either in England or abroad or where exactly the shipment originated.

Sean Mor considered this sensible. He was only too aware of the real risk of treachery and betrayal from within the movement. He had served twelve years incarceration to date because of an informer. But at least now, there was one less tout to worry about.

Once consulting with the Army Council, Sean Mor would meet with Felix again, to finalise arrangements for payment and delivery of the goods. Business completed, they parted company. Walking just a short distance back along the beach, a shout from behind had Sean Mor turning again to face Felix.

'I just want to know how my friend Anthony is keeping?' Understanding the other's interest still, Sean Mor replied reassuringly, 'He's very well. You know, he is due to marry my daughter next spring ... April in fact.' Felix smiled in approval. 'That's grand news. I hope it all goes well for you and your good wife. Anthony's a good lad. He deserves a woman such as Sarah. Let us hope their life together will be in more peaceful times.' Sean Mor nodded in agreement. Felix turned and carried on his way.

Felix's sincere words had Sean Mor thinking of the loving young couple, and was even more determined to see that their life together would indeed be a happy and peaceful one.

Number 72 Leger Street was crammed tight with invited folk as the official engagement party for Sarah and Anthony got underway. And what a party it promised to be with it coinciding with Halloween night. The good humoured row rising in the street beyond with the bonfire at its mouth being lit and the exploding fireworks echoing along the hallway of the McParland home, brought an air of excited calamity to the occasion. As another rebellious jig blasted out on the relic of a gramophone - passed down through the generations - mill girls, carpenters, neighbours and relatives on Sarah's side, all queued up to catch a glimpse of the beautiful ring which Sarah displayed proudly, leaving many a girl envious, and Anthony's workmates determined to go one better when their day came around. Anthony's other invited guest, McNab, congratulated his friend on a 'wise choice of ring', and struggled to ask permission to kiss the bride-to-be. Anthony gave the nod and McNab, yet to find himself a girl, sheepishly kissed Sarah on the cheek and wished her 'good luck' for the future.

Sarah's parents and sisters were busy in the scullery, ensuring platters and drinking glasses were well topped-up. Aunt Bella, her ulcerated legs a little better that day and content with her glass of sherry, sat up one corner of the kitchen surveying, with amusement, the goings-on all around her, in particular the antics of the younger generation.

Seeking to remain in the background as best as possible, Anthony was a little saddened that his best friends, Con and Felix, could not be part of it all, nor anyone from home. Mother's last letter had worried him greatly. It was clearly evident to him that Seamus and Owen's loss was slowly beginning to hit hard those at home. The fact also that there had been no contact from Christy was not helping matters. With the tragedy extensively reported by the press and media, Christy was sure to know of it. This obviously added to the family pain; mother and father no doubt left feeling that their eldest son cared not.

Anthony had his own thoughts as to the reasons for Christy's non-appearance. He suspected Christy still held bad memories - as Anthony once had - of home: that meagre, painstaking existence, and not least fears over having to face father again. Anthony only hoped that Christy would find the courage to do so one day, and soon, before it was too late. A voice calling out to Anthony from among the throng drew him back to the moment in time. It was that of a workmate. 'C'mon Anthony. Get yourself over here! There's a girl dying to be introduced to me.' Anthony did not wish to be a spoilsport and so found himself involved in a little matchmaking.

Apart from Sean Mor and Anthony, all others in the household had gone to their beds, Sarah to Aunt Bella's as routine. The clearing up had been left until morning; the presence of some fifty to sixty party revellers having been in through the house, much in evidence. It had been a truly enjoyable night, and both Anthony and Sarah were left delighted by it all. None had enjoyed themselves more than Sean Mor, the life and soul of events all evening. He was so happy for Sarah and his future son-in-law.

Now, alone together in the small hours, both men sat by the glowing coals in the front room, easy with the other's company and content with a half bottle of Irish whiskey still to be drunk. It was the first time both men had opportunity to talk privately to one another, what with Sean Mor always darting off to one GAA meeting after another.

'The summer months are always a busy time of the year for the association' assured Sarah many a time, not wanting Anthony to think her father was cold-shouldering him. The late night conversation convinced Anthony he hadn't been. It was free and easy. Anthony was impressed and surprised somewhat by the other man's humour - intelligent as it was. They reflected on and shared life experiences, for Sean Mor, those safe enough to talk about, leaving some nineteen years of his life out of it; the years spent lying in wait behind stonewalls and in ditches along the border in ambushing British soldiers and policemen; the days and nights on the run, sleeping in hay sheds and at times under the stars between moving from safe house to safe house; the years interned in the Curragh Camp by the Free Staters, then Derry and Crumlin Road Jails in the North. Ironically, it had been while interned in the South that had proven to be the most difficult for him. The conditions in the Curragh had been appalling and the treatment of republican prisoners brutal, administered by fellow Irishmen, once active IRA men years earlier before Collins had signed the Treaty.

That which he could talk about, Sean Mor did so passionately and humorously accordingly. Between military campaigns he had walked from Belfast to the Hill of Howth and would never forget the wonderful people he had met, ordinary decent folk, Protestant and Catholic alike, who had fed and watered him along the way, and they themselves with very little to spare. It had been a blissful summer that year. He had seen such beauty, set in glens and valleys, by riverbanks and streams, from mountaintops and seashores, in fields of barley, and all along the endless winding roads. There had been misty dawns and foggy dews and sunsets so spectacular they had moved him to tears. He'd had a love affair that summer. It had been with that splendour all about him. And his love for his country had only grown more intense, so much so, he had been, and remained, willing to die for it.

Anthony had seen the passion in the face of the man opposite as he had spoken of his country. A country the elder obviously loved a great deal more than he. This was evident from the fact that not only had Sean Mor tread the long road in determined discovery of its beauty, but seemingly had an insatiable hunger for its culture and traditions, its language, music and dance. Each and all of which the elder held an envious appreciation for, and discipline in.

Anthony felt somewhat in the shadow of the man's experience - only partly revealed - when telling of his own, hoping Sean Mor would find even half the interest in his life story.

It was Anthony's revelation of his experience at Edenderry Abbey which had Sean Mor most interested, though not in the bizarre behaviour of the Englishman, Colonel Cartwell, but rather the fact that the same man had possession of such an impressive collection of war memorabilia: revolvers, pistols, and rifles in particular. Anthony commented innocently on how the old soldier would spend endless hours cleaning the weapons, and how the workforce had all been uneasy consequently in view of the old boy's odd murmuring and antics on occasion. Sean Mor laughed along with Anthony, who saw the silly side of it now, but with alert ears Sean Mor had heard every word. Weighing up the risk of someone misinterpreting - innocently or otherwise - his future son-in-law's 'involvement' with the Englishman, a former soldier in his Majesty's forces, Sean Mor felt the need to casually ask, if Anthony had revealed the same to anyone else? Anthony said, 'No.' Sean Mor now sought to impress on Anthony, rather candidly, the need not to disclose *that* which he had just revealed, to another living soul.

'It is in all our interests Anthony, that you breathe not a word of this to anyone.'

Not fully appreciative of the implicit warning contained therein, Anthony promised he would not.

They had drunk the bottle dry and the fire had died a death by the time Sean Mor went to his bed. Anthony, at the behest of the man of the house, stretched himself out as best he could on top of the big comfy sofa in the front room, and with Sean Mor's heavy winter coat draped over him, fell asleep without effort.

Arriving in Dublin by train a week later, Sean Mor knew the procedure well. He would spend the first hour casually wandering through the large shopping stores on and around O'Connell Street, careful to watch out for possible tails, and not only those locally based. It was known to the IRA that RUC Special Branch would pursue a lead over the border and far into the South. It was also common knowledge to their own intelligence for the Special Branch at Dublin Castle to look the other way in face of such incursions - such was the tacit collaboration between the two states who had a common enemy in the IRA.

Confident he was not being tailed, Sean Mor made his way leisurely to the select bookshop in a side street, only a short distance from where, thirty-four years earlier, the republican leadership had proclaimed themselves the Provisional Government of the Irish Republic; an Irish Republic to which he and his comrades awaiting him deemed themselves to be the rightful inheritors. The men were the successors in hiding to the Dail Eireann of 1918.

Reaching the side entrance, Sean Mor knocked the Georgian-style door five times in rapid succession. He was ushered into a back kitchen room by a familiar face who quickly checked the alley, left then right, before closing the door. Sean Mor was the last to join the others gathered, having journeyed the furthest distance. He took up his place at one end of the long wooden table to complete the eight man Army Council staff.

Seated at the head of the table, the Chief of Staff, small, stout, and bespectacled, his golden wavy hair rapidly receding, was a local man and was the owner of the bookshop. Being in his late fifties, he was a veteran of all the major military campaigns against the British since 1916. He had been only a few years short in age in order to play a fighting role that historical Easter day, but nonetheless had been recognised for his steadfast contribution to the fight over the ensuing days. As a Fianna boy, he had steely dodged bullets and shells to run the line in passing messages between the G.P.O. and outlying posts. He had known them all: Connolly, Pearse, MacDonagh, and Clarke among them. He had fought the Black and Tans as a lieutenant in the Dublin Brigades under Collins' command. During the civil war he had hid in the Dublin Mountains alongside his comrades Lacey and Breen. They had been hunted mercilessly by the Free Staters and he had only been spared summary execution when captured, as the captain leading the enemy forces had been his elder brother. Nevertheless, he had been imprisoned for the last year of the war; his brother being shot dead in an IRA ambush three days before hostilities ended.

The veteran had rapidly risen through the ranks over the years and had been Chief of Staff for the last five, which had been a period of reforming and re-organising the movement, much depleted and demoralised after what was considered largely, a non productive '30s campaign - the bombings in England bringing the wrath of public condemnation at home and abroad down heavily upon their shoulders. Under the present leadership, a new campaign was yet to be launched. They all had an active part in planning and preparing it. They all eagerly anticipated the day of its commencement. One of them though, knowing what he did, knew that day was not yet near, despite the good news he carried.

Sean Mor and the other six subordinates, a mixture of school teacher and student priest look-alikes, finely rigged out in their Sunday best, and who held rather mundane jobs or none at all, all attended attentively on being addressed by the Chief of Staff, who had all their respect and recognition. His soft, deliberate voice, the calm collected mannerism and grandfather state of dress, were so disarming to others but so intense for these men, for they knew of the deadly potential behind it all.

'Comrades, let us proceed with business.' The Chief of Staff was keen to attend to such directly. 'Sean, I believe you have some news to share with us.'

Sitting at the opposite end of the table, Sean Mor held court. On delivering his brief on his most recent communication with Felix Gresham - whose name remained anonymous with acceptance to the Chief of Staff - all others shifted excitedly in their seats and there were utterances of 'Well done' and 'We're on our way.'

The Quartermaster General, a squat, quietly spoken fifty-something father of eight, was a little dejected. The prospect of obtaining flame-throwers and bazookas as part of the arsenal appeared remote. However the much taller Adjutant General sought to reassure him and spoke ever so seriously. 'Fear not comrade, there will be enough explosives regardless to shift that missus of yours out of bed in the mornings.' They all laughed then, a little humour not going amiss even with the Chief of Staff, who had difficulty keeping a serious face. But the merriment was short-lived on Sean Mor completing his report with a strong recommendation to all. 'In view of the dire state of the northern brigades, I call for any new military offensive to be put on hold until such time that there are sufficient numbers of volunteers available to fire the very guns of which we are about to take ownership.'

With the earlier uplifting news brought into check somewhat, all others were in agreement with Sean Mor that the resumption of the armed struggle be delayed until such time that the northern brigades were fully ready for war. While a major recruitment drive north of the border was essential, what was now of prime importance to the IRA leadership, was acquiring the finance to pay for the military hardware on offer to them. Tentative groundwork had already been undertaken with a view to a number of armed raids against banks and post offices in the South.

The Chief of Staff ordered the raids to go ahead at the earliest opportunity, stressing that only 'the best of men' be used, who were to deny any IRA involvement if captured. All monies seized were to be deposited with the Director of Finance in preparation for payment. No operations of this nature were to be carried out in the North as it was considered to do so might overtly raise the suspicions of the enemy there.

The Quartermaster General was instructed by the Chief of Staff to pinpoint potential locations for arms dumps throughout the twenty-six counties. All dumps were to be solidly constructed bunkers beneath ground level on accessible land adjacent to primary and secondary routes, so to allow for easy and swift transportation of weapons northward for use along the border. A tunnelling team of highly trusted men was to be selected from the battalion staff ranks south of the border and work was to begin once the worst of the winter was over. Although twelve months seemed a long time, all knew it would not be long in passing and agreed unanimously that preparations to receive the shipment be made ready as from that day.

Sean Mor was instructed by his senior rank to liaise with the Director of Intelligence to establish suitable landing sites along the east and/or west coast. The QM General was also to be consulted with regards to the hasty transportation of weapons away from landing sites. The Adjutant General and the Director of Propaganda and Education were to place themselves at the disposal of their comrades. There was much to be done. Everyone would be kept busy. Seeking to maintain the momentum of developments underway, the Chief of Staff assured all that the proposed border campaign would commence as soon as everything was in place - men, weapons and munitions. This was a further boost to morale and all voiced support to it, while acknowledging that there remained much to be undertaken meantime.

Bringing the meeting to a close with no other business being raised, the Chief of Staff had the final word. 'It is imperative that there be no leak as to the arms shipment, nor the proposed border campaign, delayed though it may be. A veil of secrecy must descend on our plot. When the time is right, information must only be given in segments to the select few. Other than us, no one should ever hold all the pieces to the jigsaw. To do otherwise, will be to give the enemy the full picture. The element of surprise is to win. Let us not compromise this at anytime.'

They left the bookshop as they'd come in, in ones and twos at intervals, leaving the host to return to his books and to tend to those customers who would call to the shop after lunch. The eight men would not meet again until the spring of the following year.

Sean Mor had deliberated long and hard as to whether to have a word with the QM General about a possible raid on Edenderry Abbey, to seize the substantial arsenal there, but decided against it. Apart from the very reason considered on that night of revelation by Anthony, he considered the risk of Anthony being traced by the Special Branch through follow-up inquiries as too great, not only in face of his relationship to Anthony, but more so in consideration for what Felix Gresham had hinted at that day on the beach in County Down, when inquiring about Anthony's welfare.

In order to fully protect his daughter and son-in-law to be, in light of things to come, Sean Mor realised the need to have a heart-to-heart with Sarah as to her role in future developments, if at all, now that the day fast approached when her loyalty and devotion would be obliged to another man, first and foremost.

Chapter Fourteen

With the Christmas celebrations of 1950 coming to pass peacefully for all, and with Anthony now feeling truly one of the McParland family through the generous hospitality bestowed on him, it did not come completely as a shock to him to hear Sarah request that the marriage be postponed until the following summer or autumn, due, not only to the deterioration in Aunt Bella's health, but equally disturbing, a seemingly dramatic and sudden decline in that of Sean Mor's. It had been evident to those closest to Sean Mor, that prior to Christmas he had appeared washed out. And despite, in particular, his wife's protestations at his ceaseless 'running about', he had run himself into the ground. Now, it was not uncommon to see the man, normally rarely seen indoors, shuffle around the house in his slippers and with a hot water bottle clutched to his stomach, for the violent bilious attacks he was having day and night left him exhausted. Yet he would not thoroughly rest as others prescribed. 'Visitors' came regularly for private audiences with him in his 'surgery' - the front room where no one dare enter when in use.

It was a casual slip of the tongue by the man's wife one day when in conversation with a neighbour on the front doorstep, which served to give Anthony an insight into the man's troubled past.

'The kickings he got when interned are the cause of this. It's a wonder he's got any stomach left after what they put in his food ... smashed light bulbs and cockroaches. Animals, that's what they are. Animals!' The neighbour sighed sympathetically. 'We can only hope and pray he'll be back on his feet soon Missus Mc, and with the help of God he will.'

Now knowing an aspect of Sean Mor's life which the man himself, and his daughter, had kept hidden from him, and assuming they had done so because they wished to leave the troubled past behind them, Anthony would simply be counting down the days until the wedding could finally be held. No event, past or present, nor the actions of anyone, dead or alive, would deter him from ultimately marrying the girl he adored.

Sarah just did not consider it right to proceed with the wedding when loved ones were so unwell. She needed her father to give her away, and he had promised to walk her down the aisle. Now, so weak was he, he could barely stand.

Aunt Bella was also determined to see the grand day. She knew it might well be the last special occasion she'd live to see. Knowing this also, Sarah and the rest of the family were determined to get her to the church. They rallied to nurse her and father round-the-clock, so that together they'd all see the day come to pass.

Anthony saw little of Sarah some weeks throughout the spring and into the summer months of 1951. She spent every spare minute with those frail family members whom she loved so very much. Not at all aggrieved at this, knowing Sarah would do the same for him if need be, Anthony admired her caring qualities and sought to lend help in whatever way he could, if it was only by staying away for the meantime.

The road to recovery for Sean Mor was not only mapped out through a determined will to walk his daughter down the aisle, but also the need to be, and to be seen to be, fit enough mentally and physically to keep appointment with other pressing business. He had somehow kept a hold on army related matters from his convalescent fireside armchair with the added and much valued help of Barratt, who had come and gone quietly, discreetly, through the back door to No72 over the long months. Now though, there was another crucial engagement he had to personally attend to. And thankfully, much recovered, he set out to keep to it with renewed steely resilience.

The IRA Army Council sat in session once again, same faces, same venue. There was an excited buzz around the table as the seven field officers in turn reported developments since they'd last met to the eighth man who sat in his place of authority.

The press in the Free State had screamed alarm over the months at the series of armed holdups that had been described by one leading newspaper as *Subversive Monetary Rape*. The Director of Communications had covertly combated the theory that *diehard republican elements are behind the holdups to finance the resurrection of the IRA*, by putting it about among certain circles in the press and media, sympathetic to the republican cause, that a new, younger breed of criminals unknown to the Gardai Special Branch had been behind the raids. This had, at first, balanced the picture, then eventually won the argument with, ironically, existent and former statesmen stating publicly that the IRA was a 'spent force' and could not organise such a series of 'sophisticated raids'.

The republican leadership had experienced quiet satisfaction over this, knowing substantial funds were available to finance the arms deal and men in sufficient number north and south of the border to carry the armed struggle forward. Preparations to receive and conceal the weapons were nearing completion also, with only a few of the more comprehensive bunkers yet to be sealed against damp and vermin. This series of covert operations over the months had placed an immense physical demand on the tunnelling teams involved. They had worked throughout the night, most often with the aid of paraffin lamps and torches, to dig and shift in total, many tons of earth, and sand, for some of the major bunkers had been ingeniously installed in sand-dunes well above the tide mark on several beaches along the northwest coastline, in Counties Sligo and Donegal.

The Quartermaster General had made ready for the transportation of the shipment from landing sites to the dumps. A hundred men with scores of vehicles stood on standby, ready for the word, which he in turn awaited from the Adjutant General and Director of Intelligence. They were yet to decide whether to use one or more of the half-dozen landing sites short-listed. For obvious reasons this information would not be revealed to the QM General until the eleventh hour, and who would only transmit the same information to section leaders at the last minute. Secrecy and security remained of paramount importance. So far it seemed to be holding well.

It was agreed then that the plan was to proceed with Sean Mor, once identifying the landing sites to be used, contacting his 'source'. The source would then travel to England at the earliest opportunity to finalise plans for delivery of the shipment.

At the Chief of Staff's behest it was accepted by all, that half the total sum of money payable be forwarded to the suppliers via the source, with the remainder to follow on delivery and receipt of the goods. But all were then taken aback somewhat by the Chief of Staff issuing directives to the Director of Intelligence and Quartermaster General, to liaise with each other and examine the potential for a series of raids on weapons and munitions stores, military or otherwise, in the six counties, and England and Wales, to be executed if 'Plan A' failed. This action, he suggested, would serve to avoid a potentially destructive outcome - the complete fragmentation and collapse of morale within the movement, and probably the entire movement itself, by enabling the proposed border campaign to go ahead as planned, albeit a year to eighteen months behind schedule. No one was left in any doubt that things were to move forward at an energetic and earnest pace. Either way, a new chapter in the bloody, violent struggle for Irish independence was about to be written.

It had been a brief meeting between Sean Mor and Felix Gresham, held inconspicuously on the seafront of the busy little postcard town of Ballycastle, North Antrim, an hour's scenic drive from Belfast. Felix was to sail to England early in July to meet up with his two contacts there, senior rank merchant fleet export/import officials. These men would, assured Felix, finalise arrangements for the shipment to be delivered and off-loaded from a cargo ship destined first for Belfast, then Dublin. The location for the proposed rendezvous, ten miles off the southeast coast of Arklow Head, County Arklow, appeared ideal. If calculations proved right, the three deep hull trawlers would take on board and bring ashore the fifty tons of stock in one run under cover of darkness. The month of September was earmarked for the drop. Only a specific date remained to be fixed, which Felix was to confirm on his return.

Sean Mor informed Felix that the down payment money would be delivered to him the day before he set sail, and left Felix with a sobering thought on taking his leave. 'If these associates of yours do not deliver, and do a runner with the money, you and I will not see the summer out.'

The bright, hot July sunshine brought a new lease of life to Aunt Bella who had spent the last three months confined to her bed. Now however, she was to be found regularly sitting on a low stool by the front doorstep to her house, seldom letting young or old pass by without a conversation of sorts striking up. Everyone was delighted to see the old girl back to form and in her expected place. Ever since she was suddenly widowed at the age of thirty, this was, as it had been each summer for the past fifty years or so, the ageing woman's favourite entertainment, particularly the antics of the street's children in whom she found much comfort - her first and only child had been stillborn a month after her husband's death from the cursed TB, all those years ago. Feeling burdened at being the reason why her great-niece had postponed her wedding in the spring, Aunt Bella urged Sarah to finalise arrangements, now that she was, as she put it reassuringly, 'on the mend and raring to go.'

At last convinced her aunt was not to give up the fight that easily, Sarah prepared the last of the invitations to be sent out. Relieved too that the big day was once again formally booked at the church, Anthony made his way along the Falls Road with a spring in his step to ask the only man he could to be his best man. Knocking upon a door, Anthony was hopeful that McNab would not let him down.

Being asked to be best man left McNab feeling a little nervous at the prospect of standing in the local church once again. It had been ten years since he had last set foot in the place, the day his father's remains had been removed from the side chapel in Saint Augustine's for burial up at Milltown. He had lost his faith that day at the graveside. He could not accept that a God of Mercy could let any child's parents die in such agony, and he first seeing and hearing it all at the age of eleven, when his mother had been sent home from the cancer ward to die. The consultant had told his father there was 'no hope' for the woman. Little had anyone known then that the widower too would be buried in the same grave only a short five years later. The loss of both parents, good living, hard working people, and so young of age, was too cruel a blow to be kind, despite the priest's efforts in vain to reassure young Joseph McNab that God only took the best early in life.

Out of a fondness for Anthony and respect for his neighbours the McParlands, in particular Sean Mor, who had taken a genuine interest in his own welfare all those years ago, McNab readily agreed to be best man. Anthony felt happily relieved. It was McNab who suggested they go to the pub on the corner for a jar, one for Anthony that was, his own pleasure being a glass of cream soda.

The drinks were on the house with McNab publicly announcing to the early evening regulars gathered in the Coat of Arms that his friend, whom he threw an arm around, was to marry the daughter of Sean Mor. It was soon evident to Anthony that he was marrying into a family whom everyone seemed to know and respect. With glasses refilled, a good-humoured McNab, holding aloft his glass of cream soda, offered a toast.

'Anthony Brennan, you are now an adopted son of the Falls Road, Belfast. Welcome, and good luck to you!' The bar echoed to a chorus of 'Hear! Hear!' and the clinking of glasses. All drank heartily.

The rapid thud of someone's fist pounding upon the door to his flat that lazy Sunday morning, rudely awakened Anthony from a drunken stupor and aggravated a throbbing headache. His head throbbed even more when lifting, what felt like a sack of spuds, from off the pillow. Apart from entering the bar with McNab, Anthony's recollection of the previous evening was lost to him entirely. Tripping over himself on racing to the door, a bare-chested Anthony prayed that he, nor anyone associated with him, had given cause the previous night to warrant such an early morning visit. On pulling the door open, he was left greatly surprised and concerned to find a distraught Bernadette Gresham, who collapsed sobbing into his arms.

Travelling on a weekend return ferry ticket and once arriving in his native Liverpool that previous Friday night, Felix Gresham had swiftly made his way to his sister's house to leave safely there the suitcase packed tight with money due to be handed over to his two contacts once he was convinced that the deal could be struck.

The following morning and keeping to a tight schedule, he breakfasted with his sister, her husband and their two boys - both highly excited at the prospect of being among the Kop later that day - before taking his leave to keep the early morning appointment across the city with those, into whose hands, he would be placing his life when handing over the money.

The early morning sun was warm upon his back as he briskly walked along that deserted cobblestone street dividing the neat rows of kitchen terraces, and where once he had played so carefree as a child, which he momentarily recalled to mind. He was on time to catch the bus on the corner that would drop him at the prearranged meeting place. Felix considered it a good omen that the major conspiracy about to unfold was to take place in the shadow of the city's main Catholic Cathedral, outside of which he stood waiting.

It was a worry for Felix however to discover that the big bear of a man behind the wheel of the car into which he climbed, was not sober on such an important occasion. The smell of alcohol was heavy on his breath as he spoke, his speech slurred. 'It's great to see you again, Felix. We have a surprise for you. Our European friends are here in town. Their ship came in on Wednesday, so we can go speak to them.'

The second contact in the back seat, a baldheaded thuggish-type, leaned forward to ask Felix, 'Did you bring the money with you?'

Felix was a little relieved to know one of the two men at least was thinking business with a clear head. There was no smell of drink on this man's breath. Not taking his eyes off the road ahead as the car pulled away, Felix replied firmly, 'The money's here in town. Once I am satisfied the deal is on, it will be handed over.'

The journey continued in silence as the car weaved its way through heavier traffic on the way to the docks. The footpaths were busy with Saturday shoppers and those Kop supporters making their way toward Anfield for the Testimonial game's early kick-off. Felix was keen not to distract the driver with idle chitchat. It was obvious to him that the previous late night drinking session had impaired the other's judgement somewhat, on missing two turnings that would have spared them half the journey. The car's speed was a source of concern also. Felix turned his head to tell the driver to slow down, when out of the corner of an eye, he spied the heavily laden lorry pull out suddenly in front of them at a short distance. Instinct told Felix to throw himself flat across the seat and was about to when there was an almighty crash. Thrown forcibly forward by the violent impact, a shower of glass peppered his face and collapsing jagged-edged metal tore open both legs, smashing and ripping through bone and muscle. Above the excruciating pain seizing the whole of his body, Felix's last thought before losing consciousness, was that he would never again see his beautiful Bernadette.

A gang of football supporters first on the scene tried desperately to stem the blood spurting from the throat of the man pinned by both legs in the back seat. The car's internal mirror was embedded deep in his neck. The football scarves applied to the gaping wound quickly turned a darker red under the steady, hot crimson gush as the man's life drained from him. He died where he sat just as the first policeman reached the scene. Anyone else in the front of the car was presumed dead. Surely no one could have survived the impact. The car, right up to the edge of its rear seat, had disappeared under the lorry, between its front and rear wheels. A twisted, tangled mass of metal, which was once two thirds of the car, was the grizzly sight was seen by all who surged round as spectators and to speculate; the traumatised lorry driver was comforted by mid-morning shoppers as he sat on the kerb edge, his head in his hands.

The small crowd remaining at the scene of the crash thirty minutes later were left totally confounded on learning that the passenger in the front of the car, itself dragged clear by the fire engine, was still alive, but only just. One leg had been cleanly severed on impact, the other, badly crushed. It was doubtful it could be saved, indeed, the man himself, such were the extent of his injuries. A young policeman was violently sick in the gutter on seeing the survivor's horrific injuries. Another, more hardened and experienced officer, held his breath to prevent himself from vomiting also on removing the severed and mutilated head of the driver from among the wreckage, so to wrap it in his tunic to spare the onlookers the gory sight.

It had been due to Felix's sister going along to the local police station later that night to report her brother's 'disappearance' that the mystery of the unidentified car passenger, critically ill in hospital, was established.

Bernadette Gresham had received a phone call from England at dawn that Sunday morning, informing her of the accident, and that her husband may not live to the end of the day.

Hearing this from the woman struggling to compose herself left Anthony feeling so helpless. What can I say, he thought, painstakingly. He knew that with both Felix's legs lost and his body so badly smashed, it would be an act of mercy if God was to take him.

With his own faith put to the test yet again, Anthony understood in that instant why McNab had lost his, all those years ago.

Chapter Fifteen

Sitting at the kitchen table at home, Sean Mor felt the blood in his veins run cold on overhearing the news about Felix disclosed along the hallway by Anthony to Sarah. She too was dumbstruck by what she heard because she realised the severity of what this would mean for her father. The near empty tea cup in Sean Mor's hand suddenly felt as heavy as a brick, his legs like cotton wool as he raised himself from the chair to reach for his jacket from the back of the kitchen door. He had an urgent call to make.

Anthony sensed the man's unease as he sidestepped Sarah and he in the hallway without even a glance, to rush out of the house. Suspecting her father had overheard, Sarah excused his lack of manners as being down to the fact that he was late for a meeting. She then led Anthony into the front room where she calmly sought more details about Felix Gresham.

Sarah sat up late that night waiting for her father to return and sighed with relief on hearing his key turn in the front door. It had just gone midnight and she had grown increasingly worried over him. He joined her in the front room where she'd sat alone, mother and Caithlin having gone to bed, Bridget to Aunt Bella's. Anthony had gone home early for he was not feeling the best. It was clear to Sarah that Anthony had been clearly upset over Felix, and on confessing to her his sorrow over a friendship lost, had painfully resigned himself to the fact that it was unlikely he would again see Felix alive.

From the beginning of their relationship, Sarah had given no hints to Anthony as to her 'relationship' with Felix, other than casual reference to his charitable work for a local orphanage. And until earlier that evening, Anthony had never mentioned his name since Felix and he had parted. Consequently, Sarah knew her man to have kept Felix's request for secrecy as to his commitments, and she privately admired Anthony's loyalty to his friend.

Pale and exhausted and totally demoralised, Sean Mor collapsed into his fireside chair, his mind racing over the day's hectic events. Sarah was anxious to discover his thoughts.

'You heard what was said?' Sean Mor nodded with a dejected look. 'Da, what's going to happen?' The reply fitted the man's expression. 'Christ knows! But I don't want you worrying. I will take care of whatever's to be done. And I'll be taking care of myself too. Understand!' Sarah was worried sick and her father could tell by his daughter's fraught face. Sean Mor forced himself forward in his seat. 'While we're talking Sarah, there's something I must ask you to do.' Sarah listened intently, not knowing in the slightest what her father was about to ask of her. 'Now that plans are set for your wedding, I want you, *I request you,* to give your full commitment to seeing that day through. And then, to your husband, to whom your loyalty and time should be given, first and foremost.' Sitting back in his chair and finding a breath, Sean Mor added solemnly, 'If only I could turn back the clock, I would give your mother so much more of my time. I've put her through hell. She has suffered more than anyone. Y'know, she reared you three single-handed. You never wanted for anything, not even a father, for she was that too when I was not around.' Sean Mor sighed heavily. 'Life's too short sweetheart; don't waste a day.'

Sean Mor left his daughter alone then and wearily climbed the stairs to lay himself down beside his wife, by whose side he had not been nearly enough over the years, such was his loyalty to others, his comrades-in-arms. He was in too deep to get out of what he was involved in, and was not sure whether he would want to even if he could. He prayed now that events unfolding would not result in a sudden end for him, one way or another.

The big man's daughter in the room below wept silently over her father's words, so true, though so hard to accept. Sarah shed tears also at the suffering all about her, and her thoughts turned to the woman who had left Ireland hours earlier to be with her husband, not knowing if when she arrived at her destination, he would still be alive.

That following morning Barratt arrived at the cobbler shop as instructed. Most of the folk along the Falls were still in their beds as Sean Mor tuned the wireless to the seven o'clock news bulletin broadcast from England. In the small workshop out back, smelling of leather and glue, and huddled close over a cluttered workbench both men listened intently as the sober-voiced Englishman read his way through the news reports on events the previous day. What the two IRA men waited for came toward the end of 'news closer to home.'

'Police in Liverpool have identified the two men tragically killed in a road accident on Saturday. Their motor vehicle had collided with a lorry close to the Anfield football ground. A third passenger remains critically ill in the Liverpool General Hospital, where surgeons were forced to amputate his remaining leg. The first had been severed in the accident. A hospital spokesman said it was miraculous the man had survived the crash such was the severity of his injuries. Police continue to investigate the cause of the accident. The driver of the lorry, who was unhurt, is assisting police with their inquiries ...'

Sean Mor switched the radio off and paused to think for a moment before addressing Barratt, his voice hushed and conspiratorial. 'Time is of the essence. This lad of yours ... Stack, is he still on the scene?' Barratt gave a nod.

'Good. Would he be up to crossing the water tonight if we fixed him up with some cash?'

'What you got in mind, Sean?'

'We need to get our hands on that money Felix took with him. We *must* get it back, and quick at that. It was in a brown leather suitcase. I'm thinking it may still be at Felix's sister's house. That is where he was planning to stay over the weekend. I don't know the address, but if yer man tailed Felix's missus from the hospital, we could be on to it.'

Knowing Sean Mor's intentions, Barratt casually asked the question, 'How is he to get into the house?'

'He'll just have to use his imagination. But whatever he does, I don't want him leaving a trail of havoc behind him. But if the money is there, he must get it and bring it back here.' Pausing for a further moment's thought, Sean Mor added, 'Might he do a runner with it?' Barratt deliberated. There was no reason not to trust the lad. 'He'll be okay.

Perhaps he can make out he is a friend of Felix, who happened to be in town ... that sort of thing.'

'Whatever. But he must get that money. Doing so may just save the day. See that he gets today's sailing.'

'Will do, Sean.'

'Now to other business,' said Sean Mor. 'It's only a matter of time before news of Felix is mentioned somewhere, somehow. I know the patience of one person in particular in this city is running dangerously thin. When he realises that plans laid for the shipment are up in the air, he might consider taking matters into his own hands. So as a precaution, I am going to stand down McHugh and appoint you brigade OC. This will formally take place tonight, but I want McHugh to be the last to know.' Barratt nodded hesitantly. 'I want you and the rest of the brigade to meet with me at the safe house at seven,' commanded Sean Mor. 'Once I've made clear the changes afoot, you and I will pay McHugh a visit. Arrange a meeting with him at the Coat of Arms for eight. Are you with me?'

Barratt had suspected that this day would come and couldn't help but think it was far from complete. He saw now how Sean Mor checked him out with his searching eyes. Barratt knew McHugh might be tempted to go over the heads of the Army Council when learning of the setback, which undoubtedly would be a sickener for all. But he knew which side he would want to be on if things turned ugly. His reply came easy. 'I am, Sean.'

Sean Mor was glad to hear it. Barratt, he knew, would carry a lot of support at grassroots with him if things did take a turn for the worst. He prayed that it wouldn't, and that his comrades, with whom he was due to meet in Dublin the next day in emergency session, would stand shoulder to shoulder and bear the grim news which he was to break to them. The next twenty-four hours would be heavy going, and Sean Mor braced himself for it.

Later that day in Belfast, several people sitting by their firesides read with an intense interest the early evening newspaper's front-page headline report: *Belfast Publican's Fight For Life*.

One of that number, Sean Mor scanned the story closely for mention of a large sum of money. There wasn't any. All his hopes rested with Stack.

Fergal McHugh sat upright in his armchair to read the same headlined story over again and let the grave meaning of what was revealed sink in. Surely the message via his missus from Barratt to meet with him at eight o'clock was in some way connected to events in Liverpool. He felt a tingle of excitement sweep over him knowing that the long-awaited opportune moment to make his decisive move against Sean Mor and others may be about to present itself. He would wait until he had met with Barratt before deciding what to do next.

Anthony read the same report with mixed feelings. In one way he was glad to learn Felix was putting up a fight, but at the same time the thought of the man's suffering depressed him. McNab meanwhile, deeply shocked by the news, considered it ironic that he had been talking of Felix only a few days before to Anthony. He wondered if Anthony knew of or would be at all interested in Felix's misfortune, in view of the fact that they were seemingly no longer friends, according to Anthony's brief and closed reply to his question as to how Felix was keeping these days. Now he knew.

'It is indeed a wonder how he is still alive,' mouthed McNab to himself, studying the list of injuries received by the publican, and was convinced more so that no Merciful God existed.

There was much speculative talk among the four brigade officers who assembled at the safe house in Beechmount, further up the Falls from Clonard. It was most unusual for a meeting to be held in the absence of McHugh. This talk ceased in an instant on Barratt and Sean Mor entering the kitchen through the back door. There was a scrape of chair legs as the four men quickly stood to attention on receiving the senior rank. Issuing commands in Gaelic, Barratt brought the men to stand easy, then to sit again around the kitchen table. The two late arrivals joining them, sat side-by-side at one end of the table. There was an uneasy silence in those few seconds before Sean Mor spoke. All eyes fixed firmly on him.

'In the long-term interest of our movement, and in particular, that of this brigade, I consider it necessary to appoint a new brigade OC, Frank Barratt, who will take command immediately. Fergal McHugh is to be stood down from all ranks. He is not to be approached on army business under any circumstances. However I wish to stress that McHugh's integrity as an Irish republican remains intact. It is his methods of promoting our cause that have been judged counterproductive to our long-term objectives. No staff officer or volunteer will be sacrificed for short-term goals. Rest assure, efforts are underway even as we meet to secure the means of taking our struggle forward. Meantime, I ask you to remain steadfast to your commitment, patient as it may be presently, to seeing our country ... our people rid of British interference, permanently. If there are no questions, this meeting is now closed.'

Not a word was uttered. After a few seconds Barratt brought the parade to attention, then to dismiss. Sean Mor was heartened to see each man filing by, stop briefly to shake Barratt's hand in a genuine sign of support. But he knew there would be no handshakes at his next port of call.

Fergal McHugh suddenly felt ill on turning in his chair to discover Barratt was not alone. He had not expected Sean Mor to be present at the meeting. He knew then what was to unfold before the other man even opened his mouth. Barratt and Sean Mor joined him by pulling up bar stools to sit among the empty beer crates stacked high in that improvised storeroom above the bar. McHugh showed no emotion as Sean Mor delivered his verdict with a calm, collect voice.

'No doubt Fergal you have heard of Felix's misfortune and are aware of the possible consequences in its aftermath, your perception being, I am convinced, that those plans laid down are now compromised.' McHugh did not speak. 'In view of developments I suspect you may attempt to pre-empt the movement's long-term objectives through renegade action. So it is my decision that you be stood down. You are to disassociate yourself from army business forthwith. There is no avenue of redress.'

For McHugh, it was a bitter pill to swallow. Sean Mor's power of insight unnerved him. He considered it wise to say nothing that may serve to dig a deeper hole for himself. Rising to take his leave, McHugh looked down with disdain on those seated and thought, The will to carry forward the fight is far from over despite this ... rest assured of it.

McHugh turned his back to those he considered to be traitors to the republican cause, and took his leave without giving a hint as to what his next move might be.

Chapter Sixteen

The woman keeping vigil by the hospital bedside had painful mixed feelings for the man lying in it - fighting for his life. They had recently celebrated eighteen years of marriage and she'd thought she had known him inside out. They had worked, lived and slept alongside each other since they'd wed. The bar had been their life. But now Bernadette Gresham questioned what the past eighteen years had been all about. It was painfully obvious to her that her husband had been living another life, to which she had not been party. In memory of that life they'd shared she loved him dearly, but her hatred for him was as a consequence of his deceit, his lies, his mistrust of her, in not confiding in her his other commitment.

Felix's secret, clandestine life had been exposed by chance. Bernadette had innocently stumbled across the brown leather suitcase in the spare bedroom at her sister-in-law's. On sitting herself down on the side of the bed, the very same bed that she had shared with Felix each year when they had come to Liverpool for their summer holidays, her high heel shoes had knocked against something under it. Casually looking there, she had found Felix's suitcase. Bernadette had questioned Felix the day he had left Belfast as to why he was taking the case with him. He had already packed a change of clothing into the grip bag. He'd said that he needed it for the football memorabilia he planned to bring back with him from the testimonial match, which was the purpose of his journey. This had seemingly been his cover to hide the true reason for his trip to Liverpool, and she was terrified by the thought of what the ultimate outcome of his visit would have been for so many people for she was experiencing a horror right now, in more ways than one.

Bernadette had been left dumbstruck on flicking back the lock snibs and opening the case in the privacy of the bedroom the previous night. She had innocently assumed that there may be something in the case which would be of some use at the hospital, not knowing at that moment just how close to death Felix actually was. To be left holding a suitcase packed tight with wads of crisp new bank notes, too many to count, and not knowing what on earth lay behind what was happening to her, had moved Bernadette to shed tears of frustration, anger and fear. Out of blind instinct she had tipped the money onto the bed in the hope that she would find a more definite clue that would put her in the picture. There had been none. Even more desperate then for a lead, she had removed her husband's grip bag from the wardrobe and tipped its contents onto the floor. On hands and knees she had searched frantically among the few clothes strewn across the well-worn linoleum. On finding nothing, she'd begun to tear apart the garments - shirts, underclothes, socks, the turn-ups on a pair of trousers, then the pockets and lining. All that remained intact was a tie, which she fingered like Rosary beads tortured in mind at not finding any clues and not knowing what to do next. Then her fingertips accidentally found it. On prising two fingers into the lining of the tie and ripping apart the stitching, a cigarette-shaped piece of paper tightly rolled, had fallen to the floor. Picking it up and unrolling it with nervous anticipation, Bernadette could simply not come to terms with what her husband appeared to be involved in. What she read then had made her feel ill. She'd knelt on the floor numbed with shock.

As she watched over her man, his face smashed and bruised, his body crushed, his legs gone, and knowing what she now knew, she prayed and prayed hard, that something, someone, would guide her in what to do with the secret she kept. In that moment, she called to mind that other secret, equally as dark and destructive: the truth she'd kept hidden from Felix down through all the years as to why she could not bear him a child.

All alone by the hospital bedside, consumed with fear, and guilt, Bernadette considered if what had befallen Felix were in some way a cruel though just punishment for her. But she had decided long, long ago, never to reveal all to Felix. To do so, she knew, would destroy him. Bernadette closed her heart and mind to the ugliness of her guilt and instead willed her man to survive.

It was the first time Martin Stack had been on a boat; indeed it was his first time away from home. Walking down the gangway he was very conscious of being a stranger in a strange land. He could not help but stare in wonder at the man walking along the quay below, the first black man he had ever laid eyes on. Following the small group of fellow passengers out through the ferry port's main gate and onto the busy main road, Stack stood to take note of his new surroundings. As dusk fell, the city of Liverpool appeared just like the one he had left behind earlier that day.

Following instructions not to waste time, Stack walked the short distance to the corner of the road, where he asked for directions to the General Hospital from the peculiar-looking newspaper seller, an Englishman wearing a cloth cap and whose cigarette butt threatened to burn his bottom lip. The friendly scouser was happy to assist the stranger and Stack was surprised by the other man's enthusiasm to do so. He not only told him how to get to the hospital but also emptied his cigarette box of its last few cigarettes to draw a little map with a stub of a pencil retrieved from behind a withered ear. Stack considered it only right to buy a newspaper from the Englishman and thanked him for his help. Eager to make the new arrival in town feel welcome, the local said, cigarette still in mouth, 'That's all right Paddy. Wouldn't want you getting lost now would we?' Stack smiled and thought, If you only knew mister ... if you only knew!

The rough drawing served its purpose. After a brisk fifteen-minute walk across a quiet city centre, Stack paused for a moment before crossing to the other side of the main road where the General Hospital stood. Binning the unwanted newspaper just inside the hospital's main entrance, Stack's leather shoes clicked noisily upon the gleaming terrazzo floor and echoed the length of the long deserted corridor as he set out in search of the Intensive Care ward. The red arrow painted on a bare plaster wall, marked the way. Stack felt compelled to complete the remaining distance leading to the double doors marked, Waiting Room, on tiptoe. Entering the gloomy room, he noted several people dotted here and there among the dozen or so chairs. All the folk appeared heavily troubled in their private thoughts. One elderly woman sobbed into her handkerchief. None of the people looked remotely like the woman he sought. He distinctly remembered her stunning good looks as she'd stood behind the bar that Christmas Eve night, almost two years before. Studying her briefly that night from a distance, he had concluded that despite being in her forties, she would still give many a woman half her age a run for their money where good looks were concerned. Looking about him, he wondered then what the landlady might look like present day. To his right, a very fat nurse, squeezed into her starched white and navy blue uniform, manned a reception point. With her head buried in some patient's medical notes, she was too busy to notice him. Ahead of him lay the entrance to the Intensive Care ward.

'Can I help you, sir?'

A little surprised, Stack was thinking fast as he approached the reception where a younger, much prettier nurse had suddenly appeared. Conscious of the surroundings, he too spoke quietly. 'I'm a friend of Felix Gresham. Y'know, the road crash victim. I was just passing and thought I would call in to ask how he is.'

The fat nurse now eyed Stack up and down suspiciously. The prettier nurse politely inquired further, 'I know you're not a local man, but I must ask you, are you a reporter?'

'No! No! Not at all.' Stack was keen to ease the other's suspicions. The nurse relaxed her gaze a little. 'That's good. Missus Gresham is understandably very distressed and just could not cope with anyone pestering her at this moment. You see, Mister Gresham remains very ill.' Stack nodded. 'I understand. I just wanted to know how he is.' As if as an after thought, Stack asked casually, 'Is Missus Gresham here now?' The nurse was too quick to provide an answer to the late night caller's inquiry. 'Yes, she is. She stays with her husband throughout the night. Do you wish to speak with her?' Stack thought long and hard before replying, 'No, I will not trouble her tonight.'

Stack thought it best to make contact with Mrs Gresham a little less publicly. He decided to take his leave but would ensure to be at the hospital first thing in the morning to follow her to Felix's sister's home. There he would make his move. Meantime he would book himself into a B&B close to the hospital. Saying 'Goodnight' to the friendly nurse and turning to take his leave, Stack's attention was drawn to those swing doors leading to the Intensive Care ward which opened towards him. A woman, appearing exhausted though pretty with it, moved towards him, a blank look etched upon her grey face. He recognised her immediately as the publican's wife. Barratt had said her first name was Bernadette. Their eyes were locked on each other at that moment and once again Stack stood out like a sore thumb in Bernadette's sharp eyes. She had clocked him that Christmas Eve night as he'd entered the bar. He had been a little too young to be a regular patron and had been too busy in his actions as he'd shifted among the regulars to be in festive mood. He hadn't stayed long and had left without having a drink. He had been the odd one out that night and was the odd one out here again.

Stack felt the woman's eyes burrow through him as she came closer. Feeling very uncomfortable, he turned away and walked back through the other swing door into the side corridor. Bernadette knew for definite then that it was one and the same man through the way he carried himself. To her thinking: a man on a mission. Bernadette's gut instinct was to follow him, to challenge him. She just knew that he had come for the money. Entering the side corridor a few paces behind the man, she called out to him. 'Wait a moment!'

Stack was halted in his retreat by the woman's command. A cry for help more than anything else, he thought, turning to face her.

Bernadette came to stand in front of Stack. He noticed the woman's eyes to be bloodshot, from crying sorely. It was she who broke the tense silence. 'I've seen you before, haven't I?' Her challenging Belfast accent, stating a fact rather than asking a question, reminded Stack of a former schoolteacher who had made his childhood years hell. He was as cheeky now with his reply as he had been all those years ago. 'Are you asking me or telling me?' His accent rubber-stamped her suspicions. Bernadette was nervous, but had new hope.

'I'm telling you! It was in my bar, back in Belfast on Christmas Eve, two years ago. You were busy that night and couldn't settle. And you're busy tonight again. I can tell. Y'see, working behind the bar all them years, you get to know people's ways, when they're on a high or feeling low, when they're feeling easy or on edge. You begin to read them, just like a book.' She stepped up closer to Stack, to look him searchingly in the eyes. 'You've come to see me, haven't you?'

The woman's bluntness and her intuition surprised Stack. But she presented him with an opportunity to get the business done. He decided to seize the chance. 'What makes you think that?' Bernadette was so self-assured. 'You've come to collect something, haven't you?' Stack was growing restless with her cat and mouse tactics. 'Such as what?' Bernadette sensed she was getting close to the truth and laid the bait. 'You tell me and I'll let you know if we are talking about the same thing.' Stack knew this was the moment of make or break. He came straight out with it. 'A suitcase ... a brown suitcase?' With a cockiness in her voice, she said, 'What about it?' She was pushing her luck. He moved closer to her to say in a hushed voice, 'Look, I've been sent here to find a suitcase full of money ... to take it back to Belfast. I don't know the full story behind it. I'm only tying up loose ends. I need to have that case. Have you got it?'

Bernadette felt so relieved to know she was finally getting somewhere near to establishing the truth, or so she thought. 'What exactly is my husband involved in? And who with?'

Stack was dreading the woman causing a scene on hearing the truth. He knew nothing. All that he had been told was that Felix Gresham was to have brought a suitcase full of money back from England to Barratt. He knew not how much, where it came from or for what purpose. All he knew was that he must find it and return it intact.

'I've told you. I am only here to find that money. I know nothing of your husband, other than he'd been holding money belonging to my people.' As soon as he'd said it, Stack knew he had ignited her interest even more so. He cursed his own stupidity under his breath.

'Your people! *Who* are we talking about?'

Stack knew he had compromised himself. He felt it best to get a commitment from the woman to meet with him in a more private place, where they could settle the matter.

'We can't talk here. We need to go somewhere more private.'

Bernadette was determined to get answers to her questions first, before she would hand anything over to the man. She took the initiative.

'Tomorrow. We can talk then.'

'Where?'

'My sister-in-law's; number twenty-seven Stanhope Street. Come early ... nine-thirty. Everyone else will be out.'

'Have you got the money? *Have you*?' Stack needed to know.

'You can have the money tomorrow. But first I need answers to questions. I must have them!'

Stack heard the desperation in the woman's words and saw it in her eyes. She was a woman on the edge and he felt pity for her, though feared she may not make life easy for him when discovering he had no answers for her.

'We'll meet tomorrow as you suggest,' said Stack. Her eyes falling closed through the want of sleep, Bernadette simply nodded. Stack turned and walked away, hoping the hours until morning would pass quickly. He longed to be going home again, and not empty-handed.

Chapter Seventeen

The head of the Jack Russell moved like the pendulum of a clock beneath the kitchen table as its master paced the floor in the wee small hours. Barratt was having second thoughts over his agreeing to send Stack to England and considered now that perhaps he himself should have gone instead. But Sean Mor had insisted that Stack go, as he was unknown to Special Branch and would therefore not be tailed either departing or arriving in port. Equally important to Sean Mor's calculation, Stack was naive as to what was planned, the intended purpose of the money and Felix Gresham's role in things. All he had been told was to find the money and bring it back to Belfast - all of it. Stack had been warned, that if picked-up by the Special Branch with or without the money, he would be a dead man if he opened his mouth or if he scarpered with the money. Such had been the implicit warning chillingly delivered by Barratt just before his departure.

Checking his wristwatch, Barratt knew that in a few hours Stack would make his move to retrieve the money, if it still existed. The senior IRA man would wait indoors all day for the word.

Stack had not slept a wink during the night in the rundown guesthouse, what with all that was on his mind and the bloody bed which he had cursed, comparing it to that piece of waste ground back home where as a youngster he had kicked ball with his pals. It too had been all humps and holes. He had skipped breakfast on seeing the measly portion of fried egg and bacon served up to another early riser. In comparison, it made an

Ulster fry look like a feast fit for a king. Gulping down the mug of sickly sweet, lukewarm tea, Stack quickly took his departure without goodbyes said. He was feeling hard done by, having paid his money up front to the scrawny landlady the previous evening.

Asking for directions to Stanhope Street from an early morning pedestrian, Stack made his way briskly in the bright morning sunshine through the maze of cobblestone side streets, not unlike those of Belfast. He stopped occasionally on street corners to check his bearings.

Stack arrived at the mouth of Stanhope Street a few minutes before nine-thirty. He was surprised to see that a chimney of a house on the opposite side and halfway along the narrow deserted street, billowed white smoke which, in the early morning still-heat, hung low over the rooftops of the terrace houses. White ash fell from the sky like snowflakes. Seeing the odd numbered doors on the opposite side, Stack crossed over and proceeded along the footpath, counting as he went. 'Seven, nine, eleven ...' Stack casually flicked the powdery ash from the lapels of his navy blue jacket with his fingers as he walked further along. An odd, peculiar burning smell filled his nostrils. 'Twenty-three, twenty-five, twenty-seven.' The front door to the house lay wide open. That burning smell was more obvious now. Stack was sure it was coming from inside the house. Out of curiosity he stepped from the pavement into the road and craned his neck to look up at its chimney. This was indeed the house which had a fire lit on such a glorious morning. Stack moved to the open door again and knocked hard against it. No one answered. He knocked again, harder. He shouted out then, 'Hello, anyone there? Hello!'

No one answered. No one stirred. Stack's instinct told him to enter. He did, and moved slowly along the hallway. The parlour door on his left was ajar. He sensed someone was in the room. He gently pushed the door open and entered cautiously. Inside the room, Bernadette Gresham, her face streaming with tears, her bedroom attire unkempt, sat forward in the fireside chair. A fire blazed in the grate, the heat from it, intense. Between her bare feet on the floor was a brown leather suitcase. Its lid was open. She reached inside and produced a tight wad of bank notes. Stack felt the panic grip him in an instant. '*Fuck*! What are you doing you stupid ...' The last word screamed by Stack had barely passed his lips when the woman, glancing Stack momentarily with red raw eyes, threw the bundle of bank notes into the fire. Stack darted across the room. Bernadette Gresham sprang out of the chair and stood defiantly in front of the fireplace. Stack snatched the case from off the floor; it was lightweight and empty. Panic turned to shock. He struggled to comprehend what she had done.

'You've burnt the fucking lot! You mad bastard!'

Stack threw the suitcase up one corner, grabbed the woman by the shoulders and forcibly flung her into the fireside chair, and was quickly down on his knees, trying to snatch the burning bundle of bank notes out of the fire. The rising flames licked his fingers, burning his flesh. But still he tried. Stack felt as though he was being scalped then as the woman's razor sharp fingernails tore into his scalp to drag him away from the fire empty handed. 'You bastard! The woman's voice was venomous. You've ruined our lives!'

Overwhelmed with anger for the woman, Stack pushed himself onto his feet, drew his right arm forward and rammed his elbow violently into the woman's ribs. Bernadette Gresham fell winded onto her knees at Stack's feet, gasping for breath. Stack turned to face her and seething hate, screamed at the woman, 'You fucking bitch!' He landed the full force of his open hand across her mouth, sending her collapsing to the floor. He bent forward, grabbed hold of the woman's dressing gown and lifted her dead weight with much effort, and pushed her hard onto the sofa against the far wall. Her body, limp and lifeless, lay spread-eagled across the three-seater. Bernadette felt as though she was dying, then felt the air find her lungs slowly. Her mouth throbbed and she tasted her own blood. She suspected that the youth had knocked every tooth out of her head. Checking to see if he had, she ran her tongue along the edge of her upper teeth. Stack loomed over her, a finger pointed threateningly in her face. 'Don't start me missus! I'm warning you! Don't start!' Bernadette didn't care then what he might do to her on speaking her mind and experienced much pain on doing so.

'My husband is lying on his deathbed through getting involved with the likes of you. I'm sure if he had known this was to happen, he wouldn't want anything to do with your cause ... with scum like you.' With her temper coming to the boil, she spat, 'Yes, I burned your money ... fucking blood money! And I'll tell you why: so that no poor soul will suffer what I'm suffering today, knowing, that if a loved one lives, they'll be crippled ... mutilated for the rest of their life. No cause is worth such suffering!'

Stack had heard every word. But his conscience had not been pricked. All he wanted to do now was to get the hell out of there, to be on the next boat home. He took in the tortured, bloody face of the woman once more as she lay in a pathetic heap, her large pointed breasts, half exposed, rising and falling erratically as she fought to compose herself. He knew in that instant that he would not forget her easily, that look of despair engraved on her face. Stack was out of the house in a flash and scurried down the street, still empty and quiet, but sensed that all eyes were on him from behind net curtains as he went on his way.

Her body aching, head thumping, Bernadette Gresham curled up into a ball on top of the sofa and sobbed loudly.

Stack felt safe among the masses as he merged with those English folk busily shuffling between the city's large department stores. He had several hours to kill before the next boat sailed. He sought to clear his confused thoughts and calm his nerves over a mug of tea and a cigarette in the High Street café. Finding an empty seat at a table by the window,

Stack deliberated over what to communicate to the man back in Belfast awaiting word from him.

'How the fuck am I supposed to break this kind of news to Frankie?' Stack quietly begged of himself, his right hand trembling on removing the lit cigarette from his mouth. He inhaled deeply, letting the smoke escape slowly through his nostrils, and with it he felt the tension gripping him, ease a little.

Sean Mor checked his pocket watch against the radio's time signal. He would be closing the shop an hour early today. He was due in Dublin at eight. He was anxiously waiting on word from Barratt so that he could give the latest update on developments to his contemporaries in the Army Council. Either way, he suspected he would not be popular with any one of them, and may well be ousted from the ranks. His main concern then, would be how he would fair with the likes of McHugh, who, seeing his demise, would surely stick the boot in.

He had sent the wire to Belfast and standing on the upper deck of the boat leaving port, Stack mulled over the likely reception he would receive on arriving back in Ireland. They'll hardly believe my story. They'll suspect I've dumped the money for collection later on, that I've betrayed them. Then they'll speak to the woman themselves. And what will they think of me slapping her about? She could say anything about me. The bitch could get me hung ... *Christ*! Looking to starboard, Stack's attention was drawn to the dilapidated ship putting to sea under some foreign flag and to the solitary figure on its deck. In an act of anger the swarthy-skinned man screwed the newspaper he'd been reading into a crumpled ball and threw it overboard. This man, searching for answers also it seemed upon the murky black water, appeared as troubled as he, concluded Stack, and wondered what awaited the seaman on returning to his homeland.

That very same seaman had just read the latest report on that road accident two days earlier and his fears had been realised. The names of the two men killed, were that of the two English shipping officials with whom he had been due to meet to complete the deal for the arms shipment. That sizeable cut from the money to be paid by the IRA was not, after all, coming his way. The arms deal lay dead along with the Englishmen.

Sean Mor knew instantly that the news was grim. The expression on Barratt's face as he entered the shop told all. The telegram slipped to him as the last customer of the day took his leave, raised Sean Mor's worst fears. His chin falling heavily onto his chest, he read it slowly to himself and it sickened him. Weighed down, he supported himself by placing his hands on top of the counter. He paused for a moment's thought before addressing Barratt, looking on nervously. 'This is the worst possible news.

It's bad enough with Felix out of the frame, but for the money to be destroyed ...'

Barratt was lost for words. Sean Mor was speaking again, his voice, menacing. 'Make sure you meet Stack when he steps from that boat. Take him to the Coat of Arms and keep him there. If I return safely from Dublin, I'll find out exactly what bloody went on in England!'

Chapter Eighteen

At eight o'clock that evening Sean Mor lay his cards on the table by requesting of the demoralised Chief of Staff and his Army Council comrades, sitting stunned and long-faced around the table in the back room of the bookshop, to indicate whether or not they had any confidence in him, now that he had informed them of the disaster. The Chief of Staff quickly quelled Sean Mor's sense of insecurity, while daring others to challenge his authority. 'We have already lost enough in the past forty-eight hours, Sean. We don't need to be our own worst enemy by getting rid of you.' The Dubliner added with gusto. 'The republican movement *is* people like you. The day we lose your kind will be the day the movement's death-knell will sound. No one here doubts your commitment nor your ability as a soldier and strategist in the field. Ever since I can remember, the army has been plagued with setbacks: arms seizures, plots uncovered, informers, volunteers caught red-handed. But the struggle goes on, and will go on, come what may.' The Chief of Staff paused to take stock before continuing. 'Here, tonight, I give the command for Plan B to be fully implemented. Raids for arms are to take place as soon as possible. The border campaign, its commencement date inevitably delayed further, will nevertheless go ahead at the earliest opportunity. And I ask you all to reaffirm yourselves to that objective here and now.'

The Quartermaster General seconded the Chief of Staff by addressing Sean Mor sitting opposite, directly. 'All of us here have a great deal of work to do ... together as one. No one doubts another. We have all walked the treadmill. We all know each other. We must see this through to the bitter end.' All heads nodded positively.

Sean Mor breathed easy as he set out on the return journey home with renewed confidence, and with firm conviction to find out exactly what had happened in England.

Dreading what lay ahead for him, Stack sat ashen-faced on an upturned beer crate in the middle of the cramped storeroom in the Coat of Arms. His right leg trembled as he drew hard and long on his last cigarette. Barratt and two other brigade staff officers sat lazily on bar stools dispersed around the room. Stack checked his wristwatch again. It had just gone two in the morning. It was four hours since he'd sat himself down. No one had spoken more than a few words in all that time. He knew it must be someone high up in the movement whom they all awaited.

Half an hour later, Barratt and the others stirred on hearing heavy feet upon the stairs. Barratt moved to open the door leading onto the small landing. A fourth man entered. He was tall and straight in stature, his face cast in shadow under the broad brimmer he wore, yet Stack sensed he knew the man who clearly held authority. With the man whispering into Barratt's ear, Stack heard Barratt order the other two brigade staff to leave the public house, which they did without question. This unsettled Stack more so. He interpreted their departure as ominous - two fewer eye witnesses to the violent deed about to be done.

As the newly arrived man stepped closer, Barratt by his side, and with the dim light from the naked light bulb falling upon his face, Stack looked up in disbelief. Hovering over him grim-faced, stood the father of the girl he secretly adored. He understood then why Barratt had since told him to be discreet about inquiring after Anthony Brennan.

Sean Mor studied Stack for a moment before speaking. 'I want the truth and nothing less, about what went on in England.' His voice cold and malicious, Stack realised that Sean Mor was the man to fear. So he told it as it had been - what the woman publican had done, what she had said. He felt his voice tremble as he spoke. When he finished, the two men standing over him said nothing. Daring to look up at each of them in turn, Stack saw their faces blank, giving nothing away. Sean Mor moved behind Stack, slowly and deliberately. Stack felt an even greater fear grip him. He closed his eyes tightly and whispered a prayer. He asked God not to let him die like this, wrongly judged a liar, a thief.

Both men hovered over him for what seemed like an eternity. No one moved. No one spoke. The silence for Stack was intolerable. His nerve gave way and he felt his body shake uncontrollably. Tears streamed down his face. He tried hard to keep his dignity by clutching tight the sides of the beer crate, but to little effect. He couldn't take much more of the torment. He expected the cold steel barrel of a gun to be pressed into the nape of his neck at any moment, to hear the gun cocked, the trigger ...

Soon, Stack was longing they would do it, to end his agony.

What Stack did feel and hear then was a firm hand on his shoulder and Barratt say with little emotion, 'Okay lad, on your way, and keep yer gob shut. I'll give you a shout later.'

Stack did not wait around for the men to change their mind. In no time he was on his feet, dashing across the room and stumbling down the stairs and exiting the public house by its back door. He ran all the way back to his home through dark and empty streets. The only sign of life being a bastard of a black cat darting across the pavement at his feet from out of a side-alley, which left his heart in his mouth.

Dawn was breaking as Stack arrived in a cold sweat and out of breath at the back entry door to his house. Pushing the rotting door open, he crossed the backyard quietly and eased open the scullery door, also unlocked as a rule. For Stack, it felt so good to smell the familiar smells lingering around the cramped, untidy house as he tiptoed through the kitchen, up the stairs and into his bedroom, not wanting to rouse his mother lying in the next room in a half drunken stupor no doubt. She was finding it hard to come to terms with life alone, now that her husband, his alcoholic father, had run off and left them. Where? No one knew. Stack lay himself down gently on top of the bed, his mind racing with thoughts of what he had been through the past twenty-four hours, and what might yet come to be.

Having dozed for an hour or so, Stack awoke to the sound of his mother clambering down the stairs on her way to work and slamming the front door shut behind her. The little cleaning job she had at the school kept her in drink money. She hadn't bothered to look in on him and most probably had not even noticed his absence over the previous few days. She was past caring about anyone, herself included. They didn't speak much to each other presently. She was more a stranger to him than a mother.

Stack knew he would never again be trusted by Sean Mor and Barratt. It would only be a matter of time before word got out that he was a failure - a 'liability' in their midst. But worse still for Stack, was how he would be thought of by Sarah. Surely she would learn of his blundering. How was he ever to face her, never mind win her favours? With his spirit broken, Stack, staring into space, condemned himself aloud.

'After my fuck up, Sean Mor won't have me anywhere near him, nor anyone belonging to him.' Stack considered his own foolishness in scheming the way he had over Anthony Brennan, not knowing until only hours earlier, that Brennan's future father-in-law, was the 'top man' himself. Sarah, he knew, was lost to him forever. Stack despised himself over his failure, and there was no running away from it, and wouldn't, even if he could. He'd heard almost every day on the factory floor, on street corners, for the past nine years, the malicious whispers, his father condemned as a 'wicked oul bastard' for running off with another 'hussy' all those years ago. There was no way his name was going to be likewise shamed. Weighing up his predicament, Stack considered that what he was about to do would - at least for one person - restore some good to his name. He knew Sarah would understand and felt some peace of mind knowing she would think kindly of him at the end of the day. Stack took pen and paper in hand.

An envelope with his dream girl's name scribbled upon it was left behind a candlestick on the living-room mantelpiece. Moving into the kitchen, Stack picked-up a chair, then the carving knife from the kitchen table, and entered the backyard, filled with brilliant sunshine. Trance-like, Stack proceeded to slice through the thin rope that normally stretched the length of the yard. The washing line was fixed securely to the brickwork of opposite walls. He had cut the rope long enough to make a noose with a sliding knot. Placing the chair against the nearest wall, Stack stepped onto it and placed the noose over his head. He then slid the knot against the right side of his neck, tight enough to feel the noose constrict his breathing and crush slightly his Adam's apple. He swallowed with great difficulty. Stack's concentration was broken then by the fluttering of wings as a brilliant-white bird descended onto the yard wall opposite. It seemed to look at him bewildered, its little head jerking back and forth and from side to side inquisitively. In all his twenty-one years, Stack had never seen such a distinctly marked bird. It was so beautiful. He was pleased to have the bird for company in the final moment. He blessed himself for the last time. The bird took flight on the sudden movement as Stack stepped off the chair.

The Falls Road was beginning to get busy when Barratt set out from his house to call on Stack. It had been decided by Sean Mor that the lad be temporarily stood down from the ranks until his story could be confirmed. This, Sean Mor would seek to have done on Bernadette Gresham's return to Belfast. He would assign the task to a third party, who as yet, he was undecided on. Meantime, Stack was not to leave the area and was to show his face each night at the Coat of Arms, where someone would note his appearance. He was to go back to work, having had a few days 'off sick'. Someone had had a word with the floor supervisor on that one, while he'd been across.

    Calling to the entry door as he always did when visiting Stack, Barratt nearly threw up his breakfast on entering the backyard, where he found Stack's lifeless body hanging limp against the wall to which the yard door opened.

    'You stupid wee bastard!' Barratt cursed angrily, the horror that greeted him, slowly sinking in. He contemplated cutting Stack down with the knife that lay on the ground beside the chair. But studying for a moment longer Stack's blue, almost black, contorted face, the swollen purple tongue protruding grotesquely from his mouth, and conscious of the stench of stale urine and death as a fierce sun beamed down on the unsightly corpse, Barratt knew he was far too late. Knowing also that at any moment someone looking out of an upstairs window could very well spy Stack, Barratt did not wish to be around when the screaming started and so wasted no more time. He searched through the dead man's pockets with haste and in one found the stub of the return sail ticket from Belfast to Liverpool. He placed it in one of his own jacket pockets and removed a handkerchief from another before moving across the yard and into the house. He was careful to use his covered hand in turning the doorknob on letting himself in. With his eyes carefully scanning shelves, tabletops and sideboards, he moved uninhibited through the downstairs rooms, knowing the woman of the house to be out at this time of the morning. Barratt's attention was soon drawn to the white envelope on the mantelpiece, bearing the name Sarah McParland. He thumbed open the envelope. Removing the single sheet of plain writing paper, Barratt silently read the few lines scribbled on it:

Dear Sarah.
I just want you to know that you will always be my girl.
I love you. Please pray for me.
Martin Stack.

Barratt did not hesitate to remove the zippo from his trouser pocket to set light to the letter and envelope, which he placed on top of the dead ashes in the hearth, also the sail ticket stub, making sure everything was thoroughly burned. Lifting the poker from the brass fire set, he dispersed the smoking black ashes among the cooled white ash of burnt coals. There was no way anyone would know of the letter, least of all Sean Mor. Barratt concluded that Stack must have taken a fancy to Sarah McParland when seeing the *stranger*, Anthony Brennan, in her company along the Falls over recent time.

Climbing the stairs quietly, not wanting to draw the attention of the neighbours on the other side of the single brick staircase wall, Barratt checked both bedrooms for anything that may cause difficulties for the IRA. It was all clear. Making his way back down the stairs in the manner he had ascended them, Barratt took his leave from the house, thanking God above that *he* had been the one to find the love letter. If it had fallen into the wrong hands, then the consequences could have been dire, with rumour soon abound that Sean Mor's eldest daughter was a loose woman – another hussy.

Barratt exited from the scullery and stepped past the hanging corpse. Without looking up, he blessed himself. He pitied the one who would find Stack next. Checking his wristwatch on exiting from the back alley onto the Falls Road, Barratt knew Sean Mor would be in his shop, so made his way straight there to break the latest concerning news.

Sean Mor reversed the shop door sign again on receiving Barratt, the first caller of the day. They withdrew to the small workshop behind the counter. The wireless there, tuned to a studio play, played low.

'Sorry Sean,' sighed Barratt. 'But we've got a drama of our own to contend with.'

Sean Mor was deeply shocked by what he learnt from his subordinate and paused to collect his thoughts before inquiring, 'Who, apart from those present last night, know Stack was connected?' Barratt reluctantly mentioned McHugh's name. Sean Mor was quick to lay down the law. 'There must be no talk of Stack being a member. Inform the others of this and put it about that the lad was questioned by me on some other matter. Perhaps, that he was suspected of crimes locally. But this is not to be shared recklessly. As for McHugh? We need to be careful. He might try to read something into the death and stir the shit. So needless to say, we need to keep a close eye on him. See to it Frankie.'

Barratt too was keen to keep McHugh in check. He knew that he might attempt to use Stack's death as a means of stirring hostility toward certain republicans in the community, through implying that something improper within the movement had led to the lad's death. And so Barratt suggested to Sean Mor that it may be beneficial to them, if McHugh was to 'overhear on the grapevine' that Stack had been seen 'molesting a minor' and was to have been 'dealt with.' But that evidently Stack had administered his own punishment. Confident in the success of his own proposal, Barratt sought to win Sean Mor's sanctioning of it. 'Surely McHugh would be compromised before he could even open his gob.' Barratt's closing prognosis of the potential developments to unfold, fell favourably on Sean Mor's ears.

'Okay!' Sean Mor confirmed, anxious to set the scheme in train. 'But be careful. McHugh must be convinced of what he hears.' Barratt reassured Sean Mor. 'Leave it with me, Sean.' Barratt's interest turned then to how Sean Mor viewed the position of Bernadette Gresham.

Although Sean Mor was aware of the possibility that Stack had revealed his identity to the woman, that consequently, Bernadette Gresham would put two and two together if finding out about the lad's death, his final analysis painted a more optimistic picture.

'In retrospect, Frankie, I'm convinced that Stack told us the truth last night. I would have known otherwise. I've been present at too many interrogations in my lifetime to know different. I've seen men breakdown even when they have spoken the truth. They break because they've nothing else to say and are pleading to be believed. That's what happened to Stack last night, even though there was no gun held to his head.' Barratt just nodded. Sean Mor added with an air of confidence, 'No, we have nothing to fear from Missus Gresham in that respect. As a matter of fact, I feel we have nothing at all to fear from her.' Barratt sought to know the reason for Sean Mor's confidence. 'What leaves you so sure?'

'If she sets out to sink anyone, she knows she will be digging her own grave. And if by chance Felix pulls through, his too, for he was the main conspirator. Anyway, considering what she's been through, what she did comes as a disappointment yes, but not as a surprise. With Stack dead there's no reason to pursue the matter any more. I'll simply inform others that Stack's story is true.' Sean Mor was a little more upbeat in his conclusion. 'Meanwhile, we've got matters closer to home to concentrate on. I need you to give me a hand to organise a forthcoming event. I only hope and pray there's no such crisis on that day.'

Chapter Nineteen

The telegram received by Anthony at his home minutes before he was due to leave to be married, left him feeling extremely happy. It read:
> Best of luck to Anthony and Sarah on your special day!
> We hope to see you soon.
> Felix and Bernadette.

Anthony had heard in recent weeks that Felix had made a miraculous recovery and despite being confined to a wheelchair, was well and strong. It was reported also that Felix planned to return to Ireland in the New Year to man the bar again with Bernadette, whose brother had part-managed it in their absence.

The tooting of a car horn signalled to Anthony that his lift to the church had arrived. Hurrying out of the converted house, he was pleased to see McNab - holding open the car's rear door for him - looking so very smart in his new suit, complete with a fresh white carnation in buttonhole. The car itself was gleaming and a white 'V' shaped silk ribbon was draped across its bonnet.

'I am at your command my dear chap,' McNab quipped, and adopting the mannerism of a court jester, bowed and waved the bridegroom into the car. In a mock posh English accent and acting out the role of royalty, Anthony joked, 'Come then, get a move on!'

The improvised limousine sped its way to the church, and backfiring, served to humour the looker-on.

Sean Mor had been keen to keep the wedding a quiet affair and at his beckoning, Sarah kept the invitations to a minimum. Sean Mor did not wish to draw undue attention to the occasion from certain sources, namely the RUC Special Branch, presently busy in the area pursuing inquiries into the most recent sudden death. Martin Stack's mother had lost her mind since discovering her son's body and had turned to the bottle with a vengeance in the months after his death. A concerned work friend had found her dead on the scullery floor of her house. The bereaved mother had choked on her own vomit. Her death, so soon after her son's suicide, had cast a cloud of gloom over the close-knit community, deeply shocked by the double tragedy in such a short space of time. Some folk held themselves at fault for not having done more to help the woman through her loss. Taking these factors into account also, Sean Mor did not wish a flamboyant wedding to intrude on people's mourning.

The low-key affair did not go entirely unnoticed though. The two plainclothes policemen sitting in their unmarked car at a discreet distance in a side street, monitored the coming and going of folk to and from the church in Clonard, in which Sean Mor, his family and friends - all a source of interest to the RUC - congregated. The policeman in the front passenger seat, Sergeant Craig, jotted down in his handy notebook the names of those attending - men, women, young and old, even the names of the children he knew.

Another man standing nearby looked on with contempt also. Fergal McHugh was biding his time. An opportunity to hit back at Sean Mor had to be abandoned, given the filth that Stack had apparently been engaged in prior to his death and the slandering of his name which had then ensued. McHugh had contemplated dropping the odd word here and there among the battalion ranks that Stack had been 'snuffed out' as a warning to those restless over the lack of activity. But McHugh wasn't giving up the quarry yet. He had new plans afoot. He was confident that his meeting planned for the following day with an old comrade as equally impatient as he to get the war started again, would soon have the tide of change coming about.

As the enthusiastically played bridal march filled the church, Anthony glanced over his shoulder to steal a glimpse of the bride, floating it seemed down the central aisle toward him. To Anthony, Sarah was a beautiful vision. His heart was filled with joy. As he turned to face the altar, a calm peace descended on him. Outside the bright autumn sun breaking through the dispersing clouds sent heavenly rays of sunshine falling through the stained-glass windows onto those gathered within.

The sacred vows of matrimony were freely exchanged in the calm aura of that holy house. With its harsh granite stone exterior and spiralling twin steeples piercing a welcomed blue sky, Saint Augustine's Church stood dominant yet protected amid Clonard's crisscross of narrow back streets. For the select few gathered, the day's special occasion would hopefully bring with it happier times for all. And none longed more for this than a quietly ecstatic Anthony. With considered determination, he slipped the simple gold wedding ring onto the customary finger of Sarah's hand, which trembled under the occasion, as they stood ceremonially side-by-side at the foot of the main altar.

Those assembled in the front pews smiled and nodded in approval toward the happy couple as they walked arm-in-arm back along the aisle with the priest's blessing bestowed on them. The entourage of bridesmaids and pageboys trooping merrily along behind, their excited thoughts turning to the rare treat of cakes and cream soda which awaited them, smiled angelically at their peers. Directly in front of them all lay open the heavy, arched doors of the church, and sweeping in over the terrazzo floor on a chill autumn breeze to throw ghostly echoes around the side altars and empty confessionals, came the escalating cacophony, pitched with guttural back street accents, tense, almost hostile, but commonplace in the ghetto beyond. Despite that new day, no one emerging from the house of prayer, which gave sanctuary to their very own prayers, their innermost pleas, would dare to predict what lay ahead for the newlyweds in the world awaiting them.

A good Irish do, with food, drink, music and mayhem being the necessary ingredients, Anthony concluded happily in thought as he surveyed the carefree goings-on around him. So far he had escaped the pandemonium on the dance floor in the local GAA club, which the committee had readily made available to their esteemed colleague, Sean Mor. Now though, he was a little anxious for the safety of the three-tier wedding cake on the table in front of him as a larger crowd of guests took to the floor - that cramped space amid the walls of tables and chairs - to dance riotously as the three-piece traditional band belted out reel after reel, jig after jig.

The alcohol flowed in plentiful supply and the air was filled with an energetic excitement. Sean Mor danced proudly with his eldest daughter amid the frenzy, and a half-dozen more men with fixed, eager eyes, stood in the wings patiently awaiting their turn to tap a dance with the prettiest girl around. Anthony feared not though. He knew that same girl was his and would offer up everything to him that night. Patiently, he was willing away the hours. His mind wandering for a minute, what was sad about the day for Anthony, was the absence of his loved ones, and dear friends. Mother would have been so pleased with the service, and father, the craic that had followed. And Con? Well, he probably would have been sick with jealously seeing Sarah look so pretty. At least mother and father will see her tomorrow and hopefully it will not be long until Felix is back in town again. McNab jabbing him with an elbow interrupted Anthony's thoughts. Looking out over the dance floor, the best man prophesised, 'You've got a fine woman there Anthony. No doubt she will do you proud and bear you a fine family.'

McHugh took his leave from a displeased wife, whose five dirty-faced children clung to her like little mischievous apes as she stood at the front door to their home in seeing him off without a smile or a wave goodbye. She was full of hate, he knew, for what he had put her through over the years, and what he was putting her through now. McHugh suspected that his wife knew he was up to something. She had warned him ominously that if he ended up inside again, she nor the children would be there for him when he got out - if he got out. That was a risk he was prepared to take as the inactivity since coming out of jail in '45 was killing him slowly but surely. He was hopeful now as he set out on his journey that his meeting with an old comrade would put an end to the days of idling in his armchair waiting for something to happen.

Both stone cold sober, Anthony and Sarah Brennan set out on their honeymoon under a barrage of shouted good wishes, clapping and cheering. A loud 'Hooray' struck up as Sarah's former school friend, Evelyn Storey, caught the bride's bouquet.

Stealing a quick kiss in the back seat of McNab's car, Sarah waved and blew kisses to family and friends as the car pulled away from the green wooden hut, which timbers had groaned and creaked on the corner of the side street under the heave and shove these past five, hectic, but fun-packed hours. Glad to have some peace and quiet at last, husband and wife snuggled up to each other, only to be reminded that they were not yet completely alone. Keeping an eye on developments in the back via his rear view mirror, McNab quipped, 'Easy on you two. Keep your hands to yourselves for a wee while longer. It's not far now.'

With eyes only for each other, Anthony and Sarah laughed mischievously.

Pre-booking the single night's stay in the honeymoon suite, the honeymoon couple thanked McNab for his kindness and bid him goodnight in the hotel foyer. But on doing so, both were left feeling highly embarrassed with McNab, mischief imprinted all over his face, and he too, stone cold sober, saying aloud, 'Well, I'll see you two in the morning bright and breezy. And you know what they say: early to bed, early to rise!' The bellboy taking charge of the newly-weds suitcases found it difficult to keep a straight face.

Alone at last in the softly-lit, magnificently furnished and tastefully decorated bedroom, in which fabrics, carpet and wall covering complemented each other superbly, Anthony slipped naked between the crisp new sheets and felt his body tremble in heightened excitement with Sarah making her much awaited entrance from the bathroom. She was so sensually seductive in appearance. Her long yellow hair fell soft and freely over her bare shoulders to nestle upon her breasts, which were fully round and firm under the short, white negligee she wore. Beneath the lace material the suggestion of the triangular patch of hair between her shapely thighs as she walked teasingly toward the bed, aroused his longing for her as never before. With Sarah sliding into the bed beside him and seeing the low-light in the room reflected in her dilating pupils, her pulsating red lips parting slightly, Anthony was fired by the urge to make love to his beautiful bride. He took Sarah in his arms and drew her close, to kiss her hot mouth gently; her warm, firm body, crushed against his as their inhibitions came undone freely and easily. Their newfound expressed love for each other drew tears of ecstatic joy from them both.

Alighting from the Ulster bus, McHugh was picked-up as arranged from the deserted market square in the heart of Irvinestown by Oliver O'Rourke. He proceeded to drive his car at speed to the remote and deserted slate roofed cottage wherein Liam Sexton and Oliver's younger brother, Dermott, awaited them. Joining them there, the four men sat around a low table. With welcomes and introductions made, as McHugh had not before met the O'Rourkes though had heard of their notoriety, the men attended to business promptly. With the meeting being held on Sexton's home ground, he chaired the meeting and got business underway.

'I'm confident that we all know why we're here tonight and the importance for complete discretion by each of us in undertaking matters in hand. Failure to do so will undoubtedly result in our deaths, and not necessarily at the hands of the common enemy, but of those closer to us.'

Their meeting lasted until midnight. The conspiracy was in place. Their aim was to 'bring-to-a-head' the mounting frustration within the IRA right across the North by sparking a state and loyalist backlash in response to their planned pre-emptive strike, earmarked for the run-up to the 'Twelfth' celebrations in Belfast the following year. They calculated that their armed action and the ensuing backlash by the Orange state, would move those brooding republicans raring to have a go, to bring out the guns - at least those precious few held by them. News of the failed shipment, which the Belfast man leaked to the Fermanagh three, served to push forward their argument for an effort to be made at home to acquire weaponry from military barracks north and south of the border. They were confident this would be forced onto the agenda once an armed commitment was undertaken. For them, the key to the success of their plan lay in the hands of the Belfast Brigade, which they readily agreed must be seen to lead the way. McHugh was confident that this would come to be through his manipulation, even though he was now judged to be an outsider by others.

It was agreed by the four to meet once again before the end of the year to undertake reconnaissance work in Belfast and to finalise details on the proposed attack there. As the three locals prepared to take their leave, leaving McHugh to bed down for the night, the Belfast man, on the spur of the moment, inquired out of mild curiosity if any of them knew of a Donegal man by the name of Anthony Brennan? McHugh had heard on the grapevine back along the Falls, that Sean Mor's son-in-law had apparently lived among the Fermanagh men a few years before. The three locals looked searchingly at each other for a moment. It was with Dermott O'Rourke that the name mentioned rang a bell. Turning to his brother he sought confirmation.

'Wasn't he the fellow who worked with yer man Con McStravick up at the old abbey?' His memory jogged, Oliver O'Rourke replied in confirmation, 'Aye, that's right. They restored the monastery for that Englishman ... Cartwell, Colonel Cartwell.'

'*Colonel Cartwell*, you say?' probed an alerted McHugh.

'Aye, a British soldier from the Great War. A mad oul bastard if ever there was one,' confirmed Dermott O'Rourke, adding bitterly, 'He parades about as if he owns the whole bloody place.' Liam Sexton butted in. 'Sure, isn't that the mentality of the English anyway.'

What McHugh had heard was sweet music to his ears. Well, imagine that, he thought. The son-in-law of the top IRA man in the North, a *lackey* to a Black 'n' Tan, and him living like a king in a sacred Irish monastery. What will the lads back in Belfast think on hearing this?

McHugh now held an ace card, to be played when the moment was right. Meanwhile, he was again laying down the poison by what he said to the Fermanagh three.

'To my knowing, most old soldiers keep memorabilia from their campaigns. Might it be the case that this, *Colonel Cartwell*, has some things that may be of interest to us? Which we could do with laying our hands on for future use?'

The three locals smiled icily in acknowledging McHugh's hunch and Sexton promised action. 'The least we can do is serve notice to the oul bastard and his kind, that this country is ours. And ours alone!'

Chapter Twenty

McNab did indeed arrive bright and early at the hotel that following morning, and engrossed in each other's bodies in the comfort of the big luxurious bed, it was a struggle for the newlyweds to be up and ready for him. But somehow they managed it, and dressed less formally that day they descended the grand staircase together with the bellboy in tow with their cases. Seeing McNab awaiting them at the foot of the stairs and sensing that he was itching to make another of his wise cracks, Anthony pointed a finger of subtle warning at him before he had chance to open his mouth. So McNab controlled his wit.

Mr and Mrs Brennan checked out of the hotel and set out on the road to Donegal and to Anthony's home place. They planned to visit Mr and Mrs Brennan senior, the girls, and not least the grave of the two boys. They would book into the one hotel in Toome and would stay the remainder of the weekend to take in some of the many scenic sights. McNab had been invited to make a holiday of it for himself and had reluctantly agreed, not wanting to be the one to make three a crowd. It had been Sarah who allayed his anxiety by stating that she wanted him to come along, as she wished to show her gratitude for his befriending Anthony in his times of need, those tragic and those joyous.

The journey south was a real adventure for Sarah, having never ventured much further than North Antrim. She looked on with a sense of wonder as the car weaved its way through the Irish countryside, at its most splendid with autumn golds, greens, browns and orangey-reds in abundance.

Their first stopping-off point on arrival in Toome was the graveyard. Retracing his steps through the maze of Celtic crosses and headstones, some ancient, some not so old, Anthony came to stand in silent prayer where his brothers had been laid to rest and was joined by his wife and close friend. They stood in silent prayer beneath a clear blue sky and much welcomed October sunshine. A chill wind blew and falling leaves rustled around their feet. In the far off distance the roar of the broad Atlantic was ever present. An old woman dressed entirely in black, her hobnail boots clicking as she came purposely along the pathway to the church to offer up her daily Rosary as the Angelus rang out at noon, threw them a hearty smile. Studying the old woman's craggy, weather-beaten face, which yet was so beautifully youthful in its own way, and noting the glint of mischief evident in her beady black eyes, Sarah hoped she'd be as fortunate in her old age.

Anthony was heartened to see an impressive cement headstone erected on the grave, to which he had readily contributed financially. He read quietly the simple inscription in white lettering engraved upon it: *In loving memory of Owen and Seamus Brennan, died 31.12.1949 aged 19 and 20yrs. Sadly missed by Mother, Father, Brothers and Sisters. In God's loving care. Our Blessed Lady Intercede. R.I.P.*

Upon the grave, Sarah left the posy of flowers she'd carried from her family home before taking their leave.

As they covered the short distance from the graveyard to the Brennan homestead, Sarah took stock of the many stone-built thatched cottages dotted across the rugged landscape, yet all uniquely different. She found it difficult to comprehend how a person, let alone families of six, eight, ten and more, lived in such confined spaces.

The generously warm welcome she experienced on arriving at Anthony's family home overwhelmed Sarah so much that she was moved to tears. It was obvious to her that a mother and father and two sisters ravaged by grief, were trying so hard to make her feel at ease and happy by placing their grieving temporarily to one side. Sarah realised the pain of others at first hand as Anthony's mother bravely fought back the tears when she embraced her in welcome. Sarah knew exactly what the other woman was thinking in that moment: that with the loss of her two youngest sons, a day such as this would never be for them. And true enough, the mother had been hoping that in time all her children would have been married and had children - her grandchildren. Sarah hoped that the woman would realise that she understood. She in turn embraced her and held her close. Like mother and daughter they stood as one, and it was an uplifting sight for all to behold.

Despite their thoughtful efforts to brighten themselves up for the occasion, Anthony could clearly see in the eyes of his father and mother that they were broken people deep inside, that their sense of loss was eating away at them. And still there was no word of Christy, which was in itself another kind of bereavement for them.

Life for them, and undoubtedly the girls too, must be pretty tough, concluded Anthony in thought. He was more in tune to their circumstances, now that he was home. And for the short time he would be, he was determined to ease the pain if only a little for those suffering most, by making it a weekend to recall fondly for years to come.

As McHugh returned to Belfast with his morale sky-high, a perturbed Sean Mor departed south at short notice. The Chief of Staff had called an urgent meeting of the Army Council. It was far into the Wicklow Hills and to the safe house of a trusted sympathiser that Sean Mor was driven. As arranged, he had been met at Dublin's Connolly Street Station by another Dubliner, the Director of Propaganda and Education, a former Trinity College Don and esteemed intellectual - a vital component in the movement's propaganda machine. Despite being closest to the Chief of Staff, the Dubliner had no inkling to what the meeting was about. This only aroused Sean Mor's fears once again. He considered the possibility that the Chief of Staff had had second thoughts on his status within the movement and was, after all, to be stood down or perhaps, face a worse fate. It was now known to others, through his earlier communiqué, that the down payment money was lost to the movement.

Sean Mor's fears were to prove unfounded, at least as to his own immediate fate. However, with his superior calling the Army Council to order and hearing him confirm the very latest intelligence reports from reliable sources, no one listening was left in any doubt as to the severity of the crisis threatening the republican movement and the new dangers presented to them all consequently. Due to increasing unionist suppression of the nationalist community, particularly along the border, and the perceived lack of response from the leadership in Dublin, there was mounting dissent among the IRA rank and file. Nowhere was this more evident than in County Tyrone, with one group of influential republicans the cause of grave concern. Sean Mor was surprised not to hear the names Sexton and O'Rourke mentioned also, and considered his last meeting with the Fermanagh Brigade to have been to good effect.

The Chief of Staff sought suggestion from among his troop of men as to how best prevent the 'boiling over' of unrest and how to stimulate, in the short-term, new faith and hope in the movement's mission and methods. Each of the other southerners had their say. Some suggested the immediate suspension of those brigades instigating unrest, with the Dublin-based GHQ staff then arresting control of battalion staff and volunteers direct. Others proposed that an 'example' be made of key antagonists. However it was Sean Mor's considered analysis and proposed action which fell most favourably on the ears of the Chief of Staff. It was similar to the course of action he had contemplated. The Northern Command Commandant simply proposed that the prime antagonists in County Tyrone, whom they had once respected as committed republicans, be quietly invited to resign from the IRA on the understanding that IRA weapons and munitions would strictly remain property of the army. By doing so, Sean Mor reasoned that the leadership would be seen to be assertive in its actions and unperturbed by the prospect of losing members rather than abandon long-term objectives. This in turn would renew faith in the leadership among those members who had up to now remained loyal to it. All were impressed by the simple though ingenious logic behind the Belfast man's proposal and the Chief of Staff was quick to endorse it.

Winning the support of his comrades, Sean Mor moved that the resignations of the Tyrone dissidents should be overseen by trusted brigade staff in Tyrone. He cautioned that to involve 'outsiders' in the present climate, may be judged 'dictatorial' by those awaiting further excuse to breakaway - revengefully so. Again the Chief of Staff and others seconded. It was agreed that the Tyrone dissenters were to be invited to resign immediately by the South Tyrone Brigade staff, which remained loyal to the Army Council.

Not wishing to undermine the role of the political arm of the movement, which was presently stagnant, the Chief of Staff ordered the Director of Propaganda and Education to initiate a more proactive political campaign of agitation north and south of the border to coincide with the border campaign once it commenced. At this point, the Director of Operations informed comrades that people and resources were being carefully put into place at home and overseas, so that a series of raids on military stores could be realistically undertaken at the most opportune moment. Regardless of the unease in the ranks, all agreed the need still for planning to remain secretive, thus avoiding the stirring-up of too much motivation and hope over what was to come, and so minimising the real risk of jeopardising everything if enemy forces picked-up on a sudden flurry of activity or rumour. A steady, measured pace toward achieving long-term goals was desirable by all. The meeting closed on that consensus.

Walking Sean Mor under the bright autumn sunshine to the waiting car nearby, the much relieved Chief of Staff confided the depth of his earlier fears over a split.

'You know Sean, to be standing amid these hills where I spent endless days and nights duping the Free Staters, leaving by the back door as they smashed their way in through the front, and living on raw energy and nerves, reinforces my determination to avoid a bloody feud. For there is surely no worse crime perpetrated against any nation, than for its sons to butcher each other in its very name.' The old veteran fell into sad reflection. 'The atrocities committed by both sides during the civil war were barbaric, equally as bad as those carried out by the Black and Tans. I never want to see that barbarism perpetrated again by comrades against fellow comrades, despite what the indifference may be. Such an abomination would set back the cause of Irish freedom a hundred years. God knows, the road to freedom is long enough without labouring ourselves any more.' With renewed vigour the ageing Dubliner stopped and turned to face Sean Mor. 'The fight is with the British Government. We must carry that fight to it with haste, effectively so. But, realistically speaking, I know, as you do, that we must keep a constant eye over our shoulder. The threat from within is a real one. Hopefully, today we have identified the means to quell the threat, but if need be, and only as a last resort, force must be applied in a disciplined manner. It must have an acceptable face. But let us pray *this* will never come to be.'

Sean Mor already prayed so, each day that dawned.

New life came to the Brennan home that weekend through music, song, dance and cheer. Family, friends and neighbours called in droves to the ceilidh house two nights in succession, and Sarah had been the star attraction. All the locals were amazed that a girl from Belfast could put them to shame when it came to dancing a reel and a jig. Old JohnJoe had given the dancing queen a run for her money though. He had taken sparks out of the flag-stone floor as young Mick Onion played hell for leather on the fiddle. Mother and father had laughed heartily and cheerfully sang along for the first time in ages, and the girls too had their spirits uplifted on witnessing such an exhibition. All were agreed that Anthony's choice of wife had been a wise one. She was judged to be beautiful, respectful, intelligent, and without doubt, talented. While obviously popular with the men folk, the local women, especially the younger ones, were enviously engrossed in the city girl's movie-star-looks. Her exciting hairstyle, fresh make-up and perfectly cut dress, so colourful and stylishly new, had them all critically evaluating their own subdued statement of femininity. Nevertheless, the women had got on together powerfully, for despite the Belfast woman's pronounced flair, she remained a down-to-earth sort. At heart one of them.

That Sunday morning the visiting trio knelt and prayed together with all others in church, with the rest of the sunny, cold day spent racing each other along sandy beaches and climbing a hilltop to sit and savour the beauty of the rugged land and vast open sea merging below, so spectacularly. Sarah came to appreciate fully what Padraig Pearse had experienced and expressed through his shared writings, giving account of his sacred visits to Ireland's rural west.

Departing the simply furnished, though comfortable Main Street hotel in the neighbouring town of Toome, the newlyweds and their close friend called to the Brennan home early that next morning to bid their farewells. Sarah knew that she was now part of a larger family and community, who had taken her into their hearts, as she had they to hers. She choked back tears on kissing those in turn who in the shadow of their common heartache, had made her feel so welcome, so loved. She left them knowing that they were, and would remain, so very special to her always.

McNab had thoroughly enjoyed himself also, and had made friends for a lifetime. And Anthony? He was full of hope that the three days of merriment marked a turning point for his loved ones. He prayed that they too would live life with new hope, which he himself sought to do, together with his new wife, and the family and friends in Belfast to whom they would return.

Chapter Twenty-One

That December, McHugh kept his engagement with the Fermanagh three, who had deliberately adopted a low profile over recent months so to avoid the scrutinising eye of suspicion from higher command. They met in Belfast under cover of darkness to undertake reconnaissance and to finalise details for the planned attack. Firstly, the 'expulsion' of the Tyrone dissidents, whom they collectively judged to be mavericks, was briefly discussed. The forging of any alliance with the Tyrone men was quickly and unanimously ruled out. Apart from doubting their true motives, McHugh, Sexton and the O'Rourkes were uncomfortable with the men being so public in their fall out with the leadership, and secondly, the three remained determined to wrestle control of the IRA from within. The one stumbling block to the execution of the planned attack, which would, they firmly believed, achieve their goal, had been the acquisition of guns, other than those that were the property of the army. They knew that to use such guns would expose them to the risk of detection by their own through the chance discovery of weapons being removed from a dump without authorisation. This, consequently, would warrant the execution of those responsible. But as a consequence of the O'Rourkes investigations, all appeared to be in hand. All that remained was waiting for the chosen time to come around.

While Anthony was outwardly grateful toward Aunt Bella for offering her home as a permanent place of residence for his wife and he, he secretly longed for a corner of his own, alone with Sarah. He felt obligated to consider his every word, his every move whilst under the elder's roof, despite Sarah's earnest efforts to make him feel at home. She doted on him at every opportunity, when not attending to Aunt Bella. The nighttime was particularly difficult for Anthony. Knowing the frail aunt lay on the other side of the thin dividing bedroom wall, asleep or not, played heavily on his mind when making love to Sarah. He could not help but be restrained in the act, which greatly frustrated him.

Under the circumstance, Sarah too confessed when Anthony broached the subject, that she felt somewhat guilty when making love, knowing her aunt in the adjoining room was at death's door. Anthony understood his wife's dilemma. She was caught between her love for him and her devotion to her aunt, who having clung onto life to see them married, was letting go of it with each passing day.

Time for the oul girl is short enough without my adding to her burdens, thought Anthony, listening to the old woman's wheezing coughs rising from the adjoining bedroom one night as he lay awake beside an exhausted Sarah.

Remaining committed to caring for Aunt Bella in those early days of married life, while at the same time seeking to honour her marriage vows fully, Sarah was forced into thinking of herself first and foremost on receiving confirmation early that December that she was pregnant, and on being warned by the family doctor to 'take it easy.' It was his considered opinion that no one could keep to the pace she was setting herself, what with working fulltime at the mill and the duties she undertook outside of it. He prescribed plenty of rest as the best medication.

The welcomed news was much celebrated within family circles in both Belfast and Donegal, where a grandchild for Dan and Mary Brennan would greatly ease the heartache over the loss of Seamus and Owen.

An ecstatic father-to-be was further delighted to learn that Christmas by means of a greeting card received from Felix and Bernadette Gresham, both still in Liverpool, that they hoped to return to Belfast the following summer. Standing at the bar in the Coat of Arms, Anthony remarked, 'What a party that will be, what with the baby's birth and my old pal Felix back in town.' Delighted by his son-in-law's high spirits, the grandfather-to-be smiled and nodded, comfortable in the knowledge that Felix Gresham was now on the outside; that the business over the lost money was dead and buried, along with Stack. Buying in a round of drinks, Sean Mor raised his glass and toasted 'Good health' to Sarah and Anthony, and the baby-to-be. Anthony acknowledged the toast and drank his drink heartily, longing for the New Year to come soon.

The death of the King of England in February 1952 had McHugh deliberating whether to target an RUC memorial parade to be held in Belfast later that month, which would guarantee a Protestant backlash. McHugh's bravado was up, having won sympathy and pledges of practical support in recent days from his former brigade staff - with the exception of Barratt of course - who had all been suddenly and unexpectedly 'stood down' in what was, in McHugh's considered calculation, a clean-out at the top by Sean Mor. It was clear to him that the big man was using the opportunity of the Tyrone dissidents' departure from the mainstream to remove any remaining threat, no matter how remote, to his power-base from within, and that Barratt was now firmly sided with Sean Mor. But guarded against any sly counter-manoeuvre by his adversary, McHugh opted to keep his new found allies in the dark as to plans afoot for July, until such time that he was convinced he was not being set-up. And if he were to involve the others, he would do so at the eleventh hour, when they would have little option but to either keep good to their word or run scared.

Meeting with Sexton to sound out his thoughts as to his own plan to attack the memorial parade, Sexton argued that such an act could well provoke a backlash yes, but by their own people, the majority of whom would not stomach the re-emergence of militant republicanism by way of such an atrocity, on such an occasion. Sexton went on to persuade McHugh to keep to the original date set for planned action. Anyhow, the firepower was not yet at hand. Only that final critical piece of preparation work remained to be undertaken, and the O'Rourke brothers were to attend to it when the time was right.

It was the night of 2nd July 1952. Sitting in the car parked in the shadows cast along the slip road directly opposite the isolated public house, the O'Rourke brothers had waited impatiently for all but one of the night's customers to take their leave from the local bar, so leaving only that stubborn patron behind after closing, as was commonplace most nights. It was that same patron in whom the O'Rourkes were interested, and with whom they now set out to have a quiet word. Entering the dimly lit barroom the brothers were not surprised to find their man perched on a high stool and slouched over the bar, an empty glass and a near empty bottle of whiskey in front of him. The thin, poker-faced barman, who had been expecting the late night callers, left an unopened bottle of whiskey and two clean glasses on top of the bar counter, then quietly withdrew, leaving the three men alone together.

A weasel-faced wiry little man with wispy grey hair, Willie Bogle was the local postman, and was finally due to retire in three weeks time after forty-five years treading the roads. He was well-known and much liked by all in the community, those Catholics in the small enclave nearby among whom he lived a bachelor life contentedly, as well as by his own Protestant folk of greater number, spread throughout the town land. Bogle was known to be a heavy drinker and baffled all as to how he managed to be up so early and sprightly each morning to do his round, not a letter known to go astray. Saying had it, that he could down a bottle of whiskey in one sitting, no bother. The O'Rourkes were intent on putting this to the test.

Bogle had not heard the brothers enter and was only aware of their presence when they casually presented themselves either side of him. Though heavily intoxicated, Bogle was able to put names to faces. He had come to know the boys from a distance, though had been more familiar with their father, a man of notoriety. For most Fermanagh Protestants, it was taboo to integrate socially with the O'Rourkes, be it their grandparents or their parents who had been the enemy years earlier. Now, the sons of an infamous IRA man who had murdered many a good Protestant surrounded him.

Unscrewing and removing the top from the full bottle of whiskey, to first pour himself and his brother a large measure, then topping up

Bogle's glass to the brim, Oliver O'Rourke sought to establish a rapport with the postman. 'Come and have a drink with us Mister Bogle. Here's good health to you!'

Sensitive to the insincerity in the man's voice and noting the glint of malice in the eyes of the other brother to his right, Bogle thought it best to accept their false generosity. He took the glass in hand and drank a large mouthful of whiskey from it, which he swallowed easily. He intended to finish his drink quickly then be on his way. But it soon became apparent to Bogle that it wouldn't be as easy as that. His glass was quickly refilled, and looking about him, he considered the barman to be conspicuous with his absence.

'C'mon, drink up!' Oliver O'Rourke sounded almost impatient.

Downing the first measure so quickly, on top of the eight or nine neat double whiskeys from earlier in the evening, went straight to Bogle's head and his resistance to accepting any more was waning. Coaxing another large whiskey into Bogle, the O'Rourkes got ready to make their move. 'That's it, get it down your neck,' mocked Dermott O'Rourke, receiving much amusement from seeing Bogle guzzle the whiskey as though there was no tomorrow.

It was simple chitchat at first with Bogle - who was just about holding his own - the weather, the harvest, the older man's impending retirement. Bogle was barely audible. He spat and spluttered in getting his words out. He was on the verge of passing out, so the O'Rourkes wasted no further time in getting to the heart of the matter in hand. Oliver O'Rourke spoke slowly and clearly.

'Mister Bogle, you call to Edenderry Abbey regularly. Y'know, where the Englishman lives. Is it true what we hear, that you have to keep the head well down, with thon crazy oul fella firing off those guns of his?'

The drink now his master, Bogle laughed aloud on hearing this. He knocked back the third glassful before slobbering, almost incoherently, 'No! Thon's bullshit!' The O'Rourkes were suddenly glum-faced. 'No, he doesn't fire the guns at all. Y'see, he tells me, they're too lethal to fire - *Ha*!' The O'Rourkes threw each other a congratulatory glance behind the elder's back before pressing on. 'How many guns would you say the oul boy has, Mister Bogle?' Bogle shrugged his shoulders in saying with a little sarcasm, 'Ack, who knows? Enough to fight another war.' Bogle went into a fit of hysterical laughter at his own humour and nearly fell off his stool. Oliver O'Rourke stretched out a steadying hand and said with mock sincerity, 'I think we need to be getting you home, Mister Bogle.' Oliver O'Rourke winked to his brother then, who smiled smugly. With a firm grip on each of his upper arms, Bogle was hurriedly led through the barroom, out the main door and across the deserted country road to the car parked out of sight. Unable to stand never mind walk, Bogle was a dead weight and slumped in a pathetic heap on the back seat on being manhandled into the car. The O'Rourkes quickly piled into the front of the vehicle that started first time to pull away quietly.

No one heard or saw the same car pull up at the rear of Bogle's remote cottage five minutes later or the two men drag Bogle into his unkempt house. Bogle was dumped unceremoniously into a fireside chair. Saliva dribbled from the drunk's mouth and off his chin. He was so far gone he could not lift his head from off his chest or keep his eyes open. The brothers stood over Bogle contemplating. It was the younger O'Rourke who was first to reveal his thoughts.

'This oul fucker could wake up in the morning remembering every word we said. D'yeh want to run the risk of being strung up or shot by our own, due to 'em opening his fucking gob?' Oliver O'Rourke did not have to reply to the question for his brother to know the answer. Walking to the rear of the tatty armchair in which Bogle sat slumped and asleep, Dermott O'Rourke grabbed a handful of Bogle's wispy grey hair, and shunted the non-resistant, sixty-nine year old forward in his seat. Bogle was sitting upright with his skinny arms dangling by his side, his head jerked back. With an almighty thrust forward, Dermott O'Rouke smashed Bogle's bony forehead against the edge of the fire range's cast iron hotplate. The crack of Bogle's skull made Oliver O'Rourke wince, while his younger brother, who had not batted an eyelid, casually wiped his hands against the lapels of his short jacket. Bogle was dead before his body hit the floor.

The O'Rourkes turned and calmly walked out of the house, content in the knowledge that the means to enable the Belfast attack to proceed was in hand, and that Bogle's 'accidental' death would leave them with a clear run.

Chapter Twenty-Two

The sudden stabbing pain deep in her hugely swollen abdomen forced Sarah onto her knees halfway up the stairs at Aunt Bella's. Clutching the bannister for dear life with one hand, she nervously lifted her maternity skirt and saw blood trickling down the inside of her thighs. She clenched her teeth tightly; her face was contorted with agony as the excruciating spasmodic pain gripped her once more and her panic-stricken screams were heard further along the street. Two women neighbours idly gossiping under a sticky July evening heat on a front doorstep three doors down, were shaken by the terrifying screams that shattered the easy peacefulness and were moved to investigate. On partly pushing open the front door of the house they found their way blocked by the body of a woman lying wedged behind the door - between it and the foot of the stairs. A helpless voice from within cried out in desperation, 'Sarah! Sarah! Please God ... someone help!' Aunt Bella had crawled out of her sick bed to the top of the landing on hearing Sarah's screams and now looked down horrified on finding her great-niece lying twisted and motionless at the foot of the stairs.

'Bogle's long years of hard drinking finally caught up with him. He simply fell over in a drunken stupor and split his skull.' This was the gist of conversation in the packed barroom of that isolated public house in which Bogle had sat the evening before. Sitting alone together over their pints of porter up one corner, the O'Rourke brothers received quiet satisfaction from hearing this on the grapevine. The local news reports signalled that this was also the theory that the RUC had reached. The brothers finished off their drinks and slipped out of the barroom without a second glance from anyone.

   'Oliver, are you sure yer man behind the bar can be trusted?'
   'I don't think we need lose any sleep over him. He won't want his missus scraping his brains off the floor.' The brothers quickened their step to the car. They were due to meet with Sexton, then journey on to Edenderry Abbey to pay the Englishman a visit.

   The three dissatisfied IRA men sat waiting in a lay-by a half mile from the abbey so to give time for the last of the servant staff to leave for home. The men had taken it in turn to lie up at night in fields overlooking the abbey with powerful field binoculars to clock out the Englishman's staff, those farm labourers and servant girls. Keeping a check on their wristwatches and at the anticipated hour, they had all looked out for the last servant girl to cycle over the brow of the hill to their left, pass them by, then disappear out of sight as she free-wheeled the fall in the road. From their combined reconnaissance notes they also knew that the last of the lights at the abbey would be going out about now. The key turned in the car's ignition and the vehicle pulled out slowly, silently from the shadows to cover the short distance to Edenderry Abbey. The car's headlights were dipped and on reaching the crotch of the 'Y' shaped junction, the car turned to the right and travelled five hundred yards further on before reversing into and down a narrow dirt track which led to acres upon acres of lush green fields of grass, property of the Englishman. The three alighted from the car and closed its doors quietly. They stood silently for a moment to listen. Only the gentle breeze ruffling the leafy trees overhanging them broke the stillness of the night. A star-filled sky cast a whitish glow and served to show the way for the three men as they moved to the rear of the car. The vehicle's driver, Oliver O'Rourke, opened the boot lid and reached inside. He passed a loaded shotgun to Sexton, who'd had secret hold of it for some years, a hurley stick to his brother, and took charge of a five gallon container full of petrol and a heavy-duty torch before gently shutting the boot lid. They pulled the scarves hanging loosely around their necks over their mouths and noses. Sexton at the lead, they proceeded up the track and darted across the narrow country road. Climbing over a low stonewall, they scurried up the field toward the east wing of Edenderry Abbey, their long matchstick shadows stretched out over the grass as they went, their hearts racing, their thoughts filled with murderous intent. They were particularly careful not to be heard on approaching and sneaking across the rear of the dog kennels wherein, they knew, half a dozen Rottweilers were housed. Only the sloshing of petrol inside the can marked their presence, but they reached the patio on the eastside of the abbey house unchallenged. They gathered around the patio's glass door, which when breached would lead them to the main panel and glass door of the abbey itself. The building was in darkness. The Englishman would hopefully be sound asleep in his master bedroom on the west wing. He would not hear the glass break, but the dogs might.

Their eyes intense, the three gritted their teeth as the hurley forced the small pane of glass immediately above the door handle. It gave way easily, with only a faint smashing of glass upon the tiled floor on the opposite side of the door. They stood silent for a moment. Nothing stirred. They slipped in through the door, opened then by a hand reaching inside to turn the key carelessly left in its lock. They used the same method on the second door and were finally inside the abbey. The torch quickly came into use and the way ahead was clear to them. On the balls of their feet they made their way unheard along the hallway to the foot of the grand staircase rising from the middle of a very spacious open quadrangle. From here all parts of the vast building could be accessed. Sexton and Dermott O'Rourke took to the stairs in search of the Englishman's bedroom. Placing the petrol container on the black and white floor that appeared as one huge chessboard, Oliver O'Rourke set out to locate the ground-floor room in which the guns were kept. Keeping the torch on his person, he selected one of the many doors around him at random so to begin his search. He glimpsed the kitchen then the dining hall and the library before feeling his patience run thin. 'Bloody hell! A labyrinth!' The scarf wrapped around his face muffled his curses. Swinging open a fourth door somewhat recklessly and taking a few paces into the room, he froze. The beam of his torch picked out two glass-like eyes, which were fixed menacingly on him. The Rottweiler sprinted silently towards him, a killing snarl gradually rising from behind its flashing teeth in the last few paces before it sprang with its bone crushing jaws wide apart and hot saliva dripping. The dog sank its razor sharp teeth around the intruder's throat as its immense muscular body weight knocked the fear-stricken man crashing onto the flat of his back, the torch skimming across the floor, its beam of light illuminating man and beast.

Oliver O'Rourke had felt the fear ooze from his pores as the dog had come at him. He'd been transfixed to the spot at its mercy. Now he was pinned beneath and eyeball-to-eyeball with the animal - spread-eagled over him - that threatened to rip his throat apart. He could smell the dog's vile breath as it tightened its grip, a vice-like grip around his throat. Luckily for him the dog had lock-jawed on a mouthful of thick woven wool and its piercing teeth had literally torn the skin from around his Adam's apple. But there was the danger of him being choked to death as the scarf, being violently yanked by the dog, began to constrict his breathing, while his head, like that of a rag doll, was pummelled against the marble tiled floor as the dog went into a frenzy.

Oliver O'Rourke was sure the others could hear the dog's snarling echo along the many passages, but knew he had only seconds to save his own life. He was determined in that moment - with all that he had been through over the years flashing in front of him - not to die like an animal in the jaws of another. In blind instinct, he gripped the dog's hard muscular head with both hands and sunk his thick thumbs deep into its black, ferocious eyes. The dog's snarling turned to hellish yelps. Oliver O'Rourke did not release his grip. Instead, he sunk his thumbs deeper as the animal - itself gripped by terror - released its grip. He pulled the dog off him while raising himself onto his knees and, mustering all his strength, threw the dog onto its back.

'Watch out Oliver!'

Oliver O'Rourke looked up to see the ghostly outline of someone standing over him with hands raised above his head and sensed the man's intended action, so was quick to let go his hold on the dog - rising on all fours again. He felt the whoosh of the hurley breeze against his face as it came down with an almighty crack, dead centre of the Rottweiler's square head, killing it instantly.

Colonel Cartwell's eyes had shot open on hearing the dog's yelping, the others in the compound beyond barking madly, only to feel the cold steel muzzle of a shotgun pressed hard into the side of his face force his head further into the pillow. A local voice, menacingly stark, addressed him in the near darkness of the room.

'We want no heroics from you old soldier. That's right, it's your worst nightmare come true. We're the IRA and your time has come to answer for your crimes against our people.'

Still trembling over his ordeal, Oliver O'Rourke was grateful his brother had arrived on the scene when he did.

'I thought my day had come there for a moment. Thank Christ for the oul hurley, eh?'

'Sure, it's never let us down yet, brother,' replied Dermott, inspecting the hurley in the grey light within the abbey for any sign of damage. The touch of light humour between the brothers served to settle their nerves a little. The commotion on the stairs drew their attention. With Oliver O'Rourke picking up the torch, they went to investigate.

The naked Englishman, in the spotlight as he descended the stairs like some pitiful character about to meet a horrendous fate in some Shakespearian play, appeared ghostlike in the eyes of Oliver and Dermott O'Rourke. They were both lost for words as a very bony, very white-skinned, grey-haired old man came towards them at the point of the gun.

Colonel Cartwell came to attention in front of the brothers and in a demanding, dominant voice, stated, 'I wish to speak to your Commanding Officer. I must protest at this obscene treatment!'

Dermott O'Rourke's outburst of laughter was almost psychotic in tone and drew a questioning look from his brother and Sexton.

'You mad Irish scum! There's not an ounce of discipline among you!' Cartwell screamed, as if dressing down misfits on parade. As sudden as his outburst of laughter had been, so was Dermott O'Rourke's lunge forward to viciously slap Cartwell across the mouth, which almost felled the old soldier. The silence in the quadrangle then, rebounded off all four walls. All took stock of the developing situation. Sexton took control.

'Move it!'

They followed a bloody-mouthed Cartwell into the study, where he came to an abrupt halt on finding the dog dead at his feet. Engulfed with rage, Cartwell swung around and screamed violently again at those strangers who had brought such barbarity to his home. 'You bloody Irish bastards! The Black and Tans should have put down your mothers!'

Taking a firm grip of his hurley with both hands, Dermott O'Rourke stepped forward to have another go. Sexton intervened by stepping between the two men and, pointing to a fireside chair, said firmly, 'Take him over there and tie him up.' Oliver O'Rourke manhandled Cartwell toward the chair. His brother Dermott was baying for blood and spoke his mind in a seethed whisper. 'Liam, let me put a bullet through the fucker's head.' Sexton considered his request for a moment, then looked across the room to see Oliver O'Rourke use his torn scarf to tie the Englishman's skinny arms and legs - heavily scarred by old war wounds - to the armrests and legs of the chair, and recalled to mind stories told by his mother of Black 'n' Tan atrocities.

'No. Shooting the bastard is too good for him. I've got another way.'

The display cabinet's glass panel in the corner of the study room was smashed through. A dozen bolt-action rifles, shotguns, and some twenty pistols, and revolvers, all in mint condition, plus many boxes of assorted ammunition were seized and piled into the centre of the large table cloth snatched from the adjoining dining hall, and which had been spread over the floor of the study.

With what looked like a large swag bag between their feet, Sexton directed the O'Rourkes to proceed with the cache to the car. He would catch them up in a short while, 'once completing business.' The O'Rourkes threw Cartwell one last condemning look before departing with their prize. Neither had a word nor thought of pity for the old man, who sat trembling, his head bowed in silent prayer. He knew his time was short. Minutes earlier, he had seen the faces of all three, the other two eventually as they'd relaxed their guard on removing their scarves when kneeling to examine the weapons under torchlight in front of him. He'd known in that instant that they would kill him, and he was prepared for it. A bullet in the head, perhaps even one of his own, would be quick and merciful. He was not afraid. But the smell of petrol filling the room then struck terror into Cartwell's very soul, for he feared a worse fate.

Working his way backwards with the petrol can from the rooms upstairs, down the grand staircase, through all the other main rooms on the ground floor and finally into the study, where he splashed curtains and upholstery, Sexton saved the last of the can's contents for Cartwell and casually poured the remaining petrol over the old soldier's head. Trying hard to retain his military stature, his stiff upper lip as a teardrop of petrol fell from the end of his hooknose, Cartwell protested. 'This is not the done thing by us soldiers.' Sexton was quick with his answer. 'Neither were the actions of your Black 'n' Tan friends. You can tell them that too, when you join them ... in Hell!' Sexton turned and walked away. Cartwell refused to let it go, his voice breaking in saying with forced bravado, 'I'll see you in Hell too then Paddy!'

Stepping over the dead dog, Sexton paused in the doorway, and without looking back, said casually over his shoulder, 'For me, Hell is right here, living in a partitioned land.'

Sexton took his leave unchallenged.

Pausing by the door leading into the patio and placing the empty container between his feet, Sexton removed a box of matches from his jacket pocket. He struck one, placed it in the box, which ignited like a flare, and threw it into the quadrangle. A loud whooshing noise was immediately followed by several trails of fire simultaneously igniting and quickly spreading in different directions. Sexton looked on in amazement as one fire-trail rapidly climbed the stairs, then the whole interior of the abbey seemed to erupt into a huge fireball. Stooping to pick up the container once more, he turned and ran back along the field away from the abbey. The agonising screams of a human being perishing in the flames, mixed with the barking of crazed dogs smelling death, would, he knew, haunt him to his dying day.

Chapter Twenty-Three

The uniformed Knights of Malta nursing auxiliaries holding their weekly first aid class in Clonard School assembly hall had been quick to arrive at Aunt Bella's on the alarm being raised. The very petite female nursing auxiliary had easily slipped through the narrow gap between the front door and its frame, behind which the heavily pregnant woman lay semi-conscious. Once in, the nurse carefully manoeuvred Sarah enough to enable her two male colleagues to also squeeze into the cramped hallway, freeing her to attend to the old woman upstairs, deeply traumatised by the ordeal.

Sarah had soon been rushed to the City Hospital in the Knights of Malta ambulance, and on arrival an urgent blood transfusion was swiftly administered as she had haemorrhaged heavily. A check of her abdomen confirmed that the baby was still breathing and the attending doctor was quick to stop the bleeding.

Making his way to the hospital with haste on receiving a phone call at work, Anthony sat holding his sedated wife's hand into the small hours. He would not leave Sarah's side until mother and child were both out of danger.

Sean Mor and his wife planned to visit Sarah again the following day. They were happy to take their leave from the hospital knowing Anthony would be by their daughter's side throughout the night. They returned home just before midnight, mentally drained and physically exhausted. The six long, worrying hours since Sarah had been admitted to hospital had taken its toll on the parents. Mrs McParland had assured Anthony that meanwhile, she would be praying hard for Sarah, he and their child.

McHugh was out of his bed much earlier than usual that following morning. Peeping through the heavy twill curtain, the bright July sunshine signalled another day of grand weather at least. With his shirt and trousers flung over an arm, he tiptoed downstairs. Once dressed, he made himself a mug of tea and sat down at the scullery table to once more go over the plan logged in his head. It was a good plan, bound to succeed. Much pleased with his scheming, he checked his wristwatch. He took his leave from the house to put the plan into action just as his wife and children stirred from their slumber.

The squat, retiring detective, rigged out in an ill-fitting fawn coloured mac, stood amid the smoldering remains that was once Edenderry Abbey and pondered. Within a period of twenty-four hours he had been called on to investigate two deaths, each of the deceased a prominent figure in the community. The first death, that of the postman, Bogle, was an accident, he was convinced. This latest one however, on studying the charred remains of Colonel Cartwell lying at his feet, was not so clear-cut. Looking around him, half a dozen uniformed men and three forensic officers in blue boiler suits sifted through the debris, from which palls of grey-white smoke eerily intermingled with the early morning mist. The scene of utter devastation led him to believe strongly that this fire may not be, as had been suggested by one of his rookie constables, 'the act of an eccentric old soldier gone berserk'. His problem, being the detective, was finding enough evidence to lay his case to rest, either way. For at first sight, anything of any significance appeared to have been incinerated.

McHugh was hoping that the flat cloth cap cocked low over the left side of his face and the long winter coat he wore on such a gloriously sunny day, would not arouse too much suspicion. He entered the park and sat himself down on the first wooden bench just inside the main gates from where, through the gaps in the park's perimeter wrought iron railings, he could look out for the car to pull up in the wide, tree-lined avenue opposite. If working to plan, the Fermanagh three would show up in less than half an hour.

Putting his scheme together meticulously, McHugh had calculated that a fast car left parked in the residential suburbs of south Belfast, home to many of the city's Protestant elite, would not draw the attention of the RUC, as it would if spotted along the Falls.

Conscious of the heavy bulk in his inner jacket pocket, Sexton started up the powerful Ford Buick that had been stolen from outside a market town hotel south of the border a week earlier and garaged out of sight ever since. He was due to pick-up the O'Rourkes at Portadown, County Armagh, from where they would carry on to Belfast to meet up with McHugh. They would arrive there at approximately 11.15am. The attack in the city was planned for noon. For Sexton, the day would mark a new beginning in the fight for Irish freedom, the end to partition.

Working to his own secret agenda, not only had it been McHugh's idea to park - what was to be the getaway car - in a residential avenue only a brisk fifteen minute walk from where the ambush was to take place, he had also contended that in terms of departing the city after the attack, it would be wise for the other three men to abandon the stolen car halfway between Belfast and Fermanagh, where the risk of running into an outlying RUC border patrol, was too great. Sexton and the O'Rourkes had agreed with him. So the O'Rourkes were to make their own car available at Portadown for the return trip to Fermanagh. Quietly confident in his scheme knowing this, McHugh checked his wristwatch again. The hour much anticipated by him, fast approached.

Sarah had awoken to the day feeling sore and a little groggy, though managed a smile on finding Anthony by her bedside. He had stayed awake all night, not taking his eyes off her. The night nurse and duty doctor had attended to Sarah throughout the night and Anthony was greatly relieved to learn that she was very much better. Her condition and that of the unborn baby was stable. He was further heartened on hearing Sarah complain by mid-morning of feeling hungry, impressing this on him by saying with a faint smile, 'I could eat a horse!' Smiling too, Anthony replied, 'I'll go and check if it's okay for you to have a bite to eat.' Sarah served Anthony a full smile. 'Don't be long love, hurry back with something nice.'

Anthony had walked only a short distance from the side ward when his name was screamed aloud. Darting back into the room, he saw Sarah's face screwed up in agony, her knees drawn up under the bed sheet covering her. A nurse quickly appeared on the scene and hurrying to the patient's bedside, lifted the sheet and peaked underneath. After a moment's deliberation, the nurse turned to Anthony and said gently, but assertively, 'You had better wait outside Mister Brennan. Your wife's in labour!'

Sean Mor worked busily in his shop in trying to keep his worry over his eldest at bay. He kept the radio switched off that morning so that he could hear the shout from the post office next door in the event of a phone call coming through from the hospital. Consequently, he did not hear the eleven o'clock news report of the major fire overnight in County Fermanagh, nor of the death in that same fire of the retired British Army war veteran, Colonel Cartwell.

Arriving on time, McHugh made a mental note of the stolen car's colour, make and registration as the Fermanagh three stepped leisurely out of the car into the quiet avenue opposite. McHugh stood up and exited the park and walked on ahead. Sexton was to follow him to the City Hall, a short distance away, where they would seemingly engage in some light conversation on one of the public benches there. The O'Rourke brothers, walking at a discreet distance behind Sexton, were to proceed to a café just along Royal Avenue, to the front of the City Hall, where Sexton would join them shortly after.

    On the City Hall's manicured lawns, Sexton joined McHugh on a bench cast in the shadow of the voluminous statue of Queen Victoria, which fronted the government building. Once checking that they were not being observed, and with only the resident pigeons for company, Sexton removed from his inside jacket pocket a brown paper bag containing the fully loaded 9mm Parabellum pistol and slid it across the wooden seat to McHugh. He quickly collected it and placed it in a side pocket of his long winter coat. 'Is it working okay?'

    Sexton was surprised by the Belfast man's gall. 'It's so good, I'm left wondering how the Germans lost the war with such firepower,' he mused. 'I test fired it last night. It's perfect. No problem at all.'

    McHugh was in no laughing mood. He was curious as to the outcome of the previous night's events.

    'How did it go last night?'

    Sexton gave a wry smile. 'Let's put it like this Fergal, Christmas came early for some folk in Fermanagh.' Sexton asked a question of his own then. 'Are we still in business?' McHugh nodded and looking Sexton in the eye, said coolly, 'Good luck.' The local man stood up and carried on his way, putting to flight the many pigeons milling about his feet.

On the strike of noon, Anthony and Sarah's first child was born in the same Victorian hospital side ward as the mother had been twenty-one years earlier. As then, this had been a difficult birth, but this anguished mother had an added pain to cope with, knowing this was to be her one and only child. He was so lucky to be alive, and how she thanked God for him. At this moment in time she coped with this knowledge alone, for the sake of one other.

Being told he was the father of a healthy son, Anthony jumped for joy and slapped his thigh in self-congratulation. When finally composing himself a little under the amused eye of the otherwise stern-faced ward sister, he was led into the room where new life had just come into the world.

Holding their son protectively, Sarah managed to smile through the discomfort at Anthony who stopped short of the bed, wide-eyed and open-mouthed at what he saw. Burdened with the knowledge that she would not bear another child, Sarah continued to force a smile for Anthony's sake. She was pleased she'd given birth to a son; she knew how much Anthony had wanted a boy. She held the child up to him like a sacred offering. A near-tearful, joyful Anthony took the kicking little bundle awkwardly in his arms and mouthed silently to Sarah, 'I love you.'

Chapter Twenty-Four

McHugh had made his way to the long established snooker rooms situated on the corner of that street directly opposite the one in which the RUC barrack stood, just off the lower Falls Road. The solidly built, three storey red-brick barrack, its ground floor outer walls nevertheless protected with sandbags, its windows barred, was a five minute walk from Belfast's city centre. Playing alone on the green baize with his mind on other matters, McHugh found it hard to pot a ball. Checking his watch against the clock on the snooker room's far wall, its hour and minute hand having just struck noon, he knew that at any minute all hell would be let loose in the nearby street.

Hands in coat pockets, their trigger fingers at the ready, the O'Rourkes walked briskly in step through the crowds of workers spilling out of the factories and offices to spend their precious midday lunch break browsing in shop windows under the magnificent July sunshine. Sexton, taking up the rear, would cover the brothers when they went into action. Now, stepping out of the hustle and bustle of the throng, they fast approached the target zone. The O'Rourkes pulled their flat caps low onto their foreheads as they crossed the lower Falls to enter the side street where their targets were to be found. Sexton crossed over behind them and took up position on the corner of the street. He had a wide angle view of the sandbagged barrack on the other side, a little further along, which appeared oppressively misplaced midway along the row of tightly packed kitchen terraces. Apart from a middle-aged woman in a flowery apron standing on a stool earnestly cleaning her windows a few doors beyond the barrack, and the brothers, who slowed their pace in approaching the formidable building, the street was otherwise deserted. Along the mouth of the Falls only a few men and women walked lazily to and from the city centre. Sexton felt the palm of his right hand sweaty around the butt of the luger concealed in the side pocket of his coat. He wondered in that moment, looking on in great expectation, how the O'Rourkes felt.

Adrenaline pumped through the veins of both brothers. They were willing policemen, any policemen, to come out of the barrack's main entrance and descend the six or so steps onto the pavement that they approached. They were twenty feet away from the barrack steps when their hopes were raised. Two men in smart plain clothes - crisp white shirts and sharp creased trousers, appeared together on the top step. The blond-haired, good-looking one had his jacket flung casually over his shoulder. The gun holster and gun tucked under an arm confirmed the O'Rourkes suspicions. This RUC Special Branch officer, sharing a joke with his close colleague, an overweight, ginger-haired detective, was about to pull on his coat on reaching the pavement when the brothers made their move. Stepping onto the pavement to face the two detectives, the O'Rourkes drew their semi-automatic pistols from their right side jacket pockets almost in sequence, and with their feet slightly apart and shoulders hunched forward, extended their arms with both hands gripping firmly the weapons held. Fixing a man a piece in their sights, they opened fire simultaneously. McHugh miss-cued as the rapid burst of shots shattered the lazy summer day's silence.

The two detectives had seen the gunmen in the split second before they had opened fire, but hadn't stood a chance. Three bullets from Oliver O'Rourke's weapon thudded into the muscular chest of the blond-haired man directly in his line of fire. The woman cleaning her windows looked on horrified as this man's broad back exploded open in a bloody pulp before he fell forward to land forcibly on his face.

Dermott O'Rourke had carefully aimed his two single shots, fired in quick succession. Full in his sights, the ginger-haired detective had still been laughing when the first bullet smashed through his brilliant white teeth to blow a large ragged hole through the back of his head. The second bullet had ripped through the man's gullet. With both hands clasped around his gaping, bloody throat, he staggered forward a few paces with a look of sheer surprise etched upon his wide, fleshy face, then fell backwards into the gutter to die.

The O'Rourkes turned heel and fled. They saw Sexton, white-faced, beckon them to hurry with a wave of an arm before he too started to run.

Looking out from one of the snooker room upstairs windows, McHugh saw his co-conspirators come racing across the Falls Road and disappear down the back alley directly opposite the snooker hall. The back alley would serve as their shortcut back into the city centre. It was time for him to take a shortcut too now. Carelessly throwing his cue onto the snooker table, McHugh reached for his coat and made his way quickly out of the snooker room under the concerned eye of its owner and down the bare timber staircase and out of the building through its back door. Scrambling into his coat, he cut a dash through an alleyway and exited onto the Falls a little further on from that side street on the far side. Fortunately for him, he judged, a bus travelling out from the city centre pulled up to the kerb only yards in front of him to drop off an elderly gent. He ran the short distance and leapt onto the bus as it pulled away. Glancing over his shoulder, McHugh saw two uniformed RUC men with revolvers in hand dash across the main road in the direction of where the Fermanagh three had run off. Now he was about to bring his very own secret agenda into play.

Unbeknown to McHugh, his sudden appearance from the back alley and dash for the bus had not gone unnoticed, neither had the sleekit look upon his face. Sitting by a roadside window on the upper deck of another bus passing in the opposite direction, Barratt had spied McHugh and read his facial expression well. He knew when the man was up to no good and he instantly suspected as much at that moment. The commotion in the side street that the bus was passing fuelled Barratt's suspicions. He decided to get off at the next stop to investigate. His shopping trip into town could wait a while.

Remembering what they had repeated to themselves earlier, over and over again, 'Don't run, walk, when among the crowd', prompted two of the three fleeing gunmen to compose themselves, to blend in as best they could with those about them. However Dermott O'Rourke, falling a little behind his brother and Sexton, failed to execute what he himself had preached to the others. The compulsion to run to the getaway car was overwhelming and such was his state of mind, he did not see the rather large, elderly woman, complete with blue hair rinse to match her ill-fitting summer dress, exit from a top High Street store a few paces in front of him, laden with expensively acquired goods. So determined was he in his stride, he knocked the enormous woman flying. She landed in an untidy heap at his feet with her goods strewn all about her. Dermott O'Rourke did not pause to offer an apology but instead stepped over the woman and carried on at an increased pace. The protests mouthed at the fleeing gunman, fell on deaf ears.

The three finally reached the getaway car. Sexton found the car keys where he had left them, on the road behind the nearside front wheel. It had been considered too risky for the keys to be carried by any of the three in fear of them being dropped in the rush to get away. Sexton handed the keys to Oliver O'Rourke, who was to drive the car to Portadown. With all on board, the car started first time and pulled away slowly. No one talked. They were consumed by their own thoughts and reflections on what had just taken place. Knowing that they were now the most wanted men in Ireland, Sexton prayed silently that they would get out of the city safely, in one piece.

Caithlin and Bridget had called to their father's shop during their lunch break to update themselves on any news received from the hospital. They waited with fingers crossed in the hope that father would return from the post office with good news. Studying his face closely as he came through the door of the shop for a signal as to what had been said by Anthony over the phone, the girls, receiving none, had to wait patiently for father to open his mouth. What he revealed resulted in them both screaming with joy.

'Go tell Aunt Bella,' ordered Sean Mor, himself thrilled at the news, and added assertively, 'Leave it to me to tell your mother.'

Barratt had left his seat on the bus to investigate what aroused the interests of those passengers sitting on the opposite side, eagerly looking out. As the bus slowed to a crawl on passing over the crossroads, he spied the agitated crowd of uniformed RUC men gathered on the pavement outside the barrack in the side street below. Looking closely through the legs of the ragged human circle, he glimpsed the bodies of two men lying in pools of clotted blood that glistened in the afternoon sunlight. His suspicion heightened, Barratt made his way along the aisle of the bus, down its stairs and alighted at the next bus stop, just past the junction. He walked uphill toward those civilians gathered on the corner to nosy at what was going on. An attractive middle-aged woman standing on the edge of the small crowd with an empty shopping bag limply hanging from one arm, turned to face him. He instantly recognised her and she him. She was a trusted sympathiser. She rushed toward Barratt, sending a message with her frightened eyes for him not to come any further. She was warning him off and he read the message well. Barratt turned about and walked back toward the city centre but at a pace that allowed the woman to quickly catch him up. Her voice was filled with anxiety as she spoke. 'Frankie, thon's two policemen lying shot back there. You daren't be seen by the RUC.'

That bastard McHugh ... thought Barratt, taking stock of events. He knew he had to get back up the Falls and quickly, but how? The RUC, he knew, would soon be out in force. If seen, he would undoubtedly be picked-up as a suspect. There was only one way. It would be risky. But maybe the woman could help.

'Sadie. I've got to get back to the Falls urgently. Will you take my arm?' The woman nodded. 'We can catch a bus up the Shankill and cut across by the mill. No one will look twice with a woman at my side, know what I mean?'

Taking his arm, the sympathiser said jokingly, 'You know they'll be talking about us Frankie.'

'Girl, I wish that was the only thing I had to worry about,' Barratt replied, quickening his step.

Alighting from the bus on reaching Clonard, McHugh checked around him. No one paid him any attention as he stepped inside the street corner phone box. Picking up the receiver he dialled that number listed in his head. On being answered, he inserted his money. An official voice on the other end of the line, said. 'RUC Belfast. How can I help you?'

McHugh spoke slowly, clearly. 'Listen very carefully and write down what I say,' he said. 'The men who carried out the shooting outside the barrack on the lower Falls twenty minutes ago, are driving a black Ford Buick ... registration UTP 326. The wheels have white trims. There's three armed IRA men on board. They will arrive at Portadown, County Armagh, in three-quarters of an hour.' McHugh did not hesitate in delivering the closing act of betrayal. 'Some others who can help you with your inquiries can be found up the Falls ... Sean McParland, Leger Street, and Frank Barratt, Mill Street. I repeat: McParland and Barratt.'

McHugh replaced the receiver, stepped out of the phone box and scurried off toward Saint Augustine's Church close by, wherein he would sit and wait for developments to unfold along the Falls before making his next move.

Chapter Twenty-Five

The anonymous 'tip-off' was being taken seriously and a word-for-word written account of it was speedily fed up the line to RUC intelligence at Operational Command - Belfast Central. A hastily prepared meeting of top brass generated a proactive plan to be immediately executed. Sergeant Craig at RUC Control - Shankill, was to coordinate and lead raids into the Falls to pick-up named suspects. The RUC Divisional Commander in County Armagh was to be alerted and his men mobilised so to intercept the reported getaway car and 'engage' its occupants. It was the opinion of the RUC top brass that the IRA had hit them suddenly and hard, leaving them with a 'bloody nose'. Consequently it had been agreed - off the record - that given the opportunity, the RUC would hit back equally as hard.

Breezing into the front room of his home where his wife sat happily hand-knitting tiny white booties, Sean Mor bent forward to embrace and kiss his wife, who wept with relief on learning the good news of Sarah.

'Looks like we'll be babysitting Friday nights from here on, girl,' beamed the proud grandfather.

'It'll be just grand,' sniffed the woman, her head resting against his chest.

'I'd better go and sort out a change of clothing,' said Sean Mor, drawing away and moving to the door leading to the hallway. Over his shoulder, he added, 'When I come down, I'll fetch in some coal. With that aunt of yours beating a trail here later, I don't want her slegging me for not lighting the fire.'

A grandmother for the first time, Rosie quietly cried with joy where she sat.

Climbing the stairs to their bedroom with newfound energy, Sean Mor heard the front door close behind him as his daughters, lost in excited chat, returned from Aunt Bella's. He considered it unlikely that they would want to return to the mill that afternoon, but knew they could not abandon their machines at such short notice. He hated having to dash their hopes in saying with authority over his shoulder, 'Ten minutes, then back to work you two.'

'Ah Da,' protested Caithlin, stomping a foot in a huff while looking up the stairs sullen-faced.

'You heard me, ten minutes!' Sean Mor smiled, knowing Caithlin and her sister were probably pulling faces behind his back. And they did.

Less than a mile away, an RUC raiding party backed up with reinforcements of B Specials set out in convoy from the police barrack standing in a side street just off the Shankill Road. The front seat passenger in the leading Black Maria, Sergeant Craig, issued directions to the driver. It was to the Falls Road they were destined, to call on the homes of two men, old adversaries of Craig.

Sean Mor had laid out a fresh change of clothing on top of his bed and the water was on the boil for a scrub-up. He was excited at the prospect of seeing his grandson within the hour. He entered the backyard of his house through the scullery door and taking the short shovel in one hand, a tin bucket in the other, crossed the yard to scoop up a shovel of coal. It was then that he heard the splinter of wood and the shattering of glass. Then came the inquisitive shouts and screams above the stampede of heavy feet.

'Where is the bastard? Where is he?'

He raised himself and turned to see them appear at the scullery door. There were two of them, eyes narrowing beneath the shiny peaks of their caps as they weighed him up, each noting the short shovel held loosely by his side. With raised truncheons, they rushed him, snarling threats and abuse. Instinctively, Sean Mor dropped the shovel as he ran, falling into the opposite corner of the yard and covered his head and groin with limbs drawn up. He knew from hard experience that in this position injuries would be minimised. The two RUC men waded in with truncheons and steel toe-capped boots. Sean Mor's arms and thighs bore the brunt of the frenzied attack. Intent on inflicting serious injury, one of the RUC men proceeded to systematically and viciously jab a baton into Sean Mor's ribs, so to get a clear stab at his kidneys. Sean Mor felt his body recoil in agony. His mind was in turmoil. Above the RUC men's screamed abuse he could hear Rosie and the girls screams, the commotion in the house and the street beyond, rising. Even the cursed dogs had been rudely awoken from their lazy slumber in the cool shade of neighbouring backyards. The air crackled with murderous potential. Someone was pulling hard on his hair now.

'Get up, you Fenian bastard!' one of the policemen spat.

I'd better get up, Sean Mor thought, grimacing, gripped by raw terror, or they'll beat me to death, for sure. He struggled to his feet, shielding himself as best he could in the melée; his every move being interpreted as hostile, for they would not relent in their onslaught.

He was on his feet now, half-lifted onto them by the RUC man dragging him upward by a fistful of hair, then thrown with no little force against the yard wall. Its rough bricks stabbed at his flesh through the flimsy white summer shirt he wore, reduced to a torn, blackened and blood-spattered rag. One was on either side of him, forcing his arms outstretched in a crucified pose. And that's just how the man felt at that moment. A third RUC man appeared in front of him, who forced his baton across Sean Mor's gullet and pressed hard, but calculated to be not enough to kill him - at least, not too quickly. He felt the grip tighten around his wrists, their heavy boots scrape the skin off his shins as they pinned him there. Transfixed, and at their mercy, he smelled the vile breath of the one in front. With his all-too-familiar face working with fury very close to his, and hate-filled eyes screaming murder, Sergeant Craig seethed through clenched teeth, 'One wrong move and I'll break your fucking neck!' Sean Mor felt the man's weight heavy across the windpipe, restricting his air flow. Darkness quickly overcame his confused thoughts. White speckles, orange and blue flashes flickered, exploded and disappeared inconsistently in front of him. Loud shrieks of despair brought him back. He recognised the voice of one. It was that of his distraught wife Rosie who despite the efforts of several struggling B Specials, had arched herself defiantly in the doorway leading from the scullery into the yard, determined not to abandon her man to their mercy.

'Murder!' she screamed hysterically. 'Murder!'

'Shut your mouth, you Fenian whore!' came the loud, venomous retort from that third man. Not taking his crazed eyes off his prey, he snarled over his shoulder, 'Get back into the house and keep those brats of yours quiet!' More orders then threats. 'If you don't move this instant, I'll shoot this bastard right here!'

As if possessed, still the woman screamed hysterically. 'Oh Jesus! They're murdering my Sean!'

Sean Mor felt faint as a wave of nausea swept over him. A clammy sweat oozed and trickled down his back, a throbbing headache stirred. His body protested in agonising pain at the onslaught, each symptom a hallmark of the vicious attack. Oddly, the truncheon under his chin now aided him as it held him up, a small mercy, for his legs felt numb, lifeless. Again he struggled to recollect what had just happened. An authoritarian voice cutting through the chaos served as a harsh reminder. The domineering, menacing voice sent a shudder through his pained body. 'You whore's bastard. I said *move*!' It was that of his most hated enemy with whom he was face-to-face, eyeball-to-eyeball. One evil bastard, Sean Mor thought, slowly finding his bearings. It was not the first time that he'd been on the receiving end of this one's endless questions or, indeed, his boot. A thug in uniform, Craig revelled in torture and many had succumbed to his sadistic techniques over the years only to end up serving long-terms in Crumlin Road Jail and worse, laid to rest prematurely in Milltown Cemetery from the kickings he'd meted out. And here he is again, concluded Sean Mor in dejected silence, dishing out his medicine ... and an overdose at that!

Still not diverting his glare, Craig suddenly stepped several paces back. Only for the firm-hold on him, Sean Mor would have fallen flat on his face. Craig was tugging at his side holster with one hand and soon produced his Webley revolver. In a swift arm action, he raised and pointed the gun directly at the forehead of his suspect and thumbed back the gun's hammer. Sean Mor did not flinch. Seeing this, Rosie McParland went numb from head to toe and fell silent. Two B Specials with a firm grip on the unresisting woman suddenly found it so easy to harass her back into the scullery; the muzzle of a rifle belonging to another disappeared into the soft flesh of her belly beneath the flowered apron she wore. More B Specials had swamped the already crowded house, some struggling it seemed with the two girls, who still screamed uncontrollably in the front room where they'd been herded against their will.

'Keep those fuckers quiet in there!' Craig screamed from the yard. Intense physical activity ensued within before the cacophony faded somewhat. Sean Mor was more aware of what was taking place now. He knew from hard experience to keep cool and his mouth firmly shut. 'As tight as a Jew's wallet' one of the lads had cracked on an earlier occasion, and they'd all laughed. But there's no laughing faces here, he mused, studying the men hard. Not among this lot.

Craig moved forward, the un-cocked gun by his side, but was quick to apply the pressure once again with his truncheon, thrust across Sean Mor's gullet. The violent jerk forced Sean Mor's head upward, his neck straining while his feet were crushed under the renewed pressure. His wrists were held in the vice grip of those RUC men on either side. He was helpless, vulnerable, as Craig loomed closer, looking down his long, sharp, investigative nose at him.

Bastard, thought Sean Mor, his eyes fixed firmly on Craig's embittered face. It was trying for him not to speak his mind such was his frustration. Sean Mor braced himself in nervous anticipation of things to come.

'We're taking you in, McParland,' Craig sneered. 'We'll kick shite out of you, until you give us their names ... murdering bastard!'

Though dreading what lay ahead of him, Sean Mor was perplexed by the other's insinuation.

'Sir. An angry mob has gathered. We could soon be outnumbered.' The nervous, rat-faced B Special who'd dared interrupt Craig, had come rushing through the house from the street to serve warning. Muscles and veins along the contours of Craig's embittered face popped and contracted under the sharp peak of his cap. He shuffled uneasily whilst taking stock of the developing situation.

'Alright men,' he barked, over his shoulder, 'get ready to move out fast.' More directives to his quarry this time. 'We're taking you out the front,' he said, his voice rising. 'If you try and run for it McParland, *I* will *personally* put a bullet in your back!' To emphasise the latter, Craig raised the revolver like a trophy for all to see.

Sean Mor was jostled into the middle of the yard with his arms pulled behind his back. He felt cold metal clench around his wrists. Truncheons were poked into his ribs and with a firm grip on each shoulder, he was frog-marched through the scullery and back kitchen. The place was littered with smashed crockery, furniture, and with personal belongings strewn to all corners. Sean Mor realised on moving through the rooms that the damage was extensive. On reaching the hallway, he heard more heavy feet thundering down the stairs behind him. It was soon apparent to him that not a room in the house had been spared the rampage. He gritted his teeth and remained tight-lipped. An ugly scene, he knew, could provoke more violence. He could see from where he stood that there were knots of young children, their mischievous faces fixed with an added look of curiosity, in the street beyond, and he wished no harm to befall them.

There was no sign of Rosie or the girls as he was led along the long, narrow hallway, lined both sides with RUC men and B Specials, whose faces appeared very white in the shadows cast. Their nervous, frightened eyes glanced at him as he was led through and their movements were unnerving in that they were as unpredictable as the crescendo of protesting noise in the street outside. Pitched together with explosive tension, the smell of stale sweat hung in the still air.

Sean Mor feared a bloodbath on being led out of the house. Half a dozen B Specials surged out in front of him on command to form a semicircle and wielded rifles and truncheons to keep the angry crowd back from the door. Familiar faces of friends and neighbours had gathered in protest at the uniformed men's incursion into the street, which had been peacefully basking in the hot July sunshine.

Sean Mor was pushed out into the open; the grip on him tightening as he went. The crowd had gathered in strength, and Craig, still in the relative safety of the hallway, was concerned nevertheless as to his own wellbeing, and that of his men.

'Prepare weapons to fire on the order!' he ordered.

As he finished saying it, the bolts of a dozen Lee Enfield rifles were thrown and there was no doubt among those who heard those rifles cocked that they would be used if necessary. All civilians recoiled in unison. Concerned mothers and fathers dragged their children from the front line.

'It wouldn't be the first time an innocent child paid a dear price for being in the wrong place at the wrong time,' remarked one panic-stricken mother, leading her protesting child indoors.

Sean Mor was rushed forwards in the midst of a heaving scrum of bodies, sweating profusely in their heavy serge tunics due more to the heat of the moment than the blistering weather. A ferocious barrage of abuse was unleashed at his captors: 'Orange bastards!' 'Murdering bastards!' A shrill, defiant cry of, 'Up the I-R-A!' rang out above it all and the crowd clapped and cheered spontaneously. It all added to the deadly potential of the moment.

As Sean Mor reached the back of the Black Maria, its doors were flung open from within. He instinctively glanced to his right and spied Rosie and the girls at the front room window. He'd seen that sad, terrified expression etched on their faces many times over the years and his heart went out to them. A deep sense of guilt stirred within him, something he'd never felt before. The man considered now, taking in those pitiful faces for a moment longer, if perhaps he'd put them through too much, had made them suffer for too long.

Craig and his men had come out of the house in a mad rush, heads sunk between shoulders in nervous anticipation. The last one out, the rat-faced B Special, did not see the empty wine bottle come spinning silently through the air with malicious intent to smash violently against the side of his head. His peaked cap was sent flying as shattered glass sprayed all around him. The crowd threw up a louder cheer as the B Special constable fell, dazed and bloody to his knees, dropping his rifle and clasping his hands to his gaping wound. The felled man was dragged to his feet and his rifle quickly retrieved by colleagues riled by his misfortune. Sean Mor was physically lifted off his feet then, the pain in his upper arms and shoulders excruciating and was thrown face down on the bare metal floor of the Maria. A shiny black boot quickly went to work in greeting him. He felt his own hot blood fill his mouth; his body consumed by unbearable pain once more. Darkness came swiftly as he lost consciousness.

The remnants of the invading force in hasty retreat, piled in on top of the human rag doll. The Maria's heavy steel doors were swung to, shutting out the sunlight but only part of the mob's fury. Bottles and bricks were hurled by the street's angry youth as the convoy moved off, slow, sinister, and deliberate. The diehard elements of the mob followed, their tempers boiling over. Feeling victimised and oppressed, more screams of abuse rolled off their cynical, acid Irish tongues like some perverse poetry, hurting those safely inside the battened-down armoured cars more than any well-aimed brick or bottle could ever do.

'Who's fucking your wives when you're out on the rampage?' screamed one poison-tongued housewife, unashamed of her own foul mouth. The men huddled inside sat silent, hearts thumping, trying hard to close their ears to the hard-hitting abuse.

The armoured convoy gradually picked-up speed as the last few missiles thrown in a futile assault crashed against armoured plate. It would not be far until the convoy was safely across the divide and snaking its way through a more welcoming community, that of the Protestant Shankill Road.

Caithlin was the first to reach the door of No72 in answer to the barrage of neighbour's fists upon it in the aftermath of the raid.

'Are you girls all right in there?' called out one of several concerned neighbours. Somewhat dazed, Caithlin nodded, but Mrs Carlin and Mrs Commerford, the neighbours from either side of No72, were already rushing in past her, arms folded over apron strings, hairnets and curlers in abundance as they went to see for themselves before the girl had a chance to answer. 'Aye, we're all right!' she replied, flattened against the wall.

'And your mother?' Mrs Commerford tossed over her shoulder.

'Ma's badly shook up,' Caithlin replied, closing out the front door.

'I'll go make a pot of tea,' declared Mrs Carlin somewhat excitedly, scurrying into the kitchen as if enjoying the pain and misery of others and the prospect of all the speculative talk which would follow in the wake of the day's events. Just then, a cry struck up from the kitchen. 'The dirty rotten bastards!' Mrs Carlin exclaimed and immediately mouthed a whispered contrition. 'God forgive me.' She had been stopped in her bustling tracks on entering the kitchen as the scene there shook her to the core. More protestations flowed from between her thin, lipsticked lips. 'Ack, God, look at what the blackguards have done to Missus Mc's wee house. It's a shame, shouldn't be allowed.'

The tea was made, but in Mrs Carlin's house. The rampaging uniformed mob had left not so much as a cup or saucer intact in No72. The women of the street gathered in the front room of the raided house, their words of sympathy and support filling the room, which had itself been turned upside down. Rosie was being comforted by her two younger daughters who were themselves in deep shock though did not seem to be aware of it. Some local men, awesome and mysterious in their presence to some but not to others, came through. 'We'll repair all the damage, Missus Mc, so don't be worrying yourself,' one of the three men assured her. 'We will see everything okay!'

'Mrs Mc', as she was respectfully referred to, nodded in approval to the men, whom she knew to be associates of her man.

Rosie and her two daughters were strongly advised by several neighbours to go to Aunt Bella's to escape the upsetting physical reminders of what had happened. But nothing was to be touched until Father Crossan had been summoned to witness the damage and had been told every detail of what had happened. Given past form, the parish priest would then contact the RUC to lodge a formal complaint. He knew the procedure well. 'As good as my Sunday sermon', he had once said, half jokingly, for this was a regular occurrence along the Falls.

Sean Mor's whereabouts would hopefully be established, although most often the forces of the state were reluctant to disclose precise information on the whereabouts of detained suspects. As part of their suppression of the nationalist community the RUC liked to sustain the anxiety among the suspect's relatives.

Rosie accepted the advice of her neighbours as wise counsel and instructed her daughters to go to Aunt Bella's at once, much to their protests. They did not wish to leave their mother's side at such a time. But the mother insisted, reassuring her daughters that she would be okay and that she would follow on shortly. Fears were also mounting among the inhabitants of the street, that the RUC and B Specials might pay a return visit at any moment, seeking retaliation for the felling of one of their number in the street earlier. Hearing this, Rosie wanted the girls out of harm's way immediately and would indeed follow on, once the house was secure.

The last remnants of the angry crowd outside the McParland home grew even more angry on learning that the day should have been a joyful one for the family, due to the new addition to it, a grandson for Mr and Mrs Mc.

'Those Orange bastards knew this was a special day for the Mcs!' snapped one harassed mother, her matchstick arms threatening to snap under the weight of her two children. The others around her also spat condemnation in the absence of those who had upset the near tranquillity of the street. Tempers were left to simmer in the blistering heat.

Aunt Bella had correctly suspected something was wrong. The sharp-eyed, well-informed, great-aunt had earlier heard the ructions rising over the rooftops from the streets beyond as she'd sat basking in the sun by her front doorstep. After half an hour of high anxiety and eavesdropping on murmured speculation and rumour spreading rife along the footpaths of 'raids' in neighbouring streets, she had spied the two harried young women rounding the corner at the end of the street at a run. Even at that distance, it had been instantly obvious to the aunt that something was indeed terribly wrong.

'Jesus save us,' whispered the old woman, blessing herself on struggling upright on her ailing legs to totter from her doorstep and out into the street to meet Caithlin and Bridget. Her voice filled with concern, she inquired, 'What's wrong, daughters? What's happened?'

At their mother's behest, Caithlin and Bridget had proceeded ahead of her to Aunt Bella's to inform the old woman of what had happened within the short time of their earlier visit with the good news. And now a tearful, ashen-faced Caithlin, supported by her younger sister, equally shaken by the ordeal, forced out between sharp intakes of breath the horrifying account of the raid. The battle-hardened great-aunt gently, though anxiously, encouraged her great-niece along. 'Easy, daughter, easy. God give you strength,' she soothed.

Chapter Twenty-Six

By the time Barratt and his female associate alighted from the bus on the Shankill, the RUC, with B Special reinforcements led by Craig, had smashed their way into No72 Leger Street to seize Sean Mor. Another force of B Specials had ransacked 9 Mill Street nearby, in the hunt for the occupier, one Frank Edward Barratt, also a former internee and known republican activist. Fortunately for him, he had not been at home when they'd called. Now, on spying the RUC armoured convoy turn into the side street from the Falls in which direction he and the woman walked arm-in-arm past the flax mill, Barratt's gut feeling was to walk on with his head down. The convoy raced past him and unknown to Barratt the last vehicle had been intended for his transportation also. Battered and bloody, Sean Mor lay unconscious on the floor of the same Black Maria.

The woman sympathiser had served her purpose well and Barratt thanked her before parting company. He'd walked only a few yards up the Falls toward Clonard when a voice of a young man called out behind him. Barratt dreaded turning to discover that he was the attention of the men in black after all. He breathed easier on seeing a familiar face, though pale and clearly worried. The young IRA volunteer spoke with urgency. 'Frankie, something's up,' he said. 'They've lifted Sean Mor and the bastards paid your house a visit too.' Barratt weighed up developments. 'Something's up all right! Quick, round-up the rest of the lads and meet me at the safe house in Beechmount in half an hour.'

'Right you are Frankie.' The lad scurried off. Barratt continued on his way, his thoughts fixed on one man. That man was Fergal McHugh.

As the Ford Buick with distinctive wheels left Belfast far behind, the three jubilant IRA men on board relaxed their guard a little on seeing Portadown signposted as five miles on. Once there, the plan was to dump the car in one of the many side streets leading onto the busy market square. Then, on foot, the three would cut through the town to its outskirts, to where the O'Rourkes had parked their own vehicle on a car park adjoining a public house. From there, they would complete the remainder of the journey home at their leisure.

The RUC Divisional Commander in County Armagh, a balding, middle-aged former military P.E. Instructor in the Royal Enniskillen Fusiliers and veteran of the IRA's '30s campaign along the border, quickly mobilized his men into strategic positions in and around Portadown. He felt stressed over the onus placed on him to 'deal' with the IRA unit, supposedly heading his way. Life of late had been fairly relaxed amid the easy-of-pace Ulster countryside and most folk had subsequently been lured into a false sense of security. Though not confessing it, his own recognised complacency of late, unnerved him. Not wishing to turn the centre of his hometown into a battlefield, he ordered a number of outlying roadblocks to be set-up on those approach roads leading into Portadown from Belfast and his men to engage the IRA unit once certain it was those suspected of the Belfast murders. The IRA men's response on suddenly being confronted by such force would determine the final outcome. He suspected that the IRA men would not give-up easily, not with the murder of two policemen to answer for,

      The road from Belfast to Portadown via Warringstown, some five miles northeast of Portadown, was considered the most likely route the IRA men would use. Fifty yards after a blind bend in the road, on the edge of the sleepy village of Warringstown, the RUC patrol dispatched threw two Crossley Tenders nose-to-nose across that point in the road. A dozen men under the lead of a foul-mouthed, vengeful section leader took up positions around the vehicles and among the undergrowth on both sides of the winding country road with Lee Enfield Rifles ready to fire. The RUC men watched, listened and waited. Some prayed quietly that the car would take another route. It was too nice a day to kill or be killed.

All in their late teens or early twenties, and handpicked from civilian life and indoctrinated by Barratt over recent months at Sean Mor's behest, the six men presently forming the new Belfast Brigade promptly responded to the call and met up in the back kitchen of an empty mid-terrace, the safe house in Beechmount, exclusively for their use. A little nervous over the turn of events, Barratt spoke soberly to his men who sat shoulder to shoulder around a cleared wooden table.

      'An hour or so ago, renegade elements played their hand. To avoid an untimely and counter-productive head-to-head with the British, we need to respond quickly, with the element of surprise being our main weapon.' All six men looked surprised. Barratt continued his brief. 'Let me remind you. Whatever resistance you may meet, you are acting under direct orders from the Army Council. There is no higher authority.' Turning first to those two men seated on his right, Barratt was issuing specific directives. 'Bonar, Carmichael, you're along with me. Our man is McHugh. We will bring him here ...'

Bonar interrupted. 'Frank, I saw McHugh enter the Coat of Arms five minutes ago.' Seizing this latest information, Barratt sprang out of his chair at the head of the table. 'We'll go straight there. McElwee, Doyle, make your way to the main dump. No one is to get near it. Cassidy, contact the battalion OCs. Tell them to hold tight ... to do nothing until they hear from me personally. It's likely that there'll be more raids tonight across the city, so they'd better get offside.' Turning to the other man seated, Barratt was soon issuing a series of further commands. 'D'Arcy, to Sean Mor's home. Check out what went on there, then return here to brief me. Later on, I'll want you in the Coat of Arms. You will be our eyes and ears. Whatever is being mouthed, you'll get it all on the grapevine there. One more thing, the Falls will be crawling with RUC, so all be careful. Let's move!'

Learning of the raids from the fearful talk among a group of concerned women gathered on a street corner, McHugh casually entered the Coat of Arms and walked straight to the bar counter and ordered his usual. He scanned the bar over the top of his glass as he sipped the thick, black creamy stout. No one of any importance except one man was in, which was a help to his thinking. Turning to place his glass on the counter, he caught the eye of the lanky, pockmarked-faced barman again and beckoned him over with a discreet nod. Staring the barman straight in the eye, McHugh, deadly serious, said lowly, 'A wee word in your ear Michael ... in the bog ... *right now.*'

The barman, the local battalion quartermaster, knew McHugh was no longer connected. But knew also the reason why and in some ways sympathised with McHugh's argument, but not to the extent that he had been prepared to break rank with the mainstream. The look McHugh had just served him, the tone of his voice, left the barman feeling fearful of what may be asked of him. Throwing a beer towel over his shoulder, he moved from behind the bar reluctantly to follow McHugh to the toilet out back.

An hour and a half after the bloody deed, the O'Rourkes had relaxed enough to laugh heartily at the joke cracked by Sexton, sitting relaxed also in the back of the car. But their laughing faces turned to expressions of sheer terror on taking the bend in the road.

'Holy fuck!'

Dermott O'Rourke, and Sexton in the rear, were both thrown forward in their seats as Oliver O'Rourke slammed on the brakes. The car screamed to a halt and rubber burned upon the blistering hot tarmacadam. The crunching of the car's gearbox as the driver fought with the gear change, was the signal to the RUC men to take aim. Their section leader smiled confidently at what he witnessed and muttered to himself, 'Like rats in a hole.' As the car began to reverse he was confident that he had reason enough to give the command. 'Let the bastards have it!' A volley of shots peppered the front of the car. The windscreen and radiator were blasted out and the car jumped to a stall. Sitting in the front passenger seat, Dermott O'Rourke died instantly with a bullet between the eyes. He slumped forward, his head - what remained of it - landing with a sickening thud upon the glass-littered dashboard. Oliver O'Rourke had been hit in the chest and both shoulders, with the bullets gorging their way through spinal tissue, muscle and bone. He screamed in agony and with the power in both his arms and legs gone, he was helpless. Transfixed in his seat he saw the enemy fix him in their sights once more and he surrendered himself to certain death. Withdrawing his revolver from his waistband, Sexton, splattered by the dead man's brains, decided to make a run for it. Manipulating the rear passenger door open he somehow scrambled out and fired blindly in the direction of the barricade as he ran crouched forward toward the line of trees, ten feet or so away at the side of the road. A second volley of rifle fire killed the wounded driver, with bullets ripping into his face and throat. Sexton was felled by a multitude of bullets. Blood spurted from his arms, hands and legs as he writhed in agony on the ground. The revolver had been shot from his hand, together with several fingers. Through the blinding pain he remained aware of his predicament. Raising his good hand in signalling his surrender, the RUC section leader, who had briskly walked from behind the safety of his Crossly Tender, came to stand astride Sexton by the side of the car. Confident that the two IRA men in the car presented no threat, the section leader bent forward and took pleasure in pressing the barrel of his Webley revolver against the centre of Sexton's forehead. With a damning eye he looked down his official nose at the gravely injured man and spat venomously, 'Fuck you!' before squeezing the trigger. In that moment the raw recruits looking on and trembling in their tight fitting boots, their nostrils filling with the smell of cordite and death, realised the full horror of war.

McHugh was shrewd enough to manipulate the barman into a corner of the backyard, where the acrid stench of urine hung heavily and sickly. This was intended to add psychological pressure on the barman, whose back was literally up against the wall.
    'There's been developments today,' McHugh spat. 'Some of us are busy fighting a war while others lie around scratching their holes. Now, it's

time for action!' The barman was growing increasingly worried over the other's volatile mood and was left greatly more concerned on hearing what McHugh had to add. 'The RUC didn't know what fucking hit 'em. You'll hear all about it soon enough. Meantime, there's a dozen men ... good men, along this road, who are chewing their nails in the hope of being able to have a dig as well. Y'know as well as I do, that if the gear was made available, we could get things moving. So you see ... yer the man who holds the key.' The barman's fears suddenly manifested. His stomach churned in saying apologetically, 'Look Fergal, I can't do that. I know what yer saying, but they'd have my ballocks!'

'They'd have my ballocks!' McHugh mocked, and added menacingly, 'I'll put a bullet through your fucking skull here and now yeh ugly cunt if you don't tow the line!' McHugh pulled the pistol from his jacket pocket and held it to the barman's right temple. 'And don't fucking doubt that I'd do it!' The barman didn't. McHugh hissed. 'The RUC will rip this town apart tonight. What are you gonna be doing ... pulling fucking pints?'

Their head-to-head was interrupted with the door leading from the bar to the toilets opening. An old man, reaching for his zipper, made an untimely appearance, but on weighing up the goings-on he'd stumbled on, he threw a salute to the two younger men in the far corner of the bog then beat a hasty retreat. McHugh quickly returned the gun to his pocket and his attention to Teer again.

'Oul Alex is all right,' assured the barman.

'Fuck oul Alex!' McHugh spat. 'What do you say?'

Any sympathy that Teer had held for McHugh had vanished as quickly as the man had pulled the gun from his pocket, but he kept a cool head. He was convinced that McHugh was on the edge. Teer decided to play along for the moment until the opportunity presented itself to grab someone's attention.

'Look, let's go inside,' suggested the barman, hinting falsely that he was about to cooperate. 'We can go upstairs and organise this properly. C'mon, they'll be spreading rumours in there about us, know what I mean?' The wee joke on the end defused the situation somewhat. But McHugh, his adrenaline pumping through his veins like quicksilver, was quick to conclude, 'Alright, but no fucking about. Time is vital!'

Eamon Bonar and Padraig Carmichael were first to enter the Coat of Arms and quickly noted McHugh's absence, also that of the barman, who Barratt, joining them, had briefed them on. Bonar casually asked the old man at the bar where McHugh was. Old Alex answered with his eyes. Deciding to stay close by the bar's front door in case McHugh made a bolt for it, Barratt nodded to his two subordinates to continue out the back. On moving through that door to the toilets, Bonar and Carmichael came face-to-face with the barman and McHugh. The two young faces were familiar to the barman. They were local lads he knew, but had never been in the pub before. He stepped back to allow both clear passage to the toilet, forcing McHugh - immediately behind him - to do likewise. When Bonar and Carmichael were in line with the barman and McHugh, they made their move. In the blink-of-an-eye, Teer and McHugh found themselves each staring down the barrel of a revolver. Caught completely unawares, his hands by his side, McHugh felt sick when demanding, 'Who the fuck are you?' The barman was equally intrigued. Bonar, who held a gun to McHugh's forehead, had his answer ready. 'The Irish Republican Army! *Who the fuck are you*?' For once McHugh was lost for words. The arrival of Barratt on the scene confirmed Bonar's claim and prompted the barman to spill the beans. 'McHugh's carrying Frankie. He was trying to force me to hand over gear!'

Bonar was quickly dipping into McHugh's pockets with his free hand and soon found the weapon, which he handed to Barratt. Checking the gun over, Barratt found it to be fully loaded. He handed it back to Bonar to pocket. Barratt knew better than to carry a gun around the Falls on such a day. He would leave such things to others. Stepping forward, Barratt threw McHugh a look of condemnation. 'A wee word in your ear Fergal.'

McHugh knew the game was up, but was determined to say nothing. Even now, he was confident he would not come to any real harm. Anyway, what are they going to do, he thought, with a smirk. Shoot me for shooting two peelers? Throwing a look of disdain on those about him, McHugh was calmly led away.

As the two IRA volunteers escorted McHugh to the safe house in Beechmount, Barratt turned his attention to the barman. Teer was fighting for his life now. 'Honest to Christ Frankie, he put that gun to my head and still I told him I wasn't interested.' Pausing for a moment to let the other sweat a little more, Barratt replied calmly but authoritatively, 'This never happened.' The barman immediately nodded. Barratt added ominously, 'I'll have a word with you later.' Teer only breathed easier when seeing Barratt turn his back to him and take his leave.

Entering the barroom himself then, Teer was greeted by a barrage of moans and groans from the dozen or so patrons dissatisfied over the bar not being manned. One very impatient customer sought to remind Teer of his obligation to his customers. 'Just in case yeh hadn't noticed young Michael, it's damn thirsty weather today.'

As old Alex brushed past Teer to have a desperately needed piss, Teer threw the hardened drinker a cautioning look and held a finger to his own lips in reminding the old boy to keep his mouth shut. Old Alex threw Teer another salute on receiving the message.

On returning to the bar, Teer poured himself a large brandy and downed it in one.

Back at the safe house, Barratt listened impassively as D'Arcy relayed the news of Sean Mor's beating and arrest on a day which should have been so special to him, now that it was known that the big man had become a grandfather. Barratt learnt also that his own home had been smashed to pieces; his dog seemingly kicked like a football around the backyard by the B Specials, according to a neighbour who cared for the animal. But it was D'Arcy confirming that two RUC men had been shot dead on the lower Falls that had Barratt working up a rage. Intent to get answers to questions by whatever method, he turned to face McHugh, who sat indifferent in a ladder-back chair in the middle of the otherwise empty kitchen. Without taking his eyes off McHugh, who in turn watched his every move, Barratt removed his coat and threw it to the floor. He proceeded to roll up his shirtsleeves with a purpose, displaying thick wrists and muscular forearms, while his hands were like cudgels. McHugh knew well the damage those same hands could do. He had seen Barratt dish out punishment beatings in Crumlin Road Jail when keeping discipline within the ranks. It was there, where Barratt had cut himself out to be the Belfast Brigade Adjutant.

Despite the impending beating McHugh was determined not to confess to having set-up the Fermanagh three to provoke the border brigades and ousted IRA men into bringing out the guns, albeit out of revenge. Nor, that he'd had Sean Mor - though evidently not Barratt - removed from the scene, so that he could have a clear run; that he had hoped a good kicking from the RUC would see Sean Mor out of the way for good. And not least, with the added information he had on the big man's son-in-law, his intention to use it to destroy all faith and trust in Sean Mor - if surviving the arrest - and all those associated with him, including Barratt. The same 'incriminating' information on Anthony Brennan, McHugh now knew, could well be his bargaining counter, his only chance to stay alive. He was intent on playing his ace card at the right moment, when the stakes would be high for everyone.

Barratt had no doubts that McHugh was at the centre of what had gone on that afternoon. Glimpsing his wristwatch before slipping it off and pocketing it, he knew he had to act quickly to get the information he needed. The leadership in Dublin would soon want to know what the hell was going on.

Considering the possibility of such an adverse act in view of the volatile climate within the army, Sean Mor had supplied Barratt with a contact telephone number in Dublin to call if he himself was indisposed, and had assured Barratt that others would advise on how to take charge of any crisis situation. Knowing the onus on him to make that vital phone call as quickly as possible, Barratt knew he could only do so when he had something of substance to transmit - some hard, sound information. Now at least, he had the source from where that information could be had. It was time to go to work to get it.

Barratt broke the uneasy calm through delivering his command to McHugh. 'Get stripped!' Taking in the serious faces surrounding him, McHugh knew it to be futile to resist. He stood up slowly and began to undress. All eyes were on him. Once naked, Barratt issued more commands, this time to those around him. 'Lash his arms and legs to the chair.' In a heave of bodies McHugh was forced back into the chair and was pinned there by D'Arcy and Carmichael, while Bonar, using McHugh's own belt, tied his hands together behind his back, then to the chair. With the laces removed from McHugh's boots, Bonar knelt to tie his muscular legs very tightly to the chair's legs. McHugh's clothes were searched, but nothing incriminating was found. In the heat of the day the room was filled with the sweet, sickly odour of all their sweat. But no one noticed under the circumstances.

With a fixed eye on McHugh, Barratt set the ground rules for what was to follow.

'Listen lads. As far as I am concerned, we have a rogue ... a fucking tout in front of us. If he wants to talk we will listen and perhaps we can come to some arrangement. If not, *we* will make him talk and there'll be no arrangement. Only those his poor missus will have to make.'

Though petrified at what was to come, McHugh was prepared to win some respect from the other men through holding out to the end. Then and only then would he tell them what only *he* would want them to know.

Knowing McHugh down through the years, Barratt knew he'd be a tough nut to crack. But crack he will, he thought, clicking a finger and pointing to McHugh's socks on the floor. On receiving them in hand from D'Arcy, he rolled the socks into a tight ball and gesturing to Bonar to force McHugh's jaws apart, shoved them into the prisoner's mouth, which was then covered by industrial tape. McHugh's very pale face quickly turned blood red and his eyes and cheeks bulged grotesquely. His body became rigid. He drew his head back in expectation. All saw his fear.

Removing a packet of cigarettes and a box of matches from his trouser pocket, Barratt left them on top of a mantelpiece. Then, without addressing anyone in particular, was speaking again, cool and collect. 'Someone fetch a bucket of water.' Barratt beckoned the three volunteers to stand back and with huge fists proceeded to attack McHugh's vulnerable head, which jerked violently from side to side under each vicious blow. Periodically, Barratt stopped to ask McHugh if he was ready to talk. Though crazed with pain, his face grossly swollen and heavily bruised, his eyes closing rapidly, his nostrils flaring frantically, McHugh gave no such indication that he was and so Barratt continued with the attack and sweated profusely in administering it. With blood gushing from McHugh's shattered nose, Bonar threw the bucket of cold water against his face to prevent McHugh from losing consciousness prematurely. Still the blood flowed in a steady trickle. Barratt paused for a breather and lit a cigarette.

He toked long and hard on the cigarette several times before stubbing it out slowly and deliberately on McHugh's hairless, thick chest. And relighting the cigarette, repeated the burning a dozen times or more.

McHugh's tortured face and muffled cries led no one to believe his pain was bearable. Barratt however had not yet seen the crack in the man's resistance that he desired, and so persisted in his methods. He was not going to stop until McHugh was broken and revealed all. The beating and burning of flesh intensified until finally it reached a point that McHugh, tears of agony streaming his face, could not take any more. He frantically shook his head from side to side to signal he'd had enough, that he wanted to talk. Quietly relieved, as he had not enjoyed the past half-hour, Barratt ordered the other men who were somewhat stunned by the ferocity of the treatment meted out, to leave the room and wait in the backyard. He did not want McHugh to say something that would in anyway compromise their loyalty by casting even a flicker of doubt into their minds over events.

Gathering his troubled thoughts, McHugh realised Barratt's method and this was as hard to bear as the physical pain he experienced. He just hoped that Barratt, for old times sake, could pull a few strings and save his neck.

Barratt yanked the gag from McHugh's mouth, then lifting the refilled tin bucket, slung more cold water over McHugh's battered face and blistered chest. Shaken by the sudden soaking, McHugh gasped for air and his body shook violently, which he could not control. He licked his lips as water, mixed with his blood, trickled down his face, and managed to wet his parched throat. Unable to see Barratt through slits for eyes, McHugh begged the question with a voice almost child-like, 'Did we ever think Frankie, banged up together all those years ago, that it would come to this? Did we ever?' Barratt knew with those words spoken that McHugh was a broken man. For McHugh had never spoken a soft word in his life, not to his recollection anyhow.

'No! And while aware of your capability of being selfishly expedient over the years McHugh, I never thought you'd go this far against the grain. So cut out the crap and let's get down to talking hard facts.'

McHugh knew it was time to play his ace card. His life was on the line. He was only forty-four years old, had a young family, and a wife. He did not want to die yet.

Chapter Twenty-Seven

An unconscious Sean Mor had been dragged face down from the rear of the Black Maria, across the enclosed barrack courtyard and down a steel spiral stairway to the basement cells. In one, his limp body was forcibly propped up in a wooden chair. Four uniformed men, including Sergeant

Craig, stood over the suspect and struggled to restrain themselves from committing murder. Craig stepped aside as a burly, beer-bellied plain-clothed detective, sweating profusely, swept into the cell in pent-up rage to begin the interrogation. He had driven at speed the short distance to the Shankill from the barrack outside of which his two colleagues and close friends had been gunned down in cold blood an hour earlier. He too, would have left the barrack with them if not being called back by the desk sergeant to take a phone call from his wife. She'd wanted to check what time he'd be home for tea. Thankfully, due to that call, he at least would be going home for tea, albeit very late that day.

Some of that pent-up rage was released in a verbal outburst riddled with abuse, though not at the suspect but those uniformed men standing nearby.

'You stupid bastards! You've nearly killed him. He's no fucking good to anyone in this state. Get the doctor here fast!' Turning to the senior uniformed rank present, the detective, his face only inches from Craig's, seethed, 'Don't lay another fucking finger on him or I'll have you good and proper. It's in our hands now, understand?' The detective stormed out of the cell, leaving Craig silently fuming and his ego deflated in front of his men. They stood with their heads bowed in discomfort over the other's embarrassment. Craig silently cursed the Special Branch man and Sean Mor more so.

Knowing he was a wanted man, Barratt had Bonar and Carmichael scout ahead of him as he cut through the maze of back alleys and side streets toward Clonard and No72 Leger Street. He wanted to call on Mrs Mc to see that she was okay and to find out the latest on Sean Mor. Meanwhile, back at the safe house, Doyle and McElwee guarded McHugh.

Listening closely to what McHugh had wanted him to know, Barratt knew the rogue's life lay in the hands of others, whom he was yet to consult. Though if it were up to he, McHugh would already be dead. He had told McHugh this, before shoving the gag back in his mouth. Surprisingly, RUC personnel appeared absent entirely on the Falls in the aftermath of the shooting but Barratt suspected it would be after nightfall when they would again show up in force. What was of immediate concern to him, were those rumours abound on the street that the IRA were at war again. The gangs of psyched-up young men on street corners, conspiring plans to ambush RUC patrols with petrol bombs later that night, all needed to be contained too, and quickly. Barratt was left hoping that Cassidy was making successful contact with the battalion OCs to avoid any rash and premature action on their part in the wake of events.

On reaching No72 Barratt observed a major cleanup underway. D'Arcy had clearly not exaggerated when saying that the damage was extensive. Neighbours and friends and three IRA men from the Clonard were all busy with an assortment of brooms, buckets and tools. Barratt was glad to see Mrs Mc brave up well under the circumstances. With the woman of the house putting aside her own anguish for the moment to ask after Barratt's own wellbeing, the IRA man was reminded of what was most likely to greet him at his own wee house a few streets away. He could not stay in one place too long, so was on his way again with Mrs Mc calling out after him along the hallway, 'Take care of yourself son.'

Checking the street from left to right and getting the all clear from the lads keeping dick at each end of it, Barratt exited the house just as a car pulled up to the kerb. McNab caught his attention on stepping out of the car. Knowing McNab to be a sound character, Barratt would spare him a few minutes.

'I hear there's been ructions, Frank. Is it true Sean Mor's been lifted?' Keeping a sharp eye out for a warning signal from either end of the street, Barratt nodded. 'Aye. And the bastards left a right mess behind them.' Concerned for his good friends, McNab inquired anxiously, 'What about Anthony and Sarah? Do they know of this?' Barratt put McNab further in the picture. 'Don't y'know? Sarah gave birth a few hours ago. Sean Mor and Missus Mc were on their way to the City Hospital, so someone could do with getting over there fast to let Anthony know what's gone on, though he'd better break the news gently to his missus.'

Fully in the picture, McNab let his anger over events boil over. 'Fucking RUC bastards want exterminating.' Barratt appeared to be the only one to keep a cool head. 'McNab, you could scoot over to the hospital to let Anthony know what's gone on ... to bring him back with you?' McNab winked an eye. 'No problem.' Barratt added, 'Grand. Then my advice is this: Anthony and Missus Mc need to get offside. I think we're in for a rough night. The Specials could well make a return visit.'

'I'll see they do that Frankie,' assured McNab. 'Any word on Sean Mor?'

'No', replied Barratt. 'Father Crossan is away to ask the RUC where he's being held. Power to his elbow, I say.'

He had chatted long enough. Barratt could see that the lads on the corner were restless. He was chancing his luck being stood in the one place so long, so parted company from McNab with a quick handshake. McNab would briefly call on Mrs McParland, not knowing how to balance congratulations with sympathy.

The front door to his humble abode had been kicked off its hinges, the contents of his house smashed to smithereens. All personal belongings were strewn everywhere. Precious, irreplaceable photographs of his long lost mother and father had been ripped to shreds. Barratt swallowed hard on taking in the scene of utter devastation before leaving. On exiting the house and seeing his old faithful friend come limping along the footpath toward him, Barratt felt as though he'd been kneed in the balls. He gently picked the dog up and kissed it softly on the head. The dog yelped lowly, though its wee stubby tail vibrated from side to side, so happy to be reunited with its master once again. But their meeting was to be short-lived. Once snatching a few minutes to grab a bite to eat and a drink of tea in his neighbour's house, while the lads still kept dick on the corner, Barratt took his leave to meet with the brigade staff. The neighbourly couple promised the IRA man that they'd see the house boarded up, the dog all right, and sought earnestly to impress on him, not to worry. Humbled by everyone's thoughts and concern, Barratt's anger for McHugh turned to hatred. He hoped that he would get the okay to put a bullet through McHugh's head.

Snatching an early-evening newspaper from the street seller's hand on the way to the nearest phone box, Barratt feared the worst was yet to come to pass. On glimpsing the very latest news, he was unsure as to how the border brigades would react in the aftermath of the shooting dead of the three IRA men from Fermanagh who had, no doubt, been in cahoots with McHugh. He only hoped that the southerners would not undermine him, but instead heed his counsel. Barratt hastened along to learn what the Army Council had to say once briefed about McHugh.

McHugh had admitted to planning the Belfast attack with the Fermanagh three in an attempt to stimulate republican violence and had revealed how - once discovering the connection between Anthony Brennan and Edenderry Abbey - they had come to be in the possession of such weaponry. McHugh had also revealed that the Englishman's death had been premeditated, not least to eliminate forewarning the RUC of things to come if discovering the theft of arms, thus the fire to cover-up the raid. But with the Fermanagh three themselves dead, Barratt knew it was only a matter of time before the 'connection' was made through the guns recovered from the scene of the ambush in Warringstown. Barratt suspected that McHugh had set-up the Fermanagh three, just as he had Sean Mor and he for arrest. But it was what McHugh had then gone on to reveal that left Barratt gravely troubled. McHugh had fired the charge that Sean Mor's claim to being a 'republican, true to the cause' was a 'charade', that he was 'not to be trusted'. He attempted to qualify his damning of Sean Mor by claiming that he must have known of his son-in-law's past dealings with a 'Black 'n' Tan', and that the Englishman had possession of a vast array of arms, so desperately needed by the IRA, but about which he had kept silent. Surely, the facts, McHugh had contested, proved that Sean Mor was guilty of 'selling out the armed struggle to see his daughter marry a man who carried a fat wallet ... the Englishman's shilling'. Such facts, he'd then boasted, had come to his attention as a result of what Barratt himself had 'carelessly divulged' about Brennan's links with County Fermanagh to 'associates' of his, in recent time. The latter charge by McHugh, Barratt soon recognised, had been a lie that was intended to pressurise him into striking a deal with McHugh, who had gone on to urge Barratt to join him in ousting Sean Mor, to seize command of the movement in the North and to pursue the struggle working to their own agenda. In that instant Barratt fully realised what a real threat McHugh presented to the whole scheme of things, to people's lives, his own included, if mouthing off to a wider audience. He was quietly relieved that he had taken the precaution of sending Bonar and company out of the room when he had.

Barratt had proceeded to condemn McHugh as a 'low life' and had dismissed his accusations as not worth his breath. He had added that even if Anthony Brennan had been an employee of the 'old soldier', it was 'insignificant'. He went on to tell McHugh that, if Sean Mor had known about the hoard of guns, he'd had good reason to keep quiet. The 'Brennan connection', Barratt counter-argued, would have undoubtedly been unearthed by the RUC, also Sean Mor's involvement in the disappearance of the guns and future use. It was then that the full danger presented as a consequence of McHugh's action, dawned. Barratt knew that Sean Mor and his son-in-law stood to be implicated in the murder of Cartwell and the policemen.

Charging McHugh with putting the lives of IRA personnel and others at risk, and dragging the republican cause into the gutter, McHugh unleashed a torrent of abuse at Barratt and had called into question his own republican credentials. With that, Barratt had been quick to ram the gag back into McHugh's gaping mouth, knowing that for as long as McHugh breathed, he would be a major liability to the entire republican movement.

Approaching the Clonard cautiously, Barratt hoped that those back at the safe house guarding McHugh would not succumb to temptation and remove his gag, with the potential for untold damage to ensue. It was with haste that Barratt cut a dash to the red phone box on the corner.

It was just after five in the evening when he made the call from the same phone box from where McHugh, unbeknown to him, had indeed instigated the arrest and killings of former comrades. Standing nearby, Bonar and Carmichael scanned the Falls Road for any sign of the RUC.

The phone rang out continuously and Barratt was about to hang up in frustration when his call was answered. Following strict guidelines laid down by Sean Mor, Barratt spoke first, using a codeword to introduce himself. The voice at the other end was that of a male, a Dubliner, ever so calm and quietly spoken. Barratt was instructed to speak slowly and clearly. Doing so, he proceeded to relay the facts as he judged them, making no reference to McHugh's claims on Sean Mor, to whom he referred in code also in notifying the Dubliner of the Belfast man's arrest. The other man had listened without interrupting and when Barratt had finished, he was simply informed to call the same number in one hour.

Saint Augustine's Church was the safest place to be on such a night and Barratt was at peace with himself as he sat in the rear pew of the side chapel. He was alone with God and prayed silently that no other innocents would suffer that day. He thought about saying a prayer for himself, but didn't. He considered his soul long since damned. A hand on his shoulder startled him. Glancing sideways and seeing the outstretched black arm, Barratt was convinced the RUC had broken all codes to seize him in a church, but felt a fool on turning his head fully to see Father Crossan standing over him.

'Christ Father, you scared the shit ...' Barratt remembered then where he was and to whom he was speaking. 'Sorry Father, I ah ...'

'That's all right Frank,' interrupted the priest, a little amused. But Father Crossan's mood soon fell serious. 'There's been a lot of pain and suffering in the North today, Frankie. Do you think there will be more of it tonight?' The question was designed to make the IRA man check his conscience and Barratt knew it. He had little time for any priest and rising from the pew he made his real feelings known over what had been asked.

'Listen, Father. For your information and anyone else who might be interested, the IRA were not behind today's killings. As for any more violence? Well, as usual, it will be the innocents who suffer most. But there is always the odd one or two who bring it on themselves. And they? They're beyond saving.' Barratt moved to take his leave. A voice from behind him prophesied, 'Through seeking God's merciful way, no one is beyond saving!' Barratt stopped and turned to face the priest. 'Did you find out where Sean Mor is being held? How he is?' The priest shook his head. 'They wouldn't say, only that he was in custody.' Barratt looked the priest straight in the eye. 'Say a prayer for Sean Mor tonight, Father. In the clutches of the RUC, he will need all of God's mercy.' His bit said, Barratt carried on his way.

Barratt met up with Bonar and Carmichael who awaited him on the church steps and walked the short distance back to the phone box. Getting through to the other source more or less straight away this time, it was Barratt's turn to listen. At the Chief of Staff's behest the IRA's Belfast Brigade was to contact the press in Belfast before the night was out to deny any involvement in the killings of the RUC men. The dead IRA men were not to be acknowledged as IRA personnel. A similar statement would be released in Dublin within the hour. A communiqué to all other brigades not to commence hostilities against enemy forces was already being circulated. The fate of the 'renegade' was in the hands of the Belfast Brigade. The Chief of Staff would approve any action taken no matter how extreme, though it was stressed this must be done quietly and with discretion. It was the Chief of Staff's analysis, that any blatant punishment of even a former IRA man for being involved in the killing of two RUC men, may be considered hypocritical by existent IRA members and could result in further upheaval.

Barratt was expected by those in Dublin to 'hold the circle' until further notice or until the release of Sean Mor - whatever came first. The telephone receiver at the other end was replaced. The line went dead.

Without wasting any time, Barratt dialled the local nationalist aligned newspaper and spoke clearly and assertively on being answered.

'This is a statement from the Belfast Brigade IRA. We would like to state categorically, that the IRA was not involved in the deaths of two RUC men in the city today. Message ends!'

Returning to the safe house in Beechmount by way of back alleys at around 6.30pm, Barratt found McHugh just as he'd left him, gagged and bound in a chair in the kitchen. The prisoner had fallen into an uneasy sleep. His face was hideously swollen and purplish-blue in colour. Both eyes had closed completely and a crust of dried blood was caked along McHugh's upper lip. Most of the blisters dotted across his chest and stomach had burst and were weeping. Barratt held more concern for his dog, than for McHugh. He considered it unnecessary to inform McHugh of the Fermanagh three's fate, convinced he was already resided to it. Barratt would decide in the morning by what means McHugh was to meet his maker.

On being briefed by Cassidy who had returned to the safe house earlier, Barratt was pleased to hear that all battalion OCs had been contacted and had responded favourably to his command. D'Arcy meanwhile, coming in on Barratt's heel, reported that the Coat of Arms had closed early as had all other pubs along the Falls as the worst was feared. A young IRA volunteer had earlier entered the bar to ask for volunteers to form vigilante groups. A dozen or so men, both young and old, had readily showed their hands and had been told to meet on the corner at ten-thirty. There had been little talk in the bar throughout the evening, only nervous expectation at what darkness would bring. Other IRA volunteers busy assuring all that 'everything was under control' were pacifying the crowds of expectant youths lingering on street corners.

Pleased with progress made so far, Barratt let all but Cassidy and D'Arcy go and relaxed a little in a scullery chair to sup tea from a cracked mug. The three of them would take it in shifts to keep an eye on McHugh throughout the night. Feeling washed-out from the day's events, Barratt got his head down early on one of the single mattresses spread out on the bare-boarded floor in the front bedroom upstairs. He would be one of a number of IRA men to sleep under another roof that night. Cassidy would take the first watch. In the downstairs kitchen, he sat opposite McHugh who was draped in a threadbare grey blanket. McHugh prayed quietly that he would live to see the dawn such was his suffering, silently endured.

Rudely awoken in the cool shade of his suburban home's splendid garden an hour earlier, the disgruntled, grossly overweight, police doctor ignored completely the prisoner's obvious facial injuries and loss of blood from a gaping head wound, and first endeavoured to bring Sean Mor out of a semiconscious state by pressing a bottle of smelling salts to his nose. Then, and only half earnestly checking the revived man's heartbeat and lung function, confirmed him as fit for further interrogation. No sooner had the doctor spoke, did the three Special Branch men move in to do their bit. With the doctor offside they felt at liberty to do as they pleased. With their shirtsleeves rolled up, they stood in a semicircle in front of their suspect to fire questions at him in turn. His body a prisoner to unrelenting pain, his vision blurred, and with the strength in his legs gone from under him, Sean Mor was closed to those voices yelling at him. They were muddled and echoed riotously in his head.

'C'mon you fucking Fenian scum, open your mouth! Tell us who murdered our colleagues, you shite?'

'We'll have you squealing like a pig, you whore's bastard!'

Sean Mor's vacant expression had the burly one of the three lash out in blind rage. A vicious punch to the right side of the prisoner's head sent him falling as a dead weight from the chair onto the floor. The other two officers ran forward to sink their boots into the man's gut with great force. Six, seven or more wild kicks landed before the burly one called the other two off. 'Leave the bastard to sweat for a while longer. We'll call back later and nail him to the wall if need be.'

Sean Mor had been knocked out cold again by the punch to the head. Unknown to his captors he was gravely ill, and would not survive another such attack.

News of the Warringstown shooting, with three suspected IRA men dead and weapons recovered, had the RUC in Belfast jumping with joy. In the barrack where Sean Mor lay captive and seriously ill, a party mood stirred. With senior ranks joining in, bottles of whiskey were suddenly produced from the bottom drawers of office desks and lockers and glasses and tea mugs were filled to the brim and soon downed. Meantime at RUC Headquarters, night manoeuvres planned were put on hold. RUC intelligence had considered as significant the fact that the three suspects shot in County Armagh had carried out the Belfast attack. To their collective thinking, it signalled that an internal power struggle within the IRA - inactive of late - was most probably afoot. Therefore it was proposed by the Inspector General that it would be wise to sit back and observe what transpired over the forty-eight hours to follow. By refraining from such action as mass raids and arrests of suspects, which paradoxically may interfere with a possible upheaval within the republican camp, the RUC top brass were hopeful that the IRA would leave itself wide open to infiltration, thus the securing of much needed intelligence. Subsequently all regular and auxiliary personnel called up earlier in the day were 'stood down'. Instead, a dozen 'feelers' were dispersed throughout the nationalist ghettos across the city to keep an ear to the grapevine. It was hoped that by sacrificing short-term goals on this occasion might in the long-term, bring about the means to eradicate the IRA from existence once and for all.

Chapter Twenty-Eight

Anthony glanced up at the clock above the double swing doors to the hospital's maternity ward and shook his head.

'My Da's probably been held up at the shop or they're trying to beg a lift,' said Sarah, holding the baby snug to her ample bosom.

'They're hours late, love,' Anthony retorted, growing impatient as the time allotted for visiting ticked wastefully away.

'They'll be here in a minute, for God's sake,' laughed Sarah, lightly. The stitches still pulled and she grinned as she bore the discomfort. 'You're more disappointed than me and *I'm* the one whose Ma and Da haven't turned up to see the baby!' Just then, Anthony and Sarah spied McNab walk onto the ward. The local Good Samaritan appeared somewhat lost and out-of-place, then at ease on spying Anthony. With a discreet nod Joe McNab beckoned Anthony to approach him.

'He wants me,' said Anthony, puzzled, as he raised himself from the low stool by the bedside. As he approached, McNab rubbed his unshaved chin disconcertingly and Anthony sensed that something serious had happened. Looking over the young father's shoulder toward the woman who sat tense and upright in bed, her ears pricked, McNab forced a smile in the hope of allaying the fears so evident on her pale face. In a secretive voice offering no congratulations, McNab spoke out of the corner of his mouth, adding contortion to his already queer face. 'Anthony, the RUC have lifted Sean Mor from the house.' McNab waited patiently for the other's response. He had not long to wait.

'Jesus!' Anthony croaked, rage firing within him, which he fought to contain amid the sterile surroundings. Anthony looked up to the high ceiling as if the answer to his troubles was to be found there. He sighed heavily, letting some of his anger escape on a slow fuse. McNab interrupted his troubled thoughts. 'You'd better come quick. 'The women could do with you there ... reassurance, and all that. Know what I mean?' And he winked an eye.

'Aye, but how am I going to tell the wife?' Anthony asked, struggling to cope with it all.

'Just break it to her nice and easy,' counselled McNab. 'She's a tough wee girl. She's been through it all before. God knows, she's probably prepared herself to hear more tragic news of her father than this, bad as it is.' McNab was reassuring with his words tough as they were to hear. Anthony closed his eyes for a moment to find a little peace, then turned and looked back at Sarah, the newborn safe in her arms. He loved them both so very much. And they so innocent, so vulnerable, he thought.

Sarah observed her husband's troubled face from a distance. She read it well, knew all the signs: that happy contented look and the harassed, worried frown. It was the latter she recognised now as he tentatively approached her.

Anthony had asked McNab to wait. He planned to travel back with him to the Falls. McNab looked on and watched the scene develop as Anthony bent low over his wife to relay the dreaded news in a whisper. McNab saw how, fighting back tears, the woman grabbed her husband's arm and how her lips moved frantically in demanding information, reassurance, desperately so. Anthony consoled the already haggard-looking woman, her eyes so heavy for want of sleep, her face lined with worry. Another long, restless night for this mother and for many others in Belfast, McNab thought, pessimistically. Anthony kissed Sarah tenderly on the forehead, then the baby in her arms. The little scrap of humanity was oblivious to all that was going on in the cruel world into which he had just been born. Its mother slumped back dejectedly into the bed, her child suddenly a dead weight in her arms. The onlooker, a witness to the misery, could only feel sorrow for both mother and child.

Sarah tried to put on a brave face for Anthony as he took his leave. She was also conscious of the other mothers around her, looking on nosily, but she was isolated and could neither relay her fears to them nor seek comradeship or sympathy from an unknown quarter. No! She would suffer in silence, and there was no medication at hand to ease the worry and real fear engulfing her.

The shrieks of a newborn cut through the uneasy, brittle silence like a scalpel. Anthony sighed, 'C'mon, McNab, let's go.'

The night air was loaded with a tense, volatile atmosphere and there was little doubt as to what the main topic of conversation would be among those narrow back streets, on doorsteps and street corners and in smoke-filled public bars set along the Falls Road. Most of it would be rumour and speculation and it was the curse of the ghettos. It caused blood pressure to rise, hearts to palpitate and untold anxiety and stress among the community. Suffering on top of suffering brought about by actual events - the hard reality of the day. The strident cries of a newspaper boy on a street corner underlined it all. 'Read all about it!' he proclaimed. 'Policemen shot dead in city! Just as quickly as parched children snapped up the ice-lollipops that sticky summer's day, so were the early evening newspapers by news-hungry adults. Urging McNab to pull the car up to the kerb, Anthony exchanged his money for a paper through the front passenger side window. He digested all the main points and it left him very concerned. What he hungrily read set his heart racing.

There had been a serious shooting earlier in the day, only minutes after his son had been born. Two police detectives had been killed in an ambush outside a barrack on the lower Falls. The gunmen (two, according to eyewitnesses) had run off towards the city centre and had made good their escape. Later in the afternoon, RUC and B Special reinforcements had arrested a key suspect in a house raid in the west of the city. Inquiries were continuing, with more follow-up raids and arrests likely. The report went on to say that the shootings had come as a major shock to the people of the city, which had seen little or no sectarian violence or subversive activity in recent years. Most citizens, leading politicians and state security sources had believed that republican subversion no longer presented a real threat to the status of Ulster. Clearly, in the opinion of the newspaper's leading reporter, this had been a misjudged belief. Now, in his analysis, high-level talks between government ministers and security advisors were most probable, with the events of the day top of the agenda. Anthony's eyes were drawn to the Stop Press item at the end of the main report. Within a pronounced border, the bold black print read: *Latest On Belfast Shooting. Reported second shooting at Warringstown, County Armagh. Several men believed killed in gun-battle at police roadblock. Police investigating links with the murder of two Belfast detectives.*

There was much activity stirring in the Clonard as McNab's car pulled into Leger Street, cast in a long shadow as the sun went down behind Black Mountain. A small, hard-line crowd still stood vigil outside No72 and suspiciously eyed the occupants of the car pulling up before those inside were recognised. Somewhat a well-known stranger along the Falls Road, men and women nodded respectfully toward Anthony as he stepped from the car to walk the few paces to enter No72, the front door to which, as usual, lay open, but bearing the dents and cracks left by the earlier, unwelcome callers. He paused first to look up and down the long, narrow, cobbled street. You can smell trouble brewing, he thought, noting the groups of scheming young men forming, their actions tense and conspiratorial. In the background, he could hear the heated conversation, aggressiveness and resistance in the voices, and the clattering of milk bottles. The tang of petrol was carried on the slight evening breeze.

On entering the house, Anthony saw people he had never seen before and others he knew only by sight. All were busy, scurrying back and forth, each thoughtful in their respective tasks. Brooms and mops were in abundance and from the back of the house came the sound of someone's earnest hammering. The smell of concentrated disinfectant mingled with that of petrol swept in through the gaps left by the open doors. On moving along the hallway, Anthony was directed into the front room by someone apparently coordinating the mass cleanup, a youngish man with a pale face and determined chin.

Through the pall of cigarette smoke in the packed room, Anthony spied his forlorn-faced mother-in-law sat in a corner, being consoled by two neighbours kneeling both sides of the armchair. Half a dozen morose women sat around in support of each other, recalling the events of earlier that day, and of days thirty years before, when it had been the Black and Tans who had been the culprits and who had received the wrath of their tongues. The embittered conversation hushed somewhat on Anthony's unannounced presence being noted and the women proceeded to leave the room in single file. The last one out grabbed hold of his left forearm to say, genuinely, though deadpan, 'By the way son, congratulations.' Anthony forced a smile before giving his mother-in-law his full attention. Tears filled Rosie McParland's eyes as Anthony placed a gentle, comforting arm around her shoulders.

As darkness fell over the city and many had taken to their beds, others, who in some way or other had been directly and brutally affected by the day's headline events, sat alone to contemplate in their respective corners, wherever they found themselves to be.

The widow of one of the policemen shot dead, gently turned the gold wedding ring on her finger while painfully recalling the moment they had shared that very morning - so precious she realised only now - before he had left the house. The baby kicked in her womb as she sat on his side of their bed, adding more hurt to her tragedy.

A disabled father, confined to a wheelchair for life by an IRA bullet ten years earlier, prayed that his policeman son was reunited with his departed mother.

A wife and mother to three youngsters, all too young to know their father was dead, lay among them on top of the bed in which they had all been conceived, asking God why? And herself how she had not known her husband to be involved in such - his readiness to go out and murder policemen. She felt betrayed. And she hated those whom she had trusted so much and who had left her on her own with three weans.

The elderly mother, both her sons shot down like dogs in her mind's eye, cursed their murderers as she prayed on her knees on the cold stone floor of her humble country home, in pleading with God that Ireland may one day be free and rid of them. The RUC had murdered her husband years before. Now, her sons also, were martyrs to the cause.

A man lying huddled under the bright naked light in his captor's cell, battered and bloody from their onslaught of an interrogation, questioned himself. Who has carried out the attack? Why, and by what means? The man had his suspicions. There were questions to be asked and answers to be demanded. He was determined to find out, when he got out - *if* he got out. His stomach churned on hearing heavy feet approach and a key rasp in the lock.

A young mother of just a day, thinking of her father languishing in a barrack cell, and of a son barely a day old, hungrily sucking at her nipple. What was to become of him?

The father of that same child sat in uneasy silence by a low-burning fire, swamped by his own thoughts, a half-empty bottle of whiskey his sole companion now.

Upstairs, half sleeping, half reliving the terror of that day lay the old aunt and Mrs McParland with two of her three daughters. All felt safer under the roof of a house other than the one raided earlier that day.

McNab, who had stayed with Anthony late into the evening, had an ear to the grapevine and had given him the latest news before getting off home. Fears were running high throughout the Catholic areas of Belfast, that the night would see a bloodbath. RUC men and B Specials were expected to descend in hordes. More homes would be wrecked. Many more men would be dragged out and arrested. Loyalist mobs would also attack, seeking revenge for the murders of two Ulster Protestant policemen. Preparations had been made for such eventualities. Vigilantes were out in force. Stockpiles of Molotov cocktails were at the ready. The banging of bin lids would sound the alarm. Those men facing arrest had since gone to ground, moved on to safe houses. There were very few trusted, die-hard sympathisers to the republican cause left in Belfast. These people would be expecting the brunt of whatever was about to unfold. They were hoping the majority of people in their community would resist any unionist inspired pogrom. If history was to repeat itself, they would.

It was an eerie silence that Anthony was conscious of now. Only the loud tick-tock of the clock above the mantelpiece and the settling of the burning embers of coal disturbed it. In the far distance the Lambeg drum had fallen silent. The Orangemen had been provocatively celebrating the deaths of the three IRA men shot by the RUC at Warringstown and claimed in the latest news reports to be the murderers of the two police detectives.

Maybe Belfast will be given a miss tonight, Anthony thought, in contemplative mood. But what would tomorrow bring? Slumped in the fireside chair, Anthony poured another slug of whiskey into the glass and raised it to his lips in an attempt to drown his sorrows on what should have been the happiest day of his life. That drink in his hand was warm comfort and a good friend, and under its influence he slipped from sorrows-drowning to reminiscence ...

Daring to look back to a troubled past, the years of feuding with Christy now seemed so bloody childish. But at the time, as only he knew well, for his heavily scarred arms reminded him each day, it had been oh so deadly earnest to those seeking to prove, if not to others, then to themselves, their masculinity, their prowess, in the belief that they would win favour, respect, notoriety even, among the close-knit local community. What bollocks it all was, Anthony thought cynically. The difference with him had been the quest for equal renown or, for that matter, notoriety, had not run riot. Instead he'd had plans to leave far behind him and at the earliest opportunity, what he'd judged 'the backward life'.

Internal feuding had not been uncommon among families - and large ones at that - who earned their crust through hard, backbreaking toil with the testing ground and against even harsher elements. With much dependant on the weather on the exposed northwest coast of Donegal, where it most often proved extreme, life, in his experience, had been hard enough without battering each other to a bloody pulp over something such as a few acres of rock-riddled ground, which, if you dearly wanted it, would make you a slave to it for all time. Many families had been torn apart by such jealousy and violence, and many a son and daughter had taken flight without goodbyes, not only from the homestead but from their homeland in the hope of finding a new life in a new land across the water.

The whiskey warmed Anthony as the memories flooded back. And how ugly they were in their crystal clarity.

Chapter Twenty-Nine

The young, conscientious RUC constable, newly assigned to the west Belfast Division, had been designated a programme of mundane barrack duties in his first two weeks with the force. His tasks included checking on suspects in their cells at two hourly intervals. Coming on duty at 10.00pm to find the celebrations over the death of the three IRA men in full swing, it was just after midnight before the constable had chance to brief himself on those in custody. Formal handover procedures had gone to the wall somewhat with the duty officers from the early shift drinking themselves sober in the barrack canteen.

Briefed on the daily log by his night-duty sergeant, the constable knew that three of the six cells were occupied. In one there was the man charged with wife-battery. It had taken four constables to disarm him of the hatchet with which he had attempted to decapitate his woman. Then there was the regular, that wino from the Shankill who, devastated to find the local wine store shut at half-past six in the morning, had tossed a dustbin lid through the store's window. Two constables had found him sitting on the kerb merrily knocking back a free bottle of Mundies. The third prisoner was a completely different kind of breed. He was a known republican, suspected of a hand in the murders of the Special Branch officers. The constable was keen to have a look at the man named Sean McParland. He had never seen an IRA man in the flesh before and wondered what he'd look like. Descending to, and moving along the dimly lit corridor separating two rows of cells, a bunch of keys jangling at his side, the constable stopped to check that first cell to his left. Through the peephole he could see the wife batterer walking his cell demented. In cell two the wino lay asleep on his bed snoring loudly. Moving to the end cell, he spied a sandy-haired man, his facial features battered, bruised and bloody, his attire torn and ragged, lying on his right side on the floor between the chair and a wall, his knees drawn up protectively to his chest. The constable couldn't believe his eyes. He had heard the republicans protest over police brutality, forced confession and summary executions, and had dismissed it all as part of their propaganda war against the state. But here he was, looking at hard evidence of such at first hand and it disturbed him. The prisoner's body appeared lifeless. His eyes were shut, his face pale. The constable feared the worst. No personnel were to enter the cell holding a subversive alone. Adhering to commands, the constable briskly made his way to the duty sergeant's desk on the floor above.

The old-timer, Sergeant Hanratty, who had been on the night shift at the barrack for the past eighteen years, and serving his thirty-seventh year in the force, drank the last of his tea before leaving his desk to check out the new recruit's concern over the prisoner in cell three. Never in a rush to go anywhere, thus the big friendly countryman's ease with his role as night duty sergeant, it seemed like an eternity to the young constable for his senior rank to make it to the cells. On looking in on the suspect, Hanratty's concerns were immediately raised also and he soon had the cell door thrown open. Both policemen rushed to the prisoner's side and on their knees, checked for signs of life. The constable checked the IRA man's wrist for a pulse while Hanratty pressed two fingers into the prisoner's neck and exclaimed with much relief, 'He's alive, but barely conscious.'

The chair was pushed up one corner and the prisoner was carefully manoeuvred into the middle of the floor. The more experienced one of the two policemen closely examined the prisoner's twisted right leg and suspected it to be fractured. 'I fear this man is dying.' Hanratty's voice shook with anger. 'Stay with him, I'll go make the call.'

The new recruit contained his own anger at the turn of events. His father had been an officer in the RUC for forty-three years and had received the King's medal for gallantry before retiring without a blemish on his career or character. The very thought of other so-called policemen acting so callously under the guise of the force and all that it demanded in character of its men, of which his father had been a shining example, left him questioning himself if he could serve alongside such degenerates.

The shrill of the bedside telephone startled the intoxicated police doctor from his slumber and he cursed aloud the intrusion. Reaching out from under the covers to first switch on the bedside lamp, he then snapped up the receiver. 'What is it?' He fumed. The doctor listened impatiently to what the duty sergeant relayed with urgency down the line before replying. 'Hanratty, I've already examined that prisoner and passed him A.1.fit! Honestly, I think you're exaggerating somewhat sergeant.' Hanratty almost ate the phone's mouthpiece in lambasting the doctor. 'If that's your diagnosis, then *you're* not fit for your post! Furthermore, if this prisoner dies, I will be forwarding a full report on your malpractice to the Inspector General. So I suggest you grab your stethoscope and get over here ... double quick!' Frothing at the mouth, Hanratty slammed down the phone and quickly made his way back to the cells with haste under the concerning eye of his deputy.

Rebounding from the verbal onslaught, the doctor slammed down his phone, rousing his secret lover by his side in the process. 'What's up love?' The doctor protested aloud. 'That fucking farmer at the barrack just spoke to me as if I was shit! I'll have his balls when I get there!'

'Oh, don't make me jealous Sidney, here ... you can have mine!' The sixteen year old boy slid his naked lithe body on top of the doctor's bloated mass and, reaching to switch off the bedside light, kissed him fully on the mouth.

An hour had passed since the phone call and still there was no sign of the police doctor summoned. Kneeling on the cell floor cradling Sean Mor's head in his lap and rubbing the prisoner's back in a circular motion to combat the chill seizing his body, Hanratty took matters into his own hands by ordering the constable to go to the desk and phone for an ambulance. Having done so, an ambulance arrived within ten minutes and the two-man crew had been quickly shown to the cells and the injured man. On seeing the condition of the casualty both ambulance men threw each other a questioning look, then one inquired bluntly, 'What do we tell the doctors at the Mater?'

    For the young constable, it was an agonising silence before his red-faced sergeant, replied flatly, 'I am led to believe he stumbled and fell down the stairs.' The young constable was gutted. How many times had he seen and heard that line reported, when the force was asked to account for a suspect's injuries.

    He followed sheepishly at the rear as Sean McParland was stretchered awkwardly up the spiral stairway and into the assembly area, where the three plain-clothed detectives - the worst for drink - had gathered to engage in some banter over the desk with the deputy sergeant. The red-eyed burly detective, unsteady on his feet, suspected at first that the drink was playing tricks with his mind on seeing his suspect carried past.

    'Oi! Oi! Where do you think you're taking him?'

    Hanratty intervened. 'Carry on lads. Get him to the hospital.'

    The detective turned to vent his anger at the uniformed senior. 'Hanratty, who the fuck do you think you are?' Hanratty faced up to the detective while all others, except the constable, looked on expectantly. The constable looked on with disbelief and thought, This cannot be happening. 'You're drunk ... move out of my way!' Hanratty demanded, moving to go past, but was caught off balance on being forcibly shoved in the chest by the riled detective and was sent crashing against a wall. The much younger, athletic deputy sergeant leapt over the desk and scrum-tackled the burly detective to the floor and kneeling on his back, pinned him nose down. Drawing his truncheon, the deputy seethed into the detective's ear, 'Any more shit out of you and I'll split your skull!' The other two detectives stepped forward to protest but were halted in their tracks by Hanratty meeting them eyeball-to-eyeball. The atmosphere was explosive and Hanratty sought to defuse the situation before it got completely out of hand. 'Hold it everyone! There's enough blood being spilt on the streets. We don't need it in here.' All took stock with Hanratty's words ringing so brutally true to their ears. The open-mouthed ambulance men carried on their way with a story to tell.

The deputy sergeant manhandled the felled detective onto his feet and sought the chief's counsel. 'What shall I do with him, Sarge?' Hanratty took a step closer to the detective and spoke with conviction. 'I want you and your sort to leave my barrack immediately. If you pursue that casualty tonight, I will have you arrested and charged with being drunk and disorderly and for assaulting a police officer in the course of his duty. I will also report to higher authority that I have reason to believe that you and your lackeys here have inflicted G.B.H. on a man in custody, held on suspicion.'

'Gone soft in your old age, have you?' snapped the burly detective. 'Don't you realise McParland was a suspect for the murder of my best friends ... *my best friends*! Whose side are you on, Hanratty?'

Sergeant Hanratty chose his words carefully. 'McParland has been dragged in here umpteen times over God knows how many years. Yes, he's been interned in the past, but never charged. He's too clever, too hard for the likes of you to break. Craig's been trying to do it for years. He can't sleep at night through scheming how he might set the man up. So every time you drag him in here, another youngster joins their ranks ... another rebel to *the cause*!' Stepping up closer to his adversary of sorts, the elder continued with a sincere purpose and much anger. 'There's only one way to get McParland, and it's not by murdering him, for a hundred or more will only step forward to take his place. No, it's all down to good old-fashioned detective work, but with an edge to it. That's your job, I suggest you go and apply yourself to it, once you've sobered up. Then a job worth doing, will be done.'

The detective had met his match and was lost for word. But Hanratty had not yet finished his lecture of sorts. 'Oh, and just one more thing! When you and your ilk were in short trousers, my brother and I were hunting IRA men along the border. He was murdered by the scum. We counted twenty-seven bullet holes through his body ... what was left of it that was. Now get out of my sight!'

There was nothing anyone could say. The three detectives sheepishly shuffled away.

Arriving just before midnight at the Victorian built Mater Hospital, situated on the lower Crumlin Road, Sean Mor was rushed to casualty. The night-duty doctor there soon diagnosed the casualty to be slipping in and out of consciousness. The man's right hand and right hipbone were broken; a deep gash along the hairline required stitching, as did his bottom lip, and his entire face was heavily bruised and severely swollen, his body, in numerous places, likewise. The doctor found it hard to believe or indeed to accept that the man had 'fallen down a flight of stairs', nor did the other professional carers who promptly went to work on him.

The new recruit had been dissuaded from writing his resignation letter on witnessing Hanratty dressing down the bad blood within the ranks. He was even more heartened on hearing his sergeant tell the police doctor where to go when he eventually turned up almost two hours after being called out.

With newfound inspiration the young constable applied himself to the task in hand, albeit mundane yet again. In view of RUC and auxiliary personnel being ordered to stay out of republican ghettos that night, he had been delegated the responsibility of contacting Father Crossan at Saint Augustine's Church in Clonard, to inform him that one of his parishioners, Sean McParland, had been released without charge to hospital. But when pressed by the suspecting priest as to the reason for the man being hospitalised, the constable, turned to his chief for guidance, and cast a slur on his deceased father's good name, by confirming the prisoner had sustained injury falling down a flight of stairs. Despite the senior rank confiding that 'to keep the peace in-house' there was no other way, that such injustice had, at certain times, to be tolerated and indeed aided and abetted, the constable hated himself for what he had done.

Calling on Mrs McParland at Aunt Bella's the previous evening to inform her that there was no further news of her loved one, Father Crossan had spent the night touring the streets of the lower Falls and among the vigilantes, who'd stood expectantly on street corners with bin lids at the ready. Rattling them upon the cobblestone streets would serve warning to all that the RUC and B Specials approached. But as the dawn sky turned to a clear blue and with the sun coming out gloriously once again, it was evident and an immense relief for all, that the expected dawn raids were not to be, nor, as the priest had feared and prepared for, the bloodshed - not so far anyway.

He returned to his presbytery just after 6.30am, tired and hungry, to find the telephone ringing. He answered it and listened without interrupting the police constable who informed him somewhat hesitantly of Sean McParland. The priest knew it to be futile to attempt to get any truth over the phone as to the real nature of Sean Mor's injuries. It would have to be him, face-to-face with some nameless government bureaucrat at the end of the day. What was of immediate importance was to contact the McParland family to break the latest worrying news.

Barratt had sat in the scullery to see in the dawn and was himself greatly surprised at not hearing the rattle of bin lids in the small hours. With D'Arcy emptying the contents of the tin bucket used by all during the night and Cassidy double-checking that the prisoner's hands and feet were secured, Barratt decided to check on the night's events and departed the house by the back door.

McHugh sat motionless, numbed by the pain and the cold besieging him. In his disorientated state, having slept very little and with all that played on his mind, he listened intently for the slightest utterance that may indicate his fate.

Walking cautiously up the Falls where a few people - up all night - mixed with those emerging cautiously from their humble abodes, Barratt noticed Father Crossan walking briskly along on the opposite side of the road. On some mission of mercy, Barratt thought, a little cynically. As Father Crossan crossed the Falls Road, he spied Barratt and waved to him in seeking a word in his ear. Thinking the priest was about to give him another lecture on God's merciful ways, Barratt was tempted to bless himself. Meeting up with the priest who appeared tired and weak, Barratt sought the latest news as to the night past. 'Morning Father. All quiet last night?'

'Yes, thank God, surprisingly so. But the news this morning is not so good.' The priest proceeded to give Barratt a full account of the phone call received half an hour earlier. Barratt quickly assessed what had been disclosed and advised the priest to return to the presbytery to rest, informing him that he would contact the McParland family and attend to matters in hand. Knowing when best not to get directly involved, Father Crossan agreed. But knowing the IRA man's lack of enthusiasm for him and the church in general, the priest assertively brought into check the other's self-perceived priorities. 'If Sean Mor or his family need me, be sure to let me know.' Barratt said he would. The priest turned and walked back toward home, praying silently for the family for whom more bad news beckoned.

Barratt called on McNab on the way to Anthony and Sarah's to ask whether he would help out again. Just in from standing lookout on the corner all night, McNab was happy to. Once splashing his face with cold water and guzzling down his mug of tea, both men set out together in McNab's car to drive the short distance to where the driver had left the McParland family the night previously, and Anthony, in the fireside chair, alone with his troubled thoughts and memories.

Chapter Thirty

Anthony's eyes shot open on hearing the loud thumping echo along the hallway of the house. He was convinced the RUC were at the front door. Fearing the door was about to be kicked in, he felt stiff and sore on struggling out of the fireside chair in which he'd fallen asleep in the early hours. He accidentally kicked the empty whiskey bottle and tumbler across the floor of the front room on stumbling into the hallway. The cacophony of words shouted through the letterbox and the fear-stricken voices rising in the rooms upstairs, stirred the tension and fear in him. Entering the hallway, he was greatly relieved to hear the mouth at the letterbox announce, 'It's me, McNab!'

A woman's panicking voice at the top of the stairs called out to him then. 'Who is it Anthony? Who is it?' Approaching the front door, Anthony shouted over his shoulder, 'It's all right! It's only McNab.'

Opening the door, Anthony was relieved to see that indeed it was, though threw a cautionary eye at Barratt who stood grim-faced by McNab's side. Anthony knew Barratt only by sight from the man's regular visits to No72, where he had engaged in hushed conversation with Sean Mor. McNab noted Anthony's concern. 'It's all right Anthony, this is a good friend of Sean Mor. He needs to have a quiet word.' His anxiety heightened again, Anthony invited both men into the house.

Mrs Mc, her face white with worry, her appearance unkempt, came scurrying down the stairs clasping the neck of her washed-out floral print dressing gown with both hands. The girls peered around the landing with frightened eyes. 'Frankie, have you any news of my Sean?'

'It's all right Missus Mc, he's safe, but he's in the Mater.' The woman blessed herself. 'He's obviously had a hard time,' Barratt added solemnly. 'The RUC are saying he fell down some stairs.'

'Jesus help him,' the woman frowned and made the sign of the cross again.

'I'm going over there now to see him,' added Barratt. 'Do you want to come along?'

'I do, I do. I'll be with you in five minutes.' Rosie McParland pounded back up the stairs barefoot to get dressed and there was a commotion up above as the girls and Aunt Bella demanded news from her.

Barratt beckoned McNab and Anthony into the front room and following them through, pushed shut the door behind him.

'My understanding is that Sean Mor is very ill. In view of what's gone on, we need to get him shifted fast. The Mater is not the safest of places. I may need your help!' Anthony and McNab each acknowledged Barratt with a nod. Gripped by a nervous excitement, Anthony felt the need to freshen up a little. He left the other two men alone together momentarily while he went out to the scullery to wash his face under the cold tap. Before doing so, he switched on the wireless to listen to the 7.00am local news bulletin. After the last time signal bleep, a sombre-voiced male newscaster caught and held the attention of all who listened.

'The RUC now believe the guns used in yesterday's murder of two Special Branch detectives in Belfast and recovered from the bodies of the three IRA men shot by the RUC in County Armagh, had earlier in the day been stolen in a subversive raid on Edenderry Abbey, Irvinestown, County Fermanagh. A murder investigation is underway following the discovery of the charred remains of Colonel Cartwell, the retired owner-occupier of the abbey, destroyed, in what is considered to have been a malicious fire ...'

Bent over the Belfast sink, his face dripping with cold water, Anthony felt as though he were about to throw up. His thoughts raced back to the night of the engagement party, when he had confided his experience at Edenderry Abbey; revealed details of the old soldier's hoard of guns to Sean Mor, who, having been snatched by the RUC within minutes of the policemen being shot, must have betrayed his trust. Indeed, that of his own daughter. Anxiety-ridden, Anthony moved to the table behind him and snatched up the previous night's newspaper. His heart thumping, he carefully scanned the front-page, the news of the policemen, and the Stop Press section on the County Armagh shooting, but there was no word of the Edenderry Abbey fire and death. Turning quickly to the next page he spied what he had missed the day before. The report confirmed the fire that had completely destroyed the landmark. The police feared the landlord had perished in the flames, along with all livestock. The initial report did not imply any suspicion of foul play, only that police investigations were ongoing. Anthony's attention was drawn away from the article on the wireless being silenced. The man called Frankie appeared just inside the scullery door.

'We're ready to go.'

Looking at the man with an incriminating eye, Anthony had thoughts to match. What hand has he had in this? What people am I involved with here? Is Sarah part of it all too?

Feeling claustrophobic in the rear of the car with Sean Mor's friend close by his side, while his mother-in-law sat in front, Anthony's thoughts were solely on Sarah and he felt the need to speak with her urgently too great to delay any longer. He demanded then to be taken to her immediately and for the others to carry on to the Mater without him. The sudden outburst had Barratt throwing Anthony a concerned look, as did McNab via the rear view mirror. A heavy frown upon her face, Mrs Mc looked over her shoulder.

Being a true friend to Anthony first and foremost, McNab swung the car left and sped on toward the City Hospital to where Sarah, with the baby, waited anxiously for news of her father. At her mother's behest, Caithlin had phoned the hospital late the previous evening to request that the nurse-in-charge inform her sister that there was no word on her father. Not wanting to create any difficulty for Sarah, Caithlin had not elaborated. On inquiring, Caithlin had in turn been informed by the ward sister that the baby was 'doing grand', while the mother, though well, appeared a little agitated and had been returned to the side ward. Nothing more had been divulged by either party.

Dropping Anthony off at the City Hospital's main entrance, McNab promised his friend that he would call back to pick him up shortly. The way

Anthony felt at that moment, he cared not if he was never again to lay eyes on any one of the three.

The night duty nurse was surprised to see Anthony present himself in the ward so early and her immediate concern was for the other heavily pregnant women and mothers. At that time of the day they were all in various states of undress. She moved to block his way.

'I must see my wife. I must speak to her!' Anthony despaired.

Seeing the new father's troubled state and noting Sarah's throughout most of the night, the nurse thought it best to let the early morning visitor proceed, but not before she went ahead of the man to pull bed curtains closed.

With Anthony appearing unexpectedly in the side ward, Sarah - breastfeeding their son – was instinctively fearful for her father. She cried out in anguish, 'My Da, what's happened to him?'

Anthony closed the door to the side ward behind him and pulled up a chair to sit close beside the bed. Anthony had never seen such a wonderful sight as the newborn sucked hungrily and hard on one of its mother's swollen nipples. In that brief moment all his concerns, worries and fears were lifted from off his shoulders. Insisting on news of her father, Sarah brought Anthony back to hard reality. Seeing his wife's anguish, her beauty ravaged by it, he sought to ease her immediate concerns.

'Your father's in the Mater Hospital. McNab has taken your mother to see him.' Sarah grabbed Anthony's wrist tightly. 'Is he all right?' Anthony shrugged his shoulders. 'We don't know. A man called Frankie called to the house this morning with McNab. All he said was that the RUC were claiming your father fell down some stairs. No one knows how badly injured he is.'

Sarah was rising in the bed then; the baby denied its feed momentarily. 'I'm getting dressed. I'm going to see him.' Anthony grabbed her arm. 'Christ, don't be silly. You're in no fit state, not after what you've been through.' Sarah turned on him. 'Don't tell me what I can or cannot do where my own family is concerned. You or no one else knows what I went through giving birth to our son. But I'll tell you this for nothing: the ordeal was nowhere near *that* which I went through lying here alone last night, not knowing if my father lay murdered somewhere. Now, you tell me how I am supposed to feel better cut off from the world ... from my loved ones in such times? Eh, tell me that! Now, are you going to help me get dressed? Or do I have to struggle on my own?'

Anthony knew Sarah meant to, and would, despite his opposition.

'Okay. But I need to speak to you about something which ...' Anthony hesitated before adding nervously, '... frightens me! I need you to be totally honest with me in what I ask.' Sarah frowned heavily, 'What is it?' Leaning closer to Sarah, Anthony spoke secretively. 'You remember me telling you of a place where I once worked? A place called Edenderry

Abbey?' Sarah nodded. 'Well, the night before last, men raided it for arms, set it on fire, and that old soldier, Cartwell, remember? He was burnt to death!'

Sarah was puzzled. 'What's this got to do with us?'

Anthony replied with recrimination. 'Three IRA men were shot dead in County Armagh yesterday afternoon ... an hour or so after two detectives were shot, killed here in Belfast. The guns used by the IRA men are known to have come from the abbey.'

Sarah's patience with her husband was running thin. 'So what's the point you're trying to make, Anthony?'

'The point I am making, is this,' Anthony snapped. 'I told only one man of the guns kept in the abbey by the Englishman. That man is your father.'

Only the sound of the child's suckling broke the brittle silence. Her loyalty to her husband on trial, she knew, Sarah looked her husband straight in the eye. 'So what are you saying?'

Anthony truly loved the woman who had just given birth to his son and did not wish to hurt her, but he had to know what was going on. Not just for his sake but for Sarah's too, and most importantly, for the sake of their son.

Anthony spoke in a flurry. 'I tell your father about the guns, the abbey is raided; the Englishman, an old soldier, is killed; two policemen are then shot; the men who shot them are shot. And then your father, out of all the men along the Falls, is arrested minutes after the barrack shooting. The guns used to kill the RUC men had been taken from the abbey in Fermanagh. A few months after telling your father about the guns, *you* informed me one night that he was away on GAA business ... in *Fermanagh*! Not so long after, I overheard your mother tell a neighbour of the years your father spent in jail ... of the way he'd been ill-treated. I never made a point of questioning you over this, nor did you ever talk of it. To be truthful, I never considered it all that important. That was, until now, because I am frightened, especially looking at the two of you lying there.' Anthony took a deep breath before delivering the final charge. 'I'm frightened, that your father betrayed my trust in him. That I have, no matter how innocently, the blood of at least six people on my hands. That the police, through their investigations in Fermanagh, will somehow trace me to your father ... will implicate me in the murders committed.'

Deeply worried by her husband's real concerns, which she silently accepted, Sarah was very frightened too then, but tried hard not to show it. She breathed in deeply and out slowly before asking gently, lovingly, 'What do you ask of me?' Anthony took a greater risk now. 'Your father ... did he abuse my trust to bring about these events?'

Ever since she had been a child, father had drilled her never to give any potentially damaging information about the family to anyone:

family, friends, strangers or foe. Though genuinely seeking to soothe the fears of the man she loved deeply, Sarah was keeping true to her word.

'Anthony, my father spent a total of twelve years interned without trial. He was never charged or found guilty of any crimes. He is a good man, who dearly loves his country, his family. He would never do anything to deliberately hurt anyone of us, nor anyone who we his children love. I understand your fears and suspicions, but you have nothing to fear. You are part of that same family, as is this child. Do you really believe my father would do anything against you, against us, for his own grandchild to be left fatherless?'

Anthony could not hide his tears and wept with relief. Sarah leaned forward and tenderly kissed Anthony on the forehead. She knew she had to speak with her father, and quickly, if he was still alive and able. Danger indeed threatened to engulf them all.

'I'll get dressed. We'll go see my father together and by the help of God, seeing his grandson will help him pull through.'

The exhausted night-duty doctor at the Mater Hospital gave way to the concerned wife's demands and allowed her through to see her husband. Dosed with various drugs during the night, Sean Mor had regained consciousness. Although having incurred multiple fractures, with cracked ribs since diagnosed also, the patient was not in any imminent danger but required much rest and peace and quiet.

While equally as eager to speak with the patient and getting McNab to first check for any sign of RUC men within the hospital, Barratt had respected Mrs Mc's right of place to see her husband first and used the spare time to have a private word with the doctor before he went off duty. Knowing Sean Mor's re-arrest was highly probable at some point, Barratt knew also that the threat of B Specials paying a visit to the hospital out of uniform to wreak direct revenge was very real. Enlightening the doctor to the urgency to secure a bed for Sean McParland at the Royal Victoria Hospital, situated at the junction of the Grosvenor and Falls Roads, the doctor, considering the circumstances under which the patient had been admitted, informed Barratt, 'I'll see what I can do.'

Emerging into the otherwise deserted waiting room on keeping to the allocated five minutes for visiting, Rosie McParland burst into tears on McNab's shoulder. They were tears of both upset and joy over her husband's ordeal and state of health, and to have found him alive.

Winning the doctor over, Barratt darted off to snatch five minutes alone with his commandant, whose counsel he urgently sought. While angry at seeing Sean Mor's bruised and broken face and body, Barratt was not surprised by it. He had seen the same man a victim of such beatings time and time again in years past, and was reminded of his very own potential to inflict such injury; the previous day's dealings with McHugh a brutal, though necessary example.

Sean Mor was as equally pleased to see Barratt as Barratt was to see him, but Sean Mor could not force a smile. Barratt sat himself down in the bedside chair and shunted forward as close as he could. Conscious of the other five male patients sitting up in their beds looking on nosily, he leant over Sean Mor's shoulder to whisper into his ear. Barratt transferred specific information, details of how McHugh had come to be arrested by the brigade and McHugh's subsequent confession, including how he'd come to be in possession of the guns from the abbey; procedures followed in contacting battalion staff and Dublin and the outcome of that contact, and an update on press reports, together with his own assessment of the events and possible developments to come. The only fact that Barratt kept hidden from Sean Mor was McHugh's claim that he, Barratt, had leaked vital information on Anthony Brennan which had proved advantageous to McHugh. Although Barratt was convinced that McHugh had instead stumbled on Anthony Brennan's past connection with Edenderry Abbey by accident, he remained inclined to look after number one.

His body numbed with drugs, his brain on a go-slow, Sean Mor had to focus his mind in order to listen carefully to what Barratt reported. With grave concerns raised for both Anthony and Sarah, knowing what he did, Sean Mor signalled that concern.

'Bring Anthony here. I need to talk with him urgently. As for McHugh, your suspicions are correct. He wanted us both out of the way. And his motive? Well, it goes without saying. We need to deal with him, for sure, but in a way that we don't make him a martyr.' As if as an after thought, Sean Mor asked, 'How old are his children?' Barratt considered the question odd but nevertheless replied to it without query. 'I'd say the eldest is six, maybe seven, and the two youngest, the twins, less than a year old.'

Knowing he was himself a grandfather and how he yearned to see his grandson who had been born into so much bloodshed, Sean Mor considered it cruelly ironic that McHugh had made his move on the very day the child had come into the world. He hoped to see his grandson soon, but did not wish to hold him for the very first time with his hands dripping with McHugh's blood. So Sean Mor thought for a moment. 'Frankie, take some money out of the pot and buy a one-way ticket to America. Take McHugh south and see him onto the boat. Make it clear to him that he is being banished ... never to return. He is and will remain an outcast. For McHugh, this will be the worst imaginable sentence. Total secrecy over this is essential mind you. Only his wife need know. She and her children are free to follow him. We will provide passage. But she too, must keep her lips sealed.' Barratt understood. Sean Mor grimaced. His badly swollen mouth was very painful now. 'Until I am fit enough, I want you to hold the fort, Frankie. I have full faith and trust in you.' Barratt nodded. 'Now, go find my daughter's man and bring him to me.'

'I don't have to do that, Sean,' Barratt replied. 'Your daughter, Anthony and your grandson, are here!'

His infant son held in his arms, and Sarah close by his side, Anthony had just walked through the swing doors onto the ward.

Chapter Thirty-One

Despite all his years of suffering such brutality, Sarah had never before seen her father cry, and unashamedly so. But his tears were tears of sheer delight, shed by the proud grandfather on reaching out with his good hand to gently stroke the milky soft cheek of the grandson, sleeping sound in the arms of his father, who Sean Mor now asked to sit close by him.

Distressed by her father's shocking condition, Sarah sat on the edge of the bed to listen intently to her father as she'd always done, for as long as she could remember. Giving Barratt the deadeye, Anthony nevertheless accepted the man's offer of a seat as Barratt withdrew to the foot of the bed, where he would await further orders from Sean Mor.

Anthony felt no pity for the man in the bed, only anger, which he fought to contain.

Speaking low, Sean Mor sounded solemn, for it was a true reflection of his innermost feelings.

'Anthony. Sarah. This is the last thing you will want to hear, the hardest thing you will be asked to accept. But it's not only in both your interests, but also that of your son, my grandson, that you do so, believe me!' Anthony and Sarah listened intently. 'It is vital that you leave Belfast as soon as possible. There is grave danger for you here presently in view of recent events, of which I cannot go into detail. Please, believe the sincerity of my plea to you both, here today.'

Anthony, and indeed Sarah's fears were realised. Anthony considered Sean Mor's plea to be a plea of guilt. He had indeed betrayed him, a 'Free Stater', and his own daughter. He was about to tell Sean Mor what he thought of him, when Sarah, speaking almost in a whisper, sought the truth by speaking the truth.

'Da, we both know. That is why we are here, and why I asked Ma to leave us alone with you, so we can speak freely with you.' Sean Mor was not surprised by his daughter's power of insight on events of the past twenty hours. 'What we want to know is, do you know how those men killed in Armagh came to be in possession of guns ... those about which Anthony told you, the night we were engaged to be married?' Anthony was taken aback by Sarah's forthright manner but was heartened to know that she was a hundred per cent with him. Sean Mor quietly admired his daughter. She was standing by her man, just as her own mother had stood by him through thick and thin over the long years in face of all adversity.

Sarah had been selective with her words, not wishing to blatantly compromise her father, and her father noted her veiled respect for him. She had not only allowed him scope to reply safely, but an opportunity to address the 'issue' directly with Anthony, whose fears and suspicions of being betrayed, he realised. And which, he knew, if not addressed and allayed quickly, would naturally place the young couple's marriage in grave jeopardy.

Sean Mor fixed his blood-shot eyes firmly on Anthony and said without conflict or contrived deceit. 'Anthony, do you recall that Halloween night, when the engagement party had ended, when you told me of the Englishman's hoard?' Anthony remembered. 'I asked if you had revealed the same to anyone else. You replied "No", and that you would not. I warned you what may come to pass if you did, what people may think. I must ask you again, here and now, *did you*?' Sean Mor was making it clear that the suspicion or belief that Anthony held, and perhaps Sarah also, that it was *he* who had abused Anthony's confidence, was unfounded.

Thrown somewhat by Sean Mor's instant dismissal of the implied insinuation, Anthony was provoked into considering Sean Mor's suggestion, that *he* must have revealed details of Colonel Cartwell's guns to someone else. Anthony cast his mind back and concentrated hard.

'Think hard, Anthony,' Sean Mor encouraged, his pain increasing.

It came flooding back to Anthony then. It had been on that very first day on arriving in Belfast, in conversation with Felix and Bernadette.

'Felix, Felix Gresham', Anthony whispered, but loud enough for Sean Mor to hear. He in turn prompted Anthony. '*The barman*?'

Lost in his own thoughts in putting two and two together, Anthony had not heard him.

'Felix knowing then breaking off our friendship. He had said things were going to …. Yes, it all makes sense now.' Realising he had absent-mindedly revealed his thoughts, Anthony focused once again on the moment in hand, knowing his fears over Sean Mor had been ill founded. Instead, it seemed apparent to him that it was through Felix Gresham that this misery had befallen them all.

Sean Mor suspected that Anthony suspected that his once good friend, Felix Gresham, had betrayed him. But knowing what he did, what McHugh had confessed to Barratt, he sought to put his son-in-law out of his misery - if only a little.

Continuing to speak secretively and in much pain, Sean Mor spoke directly to Anthony but loud enough for his daughter to also hear what he had to say.

'Felix Gresham did not betray your friendship, Anthony. He would not have spoken so carelessly. No! It's simply due to another man and his treachery that has brought this terrible day on us. I'm aware of his motives, but that's another story. All you need know is that you were not his prime target. But what is of concern to me now, Anthony, is that the

RUC in Fermanagh may come across your name somewhere as having worked at the abbey and may seek to speak with you.' Anthony had already considered the point. Sean Mor removed any lingering doubts as to the real threat to Anthony's safety. 'Once you're traced to the Falls Road and seen to be associated with me, a former internee - thus my arrest on suspicion of being somehow involved in yesterday's shooting - may well be enough for the RUC to implicate you in events. The repercussions as you know, could be terrible for us all. That's why I feel it best for you both to get offside. Even if just for a little while until things settle. As the saying goes: out of sight, out of mind.'

Though convinced he had judged Sean Mor hastily, and relieved to discover that Felix had not betrayed him, Anthony was very worried by the fact that Sean Mor's fears mirrored that of his own. Anthony weighed up his predicament. Sean Mor's right, we have to get out of here as quickly as possible, he thought, despairing. But where do we go? Where do we run to? There were no opportunities south of the border. Work there was chronically scarce. Scotland, with all its bittersweet memories, did not appeal to him either. The only logical place for he, Sarah and the infant to go, was London, where they could lose themselves among the masses. Anthony knew it was not realistic to expect Sarah or the baby to go with him immediately. He would carry on ahead on his own, find work, a place to live, and then they could follow. Though he knew it all made sense, the thought of leaving Sarah and his infant son, gutted him.

'Okay, I know what must be done,' Anthony said, with resignation.

'There is no time to lose, Anthony, it must be today.' Sean Mor's sense of urgency only added to the young father and mother's agony. Anthony saw the pain etched on Sarah's face. He felt it too. His heart was breaking. He looked down pitifully at the child asleep in his arms, so sweet, so innocent of it all, but yet already a victim of Ireland's troubles.

Anthony silently cursed his country. His voice rising, caring not who heard, he spoke his mind, not taking his eyes off his son. 'I'll go across the water today. Sarah and the baby can follow once I get settled. I'll find work and a place to live. We'll be all right. But I want to make it clear here and now: this child, my son, will never again set foot in this cursed country for as long as I am alive. It is no place to hold hope. It's beyond that.' Anthony stood, and with his face blank, looked Sean Mor straight in the face. 'Goodbye, Sean. Look after yourself.' Anthony turned and walked away, leaving a father and daughter alone. Watching him leave, Sarah wept silently over what was happening to them. Knowing Anthony had meant what he'd said, Sean Mor would gladly have given his life to change it all, to save his daughter and his grandson from exile. But he feared a worse fate awaited the family, if they stayed.

Barratt saw at first hand that greater pain heaped upon the family through McHugh's actions. The scene at the old aunt's house on their return there, with Sarah informing all that Anthony had to leave Belfast that very day, and she and the baby shortly after, had the women, spanning three generations, crying hysterically. The anguished cries had startled the child into crying also. It all served to remind Barratt of the tales told by his granny when a child himself, that the wailing of Irish mothers burying their young during the famine years could be heard the length and breadth of Ireland. So much so, it had struck terror into one's very soul. Slipping away from the house unnoticed, Barratt knew exactly what his grandmother had meant.

It was a different type of pain that Barratt saw expressed by McHugh's wife, who looked as though she did not know what sleep was, for hers was a bitter pain. She had willingly opened the door to him, knowing he was an associate of her husband. The elder kids played riotously on the street's sunny pavement, seemingly oblivious to their father's prolonged absence these past two days. The twins lay fast asleep in the big cot in one corner of the front room, which looked as if it too had been visited by the RUC such was the woman's apathy with life.

The man and woman sat in opposite fireside chairs, she, on the edge of hers biting her bottom lip, her fingers wrestling with themselves in her lap as she waited in dread of what he'd come to tell her.

'It's about your husband, missus. He can't come back. Ever!' Barratt affirmed. 'He'll be leaving the country shortly for America. What I want to know is, do you and the little ones want to join him?' Barratt saw tears well in the woman's eyes, her bottom lip tremble. She breathed deeply and composed herself. A look of self-pity turned to one of bitterness again, which was evident in her words. 'You know, when Fergal went out so early yesterday morning, I knew that he wouldn't be coming back. And no, we won't be going anywhere. This is my late mother's home. She left it to me and I am not leaving it for anyone. I've managed before on my own. I'll manage again.' Pausing to take a deep breath, she added with a trembling voice, 'Tell him from me, *Good riddance*!'

Barratt stood to take his leave. He would take pleasure in passing on her message, personally. But he had another, very important message for her, and his voice emphasised its importance.

'There is to be no talk of him anywhere, to anyone! Make something up to tell your children. You'll hear no more of him or have any more contact from me.' A moment's pause. 'I'll take my leave now.'

The woman followed Barratt to the front door. Barratt took in her face once more. Her eyes were cold and hard, her chin determined. He was going to wish her Good Luck, but knew she would not have need of it. He turned and walked away.

Setting off along the Kashmir Road and covering only a short distance, Barratt was abruptly halted in his stride by a dirty-faced child, no more than seven years old, who'd jumped out from behind a garden wall to point a toy gun made of bits of wood, straight at him. 'Bang! Bang! You're dead mister!' shouted the youngster, before scurrying off. A chill ran down Barratt's spine, for he recognised the child as being one of McHugh's. He couldn't help but wonder whether the child's prank was, for him, a bad omen.

Returning to the safe house and entering the kitchen stinking of McHugh's obnoxious body odour, Barratt ordered McHugh to be dressed by Cassidy and D'Arcy. Ravaged by migraine and cramp and appearing like a battlefield casualty, McHugh's hands and feet were temporarily untied during the process, but his mouth remained gagged throughout. Once ready, McHugh was to be placed in the boot of the car and driven south.

With Cassidy parking the car at the rear of the house and leaving its boot lid ajar, McHugh, unable to walk, was covered with a blanket and physically carried out of the house into the yard. Checking the alley from the safety of the back entry door, Barratt gave the all clear with a thumb up. McHugh was quickly bundled into the car boot and its lid slammed shut. Barratt joined Cassidy in the front of the car. D'Arcy was to lock-up the safe house before getting off home. The loaded pistol retrieved from McHugh the day before was tucked into the waistband of Barratt's trousers. On getting the nod from Barratt, the driver set out to take the back roads south.

Chapter Thirty-Two

No one knew better the need to be left alone with one's man on particular occasions than Rosie McParland. Knowing it to be such an occasion for her daughter, she succeeded in coaxing the girls and Aunt Bella, who all doted on the baby, to come out of the front room to leave be Sarah, Anthony and the child. Time for them to be alone together as a family was short, and precious. McNab was to call back to the house in a few hours to drive Anthony to the docks. He was to catch the midday sailing to England.

Alone, a mother, and father, clasping each other's hands tightly as they sat on the sofa, looked on with mixed emotions at their son, his blue eyes in wonder at the dancing shadows all about him as he lay upon the blanket between their feet. Anthony now knew there would be only one child. There had been complications. He was just so grateful to Sarah for bearing him a healthy son. They had not had chance to talk of this to anyone else; other events had taken precedence. In time, Sarah would have a talk with mother, so that expectations of many grandchildren from the first daughter married would be understood as not being possible. What was important for both Anthony and Sarah was to know that they would be reunited again as a family, and as soon as possible.

'Everything will be okay, Sarah. We won't want for anything. We've got a few pounds behind us. There'll be no shortage of work in London and I'll soon find us a place. It may not be much of a home to start with, but in time we'll find something permanent. No doubt it will be a big change to us. But one thing's for sure, we'll be able to live in peace and that is the best thing we can ever wish to give our son.'

Sarah knew this to be true. She had listened to Anthony attentively and had pictured it all as he'd spoken. She'd seen good times and hard times ahead. While she knew she would not be living in dread as her own mother had and still did, of the RUC kicking in the door in the early hours to drag her man from his bed, nonetheless she felt it hypocritical to her whole upbringing - her faith, culture, political beliefs, and her own identity as an Irishwoman and now a mother herself, to have to run off to England with her child under one arm, a suitcase under the other, in seeking peace in a country which she held ultimately accountable, fundamentally, for the conflict in her own country. For Sarah, the paradox in that same country holding out a rescuing hand, a lifeline to them both and their child in their hour of need was a bitter pill to swallow. But she knew and accepted, albeit reluctantly, that there was no other corner for them to run to.

The Fermanagh detective repeated his thanks to Mr and Mrs McStravick for their co-operation and bid them both goodbye. To assist any future follow-on investigations, he had called on Mr McStravick to obtain the names of those he had recruited some years ago to undertake the restoration work at Edenderry Abbey. The gentleman had readily supplied the names to him at the expense of again being sadly reminded of his son Con's tragic death. The fire at the abbey had left the couple devastated, as the only hallmark of their son's highly skilled work locally, was lost forever.

All the names logged in the detective's pocket notebook, bar one, were local men. The odd one out was a Donegal man by the name of Anthony Brennan, who was believed to be living in Belfast. Both Mr and Mrs McStravick had obviously taken a strong liking to their son's closest friend, having spoken so highly of him.

Climbing into his car, the detective glanced the list of names once again. All but the Donegal man would be easily contacted. He would have a word with his colleagues in Belfast, who could then pick-up Brennan for interviewing and at the same time spare him the journey up to the city. Sifting through his pockets for the stub of a pencil and finding it, the detective circled the odd name out. He would call Belfast on returning to the barrack.

Cassidy had wondered why Barratt had asked him to pull up outside the hardware store in the last little town they had just travelled through, to buy, of all things, a spade, what with them driving to the Free State to put their man in the boot onto the boat out. But with Barratt telling him to turn off the mountain road, down a dirt track and into bog land which lay in a low valley amid the green Sperrin Mountains and out of sight of the main road, Cassidy had his own suspicion of what was about to take place and prayed silently to God that he would be proved wrong. Barratt signalled to the driver to bring the car to a halt and then to get out. They both walked to the rear of the car and Barratt gestured to the volunteer to open the boot. Drenched in sweat McHugh grimaced under the brilliant sunshine cutting into his swollen blackened eyes as he was manhandled out of the boot and onto his feet. He struggled to straighten himself. Barratt ordered Cassidy to untie the prisoner's feet, then to fetch the spade from the back seat. McHugh seemed to come alive on hearing this. Breathing erratically through flaring nostrils, he looked at Barratt anxiously. Barratt moved behind McHugh and ordered him to walk on ahead, further into the bog. McHugh limped on.

It was a beautiful day in no-man's-land. Bumblebees and butterflies hovered and fluttered amid the scented lavender heather. A gentle breeze blew. After thirty yards or so, Barratt ordered McHugh to stand still. Removing the pistol from the waistband of his trousers to press its barrel hard against the base of McHugh's spine, Barratt grabbed McHugh by the scruff of the neck and marched him off the track and into the bog land. After a short, brisk walk, Barratt jolted McHugh to a halt.

Cassidy had fetched the spade and was about to cut across the bog towards the two men when Barratt shouted to him, 'Wait there!' Cassidy halted abruptly and looked on anxiously from a distance. Barratt turned his attention to McHugh again. His adrenaline flowed in giving the command.

'On your knees McHugh!'

McHugh fell to his knees due more to exhaustion than obedience. He knew he was about to die. He began to weep silently. Unmoved, and standing close behind his prisoner, Barratt spoke down to McHugh as if chastising a dog; the gun in his hand pointed at the back of his head.

'Y'know McHugh, others were prepared to let you live ... to put you on a boat to America, an outcast, never to return. I think that's too good for you. You've left nothing but a trail of disaster and misery in your wake. That's your contribution to Ireland's cause. We'll, know it here and now McHugh, your name's already forgotten.'

McHugh shook his head. A death cry fought to be released from behind the gag in his mouth.

'I went to your wife this morning to ask her if she and the kiddies wanted to join you there. She hadn't a good word to say about you. And do you know what her last words for you were? *Good riddance*! And so say I!'

From a distance of some thirty yards, Cassidy saw Barratt grab McHugh's hair and yank his head back violently, then put the gun's barrel to McHugh's right ear. Cassidy winced with each of the two shots fired in rapid succession and the shovel in his hands suddenly felt a ton weight, his legs like jelly. He watched as Barratt let go his grip on McHugh, the lifeless body fall forward as if in slow motion to disappear among the heather. Barratt turned away and walked casually back toward him, the gun by his side, his pale face expressionless. Reaching Cassidy, Barratt spoke calmly to the astonished youth. 'The story about taking him to a boat was a decoy for security reasons. This is what happens to touts!' The volunteer felt weak with fear. 'Now go dig a hole and bury the fucker. Make sure there's nothing on his person that can be traced back ... *nothing*! And here, wipe this well and bury it with him. I'll wait for you up at the car.'

Cassidy took the gun in hand and felt the clammy sweat from Barratt's hand around its butt. Barratt casually walked on and left him to it, but after a few paces stopped and turned to face Cassidy, still trembling. 'By the way, don't leave the spade. Y'never know, it might come in handy again.'

On returning to his cramped office and sitting down behind his cluttered desk, the Fermanagh detective was handed a sheet of paper by the young uniformed constable breezing in, having first knocked the door. The detective snatched the report from the constable's hand and cracked, 'No rest for the wicked, eh?' The constable smiled and replied heartily, 'No sir, but it won't be long now.'

'Aye, and not a day too bloody soon! Now on yer way lad.'

Still smiling, the constable heeled and marched out of the room.

'Not a day too bloody soon, true enough,' repeated the detective to himself, studying the latest report on recent events from Divisional Command. It made interesting reading. Forensic officers at the scene of the Armagh shooting detected a strong smell of petrol on the hands and clothes of the dead man, Sexton. An empty petrol container had also been found in the boot of the O'Rourke's car, discovered parked up in Portadown. But more importantly, a large tablecloth found in the car had since been identified by the late colonel's housemaid as the very one from the abbey's main dining hall. She was certain it was one and the same, for its corner was slightly marked, where she herself had accidentally burnt it while ironing it only days earlier. And not least, two of the farm labourers questioned also, were confident that the guns recovered from the three dead men were the same as those Colonel Cartwell had been seen to clean on regular occasions.

As far as this detective was concerned, it was an open and shut case. It was clear to him that Sexton and the O'Rourkes had been directly involved in the whole bloody escapade. He suspected also, that they might well have had a hand in old Bogle's death, indeed murder. The postman would have been a good source for information in their eyes as to the lay out of the land and the pickings to be had at the abbey. To launch the attack in Belfast, the detective concluded that Sexton - who had once worked and lived in the city during the war years prior to being interned there - had calculated that the attack would inspire the IRA's Belfast Brigade into action, which in turn would most likely trigger the IRA north and south of the border to do likewise. But it was now a case of wait and see. He at least was never happier to be leaving it all behind him. The detective would submit his own conclusions in his end of day report to the Divisional Commander, whom he knew to hold his judgement on such matters in high esteem. With, in his book, the case now closed, the detective removed from his pocket that notebook which had served him so well over the past year, raised himself out of his desk chair and walked to the 1952 calendar pinned to the notice board. He ran a finger along the dates circled and counted. There were six days to go before he retired and hung up his mac. He considered it would take him that long at least to clear out his office. So he opened his notebook, fingered through its creased pages and finding the page listing the names supplied by Mr McStravick, tore it out. He crumpled the piece of paper into a tight little ball and, testing his aim in his old age, flicked it into a wastepaper bin up one corner. The detective felt quite good in himself; he had left no loose ends.

Saying goodbye to the family who had accepted him as one of their own, even before he'd married into it, had been heart-wrenching for Anthony. He knew that saying farewell to his good friend McNab, would not be any easier, and to his wife and child, more painful. McNab had driven the Brennans to the docks and they all stood now on the quay as the last of the passengers climbed the gangway to board the midday ferry.

    Anthony reached out to shake McNab's hand. 'Goodbye McNab. Thanks for everything.' Braving a smile, McNab took Anthony's hand in his and placed his free hand on Anthony's shoulder. 'You'll always be a good friend to me, Anthony. Good luck.'

    McNab returned to the car nearby, leaving a husband, wife and child alone together. Sarah was ashen-faced and tears fell from her cheeks. The child in her arms looked up at both parents wide-eyed, oblivious to the pain and suffering all around him.

    Anthony drew mother and son close. 'Take good care of yourselves.' He kissed Sarah gently on the lips, felt her warm tears against his face. He bent forward then to kiss his son upon the forehead and a truth dawned. With a forced smile, Anthony said, self-consciously, 'We haven't thought of a name for him yet.' Sarah choked back more tears and managed a little smile also in acknowledging their oversight.

    'Well, now's the time,' she said. 'I'll leave it to you to decide.'

    Anthony thought for only a moment and looked Sarah in the eye. 'We'll call him Sean, after your father. He's a good man.' He saw a broad smile break on Sarah's face; more tears fill her eyes, tears of joy and pain.

The last call for passengers to board beckoned them to part. Sarah opened her heart to the man she loved and proclaimed to the world, 'I love you, Anthony Brennan! I love our son! God bless.'

Anthony ran the palm of his hand slowly and softly down the side of Sarah's beautiful, tortured face, then stroked his fingertips ever so gently along the contour of his son's little face. Finding the moment to part so difficult to handle, Anthony turned and climbed the gangway, which was hauled away once he had boarded. The main rope securing the boat to port was released by the merchant deckhand and cast overboard onto the dry dock.

Walking along the boat's deck to its stern, the huge turbine engines below Anthony kicked into start. With the rising wind beating hard against his face, he stood and looked on with an aching heart, not taking his gaze off those he loved as the ferry eased out onto the dark, choppy waters of Belfast Lough.

Cast against an ominous Belfast skyline, the lone, solitary figure of Sarah cradling their son close to her breast and standing as a pitiful sight, gradually became only a treasured though painful memory.

Looking on still as Ireland faded slowly on the grey, misty horizon, Anthony was left wondering, what the country he was being ferried to, the one he had consciously decided to avoid all those years ago, held in store.

Book Two

Chapter Thirty-Three

The strike of a match broke the calm silence as the solitary man lit the penny candle. Beholding the Lord's sad, compassionate eyes, he whispered a heartfelt prayer. 'Sweet Jesus, bring my wife and son safely to me.' Sighing with relief, the candle's bright white flame flickering under his escaping breath, Anthony Brennan made the sign of the cross, turned and genuflected toward the main altar before leaving the Catholic church to exit into the boding city, slowly awakening.

Walking one of the East End of London's many frost covered streets, so eerily deserted this Christmas morning, Anthony turned up the collar of his winter coat against the bone-chilling wind and was reminded of that Christmas in Belfast two years before, when he had walked merrily home from the Gresham Bar. Seeing the girl of his dreams for the first time, he had known in an instant, *she* would be the girl he would marry, and he had. He tried to imagine what Sarah and his son may be doing at that very moment back in Belfast, but could not. Bitter memories of life experiences since that day were again to the forefront of his mind. A catalogue of nightmarish events you would only hear tell happening to someone else. He vividly recalled the moment when he had learned of Seamus and Owen's drowning, and the run-in with the sadistic bastards on the border as he'd travelled home to the wake house; running for his life from the shipyard in east Belfast only hours earlier, his brogue having betrayed him to the two bigots with murder in their eyes. Felix Gresham terminating their friendship and the barman's tragic accident shortly after. Colonel Cartwell's murder and the burning of Edenderry Abbey; the guns stolen from the abbey used to murder policemen on the very day his son had been born, and Sean Mor's arrest on suspicion of being involved in the double killing; the IRA men's deaths, and his own suspicion then, of being betrayed by those close to him. He had innocently revealed details of the colonel's arsenal to Sean Mor, and to Felix, whom he both knew now to be IRA men. He had been assured by Sean Mor that he had not been betrayed, but in the same breath Sean Mor had warned that through follow-up police inquiries, he may be dragged into the whole bloody mess and judged an accomplice to it all and had pleaded with him to flee Belfast as quickly as possible. Knowing himself the very real risk presented, he had agreed, reluctantly so, leaving Sarah and a day old son behind him.

He had not written to Sarah these past six months. As a precaution Sarah had agreed that he should leave no possible trail of pursuit for the RUC. The lack of communication had been torturous for him, not knowing for sure if he was a wanted man. He had religiously scanned the newspapers and had listened to the wireless for mention of his name in connection with those bloody events back in July. Thankfully, and serving him some relief in the process, there had not been. Nevertheless he had been anxious for confirmation from the grassroots in

Belfast. He had known that Sarah would answer all his concerns, hinted at, on receiving that first letter which he had been itching to write these past months. And she had.

Stopping midway on that canal bridge and leaning over one of its smoothed parapets to seek further reassurance in Sarah's letter once again, Anthony felt a little more at ease and acceptant of its content - good and bad as it was. Aunt Bella had sadly died on the eve of their first wedding anniversary. With the old aunt's ailing health fast deteriorating in the aftermath of those same bloody events, she had taken to her bed only to fall victim to pneumonia. All the family had been by her side when she'd breathed her last. Characteristically, Bella had kept her dignity right up to the end. Now, Sarah and Sean lived alone in the house, for which Sean Mor had secured the rent book. Sarah was obviously missing him as much as he missed her. She too was counting the days until they were together again. Meanwhile, apart from mothering their son, who was thriving, Sarah was helping to run her father's cobbler shop. These days, Sean Mor rarely ventured outdoors, such was his sorry state of health. Reading between the lines, Anthony sensed that the beating the man had received that cursed July had done irreversible harm. While saddened by this, Anthony was pleased to learn that Sean Mor had been released by the RUC without charge. Evidently Sean Mor had proven himself not to have been involved in the killing of Colonel Cartwell or the policemen.

On the last page of the letter, Anthony read *that* which he had hoped and prayed to hear and it pleased him immensely. Sarah revealed, that following his departure, only neighbours had inquired as to his whereabouts. The story put about was that he was 'away across the water working'.

To learn that Felix and Bernadette were back behind the bar at the Gresham also came as welcomed news to Anthony. Although confined to a wheelchair, Felix was reported to be managing quite well as the bar had been adapted. Though heartened by this, Anthony wondered whether Felix continued with a role in the conflict in Ireland. Knowing Felix as he did, he suspected there was much fight left in him. As for Sean Mor, Anthony feared the man's days to be numbered.

At last, Sarah planned to join him in the spring, with Sean that little bit older and stronger, and more up to the journey. She closed by assuring him that he was forever in her thoughts and in her prayers. She stressed her love for him. He did not doubt it for an instant.

Pocketing the letter, Anthony saw only the faces of Sarah and Sean, innocent and sad as they had been on that last day, reflected upon the murky, dark water below. The dead leaves carried away with the gentle flow, served to remind him that a change of season was yet to pass before he would see their faces for real once again.

Chapter Thirty-Four

With Christmas and the New Year celebrations over, Anthony was one of the many thousands in the madding crowd who pushed and shoved their way along on that first morning back to work. At first the tube had terrified him and only now was he accustomed to it. But he knew that he would never be able to relax his eye as the train, packed tightly with folk, shot through the tunnel at tremendous speed. The thought of missing his stop panicked him. With a sideways glance periodically between stations, he marvelled at how people, intense in their morning newspapers - a crossword perhaps - would seemingly know subconsciously when to alight. Down to years of hard, though accepted experience, he concluded in thought. However, he was left puzzled over how such a coming together of people could result in those same people being so indifferent to each other, underground. No one dare speak so it seemed. An unspoken agreed silence prevailed. Even the roguish Celts among the throng, easily identifiable with their ruddy complexions and red glazed eyes, were compelled to abide by the way of the masses; their natural art of conversation, a wisecrack or a song maybe, suppressed by the silent ones icy stares.

There were tens of thousands of Scots, Welsh and Irish in the city, all hungry for work and all in great demand. Even after some seven years since the war's end, with much work undertaken and completed, still as much remained to be done, before the City of London would be returned to its former glory and much more. Splendid buildings of all shapes and sizes, comprising of various stone imported from all over the world, were springing up in abundance across the capital; the vast network of main routes and side roads, pedestrian walkways and underpasses, all coming together to make an amazing conglomerate of concrete and people. City life in Glasgow and Belfast had in no way prepared Anthony for life among the push and shove, which was London. He had often wondered since arriving in the capital, if a lifetime was ample enough for him to get accustomed to it. But that day, he had little else to choose from and was left thinking, How on earth will Sarah, a mill girl from Belfast, cope with it all?

A black man, as black in skin as the work boots on his feet, squeezing in through the electronic doors of the tube train to join the throng of workers en route, provoked Anthony to think with all innocence, If a black man from out of the bush is willing to come to terms with it all, then so shall we. Catching Anthony's eye with his, the black man dared to smile warmly, his pearly white teeth gleaming brilliantly. Anthony smiled in acknowledgement. Not only was this friendly encounter heartwarming, but with the black man looking about himself briefly with a concerning eye, then establishing eye contact with Anthony once again, it proved soul inspiring. To Anthony's thinking, the black man said with his eyes what he himself had thought on many an occasion since arriving in a strange land: Don't despair. We exiles have a good friend in the memories we hold of happier times among our own.

    The black man was gone in the blink of an eye amid another heave and shove of bodies. Anthony wondered if he would see the man among the thousands ever again? If not, he knew he would never forget that broad beaming smile, and thought, smiling, Precious are the memories true enough.

    Preparing himself to step out at the next stop, feeling as though he were about to enter the lion's den, Anthony studied the expressionless ring of faces about him one more time. They were the faces of those mainly akin to the capital. In that moment, he asked himself the question, Is their moody silence because of us outsiders swamping their city or is it just their way? To his knowledge, acquired from all those newspapers read of late, there was no disputing that the locals were indeed growing uneasy over the influx of such workers, ironically, bought in largely by the government to undercut the English workers rate of pay, and to which, in his analysis, the local populace was ignorant. But anyway, Anthony was convinced that most English folk could not see beyond the black man's skin nor that of the swaggering Paddy - niggers all.

    Catching the eye of a very pretty young girl getting on and hungry for some female attention, innocent though it be, Anthony was forced to let his smile die an instant death under the woman's look of daggers drawn. Alighting from the train, he felt her damning eyes burrow deep between his shoulder blades. Christ Almighty! thought Anthony, If that one smiled, her face would crack!

    He forged his way onward, intent to do his bit in putting right what the German bombers had laid waste. Today, he walked with his shoulders back and head aloft. He no longer felt as though he was running scared. To know all was quiet back in Ireland left him feeling lighter on his feet, and of mind.

    For the sake of his mother and father, a New Year's resolution had been to trace Christy. Anthony still firmly believed that Christy had shunned their younger brothers' funeral out of fear and possibly a sense of shame at fleeing the homestead in the dark of night, leaving others to fend for themselves when times remained so hard. Anthony hoped to impress on Christy that he no longer need hold such fear of returning home or such shame, for all others had painfully learnt how precious life was, and how little time there was to be as one, if only in spirit.

    Anthony had forwarded a letter to his mother soon after arriving in London to let her know of Sean's birth, but had made no reference to the reason why he himself was now in England. All that he had said was that work in Belfast was scarce and that Sarah and the baby would be joining him in the New Year. He had stressed to mother and all others at home, not to divulge to anyone that he was in England. He was intent on finding

Christy and did not wish to risk compromising this through word getting to him beforehand. Anthony had reasoned, that if learning that he was in England - on the lookout - Christy would go to ground. At the same time, Anthony was of course considering his own safety. Living in dread of being publicly named by the RUC as wanted for murder, he did not wish his presence in London to be common knowledge among those Donegal folk flocking to the city, foolishly believing the streets to be paved with gold. He had been fearful that one of his fellow countrymen would, if identifying him, readily give him up for the Saxon shilling. So, he had kept his distance from the capital's broader Irish community in the first six months. Now, thankfully, all the precautions taken were burdensome baggage he could offload. As for Christy? Studying the sea of faces all around him as he emerged from the underground into the hustle and bustle of the early morning rush hour, Anthony knew that in order to stand any chance of tracing him, he would need help. Without it, he also knew, would be like trying to find the lost boy in the Fairy Ring.

Knowing that he could now come out into the open to begin the process of searching out his long, lost brother, Anthony stepped forth with new hope and faith; the forlorn words of a fireside song sung often to them all by mother on cold winter nights, lingering hauntingly in his head.

In the Green wood by the river
Where my child did often play
Where the flowers bloom in springtime
Where I wander day by day
Where I wander growing fonder
Of the child that was my joy
Why for steal a mother's blessing
Therefore steal my baby boy

Morning comes when stars are gleaming
Gleaming o'er the lonely spring
Where I cry, my tears a'falling
Falling on the Fairy Ring ...

Chapter Thirty-Five

Arriving in London intent to keep a low profile among his own, who had swarmed into certain parts of the city in such numbers they had become Irish town lands, Anthony had sought and found lodgings in the heart of the East End, among the clannish locals, who in recent years had borne the brunt of the nightly air attacks by German bombers. The wasteland further along that street in Whitechapel in which he resided, marked the spot where one of the last V8 rockets fired across the channel had nose-dived and exploded. All eight occupants in the end terrace, the youngest child, only six weeks old, had perished in their beds at dawn that fateful day.

Comradeship born out of singsongs down the tube and in garden air raid shelters as the bombs and incendiaries rained down had seen his hardy neighbours through. They had remained clannish folk, friendly to outsiders, and Anthony was no exception. The fact that the original owners of the large Victorian-style lodging house had been a well-to-do family from Dublin, who had mainly dealt in buying and selling antique furniture, helped too, he thought. That same Irish family had lived in the street for over one hundred years and presently an English-born niece to the last of the three sisters, who had only recently died from old age, ran the business as it was present time - the renting-out of the upper four floors in the very spacious five story dwelling. So here, the Irish were not entirely out of character with the place.

With his life consisting of rising at half past five each morning, six days a week, to put in a twelve hour working day before returning to his humble abode in the converted roof space of the house, most often to collapse into bed exhausted, Anthony felt safe and relatively content amid his surroundings. No one paid him any undue attention. He could count on the fingers on one hand the amount of times he had caught a glimpse of his immediate neighbours, all working people, and indeed all a little odd in their ways - particularly the eccentric landlady. She appeared to be fifty-something and seemingly trapped in a time warp. The woman was forever rigged out in Charleston-style dress and with her outrageously long cigarette holder and imported cigarette held gracefully in hand, would glide along the gloomy hallways of the house seemingly in a world of her own. With a rather forlorn, abandoned expression etched upon her cow-shaped face, she appeared a tragic romantic type who had lost her heart to some silent movie star, and sworn never to love another.

Anthony's only irritation with the household was that cursed piano played so melodramatically in the landlady's basement flat at all hours of the day and night. But who dare complain? With accommodation in the capital so hard to come by, Anthony was thankful for his lot, though knew he would have to eventually find somewhere much bigger and more practical for when Sarah and Sean arrived in the spring. Until then, he was only too glad to have a roof over his head, a place to lay down his weary bones after another long day's graft.

Such a day lay ahead of him as he arrived at the small, select back street workshop in the centre of London to take up his place at his workbench alongside a dozen other master craftsmen, busy setting about their skillful production of individual pieces of hand-crafted furniture. Once completed, the furniture would grace the magnificent homes of the socialites in the West End and of rich folk overseas.

On searching for work during those first days in London, Anthony had consciously shied away from the many building sites where Paddy formed the bulk of the workforce. Instead, as when seeking a roof over his head, he had checked the small ads in the daily newspapers and had struck lucky on both occasions. The hours were long, the work very demanding, testing fully the skills he held. The twelve-man workforce worked with only the most sought after and expensive timbers. In return, the pay was good and Anthony managed to save a little at the end of each week to add to the tidy sum he had put by. Once securing a suitable home, setting-up in business was still a possibility. But for now, with barely time to get out of his winter coat and to get busy at his workbench, the only plans he proposed to put into action was to journey up to north London later that night to check out the Irish pubs for sight or sound of Christy. With those days of walking with his head to the floor behind him, he would be looking straight ahead, from left to right and over his shoulder for a familiar face who may help fulfil that New Year's resolution.

In his mother's letter of reply the previous summer, she had first forwarded congratulations on Sean's birth, and had acknowledged his request for discretion as to his whereabouts in London before writing of the sad passing of father's lifelong friend, old JohnJoe. Then at the close of the letter she had revealed that young Mick Onion had recently left home for London and that she and father had asked him to keep an eye out for Christy.

Taking his tools of the trade in hand to set about completing the elegantly carved, dark oak drinks cabinet destined for a rich yank in the States, Anthony paused to say under his breath, 'Sure enough, I wonder who I might meet tonight.'

Witnessing the crazy pub scene from just inside its smoked glass doors, Anthony's thoughts were drawn way back to when, at the age of seven or eight, he had risked a belting on stepping down from that horse drawn cart one hot summer's day in the market square in Toome, to spy on the antics of father over the half door of the Corner Bar, one of many public houses dotted along the Main Street. Father had had some 'business to settle' with one of the notorious Noone brothers. Even at such a young age, he had known something untoward was about to unfold by the way father had determinedly rolled up his shirt sleeves before entering that infamous drinking hole. And sure enough, on disobeying his father to stand on tiptoe to steal a peep, wide-eyed and aghast over that half door, his virgin instinct was to be proved correct. He had seen father walk boldly up to Noone senior at the bar, tap him on the shoulder and proclaim aloud, right up close to the hard man's face, 'I can fuck and I can fight! Which is it to be?' Noone senior had been too slow in his attempt to glass his father that day. But father had been quick to lay Noone out cold with a powerful uppercut that left the other's jawbone shattered. Rubbing the knuckles of his right hand soothingly with the palm of the other, father had stepped up to the bar then to order a jar; his broad back slapped frantically by the half dozen resident piss-artists swarming around. They had been in awe of his bravado for having KOd the reputed hard man of Toome. The drunkards had all heaped their insincere praises onto his father in the hope that he would buy drinks all round. But father knew their form, condemning them on numerous occasions as the 'shower of shite who would sell their own grannies for the price of a jar.' Father had raised the pint tumbler to his mouth with deliberate showmanship while the others licked their lips in silent anticipation as he downed the cool, creamy black porter in one. Placing his empty jar down gently on the counter top, father had drawn the back of his huge hand across his frothy top lip before turning to face all, drooling at the mouth like dogs in heat. As if possessing not a care in the world, he had said, 'I'll be on my way. I've got other animals to see to ... those more friendly, four legged kind.' Rolling down his shirt sleeves, his father had calmly stepped over his felled foe and had made his way back leisurely to the horse and cart, wherein Anthony had quickly found his seat again, pretending he'd seen and heard nowt. He had admiringly looked up to his father for days and weeks after, up until that was, he too had felt the same force of his father's open hand across his little arse, for little or no reason.

Anthony had soon discovered why Charlie Noone had come into contact with father's knuckles that glorious day. Charlie had been seen by a good neighbour to rob turf from father's turf stack at the rear of the family home at dawn a few days before. Seeking to have this confirmed, his father had lain in wait behind a briar bush that following morning and sure enough, witnessed the dirty deed repeated. He had been tempted to jump the thief there and then, but instead had bided his time for the opportunity to present itself to make an example of Charlie in public. And it had not ended there. On the way back home, father had stopped off at the Noones' homestead to fill a dozen potato sacks with turf, his turf, stolen over the previous days, and tossed them effortlessly into the cart under the damning eyes of the other two notorious Noone brothers, who dared not make a move. Father had warned them off by saying in all seriousness, 'Take one step forward and I'll break your fucking necks!' The Noones had known he meant business. They too had met their match in him that day.

Yes, it all came flooding back to Anthony on spying a man flat on his back and out cold on the floor of the north London pub, which could easily be mistaken for a pub on any night of the week, anywhere in Ireland. The other patrons, all paralytic on first appearances, seemed oblivious to the man down as they cumbersomely stepped over him and swaggered up to the bar for yet more alcohol. The sole barman struggled to keep up with demand, but was hardened enough to his trade to ride the storm of cynical banter fired at him by those dying for a drink.

'Fuck sake, Geordie, get your act together.' Another heavy boozer chipped in, 'Aye, get a move on is right. At this rate, it'll be next New Year before we get a bloody drink!'

'Hear! Hear!' A comradely chorus struck up to fill the barroom, packed to the rafters by thirsty, worked-hard Irishmen, drawn from most, if not all of Ireland's thirty-two counties.

A passer-by sporting a thick Mayo accent had told Anthony minutes earlier, that this pub was, 'thee pub for a good drink'. But on studying the sea of haggard, stoned faces, the chaos reigning, Anthony was relieved to see no one familiar and beat a hasty retreat. He would try one of the other bars, all the other bars sited along Camden Town's High Street if need be. He was determined to get some word of sorts about Christy from someone, somewhere. There was little over an hour's drinking time left and feeling the night's bitter cold seize his bones, a wee drop of the hard stuff in a quiet corner - if he could find one - urged him further on his way.

Calling into that second pub along the route, thankfully a little quieter than the first, and ordering a drink, Anthony casually asked the more relaxed barman if he had ever heard of a Donegal fellow by the name of Christy Brennan? The much older, friendly-faced barman paused to think for a moment and weighed up the newcomer with a suggestion of doubt in his eye as to who he might be, what his business was? Sensitive to this, Anthony assured the barman that he had just come off the boat and was a 'close friend.' But the barman, knowing what he knew, and still not convinced, was saying nothing, but rather played safe in replying with an Irish accent which Anthony could not place. 'You're in the wrong place, lad. All the Donegal men in this part of town hang out at Donegal Danny's.' A naive Anthony - as far as the layout of the land in north London was concerned - inquired innocently, *Donegal Danny's?*' Knowing the inquirer to be a stranger true enough, the barman sought to enlighten Anthony further.

'Aye, Donegal Danny's. It's thon big pub on the corner of the High Street, about half a mile down the road. Known as the Stag's Head to those English folk here about, few as they are.'

Anthony downed his large measure and was on his way again. He was urged on by the barman shouting after him, 'You'd better get a move on. It'll be chucking out time soon!'

Exiting onto the busy street as a cutting, icy sleet fell, much to the annoyance of the night revellers shuffling by, Anthony set out to briskly walk the half-mile with expectation raised.

The rowdy, brightly lit public house appeared to Anthony more like a main street hotel than a pub. Shivering a little under a cold sweat and feeling a little nervous, he proceeded up a short flight of steps to enter the big pub by its front doors. Reaching the top step, he was met by three happy-go-lucky sorts exiting under a loud boisterous din from within as desperately sought last orders were yelled across the crowded bar room.

'Two more pints over here, you oul whoor!'

'Another five pints when you're ready,' bawled another impatient drinker, before the pub's swing door swung to.

'*Anthony*!'

With his own name proclaimed aloud, Anthony fixed his eyes on the faces of the three men in front of him, cast in shadow beneath the canopy above the pub's main door.

'Anthony Brennan! Bejasus, 'tis the very man himself!'

Anthony was quick to put a name to the mischievous face of the man standing between two associates - strangers to him. 'Mick! Mick Onion! I don't believe it!'

The bottle of whiskey left over from the New Year celebrations was tipped in equal measure into four large tumblers and topped-up with hot water. The four Donegal men settled down on upturned wooden beer crates pulled up to the paraffin heater, which struggled to heat the large, open room, its walls coated in a bilious green distemper. What a pitiful sight, thought Anthony, casually looking about him between careful sips. It was clear to him that the other three men were at ease with or seemingly blind to, their own squalor. Mud-caked work clothes and boots, dishes thick with grease, old newspapers and empty beer bottles, to name but a few of the more recognisable items, lay strewn across the room's bare boarded floor. On every breath a stale, sweaty stench hung heavy and sickly together with the fumes of the paraffin heater. It was the first time the others had been away from home, so Anthony was prepared to put up with the discomfort in the hope this chance meeting might bear fruit.

The two associates of Mick Onion, Cathal and Pius, natives of the Gaeltacth on the extreme northwest coast of Donegal, both fair-haired and swarthy skinned and enormous in build unlike their thin, wiry, friend, his sharp face wearing an unhealthy pallor, were obviously well steamed in Anthony's sober eye. Once downing their hot tonics as if simply drinking tea, Cathal and Pius swaggered off to the adjoining room wherein single beds in separate corners, allowed each to throw down their bull-worked bodies.

From the brief chitchat beforehand, Anthony had established that the three workmates were tunnellers, who burrowed deep beneath the streets of London as its tube network continued to expand. To Anthony's thinking, it was true to say that the men risked their lives each day when picking up a shovel and pick. Like the multitude of Irishmen in town, they knew no other than hard work and sleep - and of course, the six or seven pints of black porter each night, the essential rocket fuel which kept them going. It was through the spilling of their blood, sweat and tears, that the great city was being rebuilt - in parts literally brick by brick.

Left alone, happy and expectant in the other's company, the conversation between the former neighbours and old friends turned to matters more personal and closer to home.

'Christ Anthony, I can hardly believe it!' Mick Onion declared, sitting hunched on his stool-of-sorts and looking Anthony straight in the face with red glazed eyes. 'And here was I talking of you to those two quare ones just the other day and asking myself when might we meet again? Well, it just goes to prove the old saying true, sure enough: 'tis a small world, even here in London, eh?'

Noting little change in the scrag of a man sitting opposite bar his unkempt appearance - a mop of curly blond hair growing out of control, vein bursting thick arms and huge, square fingered hands, out of proportion to the rest of his thin, wiry frame, Anthony threw Mick Onion a smile and raised his near empty glass. 'How right you are, Mick.' Anthony drank the last of his hot whiskey and swallowed hard. 'Tell me, how do you find life in the Smoke?'

'Ack, God almighty Anthony, sure y'know it's damn hard. I was lucky to find work ... and digs. Though the place is a hole, it sure beats lying out on a night such as this or lying up in one of them there dosshouses, where I hear you have to sleep in your clothes and with a firm grip on yer wallet. Sure I heard only the other day they stole the very boots from a man who'd slept sound.' Anthony nodded and commented, 'I hear, with the oddballs you get in them places, it's not only yer wallet they're after!' Mick Onion shuddered where he sat and slapped his knee. 'Aye, too true. Sleep with yer back to the wall is right.' They both laughed. Mick Onion took a hearty slug from his tumbler. It was Anthony who drew a more sombre tone to the conversation.

'I heard from home about old JohnJoe.' Mick Onion sighed heavily. 'Ah Jasus Anthony, that was tragic sure enough. Y'know, he never got over the deaths of Seamus and Owen. His poor mind went y'know. He'd been found wandering the shore road at all hours, crying like a wean. He hit the bottle hard, and some say he drank himself to death. He'll be sadly missed, sure enough,'

'He will that,' confirmed Anthony. 'He was a sound oul character.'

'Sure Anthony, we all miss the boys terribly. I don't think a small community like that can ever get over such a loss. It devastated everyone.'

'True enough Mick. True enough,' sighed Anthony, adding with a hint of hope in his voice, 'But they say time's a great healer.' Mick Onion was not so hopeful though. 'I'm not so sure about that Anthony. Y'know, my younger brother died at the age of four from the cursed TB and yet to this very day my mother weeps for him.' Anthony knew well of the mother's loss and was thinking of his own mother in saying, 'I know, I know. I suppose that for some folk there is never enough time to allow memories and heartache rest.' Anthony paused for a moment, his mind wandering again. 'Thinking about it, how true this is for my own mother and father. They remain brokenhearted though show a brave face. The heartache is made worse not knowing if Christy is alive or dead. Not a single word have they heard from him in five years. In some ways, this must be even harder to accept, not knowing anything at all.'

Anthony saw the expression on the younger man's face become even more sombre, the lines in his forehead deeply furrowed as he sat forward, hand to chin, to seek confirmation. 'D'yeh really think Anthony, that not knowing is as painful for your folk, than perhaps learning that something terribly tragic happened to Christy?'

Anthony sensed immediately that Mick Onion knew something vitally important about Christy; that he was unsure whether he should offload the information. In a firm, confident voice, Anthony prompted Mick Onion to open up. 'I know a great weight would be lifted off my folks shoulders, off all our shoulders, if we knew what has become of him ... good or bad as it may be.'

Mick Onion had got the message. He finished off the last of the hot whiskey before begging. 'You must understand Anthony, I've been in London less than a year. All that I know has come to me secondhand ... a word here and there from the mouths of nameless people. But it all adds up to a story of substance.'

'Go on,' urged Anthony gently, sitting forward on his crate.

Sitting close by, Mick Onion spoke with a hushed voice.

'What I know is this. About six months after arriving here, Christy got mixed up with some shady character involved in ... well, bare-knuckle boxing. Down on his luck, Christy fancied his chances, and it is said he flattened every challenger. Anyway, just before Christmas of that year, this character arranged for Christy to fight the street champ, Billy Wether, a Scot going by the ring name of *Stormy*, a proper nutcase if ever there was one. There was no song or dance about him, I can tell yeh. Anyhow, the fight took place in a warehouse in docklands. Hundreds - in the know like - turned up. They say a fat purse was up for grabs ... that there has not been a scrap like it since. Both of them had been on the floor a dozen times or more. It is said, you could see the white of their knuckles.' Mick Onion nervously licked his lips. 'Christy lifted the title that night, and the purse. The Scot had been carried away unconscious ... a right mess, they say. Anyway, about a week later, while out on the town celebrating, Christy was jumped on by a gang of Scots wielding pick-handles, razors, and God knows what else. They left him for dead in the gutter.' Anthony was in dread of what he might hear next. 'Christy pulled through though, but they say he'll be scarred for life. The bastards knifed him in the face, time and time again.' Mick Onion hesitated. On the edge of his seat, Anthony urged him on. 'C'mon, out with it!'

Mick Onion had heard the anxiety in Anthony's voice, saw the eyes alive with fear, just as they had been on that night he'd walked into the wake house back home. He knew he could not hold back anything now.

'Christy believed Stormy to be behind the attack. Once recovered enough, Christy pursued yer man north. Y'see, the wee cunt had left for Glasgow the day after the attack. Before Christy departed, he put it about town that he did not want word of what had happened, leaking out. With the nature of what he had been involved in, being illegal, it had all been kept quiet. When word came through from Ireland of Seamus and Owen, it had been considered best by those who knew of this business to keep their mouths shut. After all, they knew Christy was not to be crossed.' Mick Onion paused for a moment and braced himself before revealing the brutal conclusion to the tale. 'Christy had been informed all right, of the tragedy at home by a contact here in London. A letter was sent to America, to where he had gone from Scotland. He is said to have sent word back to London, to say that those in Ireland had enough trouble of their own, that it was best if nothing was ever said about his circumstances or whereabouts.' Anthony lowered his head. Mick Onion twitched nervously. 'Anthony, the story ends with news coming down from Glasgow, that Stormy Wether was stabbed to death in a street brawl by a person unknown, the day before Christy left for the States.'

Anthony's stomach churned and his head fell into his hands. Mick Onion sought to give food for thought out of concern for others absent.

'Anthony, is it not best that your folks carry that heavy weight ... that they know none of this?'

Clenching his eyes tightly closed and hoping that when he opened them, he would awake from a bad dream, Anthony said despairingly, 'Maybe. Maybe.'

Chapter Thirty-Six

Anthony and Mick Onion met up a week later in Donegal Danny's. Mick Onion had willingly agreed to Anthony's request that first night to dig out in between time, the name or names from among those 'in the know' who may be able to tell Anthony one thing, how he could contact Christy? Meeting much earlier that Saturday night, Anthony and Mick Onion - the latter a familiar face in Camden Town - found a quiet corner in the spacious barroom steadily filling up, and over their pints discussed what had since been unearthed. It soon became apparent to Anthony that Mick Onion had indeed been busy, but thankfully, discreetly so.

'I'll tell you something, Anthony, it was like trying to get the name of the man who lives on the Moon.'

Anthony eagerly received the scrap of paper slipped across the tabletop by Mick Onion, behaving as if he were a spy on a mission.

Anthony glance read and memorised the scribbled name and address, then discarded the note among the overflowing ashtray in front of him. Anthony raised his drinking glass to his lips while Mick Onion earnestly attacked his pint.

'Drink up Mick. We're going to pay someone a visit!'

Mick Onion swallowed hard a mouthful of porter on hearing the pronouncement.

They had caught a tube train south and alighted at Elephant and Castle. With the last of the late night traffic racing homeward bound, Anthony and Mick Onion walked briskly in a fine drizzle towards The Old Still public house. Reaching it, they turned right into a deserted side street, then left down an alleyway partially illuminated by the garish neon light overhanging a steel plated door, which ominously informed those who approached what to expect if they entered. Mick Onion's nerves were shattered at the prospect of what may await them inside JACK KILTY'S BOXING CLUB and was moved to voice his concern, hoping Anthony might get a grip.

'Jasus, Anthony, I don't know. Don't you think it would be better to leave it until tomorrow say, when it will be a lot quieter? When yer man might be on his own like?'

Anthony already had his mind made up. The time had come to get his hands on that information which would put to rest the family dilemma over Christy once and for all. His thinking was clearly made evident in what he said in reply. 'As they say Mick, why put off till tomorrow what you can do today?'

Mick Onion faithfully followed his friend through the unlocked steel door, feeling like a lamb to the slaughter. They did not get very far along that grim hallway, dimly lit by a naked light bulb, before they were stopped in their tracks by a flat-nosed, cauliflower-eared man mountain, blocking their way. His speech slurred and wearing a somewhat docile expression, the bouncer inquired, 'What you wantin', boys?' Anthony felt pity for the man more than anything else. But Mick Onion, at the rear, was more fearful.

'The gaffer, is he in?'

The punch-drunk hulk eyed Anthony contemptuously, before hissing, 'Mister Kilty to you! What if he is?' Anthony was not in the mood for any bother, not least with this old hand.

'Tell him the brother of Christy Brennan wishes to see him. He'll understand.' Anthony saw the man's battle-scarred face, light up.

'Christy ... *the Paddy?*'

Anthony nodded.

'No problem! You follow me,' winked the bouncer, throwing Mick Onion, lingering nervously behind Anthony, an inquisitive look. Anthony intervened. 'It's okay. He's with me.' The bouncer gestured with his head for them to follow. Anthony and Mick Onion did so, cautiously.

Approaching the gym at the far end of the hallway, the sound of leather and muscle being pounded relentlessly gradually filled the visitors' ears, the potent sweaty odour, their nostrils. Making their unannounced entrance into the cramped, hectic surroundings, wherein perspiring, muscular and fit young men of all sizes and weight, style and skill, let loose with both hands on a mixture of hanging punch-bags, target gloves, punch-balls, and the kidneys and exposed heads of sparring partners, Anthony and Mick Onion felt a shiver of both fear and excitement run down their spines at witnessing such a disciplined exhibition of human strength and raw determination, all in the quest for glory and pride, personal and public.

The over-the-hill ex-pro, who'd found neither, pointed Anthony in the direction of the central attraction - the full size boxing ring in which two young sparring gladiators tried to do each other serious damage under the manipulative eye of the smart dresser at ring side. The tanned, fit-looking, middle-aged gym owner cum professional boxing promoter, rigged out in a very expensive Italian suit and crisp white shirt, was standing in judgement. The man's slick grey hair, the gold cluster rings decorating every second finger, confirmed Anthony's suspicions. He thought aloud, though quietly enough for the bouncer to miss it, 'A gangster if ever there was one. This isn't going to be easy.' Turning to an extremely nervous Mick Onion, Anthony made his friend even more nervous by saying out of the corner of his mouth, 'Whatever happens, don't move from here. And don't let anyone get between me and that door behind you.' Feeling and looking so inadequate in stature, Mick Onion nodded and gingerly removed his huge hands from his trouser pockets to make ready formidable fists by his side.

The bouncer led the way. Anthony followed with shoulders back and chin up, and was thinking, If Mick only knew how I felt he would run for his life. Anthony was sweating under his clothes as fear gripped him, but he put on a brave face as he stepped up closer to the man himself. Whispering into Jack Kilty's ear in announcing the unexpected and surprise visitor, Kilty peered over the bouncer's shoulder with a fixed, cold eye and studied Anthony long and hard. Anthony saw Kilty mouth a comment to the bouncer, who then turned and walked back toward him.

'Mister Kilty sez follow 'em to his office.'

Anthony watched Kilty move casually to the door of a makeshift office on the opposite side of the ring. Mick Onion felt as though all eyes were on him and tried to disguise his fear. He relaxed his shoulders a little and controlled his breathing, but was quietly cursing himself for not having Cathal and Pius alongside him now.

The craggy-faced, sharp-eyed coach at ringside studied Anthony closely as he moved to go past. An equally watchful Anthony threw him a cautionary glance and he noted the man's cancerous, feeble appearance. Looks as though he hasn't one decent punch left in him, thought Anthony, turning his attention quickly again to the man he was about to meet.

A hard-faced fifty year old, a middleweight contender in his younger days, Kilty was already sat protectively behind the cluttered desk in his seedy office by the time Anthony entered. Kilty was a very busy man with much on his mind, and didn't waste time in doing business.

'What Christy Brennan are you talking about, sonny?'

The man's abrupt, demeaning manner instantly triggered anger within Anthony, which superseded his fear. Normally quiet and accommodating, the life experience of Belfast had hardened Anthony. He too had urgent business to attend to and it began right there and then for him. He was determined to see it all complete before his family joined him in a few months. He wanted to devote himself to Sarah and Sean body and soul and was set on leaving all bad times behind. No one would intrude so oppressively into his life ever again. Looking down at the man's Jewish features, the solid gold, thick cluster rings decorating his fingers, Anthony concluded easily that he wasn't taking any shite from Kilty, nor anyone, anymore. Leaning his formidable frame over Kilty's desk to leer into the cockney's battered, tanned face, Anthony was challenging and demanding with his response and it unnerved the host, not easily intimidated - and on his own manor at that.

'The Paddy who came to London and beat the shite out of all takers, only to be Judased by half a dozen yellow bastards who left him scarred for life, and his folk back in Ireland, heartbroken. And me? Very angry, but determined to find out where my brother is today.'

Kilty did not take lightly to being spoken to in such a manner by anyone. He had a reputation to keep, an image to uphold, and could easily have the Irishman nailed to the wall. But instead, he quietly admired the man's gall, not least because he had fond and vivid memories of his brother, who had indeed beaten the shite out of all takers, to earn him, as manager, big money in the process. Kilty thought it best to defuse the heat of the moment. He reached for the bottle of scotch and two glasses on his desk, and said, politely, 'Pull up a chair Anthony.'

While not dropping his guard completely, Anthony sensed Kilty had got the message and was willing to let the cockney prove him wrong. Kilty unscrewed the bottle top to pour a generous measure of Jack Daniels into each glass and, stretching across his untidy desk, offered Anthony one of the drinks. Sitting down a little hesitantly and accepting the drink from Kilty, Anthony listened as the now bona fide boxing promoter relaxing in his swivel chair, drink in hand, gave him an insight into the events of that year when Christy had definitely made his mark on the back street fight circuit. It had all tallied with what Mick Onion had said, up until Christy's departure north that was, then Kilty dried up. Anthony persisted.

'Christy, what became of him when he left London? What happened to Stormy Wether?'

Kilty sighed before answering. 'The least said about Christy the better. All I'll say to you is, he vowed to get even with the Scotch mob. One day I hear Stormy is dead, the next, that Christy is in the States. He sent a note to me soon after. It reinforced what he had asked of us all before he left. He wanted no one to know what had happened or where he had gone.'

Anthony considered what Kilty had said and doubted not that Christy had killed the Scot. He was shocked. While only too well aware of Christy's potential to do grievous harm to his opponent, he had never seriously considered him to be a killer.

'When did you last hear from him?' Anthony probed, before taking a slug of the quality malt.

Kilty was honest in his response. 'Last Christmas.' Kilty sat forward in his swivel chair. 'Despite what you may think of me, your brother became part of another family when he was on the scene, and we tend to take care of our own sort, through good times and bad.' Anthony still had his guard up. Kilty was speaking again. 'Christy is doing okay for himself in the States. He took it bad when he learnt of his kid brothers' deaths, and though he knew the silence would not be easy for others to accept, he did not wish to bring the family any more pain. When he left for America, he had no intention of going home, nor of coming back here.'

Anthony felt relieved and saddened by what he had heard and was thankful for Kilty's concern, indeed, his loyalty to Christy, though did not say so. Still judging Kilty to be a dark horse of sorts, Anthony also judged it best not to compromise Kilty by asking for Christy's address in the States. But out of concern for his mother and father, Anthony felt compelled to ask Kilty for a favour.

'Next time you write to Christy, will you ask him to write home to his folks, just to let them know that he's okay? He need not say anything as to what happened here.' Kilty thought for a moment. 'I'll drop him a line,' he said, genuinely. 'And where can I contact you?'

'Donegal Danny's,' replied Anthony. Kilty nodded. Putting down his drink, Anthony stood to take his leave. Kilty was rising out of his chair to see Anthony out, then had a thought. 'Hold on. I've got something you might like to see.' Kilty pulled open a desk drawer and removed a hardback photograph album. He quickly flicked through it. Finding what he sought, he handed the open album to Anthony. Taking it in hand, Anthony found himself looking at a bare-chested, hard-chinned young man, standing with fists raised and with malice in his eyes. He was looking at a pre-fight photograph of Christy, back in his heyday.

'Your brother could have made it big time only for that bastard Scot,' Kilty mused. Studying the photograph, Anthony didn't doubt it.

'If you're curious, there's also a pre-fight photo of the Scot.'

Kilty's invitation stirred Anthony's curiosity to see the face of the man who had brought such misery to the Brennan family. Anthony knew immediately who Stormy Wether was on seeing his narrow, granite-hard face for the first time. The eyes, void of any emotion, were representative of all he had come to learn of the man. Anthony would never forget those eyes. He slammed the album shut and handed it back to Kilty, who noted his unease.

'Justice was served that day in Glasgow,' affirmed Kilty. 'The Scot was evil. He had it coming. A lot of people live easier knowing Stormy Wether is not around today.' Kilty's brutal words served to remind Anthony that it was indeed a cruel world in which they both lived. He took his leave then without goodbyes.

The sharp-eyed coach, seeing a prospective heavyweight in the one leaving, for the build, the power was there, questioned Kilty as to who the visitor was.

'Believe it or not Pop, that's the very man our Christy said he would never get into the ring with ... Anthony Brennan, his kid brother. Christy had come to fear him showing up one day, for when young, Christy had made his life a fackin' misery.'

During the train journey back across the city with Mick Onion asleep at his side, Anthony, knowing what he did, pondered earnestly over what Mick Onion had said that first night: that maybe it was best for his mother and father to continue carrying that heavy weight by not knowing any more about Christy than they did presently. After much private deliberation, Anthony concluded that Mick Onion was right in his thinking. To reveal that Christy had killed another man, no matter how justified, would, he knew, send one, if not both his parents, to an early grave. So he decided, that if Christy opted to stay quiet, and in exile, he would be saying nothing about what he knew - not ever.

With no news of Christy in the weeks that followed, Anthony was delighted to receive a letter from Sarah each fortnight, informing him of every noticeable development with Sean. The letters also told of a mother in full bloom, enjoying each new day with their thriving child. A first photograph of his son now took pride of place upon the ornate mantelpiece in the attic room. Despite Sarah's claims to the contrary, Anthony was convinced his son was the double of his mother, not he. Each letter, mentioning briefly family and close friends, all seemingly in good health or at least making steady progress toward it, ended with the sender's declarations of undying love for him. And this warmed his lonely heart.

During those bitterly cold winter days that followed, a solid friendship was forged between Anthony and Mick Onion. Most Friday and Saturday nights were spent in that pub where a great number of those Donegal emigrant workers in north London met up to drink alcohol - the navvy's salvation – in vast amounts, and the craic was good. Songs, stories - true and imagined - even the odd dance, jig and reel, and not least, the occasional scrap, were in no short supply. It was not uncommon for Anthony to awake on Sunday mornings with a head feeling like a sack of spuds. Long walks on a nearby common were found to be the best cure. On those quieter evenings, Anthony would sit on his single bed with a steaming mug of cocoa and scan the evening newspaper's ad columns with a keen eye, in search of more suited accommodation. April fast approached and those he awaited longingly, would soon be joining him.

Chapter Thirty-Seven

It was a chaotic scene in Donegal Danny's as the good-humoured birthday celebration for Mick Onion reached a peak. Men eagerly queued to arm-wrestle the birthday boy who had a rare knack of beating all challengers. The secret was in the wrist technique, though possessing hands the size of shovel pans helped too. The fact that the lightly made-up man, appearing in need of a good feed, was able to put the biggest of men to shame caught everyone's attention. All in the straggly circle hovering over that makeshift arena in the middle of the floor - two combatants at a table - craned their necks to see another teeth clenching, muscle busting exhibition of showmanship as yet one more contender fell defeated, the twelfth in succession, but who had come closest to victory, for the victor's arm was tiring.

Himself one of the defeated, Anthony had thoroughly enjoyed the craic despite being left to nurse an aching arm in a quiet corner. But his mind was soon distracted from the nagging ache on spying Jack Kilty enter the bar – his expensively flash attire leaving him appearing totally at odds with his surroundings, but obviously unperturbed by the circus-of-sorts in full swing. Seeing Anthony sitting alone, Kilty threw him a friendly smile and made to join him in the corner. Kilty had kept to his word and had journeyed across London to let Anthony have sight of the letter he'd received from Christy a few days earlier, and which he assumed confidently, would be welcomed news for Anthony.

On being received by Anthony with as equally a friendly smile, Kilty readily handed the airmail letter to him. Anthony read it hungrily and Kilty received much satisfaction on seeing Anthony consumed with sheer delight. With Kilty the bearer of such good news, Anthony ordered another round of celebratory drinks, this time in light of what the letter had revealed.

Christy had responded positively to Kilty's written word of counsel to do as Anthony had suggested, to write home to his mother and father and ease their burden of pain, though Christy had wisely not revealed details as to his near-death experience in London. Best of all, Christy had hinted at returning home some day to visit. For Anthony, this was the best possible news, knowing the joy at home over this grand turn of events. And he had the south Londoner to thank for all of it.

That night's party in Donegal Danny's would not be easily forgotten by any of those present, least of all Jack Kilty. Thinking that there was nothing knew to discover about the Irish and how they could party, Kilty considered the saying 'You learn something new every day' as very true, on waking up stiffly and with a big sore head the next morning on top of two barroom tables pushed together.

Upstairs, in a guestroom over Donegal Danny's bar, Anthony slept sound knowing Christy had done the right thing by his mother and father, thank God, and that for him, another special prayer had been answered. Also a property dealer of sorts, Kilty had informed Anthony in friendly barroom conversation the previous night, that if he wanted it, a modest, three bedroom family terrace in Clapham Common - one of many south of the river which he'd bought cheap after the war - had become vacant suddenly. The rent was fair, the street quiet and friendly, and the house came complete with a back garden.

Anthony had agreed to journey out to the house with Kilty the following evening to view it. But with only two weeks to go before Sarah and Sean arrived, Anthony knew it was unlikely that the offer of another house - much more than he'd expected to have a chance of securing through his own efforts - would come his way in the meantime.

As Jack Kilty attacked the cure at the bar below, Anthony slept sound for the first time in a long time.

Chapter Thirty-Eight

On the eve of leaving Ireland for England, Sarah stood by Aunt Bella's graveside in a windswept Milltown Cemetery lost deep in thought. The prospect of leaving family and friends, life around the Falls far behind her, left her heavy of heart. Though she knew that being reunited with Anthony was less than twenty-four hours away, she was not looking forward to life in London, nor to raising her son in a foreign land, the successive royals and governments of which, she had come to loath and hold responsible for the persecution of her land and its native people over the centuries; the stories of such had been told to her with a fiery passion since early childhood by the very woman for whom she had just prayed.

Surrounded by centuries old headstones and Celtic crosses, and those of more recent times, the ghostly images of all those would-be leaders: trade unionists, scholars, farmers' sons and daughters alike, revolutionaries one and all, and who had perished at the hands of the

English, evoked a spirit within Sarah that was nothing less than damning of the same colonial regime, under which, as a resident immigrant, she would be expected to be subservient. For her, this was an abomination. To Sarah's thinking, she, at the age of twenty-one, and her son, barely ten months old, like the many thousands before them, were victims of the oppressor's continued presence in Ireland, and consequently, were forced to leave it behind them.

    Remaining defiant in the face of looming danger in the aftermath of that bloody July day, Sarah had considered writing to Anthony on several occasions to implore him to return, but each time had clearly called to mind his determined mood that day at her father's hospital bedside, when he had vowed never to return to such a cursed place. Though events had cooled somewhat since the sudden explosion of violence in the summer of '52, and her father had been left with little option but to take a back seat of recent, due to his poor health, she could not deny that danger could well be presented to them all yet again, if Anthony was to return. It was out of love for Anthony and loyalty to him therefore, that she would join him the very next day, but was unsure as to what life in England could offer her, her son, and they as a family. Even that peace that she and Anthony had sought was for her, not so certain any longer on realising the strength of her deep-rooted emotions. But in consideration of her marriage and her own family, she would go, but with no great expectations or fixed designs.

    Sarah received a little comfort in knowing that she would carry with her to England those memories of her twenty-one years of Belfast life, good and bad as it had been. Those more pleasant times she now called to mind. Playing out on long summer evenings, her first day at school, sleeping Friday nights at Aunt Bella's after devouring a delicious pasty supper. Watching father hang up stockings at the foot of the bed on Christmas Eve. Those wartime, summer nights, the nervous excitement which came with sleeping out on the Black Mountain during the blitz. The lazy walks on Sunday afternoons along Cave Hill. Stories told by the open fire. Baby-sitting her sisters. Making one's first Communion. That first Saturday night dance, and that first kiss behind the GAA Club ... whatever became of him? The importance of stitching flints into the corners of handkerchiefs to be smuggled into the Crumlin Road Jail to father; winning the Down and Conor Irish Dancing Championship and coming runner-up in the Under '14 All Ireland, and her first days as a doffer. And more recently, meeting and falling in love with Anthony, their marriage, and the birth of their son.

    While for every happy occasion recalled, Sarah knew she could very easily equal each with a dark, tragic one, most often brought about by the state's oppressive hand. But trying to put herself in a healthy frame of mind for the remainder of the day ahead and those to soon follow, it was the former memories she allowed to predominate.

Sarah bade farewell to Aunt Bella, then set out to walk back along the Falls to make ready final preparations. Tomorrow, she knew, would not be long in coming.

Sarah had decided to spend her last night in Belfast with her baby at her parents' home. She put Sean down to sleep in his pram in that bedroom where she had shared most of her life to date with her two sisters. Sitting up late chatting with loved ones about times past, it was midnight when mother, Caithlin and Bridget retired to their beds. Sarah was left alone with father by the cooling coals in the front room. While close to mother and loving her with all her heart, it was father whom Sarah could confide in best. Sean Mor read his eldest daughter's disconsolate face accurately and sought to comfort her.

'I know what you're thinking Sarah. You consider it hypocritical to be leaving here ... to be going across the water. Don't, my love. It's meant to be for the good of us all.' Looking across the dimly lit room at her father, sat in his armchair, Sarah studied his face. Weary and sallow was it, with those once smiling brown eyes somewhat vacant and sunk far into their sockets. Seeing this, and his body unhealthily thin, provoked her to conclude in thought, Christ you have suffered for your country. Once again, father had read her thoughts to the letter. 'You're right, Da. After what this family has been through, I find it so hard to accept. And I know it's not over yet.'

Sean Mor sat forward in his chair with long fingered hands resting on bony knees, to say passionately, and more ominously, 'Listen Sarah, and remember my words well. You and Anthony are only young; you've a young child. Your life together is only beginning. Now, I know as sure as I'm sitting here tonight, that life here is going to get a lot worse before it gets better. There are many years of trouble in store and it will not be the men and women of my generation that will see it to an end.' With an air of sad resignation evident in his croaky voice, the elder continued. 'When your age, I thought I'd live to see my country free. I now know this is not to be. I only hope you see it in your lifetime ... that my grandson will return someday to a peaceful Ireland, where Protestant and Catholic alike, know what justice and equality are. But while holding dear this hope, I must confess to you, that I fear that day will never come. Not because the British are here for good, that the unionists will never see the way forward, but because those treacherous bastards who hold power down in the Free State, will always sell us out. In many ways girl, they are the true enemy.' Sean Mor slumped back into his chair exhausted but had not yet finished his lecture-of-sorts. 'So don't have any hang-ups about going to live among the English, Sarah. The truth of it is, you'll be treated far better by strangers than by those across the border. I know. I've been among them. As for staying here, you don't want to bring your son up amid a bloodbath do you? For that's what it's coming to, mark my words.'

Sarah was holding on to each word parting her father's lips. Never before had he served her poor counsel and she suspected he was not about to. There was almost an apocalyptic tone to his voice now. 'So, get out of it while you have the chance, girl. Don't feel you're running away ... that you're abandoning your people. This family has suffered enough. One martyr to the cause out of any house is plenty. For I'm sure that's what they'll call me when my day comes. Then, after a week or two, that will be the last of my name mentioned. For the war goes on.'

Sarah knew the hard truth of this and it hurt.

'My days as a frontrunner are over,' Sean Mor sighed. 'The last kicking I got knocked the stuffing out of me, but the spirit of freedom is still there. I'll continue to do my wee bit, albeit as an armchair general.'

Eyes falling closed, Sean Mor fought the sleep creeping up on him. The moment's silence that ensued gave both young and old time to take stock of what had been said. Sarah knew her father would be a diehard republican to the very end. Sean Mor wondered just how long he had left as he felt as if he were already at death's door. Keen to show a brave face in that moment in time, he spoke with forced zest. 'I have a great woman upstairs who's never had much of a life with me. But I'm intent on making it up to her before we both get too old. So don't despair. What's important Sarah is that you go to Anthony and live each day to the full, and give my grandson a fair chance at life. If you do this, you will do me proud.'

Sarah had heard every word and would remember them to the day she died. She stood and crossed the room to kiss her father on the forehead. 'I'll do my best by you, Da,' she said with feeling. Clasping his daughter's hands in his, Sean Mor impressed, 'Go in God's name Sarah, and be together as a family. And remember, whatever comes to pass, either here or across the water, do not get involved. Just carry on with your lives.'

Sean Mor had said his piece. Sarah knew she was being warned of things soon to come and recognised her father's real concern. To make him happy, she sought to allay his fears through a light-hearted comment. 'Don't worry, I'll have enough on my hands looking after a husband and child.' But in reality, she would worry, and she knew that her father knew she would, and he did.

Father and daughter went to their beds with their thoughts racing and lay restless through the night, as did all others in the household, knowing the day ahead would be hardest on them all.

The following morning, with the Belfast sky thick with gloom and laden with April showers soon to fall, loved ones gathered together on the doorstep of No72 to say their heartfelt goodbyes. Hugs, kisses and tears were freely shared. Then Sarah, weighed down with Sean in her arms, climbed into the back of McNab's car and set out from the street looking straight ahead. She could not bring herself to look back. As the car progressed down the Falls, Sarah took in all the familiar street names, shop fronts and the faces of those walking past - oblivious to her pain but no doubt each carrying a cross of their own - and would savour these last images of her home town.

Bidding goodbye on the quay to a sad looking McNab, Sarah experienced not only her own pain on leaving all that she loved dearly, but that which Anthony had experienced too that July day.

As Sarah climbed the ship's gangway, conscious of Sean so heavy in her arms, his hungry blue eyes searching hers, the thought of being in Anthony's arms once again before the day's end, was her light at the end of a very long, dark tunnel.

Chapter Thirty-Nine

The couple reunited on the railway station platform stood as one in loving embrace, oblivious to everything and everyone about them. No words were ample for either Sarah or Anthony to describe how good it felt to be in each other's arms again. Cradled snug in one of his mother's arms, their son was sleepy-eyed and oblivious to the event. Once aboard the train, the gentle rocking of the railway carriages soon saw the child to sleep. In the privacy of their own carriage, Anthony and Sarah were left undisturbed to hold each other close, to kiss passionately. It had been so long. As the train rolled south and with a sense of parental responsibility predominating, Anthony and Sarah turned to talking in near whispers, side-by-side, hand-in-hand, of troubled times past and left far behind.

'I'm so glad you're out of that place,' affirmed Anthony.

'It's all right. We've nothing to fear,' Sarah soothed, her hands clasping his tightly.

'Your father, how did he take your leaving?' Anthony asked, relaxing a little.

'Father and I talked last night. He still wished me to go. He said our being here would make him happy.'

'We should thank God we got out. It's no place for Sean.' Drawing Sarah closer to him, Anthony added with a passion, 'Never ask me to go back there ... not ever!' Anthony saw Sarah's face harden a little; her eyes fall away. He knew it would be difficult for her to accept his word of never returning to Belfast with their son. A whole new life together lay ahead of them both. He did not even wish to look back into the past any more. And Sarah? Though she looked out forlornly over the English landscape, kissed by a breaking sun, her mind's eye saw only that which she'd left far behind.

Dusk was falling as the Hackney cab pulled up to the kerb in a south London side street. The exhausted family alighted onto the pavement outside their new home. With Sean sound asleep in his arms, Anthony was quietly excited. He knew of the surprise that awaited his wife, thanks once again to Jack Kilty.

Pausing for a moment with suitcase in hand to study the street, so quiet with curtains drawn and doors closed out, to Sarah Belfast seemed to be in another world by comparison. Here, even the neighbouring houses seemed indifferent to each other, the families within, in hiding from all others it seemed. A depression descended upon her with the night sky falling.

Anthony led the way up the short garden path to the ordinary looking terrace, newly painted white. A heavy brass knocker, centre of its black Georgian-style door, gave it a slight added stylish feature compared to most of the other houses in the street. He had sweated buckets these past two weeks decorating into the small hours and moving in furniture whenever free time allowed. He'd wanted the house to look a little palace for his wife and son and was proud of the end result, especially Sean's room, complete with brand new cot.

Once inside, and with Anthony switching on the house lights, a bright, brand new beginning confronted Sarah for the very first time since setting foot in England. Realising how much Anthony wanted to make it a happy new life for them all, Sarah burst into tears. Falling against Anthony's chest, Sarah found the comfort and reassurance she so much needed that everything was going to be all right.

With Sean snug amid his new surroundings, Anthony and Sarah fell naked into the spacious new bed in the adjoining bedroom and willingly let their hunger for each other escape through the raw sex to which they freely exposed each of their own bodies. There was an erotic liberation in their lovemaking and both savoured sexual bliss never before experienced. Fears and anxieties as to the past and the future were soon abandoned.

It was the early hours before they fell sound asleep in each other's arms, their sweat intermingling, their bodies tender and sore, but pleasantly satisfied, on this their first night together in England's capital.

Sarah tried so hard to settle into her new surroundings and an ordinary routine as a mother and housewife in those first days and weeks. And while those few neighbours she caught sight of first thing in the morning and last thing at night as they quietly left for and returned from work, and local shop proprietors and market traders were friendly enough with their hearty 'Good Mornings' and light and easy conversation, Sarah knew it would be especially difficult for her to establish even the most casual of relationships with the locals and to grow accustomed to the environment itself. This challenge manifested during the last days of May as the street and city, the entire nation, prepared to joyfully celebrate the Coronation of the new Queen of England, Queen Elizabeth II. Knowing that the day itself, what with the street party planned and everyone expected to join in, could well compromise both her and Anthony's future standing in the immediate neighbourhood. As Anthony and she had no interest in, nor intention to participate in the day's calendar of celebrations, Sarah thought it best that the family not be around on the 2nd June and so propositioned Anthony to take both her and Sean out for the day. She suggested they spend the day at the coast, where she hoped she'd find some peace of mind in more ways than one.

Sarah had been anxious about whether they'd be accepted by the people they were going to live among; Sean's christening, schooling, and if she would settle, make friends or work again. And not least, if Anthony was truly out of danger as she had felt that a new, even more serious threat was posed to him, to them all.

Anthony had informed Sarah of events surrounding Christy's departure for the States. He had thought long and hard as to whether he should tell her all, and on the first day of their being together again. But he wanted his marriage and relationship with Sarah to be based on trust. He knew the importance of this from his experience of life in Belfast. Believing his sharing of life experiences with those he had come to consider family, had been betrayed, Sarah and her father had been suspect in his mind that July day, when he had been urged to leave the city in the aftermath of all the killing, which he had suddenly found himself to be possibly party to, and in the eyes of others, responsible for. Yes, his trust and confidence in those closest to him on that day, Sarah, her father, the whole McParland family and close friends, had lain in tatters. Only by direct and open challenge to, and demanding the same from those closest, had the truth been realised and his faith in others restored. But nevertheless danger as an indirect consequence of his relationship with the McParland family had still loomed and the subsequent anxiety was no less real.

Yes, Anthony had come to know the real importance of truth that July day, and while acknowledging he could not have sight of all the facts, that not all the story had been told or indeed known even by those central to it, he had been determined to ensure that such honesty would continue to be shared between Sarah and he, and among those claiming to have their interests at heart.

It was in keeping faith with this newfound hope in others, that Anthony had shared his fears and hopes with Sarah on being reunited. Through holding no fear of the Scots vendetta continuing, much due to reassurances given by Kilty, Anthony had been able to allay Sarah's anxiety over further violence. As for all the other issues raised that day, they had come to accept that by tackling them together, when the moment presented itself, all fears could be overcome and hopes realised.

Determined to enjoy the welcomed day together, Anthony and Sarah and Sean set out early that morning before the day's historical event got underway under the glare of millions. As the family spirited out of the sleeping street, Sarah paused to take in all the Union Jacks and buntings fluttering overhead, particularly that one depicting the face of the Queen-to-be fastened to the drainpipe of their home and to that of the house opposite, and could not refrain from remarking cynically, 'It's like walking up the bloody Shankill on the Twelfth morning!'

Walking barefoot along the deserted beach with a fresh sea wind pleasantly beating against their faces was a welcomed experience for Anthony and Sarah. Held aloft in his father's arms, Sean seemed to be under the spell of the choppy water splashing around the feet of his parents, while the sea wind took his breath away when it came in gusts.

It was the first time that day that the family had escaped the excited interest of the masses over the Coronation. Apart from the endless streets decked out in red, white and blue all the way out from London, talk of it had been on the lips of those men and women and even children old enough to understand, encountered along the way, on trains, buses, and in the back of taxi cabs. Even on a deserted seafront normally black with folk, and despite the weather not at its best, one was still aware of something spectacular taking place elsewhere.

Torrential rain had put a premature end to the London street parties, and now the public houses dotted along Clapham High Street were doing brisk business with those parties moving indoors, the Londoners spirit, not easily dampened. As Sarah and Anthony - Sean deadbeat and a dead weight in his father's arms - walked the short distance home from the underground with the rain easing, the late evening breeze carried the cheery voices of those gathered around the piano played thunderously in the street corner pub. *'Roll out the Barrel ...'*

Sarah smiled at Anthony. 'I have enjoyed the day. Thanks love.' She stood on tiptoe to kiss him on the cheek. Brimming with joy, Anthony looked at Sean, rousing in his arms, and said with a note of warning, 'We'd better see this wee fella to his bed before he brings the partying to an end.'

Mother and son went to bed early that night, the long walk and sea air having done them both the power of good. Kissing Sarah goodnight, Anthony promised to be home again in a few hours. He was off to Camden Town to see Mick Onion and friends for a planned drink.

'Be careful Anthony and hurry home!'

Anthony stopped at the bedroom door to look back. The streetlight seeping through the chink in the curtain illuminated that warm smile on Sarah's sweet face, and knowing her to be naked beneath the sheets, Anthony was tempted to stand-up his friends. 'I won't be long love,' he assured her. Then he left to keep arrangements made. It had been a month and a half since he'd seen his friends. He had been so busy with the house and in reassuring Sarah through those first weeks by not leaving her side once home from work, and was much looking forward to a badly needed drink.

On arrival at Mick Onion's, Anthony was pleasantly surprised to discover Kilty in attendance. A private function of sorts was already underway. Apart from the south Londoner, the hosts and himself, a half dozen other friendly faces from Donegal Danny's had gathered for the session. Crates of stout and bottles of whiskey were in plentiful supply and were all being merrily downed. A steaming Mick Onion had opened the door to Anthony and literally dragged him indoors, proclaiming at the top of his slurred voice, 'Look y'here. It's yer man, himself. It's been so long since I saw him last, I've forgot his bloody name!'

    Anthony enjoyed the craic nearly as much as a well-liquored Jack Kilty. 'I've been here all day, Anthony. I wanted to escape all the razzle-dazzle. And where better to be on such a day than among a bunch of mad Paddies?' Though was quick to add, 'No offence intended.' There was no offence taken. For Anthony, there was indeed no better place to be on such a night, particularly when Mick Onion introduced him to Finn Spiceland, a Derry man who had been found labouring on the new building site close to London Bridge, where Mick Onion and his gang had recently got a start. On coming to stand in front of Anthony to shake his extended hand, Spiceland, a tall thin man with an amicable face, on hearing the name Brennan mentioned, was quick to place Anthony's face from their brief encounter years before. Anthony's mind was left racing when this was put to him.

    'Five years ago it was ... back in Ireland. It's not surprising you don't recollect. You must have shaken a thousand hands over those few days.' Anthony knew now the occasion of which the other spoke and the Derry man saw this in his eyes. 'That's right. At your brothers' wake ... God rest them. I came to pay my respects. You know, it was a big loss for the people of Derry too. We are all family at the end of the day.'

    While stirring painful memories the Derry man's words moved Anthony to embrace his neighbour from back home in a spontaneous act of gratitude. With Finn Spiceland taking his leave of the party early, to keep a prior arrangement, neither man was to discover just how small a world they truly lived in. Unknown to them both, a certain man back in Ireland, in Belfast, whose name had not passed their lips that night, for even in his absence he commanded a certain protective respect, and whom they knew personally through their respective relationships, had by the sheer nature of their contact with him, brought them together, and yet, again as a consequence of their relationship with Sean Mor, would never again lay eyes on each other.

Mick Onion was on top form and as the night wore on his patter in storytelling got better. He had all in his company in hysterics, including Donegal Danny, who'd since joined them. He had left the missus to run the bar so as not to miss the craic. The joker would not let up and as all others fought to catch a breath and wiped away tears of laughter, was off again.

'Did I ever tell youse of the experience I had coming over on the boat? Well, bejasus I only ended up sitting beside an oul Jackeen whoor in a fur coat ... her sour bake plastered in war paint. Anyway, she breaks wind and turns to me with a look of mild surprise and in a posh Dublin accent, says: "Rip goes my stocking dress!" Says I: Rip goes your arse! Says she: "Oh! I think I shall faint!" Says I: I think you'll shite first!'

Only when folk ached so much that they could laugh no more, and with Mick Onion paralytic up one corner, Anthony got the chance to have a quiet word in Donegal Danny's ear on a matter of great importance. Getting a handshake on it from the publican, a big friendly bear of a man, a delighted Anthony, himself well liquored, seized the spotlight to announce to all the special news.

'There will be another party in a few months time, over at my place. On the day my son is christened. Danny here, and on behalf of his good wife Maureen, has agreed to be godparents. So you are all hereby invited to a grand occasion!'

The 'Yahoos' and 'Good on youse' filled the room and glasses were refilled one more time - even that of Mick Onion's.

Finn Spiceland had not touched a drop of the hard stuff all night. The true reason for his being in England demanded that he in no way compromise himself and thus put at risk the crucial planning of those other men back in Ireland, who were depending on him to achieve so much. He had ensured to put distance between himself and the demon drink, which in his judgement, next to the cursed English, was the greatest enemy of the Irish people. So in recent time he had simply and solely applied his mind to that essential purpose of being in England. He had endeavoured to be meticulous in his planning. Those other IRA volunteers seeded across the city had faith in his leadership, but despite all this, there had already been one major setback in the aftermath of the first raid for arms, with both the arsenal recaptured and good men seized. But this time around, he was determined that all would go according to plan. Faith had been restored among those men remaining and who awaited his commands. Everything was in place. He had not lied to the Donegal man, Mick Onion, earlier that evening, when saying he had to leave the session early to keep a 'prior arrangement'.

Keeping the prior arrangement - the final reconnaissance of the military barrack on the outskirts of north London now clear to be raided in ten days time - Finn Spiceland was confident that he would be back in his native Derry in less than two weeks, his masquerading as another Paddy seeking his fortune in London at last over. He would be returning to Ireland with a different pot of gold, and to take up a leading role in events planned there.

Somehow Anthony made it to the underground and just caught the last tube train south. With a bellyful of drink taken, his head swimming, he had to concentrate hard at each stop, so as not to miss his. He was relieved to get off when he did, to escape the late night revellers further along the otherwise deserted carriage, breaking into spontaneous song in still celebrating the day's big event.

'God-Save-Our-Graaaacious-Queen...'

Tripping over himself on climbing the steep stairwell to the real world, Anthony was cursing as a blustery wind drove the pelting rain hard against his back as he staggered, head down, hands in pockets, the short distance home through empty rain-soaked streets with the deadpan lyrics of *God Save The Queen* echoing torturously in his head. Approaching the front door of his house cast in darkness as was the neighbouring houses, with those indoors sleeping off the day's celebrations and over indulgence in food and drink, song and dance, Anthony's attention was drawn to the rain-sodden bunting hanging limp overhead and which flapped irritatingly in the wind. In his mind's eye - under the influence - the condescending face of the new Queen of England looked down upon him, a mere subject, and a Paddy at that, with scorn. Looking back with a similar eye, Anthony spat, 'I'll soon sort you out ...'

He staggered up the garden path fumbling in his jacket pockets for his house key. On at last finding the keyhole and turning the door key ever so quietly, Anthony slipped into his own house like a thief in the night. In the greyness cast indoors, he hastily stripped off his saturated clothes and felt his nakedness shiver a little under a damp chill air. He proceeded quickly to the kitchen and rummaged through a cupboard drawer for the razor sharp bread-knife. Once distinguishing the knife by running his fingers carefully along its cold steel blade, he scurried back through the living-room and climbed the stairway on tiptoe. On reaching the landing, he gently pushed open that bedroom door, slightly ajar, and entered. Pausing for a moment to listen, to hear the heavy rain pelt the windowpane, the wind catch the sodden material just beyond, he marvelled at Sarah's naked back, which was turned to him. In the grey-blue light, he could just make out the ripple of Sarah's spine beneath her taught, silky skin; her peaceful, serene face, partially covered by her mane of thick, yellow hair falling over her round, provocative shoulder. He was fine-tuned now to her little rasps of breath rising and falling. Anthony became aroused so would waste no further time. He moved across the room like an abandoned soul and with his free hand, prised open with ease the smaller, middle window. He reached out with the hand that gripped the knife. With eyes strained to the starless night sky and feeling the chill wind and rain drive against his nakedness, he began to hack at the thick rope securing the bunting to the down-pipe of the house. The bunting had been torn and battered under the day's heavy downpour and blustery winds and at Anthony's fourth attempt with the knife it tore free in a whiplash. A sudden gust of wind catching its weight carried it away as its fastening across the street gave way under the drag. After being held for an instant in midair like a large sweet wrapper by the swirling wind, the bunting fell to the ground with a loud slap and was tossed and turned as the rising wind blew it effortlessly down the street and out of sight.

'What in God's name are you doing, Anthony?'

Woken by the cold air sweeping into the room, Sarah looked on amused and slightly concerned on seeing Anthony turn to face her in such an excited state, and with knife in hand. Stumbling toward the bed but careful to put the knife down before climbing in beside Sarah, to snuggle up against her warm, firm body, Anthony, his lips close to hers, declared in all seriousness, 'There's only one woman's face I want to wake up to in the morning.'

He saw an inviting smile break on Sarah's face. They kissed then, drawing each other into a tight embrace.

Chapter Forty

The long awaited christening of Sean that July, nearly a year to the day since his birth, came to pass as the grand occasion desired by both parents, though set against a backdrop of renewed Anglo-Irish tension. Breakaway republican agitators and the IRA were once again physically active both in Ireland and in England. With this, past anxieties not long eased, were once again resurrected for Anthony and Sarah.

Anthony was quietly concerned by the IRA's activity in England. Their daring, though somewhat desperate raid for arms on a military barracks further north, left him in nervous anticipation of an unwelcome visit in the small hours. He calculated that the police, supplied with information by their counterparts in the RUC, would be looking to the Irish community and in particular those recent new arrivals for members of the IRA and those aiding and abetting their actions. Suspecting Sean Mor still to be a key figure in the IRA, Anthony concluded easily that the man, and anyone clearly associated with him at home or abroad, would be suspected of having a hand in present developments.

Sarah knew this too, and knew also that Anthony would be weighing up matters in his own mind. Seeking to alleviate her husband's fears, while her own over events would remain, she had waited for an opportune moment to approach Anthony openly and honestly over their common concerns.

Clearing away the dishes after a pleasant Sunday lunch and putting Sean down for his afternoon nap, Sarah sat herself down beside Anthony on the living-room's comfortable sofa. The house, and street, despite the glorious sunshine, was peacefully quiet, perfect for an afternoon's lovemaking on any other Sunday. But both lovers knew that there were matters of grave concern to be discussed. It was Sarah who spoke first. 'I know you're worried Anthony ... about what's going on. But I think if we both know how the other is feeling then together we can best work at helping each other. Just as we said we would, remember?'

Anthony seized the moment to offload his very real anxiety. 'I remember. But what makes it difficult for me, is knowing your father is involved ... that, no matter how unintentional on his part, we, even our child, *his grandson*, may yet be badly hurt?'

Sarah knew well Anthony's anxiety. She had never fully denied her father's involvement in the struggle, and wasn't about to. And while some things were best kept secret, she did not wish to lie to him.

'Believe me, I know what your fears are. I carry them too, for us all. But regardless of what my father's role in all this may be, life is full of hardships. No one should know this more than you. Look at what your own family has been through.'

Sarah left Anthony to absorb and interpret this truth. Looking deep into his eyes, she saw that he realised it and sought to reassure him, just as he had her during those first months in England, when her own concerns had lain heavily on her mind.

'We are hurting no one. We are not involved. We are simply trying to get on with our ordinary lives, and if we stand together in the face of whatever comes our way, we will have nothing to fear.'

Her words of confident determination and an added warm smile, soothed Anthony's anxiety. Sarah's sweet tasting lips, pressing passionately against his then, brought healing to them both.

At that very same hour in a restless city back across the water, a housebound Sean Mor received his expected visitor in the privacy of his front room. Rosie and the girls were out walking, so both men would talk a little easier. Finding all the scurrying between Belfast and Dublin hard going in the blistering heat of the last few days, Frank Barratt welcomed the tall glass of chilled cream soda offered by his host, who sat on the opposite side of a cold fireplace awaiting the opportunity to speak, once Barratt had quenched his thirst. With half the cream soda downed, himself refreshed, the trusted courier prepared to reveal what had been decided at the Army Council meeting in Dublin the night before (Barratt had stood-in for Sean Mor, too ill to travel such a distance these days) but Sean Mor seized the moment to reveal a major decision of his own, and which he had only reached the day before.

'Hold your tongue Frankie a little while.' Barratt was a little perplexed. Sean Mor dropped his bombshell. 'Laid up here these past months, I've had time to think about a lot of things. And consequently, I've made one or two difficult decisions. I have to tell you Frankie, that I am to resign my command ... to stand down from the army.' Barratt was speechless. 'Not only does my health dictate that I do so, but I've come to conclude, that to launch a military campaign at this time, will do the republican movement, the republican cause, grave damage. The people, y'see, are not with us. The popular support is not there. To put it simply, the armed struggle is going nowhere. It's time, Frankie, for an urgent rethink. The gun, is no longer the answer.'

A deafening silence prevailed in the front room of No72. Sean Mor had said his piece. All that he now sought was for Barratt to communicate his message to Dublin for him. He awaited Barratt's response, but Barratt sat in shocked silence; the important news that he had carried from Dublin, now, not so important. Barratt just could not imagine the struggle going anywhere without Sean Mor at the lead. And for the big man to reach such a decision at such a crucial moment in time for the IRA, would, he knew, throw all that was planned, up in the air.

Only hours earlier, it had been agreed in Dublin that the long awaited border campaign get underway as quickly as possible. There had been much concern that the breakaway republican element, what with their daring exploits of late in the border counties, would steal the limelight from the IRA if it were to remain inoperative much longer. So further raids for arms were planned for England and the North. Barratt had departed the secret meeting an extremely happy man. Not only were things moving in earnest, the leadership had agreed to both Sean Mor and his own tabled request. Fearing a Protestant pogrom against Catholic ghettos if the IRA in Belfast became active, and which the Belfast Brigade would not be able to fight off given its pathetic numbers of volunteers and guns held in the city, no immediate IRA action was planned for Belfast. But by way of appeasing those few, hardened IRA militarists in the city, the leadership had further agreed with Sean Mor and Barratt, that their men could operate along the border wherever practicable.

Now, Barratt was devastated. But with his own health thankfully intact, and no wife and children to worry over, and knowing no other life than that on the run and sleeping with a gun at his side, Barratt remained committed to seeing the armed struggle through to a successful end.

Not entirely at odds with Sean Mor's analysis of the situation and respectful of the fact that his good friend and comrade was indeed in poor health, and knowing when Sean Mor had his mind made up, Barratt did not even contemplate challenging Sean Mor's decision, but rather placed himself at the man's disposal one more time in order to see outstanding matters complete.

Sean Mor talked a little longer and Barratt listened obediently - as before. His respect for Sean Mor would never diminish.

Barratt took his leave of No72 discreetly. He did not stay in one place long these days and had seldom slept in his own home since the B Specials had left it for firewood. A small mercy for him at least, was that he no longer needed to worry about Spike, his faithful wee dog. With Spike not recovering from the kicking meted out by the B Specials, he'd had him put down before the mad month was over.

Moving cautiously towards the Falls Road and seeing the two scrawny youths playing pitch and toss on the corner nervously stoop and scrape their pennies from off the pavement, was warning enough for Barratt. He casually stepped into the open hallway of a house a dozen or so doors above No72 and observed, by stealing a peep up Leger Street, an RUC patrol car cruise along the Falls. Street gambling was a finable offence he knew. But for what he was involved in, the sentence would be much more severe, if caught. Barratt slipped out from under cover and continued on his way, determined to stay one step ahead of his cursed enemy.

Chapter Forty-One

The news of a bomb exploding in the grounds of the Northern Ireland Parliament building on the 4th July, 1955, the day her son, Sean, celebrated his third birthday, left Sarah extremely anxious for the safety of her father. History told her that it was only a matter of time before internment was reintroduced back home. She knew that her father, a former internee, would be one of the first to be rounded up. Despite one of mother's discreetly worded letters informing her that father was no longer involved, Sarah knew this fact would not necessarily save him, an ill man. Being interned would kill him, she was convinced. Privately, she was worried sick and dreaded switching on the wireless each morning to hear the worst possible news.

While Anthony aired his concerns over developments also and sought to comfort her, Sarah did not reveal the full extent of her real anxiety to him. She did not wish for Anthony to worry over her as she did over her father. She felt guilty too that she was not confiding in Anthony as she'd promised, as they'd both promised each other, but she continually begged the question of herself, 'How can I tell him?' Sarah feared that to do so would leave Anthony feeling that she was pressuring him to go back to Ireland, so that she could be close to her father. And the truth of it was, she wanted to be. She was caught between her own sense of loyalty to her husband and her father. It was her son, Sean, who dictated where her proper place was presently, but she could not predict what she would do if learning of her father's internment.

With Anthony off to Donegal Danny's for a pint as routine on a Sunday evening, Sarah was itching to write another letter to mother. She was forever hungry for news from home. Once checking on Sean, sound asleep in his cot, Sarah fingered the stationery and pen from her bedside locker and descended the stairs to sit at the dining table in the kitchen, which was fanned by the cool evening breeze blowing in through a wide-open window. Only the rustling of leafy trees in the dense forest that the house backed onto, disturbed the otherwise peaceful early evening. Slipping off her summer shoes and placing her aching bare feet on the cold tiled floor, Sarah pursed her lips and savoured the bliss, which was short-lived. An unexpected knock - a little frantic - on the front door, left her questioning who it may be. With Anthony normally using his key to get in, and Sean's godparents, Danny and Maureen, never before calling this late on a Sunday, she doubted it was either. Slipping into her shoes, Sarah moved to the door and opened it cautiously, her heart racing a little.

While surprised at who the caller was, Sarah was pleased to discover that it was Frances Malpass, her work colleague of only a few weeks, and who lived not too far away. They had become acquainted at a local workplace nursery, where recently they had both been employed as nursery assistants. Sarah had made friends with Frances easily, judging them both to have a lot in common. Frances was also married, was Catholic Scots-Irish and had a little boy just a few months older than Sean, who were both placed in the nursery while their mothers worked. On being wed, Frances too had recently arrived in London from her family home in Scotland.

Ushering Frances through - young Drew restless in her arms - Sarah noted that Frances appeared somewhat erratic and quickly concluded that all was not well. Her suspicions were soon proven to be correct. Sitting on the sofa beside Frances, her normally healthy country girl features now sullen, her lively, free flowing chestnut hair, lank and matted, Sarah's cosy perception of her new friend's happily married life was shattered in a few short minutes by those disturbing revelations spurted out between mournful sobs as the sheep farmer's daughter opened her heart over her silent suffering. Frances had anxiously waited for her husband to complete his week's shore leave, and once silently cursing him off under a forced smile, had snatched Drew from his cot and fled across town to Sarah, her one and only friend. Frances simply wanted to talk; to tell the truth of her ordeal, to share her new found sense of determination to save herself and her son from future years of torment. She did not want to live a lie any longer. And through Sarah's much welcomed support, another woman's understanding, she was greatly more determined to see her hopes for the future realised.

Sarah listened intently, giving the other woman time and space to get it all off her chest, and comparing her own concerns to that burning her ears, was left thanking God for the cross she carried.

Chapter Forty-Two

Anthony was quick to lend unconditional support to Sarah in her efforts to help Frances through her crisis, both practically and emotionally. With Frances baring her soul over her 'sham of a marriage' and brave enough in Sarah's mind to reveal the sadistic, at times perverted suffering and humiliation she had endured over the years at the hands of her husband, Sarah had been left torn asunder with mixed emotions of pity and an urge to exact gruesome revenge on the same bastard of a husband. Such had Sarah been affected by her friend's horrendous experience of married life, her own faith in men would have easily evaporated if not knowing that her man at least, was one in a million. And Anthony's support reinforced that belief.

Anthony had taken a liking to the wafer-thin Scots lass that very first day on Sarah bringing her home for a cup of tea and a chat after work. In his opinion Sarah could not have made friends with a better person. Now, with Sarah giving Anthony a fair insight into the woman's suffering, Anthony realised that Frances had given so much joy and comfort to Sarah at a time when Frances herself had been silently going through hell.

Knowing that Anthony was prepared to help her in whatever way he could, Frances found her faith in men restored, if only a little.

The south London solicitor had come on the recommendation of Jack Kilty, to whom Anthony had turned for advice as to how Frances could best be helped legally. Arranging to finish work earlier than usual, and for Sean and Drew to be minded by a work colleague, Sarah and Frances arrived promptly at the sparsely furnished solicitor's office, situated on the second floor of a large converted High Street terrace. Sarah held her friend's hand throughout as the immaculately dressed, silver-haired solicitor, gently coaxed the sickening details out of the prospective client. Frances trembled in her hard chair as she spoke, at times only through great effort, and she broke down periodically. But with Sarah's support, Frances bravely relived the hell of the previous eight years. The solicitor showed no emotion as he made notes and stared Frances straight in the eye as she struggled through her hellish account of the more harrowing, sadomasochistic experiences at the clutches of her husband - leaving nothing to the imagination. Sarah wept silently through it too.

The solicitor sighed heavily when the woman had finished. In all his years of legal practice, he had difficulty calling to mind any case remotely similar or so distressing to listen to, to comprehend. After a minute's silence - which for both women seemed like an eternity - and taking time to weigh up all the physical evidence - the lumps, bruises and bite marks extensively covering the woman's breasts, groin, buttocks and thighs, as confirmed by her doctor in the enclosed medical report, the solicitor was confident that he could do justice to the woman's needs.

'I must thank you Missus Malpass. I know it has been extremely uncomfortable for you to relive your ordeal.' A nervous rattle at the back of his throat signified the solicitor's discomfort over what he'd heard. 'I am prepared to fight this case for you ... if that is, your husband makes a fight of it, which I doubt he will.'

Sarah and Frances looked at each other somewhat bewildered. The solicitor sought to dispel their confusion.

'What you've got to understand Missus Malpass is this. Your husband holds a very prestigious position in Her Majesty's shipping. With the information and solid evidence I possess, I doubt very much that your husband will contest your grounds for divorce and sole custody of the child, simply because, I feel his career will be of more importance to him. He will want to avoid bad publicity at all costs. Of course, you may well have to vacate your present home as this came with his posting south. Financially though, the boy will be provided for. Your legal costs will be recovered largely from your husband's purse.'

Sarah threw Frances a reassuring smile.

'However, what I feel you should be guarded against, is the possibility that your husband may attempt to talk you out of your course of action by means of letter-writing personally to you to display remorse and beg forgiveness. If so, and you are determined to see this through, as I believe you are, you must inform me of such without delay.' Frances said she would.

'Missus Malpass, in view of what you have told me, may I say, that for your own safety and that of your child, you must be rid of this man. I dare to conclude confidently, given the nature of your husband's sadistic, indeed beastly treatment of you, that he is indeed sick of mind.'

Frances showed no emotion. Nothing shocked her any more. Fearing his client was on the brink of a major breakdown, the solicitor felt compelled to say no more and not propose that she have her son closely examined by the doctor. The mere suggestion that the child too may have fallen victim to the man's evil ways, when her back was turned, may, he suspected, just be that which would push Mrs Malpass over the edge.

Making eye contact with the solicitor as Frances closed her eyes in whispering a short prayer, Sarah knew what he was thinking and she reinforced his discretion by shaking her head discreetly. He knew she knew his fears. They were her fears too.

Though she felt herself tremble, Frances spoke with a gritty determination that Frances said, 'Do what ever has to be done. I want that dirty bastard out of our lives!'

The solicitor assured his client that he would attend to matters at once. A comprehensive letter, filing grounds for divorce, would be sent ahead to the husband's next port of call. He would have three months at sea to stew over his predicament. Meantime, Frances and Drew would seek a new home. Sarah and Anthony would help her find one, hopefully close to where they lived.

It came as sad news for Anthony to learn from Mick Onion in Donegal Danny's that following Saturday, that Finn Spiceland had since returned home to his native Derry, due, it was said, to an illness in the family. Finn had not said when or if he would return to England. They all wished him well in his absence and toasted him a lifetime of good fortune.

Not one of the four Donegal men studying closely their evening newspapers a week and a half later, suspected the connection between the Derry man's sudden departure and the latest commando-style raid on a military barrack on the outskirts of north London. From the headline account, the raid had resulted in the armoury being completely cleaned out of its arsenal of heavy calibre machineguns, rifles, sub machineguns, small arms, explosives, and a vast quantity of ammunition.

Given the close proximity of the raid and taking more of an interest in the report than others, Anthony was left on tenterhooks by what he read as he sat in his rear garden, the last of the evening light fading fast. A thorough military and police inquiry was underway into what was being claimed by red-faced senior government ministers as the IRA's biggest seizure of arms from a British military barrack since the Magazine Fort raid of 1939. Despite extensive follow-up searches of motor vehicles, land and premises within a five-mile radius of the depleted barracks, no one, nothing associated with the raiders had been found. The police had vowed to extend their searches and inquiries comprehensively and the public had been advised to be vigilant.

Though neither said it, Anthony and Sarah went to their bed that night dreading the early morning knock.

Since the IRA raid on the military barracks in north London, Anthony had rarely set foot outside the front door once home from work. But reading in disbelief two weeks later the very latest headline news, he felt compelled to make his way to Mick Onion's where he knew, if not already learnt, this news would come as a major shock and upset for all there too. Leaving a scribbled note for Sarah - lending Frances a hand over at her new council flat - Anthony set out in haste with the evening newspaper tucked under an arm. Seated on the tube train, Anthony buried his face in the front-page once again and still struggled to come to terms with what was printed.

Police in Northern Ireland today confirmed that weapons seized in a van stopped at one of their border checkpoints yesterday evening, are from among the huge arsenal stolen from Disraeli Barracks, north London, a month ago. The RUC have named two men arrested at the scene as:

Columb Kinsella, 27, and Finn Spiceland, 35, both from County Derry. London police are hopeful that someone among the English public may be able to place one or both men to a location or event in England in recent times and are appealing to anyone with such information to come forward at once to assist further inquiries ...

For Anthony, there was only one Finn Spiceland. It all added up. He felt gutted knowing the man would most probably spend the rest of his life behind bars. He also wondered, if Sean Mor knew of the man; if he'd had a hand in his fate.

Turning into the street on the final approach to Mick Onion's place, Anthony was halted in his bustling tracks on seeing uniformed policemen exit from that front door leading to the home of his good friend. The policemen carried bulging cloth sacks, which they placed carefully in the boots of several cars lined up at the kerb. Anthony had seen enough. He quickly turned and made off towards Donegal Danny's. There, he hoped to find safety among friends. Entering the subdued barroom a little later, the barman immediately caught Anthony's eye and gestured to him to come to the quieter end of the bar where he served Anthony warning of looming danger.

'I had a notion you'd show up. Have you heard the news?'
'Of Spiceland?'
'No! About Mick O' and the others?'

Anthony begged more information. Leaning across the pumps, the barman whispered, 'They were arrested on site today. They're saying it's over the head of this Finn Spiceland character ... their association with him. I'd be careful Anthony. Know what I mean?'

Anthony simply acknowledged Danny's advice with a nod and hurriedly left the bar. He knew in that moment what the police were doing at his friend's flat and couldn't help but think that his own home was presently being paid a visit. Anthony's concerns lay only with Sarah, due to return home about then, with Sean.

Chapter Forty-Three

Though relieved to discover Sarah putting Sean down to sleep on returning home in a sweat that night, Anthony was certain it was not a question of if, but when the police would pay him a visit.

Having slept with one eye open, the sound of the car pulling up at the kerb outside his home early that following Sunday morning, had Anthony leaping out of bed and tripping to the window. Startled out of her sleep, Sarah protested. '*Jesus*! Anthony Brennan. What are you trying to do ... scare the life out of me?'

Peering through the parted curtain, Anthony was relieved to see a familiar face come up the garden path. Rising up in the bed, Sarah badgered him further. 'What the hell are you doing? What is it?' Pulling on a shirt as he moved to the bedroom door, an already stressed Anthony snapped. 'Oh, give over for Christ sake! Donegal Danny's at the door!'

Sarah was enraged. He'd never spoken to her like this before and it triggered dark images of another's suffering in her mind.

'You bastard! Don't talk to me like that! I'm not another Frances Malpass you know!' Anthony halted in the doorway. The damning words pricked his conscience. He turned and moved to Sarah's side of the bed with his palms up. 'I'm sorry love. I didn't mean to ...' Sarah silenced him by putting a finger to her lips and reflected for a moment.

'It's okay. I know, I know. Go answer the door before Danny wakes Sean.' Anthony bent low and kissed Sarah on the forehead and smiled before leaving the room.

It was a rough-looking Danny Clarke to whom Anthony opened the front door. In between making the tea for the early morning caller, Anthony listened closely as Danny, hung over and slumped in a kitchen chair, gave a slurred update on events.

Mick, Cathal and Pius had been released without charge from a local police barrack late the previous evening. Danny had just called in on the heels of the men returning home from the cells and had been given the full story by an irate Mick Onion. Tempers had been calmed through a bottle being opened and some serious drinking.

'I was shocked to hear Mick O' tell me the police had suspected them of being IRA. But of course it's all crap, ain't it? I mean, it's not like someone of Mick's character to be caught up in something like that. The Old Bill must have their heads up their arses.'

Anthony didn't answer Danny's charge directly, but rather inquired curiously whilst pouring the tea, 'Did Mick say how they'd come to be arrested?'

'Yeah. He says his site foreman pointed them out to the police. I know one thing. Mick's livid. He won't settle until he gets even with that man. There'll be a showdown in the morning, that's for sure.' Sliding the steaming mug of tea across the table toward his visitor, a concerned Anthony spoke with urgency. 'Danny, I need to see Mick quickly, before he does something that he'll regret for the rest of his days.' After slurping a mouthful of tea - this Irishman's cure - Danny had Anthony reaching for his coat. 'The sooner you get that tea down your neck, Anthony, the sooner we can hit the road.'

Anthony left his tea to go cold. Wasting no time in getting washed and dressed, he joined Danny in his car. Sarah waved Anthony off at the front door. The talking would come later.

On being dropped at Mick Onion's - Danny committed to the bar - Anthony's knock was received by a barrage of muted curses aired by those disturbed from their mid-morning slumber. 'Who is it?' Mick Onion demanded. Learning the identity of the visitor, the moaning fell silent.

Once in, a shattered-looking Mick Onion threw a bulging cloth sack labelled *Police Evidence* from off a rickety old chair onto an already cluttered floor to allow Anthony to sit gingerly in the same chair. Seated, Anthony listened to a fuming, vengeful Mick Onion. He paced the bare timber floor like someone demented, while others tried to sleep in the adjoining room.

'Those bastard policemen accused us of being IRA men ... associates of Finn Spiceland. I take it y'know all about him?' Anthony nodded. Mick Onion blazed on. 'They told us they'd received a phone call minutes after yesterday's midday news, saying that associates of Spiceland could be found on site. I saw them arrive ... in plain clothes they were, six or seven of them. I knew instantly from the way they carried themselves that they were on official business. I thought that they were from the Labour. They went straight to that bastard from Mayo.' With his face working with fury, his sharp blue eyes glinting with devilment, the aggrieved tunneller loomed over Anthony with arms very theatrical. 'I saw him with my own eyes point them in our direction. They came marching over, hands in pockets and called out to us by name. *By our fucking names*! I was suddenly staring down the barrel of a gun. They handcuffed us and marched us off site. Y'know, one of the bastards poked a gun into my ribs and said, with a cocky smile, that he'd take great pleasure in putting a bullet in my head, if I made a run for it.' Mick Onion made a fist and shook it in the face of no one in particular to spit ominously, 'I tell you something. When I get my hands on that cunt in the morning, I'll rip his fucking tongue out!' Mick Onion paused to catch a breath, then continued with a wry laugh breaking, 'And do y'know the first question the fucking peelers asked me?' Anthony shook his head. "What's your name, *Mick*"?'

The seriousness of it all put Mick Onion's black humour in the shade.

Mick Onion had not shut up for a solid ten minutes. He had gone on to inform Anthony that on reaching the cells, they had all been stripped bollock naked, fingerprinted, and questioned separately for hours as to their identity, period of stay in London, and movements, particularly over recent months and, not least, their relationship with Spiceland. They had all been truthful with their answers. In response to those questions centred around Finn Spiceland, they had all told it as it was: that they had befriended Spiceland at work, with the conversation being Gaelic football, what with Derry and Donegal being friendly rivals on the pitch back home. Sticking to this story, the police had given up on the three of them and had thrown them out, literally. Only on returning home had they discovered that they had been raided also - the law, seemingly using one of their keys to get into their digs. All their belongings had been returned intact shortly before their arrival back, according to one nosy neighbour.

Anthony's name had not been mentioned by anyone at anytime. Pleased to learn this, to know that it had all seemingly ended with their release, Anthony was keen to impress on Mick Onion to keep a cool head and to at least wait for a more opportune time to even the score with the Mayo man. For there was no doubt that the mouthpiece had it coming. Mick Onion confirmed his intentions by promising, with a finger raised, 'Fucking too right! That culshie is going to pay a heavy price for opening his gob. I'll button his lip ... *permanently*!' All who heard Mick Onion's promise to himself did not doubt his intent.

Anthony took his leave only when his good friend had made a second promise to keep his nerve meantime. Feeling a little less pressurised, Anthony returned home to answer to Sarah. He had a lot of apologising to do, a lot to tell her. With all she'd had to cope with of late over her friend Frances, he had said nothing of Spiceland or Mick Onion's arrest. After the verbal fracas that morning, he was anxious to show Sarah that he loved her as on that first night, with that first kiss.

He returned home a little sheepishly to find Sarah waiting for him - in bed.

Anthony seriously contemplated having the day off work. He convinced himself that his name too had been circled for arrest. If the police were to pick him up, he would rather it be from his own home, where he hoped it would be a discreet affair, with a forgiving Sarah, now abreast of developments, prepared for it. But in view of Mick Onion's assurance that his name had not been mentioned, that even Donegal Danny had since been briefed on what to say if visited by police, Anthony carried on to work that Monday morning, his only concern being, if Mick Onion had indeed awoken to face the same day and others with a cool head.

The three tunnellers arrived at work to a surprise reception of clapping, whistling and cheering. Their fellow workmates were glad to see them vindicated and back safe. Only the site foreman was conspicuous through his absence, but never missing a trick, the heavily-built Mayo man, six foot six tall or more, looked on with an incriminating eye from a discreet distance. He had already decided his next move.

As with every morning, Pius - the nominated cook - set about the first and most important task of the day: frying-up a big hearty Irish breakfast for all three on the makeshift stove rigged up within the confines of one of the huge concrete tunnel rings. The tunnel rings were destined to form part of that vast new underground sewer system which they were installing, but which, in the meantime, served as their den, to where they would retreat for a quick break between shifts. As Pius greased the huge black frying pan, Mick Onion and Cathal sat silently alongside each other just inside the tunnel ring, warming their chapped fingers by clasping both hands tightly around their steaming hot mugs of tea. Looking out over the bleak mucky landscape, both men were lost in their respective thoughts as to the fate of Finn Spiceland. None of them were in agreement with the man's methods in pursuit of Ireland's freedom, which they all desired, but knowing what they did of him, they were devastated in knowing his plight that day.

The squelch of heavy boots through the mud had them all looking up from their steaming mugs. The grey, murky daylight falling into the mouth of the tunnel ring was closed out by the giant of a man coming to a halt just outside of it. The Mayo man, as broad as he was tall, a hardhat sitting askew his large grey head, supported by a tree trunk of a neck, stooped forward with hands on hips and looked damningly on those sitting inside, cast in his shadow. His piercing blue eyes, set in a face blood red in colour, stared each man out when mouthing in a thick Mayo accent, barely audible. 'Right you three. Gather up your tools and collect your cards. I want you off site fast. There's no room here for troublemakers, so you'll be on your way now ... do you hear!' The man-mountain stared the three tunnellers out, daring any one of them to challenge his command. Dumbstruck by what they'd heard, no one did. The firing site foreman turned cautiously and struggled back toward that makeshift wooden hut, his work's office.

The three men with tempers brewing eyed each other silently for a moment. It was Mick Onion's that boiled over. Scrambling to his feet he snarled, 'That bastard's asked for it now.'

Pius, the elder of the three and the brains among them, tossed the big black frying pan to one side and sprang to his feet to stop Mick Onion from chasing after the foreman.

'He's not worth it, Mick. The man's as thick as a pig!'

'Aye, Pius is right, Mick,' interjected Cathal, rising also. 'Yer man's only a gobshite! Let's go and get our cards and be off.'

Mick Onion was hearing none of it. His blood was up. Reaching to pick up his shovel, propped up against the tunnel wall, he made his intentions clear on taking it firmly in hand like a prized hurley.

'God help me Pius, but if you don't move out of my path this instant, I'll take your head clean off!' Studying the man hard, Pius knew he meant it. And Mick Onion did. Pius stood aside and Mick Onion set out in hot pursuit with murder on his mind. Shaking in his rubber boots, Cathal implored Pius to join him in going after Mick Onion. 'For fuck sake Pius, we must stop him! He'll kill that bastard!' Pius grabbed Cathal's wrist. 'If you get in his way, he'll kill you! The devil's in him for sure.' They both looked out, hoping their friend would get wise before it was too late.

Mick Onion determinedly dragged his feet through the mucky swamp, turned to such with the cleared ground saturated by the overnight rain. He was blinkered to all else and everyone around him. He only had eyes for that man standing with his back to him at that moment, hands still on hips as he critically inspected the recently dug twelve foot deep, eight foot wide trench, where the main sewage pipes would be laid between the proposed new buildings. Those other groundsmen dotted around, busy in preparing to commence their shift, paid Mick Onion and the foreman little or no attention. But seeing Mick Onion's pace quicken through the mud, Cathal could not stand idly by any longer to see murder done. He set out to give chase, prompting Pius to do the same, out of concern for Cathal's safety.

On hearing the footsteps of someone approach through the muck behind him and wrongly assuming it was the gangerman in charge of the groundsmen, the site foreman barked over his shoulder, 'I don't want this trench shored up today. The grounds too wet.'

Mick Onion was deaf to all that had just been said, such was his state of mind. Swamped with pure hate for the Mayo man he wielded the shovel up and over his right shoulder like a hurley about to strike for goal and with tremendous force, landed the flat underside of its steel pan against the back of the Mayo man's head. There was a hollow, dull thud as the shovel connected. The site foreman's hardhat was sent flying, the man himself, stumbling forward to fall a dead weight into the trench. With a loud splash, the Mayo man hit the base of the trench headfirst and lay motionless and nose down in twelve inches of thick brown water. The powerful blow had been intended to kill and Mick Onion stepped up to the trench's crumbling edge to look down into what was in his mind, a ready made grave. He convinced himself that the Mayo man was still alive and like someone possessed, he leapt into the trench without thought for his own safety. With a firm grip on his shovel, Mick Onion landed with a splash on the balls of his feet before stumbling and falling across the other, very still man. Quickly picking himself up and cursing himself blind for dropping the shovel, which was lost momentarily in the mucky water, he again raised the shovel skyward to deliver the finishing blow. The screamed plea from above him just then, prevented Mick Onion from bringing the shovel crashing down on top of his quarry's exposed head once more.

'Sweet Jasus! Don't do it Mick!'

Looking down in disbelief, Cathal squatted and slid from the trench edge. He landed on the seat of his pants in water up to his waist when finally coming to a halt between Mick Onion and the Mayo man. Mick Onion stood transfixed, his eyes bulging in his head. Glancing the Mayo man, noting the trickle of blood running from his left ear to intermingle with the watery muck, Cathal feared the man, if not already dead from the blow to his head, had drowned. But if not, he wanted the chance to save life, if a chance existed. Cathal was soon on his knees and rolled the Mayo man onto his back and lifted his head onto his lap. The Mayo man's eyes were wide open and motionless, his mouth full of muck. A terrified expression was fixed on his dirtied face. He was dead all right, and Mick Onion felt pleased about it.

'Good riddance to the oul cunt,' he spat. 'He had it coming. If he'd been at home, they'd a dragged him out and shot him ... fucking tout!'

Reaching the edge of the trench, Pius felt the ground give way beneath his feet and was sent tumbling toward the others below. The sudden and massive landslip, triggered by the workmen's combined weight as they'd churned through the mud towards the trench edge, buried all four of them in an instant under tons of shifting earth as both walls of the trench collapsed inward.

The alarm raised, the wide-eyed, disbelieving workforce abandoned their tasks and with shovels and picks in hand, came running from all over the site to wade knee deep in mud and dig frantically at that spot where men had been buried alive - and dead.

The bodies of Pius, Cathal and the Mayo man had been recovered shortly after. Their corpses lay side-by-side in the mud, their blue, almost black contorted faces hidden under workmen's donkey jackets as the summoned police began their inquiries; the shocked, silent workforce in no mood for their questions.

The balding, portly-built senior detective, appearing more of a crook than an upholder of the law, and who had accompanied the Scotland Yard crew to the very same site three days earlier, had his suspicions of a dirty deed committed on learning the identity of the workman who had survived. To his thinking, the critically ill man who had been ferried to the hospital in the back of a colleague's car was the same cocky little Irish bastard who'd had all the answers three days earlier.

Spying Donegal Danny's car parked outside his house again on returning from work, Anthony quickened his step. He was awash with apprehension on reaching the front door, opened to him by a concerned looking Sarah.

In the devastating aftermath of the 'tragic accident' - as referred to by all on site - the labour force had called it a day. As a mark of respect for the dead, the workmen had laid down their tools for the remainder of the shift. Most had headed to the pubs nearby to talk of the day's horror over a pint. Some had found a little peace of mind in the Donegal man's pub. Danny, a good friend to the deceased and injured, had poured himself a large whiskey and had downed it in one on being told of the tragedy, which he now broke to Anthony.

Despairing in silence, Anthony let his grandfather's old tool bag slip from his shoulder and clatter to the floor.

Chapter Forty-Four

Armed with the police coroner's report, Detective Sergeant Rigsby arrived back at the hospital at nine o'clock that following morning determined to win access to the survivor of the trench collapse, Michael Doherty. As far as Rigsby was concerned, Doherty had some serious questions to answer. While it was made clear by the same report, that the two younger men had died of suffocation on being buried alive, it was the considered opinion of the esteemed coroner, that the elder had died as a result of a massive brain contusion, together with multiple fractures of the skull being apparent. Though there was no conclusive evidence to support the theory that the same man had suffered a heart attack or fit to cause him to stumble and fall, the fact that there had been a high level of alcohol present in the man's blood, gave credence to the suggestion that he had fallen over in a drunken stupor. As for the cause of the severe head injuries sustained, forensic evidence gathered at the scene highlighted that hardcore rock had been discovered beneath the man's body, thus the coroner concluded that the elder's death could well have been instantaneous on his head hitting the bed of the trench.

Despite all the theory, this investigating detective held faith in his own suspicion as to what had truly occurred the previous day. On being informed by the pleasantly mannered night duty sister coming off shift, that the patient in question remained critical and was in no way fit to receive visitors, D.S. Rigsby was left disappointed but he decided to wait around a while, out of interest to discover the identity of anyone turning up to visit his suspect.

Returning jubilant to his East End gym to celebrate his star fighter's big win up north the previous day, Kilty was much saddened by the news received via the phone call from Anthony to the gym hours earlier. Mick Onion and his good friends Pius and Cathal had welcomed him into their humble abode and had served him some of the best nights entertainment ever, but more importantly, a sense of genuine friendship.

Kilty wasted no time in telephoning the hospital to inquire about his friend's condition. On being informed that the patient was 'very ill' and under close medical observation, Kilty was in no mood to celebrate his budding middleweight's victory and left the others behind to party while he continued home alone. Arriving at his secluded Manor House, standing on the edge of Epping Forest, Kilty retreated to his bedroom with a bottle of French brandy to drown his sorrows over the news of the three Irishmen. Their friendship, as with Anthony's and Donegal Danny's, had helped him rediscover the fun and excitement he'd experienced outside of the cruel world of bare-knuckle fighting years earlier, simply through being in the company of Christy Brennan, who had liked to party in style after earning their crust. The good times shared with Mick Onion and company, good times which money could not buy, had greatly helped Kilty to keep his sanity in a world of shady wheeling and dealing, which paid high dividends, yes, but which also exposed him to great risk.

Victim to the brandy, Kilty somehow mustered enough energy to reach for the bedside telephone later that day to make another phone call.

Donegal Danny passed Kilty's message to Anthony, who called to the bar directly from work that evening as arranged. Both men were pleased that Kilty planned to arrive at seven and journey to the hospital with them, where they hoped to at least hear some good news as to Mick Onion's condition. With a reliable source entering the public house on Anthony's heel informing all that the work's contractor was satisfied the disaster of the previous day had been a 'tragic accident,' Danny threw Anthony a doubting look. But their lips were sealed and would remain so to certain others for all time.

Danny suggested to his closest friends that a collection be made in all the Irish pubs in Camden Town to help with the cost of having the bodies of Cathal and Pius returned home to Ireland for burial. The families of the dead had been contacted and relatives would be arriving in England shortly to make arrangements for the transportation of the corpses home. It was reported too that Mick Onion's parents had been informed of their son's condition and that his father was to arrive in England the following morning. Meantime the wife of the deceased Mayo man, an Offaly woman who lived in London, had made it known that she wished her husband to be buried in the local borough cemetery. In the hearts and minds of informed friends of the three tunnellers, the man from Mayo could be re-buried in the trench for all they cared.

Hoping that when he arrived in England, old Mick Onion would not be in need also of such a collection of money, Anthony took an empty pint tumbler in hand and contributed his own generous donation before going among the barroom folk gathered. Without hesitation, they dipped deep into their pockets to give as much money as they could genuinely spare.

Sitting in the hospital's not-so-busy Intensive Care waiting room these past ten hours, the stiff and sore detective was himself thirsting for a pint. It had been a long day and yet no sign of a visitor for Doherty, who, if opportunity presented itself, he would be arresting on suspicion of murder. The evidence to support such action was circumstantial, he knew. But he was confident that when he got access to Doherty, he'd force the truth out of him, including that as to his true involvement with the IRA man, Spiceland, and those other members of the IRA unit responsible for the series of raids around the country, and who, Rigsby was convinced, were still at large in the capital itself. It was rounding up those same bastards that Rigsby was set on achieving, even at the expense of striking a deal with Doherty over the site foreman's murder. If capturing the remaining members of the IRA unit, Rigsby was confident he could secure a greatly reduced sentence for the IRA man turned informer.

With the onset of cramp, Rigsby decided to risk the short walk to the hospital canteen for a bite to eat. He was starved, and thirsty, but the pub on the corner was too much of a temptation. He departed the hospital waiting room with the intention of returning shortly. He knew there was every chance of an associate of the suspect turning up at any moment. As Rigsby left the waiting room by one door, Anthony, Donegal Danny and Jack Kilty, entered the same room by another.

'The patient, Michael Doherty, died at seven-fifteen this evening,' revealed the softly spoken Negro doctor, checking his wristwatch. 'About twenty minutes ago in fact.' Anthony, Donegal Danny and Jack Kilty looked at each other blankly. 'Mister Doherty had been in a deep coma,' the doctor explained. 'He had sustained serious injury to numerous internal organs. His chances of surviving had been minuscule.' Judging what he was about to say next to be of little comfort to the friends of the deceased, the doctor added, 'If your good friend had survived, he would most certainly have been left paralysed from the neck down and severely mentally handicapped. He would have been dependent on others for the rest of his short life, for undoubtedly, his condition would not have prolonged it.'

What the doctor had just revealed had indeed been of little comfort to the three men, but each understood his motive. They proceeded to file out of the empty side ward in silence. At a shuffle, heads hung low, the three made their way to where Kilty had parked his car.

Rigsby returned to the busier waiting room ten minutes later. It was the sister-in-charge who broke the news of Mick Onion's death to him as he found his seat again. Disappointed that a possible trail to cornering the IRA unit at large had suddenly gone cold, Rigsby took his leave from the hospital not knowing of the three visitors who had been and gone in the short time it had taken him to stuff his belly. Sickened by the turn of events, Rigsby beat a path in the direction of the local alehouse that stood in the shadow of London Bridge, where he would satisfy his hunger again, but with alcohol this time.

The conversation among the Irish exiles gathered in Donegal Danny's that next day was subdued. It mainly focused around arrangements made ready for the bodies of the deceased to be taken home. Relatives of the dead had arrived in England earlier in the day to formally identify their kin and to complete the necessary paperwork to enable the bodies to be released for passage to Ireland.

Donegal Danny had accommodated free of charge all of the relatives above the pub's bar and lounge rooms - Mick Onion's ailing father, Cathal's younger brother, and the elder sister of Pius.

Apart from Mick Onion senior, the relatives of the dead politely declined the publican's invitation to join friends of the deceased in the bar.

Each indicated that they were tired at the end of a long day, though promised to thank those who had befriended their kin before returning to Ireland. Danny would hand over what was already a generous amount of money collected to the relatives on the day of their departure.

Remembering how the grieving father's only son had supported his own parents and sisters in their darkest hour, Anthony was the other good companion to old Mick Onion that night as the brokenhearted man sat in a corner of Danny's place, steadily knocking back the Irish as if it were tap water. His naturally watery eyes overflowing with tears, old Mick Onion was inconsolable in his grief. Studying the elder's painfully thin body all twisted and bent, Anthony was quietly amazed that the man had survived the journey, but at the same time, knew the same man to be as tough as nails. Just like his own father.

'I'll be okay,' slobbered Mick Onion into his half glass. 'I will take my boy home and see to it that he has a burial fit for a hero.'

'You do that, Mick,' Anthony consoled, placing a comradely arm around the elder's shoulders. 'Young Mick was indeed a hero in his day.' Anthony affirmed, knowing that if old Mick knew the truth behind his son's death and that of the other three men, it would surely kill him.

Mick Onion sniffed back tears. 'I'll tell your folk of your kindness this night, Anthony Brennan ... be sure of it.'

'Just tell them, that I'm okay ... that I'll be seeing them again someday.'

Anthony went home to his bed that night feeling somewhat guilty. He knew in his heart that his rightful place should be with Mick Onion senior in two days time when taking his dead son back to Ireland. But he hadn't even offered to be at the old man's side that day, simply for his own reasons. Anthony knew he could not cope with all the pain and heartache that would be resurrected again for the Brennan family on the return home of Mick Onion's body. Nor was he willing to run the risk of falling under the eye of suspicion through being seen to be acquainted with a man, who, only hours before his tragic death, had been in the clutches of the police on suspicion of being involved with the IRA. No! Not in the wake of those dark events of July 1952. And not least, Anthony did not want to be the one to have to lie to his mother and father as to the truth behind Christy living in America. He hoped Christy would be the one to tell that story, and soon.

Anthony had left old Mick Onion sobbing into his whiskey glass, having decided to withdraw to the safety of family life in the suburbs, once the body of Mick Onion departed England's shore.

The north London Irish turned out in droves at London dock to bid a silent final farewell to three of their own, their bodies loaded aboard the night freight ferry, Dublin bound.

Knowing life would never be the same, Anthony, Donegal Danny and Jack Kilty, stood shoulder to shoulder on the quay looking on sadly as the ferry left port and promised each other to meet up again sometime soon, if only to talk of the good times shared with friends lost forever.

Sitting in his car at a discreet distance, D.S. Rigsby scribbled in his pocket notebook the names of two of the three men he observed, including that of the well-known face, the gangster, Jack Kilty, who all left docklands together, in his mind's eye, up to no good. But it was that third man in whom Rigsby was more so interested. The man whose identity he was yet to establish.

Chapter Forty-Five

Leaving her doe-eyed, four year old son at the main entrance to the local school nursery on that first day of the autumn term, 1956, was particularly hard on Sarah Brennan. To this mother's critical thinking, all that would be seen and heard by her son in his new surroundings, in the company of establishment peers from this day forth, had the potential to corrupt his innocent young mind. Letting go of her son's hand reluctantly, Sarah bent low to plant a kiss on Sean's blond head.

'I'll see you later, Sean. Be good.'

The friendly-faced nursery teacher taking charge of Sean was eager to get to know her class and inquired, cheery voiced, 'And what's your name, young sir?' Wishing to appear brave, Sean replied boldly, 'Sean Brennan.'

In the early days, Sarah had judged it somewhat odd to hear her own flesh and blood speak with an accent that was more English sounding, than Irish. But she had quickly become reconciled to the fact, taking comfort in the knowledge that it was not the English tongue, nor the ordinary English people with whom Irish republicans were in conflict with, but their imperialist institutions and their army of occupation.

Despite his bravado, Sean appeared a little anxious as he was led by the hand into the nursery. Though the same, friendly-faced teacher helped to allay some of his fears, he still wished to be returning home with his mother. Sean looked over his shoulder with self-pity etched on his face and his mother would have sworn that she'd seen tears well in his eyes.

Sarah waited by the nursery gate and continued to look on until her son disappeared through the main doors of the nursery. With the playground falling silent she set out for home, separate in more ways than one from all the other excited mothers milling about her. This mother was determined that her young son's developing mind would not be corrupted so. Just as her father had not sought to, she too, would not be seeking to poison her own child's mind but rather, in time, to enlighten Sean to how the greatness and might of one nation can come to be built on the suffering of another; why some men possess all, while others become dispossessed of everything, except their spirit of freedom. As she'd grown older, her father's stories had become more thought provoking. He had spoken of man's injustice to man, prosecuted by imperialist soldiers of fortune and gluttonous Kings and Queens across seas and land, and the struggle of native peoples in the face of it. She had not been poisoned by hate for those warmongers, but rather afforded the awareness to their existence and their corrupt methods. So she too would be careful, given the family's circumstances presently, not to leave Sean in conflict with all that and those around him. She would not make him bitter, but a son of whom she would be proud; a grandson who would carry his grandfather's good name forward in a similar vain, an inheritance of substance for the generations of Brennans to follow.

Victor Stanley Craig revelled in the admiration and praise showered on him by his good Protestant friends and neighbours in the days following his promotion to Inspector, Belfast Central Division, Royal Ulster Constabulary. All in his life presently was blissful. Ever since early childhood his dream had been to become a policeman one day, and here he was steadily climbing through the ranks in a job for life. And the icing on the cake? His lovely schoolteacher wife Heather confirmed as pregnant with their third child. The sanctimonious Reverend Beatty called on Inspector Craig and his family at their suburban detached residence standing along a leafy residential avenue on the outskirts of south Belfast, and first blessed the most recent good news befalling the well respected family, then offered more prayers for the safe passage of the Inspector on his return to new duties. Seated around the grand dining-room table with heads bowed and the palms of their hands pressed together, the Craig family joined with their esteemed visitor as he beseeched the Blessed Lord to watch over his servant and loyal member of the community, in serving 'Her Majesty the Queen, God and Ulster.'

Feeble in body only, Sean Mor learnt of his old adversary's promotion via word on the street. Subsequently he had fears that Craig would let his newfound status and power go to his head and would make life even more difficult for local republicans - even those who had put away their guns. Sean Mor was not alone in thinking this way. The newly appointed Northern Command Commandant had already decided what action to take to prevent Craig from wreaking such havoc. With final preparations for resuming the armed struggle almost complete, and with a date firmly fixed in place for the commencement of the border campaign, albeit another twelve months in coming, Frank Barratt would not delay in seeing Craig removed from the scene by way of an unofficial action, the execution of which he'd personally oversee. Craig would have to be eliminated in this way because Barratt had faced up to a hard reality. The nationalist people in Belfast, among whom existed the backbone of the republican movement, would abandon the armed struggle entirely if the local IRA were not able to protect them from a Protestant backlash, which could not be ruled out if Craig was seen to have been killed by the IRA. Meeting up in a quiet corner of the Coat of Arms with Bonar, who had succeeded him as Belfast Brigade OC, Barratt set about giving the order that would see the senior RUC man dead.

'This bastard Craig will no doubt run riot. With him better placed now to put even greater obstacles in our path, I want him taken off the scene – permanently. But it must *not* appear to be at our doing.'

Bonar thought how this might be, for he did not question the other's logic.

Later that night Barratt retired to his bed in a safe house in Ardoyne, in the north of the city, wondering what the remainder of the year might bring. He knew what others had planned, what he would like to see happen. But he knew from hard found experience, that what was desired and what came to pass could often be worlds' apart if not enough attention was given to detail - to planning the achievement of success. It was such a time for meticulous planning and extraordinary effort by all. Never more so than by those who were to go after Craig, if to succeed in making the kill and to escape the wrath of not only Craig's cohorts in and out of uniform, but that of the IRA leadership in Dublin. Such a deliberate action would be judged by them to be a clear breach of a specific army directive, the penalty for which would be certain death. Though considering all such risk, Barratt held every confidence in Bonar. He knew the man would be meticulous in his planning and execution of that unspoken order.

Sitting down gently on the edge of his bed to catch his breath - the stairway a mountain to him these days - Sean Mor longed for a peaceful night's sleep. But he knew that with Inspector Craig on the loose, such could not be guaranteed. Eventually Sean Mor drifted into an uneasy sleep, regretting that he hadn't succeeded in seeing Craig dead when he'd had chance to.

On his return to work to take up his new posting, Craig was summoned by his superiors to the Operations Room, the nerve centre of RUC intelligence in Belfast. He was one of six uniformed and three non-uniformed men to assemble in that basement room around a large oval table laden with hard-back files marked 'Top Secret'. The grey, bare plastered walls of that cold, inhospitable room had been covered with large land survey maps of the six counties of Ulster. Craig recognised three of the uniformed men present, including the Chief Inspector of the Belfast Constabulary, who then asked each man present to introduce himself by name and rank. By the end of this exercise, Craig realised he was among highly esteemed and celebrated members of the force, drawn from all over the province. The Chief Inspector proceeded to enlighten those gathered as to the purpose of the meeting and left all in no doubt that each of them were to play key roles in 'operations' to be revealed, which, if successful, could well save the Northern Ireland State, the union with Great Britain, from collapse. Speaking with an ominous tone the Chief Inspector informed his colleagues, that a major threat from Irish republicans was looming. From intelligence gathered in the field, scarce though it had been, a major IRA offensive had been confirmed as imminent. Despite the latest violent attacks carried out by republican splinter groups, in which police barracks, customs houses and government buildings had been attacked, RUC feelers on the ground concluded that this was only a taste of what was to come from the reorganised, rearmed, and highly dangerous, IRA.

It was now accepted that it was the IRA who had masterminded and carried out a series of daring raids on military barracks over recent years, both in Northern Ireland and Britain. And while both police forces had been fortunate enough to recapture seized arms and arrest a number of the culprits within hours and days of the raids, a large number of those weapons and the IRA planners were yet to be discovered and apprehended. The RUC high command were proposing that *they* go on the offensive and nip the IRA's planned action in the bud, by first securing a more definite lead as to their strategies and structure present day. Thus the gathering of such men as all at one time during their careers had been to the forefront of the fight against the IRA of old. It was these same men, handpicked by the Chief Inspector himself, who were to lead the fight against the newly re-grouped IRA.

Craig was in his element over his charge in face of the IRA threat. In recognition of his years of steely service on the streets of the Falls and the wealth of knowledge and expertise gained consequently, he had at his disposal a vast array of resources to carry the fight to the IRA. Those files marked 'Top Secret' contained intelligence reports collated over the past four years since the Belfast shooting of two RUC detectives by renegade IRA men, themselves killed in an RUC ambush later that very same day. Inspector Craig had glanced through the reports at the briefing the previous evening with a keen interest and now mulled over their content once more in the seclusion of his own office. It all added up as disturbing reading. To RUC intelligence it had soon become evident, not only from the IRA's denial of involvement in the Belfast attack, but more so by the obvious standoff by hard-line republicans from events immediately following, with the renegades wakes and burials attended only by close friends and family, that the murders had indeed been the act of ruthless men working in isolation and without the sanction of the IRA leadership. Any lingering doubts over the truth of this had disappeared in an instant when it became common knowledge that the IRA had even contested the draping of the Irish Tricolour over the coffins of the Fermanagh three - the ultimate denial of the deceased. Ever since, intelligence on the IRA had been very hard to come by. This was particularly the case in the border counties despite signs of marginal dissent within IRA ranks, which the IRA had been quick to put the lid on, once getting rid of those stirring it up. It was subversives such as the renegade IRA element in Tyrone on which there was no shortage of information forthcoming for the attention of the state authorities. The renegades had been quite public in their fallout from mainstream republicanism and their sporadic violent acts, perpetrated without the consent of the broader republican community was thus easily detectable. In Belfast meantime, despite some noted shuffling around in the IRA's ranks, little or nothing was known, not even the whereabouts of the city's once leading IRA man, Fergal McHugh. He had literally disappeared within hours of events back in '52. The thinking of the RUC present day, was that McHugh had had a hand in the murder of the two RUC men and that to avoid major dissent and a possible split in the Belfast Brigade ranks, the IRA, furious at his ways, had spirited McHugh out of the city and was more than likely living anonymously somewhere in the United States. The possibility though, that McHugh had been quietly executed as an ultimate deterrent to would-be fellow travellers, had not been entirely ruled out. But what had become evident out of all the events of recent years, and most alarmingly in the mind's eye of the RUC command, was that the IRA had not gone soft, had not given up the struggle but rather, and to the extreme opposite, had applied their minds and energy to re-organising, rearming and retraining their men for a campaign of terror soon to be unleashed against Northern Ireland. From evidence to hand such preparation had long been in the making and, in safeguard of, the IRA had been prepared to lose good men but impatient men, pursuing short-term goals as opposed to the leadership's long-term plan of action.

For Craig, the most worrying fact had been and remained, that the actual plot itself - when, how, where, the IRA would attack, had remained secret, intact throughout. Paradoxically, it was the silence emanating from within the ranks of the IRA, matched with those little snippets of information passed back from, in the main, RUC moles in high places, especially their key man in Dublin Castle - the nerve centre of the Gardai Special Branch - of IRA men on the move, manoeuvres in the Dublin mountains and reports of heavy gunfire there, which had left RUC Chiefs in nervous anticipation of things to come. Collectively, RUC and Gardai Chiefs were pointing to Easter of the New Year as the most likely date for the IRA to commence their new campaign of violence. Craig realised time was not on his side. It was now in the hands of 'invaluable' men like him, to smash the IRA.

Concluding from the information at hand that the IRA were one large step ahead of him and his counterparts, Craig decided to even matters somewhat by employing his own method. Angry that his silver-haired superiors safely tucked away in concrete bunkers had made a bollocks of intelligence fed back from those on the street with their ear to the ground, including that of his own, Craig was determined in his intent. He wasn't about to let the 'wined and dined, bridge playing mob' - as he judged the RUC high command to be - expose him or his men to the sights of IRA gunmen through being slow on the take-up of information passed on in the future. He would ensure that such information would be of the calibre to make his superiors to get off their fat arses and take note.

Sitting scheming behind his new desk, Craig put the finer details to the plan of action in his head. With only limited time to get positive results, he would be taking a few shortcuts in getting some fresh, up-to-date information on what the IRA had planned. The method for which was far removed from the more orthodox approach recommended. Thus he would need the help of experienced, trusted men, on whom he could risk his whole future, indeed his life. He knew of such men and would make contact with them shortly. First though, he would attend to that other business in front of him, which due to someone's incompetence and lack of foresight remained outstanding, despite being of prime importance four years earlier. Flicking open that file and fingering through those many submissions of intelligence he himself had gathered over recent years, Craig felt the blood rush to his head on seeing his report, dated 13th July, 1952, reference Anthony Brennan (son-in-law of Sean McParland: suspect No 732) and his sudden departure from the Falls Road to England in the aftermath of the murders of the two policemen, marked in bold red ink 'NO ACTION TAKEN'. The mentality of the then assigned Intelligence Officer at Central HQ being that Brennan had simply left for England in search of work to provide for his family as rumour had it on the street at the time. This had been the I.O.'s conclusion despite the added observation by the submitting personnel, that the named suspect had departed the city only hours after his first child had been born. In view of recent developments on the mainland, Craig suspected that as a consequence of a colleague's lack of will or plain negligence, triggered by the thought of the additional administration involved if passing on to Scotland Yard that same report, the son-in-law of the IRA's top man in the North, the husband of the same man's daughter, who was herself a well-known activist, living in England too now, could well be at the centre of IRA operations on the mainland, which consequently placed the IRA dangerously at the back door.

With his voice being heard that day, the stroke of his pen read closely, Craig would personally ensure that a full, up-to-date report on Sean McParland's role in the plot simmering, be forwarded to Scotland Yard immediately, with a strong recommendation they 'check out' one, Anthony Brennan, of whom little else was known; to Craig's thinking, the perfect material for planting in England's capital to plan, organise and direct such IRA operations as witnessed these past months under the very noses of the unsuspecting public about him. Craig had not been fooled into thinking as others had, that Sean Mor, given his poor state of health, had dropped out completely from advancing the IRA's cause. Craig set out to prove as correct his suspicion that the Falls Road man still played a leading role in the IRA and their efforts to destroy Ulster.

Craig knew his world would not be complete until Sean Mor and his breed were utterly destroyed.

Chapter Forty-Six

Anthony and Sarah were intent on having a great Christmas, one that Sean, of the age to experience the real excitement of the occasion, would hopefully remember for all time.

The first Saturday in December was spent Christmas shopping in the West End, a rare act of extravagance for Sarah and a joyful occasion for Anthony on seeing his wife happy outside of the home at long last. The grand day out culminated with the picture portrait of Sean, taken in a High Street photographic studio, turning out magnificently. A framed copy would make an ideal Christmas gift for the grandparents and aunts back in Ireland, especially for Anthony's family who had never laid eyes on the child in any shape or form.

With Christmas fast approaching, fond memories of family and dear friends sadly missed were very much in Anthony and Sarah's thoughts. Conscious also, that a close friend and neighbour stood to be as equally isolated at Christmas despite her newfound freedom, Sarah and Anthony easily agreed to invite Frances together with Drew to spend Christmas with them.

That same night at a prearranged secluded spot north of Belfast and under cover of dark, Craig met up with those three steadfast loyalist men from the heart of the Protestant Shankill, whose thinking was like that of his own where the IRA were concerned: expect no mercy, show no mercy. The two serving and one non-serving B Special, his career ended prematurely back in then 1940s when an IRA landmine had ripped his Crossley Tender apart like a tin can, part of his left foot off, and another colleague to pieces, knew the extremity of what was being asked by the regular with whom they had executed some of the more outrageous actions against Fenians whilst in uniform.

The proposed 'operation' as described by Craig, instilled a quiet excitement in all three men, who were to 'see it through'.

Belfast of late had been gripped by an uneasy peace, *A calm before the storm*, one local pro-unionist newspaper editor had described it and the prospect of a little action appealed to them all now. They knew who their target was to be, when, where and how they would pick him up, and what was to be done. They agreed to meet up again with Craig that following Sunday at the predetermined venue to update him once they'd executed the operation. Meantime they would be busy collecting together the tools of the trade, quietly, discreetly.

Two nights later in that safe house in Beechmount from where Fergal McHugh had set out on his last journey, Barratt held court over three of his most trusted men. Together with the three other brigade staff members not required that night, they shaped the restructured IRA leadership in Belfast. With Sean Mor stepping down from the ranks and returning to civilian life, a number of the old school, war-weary republicans in the city had resigned from the IRA both in disillusionment at losing a much trusted and respected leader in Sean Mor, and in seeking an alternative way to drive the British out of Ireland.

Keen to remove even the remotest threat to his wellbeing in the aftermath of the bloody episode surrounding McHugh, Barratt had gradually replaced the entire brigade with his younger, trusted blood. While there had been animosity in the voices of those 1940s activists stood down, Barratt slept easier at night knowing that he was surrounded by those he could trust. He lost no sleep knowing former comrades now turned their backs on him in the streets.

That night the talk among the newly formed brigade staff was of one man, Inspector Victor Stanley Craig, and how to kill him without the finger of blame being pointed at the IRA. They all knew where Craig lived, the car he drove, the last leg of the journey home despite taking the precaution of changing his route periodically when heading out of Belfast.

Bonar, Carmichael and young Cassidy, who had all come a long way within the army these past four years, all aired ideas on how to be rid of their target. But none came close to what Barratt was tossing around in his head. It was difficult to get the balance right between the violence to be used and the outcome appearing to be the result of an accident. Barratt was confident his scheme would work and to ensure that it did he would personally have a hand in executing it on the night. There was no time to lose. Craig had to be dead at least a week before other events unfolded of which, in Belfast, only Barratt was currently aware - so he hoped.

Informing the other three IRA men what their respective roles in the killing of Craig was to be, the meeting closed with the date and time for the planned action set for the approaching Friday night.

Friday night soon came around. Craig negotiated his car carefully out of the heavily fortified central barrack as darkness fell, a light frost descending with it. He was much pleased with himself with a good week's work behind him. His intelligence brief on Anthony Brennan was on its way to Scotland Yard. The update on Sean Mor was pending the outcome of the meeting in two days time with a local man, whose name he had been shrewd enough to add to that list of names of known and suspected IRA personnel earmarked for arrest in the event of major hostilities breaking out. Everything was in hand, and that night Craig was a happy man looking forward to getting home and joining his family around a blazing fire. More alert to the rush hour traffic in front Craig did not suspect he was being followed, and so the car shadowing him at a discreet distance, its co-passenger one of the top six IRA men in Northern Ireland who headed his list for arrest, went unchecked. The route that Craig took that night was not a complicated one. Barratt ensured that Cassidy, driving, kept up with the quarry as Craig headed for the suburbs. But a sudden unexpected right turn by the leading car had the hearts of both IRA men in a flutter.

'Where the fuck's he going?' Barratt demanded to know.

Cassidy turned to Barratt to seek permission to follow. Barratt nodded. They had not to travel far along the wide suburban avenue to establish the reason for Craig's apparent detour. Fifty yards ahead of them, Craig's car pulled up at the left hand kerb, just past the main gate to Bourneville Girls' High School, its wall-mounted billboard picked out by the car's headlights.

'Drive on and look dead ahead,' Barratt ordered, pulling the flap of his flat cap lower onto his forehead. Further on, before the crest in the road, Barratt instructed Cassidy to pull up and check behind using his rear view mirror.

'Fuck no!'

'What is it?' Barratt demanded. Cassidy's heart sank. 'His wife and weans are getting into the car. What do we do now?'

'What the fuck do you mean, *what do we do now*?' Barratt snapped. 'This isn't a game we're playing! It's a fucking war we're fighting and it's tough if his wife and kiddies get caught up in it! Now check what they're up to.'

Cassidy knew from the experience of McHugh's execution that Barratt did not fuck about, but never thought the man would wage war on women and children. But as with McHugh, Barratt was evidently full of surprises. A real dark horse, Cassidy thought, checking his rear view mirror again. Craig had completed a three-point turn and was headed back toward the junction. Barratt had Cassidy do the same. They were only minutes away from executing the plan. Barratt had not got time to check out his conscience as to the morals and ethics of what was about to unfold as far as the civilians in the target car were concerned. All that mattered to him was for Craig to die that night.

Keeping to his word Craig had picked-up his family from their school rehearsals. The Christmas pantomime that year was Dick Whittington and he was prepared to put up with the excitement of it all as the row of sorts between the budding starlets in the back seat over who had the best role transformed into a drama of its own, which he viewed with quiet amusement in glimpses through the rear view mirror. But again he did not pay any particular attention to the car further back, dipping its headlights.

Heather Craig, exhausted and oblivious to the racket in the back, tried to steal forty winks in the front passenger seat. Craig was hoping his wife - two months pregnant - was not overtired. He had designs on her for later that night.

Dipping the car's headlights once turning right into that narrow country road several hundred yards behind the target car, Cassidy served to signal Bonar, positioned on a sharp bend in the road half a mile further on. Receiving the signal clearly through the aid of binoculars, Bonar shouted the command over his shoulder. 'Start her up!'

A restless Carmichael who sat listening intently behind the steering wheel of a builder's truck, heard the command first time. Parked out of sight a little beyond the bend, the lorry's powerful engine kicked noisily into start. Only the lorry's sidelights were on. Psyching himself up, Carmichael revved the engine torturously, breaking the otherwise frosty stillness of the night. Bonar waited until the leading car was less than a quarter of a mile away before turning heel and dashing back to climb into the cab beside the driver. Carmichael's eyes were fixed on the bend in the road ahead and his hands firmly gripped the steering wheel.

'Put your boot to the floor as soon as Craig hits the bend,' Bonar commanded, bracing himself in his seat.

Aware of the notorious bend up ahead and the black frost falling, Craig dropped a gear and braked slightly on taking the bend. He felt his stomach churn on catching sight of the lorry - its sidelights poor warning - in the split second before it shot over the white line to slam into the side of his car, ripping the driver's door clean off. Craig was fighting for control of the steering wheel as the car shunted effortlessly over to the left. But he knew it was a lost cause on realising the front wheels of the car had left the road. Carmichael, managing to keep his heavy charge on the road after the impact, heard a howling he would never forget. It was the sound of resignation to a violent death as the car disappeared over the edge and out of sight. Suddenly the starless night sky was illuminated by a bright yellow glow, which reflected in the lorry's wing mirrors. Bonar slapped his thigh hard with delight, knowing Craig's car had exploded into a fireball.

'May the fucker roast in Hell!' Bonar declared, revelling in their night's efforts.

Seeing the car explode as it careered down the embankment over to his left, Cassidy slammed his foot down hard on the brake pedal. The hellish sight sent a tidal wave of guilt washing over him. He knew no one would survive it. The children, all sweet and innocent in their maroon coloured berets and blazers, would have perished to.

Barratt spoke calmly. 'Turn around fast and head for the Falls nice and steady.' The man's coolness did little to ease the driver's private pain.

With the road back to the city stretched teasingly in front of him, and Barratt and company making good their escape in the car in front, Carmichael switched the lorry's headlights to full beam, not wanting to attract any unwelcome attention on the return journey back to the Falls, where on arrival the lorry would be garaged for repairs at the hands of trusted men; its work, as with their own, complete for the night. This IRA man looked forward to the following day's newspapers and learning of Craig's decease, due to the reckless driving of another, unknown driver.

On being thrown clear from the exploding car as it hurtled out of control at tremendous speed down the steep, rocky embankment, the squeals of the terror-stricken children trapped inside the fireball on wheels struck the fear of Hell into their father's very soul. Craig's despair at what he saw and heard was greater than the pain seizing his broken and torn body. With the car crashing violently into the ragged jaws of a gorge many feet below, a deafening, eerie silence, gradually filled the night. Raising himself onto an elbow halfway down the rocky embankment, Craig could only look on helplessly as fierce flames shot out of the wreckage and licked the night's sky. The acrid smell of burning rubber filled his aching lungs, and the only sound now was the roar of the flames gaining momentum. Realising he was also choking on the smell of his children's burning flesh, that of Heather, a child in her womb, Craig rolled onto his side and vomited violently, silently begging God to take them quickly. Lifting his face from out of his own vomit to reluctantly look back over his shoulder, Craig considered himself dead and in Hell itself, when seeing his daughters, one to each side of their mother, their hands joined, walk casually toward him engulfed by fire and their burning flesh peeling and falling from their bones.

'No! NO!'

At a hand's reach away lay Craig's police-issue revolver. Desperate to escape the torment of his living nightmare, he reached out, the pain excruciating for him. Taking hold of the gun, he drew it close to him and with a badly charred hand he somehow managed to hold it to his head, its barrel, pressed against his left temple. A withered finger, burnt to the bone almost, clawed the hair trigger. But Craig had not the strength to squeeze the trigger. He slumped back and gasped a last rattled breath.

That following night Sean Mor read the evening newspaper's headline report with a genuine heavy heart. With innocents tragically lost, he had not wished to see Craig die in such a way, but nevertheless, wouldn't shed any tears for him. Craig indeed, had been one bad bastard.

Despite the newspaper's article and radio reports describing the family tragedy a consequence of a 'tragic accident', with the RUC seeking information on any vehicle seen in the area that evening, Sean Mor feared that Craig's cohorts, both in and out of uniform, may read something more sinister into his death. Therefore, he decided he would take a few extra precautions where his own and his family's security was concerned.

Reading of the same 'tragic accident' in her English newspaper and accepting it as such without a second thought, Sarah, while regretful over the woman and her children's horrific deaths, felt no pity for Craig. Her childhood memories of the man haunted her even to that day. He had been an animal in her young eyes. Scary flashbacks to him and his men laughing crazily as they stood in line to urinate over her and her sisters cowering in bed when they were children, as father was dragged out of his bed, came screaming back to her regularly. This was one of many terrifying experiences she'd endured over the years as a consequence of the campaign of terror that Craig had waged against her father and her people back on the Falls. She couldn't help but think in that moment, that God had punished the man who had made her life and that of so many others, a living Hell. And Sarah cursed him to it without shame or guilt.

Craig's three co-conspirators had psyched themselves up so much for the covert operation that it was impossible for them to pull back in light of Craig's sudden death, of which they were highly suspicious. Indeed, suspecting the IRA had finally made their move on Craig, the men easily agreed to make their own move. There was too much at stake not to.

That Sunday night the three loyalists, dressed in dark winter clothing and flat caps pulled low, and with the use of a borrowed car, took up their position in the shadows of a darkened alleyway, close to Belfast's city centre. Along the adjoining street in approximately ten minutes, their target would make his way to the local brewery's office to deposit the week's takings from the bar he part managed. From their hard experience on the streets of the Catholic Falls, only several hundred yards from where they themselves lived in the heart of the Protestant Shankill, the three had come to know who was who, and they knew well that Michael Teer, the barman from the Coat of Arms, 'that republican pub up the Falls', was a leading member of the IRA, holding rank at battalion level at least. Their information had come via hard intelligence collected over the years, and at the other extreme, from the tu'penny touts who would swear their own mother's lives away for the price of a drink. It had been known that the rooms above the bar were used periodically for IRA and Sinn Fein meetings and that Teer had played host, giving free drinks out all round. That night, if he showed, they would be making him pay up for it all at long last.

The click of Teer's shoes echoing along the street, dead quiet otherwise and blanketed by a heavy frost, signalled his approach. The two serving B Specials seated in the front of the car, Lenny Dean and Walter Black, waited for their man to pass the alleyway before alighting from the vehicle, each pulling black handkerchiefs over their mouth and nose on doing so.

With a swag bag full of money tucked under his short jacket, the two masked men suddenly appearing on each side of him led Teer to believe that it was a holdup. Teer turned to run back in the direction from which he had come, but one of the two shadowy figures was quick to block his escape and he was felled by a heavy blow to the head. Landing forcibly on his knees heavily dazed, Teer clasped a hand to the egg-sized lump rising along his hairline and felt as though his skull had been split open. The swag bag fell to the pavement and one of the two masked men quickly snatched it up. Teer felt himself dragged onto his feet again to be pushed and pulled in one direction with urgency. With his thoughts thrown into confusion and feeling weak, he could not resist. It was easy for his assailants to bundle him into the back seat of the car. The retired B Special, Silver Wallace, seated beside Teer, rammed the barrel of his revolver into his ribs to say earnestly, his voice muffled, 'Keep yer mouth shut or you're a dead man!'

With the other two slightly younger B Specials back in the car again, the four men set out on a journey with only three of them knowing their destination.

Teer had soon realised he wasn't a victim of a mere holdup once bundled into the car, which sped across town, up a deserted Crumlin Road in heading north out of Belfast to negotiate a treacherous Horse-Shoe-Bend and along winding, deserted country roads. This was more serious, and Teer's mind was a riot as to who the men might be. But the earlier warning was still fresh in his mind. No one had spoken for some twenty minutes. The driver, Black, still masked like his two cohorts, threw Teer a murderous glance every so often via the car's rear view mirror.

Glancing sideways at the man at his side, who poked the gun into his ribs, Teer could just about see in the dim glow from the car's dashboard lights that this man was advanced in years - the silver sideburns, the crow's feet around the eyes, the telltale signs. Teer sensed he knew the man despite the disguise, but could not place him, and he could only see the back of the heads of both the front seat occupants.

The car turned off the lonely country road and negotiated at a crawl a bumpy narrow track. Outside, it was pitch black. After a few minutes drive the car's headlights picked out an old, stone-built byre with a rusting corrugated roof and door, outside of which the car pulled up.

'Step out behind me. And careful does it.' The gunman had jabbed his weapon into Teer's ribcage on giving the command.

Once out, and being led by the collar of his jacket, gripped tight by the one with the gun, Teer found the way ahead illuminated by the handheld torch operated by one of the other two men in front. The four men filed into the byre, colder inside than it was out, its rough flagstone floor strewn with straw. A lingering smell of pig shit clung to the air. The beam of the torch picked out a solitary ladder-back chair in the middle of the small open space and Teer was told to sit by an authoritarian voice. A match was struck and the smell of paraffin was a welcomed change for all. An old lamp hanging from a nail in the wall just inside the door gradually illuminated the grim environment, its interior almost medieval. The three kidnappers appeared even more sinister then, cast in long shadows. Teer felt his body tremble and it wasn't down to the cold, damp night air captured within. He was petrified in face of his circumstances, not knowing what was to come next.

The three men closed in around Teer. The gun in the hand of Silver Wallace was raised slowly until its barrel came level with Teer's head. Teer felt its cold steel tip pressed firmly against his right temple. The voice of Silver Wallace, muffled under the mask, came a little gentler in tone but more menacing to Teer's ear. 'I'm not going to fuck about, Teer. We know who you are, what you are. We want you to tell us, here and now, what the IRA leadership has planned; where we can put our hands on all the gear. Y'see, we're fucking sick sitting around waiting. So, c'mon, open yer trap. Then we can all go home, nice and quiet like, not another word said, eh?'

The Shankill three were hoping Teer would be duped into thinking that he was merely in the hands of dissatisfied IRA men seeking, along with others, to go it alone. For splits in the ranks had been widely reported. Shit-scared, Teer realised that whoever the men were, they were on to him. Despite displaying an ignorance to the fact that in recent months he had been stood down; that whatever gear he'd had under his control had long since been shifted, Teer knew it could all be a ploy to lure him into a false sense of security, to get him to say more than he should, than he need to, to get out of his predicament alive. What concerned Teer uppermost was not knowing if he were in the hands of three genuine renegade republicans or authentic IRA men sent by a distrusting Barratt to test his steel, to probe if he were truly dissatisfied over McHugh's fate, his own recent dismissal, thus a potential traitor.

Perhaps it's the Branch out to trick me ... to entice me into some sordid deal. The possibility that he was in the company of enemy moles could not be ruled out either, Teer knew. It would not be the first time that they had been operational within the ranks. There had even been whispers that this had been the case with McHugh - long since seen or heard.

'We're waiting Teer, and it's turning fucking colder in here by the minute!' Black snapped, who with Dean and Wallace, formed a half-circle in front of Teer.

Thinking fast, knowing he could well be fighting for his life, Teer also knew he had little choice but to take the three at their word. He would try and win them over by persuading them to do a deal with him, which he had no intention of keeping. Once out of their clutches, he would scream blue murder.

'Listen lads. I'm a non-player. I don't know what's planned or where any weapons are kept. But, there's something brewing, all right. I don't know what, but I'm willing to do a deal with youse.'

'What fucking deal?' Silver Wallace demanded. Teer acted out the maverick role with all his heart, though played his hand carefully, still not knowing who he was truly dealing with.

'I'm fucking sick of it myself. They got rid of me because I was restless also. I'll tell you everything I come to know. There will be opportunity for me to do this, for meetings are planned. I can listen in.'

'What meetings? Where? When?' Black probed menacingly. Teer felt he had the others eating out of his hand, could string them along easily by keeping them on the promise of something spectacular being revealed in time.

'Men are due to arrive from Dublin. They'll be meeting with local men above my bar. I can keep an ear to the wall, so-to-speak.'

Seeking to test his prisoner's worth, Silver Wallace seized the initiative from Teer. 'Are you so fucking sick of it all, that you would pass information to the police?' Knowing he would lose his life instantly if answering 'Yes' to either genuine IRA men or renegades, Teer replied with a firm 'No!' He did so assuming that, if in the hands of an IRA unit, at worst he stood to receive a severe beating for being willing to side with more extreme elements. But if the three revealed themselves to be Special Branch, Teer knew he would ultimately have to promise the world to be free of them.

Keen to keep himself one step ahead of his captors, whoever they be, Teer spoke with a steady voice in trying to call their bluff.

'Y'told me youse are tired of waiting. I believe you. I understand your impatience. But I'm more of a help to you by remaining close to those who are patient at the moment. They are the ones who will have the means of pursuing the fight ... arms, munitions. If this is what you need, I can deliver!'

But Teer was not in the company of either. The three men surrounding him were Protestant extremists, who detested anything remotely Irish republican and who bore a burning, deep-rooted hatred for all Catholics. They had all joined the B Specials so that they could wage terror on the papists through their formal positions of power and control, while at the same time receiving handsome payment for it.

Silver Wallace had always known that there was no way he could strike a deal with Teer, even if continuing the pretence. For there could be no guarantee that Teer would honour any such deal. Even allowing for the remotest possibility that he would, the more than probable fact that their true identity would be discovered at some point, would have Teer running for his life or indeed, taking his own, as Teer would know that their hatred of him ran as deep as his hatred for them and their like. No, Silver Wallace knew they would have to keep to the original plan. Despite Teer's mouthing, he was not convinced the IRA man had been truthful with him. There was only one way to get the information he sought from the republican scum, and Wallace set about doing so.

'The only deal we will do with you, Teer, is this. You tell us what we want to hear or I'll blow your fucking brains out! Now, where can we find the dumps?'

Teer's voice was almost hysterical in pleading the truth.

'I tell you, I don't know! Whatever gear there was, has been shifted.'

His plea fell on deaf ears.

Convinced he was at the mercy of deranged republicans, Teer felt a strong hand clasp the back of his neck and throw him forcibly out of the chair. Landing face down on the rough floor, he was pinned there by Dean and Black, forcing his arms outstretched and standing on the back of his hands and forearms. Shoving the revolver deep into a coat pocket, Silver Wallace was kneeling astride Teer's upper back, and from his other coat pocket, produced a flick knife. Teer's head was yanked back forcibly and he saw the glint of the long, thin, razor-sharp blade wielded an inch away from his face. Silver Wallace moved the knife closer to Teer's right ear and with a steady hand manoeuvred the tip of the blade inside its orifice, then applied a steady pressure. The cold steel point slowly pierced Teer's eardrum.

Outside the byre, Teer's agonising screams went unheard as the torture proceeded mercilessly. Crying out to 'Jesus and Mary' for help, Teer released an almighty cry of despair on hearing, through his left ear, one of the three laugh cynically, 'Fuck you and the Mother of God, you Fenian bastard!'

Teer knew then in whose hands he truly was. There would be no escape. Only through death, which he prayed, would come quickly to him.

Death came slow and torturously to Teer. His captors kept true to their threat. First, with the use of the knife, Silver Wallace ruptured both of Teer's eardrums, then, gouged out his eyes, one at a time. After a brief pause to deliberate how he could go one better than Wallace, Dean took great delight in hacking off Teer's penis and shoving it into his victim's mouth, then ramming it far down Teer's throat with the knife's long, thin blade.

Black, keen to outdo the other two, took his turn with the knife. Kneeling over the victim, now lying on his back and barely breathing, he proceeded to cut Teer's throat very slowly and with great care, as if slicing through prime meat at the family table, before stabbing him repeatedly in the chest in a frenzied action, only stopping when the knife's wooden handle snapped under the force of his thrusts, leaving six lethal inches of hard steel buried deep in the breastbone of the dead man. The three, dripping in their own sweat and Teer's blood, laughed hysterically at this until their sides ached. Once stepping outside the byre to catch a breath of fresh air they settled their nerves by sharing a cigarette. But a depression soon descended for despite their hard work, Teer had told them nothing they didn't already know. He had been a poor choice of victim. He'd known fuck all.

As a team, the three men spent a further half-hour working silently, methodically, in hacking to pieces Teer's remains with the hatchet and spade carried in the boot of the car. Body parts and entrails were scraped into a large potato sack, which was dumped into a disused well nearby. Teer's clothes, personal belongings and swag bag, were to be burned, the money, split between the men as a substitute reward for their labours. Silver Wallace had retrieved the knife blade when splitting Teer's chest apart with the spade, and decided to keep it as a souvenir.

The three men stripped off their own clothes and shoes and washed themselves vigorously in a nearby ice-cold stream. Lighting a fire on the bank with Teer's personal things and their own bloodstained clothes, they dried themselves by the fire. Once dressed in the change of clothing they'd each loaded into the car earlier, they set out on the road again in time for a quick drink in their local bar on the Shankill Road. For they had each worked up a thirst through their efforts.

Chapter Forty-Seven

On the night of December 11th 1956, the IRA launched its new-armed offensive against the Northern Ireland State. From Antrim to Derry, a ring of bombs and incendiary devices exploded throughout the night and into the early hours of the twelfth morning. Police barracks, customs houses, post and telecommunication offices, railway stations, lines and bridges, power stations and pylons, main sewers and transport fleets, were among the targets attacked in a series of coordinated commando-style operations by up to a hundred armed men dressed in paramilitary clothing. The majority of the attacks were concentrated along the border and at a number of locations the RUC and the IRA exchanged heavy gunfire. Miraculously, by dawn, no one had been reported killed or seriously injured. The RUC, caught largely unawares, failed to capture any IRA activists, as they were slow to deploy men in follow-up sweeps of the surrounding terrain.

The newspaper headlines on the night of the twelfth screamed alarm and condemnation. The Northern Ireland Prime Minister, RUC chiefs, politicians and church leaders from both sides of the religious divide queued up to hurl damnation on the 'evil men of violence', as described by one leading statesman. While those in high places of authority smarted in discomfort subsequently and the RUC hastily drew up emergency counter moves to thwart a continued IRA blitz, those who had masterminded the offensive rubbed their hands in glee over such an opening success and their spirits were sky-high at the prospect of what was to come, for this was just the start of it.

One of the architects behind the campaign received quiet satisfaction when reading of the events in his evening paper. Sitting safe in the home of one of his most trusted sympathisers, Barratt was pleased also that all appeared sound for the way ahead. And with Craig out of the way, the Belfast Brigade could - in between waging war along the border - keep in check those local Protestant extremists whom he suspected to be active. While most Falls Road folk were accepting the theory put about that Teer had 'done a runner' with the breweries money - having got cold feet over his impending marriage - Barratt strongly suspected foul play. Prior to meeting his death Barratt believed Craig had arranged for Teer to be abducted and tortured in an attempt to gain much-needed information about the IRA's plans. Thankfully, Teer had known nothing, but unfortunately for Teer, this had sealed his fate. Barratt was confident that Teer had been murdered, his body disposed. Barratt feared that Craig's henchmen, having killed one 'republican', would want to kill more. He and his men were taking extra precautions, especially now, with the war against the Orange state resumed.

Barratt and his men were not alone in realising the threat from Protestant extremists. His ear to the grapevine always, Sean Mor had his daughters under night curfew, much to their disquiet, as they had started courting of late. Rosie McParland considered her husband's actions as merely protective in view of the renewed violence, causing her to be extremely worried about them all. And, like her husband, she was so relieved that Sarah and Anthony were clear of it at least, her grandson, not witnessing the horror unfolding.

The Chief Superintendent at Scotland Yard studied closely the RUC intelligence report received in recent days from Belfast, which named Anthony Brennan, formally of the Falls Road, Belfast, as an IRA suspect, and who was believed to be residing somewhere on the mainland, together with his wife Sarah McParland, a staunch republican activist. The signatory to the detailed report, the recently deceased Inspector Craig, Intelligence Division, Belfast Central, had strongly recommended that the Brennan couple, once traced, be placed under close surveillance and that an update of developments be forwarded to him with haste, so that the RUC could monitor the movements of 'known associates' in Ireland.

Knowing that those who had masterminded the recent spate of raids against military barracks across the country were still at large, possibly in the capital itself, this senior police officer accepted that the involvement in such activity by the Irish couple in question - in view of the attached intelligence - could not be ruled out. Dispatching a memorandum to those subordinates leading the fight against Irish subversives to meet with him shortly, he would issue new directives for a covert nationwide manhunt to commence in order for the Brennans to be located, their every move closely observed.

It was plainly evident to those devastated relatives and friends who gathered in sombre silence amid the bleak surroundings of a suburban church graveyard, blanketed white by the previous night's heavy snowfall, that the same minister who had blessed the Craig's marriage, the heads of their girls when christened, was struggling to officiate over the multiple burials of the once very popular members of his congregation - and only days after having visited the Craig family to offer prayers for their father's safe passage through life. Indeed, as the four coffins were lowered into the hard ground, the man mouthing the Gospel found it difficult to look any one of the people assembled, in the eye, to speak the true word with a passion, such had been the enormity of the loss.

Soon enough, the minister was left alone with his God to ask some soul-searching questions in the aftermath of such tragedy.

Three days after the IRA's concentrated attacks across the six counties, the Protestant dominated government at Stormont Castle reintroduced the Special Powers Act, which armed the RUC and B Specials with additional unlimited emergency powers in fighting the IRA. In the wake of the announcement the talk among the republican community was that internment would soon follow and precautionary measures, already considered fully, were set in train. Knowing they were well-known to the state authorities, those more prominent members of the movement went to ground, only to resurface when fulfilling an active part in ongoing IRA operations.

One man who would be doing neither was nonetheless a target for arrest, he knew. Sean Mor, virtually housebound due to brittle bones and slowly wasting muscles was not going anywhere, and from the relative comfort of his fireside armchair, prepared himself mentally for the worst. His only hope was that his wife and daughters would remain strong no matter what lay ahead. But meantime he would savour for a little while longer the splendid framed photograph of his grandson Sean, received from across the water that very morning.

Chapter Forty-Eight

The short walk from home to early Mass that following Sunday morning left Sean Mor feeling as though his time had come. Gasping for breath, the sweat dripping from his brow, he let himself slump untidily into one of the front pews. Only for Rosie and the girls taking hold of his arm up the central aisle, he would never have made it that far. Those friends and neighbours dotted in the pews behind raised their weary heads from off their chests to investigate the commotion, as the big man's anxious wife and daughters flocked around him to check that he was okay. Catching his breath and mopping the sweat from his brow with his handkerchief, Sean Mor assured all that he was fine and beckoned them not to fuss so. Feeling a little more composed, he eased himself onto his knees to pray quietly during those few minutes remaining before the Holy Mass commenced. With eyes cast sideways, Rosie, on one side of him, the girls to the other, watched his every move. They were all growing increasingly concerned for their husband and father, for he was not the same man at all.

The empty pews in the rear of the church were quickly filled with dozens of young men and women filing in at the last minute. Most did not wish to spend a moment longer than necessary in the place. They'd had their fill already of priests, nuns and Christian Brothers, who'd rammed the catechism down their throats at school. The only reason they were in attendance that morning was due to the pressure from parents to keep good the faith and the threat of neighbours reporting back if not seen at the early Mass. All stood upright now as the stand-in, fiery-faced priest up from the Free State took to the altar. The eyes of the curious congregation were firmly fixed on the stranger. It was the first time in all his years in the parish that Father Crossan had not served the early Mass. The hierarchy had arranged for the two priests to exchange responsibility for their respective parish for several weeks as part of promoting 'cross border harmony and understanding'. All parishioners gathered, wondered if this priest was in any way in sympathy with their grievances; whether, like good old Father Crossan, he would come among them to see for himself the poverty and injustice they experienced living under a Protestant Parliament for a Protestant People.

The Holy Mass began. This Free Stater's voice fell harsh and cold on sensitive, critical ears. With two thirds of the Mass recited, the well fed priest left the altar and climbed into the pulpit to deliver his sermon, those personal reflections and observations as to the city of Belfast and its people, acquired since arriving five days earlier - the 11th December. The priest looked down on the meek with marked indifference. The excess flesh overhanging his dog collar wobbled slightly on clearing his throat before beginning; his thick-fingered hands gripped the pulpit as if hanging on for dear life. All eyes remained firmly fixed on him. This was the moment of truth, when the people would either endear him to their hearts or reject him, though quietly, with any respect bestowed onto him only forthcoming out of polite acknowledgement of the position he held.

'It is ironic to say the least, that on the very day I arrived here in the North, my very first visit I may add, men, who proclaim to be Irishmen, seeking Ireland's freedom, set out with gun and bomb to kill and maim fellow countrymen and to destroy property which served the needs of the greater public.'

No one among the startled congregation listened with a more critical ear than Sean Mor, sitting upright, his eyebrows raised in mild surprise. He'd heard it all before, but never in this house and not from the mouth of a stranger, a guest in his community. The priest continued with an air of chastisement all about his manner and in his words.

'How on God's earth can these evil men perpetrate such vile actions against their fellow man in the name of Ireland? Indeed, in the name of God? For their rallying cry is, God save Ireland!'

Just then the priest fell silent as the eyes of the congregation turned away from him to focus on that other man among them who dared to stand up without fear or hesitation, to no doubt speak his mind in challenging this man of the cloth - God's holy ambassador. Sean Mor had mustered all his zapped strength to raise himself onto his feet, which silenced the one above in full-flow. Looking the priest straight in the eye, Sean Mor spoke, confidently, assertively, in putting the priest in his place.

'Excuse me, Father. But I take grave offence at your ignorance of the truth, and seemingly your *confidence* in assuming that *we* gathered here, who know all there is to know about injustice, are going to sit back and listen to your rhetoric.' Hearts raced, faces became instantly flushed and Rosary beads were fingered nervously as 'Big Sean' continued unabated in unleashing an articulated barrage of unsettling facts, which left the priest's already blood-red face turning blue, he, himself, fired with rage, barely contained.

'You and your like down in the Free State presently enjoy the pleasures of freedom and independence, achieved by the blood sacrifice of those same men the church once condemned as evil-murderers and terrorists, but who you now wine and dine down in Manooth.' There was no stopping the Belfast republican. The priest was dumbstruck by the man's sheer nerve, never before encountered in the house of God. Sean Mor felt a new lease of life fill his veins in delivering another verbal blow to the hypocrite in the pulpit. 'Your present day leading statesman was himself once one of those very terrorists, who then proceeded to murder better Irishmen than he or for that matter, you or I...'

'I, I must ask you...' The priest's fumbled attempt at interrupting Sean Mor failed. Determined to be heard, Sean Mor raised his voice above the other's. 'As for the North, of which you evidently know little, we are not yet rid of the Black and Tans. Thus our fight goes on, while others, appearing to have short memories or none at all, are quick to condemn us for seeking that which they themselves hold dear and cherish. If Jesus Christ was truly a man who sought justice for those who suffered, then I say, confidently, and with pride, God-Save-Ireland!'

Among the flock growing a little rebellious there was mutterings of 'Hear! Hear!'

Sean Mor dared the man to challenge him with a long hard look, which the other could not hold. The priest let his head drop to his chest under a heavy sigh. A pin dropping to the floor would have been heard by all in that moment. Sean Mor wasn't finished though and with a determined chin, said in conclusion. 'I've attended Sunday Mass here, since I was first a child. But I for one do not need to come before *you* in order to communicate to God. So I bid you good day.'

Sean Mor struggled out of the pew, loyally followed by Rosie and the girls, half genuflected toward the altar through feeling so weak, then braced himself before walking in a near march back along the aisle, his eyes fixed straight ahead, his head held high. Those locals gathered in the pews nodded and smiled toward him in admiration as he went past. There was a rush of bodies behind Sean Mor as a sizeable number of the younger generation streamed out of the pews to register their support for their man with their feet, without throwing the silenced one in the pulpit - head still bowed - even a mere glance. This congregation was suddenly not so meek. The Falls Road youth showed the way for their elders to follow, and most did. Only a handful of the older souls remaining in their seats were left either confused or amused by it all. The Free Stater was left to brood over his own shortcoming while struggling through the remainder of the Mass, the likes of which he'd never experienced before, and prayed silently, he never would again.

Reaching home exhausted and appearing gravely ill, Sean Mor was literally carried into the front room by Rosie and the girls, who eased him into his armchair. Taking one long concerned look at her husband, Rosie had Caithlin running for the doctor and Bridget scurrying into the yard for a shovel of coal to stoke up the fire. She herself stayed with him and kneeling in front of her husband, rubbed his ice-cold hands each in turn, eager to get some heat into them.

Sean Mor felt his mouth parched, his lips chapped by the freezing wind outside. His shivering body felt so weak and for the first time he was aware just how ill he truly was. He sought to soothe Rosie's fears and looking deep into the woman's tear-filled eyes, said, with a touch of humour, 'If anything happens to me girl, whatever you do, don't get running for that priest.' Rosie gently squeezed her husband's hands and said lightly, 'You're so stubborn, Sean McParland.' Then, passionately, 'Just get better love. Just get better.'

It was a cry from the heart and Sean Mor recognised it as such. Again he sought to lift the woman's spirits, if only a little. 'I'll get through this Rosie ... so don't be worrying yourself. Keep strong for the girls. Everything will be all right.'

The no nonsense family doctor examined Sean Mor closely from head to toe and did not hesitate in recommending that he be admitted to the local hospital that very morning, prescribing a long period of complete rest and recuperation under medical observation, as essential.

Feeling as he did, and knowing the doctor's determined way, Sean Mor was in no position to argue. His wife and daughters, while sad to know he would be leaving them for a while, were relieved to know he would be receiving the proper treatment in the safe hands of the right people. With the doctor leaving the house briefly to summon an ambulance by way of a telephone call from the corner shop, Sean Mor called his family around him and sat upright in his fireside chair to serve warning.

'Listen closely,' he began. 'No matter what happens, I don't want Sarah hurrying back here over the head of me. There are rough times ahead and danger still remains for her and Anthony. So don't let me down.'

No one disputed his concern and would respect his wish right to the end if need be. And no one among those who listened obediently dared even to contemplate that that day may soon come.

The Chief Inspector of police in north London, receiving a formal request from the Yard that all personnel check their records for an Anthony Brennan, was pleasantly surprised to discover that the 'suspect' was one of the local Irishmen that his very own D.S. Rigsby had been investigating. Rigsby, having proudly come forward with the suspect's name, address, known associates etcetera, revelled in his senior's praise for a job well done.

Four senior Scotland Yard officers, well groomed and expensively clothed, their light coloured macs a bit of a giveaway as to their occupation, wasted no time on their arrival at the north London police station in debriefing Rigsby and drained every drop of information out of him about the suspect. By the end of it all, Rigsby himself felt as though he'd been put through the third degree. But his greatest annoyance over the Yard's eagerness to push ahead with the job at hand, came when being told, in no uncertain terms, that they would be taking sole control over further investigations on Brennan; that he, Rigsby, was not to show his face anywhere near the Irishman in case of arousing his suspicion. This was a bittersweet pill for Rigsby to swallow and both he and his Chief Inspector were left fuming in the wake of the Yard's departure.

Knowing that Anthony Brennan had been an associate of Finn Spiceland - recently sentenced to twenty years imprisonment in Northern Ireland for gun running - the Yard's Chief Superintendent wasted no time in ordering Anthony Brennan and his wife to be placed under round-the-clock surveillance.

With only five days remaining before Christmas, Anthony and Sarah took great delight in decorating the Christmas tree. With permission to stay up late that night, Sean sat on the floor looking on excitedly as two grownups playfully wrestled with each other over by the tree, which stood centre of the front sitting-room's bay window. The adults childishly argued as to who should put the finishing touch to the fabulously furnished fresh pine, which reached from floor to ceiling. Sarah had her own way and Anthony held the dining chair steady as his wife, stepping onto it, reached up at a full stretch to hook the silver-painted, cardboard cut-out star onto the point of the tree. An exhilarated child joined his father in giving the wife and mother a rapturous handclap in recognition of a job well done. Neither of the joyful adults noticed the big black car - with its headlights off – silently roll to a halt on the opposite side of the street nor the two official-looking men sat inside, who eyed-up their home, and who would do so until midnight before being relieved by two other detectives.

In the early hours of that following morning, hundreds of RUC men backed up by equal numbers of B Specials, visited the addresses and known haunts of republican activists and sympathisers throughout the northeast of Ireland. While wives and mothers tried in vain to fight off the marauding intruders and terrified children screamed in fear, some soiling their beds in witnessing a real life nightmare unfold, dozens of men, fathers and sons alike, were dragged from their beds, beaten and thrown like carcasses of meat into the back of waiting Black Marias. They were then driven off to nearby police barracks for interrogation, processing, and finally, transportation to a prepared wing at Crumlin Road Jail to commence their imprisonment without trial.

    Just before midnight, the Northern Ireland Prime Minister had signed the 'Internment Order' authorising mass arrest and detention of those suspected of seeking to undermine the state through the use of violence or by supporting those using such means. By noon, the last of those rounded-up arrived battered, bloody and disorientated in the cold, grey cells of that oppressive Victorian prison, which stood a mile or so away from Belfast city centre. Not all of those listed for 'round-up' had been seized. A considerable number had obviously been expecting such a raid and had gone to ground. Nevertheless, rank and file republicans, numbering sixty-six in total, were behind bars. Large-scale searches for those on the run, weapons and explosives, would remain ongoing across the province. Three thousand regular police and twelve thousand B Specials had been deployed to thwart further IRA attacks. Along the border the RUC gave cover as British Army sappers blew up and cratered all secondary crossing points leading into the North from the South, which were deemed as likely routes for the IRA to transport men and weapons back and forth across the border. Northern Ireland was gripped by a siege mentality and was subsequently being turned into a fortress.

    In the last few days, indeed hours, leading up to the swoops, RUC Special Branch had been carefully sifting through every snippet of intelligence collected in order to monitor the sudden and last minute movements of top IRA suspects, so they would not escape the dragnet. In Belfast, as a result of information passed on by their tout up the Falls, the Special Branch knew that their main suspect, Sean Mor, was not to be found at home on the morning of the 21st. It was common knowledge that 'Big Sean' was now a patient in the R.V.H., that hospital standing on the corner of the Falls and Grosvenor Roads. A Detention Order was to have been served on him at the same time those selected front doors along side streets up the Falls gave way under shoulder charges and heavy feet lashing out. But dedicated, protective and earnestly determined hospital staff had threatened legal action if need be, to prevent one of their patients - very weak and in constant need of medical attention - from being removed from their care. The leading rank among the arresting party of expectant RUC men had weighed up the potentially damaging publicity the force may well encounter if persistent in their charge on this particular occasion and had hastily withdrawn his men. Sitting up in his hospital bed, Sean Mor had not been at all surprised at the attempted incursion and had listened, while bracing himself for the worst, to the raised voices beyond the entrance to his side ward as night duty staff had squared up to those most unwelcome visitors. Keen to capitalise on the outcome of this humanitarian act and to exploit his newfound status as a 'very ill man' - although mentally he remained sharp and alert - Sean Mor had managed to win the cooperation of one of his protective carers when requesting that before going off duty, she telephone a leading Belfast solicitor, to inform him that one of her patients urgently required his services.

Receiving the duty sister's phone call just before leaving his suburban semi for his city centre office, the small, tidily dressed, professional man, nearing retirement, assured the nurse he would call to the hospital first thing. Sean Mor was sincere in saying 'thank you' to the nurse, and cleared his thoughts in preparing to meet the man of whom he had come to hear so much; a man who functioned successfully within the state's oppressive judicial system.

The two hawk-eyed Special Branch men sitting slouched in their unmarked car, one of many parked in the hospital car park, monitored the comings and goings through the main entrance of the R.V.H. as the early morning staff arrived for duty. With their uniformed counterpart arriving back at Belfast Central HQ hours earlier - minus the top IRA suspect as a consequence of the circumstances which had confronted he and his men when attempting to execute the Detention Order - it had since been decided by those coordinating the swoops from the safety of their bunker, that to seize McParland from his hospital sick bed, could well indeed backlash against the force, if provoking the more moderate element among the nationalists. So, for now, the suspect was to be kept under round-the-clock surveillance. An attempted 'rescue' by republicans could not be ruled out. At least then, if McParland and his associates were seized under such circumstances, any such sympathy for his plight would be lost. His action would confirm his guilt. The two watchful detectives were to radio through for backup if suspecting such an attempt at rescue was afoot. With their eyes focused sharply, though not on McParland's harried-looking wife entering the hospital by its main door, but rather on the ageing, ineffectual-looking man following her in moments later, the two detectives were soon sitting up to take notice. They recognised the man instantly from their attendance on occasion at the courts. Despite his nondescript appearance the detectives knew him to be one of the best in his profession, a thorn in the force's side over the years. Putting two and two together, they suspected he was about to make life awkward for them yet again.

Sean Mor was pleased to see Rosie arrive safely and she was greatly relieved to find her husband where she'd left him the day before. This sense of relief was evident through her words, which slipped off her tongue freely as she came to sit by his bedside.

'Thank God you're safe. It's been a terrible night.'

Talking in a near whisper so as not to be overheard by those other men sharing the ward, the devoted wife proceeded to give her husband a full run down on events overnight. The Falls had been turned 'upside down' and at least twenty local men had been 'lifted'. Most of the names mentioned were familiar to Sean Mor. They were mainly that of battalion staff and volunteers. Those of higher rank had wisely gone to ground some days earlier, no doubt. It appeared that Barratt was still at large, thankfully. Sean Mor was confident the man would hold the show together. One thing was clear to him though, the RUC had known not to trouble themselves by calling on No72. Evidently, news of his admission to hospital had travelled far and wide. He waited until Rosie had given him all the scéal before informing her of his uninvited visitors during the night and the bravery of others. The woman's fears had been heightened once again consequently, and she fretted. 'They'll come back for you. We should get you moved fast.'

Spying over his wife's shoulder the harmless looking soul entering the ward and recognising the man from newspaper photographs, Sean Mor assured Rosie that all was in hand.

Acting on the directions of the duty sister, the solicitor knew which patient to approach. Stepping up to that bed, where an anxious-looking woman sat nervously fingering the bony hand of her man, the invited visitor extended a warm hand in introducing himself to his client-to-be.

Roderick O'Hagan was nearing the end of his forty-second year as a locally born and bred solicitor, whose legal expertise and willingness to take on the most impossible of cases was well-known. This high-profile legal professional was regarded as a 'local hero' by many working class Catholics who held every faith in him, in recognition of his bold determined stand in the face of state injustice and through drawing such thought provoking attention to it from among those who in consideration of their own selfish interests, had for years shied away from questioning those in authority. Bishops and priests alike found great difficulty in dispelling this man's outcries over the state's oppressive sentencing of Northern Irish Catholics and the chronic prison conditions they were forced to endure as exaggerated claims of victimisation of the minority community. In the mind's eye of judges, queen's counsel, unionist politicians, policemen and prison governors alike, and not least those remaining green Tories in privileged positions north and south of the border, this man was as dangerous as any IRA man. In their eyes he could undermine the state more so through that medium which his own privileged position in society afforded him, and at his convenience.

While knowing all of this, Sean Mor still cast caution though to what he disclosed to the man who rubbed shoulders with the enemy in the cold corridors of the state's oppressive institutions. Although accepting that he would need to disclose to O'Hagan *that* of himself which would serve to give a fairly accurate picture of his treatment over the years at the hands of the RUC, Sean Mor knew that some facts would have to remain untold. His case was simply this: he was a sick man, whose body could not take any more punishment. From what the medical staff had told him in recent days, he would be laid-up for the rest of his days, tied to the house, its front door being the cutoff point from the world beyond. A batch of pills and medicines would always be at hand's reach. Being interned again would kill him. The doctor had said this also, thus the nursing staff's gusto in protecting him the previous night. And not least, his wife and family could not take his suffering in prison any more, for it brought even greater suffering on them. In Sean Mor's considered analysis, O'Hagan stood between he, his family, and a tragedy.

O'Hagan gave precedence in attending to the needs of his new client. Listening intensely to Sean Mor's brief, it was clear to him that it was yet another case of state persecution of an individual who, because of his cultural and political affiliation, had been made to pay a very heavy price. Twelve years of imprisonment, running the gauntlet of numerous beatings and interrogations, the threats, abuse, and the constant fear of being dragged out again, had taken its toll on the man and his family, who were living on their nerves in the aftermath of events these past twenty-four hours.

Not knowing what the next twenty-four hours would bring, O'Hagan wasted not a minute in setting in motion a series of precautionary and indeed drastic measures to safeguard his client's welfare. With Sean Mor's approval sought and acquired, the solicitor's first move was to convince his client's doctor - then summoned - of the urgent need to transfer the patient to Intensive Care, so as to reinforce the rationale that the patient was indeed a 'very ill man'. Through employing all his powers of persuasion, O'Hagan succeeded to impress on the medical staff that there remained a real threat of the RUC returning in force next time. This achieved, O'Hagan politely demanded and received into his hand, a copy of Sean Mor's medical history, detailing his injuries and illnesses over the past years, which read like a horror story in itself. This, together with the specialist's most recent diagnosis as to his client's concerning condition, medically irreversible, would form the basis for contesting the existent Detention Order served. Preparing his case would take up little but precious time. So, in calculating the odds of the RUC turning up again, O'Hagan knew he would have to create some space in which to manoeuvre in the immediate future. Pausing for thought, to consider all the options open to him in making it greatly more difficult for the government to pursue the detention of McParland, the scheming solicitor proposed that the local, sympathetic newspaper be 'anonymously' contacted and informed of the RUC's unethical methods in attempting to detain a sick man. A little shaming publicity would help apply the pressure on the government to withdraw the D.O. or at least to deliberate longer over whether to execute it presently. Assuring his client that a reporter would not call on him, it was left to O'Hagan to have a quiet word with his contact at the newspaper's offices.

Mrs McParland had a very important role to fulfil in the solicitor's scheme also. She was to contact the local parish priest and request that he draw her husband's plight to the attention of the Bishop, who would then be expected to voice his concern over the treatment of the family to the highest state authority.

Thankfully, in light of the visiting priest's 'unpopularity', Father Crossan had been promptly recalled to his parish. To Sean Mor's thinking, it was somewhat comically ironic that the Bishop was being called on to advocate on behalf of that member of his flock who had wandered off somewhat, having first upset the cart as far as the same Bishop's latest initiative to promote cross-border harmony and understanding was concerned.

Giving O'Hagan the benefit of the doubt as to his wisdom on this aspect of the scheme, Sean Mor decided not to interfere in the other's judgements.

Renewed faith and hope had been restored in the heart and mind of Rosie McParland, knowing one man at least had her husband's welfare at heart. Sean Mor was much grateful to O'Hagan for taking on his case and voiced his appreciation. Uncomfortable with such applause and knowing time was of the essence, O'Hagan took his leave once seeing his client safely placed in Intensive Care. An understanding and helpful medical consultant assured all that the patient would remain in the IC ward for the duration of his treatment, which would continue early into the New Year. Though saddened at the prospect of being apart over Christmas, both husband and wife accepted that the hospital was the safest place for him to be during that time. O'Hagan too, carried both their hopes and desire for a peaceful night. To raise their hopes on anything more than this - the couple knew from their own hard experience - would be tempting fate.

Silver Wallace felt as though he had been kneed in the balls on reading the front-page of the *Irish News* - the Catholic daily he normally shunned. Interested to know how the nationalists were reacting to the reintroduction of internment, he could not believe his eyes when reading that additional report titled:

Caring Hospital Staff Save Patient From
Detention On Morning Of Mass Arrests

In short, the article, which to Wallace's thinking, was typical of the newspaper's sympathy for the republican cause, detailed how *alarmed and highly distressed medical and nursing staff, very concerned for the health of one of their Intensive Care patients, prevented the RUC from serving a Detention Order in the early hours of the morning on that same patient undergoing vital treatment.* That patient was non-other than *Sean McParland, a middle-aged family man.*

The report went on to inform the reader that leading Belfast solicitor, Roderick O'Hagan, was to raise the matter with the Inspector General and government ministers, and would be seeking the *lifting of the Detention Order in view of his client's poor health, and the absence of incriminating evidence.*

Fired with fury over this development, Wallace wasted no time in telephoning his two associates, Lenny Dean and Walter Black. To his thinking, it was time to carry the war to the IRA scum and their supporters.

Sarah had been biting her nails ever since learning of the round-ups back home. While internment did not come as a surprise, nonetheless the thought of father being one of those dragged out worried her sick. And so the telegram received from Belfast two days after the raids, left Sarah offering a prayer of thanks to her favourite saint.

Rosie had known that Sarah would be anxious for news of her father and had wasted no time in having the discreetly worded telegram sent to London. Consisting simply of two lines, it had left Sarah knowing her father was safe and that mother would write soon.

It was in keeping with Sean Mor's wish, that Sarah had not been made fully aware of the fact that he was in hospital, for this, he suspected, would have his eldest daughter racing for the first boat home.

Christmas Day was excitedly received by young Sean; he was up at the crack of dawn to rip open his presents as sleepy-eyed, though thrilled parents sat up in bed to look on as their child went into a near fit with each of his wishes coming true.

The two men from Scotland Yard who sat freezing and aching from head to toe in the unmarked police car on the opposite side of the street, had seldom taken their sleepy eyes off number 101 these past six hours. Now, with their shift thankfully coming to an end, they emptied the flask of the last of the black tea, totted up with a drop of brandy, and mustering enough good spirit, wished each other Happy Christmas.

Sitting upright in his hospital bed enthusiastically bidding all those dedicated nurses and doctors scurrying about him 'Happy Christmas,' Sean Mor sipped his early morning brew cheerily. He was looking forward to seeing Rosie and the girls later in the day and while not feeling the best physically, in mind and heart he was in top form. O'Hagan, who had called on him again the day before, had made that Christmas a very special one. Through the other's grit and determination, the visit due, the coming together of a family, had been made possible.

Silver Wallace sat alone and dejected in a fireside chair amid his cold and grey terraced surroundings. He could not bring himself to believe, to accept, that in face of all the damning publicity, the persistent harangue from that solicitor, the pleading by the Fenian priest, that the state authorities had caved-in and had let Sean Mor slip the net.

It had been agreed by those in high places, that to continue the hot pursuit of McParland under the circumstances, at the expense of turning moderate, law abiding Catholic support against them, was too great a risk.

Now, with his own government failing him, Wallace would spend Christmas scheming as to how best serve 'justice' on an old enemy, his way. In Wallace's twisted mind, the only way remaining.

Chapter Forty-Nine

The New Year saw intensification in IRA attacks on RUC barracks across the border counties, this time resulting in death and injury on both sides. In face of mounting pressure from the British and Northern Ireland Governments, the coalition government in the Irish Republic threatened the IRA with internment. Undeterred, the IRA's campaign saw the weak government out of power and the dissolving of Dial Eireann. As part of the republican movement's overall strategy, Sinn Fein were to manipulate the political vacuum in the South, and would contest the elections there.

Within days of leaving hospital in that first week of spring, Sean Mor, a little fitter and stronger but still much dependant on his medications and regular visits from the doctor, received a surprise visitor to his home one sunny afternoon. With hostilities between the IRA and Crown Forces at a height, Barratt had taken to moving between secret destinations after dark. So it was daring for him to do otherwise, though Barratt considered the risk worth taking on this occasion.

Although Sean Mor was a non-combatant now, the twenty-five years of living a life consisting of secrecy, great danger, much personal sacrifice and indeed, constant fear, left him knowing only too well the high risk that Barratt had taken to steal a little time with him and was moved to voice his concern. 'You're sticking your neck out, Frankie, coming to visit me at such a time.' Barratt was having none of it and was quick to interrupt Sean Mor. 'Away with that! You'd do the same for me, and don't tell me you wouldn't!' Sean Mor knew it to be a waste of his breath to argue with Barratt. Anyway, the truth of it was, he was very pleased to see his good friend. With Barratt making himself comfortable in the matching armchair in the front room where they'd often schemed and plotted, the conversation which followed between both men was light and easy; Sean Mor careful not to pry into army business as it was not his to know any longer. But Barratt would have told Sean Mor anything, if asked. He still trusted the man with his life.

On taking his leave from No.72 an hour or so later, Sean Mor followed Barratt out into the narrow hallway of his home and placed a friendly hand upon Barratt's right shoulder. 'Thanks for calling Frankie. It's much appreciated.' Barratt turned to face Sean Mor. 'Thank you for your comradeship down through the years, Sean, and for remaining a good friend.' Sean Mor and Barratt exchanged a bold handshake. Sombre-voiced, Barratt seized the moment to reveal an ugly truth. 'It was unfortunate that Craig's wife and kiddies were in the car that night, Sean. But I was determined to see the bastard dead.' Barratt had confirmed a long held suspicion for Sean Mor. Knowing the man's regret to be genuine, Sean Mor added, 'The conflict at times gives meaning to the saying, Suffer little children.' Barratt could only nod in reply. Getting the all clear from the lookout on the street corner, the IRA man departed the house, not knowing when or if he would see Sean Mor again.

With the Brennan couple - under constant surveillance - continuing a very ordinary and indeed predictable lifestyle, the top men at the Yard overseeing operations on the ground, were forced to re-examine the possible fruits to be had from the late Inspector Craig's report and concluded easily that there were none. In their judgment, it was the case of a paranoid RUC man wrongly judging the young couple to be a splice off the old block. What had made this analysis conclusive, was the fact that before, during and after a recent failed attempt by the IRA on yet another military barrack in the southwest of the country, none of the couple's movements or contacts led anyone to suspect them of being in any way involved. All that had caught the Yard's attention was Anthony Brennan's occasional meeting with the well-known and former south London criminal Jack Kilty. Discreetly acquiring information as to the reason behind their association, and knowing of Kilty's previous illegitimate business interests, the Yard concluded that their infrequent relationship had arisen out of Christy Brennan's involvement with Kilty years before.

Anthony's visits to the pub in the north of the city had become rare, and once establishing the publican and his wife as godparents to the Brennan child, the publican and his wife's return visits on occasional Sunday afternoons to the Brennan home were not, as first suspected, the coming together of terrorists planning the IRA's next move on the mainland. It was accepted consequently that Anthony Brennan and the publican's association with Spiceland, had simply been coincidental.

By the end of April, the Yard had no doubts when deciding to end their surveillance on the couple. The Brennan file was closed and relabelled 'Non Suspects'. Scotland Yard had been so discreet in their surveillance methods that Anthony and Sarah had suspected nothing untoward.

D.S. Rigsby was greatly disappointed to learn that the Brennans had been given the 'all clear'. He had been of the firm belief that he had stumbled on something of substance where Anthony Brennan was concerned, and despite the Yard's conclusions, he still had a nagging doubt that they had missed something, somewhere.

Receiving her mother's latest letter, Sarah was able to read between the lines easily and was greatly more content knowing mother was too. Her father, it was reported, was keeping fairly well in health and was spending most of his time at home. On his better days her mother and father would go out together for a wee walk. The money coming in from renting out the shop kept them both in pocket. There was even the possibility of them both snatching a short-break in the summer, in County Down, where they'd honeymooned years ago. Caithlin and Bridget meanwhile, were doing just grand at the mill and were both courting local lads. Indeed, all the family was well, and Belfast was quiet.

Sarah knew the latter to be so as she closely followed the news of the IRA's border campaign. She also knew that her father had not returned to any role in the republican movement. So frail had he become, he'd even been forced to give up his commitments with the GAA, and from running the shop. To Sarah's thinking, someone with a conscience in the RUC top brass must have known this too and had left her father's name off the wanted list on internment morning. Knowing mother was happy to have him around her day and night, and that all was well, and Belfast quiet at least, left Sarah feeling much happier. She could focus her time and energy on rearing Sean and tending to her marriage with a clear head. With spring all about her, she was determined to make the most of life.

Anthony too, was feeling more content through seeing Sean grow up a healthy, bright child, with a mother who loved him so very much. He judged himself fortunate to have such a beautiful wife, who was always there for him, and who loved him so too. A steady job and a fair wage helped to make life a little easier, and knowing from his mother's letter that all at home in Donegal was well, served to give added comfort. Mother and father, his seventy-fourth birthday just celebrated, were in good health. Anne-Marie was going steady with one of nine brothers from a neighbouring family, good in name, while Colleen was content to sit in each night. She had always been the shy one, a proper home bird. And there had been the added good news. Christy had written to mother twice since, to say he was fine and that he was hoping to return home for a visit, but had not said when exactly. Evidently, life in America was so hectic it was difficult to walk away from it, even for a short time. There had been news also about old Mick Onion. Out in all weathers is he, mother had written, with the sweat beating his brow on a good day, the steam rising off his back on a wet one.

Anthony understood the old man's crusade. Keeping busy would help to keep him sane.

The three UVF men met as planned in a staunch Protestant bar close by the Harland and Wolff shipyard wherein, in the privacy of a snug, final plans for the killing of one man was finalised. Sean McParland was their intended target and a difficult one at that. Knowing from first hand accounts that he seldom crossed over his front doorstep, Wallace had little option but to approve Black and Dean's plan to venture deep into the republican heartland after dark, and once drawing Sean Mor to the front door of his house, to shoot him in the head at point blank range. Wallace would cover the street from a nearby corner. Once doing the job, all three would make their way with haste back towards the Falls Road from where, using back alleys as a means of escape, they would sneak back into the Shankill unnoticed. The three men knew the lay of the land across the divide as good as their own, for they had patrolled its streets daily. The way out would be easy and they were confident all would go according to plan.

Though enthused by Dean and Black's determination to get in close to McParland to ensure a kill, Silver Wallace was left a little dejected at not doing the killing himself. But with his own notoriety along the Falls still fresh in the minds of those living there, even after all these years, Wallace knew that there existed a real risk of him being recognised even at a glance by Sean Mor or one of his family. Having said so, Silver Wallace found himself being cynically teased by Dean, mouthing off recklessly. 'Anyway, at your age Silver, and with that dodgy leg of yours, you couldn't run to save your life!'

If looks could kill, Dean would have dropped dead under the fixed, spine-chilling glare from Wallace, nicknamed Silver due to his distinctive head of silver-white hair, Brylcreemed back from a face that told of a hard life lived. Black broke the icy silence with a hushed voice loaded with impatience. 'Cut out the fucking messing. There's unfinished business to discuss.'

Silver Wallace was to supply the weapons to be used, two old, but perfectly working .38 Webley revolvers, complete with live rounds long since acquired from a former UVF man, many years dead. The attack was set for Wednesday night of the following week. It was Wallace's hope that McParland's killing may be viewed by his close followers as an act of revenge for McHugh's disappearance, carried out by those renegade elements thrown out of the IRA twelve months earlier, thus a bloody feud may ensue with republicans left busy slaughtering each other.

With plans for murder in place, Wallace bought in a round of drinks to celebrate, quietly, in advance of events to come.

The secluded stretch of beach on Donegal's extreme northwestern peninsula was ideal for firing off the Thompson sub machinegun, the Belfast Brigade's prized weapon, one of only a dozen assorted and much valued weapons held in their possession. Barratt was expert in using the gun in every way. The night before, back at the centuries old and remote fisherman's cabin, under the glow of a paraffin lamp and kneeling over a blanket spread out on a stone floor, his trusted associates, Bonar and Carmichael, had looked on in awe as Barratt stripped down and reassembled the weapon with such ease. After each fumbled an attempt to achieve the same, the younger men had gradually got the hang of it, but nowhere close to the sort of time or with the same minimum effort as Barratt.

Now though, both Bonar and Carmichael released their frustrations over this in turn by letting loose with the ear-shattering weapon as the rolling Atlantic waves crashed against the rocky shoreline, drowning out the gun's blazing thunder. An old, rusting, washed up oil drum filled with sand, standing at a distance of one hundred yards, was on the receiving end. It quickly came to appear like a large sieve as the fifty rounds from one fully loaded drum magazine peppered it with neat round holes. A shower of spent cartridge cases fell silently upon the white sand around the feet of the gunmen, taking it in turn to get some much-needed practice with the gun. There was no one for miles around to hear the muted din. Between the three IRA men, hundreds of rounds of ammunition were expended at their leisure and the three republicans enjoyed every moment. They were like children with a new toy. But come the following day, they would be deadly earnest in using it. The gun would prove itself to be no toy, and themselves, no children. With the oil drum blasted apart under the ferocious assault the three IRA men called it a day and set out to return to that cabin wherein final plans for the day to follow would be sounded out and agreed.

As the night sky crept inland over a calm sea, the three IRA men set out from the remotely situated cabin in a fast black Ford Pilot car, borrowed from a trusted sympathiser in Belfast the day before. The men were intent on slipping across the border into County Derry and, taking the north coast route through Portrush and Ballycastle, arriving unnoticed back in their native city in the small hours. Carmichael, driving, Bonar, up front beside him, each carried a loaded revolver tucked into the waistbands of their trousers. Barratt sat on the back seat with his hands caressing the loaded machinegun's cooling metal and well polished hickory stock, hidden beneath the overcoat over his lap. The journey would take longer than usual, but the back road was considered the safest route, with large numbers of RUC and B Specials known to be concentrated along the border. If encountering an enemy patrol however, they would try and bluff their way out. What was for certain, none of the three IRA men were prepared to go to jail for twenty years or more.

Gathered around a scullery table in a safe house close to Belfast's New Lodge Road early that following morning, Barratt quickly ran through the plan of action once more for the benefit of Bonar and Carmichael, both in nervous anticipation of things to come. Checking his watch, Barratt nodded to both men to be on their way to the place of ambush. The assassin elect, Bonar picked-up the unloaded Thompson from the tabletop and slipped it under the light fawn-coloured mackintosh he wore. The gun's butt was snug under his armpit, while a sweaty hand in pocket cupped the stock tightly as he prepared to take his leave. The fully loaded magazine drum was tucked inside his shirt. With the coat buttoned up, only a suggestion of something bulky under it was evident. Gesturing with a finger for Bonar to turn full circle on the spot, Barratt checked his man up and down with a sharp eye and nodded his approval. 'Remember! Walk as casual as you can. But whatever you do, don't let the gun slip.'

With the occupier of the house - a short, skinny, toothless man, appearing much older than his forty odd years - entering the scullery by the back door to inform the IRA men that the way was clear, Carmichael moved ahead of Bonar on following the sympathiser out back. Carmichael would scout Bonar to that elected spot, where they would lie in wait for their quarry. They were to walk to the Ardoyne, about twenty minutes away, by way of the maze of residential side streets and back alleys that lay between the two ghettos. The stopping and searching of vehicles by the RUC was a common feature of life in the city present day. The car used in the last few days had been safely parked up outside the house to where they had returned unseen just before daybreak. They would not be in need of it now. Its owner, the man of the house, had been expecting them and had left the snib off the front door. They had entered the house at dawn unheard and had bided their time until the appointed hour by drinking mug after mug of piping hot tea in chasing the early morning chill from their bones.

Barratt knew all hell would break loose in the aftermath of events to shortly unfold, so did not intend to hang around that part of the city for too long. Once getting the all clear from the sympathiser, who would check that the area remained clear under the guise of walking the two prized greyhounds, Barratt planned to walk the short distance into town, then to the safe house in the Markets area, the tiny republican enclave in the east of the city. Once there he would lie up for a few days until the situation had cooled. Then he would meet with the brigade to discuss 'developments' before returning south of the border, from where he would continue to oversee the war along the border.

After fifteen minutes or so, the sympathiser returned by way of the back door and informed Barratt that the two lads were safely on their way and that the area was indeed clear. Pulling on his short jacket, Barratt followed the other man out into the backyard where two greyhounds, one black, the other sand-coloured, lashed to the handles of a battered dustbin up one corner, eyed him nervously. The dog owner untied their leads and led the way into the back entry. Peering around the back entry door, Barratt waited until the bandy-legged wee man and his animals reached the bottom end of the entry and for the signal before stepping out and following his trail, careful to negotiate the piles of baking dog shite that littered the way. As he walked the bright early morning sunshine was warm on Barratt's back, a nice feeling, he thought. Before reaching the end of the entry, the doggy man turned right and carried on along that street running horizontal to the bottom of the entry, on toward that next street corner, where he paused to check the main road up and down before giving Barratt the okay again.

With the children still in their beds early Saturday morning, the streets were deserted except for the old women clad in black shawls returning home in ones and twos from the early Mass, and those scrawny stray mongrels roaming here and there, sniffing their own trails of piss sprayed against gable ends in marking out their territory. Barratt progressed across a further two junctions on receiving the other man's signal. It was a risky exercise as an RUC patrol could be rounding the very next corner they approached. Barratt frequently glanced over his shoulder also, just in case. He would not be safe until reaching the city centre, where he would be Mr Nobody blending in with the masses.

Approaching that third junction, the last before the busy main road that led straight into the city, Barratt was halted in his tracks on hearing the strays behind him bark riotously. It was a well-read warning and glancing back to investigate, had his worst fear confirmed. An RUC patrol car had turned into the street behind him and was headed his way. Frothing at the mouth, the hair standing on their backs, the strays chased after the car's rear wheels. Gut instinct told Barratt to run for it. He raced for the corner up ahead. The doggy man on its far side turned very white in the face on realising the situation unfolding. His feeble body worked hard as the nervous greyhounds strained on their leads. Reaching the corner, the man running scared made a sharp right and continued at full stretch up the street's steady incline, checking for an open doorway to one of the slum terraces on his right as he went. He almost gave up hope on finding the first six or seven doors closed shut on him, but the next one, outside of which an old black bicycle stood propped against the wall, lay open to him like a gateway to Heaven. Dashing into the small hallway, Barratt threw a sideways glance and spied the long bonnet of the pursuing car cutting the corner. He calculated in an instant that they had not seen him disappear into the hallway. Thinking quickly, he closed the front door out behind him. Simultaneously, the inside half-glazed hall door opened to him. A craggy-faced old woman dressed in black eyed him up and down suspiciously. A gruff male voice from the room behind the woman put her in the news, Barratt too.

'Maggie-Anne. The street's black with peelers!'

Barratt saw the harsh, inquisitive look on the woman's face soften. Her gentle voice revealed her thoughts. 'Hurry in, son. They'll soon be at the door.' Barratt smiled and nodded and stepped into the woman's humble abode. He found himself treading newspapers spread out over the lino floor and soon knew why on seeing two white eyes blink in the head of a blackened face. The chimney sweep had been the one to alert his customer and the unexpected visitor to developments outside. Hearing more cars screech to an abrupt halt, Barratt knew he had not a second to lose.

Outside, two more police cars had braked hard in pulling up to the kerb and half a dozen RUC men alighted with revolvers drawn. They proceeded to run back and forth along the street like headless chickens checking for open doorways and peering through windows on the lookout for the suspect. Excited orders were barked between the men, knowing their quarry wasn't far away. Someone was taking control of the search by ordering some of the RUC men to 'double quick' to the alleyways at the rear of the kitchen terraces, standing in long rows on both sides of the street. A methodical house-to-house search was proposed as soon as more reinforcements arrived. Barratt realised that there was only one way out. He reached for the loaded pistol tucked into his trouser waistband and made his move.

The chimney sweep hadn't argued over Barratt's firm but polite request to 'Strip off!' Having both moved into the scullery, Barratt had quickly stripped off his own clothes to don that of the chimney sweep, left standing in his LongJohns, which were as black as his working clothes. The old woman monitored the antics of the RUC from behind her front window net and reported back in a low, anxious voice. 'There's more of the buggers arriving by the second.'

To add the finishing and hopefully, convincing touches, Barratt frantically dipped his hands into the sweep's soot bag and covered his face, neck and hands with soot, cleaned from the woman's chimney earlier. The scullery floor, scrubbed spotless a few minutes previous, was now a sorry state.

'Here, have my cap,' the original sweep said, flipping the well-worn rag onto Barratt's crown. 'Your boots ... they're too clean!' That said, the sweep scooped up a handful of soot from out of his soot bag and slung it around Barratt's feet.

'Will I get away with it?' Barratt pleaded. Looking the impersonator up and down, the dispossessed, genuine sweep, nodded. Thankfully for Barratt the sweep's physical make-up was not at all unlike his own, short and stocky, and about the same age too.

Minus the revolver now buried deep in that soot bag to be soon dumped in the woman's rubbish bin, Barratt emptied his own pockets and gestured to the sweep to have his clothes in replacement for those borrowed, and sought to assure the sweep that if all went well, he'd get his belongings and tools of the trade returned to him somehow soon. That said, Barratt moved through to the front room to collect the chimney rods and brush, tied up in a neat bundle by the hearth, and tucked them under an arm. He paused then to say to the old woman, weighing him up with an approving eye, 'Sorry for the intrusion missus ... and the mess.'

The old woman shook her head. 'Go in God's name son, and God bless.'

The old woman followed Barratt out into the hall and opened the front door of her house for him. Stepping out into that street was the greatest challenge Barratt had ever to rise to. He saw three RUC men standing in a tight circle in the middle of the road break off their conversation to eye him up suspiciously.

'Thon's a grand job done today, sweep,' praised the old woman from her doorstep.

Playing out the masquerade to the full, Barratt turned to the bicycle and manoeuvring it away from the wall, placed the chimney rods secure in the clips fixed across its handlebars. Daring to look up at the old woman once more as she stood waiting nervously on her doorstep, to see if her face had confidence in him, Barratt was encouraged to see that it did, and he smiled at her. She winked back. Turning to face the enemy, Barratt was greatly relieved to see that few, if anyone, paid him any attention. Wheeling the heavy bicycle off the pavement, Barratt chewed nervously on his bottom lip as he swung a leg over the crossbar for it had been many a year since he'd last ridden a bicycle. Mounting the saddle and quickly finding his balance, Barratt pedalled, wobbly at first, down the street as a dozen RUC men forming a raiding party, stepped aside to let him pass. Not wishing to make eye contact with any one of them, Barratt looked straight ahead and cycled to freedom.

Chapter Fifty

Barratt could have ordered the notorious B Special and UVF man, Walter Black, killed on any one of a number of occasions in recent time. Those other handpicked IRA men, D'Arcy, Doyle, Cassidy and McElwee - unknown to the RUC as being IRA - had each in turn stalked Black many a day and night. They could easily have walked up to an unsuspecting, vulnerable target to shoot him at arms length as he'd walked the dog in the park close to his home or as he'd staggered home full from the pub on those evenings when not officially terrorising the people of the Falls. With Black succeeding Craig as the popular bastard among that same community and being at the forefront of the latest raids on the homes of republicans, Barratt was confident that the killing of Black would be acceptable to those who were once again witnessing and experiencing at first hand, Black's brutish methods. Rumour had it also, that Black had recently teased Teer's former girlfriend in the street over his disappearance, mouthing such sick claims as knowing Teer's cock had been cut off, before his throat was cut.

As for the leadership's ruling on IRA action in Belfast, Barratt had won the argument when directly appealing to them to sanction the killing of Black. To do so, he had contested, would win over much needed support from among the nationalist community in Belfast, particularly along the Falls, where the people had come to believe Black to be Teer's murderer. The IRA therefore, would be seen to have pursued justice for crimes perpetrated against the Catholic people by sectarian bigots such as Black. If anything was to boost the IRA's ranks, it would be such an action, claimed Barratt, confidently. The leadership had given way and had approved the one-off action, though knowing the risk they took in doing so. A Protestant backlash had not been ruled out, despite Barratt's assurance that there would not be.

'The Orangemen will be afraid to attack the Catholic ghettos', he had said. 'When seeing how we dealt with Black'.

Bonar and Carmichael reached that chosen place for ambush safely and on time. Once checking that they had not been followed, they took up crouched positions behind that perimeter wall, topped with high spiked railings, enclosing the wooded grounds of the Catholic Girls' Secondary School. The school stood on elevated ground on the edge of nationalist Ardoyne. Behind the school, a not-so-busy main road swept down from the outskirts of north Belfast and into the Protestant Shankill, less than half a mile away. On the other side of the Woodvale Road, in a grand, semi-detached, pre-war house lived Black's widowed mother. Barratt's men had come to identify and locate Black's mother, having followed the ageing woman home on several occasions from her son's own home further down the Shankill.

Through stalking Black, Barratt knew that he paid his mother a visit at home every Saturday morning at around eleven o'clock. The school ground was the perfect cover from which to ambush the target. It had been calculated that Black, once pulling up in his car outside his mother's, would be a sitting target for Bonar.

Safely reaching his destination under the cover of his disguise and once convincing the woman sympathiser that it was *he* who called to her back door, Barratt quickly washed and changed before settling down with a much welcomed mug of tea in the woman's front parlour. And just like the gunmen lying in wait over in the north of the city, he waited patiently for the hour hand to strike.

A single man in his late forties and born and bred on the Shankill, Black was a popular figure among his breed - those loyal to Queen and Country and true Defenders of the Faith. As a B Special, known to keep the Fenians 'in their place', he was a local hero. On the way to his mother's that morning, he stopped off at the Shankill Road butcher shop to collect her meat for the weekend. Sam Vickers, the UVF's second in command in Belfast, slipped an extra pound of best bacon into Black's shopping bag and over the counter had a brief chat with his fellow UVF man about 'the situation'. Out of earshot of several women shoppers, Black casually informed Vickers that Wallace - the overall commander of the UVF in the city - had finalised plans for an offensive against known republicans in Belfast. That said, Black walked back to his car and set out on the short drive to his mother's. The house in which she lived had been purchased by him in recent years so that she could enjoy more comfortable and pleasant surroundings in her old age, as opposed to life in her former home, that rundown two-up two-down end terrace on the Shankill Road, where Black now resided. It was in that same house where his mother had single-handedly reared four children - three girls and a boy, in between holding down odd jobs over the years after her husband's death at the age of twenty-nine during the war in France in 1919.

The location of the new house, most often cast in the long, pointed shadow of the papist church opposite and just below the girls' school, was a bone of contention between Black and his mother, a fair-minded lady, whose motto was: live and let live. She herself had chosen the house when taking an immediate liking to it on stepping into it for the very first time. Black had wanted to please his mother, so she'd had her way. Black's three sisters had all since emigrated to far off sunnier places and he had been left to look after the old girl, which he considered a privilege. She was his best friend and confidant, whom he loved dearly.

With it being a Saturday morning Black planned to spend an hour or two with his mother before visiting the bookies, then the pub where he'd spend the rest of the afternoon drinking and playing poker.

Carmichael checked his wristwatch and mouthed obscenities under his breath. It was 11.10am and cramp was setting in. But to stand to stretch his aching limbs would be to give himself and Bonar away. There was no sign of Black and time was indeed getting on. Squatting alongside with eyes peeled and holding the loaded and cocked machinegun across his knees, Bonar was growing itchy with unease also. Both IRA men sweated profusely under a baking hot sun. Its heat was fierce upon the top of their uncovered heads. Beads of sweat trickled and fell from their brows. The soles of their aching feet felt as though they were on fire.

'Where the fuck is he?'

Bonar's impatience showed in a shaky voice and Carmichael wondered if the man at his side was up to the job in hand. Just as he was about to assure him, though his own thoughts had been mirrored through that same question, a car, with Black behind the wheel, pulled up to the kerb directly across the road.

'About fucking time,' sighed Bonar, bracing himself. Both men studied Black hard. Looking up, Carmichael saw Black step casually from his car. Locking the driver's door and with his back turned to them, Bonar made his move. Rising the barrel of the Thompson in line with his aim through the gap in the school railings, Bonar drew the gun's smooth hickory stock tight against his right shoulder and curled his index finger around the hair trigger. Carmichael wisely poked both index fingers into his ears. With Walter Black's broad back full in his sights, Bonar squeezed and held the trigger. For Bonar, it sounded as if the gun was being fired inside his head as he emptied the magazine drum. The tail of fire spitting from the gun's spout blinded his view momentarily, but knowing where Black had stood, concentrated his firing in that direction, spraying a relentless rain of deadly red-hot lead across the road. Bombarded by the salvo of ejected spent cartridge shells, Carmichael saw the carnage brought with it when Bonar opened up. Black's back was peppered in an instant as a multitude of bullets hit their target, gorging their way through his torso with such ferocity that the doors and windows on both sides of Black's car were blasted through. As Black slumped to his knees gravely wounded, his face transfixed with a look of sheer horror on seeing his own steaming guts spill from a gaping, ragged hole, he was catapulted forward as more bullets riddled his upper back. Black's head, smashing forcibly against the driver's side door, came apart as high velocity bullets flew blindly through the air. Carmichael was forced to look away then, wondering when a trigger-happy Bonar was going to relent. He did, but only when the magazine was emptied. Removing his fingers from his ears, Carmichael heard a mother's desperate cry, a dog yelp with fright. Ashen-faced, Bonar wore a look of wonderment as he took hold of the fruit of his labour. The few words uttered from between his thin lips told of his amazed state of mind, 'Fucking hell! Did you see that?'

In tune with the reality of the moment, Carmichael said simply, 'Let's get outta here fast.'

Bonar was way ahead of Carmichael in a flash. But Carmichael could not straighten himself, never mind move. The cramp had seized him good and proper. 'Hold on for Christ sake!'

Bolting across the church grounds with the machinegun still smoking under his mac, Bonar stopped suddenly to look over his shoulder. He could not believe his eyes on seeing his comrade stagger from out of the bushes and hobble toward him, his right leg rigid and dog shaped, and appearing as though shot himself.

'Get a move on, fuck sake!' Bonar raged. 'This place will be crawling in a minute!' Bonar's warning propelled Carmichael onward. The thought of a noose tightening around his neck made the tight throbbing balls of pain in the back of his leg disappear in an instant. Joining up with Bonar, both IRA men ran for their lives. It was Carmichael who first spied the figure in black coming through the break in the trees up ahead and reached for the revolver under his jacket. There was no way he was going to be taken alive. Two paces in front, Bonar stopped suddenly on seeing the same figure lurking in the bushes. Joining Bonar at his side, Carmichael raised his gun to fire in that direction once the RUC man had shown himself.

'Hold your fire!' urged Bonar, clasping a hand tightly around Carmichael's raised wrist. A grey-faced, nervous-eyed priest, no older than either of the IRA men, appeared in front of them with arms raised. His very soft, compassionate brogue, from south of the border, reinforced his body language.

'In the name of God lay down your arms,' the priest pleaded. 'You stand on trial in the shadow of Our Lord's house!' Bonar and Carmichael threw each other a disconcerting look. Bonar released his grip on Carmichael's wrist, and the revolver-wielding man knew what had to be done, and quickly. He served a chilling warning to the priest on stepping forward to level the cocked revolver at his face.

'Listen Father! We don't want to hurt you, so step aside.'

Taking a cautious step back, the priest pulled a determined face and began to roll up the sleeves of his soutane and with confidence said threateningly, 'Is that a fact? Over my dead body will you go any further!' Just as the last word slipped from his tongue, Carmichael lunged forward with arm raised and brought the butt of the revolver down forcibly in a slicing action. The priest staggered backwards and fell in an untidy heap among some bushes, blood streaming down his very white face.

'Mad bastard!' Carmichael spat, looking down with disdain on the priest lying groaning at his feet and clutching his hands to his head, streaming with blood.

'Let's move!'

Bonar shunted Carmichael forward. With all guns tucked out of sight and at full stretch both men quickly covered the remainder of the school grounds without further difficulty. On exiting the main gates they dodged traffic on darting across a busier Crumlin Road. Both IRA men let their heads fall to their chests so to avoid eye contact with those small groups of anxious men and women gathered in idle conversation on street corners, having been rooted to the spot moments earlier by the sudden terror-striking gunfire which had seemed never ending. The gunmen made it safely into Ardoyne, another ghetto festering from dire housing conditions, chronic unemployment and poverty. Here, support for the IRA was deep-rooted. Those who saw the two gunmen flee, had seen and heard nothing.

Bonar and Carmichael disappeared into an alleyway from where, at a gentle run and keeping to the back alleys, they made it safely to a derelict house standing in the heart of 'Old Ardoyne'. On entering the condemned building by way of the large man-made hole in a partially bricked-up back entrance, Bonar recalled to mind his much practised skills in that fisherman's cabin and proceeded with haste to strip down the Thompson. He dispersed its various lethal components by dropping them into a number of holes in the main downstairs walls, where they would be concealed between the cavity. This done, Bonar and Carmichael removed their coats and tossed them into a corner of the backyard. Using his zippo, Bonar set fire to them. Different coats, planted in the house two days earlier, were pulled on before both men slipped away in separate directions, but with one destination fixed in their minds. They planned to be back among their families on the Falls within the hour, having spent the last few days away 'river fishing' down in the Free State.

Cut to pieces by flailing red-hot lead, Black's body had been unceremoniously loaded into the back of a passing motorist's car - flagged down by those distraught neighbours first on the scene - and was rushed to the nearest hospital, but had been beyond saving. The experienced surgeon attending counted a clear thirty-seven bullet holes in Black's head, back, arms and legs. In the professional's analytical opinion, Black's body had been 'butchered.'

Back at the scene of the shooting, shocked, disbelieving women folk tried hard to comfort a highly distressed mother, who'd witnessed her son's slaying from behind the net curtained window of her upstairs bedroom, which overlooked the killing ground. Several of the retired men living on both sides of the widow's house, which had had its front downstairs windows blasted through by gunfire, threw endless buckets of water over the road to flush the dead man's spilled brains, pools of blood and intestine into the gutter. They received a little consolation knowing, that if the dead man's mother had been sitting in her fireside chair, they would most probably be scraping up her brains too.

White-faced RUC men scanned the location from where the gunman or gunmen had opened up. Eagle-eyed forensic officers sifted through that pile of spent cartridge shells lying scattered in the school grounds. The grounds to the neighbouring parish church, and the parish of Ardoyne itself, had been saturated within minutes of the shooting by many more RUC and Auxiliaries, all baying for Fenian blood. Men and women going about their ordinary miserable lives were stopped and harassed. Before nightfall the ghetto would be ripped apart and innocents dragged away for interrogation. Those 'connected' were already well offside, the handful of useable weapons held by the local company, long since shifted.

The priest who'd faithfully believed his dog collar would have had evil men succumbing to his will, had withdrawn out of sight back to the Presbytery with a very sore head. His awakened common sense, knocked into him literally, told him not to get further involved. He knew from looking searchingly into the eyes of the gunmen, their hearts, that he was lucky to have come away with just a split head, which he would put down to having simply stumbled over whilst out walking. Meanwhile, he would let his Rector handle any follow-up police inquiries.

Those people persecuted by Black over the years greeted the news of his execution with sheer delight. While no one had yet claimed responsibility for shooting Black, the boys had done a grand job in the opinion of the oppressed. Life for those same people would be that little more tolerable with Black now dead too.

Chapter Fifty-One

The holiday postcard received from Newcastle, County Down, confirmed for Sarah that her mother and father were indeed endeavouring to find some normality in their lives once again, if not for the very first time. For as far back as Sarah could remember, her parents' lives together had been riddled by trouble, much of it brought on through Craig's vendetta against father. While enthusiastically embracing the prospect of her parents finding a new lease of life, she was constantly praying that the RUC would give them chance to. And so far they had not laid a hand on her father since his release from hospital. Such had been the stir caused by O'Hagan, even the family home had been spared a raid in the couple's absence, while others the length and breadth of the area had been turned upside down as Black's mob had gone berserk in searching for his killers. Large areas of nationalist Belfast had run the gauntlet as hordes of B Specials had descended in the dark of night to prosecute their vengeful ways in the weeks that had followed Black's violent death. But no sooner had the forces loyal to the Crown turned their backs had the resisting youth lit celebratory bonfires and daubed slogans on gable ends to proclaim their joy over Black's comeuppance.

Wallace had been forced to abandon the plot to shoot Sean Mor. Ironically, with the Falls saturated by the RUC and B Specials ever since Black's murder, it had been impossible to launch the attack. Anyhow, even if they had set out to do so as planned, it would have proved a futile assault. The UVF had discovered only recently that Sean Mor had not been at home, but instead, away at the seafront living it up. But Wallace remained determined to see Black's death avenged, his way, some day, when McParland and his like would least expect it.

The IRA leadership was pleased to learn that Black's killing was indeed considered a good deed done by their people in the North. Barratt however, was reminded in no uncertain terms that the 'one off' would not set a precedent for further such IRA action in Belfast. Happy with the situation, Barratt gave assurances to the same effect before departing Dublin. But his ducking and diving the enemy was to come to an abrupt and untimely end three days later. As dawn had broken, Gardai, supported by a company of Free State troops, swooped on a remote farmhouse in Co. Monaghan. Barratt and five other leading IRA men, drawn from neighbouring border counties, were caught in possession of incriminating documents pertaining to the IRA's border campaign. Hours earlier, the recently elected Taoiseach, a former IRA commandant, had signed the 'Internment Order' and had personally authorised the reopening of the notorious Curragh Camp, which had once housed British soldiers of occupation. A series of weather-beaten corrugated huts, standing remote in a bleak, windswept bog in County Kildare, was to be home to Barratt and his comrades for the duration of the IRA border campaign.

Barratt's capture marked the beginning of a series of major setbacks for the IRA. Further detentions of prominent IRA men quickly ensued on both sides of the border, while others were killed, either at the hands of the RUC or through premature explosions, as inexperienced, nervous volunteers prepared bombs for use along the border.

By the end of the summer of 1958, the IRA leadership, largely intact, began to realise its worst fear. They judged an apathy to have taken root in the psyche of the majority of Irish people in face of those issues on which the IRA, through armed struggle, were trying to focus minds - the social, economic and political ills that came with the island of Ireland being partitioned.

Dejected republican sympathisers and radical nationalists in the North, realising the Free State had cut them adrift, accepted finally that they stood alone. And while it was hard enough for them to have to endure the battle against those unionist bigots in and out of government, the bemoans of the Catholic clergy and the TDs down south despite their genuine grievances through living under the Orange jackboot, proved, for many, to be the ultimate kick in the teeth, when already fighting against the odds. Consequently, for many republicans, the battle fought daily became one of a more immediate cause, to simply find the means to feed the hungry bellies of crying children.

Steadfast in the determination to redress the fundamentals first and foremost, British colonialism in Ireland, the IRA continued with the border offensive in the vague hope that the minds of the Irish people may yet be stirred, their awakening transformed into popular support for the cause that would see republicans achieve their goal.

By the time Barratt was released along with the last of the Curragh detainees in 1959, due to what the southern government described as 'minimal threat from subversive elements,' the IRA's border campaign had been greatly scaled-down. The anticipated popular support had not materialised. Instead, the IRA were left a spent fighting force much condemned not only by the unionists and British regimes, but also by the Catholic Church, the Southern State and leading nationalist politicians in the North, who all conspired to erode any credence to the claim by the republican movement that the border campaign was justified in seeking to end British involvement in Ireland. Hard evidence of the impact from such condemnation was mirrored by Sinn Fein's momentary increased support in 1957, falling by half. By the spring of 1960, it was generally felt within republican circles that the movement, politically and militarily, was going nowhere. A major debate was soon underway within the leadership as to the future direction of the military campaign. Soon whispers were abound among the rank and file that it was to be abandoned.

Keeping his own morale high and that of his fellow Prisoners of War as Camp OC, Barratt had been raring to go on his release, only to find his enthusiasm to carry the fight forward frustrated by the younger, more politically-minded generation rapidly rising through the ranks of the IRA in his absence. The 'politicos in waiting' - as Barratt cynically judged them to be - were pushing for an ending of the present campaign in favour of a complete revamping of the movement's political and military strategy. They argued for a more 'imaginative, energetic push on all fronts' to be made when the opportune moment presented itself, which they would covertly engineer meantime, through social and political agitation at grassroots.

Much stripped of any real influence in the shaping of things to come, Barratt had little option in the climate prevailing but to stand largely inactive on the sidelines while the debate raged. Still at the top of the RUC wanted list, the homesick Falls Road man, much to his reluctance, was forced to rent a dingy-room above a public bar in the staunchly republican border town of Dundalk, in County Monaghan, from where, on strict orders, he was to simply 'coordinate' any future operations along the border.

Discovering that Barratt had over indulged in physically partaking in military action along the border prior to his detention, the Army Council were keen to keep him safe. Whatever their final decision, come the end of the talking, they were keen to have another popular figure - as Sean Mor had been - to carry the northern brigades with him, in seeking to keep them on-side, come what may.

The internal arguments and counter-arguments within the republican movement was to drag on for a further two years while militarily the IRA surfaced periodically to make a defiant gesture in arms before the young, educated idealists won the day.

On the 26th February 1962, the order came through from the IRA High Command to its volunteers to 'dump all arms.'

With the uneasy peace of that summer warmly welcomed by most in Belfast, those more prominent IRA men from the city who had gone to ground over the past few years cautiously trickled back to their local haunts to resume some kind of normal life, in limbo. They were caught between living in an Orange state and those in authority down south who continued to turn a blind eye to ongoing injustices in the North, which left the republicans' spirit of freedom much subdued, but not broken. From a discreet distance the RUC Special Branch noted the return of those activists long absent. By fooling the brooding republicans into a false sense of security, inroads could be made in gathering vital intelligence as to what was manifesting within the ranks, for the powers-to-be were in no doubt that the IRA threat to their very own being, while cooled, was far from removed.

Though taking a major risk in crossing the border into Northern Ireland, Barratt was not about to drop his guard. Heavily disguised, with his greying locks dyed black, and bespectacled, his now much slimmer frame - down to the lean, hungry years shut away in that hellhole in Kildare - fooling even those closest to him over the years, he set out for his home town one June morning, confident with his new look and forged documents, and determined not to miss the grand affair.

Despite it being one of the happiest days of Sean and Rosie McParland's thirty odd years of marriage, this glorious sunny June morning was nevertheless haunted with the ghost of events ten years earlier. While both so proud and delighted to see their two remaining daughters wed together on the same day to the two Fitzsimmons brothers, sons of much respected parents from up the Falls, Sarah's absence and that of her husband and grandson Sean, left the doting couple quietly torn asunder.

Braving up under the nagging pain gnawing away at his bones as the tumultuous occasion got into full swing, Sean Mor still feared that

Sarah and Anthony's return to the city, even for a rare family occasion such as this, was fraught with danger, due to those same dark events ten years ago. And though heartbroken at not laying eyes on his one and only grandson in the flesh these past years, there was no reason on God's earth why he would put at risk one hair upon the child's head. It had been so damn hard for both parents to tell the then brides-to-be, that it was best for all if their elder sister did not return home, and even harder having to write to Sarah to say the same (between the lines) for in doing so, a mother and father were left wondering when they might see their own flesh and blood again.

Sean Mor's heavy heart over his elder child's forced absence was eased a little later that day at the packed reception in the local GAA hall, with the 'stranger' shaking his hand in extending congratulations, revealing his true identity. All heads turned to witness two old comrades embrace in the middle of the dance floor on being reunited. It was a marriage of a different kind and the band struck up an old favourite which had the happy revellers singing along defiantly.

> 'Twas early, early, in the spring
> The birds did whistle and sweetly sing
> Changing their notes, from tree to tree
> And the song they sang
> Was old Ireland free!'

Long after the newlyweds had set out for the seaside town to begin their joint honeymoon and the band had packed-up and gone, and as the last of the guests staggered off into the night, the brides' mother to her marriage bed of many a year, two soldiers of yesteryear sat with drinks in hand in the front room of No72 to deliberate on events past, present and future, to which they were well attuned in their respective capacity. The housebound civilian, burdened with aching bones and an ulcerated stomach, and the visiting, disfranchised IRA man, not knowing what his next move on the inside should be, had never been happier in each other's company. Though drink had sweetened their tongues and soothed their pain and fears a little, it had not yet gone to their weary heads. They conversed knowingly and with clarity of thought.

'Tell me Sean, where did we go wrong?' Barratt considered himself to be in much need of the experienced man's counsel. Flat-voiced, Sean Mor replied. 'Sad as it is to say, Frankie, I was right. The leadership misjudged the mood of our people. Y'see, they've fallen for the empty rhetoric churned out by moderate politicians and that from the pulpit, which succours the unionists by keeping the conscience of the nationalist people in check. Needless to say, they've succumbed to the measly handouts from the state, for it's more than what anyone down in the Free State is offering them.' Barratt felt his morale sink further on hearing Sean Mor add with a hint of despair. 'I am becoming ever more convinced that those Free State bastards are the real enemy. Their lack of will and spirit to pursue unfinished business and their paranoia over Irish republicans, greatly handicaps our striking arm. The period of reflection which lies ahead for republicans, even washed out ones like me, is for the best.' Sean Mor paused to take a hard slug of whiskey from his glass. Then was speaking again, a little more upbeat. 'Our next move must be the right one. It may take five years, ten years in coming. But come it will, and it will be a turning point in history. It will mark the beginning of the end of British rule in Ireland.' Sean Mor raised the glass to his mouth again to down the rest of his whiskey. 'Believe it or not Frankie, it will be the younger generation who will bring about change, for the world is slowly changing. People will become more resistant to injustice. But dare I say ...' Barratt, hooked by the other's insight and prophetic words, sat forward in his seat to receive the all important word '... in order for change to come about, we in the North need to take the lead. The days of far-removed republicans down south dictating how the war of liberation in the North should be fought are long since gone to my thinking. No! Northern men, those who live under the Orange thumb, who know the mood of folk on the day, need to prepare to fight a different fight. A political one! One which will capitalise fully on the situation when the people themselves are up in arms.'

Barratt had thought that he would never hear Sean Mor advocate a political fight over armed struggle. And Sean Mor knew it. But he had firm conviction in what he now believed to be the only way to see the British out of Ireland and to secure a lasting and just peace between all of its people.

'It's the only way, Frankie, otherwise the blood sacrifice will have been in vain.'

Barratt slipped away to a safe house later that night with Sean Mor's closing words, much food for thought.

Chapter Fifty-Two

Young Sean was sensitive to the tension between his parents, and although they put on a united front that day in endeavouring to make this his best birthday yet, it troubled him. Frances and her son Drew, licking his lips by Sean's side at the kitchen table, were both oblivious to any suggestion of a fallout between the parents of the birthday boy as Sarah enthusiastically lit the ten candles topping the iced cake, while Anthony poured generous measures of cream soda into five tall glasses.

Two nights before, as he'd tossed and turned in his bed in excited anticipation of his tenth birthday, Sean had overheard muted, though raised voices come from the adjoining bedroom. Mother had sounded very disappointed at not being able to return to Ireland for Aunt Caithlin and

Bridget's wedding; his father, annoyed that she should even contemplate returning to that 'God forsaken place'. Tears had flowed and his father had tried to console her. Father had revealed his own frustration too then over not returning home for his own sister's wedding, Aunt Ann-Marie's, two years earlier. But mother had shunned his sympathy with her retort, 'Well, when will we see our folks again ... *when they're dead*'? There had been a long silence then, broken only by mother sobbing into her pillow. Sean had finally fallen asleep, wondering what reason existed for his father to refer to where *he* had been born, as a 'God forsaken place'.

The following night, cosy by the fireside, Sean had had his curiosity over his father's concerns satisfied, though not by his mother explaining that his grandparents were 'not up to making the journey to England' for his birthday, but instead through being told that they in turn could not go to Ireland just yet because of 'the troubles'.

With his imagination and curiosity stoked through mother's fireside storytelling, Sean had hoped a trip to Ireland would not be too far off. Now, knowing the troubles there to be the cause of his father's concern for their safety if going, Sean accepted without complaint, that his chances of visiting Ireland were doomed for as long as the troubles - of which he'd heard his parents speak in hushed whispers on occasion - continued.

With his mother urging him to make a wish before blowing out the birthday candles, Sean closed his eyes to request silently of whoever listened, that his mother and father would kiss and make up. This, for Sean, was more desirable than anything else he could possibly wish for. All the candle flames were blown out at the first attempt. All others gathered broke into song simultaneously on a mother's prompting. The ten year old was happy at heart just to see his mother and father embrace to sing to him. Nothing else in the world mattered now.

Sean and his best friend Drew Malpass had been inseparable over the years and as with summers past, the summer of 1962 was no exception. They spent each day of the holiday playing late into the evening in the dense wood backing onto 101 Forest Park. Sarah was hoarse from calling them in at dusk each night. Never once did they answer her first time and would eventually timidly turn up just as she was about to set out in search of them, her fears falsely raised once again.

With faces and hands caked in mud, their knees scraped and legs blistered by stinging nettles, a hot soapy bath shared was most commonly the order of the day before either boy was allowed anywhere near the kitchen table to stuff his protesting belly. As they scoffed, their eyes, normally filled with innocent mischief, would be heavy for the want of sleep. The fresh air from playing out guaranteed to see both boys to bed without protest once filling their bellies.

On the nights when Drew did not stay over, Anthony would put his newly acquired driving skills and reliable second-hand car to good use. On carrying a sound asleep Drew to the car and placing him on the back seat with great care, he would drive the child the short distance home to his mother.

Sarah and Frances - their friendship cemented as like that of their children - always had the school holiday weeks off from work to ensure that the children did not come to any harm. While always reminding the boys to be careful in the wood, they were happier knowing they played more safely there as opposed to the streets, where the road traffic was steadily on the increase, and with it, tragic road accidents with scores of youngsters mown down.

For Sean and Drew, the wood was a child's ultimate adventure playground, with a thousand and one places for building secret dens and acting out the roles of their favourite film stars of the big screen - cowboys, fast on the draw, caped crusaders, and swashbuckling sword-wielding Knights of the Round Table. It was while re-enacting one such Hollywood scene in their own boyish playful way that the summer holiday of '62, but for the real heroics of one young adventurer, ended in near tragedy.

Skillfully managing a balancing act between the leafy branches high up the ancient oak down by the riverbank, in preparing to spring the surprise capture of his foe, the evil sheriff of the wood, Sean braced himself on spying Drew appear below on tiptoe, his wooden sword drawn at the ready. In glee at seeing the unsuspecting sheriff walk straight into the trap, Sean, prince of thieves, defender of the poor, drew his handmade wooden dagger from the elastic snake belt holding up his khaki shorts, and waited with bated breath until the enemy was immediately below.

'Death to the sheriff and his men!' was Sean's battle cry as he leapt out of the tree.

Slight of frame and nimble on his feet, Drew side-stepped the surprise and saw Sean fall and land on the balls of his feet, then spring forward head over heels without effort to tumble untidily down the steep riverbank and into the dark and deep calm water below, where he went under in the blink of an eye. It would all have been hysterically funny if not knowing that Sean could not swim to save his own life - literally. The endless notes excusing Sean from partaking in the school swimming lesson, mostly forged by classmates, had since become a standing joke among pupils on seeing a gullible teacher fall for them each time.

Seeing Sean's ashen face poke out of the water, his arms flailing, and hearing him scream a gurgled 'Help!' before disappearing suddenly again, Drew dropped his sword as he ran forward to dive into the uninviting water's decreasing circle. It was a dark, murky world below the water's surface, and despite the weeks of endless sunshine, the water was ice-cold. Drew reached out searchingly in the icy pitch black and kicked his legs violently in signalling his presence. He was sinking deeper into the murky depths and his oxygen was fast running out when he felt his right hand brush against something that he instinctively sensed as being human. With a concentrated effort, Drew ringed his right arm around and under what he was convinced was Sean's head, before fighting desperately with his left hand, his heart and lungs about to explode, back to the top. With his head at last breaking the surface, Drew gasped the fresh air far into his aching lungs and cried out in joy and despair both on seeing Sean's face re-emerge beside him. With Sean's eyes closed and his lips turning blue, Drew knew he had not a moment to lose. Manipulating Sean's limp body so that his best friend's face was facing the sky, and with his will-power and skinny frame mustering the strength of two boys his age, Drew kicked out for dear life - that of his friend he prayed - and began to swim the short distance but what seemed to him to be an ocean's width, to the edge of the riverbank. Reaching it, exhausted, he somehow found that reserved strength to drag Sean, a dead weight, out of the water. On the riverbank Drew wasted no time checking for a pulse – no pulse, then putting into practice those life saving techniques he'd observed his movie star heroine perform on the big screen only the previous Saturday. Sobbing uncontrollably and with the penetrating chill of the water seizing him, the fight to save a life was on. Drew mumbled the procedure to himself in between applying mouth-to-mouth and chest massage. After a few moments, Sean's eyes shot open, but he struggled to breathe. Rolling Sean onto his stomach to sit astride the small of his back, Drew thrust the palms of his hands under Sean's wet t-shirt and began to forcibly work his upper back in an attempt to pump water from Sean's lungs. After a few anxious seconds it came in violent spurts and Sean fully regained consciousness. Realising the severity of the moment, Sean began to weep and shake uncontrollably. Thrusting his face to the sky, a shriek of sheer delight escaped Drew's aching lungs. 'YEEEESSSSSS!

   Gathering themselves together finally, the two boys scrambled up the riverbank and darted through the trees into a clearing, where they hurriedly stripped naked before collapsing exhausted onto their backs, the blistering hot sun beating their bellies and chasing the chill from their bones. Side-by-side they lay silent and still, with the gigantic clear-blue sky overhead engulfing them. Suddenly they were very conscious of every sound, movement and smell about them, the bees buzzing over the honeysuckle, its sweet scent mixing with that of a hundred or more other wild flowers in full bloom in the meadow, the fluttering of butterfly wings, and their own, almost desperate, rasps of breath. The realisation of life being so precious dawned as never before. After a few moments of golden silence, and each whispering a prayer of thanks, frets over what lay ahead of them were voiced in turn.

'Our mums will kill us when they find out,' Sean warned. Drew, his voice high-pitched, lambasted his friend. 'Who's gonna tell them? I'm not, are you?'

'How can we keep such a thing secret?' Sean begged. 'I nearly died for flip sake!'

'Listen, if we tell, *if you tell*, we will never be allowed to come here again ... right? So where else can we go?' Sean thought for a moment before giving a reply of sorts. 'What about my sandal?'

'*Your sandal*?' Drew echoed, flabbergasted.

'Yeah! My sandal! What am I to say?'

Drew sat up like a Jack-in-the-Box and felt the sharp crisp grass crease his buttocks. 'A minute ago you were drowning, and now you're worrying about an old shoe.'

Still flat on his back, Sean was quick to correct Drew. 'It wasn't an old shoe. My Mum bought them only the other day. I shouldn't have been wearing them. They were for best.' Not believing what he was hearing, Drew sounded just like the evil High Sheriff issuing orders. 'I don't give a frig about your sandal! I just know if my Mum finds out about this, I'll not be able to sit down for a week. So you can just make up some other story!'

Sean knew he owed Drew everything now. He had saved his life. The least he could do was save him a good tanning.

'Okay. I won't say anything. I'll think something up.'

'Good!' Drew said satisfied.

They both stayed silent for a moment and took stock. It was very easy for Sean to say what he felt he ought to say, with sincerity and feeling.

'Thanks Drew ... for saving my life.'

Drew shuffled uncomfortably on his bum. 'Ah, that's okay. What was I supposed to do?'

Realising what the outcome would have been if it had been Drew who had fallen in the water and couldn't swim, Sean presented himself with a real challenge.

'I know one thing, when we get back to school, I won't be skipping any more swimming lessons.'

'Bully for you, Sean,' Drew said, with not a hint of cynicism. Sean sat upright and looked his best friend straight in the face. 'I won't forget what you did today, not ever. You're a hero!'

Embarrassed by the praise, Drew leapt to his feet and looked away shyly while massaging his bum earnestly. 'C'mon,' he said. 'It's time we were getting back.'

Compelled to demonstrate how real his gratitude truly was, Sean felt a tingle of fear and excitement combined sweep over him.

'Pass me your knife, Drew. There is something we need to do.'

Having sensed the feeling in Sean's voice, Drew reached for his shorts nearby, dug into a deep pocket to find the prized penknife - its existence unknown to all others - and gingerly offered it to Sean.

'What you gonna do, Sean?' Drew asked, feeling a little uneasy. Standing to take the knife in hand and opening out its larger blade, Sean looked Drew in the eye. 'Don't be afraid.'

Sean held out his left hand and without hesitation, though careful not to cut too deeply, sliced open the middle of his palm with the knife's blade.

'Just like our heroes, we too will be blood brothers,' said Sean, handing the knife back to Drew and gestured with his eyes that he do the same. Feeling a little nauseated at the sight of Sean's blood glistening in the sun as it trickled down his deathly-white skin, Drew knew he dare not run scared from the challenge, even if he wanted to, which he didn't. Experiencing a little excitement over what was expected of him, Drew took the knife in hand and he too, slowly, cleanly, drew it across the middle of his left palm. With a trickle of bright red blood running down the inside of Drew's left arm, it was Sean who stepped forward to place his bleeding hand in Drew's. They each looked searchingly into the other's eyes without feeling the need to utter another word as their young blood flowed as one.

In continued silence the two boys dressed in their dried out clothes, and with their socks and shoes tucked under an arm, their self-inflicted wounds congealed by a baking sun, they set out for home with an arm thrown across each other's shoulders. Like soldiers returning triumphant from battle, Sean and Drew marched across the meadow, a blaze of amazing colour kissed by the summer sun and blessed with God's small creatures.

For both boys, their friendship had been baptised as sacred in the river that day, and had been sealed for life through the sharing of their blood - a secret, never to be told.

Chapter Fifty-Three

On a sultry summer's night in 1964, a loud knock on the front door at 101 Forest Park, had a restless Sean rolling out of bed and scurrying on tiptoe to the top of the stairs, cast in darkness, to investigate who called. Stealing a peep over the landing banister, he watched his father open the door and heard him exclaim aloud, '*Christy*! God Almighty!' Sean was left in wide-eyed wonder as a heavily scarred and powerfully built man, much fairer and a little taller than his own father, stepped into the house to throw his arms around his brother. Under the dim glow of the hallway light the two men held each other close in complete silence. The look on his father's face, said it all for Sean, whose sleepy eyes suffused with tears.

Much excited by the night's events, Sean quietly descended the stairs halfway, to sit and listen as best he could to the muted conversation rising from the sitting-room. It sounded to Sean as though everyone was speaking at once. After a little while, and struggling to keep his eyes open, Sean climbed the stairs silently and staggered to his bed, wherein, with his sleepy head hitting the pillow, he fell into a deep sleep.

With pleasantries exchanged, Christy correctly sensed Anthony and Sarah's unease with his facial scars. It was never easy to broach the subject, but suspecting that Anthony - and possibly his wife - already knew the hard, brutal facts, Christy spoke with a Donegal brogue as strong as his brother's. 'I take it you know why I look the way I do?'

Christy had addressed his question directly to Anthony who sat beside Sarah at the opposite end of the kitchen table. A moment's silence followed, before Anthony replied. 'Kilty told me all there was to know. I in turn, told Sarah. It's the way our relationship works.'

'I didn't murder Stormy Wether,' said Christy, falling sombre again. 'I'd cornered him on his own ... challenged him to a fair fight, but he pulled a knife. As we fought, he stumbled and fell. The blade, the very one he'd used on me, went straight through his heart.'

Christy opened his own heart for the first time in years and went on to reveal how he'd then fled to America, and why he had not made contact with the family for so long, even though he had known of Seamus and Owen's deaths. Knowing their own fears and anxieties of recent years, Anthony and Sarah knew that Christy spoke the truth. Knowing also that Christy was off-loading a great deal of personal pain in the process, Sarah admired her husband's stance when informing Christy, sincere of voice, that it was best he put his troubled past behind him. His anguish eased by Anthony and Sarah's sympathetic response, their gentle words, Christy revealed his wish to be likewise received when returning to his homeland.

'I'm flying to Ireland the day after next,' he quietly informed. 'I hope and pray my mother and father, the girls and ... Seamus and Owen, God rest them, will forgive me.'

Exhausted after such a long journey, Christy, and his hosts for the night, retired to their beds, only to lie restless with vivid bittersweet memories of yesteryear to the forefront of their minds.

Sean found himself the centre of attention once descending the stairs that following morning with his mother proudly presenting him in the kitchen to his Uncle Christy, whose tanned, otherwise handsome features made the pencil-line scars crisscrossing his squarish face appealing in a strange sort of way. Already forewarned by his mother not to ask any questions as to Uncle Christy's car accident, Sean craned his neck to look up at the newfound uncle and felt two huge hands clasp his bony little shoulders. He saw his Uncle Christy eye him up and down as if proud to be an uncle, and heard him proclaim, 'A true Brennan if ever there was one!'

Over a hearty breakfast of bacon and eggs, Sean spoke excitedly as he answered his uncle's questions, revealing details about the more exciting events taking place in his life - bar events in the wood two years earlier of course - and of which Uncle Christy seemed genuinely keen to hear. Sean felt easy with himself in asking some safe questions of Uncle Christy in turn.

'Sure I've seen film stars for real,' bragged Christy. 'I see them cruise along the boulevard each day in their big, swanky cars. When I come back later, we'll talk some more, okay!'

Sean was left greatly excited by what was proposed and would be sure to learn all there was to know about life in America.

As far as Sean gathered from the conversation around the kitchen table, Uncle Christy would be travelling to Ireland the following day to spend some time at home with Gran and Grandad Brennan. Sean heard his mother suggest to his father that he should travel with Uncle Christy as their presence at home together, she opined, would give their parents a wonderful surprise. Holding his breath, expecting his father to erupt in fury over such an idea, Sean was both surprised and happy to see him lean across the table and plant a kiss on his mum's cheek. He would go as she advised. Sean suddenly held a little hope that he at least, might accompany his father and Uncle Christy on the journey, and would at last see that beautiful land, his homeland - as mother often reminded him - with his own eyes.

Studying with inquisitive eyes the battered faces of the big intimidating men in well cut suits, who swarmed around Christy in Donegal Danny's that Saturday afternoon to proudly shake his hand, Anthony considered the innocent faces of his wife and son, both dwarfed among the local men, to be the odd ones out in a rogues gallery.

Sean was in awe of the mean-looking men, friends of his father's friend, Mr Kilty, who himself, in Sean's calculating eye, would not look out-of-place in a gangster movie. He was left greatly excited by the fact that his father had such acquaintances who queued to shake his hand and that of Uncle Christy, close by his side. His schoolmates would be sorely envious when knowing that he had been in the company of such a bunch of shady characters - gangsters all, Sean was convinced.

The south London boxing fraternity from years past and those making a name for themselves present day, had turned out in strength to welcome home to the Smoke one of their own, even though not locally born and bred. Jack Kilty had rallied old and new together for the grand occasion and presided over the handshakes when introducing each of the faces to Anthony, and those newcomers to Christy. Anthony was not at all surprised that Christy was still held in such high regard by Kilty, who had always spoken fondly of him down all the years.

Sean's excitement over the scene to which he was witness, turned to disappointment on his godmother offering to drive mother and he back home. His father, Uncle Christy, Jack Kilty and company were all headed to a club up West. Never before did Sean long so much to be a grownup. The adult world seemed much more exciting to him - albeit a dangerous one.

Anthony assured Sarah that he would not be long in returning home. She kissed him on the cheek. Anthony climbed in behind the wheel of his car to drive Christy to an old favourite haunt.

The glitzy West End club was packed to the rafters as invited Irishmen and Cockneys of influence and power came together as one, to drink in celebration of Christy Brennan's return. Seizing the first opportunity to do so, Kilty manoeuvred his good friend Christy into a corner of the lounge bar, where he set about lavishing Christy with attractive inducements to remain in London. There was the generous offer of money, a house, a car, anything Christy wanted, in return for helping Kilty prepare a budding southpaw for his first fight, the first of many before the big one. Christy was the perfect coach in Kilty's considered opinion. While knowing Kilty had good intentions at heart, it was a painful experience for Christy. Talk of the boxing world brought bittersweet memories of bygone days flooding back. Christy verbally fought his way out of the corner by steadfastly refusing Kilty's offer, though accepted the cockney's hand finally. Gripping Kilty's hand firmly in his, twice the size, Christy pulled his former gaffer close, so to be heard under the din, and delivered a message straight from the heart.

'I know what you're thinking, Jack. You believe that if it hadn't been for you, I'd never have ended up with a face like this. Well, let me tell you something. You were a good father to me in those days. I haven't forgotten it, and I never will.' Christy had hit the truth on the chin. The scarring of Christy at the hands of the bastard Scot, Stormy Wether, had been gnawing away at Kilty's insides for years. But the Irishman had just knocked his burden of guilt out cold, and Kilty was so glad. The cockney's voice trembled with emotion. 'God bless you, Christy Brennan. You've made an old man very happy.' Christy forced a smile and nodded toward the bar. 'C'mon. Let me buy you a drink for old times sake.' Both men paraded up to the bar under the rapturous applause of the regular patrons and those dedicated followers of a cruel sport gathered together. For most, it was just like the good old days.

Arriving home steadily just before midnight and parking the car outside his home, Anthony knew Sarah would be waiting up for him, as she always did when he went out for a drink, a seldom event these days. Nights at Donegal Danny's had truly never been the same since the death of Mick Onion, of which Christy now knew. With Anthony telling his brother of those troubled events leading up to the deaths of their good friend and acquaintances, Christy had whispered a prayer for the repose of Mick Onion's soul.

It had been a long day, and Anthony was relieved it had gone smoothly. He had been dreading any fallout between his own and the cockney crew, for when drink flowed in such supply, anything was possible. Thankfully, his prayers had been answered. Even Christy, whom he knew to have been crazy for the drink, had held himself very well, despite drinking a bucketful. Asleep at his side, Anthony nudged his brother awake and proceeded to help a rousing Christy out of the car and up the garden path. The long flight, too little sleep, and the drink, had got the better of Christy. All that Anthony wanted to do now, was to get his brother safely to bed and his own head down. On reaching out with door key in hand, the front door was opened to him by a uniformed policeman, long in face, his helmet tucked under an arm. Anthony's heart sank.

From two miles up and with not a cloud in sight that Sunday morning, Ireland indeed appeared below like a patchwork quilt of forty shades of green. Anthony was filled with mixed emotions as the plane touched down on the tarmac at Dublin airport; Christy, more so apprehensive, just as he had been two days before, when his trans-Atlantic plane had flown over Ireland.

It felt indescribably odd for them both to be back on Irish soil, visited once again in the aftermath of yet another family tragedy. As Anthony had spoken in whispers to Christy the morning after his arrival to tell him of Mick Onion's death, their sister Colleen had set out over the potato field back home in search of their father. She had found him lying face down among the potato tops, which he'd religiously inspected each morning. He had not been long dead, his body still warm. The parish doctor had diagnosed the cause of death to be a massive heart attack. Their father's death, while not unexpected, as his health had not been the best lately, nevertheless came as a bombshell. Anthony and Christy's main concern now, was for their mother. They knew her sense of loss was immeasurable and that it would certainly test her resilient character to the limit. They wasted no time in hiring out a car and hitting the long road northwest, each lost in their own private thoughts over the tragedies to have plagued their family.

Throwing his older brother slumped in the passenger seat an occasional sideways glance, Anthony knew Christy to be churning inside with guilt, having left his visit home too late. Anthony had been through the pain of it himself and his heart went out to Christy, who stared blankly at the road ahead while fingering nervously the Saint Christopher medal hanging from around his neck.

Sean had been packed off to school that day minutes after his father and Uncle Christy had left for the airport. Sarah and Anthony had thought it best that Sean keep his mind positively occupied at a time when a death within the family was once again an unwelcome reality. Coming with the death of the boy's grandfather, Anthony was reminded of the heavy price they'd all been made to pay, were still paying for the actions of others twelve years earlier, when deciding not to risk taking his son to Ireland to meet his grandparents. Anthony shuddered still at the mere thought of yet being dragged into the bloody events of that July day, if ever venturing back to Belfast, to any part of Ireland for that matter. It was such a small place and news travelled like wildfire. Thus Sean and Sarah had been left behind.

Not wishing to raise Sean's anxiety through explaining those black events of twelve years before, Anthony had not told a lie when saying that it would not be appropriate for Sean to meet his relations at such a time, when thoughts would be of those passed away.

Sarah meanwhile, while not totally dismissing the possibility of questions being asked if returning to Belfast, considered this very unlikely, given the violent occurrences in between time, which had no doubt put the killings that July day, into the shade. But Anthony had not been entirely convinced by her reassurances over recent years. In Sarah's mind, Anthony's initial fear had manifested into a deep-rooted paranoia about Ireland, and was subsequently being overprotective of them all. She prayed silently that in the event of her receiving a likewise call from Belfast, he would not stand in her way. She already had her mind made up on what she would do. Indeed, on witnessing Christy's silent heartbreak at not having made time to say goodbye to his father, Sarah had a yearning to return to Belfast as never before. She was set on a heart-to-heart with Anthony on his return, and was hoping that his time spent in Ireland would relieve some of his anxieties over returning there again some day, in the not-too-distant future.

The grey, uninteresting teacher with the monotone voice, going through the motion of lecturing home economics to the final year pupils assembled, should have stayed in bed that morning as far as young Sean was concerned. His thoughts were for a different world entirely. Looking out of his classroom window at the billowing plumes of thick, dirty, black smoke escaping from the chimneys of the many factories and town-houses standing gloomily at the foot of a man made hill, and for as far as the eye could see, the disinterested pupil tried hard to imagine walking free and without concern in lush fields of green and gold. He wondered too, when or if, he might ever see Uncle Christy again. They hadn't had time to have that chat. Sean was still none the wiser as to what life in the land of film stars and movie making was truly like.

In the eyes of both returning brothers stepping out of the car, the old home place looked just as it always had - grim and poor. Even under a warm summer sun and despite the breathtaking scenery, impoverished childhood memories came flooding back. Sad too, was the absence of old Jack, the family Collie. Old age had at last caught up with him.

Colleen, now a mature young woman, showing marked signs of the strain endured these past days, was first to greet the brothers at the half door, complete with black bow once again.

'*Anthony*! *Christy*!' Colleen fell into the arms of her brothers and sobbed her heart out. The muffled cries of a newborn had Anthony and Christy lifting their heads from off Colleen's shoulders to see their married sister, Ann-Marie, standing in the doorway, cradling an infant wrapped protectively in a blanket. This woman, appearing much older than her thirty-three years, braved a smile and said, 'My son was born an hour after Da died. I'm going to name him Daniel.'

Very frail, her pointed face deathly grey, and with a mane of hair the same colour falling carefree over her narrow shoulders, mother appeared like a Banshee as she came to stand alongside Anne-Marie. Seeing her last remaining sons standing shoulder to shoulder in front of her, the mother, empty of tears, drew the palms of her hands over her tortured face and began to keen.

Barely coping with the agony of the moment, two brothers and two sisters slowly filed into the house. All followed their mother through the silent throng of mourners toward that room wherein her husband, their father, lay in wake, just as Seamus and Owen had, some fourteen years before.

Chapter Fifty-Four

Christy's overwhelming sense of guilt at having contributed to his father's death despite a loving mother's assurances that father had not held a grievance against him, took its toll on the day of the funeral. With Christy going to pieces at the graveside, Anthony was quick to reach out to save his brother from collapsing and falling into the gaping hole as their father was lowered into the ground. Slumping into Anthony's arms under the spontaneous gasp of the hundreds gathered, Christy was led away to recover his composure under the glare of all others, intrigued to know how Christy Brennan had come to be disfigured. But they would never know.

Herself barely coping with the ordeal of losing a husband, Mary Brennan thanked God that Christy had not been killed in the street fight. Christy had told her everything, and she, like his father, held no grievance against him. Seeing her eldest boy comforted in a corner of the graveyard by his younger brother, she experienced a little peace of mind, knowing her sons had made their peace.

Somehow the bereaved family got through the remainder of the day, and with Christy also succumbing to the loss of three consecutive nights sleep as darkness fell, only Anthony and Colleen were left alone by a low burning turf fire, to reflect over the week's sad events.

'It's a hard life sure enough, Anthony, what with father dying the very day before Christy's return. It makes you wonder if there's a God at all.' Though not surprised to discover Colleen - the once little angel in all their eyes - questioning her faith, Anthony was not so sombre in his reply. 'I've asked myself that very question many a time. I've doubted his being too. But I believe he exists, for he has comforted me in my despair.'

It was Anthony's faith, bold in the face of all their troubles, which rekindled a little faith in his sister - still that little angel in his eyes.

Brother and sister sat until dawn, not speaking much, but hoping their silent prayers would be answered; neither sought anything extraordinary, only peace of mind.

With the small, close-knit community gradually returning to normal rural life over the following three days, the remaining Brennans and extended family found themselves assembled once again in the parish church to bear witness to the christening of baby Daniel, grandson of the late Daniel Brennan. With all reaffirming their own vows of faith, their renewed hopes of receiving a change of fortune were soon realised with Christy requesting the permission of all to stay at home, permanently. Tears of joy were shed by the women on hearing this, and Anthony showed his delight and approval by taking Christy's hand in his, to say with a good heart, 'God bless you, Christy.'

The rest of the day had been celebrated quietly, and to see mother smile through her sorrows, made everyone's day.

It was Anthony who was first to retire to his bed that night to catch his first full night's sleep in nearly two weeks, but was soon disturbed from his slumber by Christy turning in also to share the big bed with him, just as they had in their childhood days. Colleen was sleeping in along with mother in the upper room. Feeling Christy's cold feet brush against his, Anthony was forced to say, jokingly, 'Jasus Christy ... the first job you need to do around here, is knock thon wall through and build a room for yourself.'

'And buy another bloody bed,' Christy interjected humorously.

'You took the very words right out of my mouth,' Anthony mused.

'Quiet in there, you two!' mother called-out lightheartedly from the adjoining bedroom, and her two boys settled down in an instant. Tugging the rough blankets close, Anthony rolled onto his side to fall into a deep sleep with a peaceful smile upon his face.

With a long road in front of him, Anthony was up as the cock crowed. Just as he had always done when at home, he washed and shaved with the use of the old enamel bowl placed on top of the stonewall at the back of the house. The same wall separated the pebbled street from that cursed potato field where he'd spent endless hours in backbreaking labour, and where his father had been found dead four days earlier. The early morning sunlight danced upon the healthy green potato tops, rustled by a gentle breeze. Will be a good crop the year, Anthony thought, recalling to mind how he'd sweated buckets working the same field in his younger day. Finishing with the razor, he marvelled at how the silver mist shrouded the high peaks of blue-black mountains set further back. New lambs bleating in neighbouring fields broke an otherwise tranquil silence. Away to his right, the shimmering broad Atlantic looked so magnificent - so beguiling. Nothing had changed. Everything was in its place.

Hearing footsteps approach from behind him, Anthony, towelling dry his face, turned to find Christy standing close by. Christy wore a serious frown upon his scarred face, though fresh from a good night's sleep.

'What is it, Christy?' Anthony asked.

Christy took a step closer, the palms of his hands nervously brushing the sides of his trousers. He looked Anthony straight in the eye.

'I just wanted to say thanks brother, for helping me through the last few days.' Christy gave a little cough before continuing, 'I, ah ... I also want to say, sorry. Sorry for the hard times I gave you, here at home, y'know ...' Anthony halted Christy in mid-flow. 'Christy, forget it. We were young then. We're wiser to the ways of the world for it.' Christy smiled. There was something equally important which remained to be said. 'Anthony. I don't want you to think that I'm worming my way ...' Again, Anthony was quick to put his brother's unease at ease. 'I don't think anything of the sort. Just remember though, that for as long as mother, Colleen and Ann-Marie are alive, this will remain their home too.'

'I understand,' confirmed Christy, and added with a purpose, 'And yours too, Anthony.' Anthony shook his head and smiled. 'No, Christy. I've made my home elsewhere. I've no interest in this place, only that it stays in the family name. That's how mother and father would want it.'

'It won't pass to another living soul as long as I'm alive, Anthony. I'll work it well, maybe as good as the oul boy did, eh?' They both smiled.

For Anthony, there was but one matter that remained a concern to him and he sought to make Christy wise to it for the good of his own future.

'Christy, be warned! Stay well clear of Belfast. It's a dangerous place. That's why I won't be travelling home too often, perhaps not at all. Belfast is too close for comfort. I wouldn't wish to put temptation in Sarah's path by bringing her here. She's got family up there still. Don't ask me to say any more. Just remember what I've said today.'

Thinking it best not to pry further, Christy could not help but be genuinely concerned for Anthony in consideration of certain situations that were obviously to one day come about. Wearing a frown, he sought to give his brother food for thought by presenting one such scenario to him.

'What if, y' know, Sarah's folks were ill, if one of them ...' Not wanting to even think about such an eventuality, Anthony interrupted Christy before he finished delivering the conundrum of sorts. 'I know Christy, I know. All I'll say, is that my son's safety, his life, comes before anything or anyone else.' Anthony realised he'd said enough already and closed the line of conversation by opening up with another, less serious in tone. 'Anyway, enough said. Your turn to cook breakfast.' The brothers walked back to the house side-by-side in a new found expression of support for each other, though Christy's concern for Anthony was no less real.

Later that morning, Anthony eased the pain of saying goodbye for himself and others by making the event as pleasant and as swift as possible. Starting up the hire car, Anthony leaned out of the driver's side window to quip, 'If Christy Brennan doesn't pull his weight you girls sort him out! D'yeh hear?' The two women of the house, joined by Ann-Marie clutching young Daniel close, waved him off with forced, though genuine smiles. Standing sheepishly to one side, Christy simply nodded to Anthony, and doing so, reaffirmed what he had said to him a moment ago: that he would come running if ever Anthony needed him. Anthony, in turn, gave a final salute before setting out on the return journey.

With one final piece of unfinished business to attend to before departing Donegal, Anthony pulled up the hire car outside the local parish school, which stood isolated on the edge of a windswept bog, about a mile from home. With school just started, all those children from miles around were at their desks. Master O'Doherty was very strict on timekeeping as Anthony knew only too well. Leaping over the low stonewall and crossing the rough concrete play area to enter the grim, one classroom building, Anthony peered through the half glazed classroom door from the narrow hallway and saw that nothing in the school had changed much in the twenty-three years since he'd last set foot in the dreary hole. Umpteen holy pictures were dotted here and there between the dusty bookshelves. Statues of the Blessed Virgin and holy saints adorned all four walls of the long, narrow room, while at its opposite end, Master O'Doherty, calling the register, was suitably cast against a well used blackboard. The black cape he wore over his stiff-neck collar shirt, the round wire-rimmed glasses perched precariously on the end of a long, thin snout, made him appear even more sinister. In Anthony's eye, he too had not changed much, a little greyer perhaps, his voice, intimidating more so still, than authoritarian.

Some thirty pupils, boys and girls between the ages of five and eleven, sat rigid and very quiet at neat rows of long tables and only dared to speak in answer to their name when called out.

'Doherty, Phillip.'

'Here Sir.'

'Doherty, Michael Joseph.'
'Here Sir.'
'Kearney, Daniel.'
'Here Sir.'

With the register complete, Master O'Doherty scanned the class to double-check for absentees and spied Anthony, who he did not recognise immediately, standing beyond the classroom door looking at him with a hard, embittered face. Anthony saw O'Doherty rise from his chair and come marching down the central aisle with fists clenched by his side.

'Eyes front!' O'Doherty commanded over his shoulder at those not even thinking about it. He added sternly, 'Kearney. Give out the morning prayers.'

O'Doherty had come out of the classroom with the intention to demand who it was who interrupted his first lesson. Unknown to him, he was about to learn a lesson of his own. One he would not forget in a hurry.

'Yes. What do you want?' Back in the classroom young Kearney began to recite the Lord's prayer. 'Our Father, who art in Heaven ...'

'So you don't remember me, eh?'

O'Doherty sensed the cynicism in the caller's voice and it irritated him no end.

'Should I?'

'Yes, you should, *you sick bastard*!' snarled Anthony. 'You beat me senseless often enough.'

Feeling suddenly ill on realising who it was that faced him, O'Doherty turned to retreat back into the safety of the classroom, but there was no escape. Anthony pulled O'Doherty back into the hall by the scruff of his neck, spun him around and pinned him against the classroom door, which shook violently under the heave of bodies. There was a pause in the prayer being recited by all on the other side of the door as O'Doherty's head was rammed forcibly against the door's frame. The wire-rimmed glasses now sat at an awkward angle on O'Doherty's nose. Fired with rage, Anthony tightened his grip on the ashen-faced man, trembling in his hobnail boots, not daring to move, nor open his mouth.

'Listen good, O'Doherty! I know it was you who put young Slattery in the grave all those years ago. You made the lives of countless others, myself included, as miserable as sin, and you, running to Mass every Sunday and bouncing your head of the chapel floor. Well know this, you murdering bastard: you couldn't educate a donkey to stand still.'

O'Doherty felt his bowels churn. Anthony stepped up closer and with his face an inch or less from O'Doherty's ghostly-white one, seethed, 'My sister's wean will be coming to this hole of a place one day. Hopefully by then, you'll be long gone. But if by chance you're still here, if you so much as lay a finger on him, I'll come back here, and so help me God, I'll break every bone in your body! Do you understand me?' O'Doherty nodded to save his life. 'Now get back in there and say a prayer for young Slattery

... you fucking hypocrite, and one for yourself while you're at it. For your soul needs saving more than his.' Anthony released his grip on O'Doherty and rubbed his hand against his own chest as if rubbing something vile from it.

Buckling at the knees, O'Doherty barely made it back to his desk and joined in the last Hail Mary. Anthony was back in his car and on the road south again before the sniggering children and the shamed schoolteacher said 'Amen.'

Chapter Fifty-Five

Sarah's faint hope of persuading Anthony to accompany her and Sean to Belfast for a short visit later that summer, was shattered, not through his undoing, but due rather to the inflammatory mouthing in public of threats of renewed violence back home. It was not republicans - still in reflective mode following an ineffectual border campaign - who made such utterances now, but Protestant extremists, riled by the newly selected Northern Ireland Prime Minister's flirtations with northern nationalists and the government of the Irish Republic. Any attempt to accommodate, if only the social needs of Catholics in the North or toward building any form of cross-border cooperation with southern politicos, was judged by those extremists as a 'sell out to Irish Republicans and Popery.' An enraged Protestant spokesman vowed bloodshed to dislodge, if need be, those elected representatives of the 'People of Ulster' if going too far in appeasing 'enemies of the state and the Satanists in Rome.' These were not idle threats and the autumn of 1964 saw the worst rioting in Belfast for thirty years, with the lower Falls bearing the brunt of loyalist mob attack.

Confronted with such a hostile climate and the threat of further violence, Sarah knew it to be futile to hold hope that even she, on her own, could return to Belfast, let alone suggest it to Anthony. While Anthony judged the latest outbreak of trouble in the North as another blessing in disguise, he was gravely concerned that the gradual decline in the health of Sean Mor may culminate in Sarah being called home by family at a time when it would be very risky to do so. Anthony though, was not fooling himself. He knew there would be no holding back Sarah the day such a call came through. He accepted the fact also that it was not a case of if, but when this could happen. Though he'd promised to stand by her during such a time, he hoped that such a time would come to pass later rather than sooner, and had already his mind made up on one thing: Sarah would be returning home alone. Anthony was steadfast in keeping to the promise made and served as a notice to others, twelve years before.

Growing increasingly homesick by the day, Sarah fell into a depression early in the New Year, which brought with it no sign of the latest unrest at home abating. And loudmouth bigots kept the potential for yet further violence in the headlines. While the occasional letter from Belfast sought to assure Sarah that the family was safe, reference, while subtle, to father still not feeling the best, though not in any immediate danger, did little to put her mind at rest over her fear of never seeing him alive again.

Though conscious of his wife's private unhappiness over this uncertainty, Anthony was prepared to accept it as a price worth paying by her and to be endured by him, if it meant no harm were to befall any one of them through not visiting Belfast at that moment in time.

By the year's end, there was much speculation in the newspaper columns over the prospect of Easter, 1966 - the 50th anniversary of the 1916 rising in Dublin - bringing with it renewed republican violence. This development in turn could well further inflame Protestant grievances over their Prime Minister's 'wishy-washy' stance in face of the new and more sinister republican threat surfacing under the guise of constitutional politics. The leading political correspondent of one Conservative and Unionist influenced newspaper had gloomily forecast Northern Ireland to be entering its darkest hour. Extremists on both sides of the divide were reported to be preparing to drag Ulster to the brink of civil war.

On Easter Sunday, 1966, the length and breadth of the Falls Road was amass with republicans from all over the North, young and old, male and female, old veterans, and Fianna, yet to pick up a gun. In the bright midday sunshine the colourfully dressed flute and accordion bands from all over Ireland and further afield, the commemorative wreaths of green, white and yellow arrangement carried proudly by the leading marchers, and the provincial and national flags boldly paraded by the IRA colour party in semi-military dress of black berets, blazers and gloves, were gloriously brought to life.

The scene of hundreds of men and women, spanning the generations, marching shoulder to shoulder with heads held high to the emotive tunes played, not least by the Irish Piper up front, rekindled the spirit and emotions of many of the thousands of spectators lining either side of the long, winding road, decked out in green, white and orange bunting.

On this special anniversary year of the Easter Rising of 1916, when, in Dublin City, a small, determined band of Irish republicans in bold defiance of the might of the British Empire had asserted arms in declaring an Irish Republic, old and new longing for Ireland as a whole to one day be rid of British interference and to be united, were evoked by the emotional, conscious-stirring occasion. While it was simply a good day out for many among the spectators viewing the vast parade to a loud chorus of clapping and cheering and exhilarated shouts of 'Up the Rebels' and 'God save Ireland', for those taking a meaningful interest in the day's event, there had never been an Easter Sunday commemoration like it.

An enthused, hopeful atmosphere of better times to come was evident in the air, but none doubted that anything to be gained would have to be fought for tooth and nail. There was a new militancy about nationalist and republican folk that day, and among the youth especially. It was evident in the way they marched along the road, the way they gathered to conspire in huddled groups on street corners. It was clear to the intelligent observer that it would be their generation who would make a final stand, for better or to die. They were not going to suffer the gerrymandered system as their parents and their parents before them had done. No, times were about to change, and dramatically so.

No one was more conscious of the electric atmosphere loaded with great expectations that day, than Sean Mor. Proudly sporting his Easter Lily in the lapel of his official GAA blazer, he had mustered all his strength to climb into McNab's car earlier that morning to be transported to a prime vantage spot in order to comfortably view the commemoration parade swing through the wide, high gates to Milltown Cemetery. It was there that those local republicans who had fought and died for Ireland down through the years and who had been laid to rest in the Republican Plot therein, would be honoured along with the nation's heroes through the graveside oration and the speeches to follow from leading and well-known republicans representing both the IRA and Sinn Fein.

In his younger days, Sean Mor had nervously delivered such a speech from the makeshift platform on behalf of the army to the brave and dedicated several thousand sympathisers who had gathered on that blustery, rain-swept day. The umbrellas shielding him from the atrocious weather had spared him the attention of the Special Branch, as there were always two or three mingling inconspicuously among the crowd, and that day would be no exception, he knew. The former IRA gunman and commandant made his way carefully along the narrow, well trodden paths crisscrossing the endless lines of gravestones and on towards the Republican Plot ahead of the many thousands streaming through the cemetery gates.

The annual Easter Sunday commemoration had become a profound experience for Sean Mor, who came to stand boldly to attention on one side of the Republican Plot, surrounded by faces familiar and new. Despite his brittle bones and wasting muscles screaming in agony, the gentle breeze sweeping down from Black Mountain, the flutter of the Irish Tricolour and Starry Plough flags held at half mast over the graves, and the emotional, inspirational charged voice of the oration official vowing that those dead comrades would never be forgotten, that the fight for freedom would continue, left Sean Mor feeling as though the spirit of those who had made the supreme sacrifice, were standing to attention alongside of him.

With the traditional ceremonial undertakings completed through the laying of wreaths, Sean Mor took the weight off his aching limbs momentarily by leaning against a headstone as the huge crowd dispersed. 'McNab. It's the beginning of something exciting. The people are at last getting off their knees to campaign for what is rightfully theirs.'

'I think you're right, Sean Mor,' came a voice, but not McNab's. Sean Mor turned to investigate. *'Frankie*!' Barratt's latest disguise of thick, dark rimmed glasses and bushy moustache, did not fool his old friend and comrade for life.

Merging with the last of the dispersing crowd, the three men walked slowly back toward the cemetery gates; McNab ahead of the two older men, who talked with hushed voices of matters not for his ears.

Still on the RUC's wanted list four years after the ending of the failed border campaign, Barratt conveyed to his trusted companion that times were indeed changing. Sean Mor's earlier prediction to Barratt that a popular uprising by the Catholic people of the North would soon come about, was confirmed as being accurate by Barratt. A major non-violent challenge to the unionists in power was indeed afoot. Barratt's dilemma however, was whether to side with those republicans who advocated the exploitation of it, by reasserting themselves through force of arms, or to join up with those whose argument was akin to what Sean Mor espoused.

Calling into the central library after school hours to return the book titled: Hollywood Stars, Sean's ears were fine-tuned on hearing the old gentleman at the head of the queue ask the lady librarian for the 1945 August editions of *The Times* newspaper. Suddenly, Sean was aware that he had the opportunity to investigate events occurring worldwide on the day he had been born. The same lady librarian eyed him up and down over the top of her horned rimmed glasses when he requested access to *The Times*, July editions, 1952. Sean's honest face and well-groomed mop of wavy blond hair and smart school attire, won the woman over. The formidable-looking woman, an ex-Headmistress to Sean's thinking, led the way up a decorative spiral stairway to the archive section situated in the balcony overlooking the main lending library. Here, alongside stuffy retiring types mentally devouring books on topics he had difficulty pronouncing, Sean, once supplied with the neat bundle of fourteen year old newspapers, their yellowy-brown colour denoting their age, sat himself down at a long table in one corner and began to carefully scan the first of the newspapers pages, filled with the news of the day - 4th July 1952.

'Researching something are we?'

'The day I was born,' Sean replied, honestly, looking up with big smiling blue eyes at the inquisitive librarian hovering over him.

'Just be careful young man,' stressed the caretaker of paper and print. Sean smiled. The woman managed a smile in turn then left the young researcher to it. With eyes wide open, Sean read intensely the detailed *catalogue of death and destruction* which had *ravaged Northern Ireland* in the twenty-four hours prior to, and on the very hour he knew himself to have been born.

Sliding his heavy school satchel from off his back in the hallway of the family home later that afternoon, and beholding in the mirror hanging there that handsome, honest face of his, now fixed with a somewhat confused expression, Sean was confident that his mother would accept his inquiry for what it was - a genuine attempt to understand the bloody and violent circumstances into which he had been born.

Entering that living-room to find his mother sitting comfortably in her chair awaiting him home safe as always, and with a warm, welcoming smile upon her face, Sean sat himself down in his father's chair opposite and seeking knowledge, truth, said, 'Mum, why all the killing in Ireland on the day I was born?' Sean saw his mother stiffen in her seat, her face become drawn.

Knowing Sean had been to the library and quickly putting two and two together, Sarah knew the time had come to tell her son a different kind of fireside story, a brutally true story, one in which she and Anthony were the central characters.

'Sean, you're a very smart boy. But what I am about to tell you, requires that you remain smart. Not a word of it must be shared with anyone else. Not Drew, not teachers at school, not even your father. For the sake of us all.'

Sean walked alone in the woods that evening loaded with mixed emotions. Knowing his mother and father had 'not harmed a living soul' left him relieved, while the price his parents had paid, and still paid, as an innocent party caught up in the violence over which they'd had no control, left him very angry. But calling to mind his mother's plea by the fireside not to be bitter over it all, Sean knew that he would have to let go of his anger.

Chapter Fifty-Six

For Sean and Drew, the summer of '66 was bliss. They spent most of it with their eyes glued to the television set in 101 Forest Park to see England to victory in the World Cup final. Later, when not trying to re-enact the majestic soccer playing skills of Moore, Charlton, and Hurst on the green at the end of the street, they spent lazy afternoons mimicking the antics of the Fab Four in the privacy of their bedrooms as the Beatles '45 played endlessly on the turntable. But it was the girls of that summer who they would remember most, especially the fashion conscious type in skirts so short that little was left to the imagination. With so much naked female flesh on parade, spotty teenage boys were prone to prolonged bouts of wishful thinking.

The danger signs of renewed violence erupting in Ireland before the year's end did not go entirely unnoticed in the Brennan household. Forever sensitive to political upheaval across the water, Sarah and Anthony followed events at home closely with mounting concern. With young intellectual Catholics grouping together across the North to organise passive, public protest at the Unionist Government's sectarian policies, the newly re-grouped Ulster Volunteer Force, the UVF, vowed to hunt down and execute known IRA men whom they judged to be manipulating the latest minority conspiracy to overthrow Ulster. Anthony and Sarah were soon to read of a series of ugly sectarian murders in Belfast, with innocent Catholics, and Protestants, slain by Protestant extremists blundering in their efforts to kill republicans.

In the wake of the UVF's violent re-emergence, Sean Mor was forced to re-examine his own personal security. He invested in several heavy-duty bolts and locks for the front and back doors of No72 and buckets of sand were dispersed throughout the house as another UVF tactic was to petrol bomb target houses in the early hours. Sean Mor had also advised his daughters and son-in-laws to take similar precautions.

As for republicans manipulating the tide of change, to Sean Mor's disquiet it was instead reported by reliable sources that the IRA was in turmoil. Two separatist camps were forming within the IRA's ranks. One, fronted with up-and-coming young socialist intellectuals, drawn mainly from college campus life in and around the main cities in the South, was pressing for the republican movement to abandon such futile acts as blowing up Nelson's Pillar in Dublin in favour of entering the constitutional political arena in order to advance the realisation of their goal - the establishment of a Socialist Irish Republic. The opposing argument, stemming largely from among the unskilled labourers, farmers' sons and the unemployed north of the border, was for a more concentrated campaign of guerilla warfare to be launched in the North at the earliest opportunity. Such a strategy, combined with renewed political agitation by Sinn Fein but strictly on an abstentionist ticket, was deemed by the militarists to be the only realistic way to dismantle the Orange state, to drive the British out, and to liberate the electorate in the Free State from the tweedledee-tweedledum two-party political state mentality, which would subsequently allow republicans to retake their rightful place in government. The ultimate prize for republicans, it was counselled, would thus be secured.

Believing the reports to be of substance, Sean Mor remained strong of the belief that the time was right for republicans and constitutional nationalists to unite and form a pan-Irish nationalist political front, which, if winning the powerful and persuasive support of Irish-America, could see the militarists' goals achieved without a shot fired.

Hearing that his good friend and former comrade was confined to his bed through deteriorating health, Barratt chanced another visit to Belfast on a bitterly cold September day, in 1968. On arrival in his hometown after dark, Barratt made his way straight to 72 Leger Street, where his own indecision as to events unfolding within the republican movement was given some clarity and sense of direction. Fighting the pain that ravaged him, Sean Mor shared his new vision and beliefs with Barratt and urged him not to squander a golden opportunity to see the people of Ireland united. His voice failing, Sean Mor beckoned Barratt to sit close by his bedside.

'With the students on the streets demanding civil rights, the world's media will soon arrive in droves ... just as in the States. And like the government there, the patience of the unionists will wane. They'll hammer the people into the ground in trying to drive them from the streets. When that day comes, our people will be looking to the likes of you for leadership. But it is vitally important that you don't introduce the gun to the scene again. No! What needs to happen, is more street protests ... for republicans to demand that the people vote them in!'

'But what if our people are being killed, Sean? What if ...'

'Hold back, Frankie! Let the bastards in the Free State be drawn across the border. Let the conflict become internationalised. Once the Dublin Government get involved on such a scale, then it will be checkmate! Believe me, it's time for cold, calculated, and ruthless decision-making. Don't let the hotheads fuck it up this time. I know. I used to be one of them in my day.'

Barratt thought for a moment.

'I need you to get fit again, Sean. If the men across the North hear what you say, I can carry them with me. Will you help me?'

It was a desperate plea and Sean Mor recognised it as such. For Barratt, it was like witnessing someone rising from the dead as Sean Mor, grimacing under the pain, mustered all his wasting strength to ease himself up in his bed. Once catching his breath, and managing a defiant smile, so typical of the man, Sean Mor gave his reply. 'What is it they say Frankie ... once a republican, always a sucker for a good fight?'

With such a man at his side, Barratt knew he would win the day. But looking deep into the other man's pained eyes, sunk deep in their sockets, and noting the gaunt look and sickly sovereign skin, he whispered a prayer for the first time in a very long time, in asking God to spare Sean Mor if only for a little while, but long enough to do what needed to be done.

Less than a quarter of a mile away, in a dingy room above a packed public bar on the Protestant Shankill Road, the local, infamous, self-appointed UVF commander and former B Special, William 'Silver' Wallace, okayed the plan for a series of bomb attacks against strategic economic targets across the North in an attempt to lay blame at the IRA's doorstep, so provoking a government crackdown on Irish republicans, the smashing of the IRA-Civil Rights Movement and their conspiracy to overthrow Ulster. There was another vitally important aspect to the UVF plot - the execution of Sean McParland in the days following the bombings in the added hope that it would split the IRA down the middle, with a bloody feud ensuing within the ranks through one side believing Sean Mor had been murdered by those 'careerist republican politicos'. The spring of the New Year was earmarked for the attacks. Silver Wallace was toying with the idea of being the one to kill McParland despite exposing himself to great risk, for nothing would give him more pleasure. He detested Fenians and their miserable perverted ways every conscious minute of the day. From the pit of his stomach, he cursed the Catholic Church and all its saints and scholars and not least, the whore sacrilegiously personified as the Mother of God. But that burning hatred of those he referred to as 'Popeheads and Demoniacs', did in no way compare with the hatred seeded deep in his soul for Irish republicans, IRA men like Sean McParland, who were once again threatening everything dear to him, his God, his people, his beloved Ulster.

'Silver, what do you reckon our chances are of getting to that fucker McParland?' Lenny Dean, personally responsible for killing several Catholics in recent years, did not have to wait long for an answer. 'Don't worry, we'll get to him one way or another,' Wallace snarled.

Dean declared, 'Then I'll go pish on his grave!'

The dramatic television pictures flashed around the world on 5th October 1968, which captured Northern Ireland policemen baton-charging civil rights marchers peacefully protesting on the streets of Londonderry, left Sarah weeping quietly in her armchair, Anthony and Sean, sitting on the settee close by, pale with shock. The harrowing, bloody scene of elderly men and women, and young girls and boys, not much older than Sean, being bludgeoned to the ground by men in uniform, was almost too horrific to accept as real. Though familiar with the student riots in England, France and the USA through following the occasional news bulletin, the family had never before seen such blatant, unprovoked violence on the screen. Anthony and Sarah were left feeling as they did five years earlier, when news of President Kennedy's assassination had broken, sickened and angry.

For Sean, the facts, as told by mother some two years earlier, had left him only too well aware that such brutality by the RUC was not uncommon. But seeing it wielded with such ferocity with his own eyes did not make it any easier to take-in. Leaving his father's side to cross the living-room and place a comforting hand on his mother's shoulder, Sean broke the brittle silence enveloping his parents, each contemplating what the events unfolding back in Ireland may bring for them all.

'Mum. Do you think Grandad McParland would have been among those protesters today?'

Sarah sniffed back her tears and wiped her cheeks dry with the back of her hand. 'Your grandad is barely able to make it down the stairs these days Sean, never mind go on protest marches. But I'm sure, if he were fit enough, he would be.'

'That cursed place is going to explode.' Anthony interjected, eyes still glued to the television screen, and added with an air of despondency, 'Thank God we're well out of it.'

Witnessing the melée, Sarah knew that there was little she could say to counter Anthony's reminder and quietly accepted that there was no likely hope of their return to Ireland for many a day to come, if at all. Her thoughts turned to those at home then and prayed silently that God would keep them safe in such troubled times. Sarah knew the day marked a turning point in her people's long struggle for justice and equality.

Sean Mor's prophetic words echoed clearly in Barratt's head as he walked through the debris littering the streets of Derry's Bogside in the aftermath of the previous day's bloody events. Although, to an outsider, seeing the blood splattered placards demanding: One Man One Vote, Equal Rights, Fair Housing and Employment, lying discarded among the half bricks and broken glass it may appear to have been a one sided battle, for this Irish republican it had been the scene of a great victory.

The RUC/B Special assault on unarmed, peaceful protesters had come at the end of 'The Long March For Civil Rights' that had set out from Belfast several days before and which had been designed to expose the Unionist Government's iniquities against the Catholic people in the north of Ireland to the gaze of a wider public. The state violence had unfolded in front of the eyes of the world, which would now be asking probing questions as to what was really taking place in Northern Ireland, a far corner of the British Empire, which until the previous day, along with its cancer of social, economic and political injustice, had been only another name on the map. In Barratt's assessment this was the essence of the victory to be manipulated by republicans.

Approaching the city's historic walls at the foot of the Bogside where the voice of reason had been met with brute force, Barratt addressed the young and enthusiastic local brigade OC - proudly escorting his visiting senior rank on a tour of the battlefield - and had his subordinate's fullest attention.

'The Orangemen had their victory here three hundred years ago, but we had ours yesterday. It may just set the scene for more of the same to come. I'm glad I came here today. There's a spirit for freedom alive in this city ... among its people.'

'You'd better believe it, Mister Barratt!' The young IRA man wore a determined look upon his deceivingly innocent face.

Inhaling the sweet Derry air through his nose, Barratt was earnestly pondering his next move.

Chapter Fifty-Seven

With Sean Mor experiencing his good days and bad days in the first months of 1969, his wife Rosie, a modern day Florence Nightingale, who sat with him throughout the day and lay awake by his side each night, felt as though she was in purgatory at times. She was caught between sending for Sarah on those bad days and abiding by her husband's wish on his better days, when his pain abated enough for him to speak coherently. Her husband was still insistent that Sarah must not be called home in such times, particularly with fear stalking the people of the Falls under the threat of further attacks by loyalist murder gangs. Sean Mor's biggest fight was convincing those about him, and himself, that he would not be laid up in bed much longer. Even the family doctor was left perplexed by his patient's gutsy will to get back on his feet.

With the first day of spring soon arriving, it brought with it a reprieve from a deathbed for Sean Mor and relief for all who'd rallied round those past six months to nurse him. Although he remained ill, with a incurable bone and muscle wasting condition, Sean Mor, turning sixty-three years of age, felt like a man twenty years younger on standing up, shakily, and walking a little further than the half dozen or so paces he'd only been able to manage when confined to that bedroom. The main reason for fighting the illness and holding on to life so was his love for his wife and children and his four grandchildren, three of whom were close by. He did not want to leave them yet, and most certainly not until he had laid eyes again on that first grandchild, his only grandson, for whom, in his heart, there was a special place. Although Sean Mor remembered well Anthony's vow never to set foot in Belfast again or to allow Sean to, he knew that as his grandson grew older and was able to decide for himself, then there existed every chance he would see him one day, though would not encourage this himself until life in Belfast was greatly more settled. Until such time, the grandfather was happy in the knowledge that Sean would not be exposed to any danger.

Apart from this intense love for others about him, there existed another major motivating factor to get back on his feet. Sean Mor had promised to be fit enough to meet with Barratt and brigade OCs from each of the six counties, who would all, by design, be assembled in Belfast on

Easter Sunday night, after the annual parade. It would be at this meeting that Sean Mor, a highly respected non-combatant in the eyes of all northern republicans and a great many southerners, would impress on the northern brigades to stand solid behind Barratt, and not compromise the progress of the Northern Ireland Civil Rights Association through armed actions.

IRA Launch New Bombing Campaign! That was the news headlines following the series of overnight attacks against essential power and water supply installations across the province later that spring. The first outcries of condemnation levelled at republicans by the media and press and the threatening undertones from government ministers of employing 'severe measures' to thwart any renewed IRA campaign, delivered the desired initial affect Wallace and his UVF accomplices had been seeking. Under the glare of damning criticism and outrage fired at the republicans and the nationalist community for harbouring such evil men, Wallace, itching for some action himself and disregarding the advice of the dead, made ready to personally execute the second stage of his plan.

No one was more surprised by events that spring than Frank Barratt, whose immediate fear it was, that the northern brigades had pre-empted Sean Mor's plea and had taken matters into their own hands. In the hectic hours following the bomb blasts, a stressful Barratt exposed himself to great risk in face of heightened RUC activity, by frantically scurrying across the province in establishing whether his fears were of substance. Through a series of meetings hastily arranged with each of the brigades throughout the North, Barratt was soon convinced by way of engaging in open and direct dialogue with his subordinates, that none of his men had been involved in the bombings, not least because the resources to launch such an attack had simply not been available. To his knowledge, the explosives which had been available to volunteers prior to the border campaign and which had not been exhausted in the campaign, had been collected in by the Quartermaster General and together with all but a few firearms and munitions, had been spirited away to those dumps far south of the border. The location of the dumps, no one knew, accept the QM General himself and those closest to him. Barratt's suspicion that some gear had been secretly held back, had been dispelled by those seeking the immediate return of the weapons as all sensed dangerous times lay ahead in view of the latest clandestine action by Protestant extremists. Consequently, Barratt discovered through those last minute meetings that the rank and file had already decided what their next move was to be. A return to armed action by the IRA in the North was definitely on. In face of such an overwhelming consensus, Barratt decided Sean Mor's intervention to be pointless and was forced to make a final and decisive decision of his own.

Days later, Barratt set out for Dublin to appeal to the IRA leadership for all weapons and munitions to be dispatched to the northern brigades immediately in view of the increasing threat of attack by loyalist extremists on a defenceless Catholic people. Having re-evaluated the volatile situation in the North, Barratt firmly believed that without arms the greatest opportunity presented to the republican movement to seize on massive public support - not experienced since the all Ireland elections of 1918 - would be lost with dire consequences. He strongly believed also, that if a movement that had time and time again professed to be fighting a war on behalf of the Irish people, failed those same people in their hour of need, then even he, who was presently held in high esteem by neighbours, friends and comrades at grassroots, would never be allowed to live down such a betrayal.

It was with urgency that Barratt made his way to Dublin from where, once attending to matters in hand, he would quickly journey north again, to Belfast. There, he would inform Sean Mor - equally inquisitive to know what went on in the wake of latest events - of the direction he had himself decided to take - an extremely dangerous and risky one, he knew.

As dusk fell the streets of Clonard were quiet and almost deserted. Only the devout elderly men and women scurried home from evening Mass, their faith a comfort to them in the face of the threat of further attack on their community by loyalist murder gangs.

The headscarved Mrs Carlin and Commerford, regular churchgoers, approached Leger Street arm-in-arm, talking in near whispers as if sharing some almighty secret.

'Wasn't thon carry on last night a disgrace, Missus Commerford ... blowing up water mains, I ask you?'

'Ack sure, don't talk. When they come to do them sort of dirty deeds on their own, it's a lost cause.'

'You're right there, Maggie. Sure it's no wonder poor Rosie next door can't show her face these days.'

'True enough Annie. God forgive me for saying it, but it'll be a blessing in disguise for her, the day that husband of hers kicks the bucket. Sure, she hasn't had much of a life with him.'

It was Mrs Carlin, who by nature didn't miss a trick along her street or much beyond it for that matter, who first spied the two shadowy figures lurking on the street corner up ahead. She drew her friend and close neighbour's attention to them by nudging her gently in the ribs with her elbow, then gesturing ahead with her eyes.

'I don't like the look of those two, Maggie,' she fretted, weighing up the two men in an instant.

'Two of the boys, no doubt! Pretend you're not taking any notice, Annie.' But Mrs Carlin did the complete opposite. With suspicion in her eyes, she eyed both men long and hard when turning into and down Leger

Street. Despite catching only a glimpse of their faces, partly hidden by upturned coat collars and the peaks of the flat cloth caps they wore, the nosy woman was left feeling very uncomfortable as she and her friend carried on their way. Mrs Carlin had a nagging feeling she knew one of the men. Whoever he was, he had her instantly concerned that something was not right. The woman's mind was racing in trying to put a name to the face, but Mrs Commerford, mouthing into her ear then, was not helping matters.

'You daren't look over your shoulder these days, girl. For if anything happened to those two, you'd end up having your windows put in.' Mrs Carlin was not listening. Focusing her mind's eye, she scanned the rogues gallery imprinted in her head. Just as she reached her own front door, No70 Leger Street, the name to the face came to her in a flash and she proclaimed aloud, 'Sweet mother of God. It's Wallace! Silver Wallace!' The woman had her friend swinging around on her arm. Suddenly turning to look back up the street, Mrs Carlin begged under her breath, 'Jesus have mercy,' on seeing Wallace, standing some six feet away, raise and point that gun in his right hand, toward her. The last words had barely left Mrs Carlin's lips when a bullet thudded into her large chest, ripping her heart to shreds. Death was instantaneous. In a grotesque manner the woman fell flat on her face in the gutter. Wallace quickly turned his expert aim on the other, much skinnier woman, turning to flee in blind panic down the street. Fixing the woman's upper back in his sights, he let off a second, then a third shot in rapid succession. Wallace saw the woman's arms thrown up into the air as she was sent careering forward to fall face down onto the pavement. He paused for a moment, debating whether to make sure the second woman was dead by putting a bullet in her head or to turn and run for his life back toward the Falls, where his nervy accomplice stood on the street corner willing him to run for it. Wallace's mind was made up for him on hearing someone's hellish scream close by.

Dozing in his fireside chair when the first shot had rang out just beyond his front door, and identifying it as such instantly and the two which followed, Sean Mor called out to Rosie in the scullery, 'Switch off the light and stay where you are!' Sean Mor expected the front door to be kicked off its hinges at any moment, heavy feet to come rushing along the hall and the door ajar to be thrown open, and the next bullet to come his way. But instead, he heard another deathly scream.

'Mammy! Mammy! They've shot my mammy dead!'

Sean Mor did not know from where he found the strength, but was out of his chair with no great effort to dart across the room and along the hallway. He considered not the danger to which he exposed himself on sliding back the heavy bolt and pulling the front door open, to then step out into the street. In the fading daylight it was a scene out of Hell that confronted him. Mrs Carlin's youngest daughter, Roisin, her sweet young face smeared with blood and sobbing uncontrollably, cradled her mother's limp head in her lap as she knelt over the lifeless woman. The street was coming alive as folk spilled out of their houses to stumble on the carnage.

'My God! My wife's still breathing! Someone phone for an ambulance quick!'

Dropping to his knees beside his good neighbour Mrs Carlin, Sean Mor turned and looked over his shoulder to see Mr Commerford, his white shirt saturated in his wife's blood, kneeling on the ground to nurse his wife in his arms.

'Christ almighty! The bastards are slaughtering our women!' The voice of one onlooker trembled with rage. As the horror of the evening took a grip of the street, a woman was heard to scream, 'The dirty cowardly scum!'

Women, children, and even the men of the street, wept openly at the bloody sight. Gently stroking the head of the motherless child beside him, Sean Mor knew he was lucky to be alive. The three bullets fired had had his name on each of them, he was sure. But he would gladly have received his killers on his doorstep, if to spare the child her suffering now.

The RUC had eventually arrived in the street to investigate the shooting and were jostled and booed by the locals, suspicious of the RUC's genuine intentions to pursue the UVF gunmen, for there was no doubt in the minds of the Falls Road people as to who had been responsible for the indiscriminate attack.

It felt odd for Sean Mor to be assisting the RUC with their inquiries. He simply told the investigating Special Branch Officer what he had heard earlier. Noting the expression of indifference, mixed with disappointment upon the faces of the RUC men, Sean Mor soon realised what was truly on their minds. Standing on his doorstep he said as much on replying to the smug-faced detective's sarcastic question. 'You know as good as I do, why the gunmen visited the street.' That said, Sean Mor slammed the front door in the face of the smirking detective. With the RUC scribbling their observations into their pocket notebooks in no great detail, they beat a hasty withdrawal from the area as darkness fell, leaving increasing anger and tension to brew among the narrow back streets, and the women of Leger Street to wash away the pools of thick clotted blood, that of their women folk, cut down on their own doorsteps.

Arriving back in Belfast and onto the Falls Road just after midnight later that night, Barratt was met by Bonar at the safe house in Beechmount and was informed of events earlier. One woman was dead, another, shot twice in the back, was in hospital fighting for her life. Given the close proximity of the shooting to Sean Mor's house, there was no doubt in Barratt's mind who had been the intended target, and was greatly relieved to hear that Sean Mor was safe and as well as could be expected. Deciding to leave his call on Sean Mor until daylight, Barratt's main concern was that the crowds of angry youth gathering on street corners signalled street riots. Barratt feared that such an outbreak of violence could deflect attention away from the night's atrocity which, he knew, would win their community a great deal of sympathy, nationally and internationally. Barratt wasted no time delegating Bonar the challenging task of dispersing the crowds.

'With the situation so delicately poised, Bonar, we don't want anything to happen which will draw the eye of scrutiny away from the loyalists. Come tomorrow, they'll be in the public eye more so. For once, in a long, long time, things may slowly be turning to our advantage.'

Barratt was convinced now, that his earlier decision had been the right one.

Chapter Fifty-Eight

The IRA's public denial of involvement in the spring bombings had the RUC re-examining their line of inquiry. Not only was it most uncommon for the IRA to make such a forthright defence of their non-involvement when normally they would relish such media attention, hard intelligence gathered by Special Branch informants affirmed a long held belief by many within the security services, that the IRA was long since a spent force, with little or no human or material resources at its disposal. It was the considered opinion of the same informed sources, that a counterproductive border campaign had sounded the IRA's death-knell.

Once briefed on developments by his security minister, the extremely anxious Northern Ireland PM immediately issued a directive through formal channels to RUC HQ, which forced Special Branch chiefs to re-deploy investigating officers in the field with a new and urgent brief of their own: hunt down those militant loyalists responsible for the bombings. It was the firm belief of a very concerned Prime Minister that it was indeed among his own community, the Protestant people, from which the recent spate of bombings had been hatched. Furthermore, there was a real fear manifesting within government circles that a potentially more damaging Protestant conspiracy was afoot, designed to oust the government of the day. The PM and his party were anxious to have the conspiracy unearthed quickly, the ringleaders rounded-up. With their energies presently stretched to the limits in coping with the increasing threat stemming from among nationalists, the government ministers were anxious not to be left exposed on two fronts.

In a calculated effort to appease the Catholic community, particularly that of the Falls Road and its people's anger and frustration over the 'heavy handed' and 'insensitive' approach by the RUC in light of the recent outrage, the PM's minister for security privately urged the RUC Inspector General to ensure that his men on the ground made rigorous efforts to arrest the murderer of the Falls Road woman, as the identity of the killer was now known. The dead woman's friend, shot twice in the back by the same gunman, had mustered all of her waning strength to splutter out the killer's name before slipping into unconsciousness as detectives had stood guard at her hospital bedside.

The calculating politicos at Stormont were hoping that with the RUC being seen to be evenhanded in administering the law when investigating murder - at least - the anger of the Catholic community may be abated, if only until the Protestant militants lurking at the back door were put firmly in their place.

Mr Commerford had also heard his critically ill wife condemn William Wallace as the killer. The devastated husband had not left his wife's side since discovering her lying face down in a pool of her own blood outside their front door. Filled with the hunger for revenge, he had served notice to the two expressionless plain-clothed RUC men standing on the opposite side of his wife's hospital bed, that if they failed to bring Silver Wallace speedily to justice, he would, in his own way.

It was this that the heartbroken husband repeated to his neighbour, Sean Mor, for there was no reason for Mr Commerford to be up at the hospital that night. Maggie, his wife for forty-two years, had died an hour earlier. Choking back tears the widower sat on the McParlands' sofa with head bowed, his voice trembling. 'My Maggie and Missus Carlin must have recognised Wallace that night. Even after all these years out of uniform, they would never forget that evil bastard's face. He was regular in running amok up and down this street in his B Special days, along with Craig ... another sadistic...' The pitiful man broke off from delivering his damnation of the dead on hearing the living-room door open, and looking up, saw a serious-faced young man poke his head into the room and gesture to Sean Mor. The man of the house struggled to his feet and on shaky legs dragged himself towards the door, where he paused for a moment to address the grieving neighbour.

'What happened to the women was an act of someone depraved. Wallace should be thankful if the RUC get to him first, for I'm sure if not, someone else will.'

They were the very words Mr Commerford had wanted to hear. He took his leave a little more content of mind knowing that one way or another justice would be served unto Wallace, whom he would curse to Hell all the rest of his days. There would be no forgiving, nor forgetting, for the widower had been cruelly robbed of a most precious gift.

With his bereaved neighbour gone, Sean Mor joined the two men awaiting him in the front room, the second man just arrived. With Rosie in the house next door comforting Mr Carlin and his family, Sean Mor could talk easy with Barratt, and Bonar, the Belfast Brigade OC.

'Missus Commerford died an hour ago, Frankie. When news of this spreads our people will go off their heads. You must keep the lid on their anger. It's best saved for another day.'

Barratt looked Sean Mor in the eye. 'I'm sorry, Sean. But I've decided to go with the mainstream. What happened here the other night reinforces my belief that only at the barrel of a gun will we bring this bastard state to its knees.'

Sean Mor was disappointed but not surprised by Barratt's revelation. He spoke his mind too then. 'I understand, Frankie. I knew it wasn't going to be easy to win people over to my way of thinking. But believe me, if our crowd rampage we will hand back on a plate to the unionists the propaganda victory won in Derry last winter. We must keep the sympathy gained, on-side.'

Barratt shook his head. 'My people have already made their minds up on what to do, Sean. I can't, and won't stop them.'

In that moment, Sean Mor knew that a golden opportunity for the republican movement to rally the nationalist people to their cause as never before had been squandered.

Barratt and Bonar moved to take their leave. Sean Mor had only one request.

'Before you go, Frankie. It was Silver Wallace who came for me last night. The two auld girls recognised him.'

Barratt winked an eye. 'I hear what you say, Sean.'

Both IRA men took their leave and left an old republican alone with his fearful thoughts for the future.

Barratt knew his next move would be dependant on the reply he awaited anxiously from Dublin. He felt relatively confident that the Chief of Staff would consider favourably his recent request for arms to be released to his charge, for use in defence of Catholic areas in view of UVF activity.

Returning to the safe house in Beechmount later that night, Barratt felt obliged to inform Bonar of the latest crisis facing the IRA in the North, and particularly in Belfast. Sitting at the kitchen table, the weight of the world on his shoulders, Barratt spoke with little gusto.

'The leadership have left us in the shit. Those who seek to lead the movement up the one-way political route, hold all the hardware. In light of the UVF threat, I have formally requested they supply the Northern Command with sufficient arms and munitions. I await a response.'

Heartened to know Barratt was not running scared from those in Dublin, seemingly holding all the ace cards presently, Bonar felt it incumbent of him as the Belfast Brigade OC, to voice how strong he felt about IRA arms being held in reserve by the leadership at a time when further Protestant pogroms against Catholics in the North was threatened.

'No one who lays claim to being an Irish Republican, regardless of rank or seniority, must ever be expedient when it comes to defending a defenceless section of the Irish people ... confronted by the common enemies of the Irish people!'

Barratt understood the profound, but yet simplistic message in what had just been said, and agreeing wholeheartedly with every word, with what was implied, said simply, 'Fair play, Bonar.'

On learning of the death of the second woman, Silver Wallace danced for joy around the kitchen floor. Safely holed up in the home of an old girlfriend in the staunchly Protestant Sandy Row area of Belfast, he had been cursing himself those past twenty-four hours for not finishing off the Taig good and proper. He was greatly relieved too that there was no suggestion of her having breathed a word. The radio news reporter's closing comment that police were still seeking 'eye-witnesses' left Wallace confident that he was in the clear.

Feeling assured that God was keeping him safe so to do what was right - for God and Ulster, the Shankill Road man vowed unto himself, that once returning to the Shankill, he would go back to the drawing board to consider how best to complete the mission of eliminating his sworn enemy, Sean McParland.

Barratt received a reply of sorts from the Chief of Staff earlier than expected on his return to his lodgings in Dundalk that following night. In the shadowy backyard of the main street pub, two burly men suddenly appeared in front of Barratt, and one, speaking with a pronounced Dublin accent, informed him that the Chief of Staff required his presence in Dublin immediately. With his suspicions aroused as to what awaited him, Barratt was hurriedly led away and bundled into the back seat of a waiting car to be driven at speed further south for the unscheduled meeting.

Two days later as thousands lined the Falls Road for the joint funeral of the two women murder victims, Silver Wallace was arrested by armed detectives outside his own home standing midway along a side street just off the Shankill Road. The detectives had been keeping the mid-terrace under surveillance. On his person, Wallace still carried a loaded service issue .38 Webley revolver, stolen by him from the barrack armoury twenty-six years earlier, days before being pensioned off due to injuries received in the IRA landmine attack.

Within an hour of being questioned over the double murder on the Falls four days earlier and the bombing of electric and water supply installations the day before that, Wallace voluntarily confessed that he had personally shot the women, who had, in his judgement, 'compromised' him while en route to execute the leading IRA man, Sean McParland. But Wallace denied involvement in the recent bombings and insisted it had been the work of republicans, though his interrogators were not convinced. Asked what the motive had been behind his actions, Wallace boasted that they were designed to 'carry the fight to the IRA and their communist inspired allies in the Civil Rights Movement,' and in defence of 'God and Ulster.' The latter he went on to describe as being in peril in the hands of a treacherous government, 'the enemy within.'

Wallace sealed his fame amongst inspired loyalists with such defiant words and with the same breath, his infamy among Northern Ireland Catholics for all time.

In the weeks following his arrest and remand to Crumlin Road Jail, Wallace's popularity among the Protestant community soared to unprecedented heights. However the province's PM's popularity steadily dwindled in the face of a mounting challenge to the very existence of the Northern Ireland State by ever greater numbers of protesting Catholics, unimpressed by his token gestures of promised social reforms and fair policing which, together with his own electorates' loss of faith in him, culminated in the PM resigning from government at the close of April, 1969.

The political circus unfolding within the unionist camp in the wake of the PM's resignation at a time when further major civil rights marches were being planned for the summer months, to coincide with the loyalist marching season, left Northern Ireland holding its breath.

Chapter Fifty-Nine

Still light on his feet and as shrewd as ever in his thinking in his seventieth year, the IRA Chief of Staff had deliberately misled Barratt to believe that there existed the possibility of arms being released to the northern brigades in light of recent UVF attacks. The truth was, the Dubliner was suspicious of Barratt's true intentions at a time when the majority of the Army Council were aligning themselves to the argument put forward by the southern-based young radicals. The call for republicans to commit themselves solely to launching a concentrated campaign of political agitation in the twenty-six counties to stimulate the electorate - pacified by conservative government over the past forty years - into a more radical mode of thought, was winning the day among republicans in the South.

With his suspicions of Barratt aroused, the Chief of Staff consulted his southern counterparts in the Army Council on his decision to have Barratt picked-up. It was the Dubliner's intention to establish Barratt's true intentions. On receiving full backing from his southern allies, the Chief of Staff had handpicked men from the Dublin Brigade set out to lure Barratt to a safe house in the suburbs of North Dublin, where he was to be held incommunicado until further notice. Though fully aware of the Belfast man's popularity among the rank and file in the North and the subsequent risk he had taken in ordering Barratt's 'detention', the Chief of Staff was prepared to run such a risk. He was confident that once meeting with

Barratt and through the powers of gentle persuasion, the Belfast man would see things his way. It was crucial, he knew, to keep the northerner on-side. A split in the IRA would be the worst possible scenario at a time when the movement's ill-fortunes of the past forty years could be about to dramatically change, if republicans explored the political opportunities opening to them. It was in acknowledgement of the risk he took that the Dubliner knew he had it all to do to win Barratt over, thus keep the movement as one.

Taking stock of the reasons why he should be held against his will for the past forty-eight hours in some grand, Georgian-style house, and his predicament as a consequence, Barratt feared the Free Staters were planning to make an example of him - having sided with those who had been fanning the flames of unrest over the leadership's plan for the movement's future. Though accepting that his life hung in the balance, Barratt had already decided to speak his mind when face-to-face with the Dubliner, whom he now knew to be coming to meet with him the following day.

On completing his O' Level exams and attending school for the last time, Sean was one of a handful of grammar school pupils seated on the upper deck of the bus destined for town, when his best friend Drew - the odd one out in a rather bedraggled compulsory secondary school uniform - made an unexpected appearance at the top of the stairwell. Drew looked searchingly for Sean among those schoolboys dressed in the smarter maroon and grey colours, which denoted their superior academic ability. Spying Drew, and sensing immediately that something troubled his friend, Sean signalled to him with a wave of the hand. Drew was soon seated beside Sean and frowned heavily as the bus pulled out again.

'What's up?' Sean asked, conscious of the disapproving eyes of his snobby school associates, though he cared not a jot. Drew spat. 'I'm proper fucked off. That prick of a careers teacher gave me some right bleedin' earache.'

'Like what?' Sean probed, turning in his window seat to look Drew straight in the face. Drew looked aimlessly to the floor of the bus when replying. 'The twat said that if my leaving results are anything like my pre-exam work, I'd be lucky to get into the army.' Lifting his head to look Sean in the eye, and with more than a hint of anger evident in his voice, Drew added, 'Can you believe it? The fucker's only a recruiting officer for those wank-offs in Whitehall!' Sean could not help but laugh at this, and found himself on the receiving end of Drew's cynical tongue. 'Oh yeah! Go on, have a good laugh. It's all right for you, smart ass. No doubt you'll pass your O' Levels with distinctions. Wot's it gonna be for you then ... next prime minister?'

In that moment Sean was moved to consider what he would indeed do with himself when faced with the choice of either returning to school to sit his A' Levels (he was quietly confident he would do well with his O' Levels) or to answer the early call to the world of work, the prospect of which left him a little more excited.

Turning to look out of the bus window once again and seeing the multitude of grey, indifferent types pushing and shoving their way home, having no doubt just put in another uneventful ten hour day in some grim office halfway between Heaven and Earth, Sean decided in an instant that come what may, he would never be one of their number.

Alighting from the bus together, Sean took his leave from an embittered Drew on a street corner. He was soon looking over his shoulder though, on hearing Drew call out to him.

'I'm gonna grow my hair down to my balls and join a hippie commune, where I can smoke dope all day and shag all night!'

Seeing the tweed-coated elderly couple out walking their Poodle stop to take issue with the foul-mouthed schoolboy on the corner, Sean thought it best not to get involved.

Sean decided not to go straight home, but instead, to take a walk in the wood. He always made for the wood when things played on his mind, but most often became distracted by the daily goings-on among its wildlife. Badgers and foxes were among his favourite. As Sean flung his weighted school satchel to one side and lay down on a grassy hillock amidst the wood, he saw a badger emerge cautiously among the trees below as the daylight faded.

Sitting alone, listening to the nocturnal inhabitants of the wood come alive, Sean was suddenly aware of his own sense of being. These past months he had been listening to what others were claiming would be best for him once completing his schooling, in half expectation that someone would come up with the perfect game-plan to secure the most brilliant of jobs. But now he concentrated his mind to seriously consider what *he* wanted to do with his life.

'Sean.'

His power of concentration broken, Sean looked over his shoulder. Appearing exhausted of late, his father came to stand over him, to look out over the wood with sleepy eyes. The wood engulfed them both, its leafy head merging with the night sky falling.

'It's a grand evening, son', Anthony announced. 'I fancied a wee walk to clear my head.' After a moment's pause, Sean heard his father sigh heavily, 'It's been a hard slog of a day.' Sean stood and dusted himself down while looking out over his childhood adventure playground. It was as if his father read his thoughts then.

'Thinking about your future, son, what with exams and school over?'

Sean was honest with his reply. 'I don't know what I want to do. It's difficult to decide.'

'You've got the opportunity to do something special with your life, the brains to go places.'

'I don't know exactly,' said Sean, sounding a little confused. It was with a more determined voice that the sixteen year old rid himself of some of that confusion. 'Tonight, coming home from school, I saw folk coming out of factories and offices. Not one of them was smiling. They all seemed so miserable. I don't want to end up like that.' Studying his father's own haggard face, Sean thought, Nor as you, Dad.

It was the first time his son had expressed his own uncertainty with life. There was much to talk about, but feeling as though he was about to collapse with exhaustion, Anthony said, 'C'mon son. Let's go home. We'll talk more tomorrow.'

Sean felt a little better in himself for at least eliminating any prospect of working in some drab office. Picking up his satchel, father and son together walked back to the house in comfortable silence.

Within minutes of meeting with Barratt, the Chief of Staff soon realised the Belfast man was not going to be easily pacified. To spare himself any embarrassment in front of the two staff officers standing over Barratt, rising to his feet, the senior rank sent the two men out of the room as it was obvious from the expression on Barratt's face that there was going to be some straight talking.

Alone together, Barratt immediately went on the offensive and pulled no punches in letting his anger be felt by that man he now held little respect for in any regard.

'What the hell is the meaning of this?'

The Chief of Staff was keen to keep the conversation orderly. 'Calm down, Frankie. Let's talk this through quietly. Take a seat.'

'*Take a seat*!' Barratt mocked contemptuously. 'I've been sitting on my arse the past three days and nights, staring at four walls, wondering if I'd see the dawn.'

'There was never any question of you being harmed, Frankie,' insisted the Dubliner. 'As you know, men like you and I have to make solitary decisions at times ... on what we think to be for the best. I had you brought here so that we can discuss what is the best way forward for the movement as a whole.'

'I think you and others have already made up your minds on that one.' Barratt said, without fear or seeking favour.

The Chief of Staff was growing a little impatient and this was mirrored in what he had to say. 'Look, Frankie. I've been around a long time. I've seen times changing. And I know that we've got to go with the flow this time. We can't be left standing on the sidelines any more. The way forward for republicans is clear.'

Barratt was equally impatient with his response.

'What about the people in the North? They're the ones ringing the changes. You know as well as I do, what's coming. There's going to be a bloodbath. What are we supposed to defend ourselves with, eh? What do I do when people look to my men and me for help? Answer me that!'

The Chief of Staff knew the crux of the matter had been reached. He was forthright in addressing the key issue.

'It won't come to that, Frankie. The eyes of the world are on the unionists at the moment. If they persist, I am confident, as are many others, that there will be an international outcry and possibly intervention. We must be ready to then present our argument for fundamental change ... for a New Ireland. That is why politically we must organise and make ready and I need you and the men and women in the North to make ready also.'

Barratt was at odds with himself. What he'd heard the Dubliner say was almost a word-for-word repetition of what Sean Mor had said to him only recently. He wondered then, if both men were in cahoots, were conspiring against him. But he was quick to dismiss such thoughts, knowing Sean Mor would not be so clandestine with him ... the volunteers in the North. Convinced that Sean Mor's thinking and that of the Dubliner was simply due to two old republicans individual weariness with the armed struggle, Barratt was sticking faithfully to his guns.

'How do you expect me to think pure politics when my neighbours, women folk, are being gunned down in their streets?' Before the Dubliner had chance to reply, Barratt revealed his real thoughts on the situation. 'Give me a gun first, then I might consider picking up your political manifesto.'

'Sorry Frankie, that is not possible.'

'So what happens now?'

'You're free to go, Frankie. All I ask is that you and the brigades in the North await the outcome of the ard fheis in January ... when it will be clear to all which path to follow. If you still decide to go your own way, so be it. But until then, there will be no split! If any IRA man or woman in the North feels compelled to breach the standing order of '62, let it not be in the name of the IRA. Until January, I see no reason for you or I to meet again. Meantime, I will be lending my full support to the growth of the political wing of the movement. If by chance you wish to join in the dialogue, you know where to find me.'

The Dubliner served Barratt a searching look before turning away and leaving the room.

Taking no chances, Barratt declined the offer from one of the other two Dubliners to be driven back to Dundalk. He instead made his own way into the centre of the capital in time to catch the last train north. Suddenly, to Barratt's thinking, it would be safer to be back among his own people in Belfast.

Much depressed over the violent deaths of the two women who had treated her as one of their own when a child; her anguish for her father's safety unknown to anyone else; and accepting that she risked destroying her marriage if returning to Belfast at the present time, Sarah felt obliged nevertheless, to keep a promise to another, despite feeling as though she was herself on her last legs.

With dinner served, Sarah left Anthony and Sean alone together at home and set out to pay her friend Frances a hospital visit on the night prior to the scheduled operation to remove her friend's womb.

Mealtime over, father and son withdrew to the comfort of the living-room. Sitting across the room from his father, slumped exhausted in a fireside chair, Sean was moved to voice his concern over how tired and weary his father had appeared in recent days.

'Dad, you said last night that it had been a hard slog at work. Is everything okay? You look very tired.'

'Aye son,' Anthony sighed. 'It's just that since the old boss passed away, his son has been accepting more work than we can handle.'

'You take it easy, Dad. Don't let him work you too hard.'

'Don't worry, son. Those years working the land at home prepared me well for hard graft. But stay smart. Get yourself the kind of work from which you can come home with a clean shirt on your back.'

'Do you think you will ever return to Ireland ... to live I mean?'

Only when he'd said it, did Sean realise what he had actually said, and was a little anxious at what his father's reaction to the question might be.

Dumbfounded at first that his son should dare ask such a question, knowing well his thoughts on the matter of returning to Ireland, Anthony found himself repeating the question in his head. Surprisingly, he did not dismiss it out of hand but rather considered it in some depth. Not able to give a definitive reply due to the multitude of worrying issues surfacing in light of his son's question, Anthony sought to substantiate why Sean had put the question to him.

'Why do you ask, Sean?'

Taken aback somewhat by his father's casual, though thoughtful reply, Sean had his mother's interests at heart when saying, 'I just want you to know, Dad, that if you ever want to go back, I would not mind. Whatever makes you happy ...'

Anthony was quick to ask the critical question. 'Say I never want to, but your mother does. Do you think you might return there someday?'

Sean did not need to pause for thought. 'I think there comes a day when most people want to at least see the land where they were born.'

Sean's thoughts shared came as a revelation for Anthony, who until that moment had not considered the extent of his son's thoughts on Ireland, having assumed, wrongly, that he hadn't any. Anthony paused to take stock. Considering his son's educated reply, he did not doubt for one moment that Sean would return to Ireland someday. This troubled Anthony immensely, knowing Belfast, on the verge of anarchy, was his son's birthplace. Noting his father's silence, a mood of contemplation descend on him, Sean quietly withdrew from the downstairs room and reaching his bedroom, threw himself on top of his bed, where he lay reflecting on what had just been said between a father and son.

Sensitive to his mother's silent anguish over recent days in the aftermath of yet more blood-letting back in Belfast, Sean suspected his mother to be tortured mentally, knowing her father - of whose politics she had told him little but enough for him to calculate that it was *he* the UVF gunmen had been out to kill - may yet be violently killed before she had chance to see him.

Considering what his father may now be thinking, what he may come to terms with as a consequence of their conversation, Sean was a little more hopeful that his father would discuss seriously with mother those agonising concerns of the heart: her needs, his own anxieties, once accepting that events of sixteen years ago would constantly return to haunt them, to cast a dark shadow over all their lives, if not examining in depth, and anew, the possible benefits, and dangers, presented to them all if indeed returning to Ireland.

It was Sean's private fear that if his mother and father were not moved to do this and quickly, they may all yet fall victim to the troubles in Ireland with the family being ripped apart when loyalties to others were put to the ultimate test.

Chapter Sixty

The Belfast Brigade staff had great difficulty in accepting as true what Barratt told them on his return to the Falls. Knowing once former comrades with whom he had fought alongside over the years in pursuit of a common, cherished goal, had evidently truly abandoned the armed struggle and the abstentionist policy of the last fifty years, in favour of recognising the validity of the status quo, north and south of the border, left them gutted. With the leadership in Dublin set on advocating constitutional political participation in the two alien states, Barratt was determined to see the split come about at whatever cost.

Barratt was to call an assembly of all northern brigade OCs as soon as was practically possible, and for him, it could not come a day too soon.

Barratt prepared himself mentally for the all-important meeting. He would be seeking the full support of the northern brigades for his own simple proposal: vote against those proposed by the present leadership in the Free State. The forthcoming ard fheis, the annual honouring by republicans of the assembly of that first Dail, of 1918, would be the time and the place to make such a stand, and to coincide the birth of a new movement, one committed to pursuing armed struggle as a means of securing a free, independent Irish Republic. Holding true to this belief, Barratt would also be calling on those same men and women to be prepared to bear arms against deserters of the republican cause and in upholding the claim to be the authentic government of the Irish people. Although confident of that support, Barratt was not so sure how he would find the ways and means of pursuing the armed struggle, now that the weapon stock was completely in the hands of the present leadership, and not least, how to defend the Catholic people across the North in face of rising tensions and the threat of increased violence to come with it. Barratt considered the matter of acquiring arms and ammunition as the next most important issue on his agenda, and once calling together those officers commanding the northern brigades, would set about the task with urgency.

Barratt's return to Belfast did not go unnoticed by another interested source. In the days immediately following the IRA man's return, Special Branch operatives in the west of the city were on full alert for warning signs of what may follow Barratt's reemergence north of the border.

While Sarah's thoughts in those early days of May were focused mainly on the wellbeing of her friend Frances - returning home in agony a few days after her hysterectomy - Anthony's thoughts were constantly wrestling over that scenario put to him a few nights earlier by his son which had left him confronted with that very question: would he ever return to live in Ireland? If the question had been asked of him just five years earlier, Anthony would have given short shrift to the one asking, but not so now. As he himself grew older and more sensitive to his own emotions, the immigrant's sense of belonging - not belonging, the call of home, those loved ones there, and mother, in her sixty-seventh year, was constant on his mind. No one was getting any younger, he knew, and most recently had found himself growing ever more conscious of his own and his family's predicament and was greatly critical of it in his own mind. The truth of this being, he had come to slowly accept that living in England both Sarah and himself were in a kind of limbo.

Anthony was concerned at seeing his wife silently grieve at being so far apart from her loved ones, and he feared that Sarah's mood was beginning to affect their marriage. While he would not conclude easily that Sarah no longer loved him, Anthony sensed that Sarah resented him for not giving her any hope of returning to Ireland for even a brief visit, when knowing her father to be ill. Fearing the resentment could turn to hate if anything was to happen to Sean Mor, Anthony felt greatly more obliged to enable Sarah to return home, although the issue of Sean going also, worried him greatly. But with Sean himself declaring that he may return some day, Anthony knew he would have to compromise somewhere along the way. So with Sean opening a window of new opportunity to him, for them all, Anthony was seriously weighing up the potential of a return to Ireland and began to take full account of factors for and against doing so. While the arguments for returning presented themselves in equal number - Sarah's unhappiness, his own with life of late - all work and seldom any pleasure, Sean's openness to change, and the absence of family and dear friends, the sole counter-argument for not doing so, was not easily dismissed. It was over this that Anthony needed reassurance and would seek it from the only person in whom he held any faith. He knew Sarah would not put at risk the safety of their son at the expense of returning to Ireland for whatever reason. If she could give him that assurance, he had a plan for returning there. A plan that could satisfy their simple desires and ease all of their deep-rooted concerns. Anthony would wait for an opportune moment alone with Sarah to put his proposal to her.

With cities and major towns across the North alive with RUC and B Special activity in light of mounting sectarian tension, Barratt - moving constantly between safe houses - arranged for the meeting with the brigade OCs to be held deep in the republican heartland of South Armagh, where enemy forces were scant on the ground presently and where the locals would resist any attempted swoop as the word had been put about.
    Slipping away from Belfast under cover of dark the previous night, Barratt and Bonar lay low throughout the following day at a remote farm house midway between the border and the South Armagh market town of Crossmaglen, where, above a much trusted sympathiser's public bar, the meeting would be held later that evening.

Skirting outlying towns so to avoid RUC roadblocks the five other brigade OCs from counties Derry, Down, Fermanagh, and Tyrone, and the host county itself, arrived within a few minutes of each other at the secret venue a little after eight-thirty. They slipped into the main street public house by its back door and climbed the stairway to the improvised meeting room above, wherein Barratt and Bonar were already sat waiting.
    Once assembled, Barratt stood to address the six sober-faced men sitting around a small table, upon which there were only drinking glasses and a large jug of water. He was determined that, unlike past meetings, alcohol would not influence decision-making that night. Barratt spoke with a steely voice.
    'Sad as it is to say comrades the leadership in Dublin are for talking, not for fighting. We are on our own. But rest assured there are a great number of our comrades in the Free State who are as equally concerned at what is proposed by the leadership. They may be the silent minority today, but once seeing the backbone of the movement make a stand, they too will stand up and be counted. And remember this: just as

when the treaty of 1921 was signed, the majority decision may not always be the right one.'

There were utterances of agreement among those sitting. This heartened Barratt, and it was evident in his words.

'We must be prepared to defend what is sacred to us true republicans. The ard fheis will be the occasion that will map out the future for us. In the meantime, we must prepare ourselves for going our own way if need be. We must not take our eye off the ultimate prize. And believe me, the opportunity to seize it will soon come our way. Despite what others may say, I know, as sure as I stand here tonight, the unionists will unleash their full might to crush the street protests. We must make ready to answer our people's cry for help ... for I ask you, to whom else will they turn? And who else will respond? There is much to do and much sacrifice to give. Are you with me?'

The young Derry man sprang to his feet. 'All the way! The men and women of Derry won't let you down.' The other five men quickly stood also to voice their support. Exhausted but exhilarated, Barratt slumped into his chair and felt Bonar's open hand pat him warmly on the back.

'The men are with you, one hundred per cent, Frankie. We will not let you down!' Bonar vowed passionately. Though heartened by the man's genuine word, Barratt knew he had his work cut out when telling the other five men that they were an army without arms.

Anthony sat alone in the living-room of 101 Forest Park awaiting Sarah's return from her latest visit to Frances, who was reported to be feeling a little better these days. He had intentionally stayed up late for it would be the night that he would reveal his proposal to his wife, whose key turned in the front door. On entering the room, Sarah was surprised to find Anthony up so late, and said so. Quiet of voice, Anthony addressed his wife. 'Sarah, we need to talk.'

Sitting down on the settee beside Anthony, Sarah looked at him in nervous expectation. Anthony continued. 'I've been thinking lately about our way of life here. I know you're not happy at heart love, not truly settled. You miss your folks, I know. For I miss mine also, if truth be told. And life here? It seems to be all work just lately. I only realised the other night how distant I've become for my own son. We talked man to man like, and it struck me just what I've been missing out on all these years.' Anthony hesitated. 'Sean asked me a question. He wanted to know if I would ever return to Ireland ... to live.'

Sarah's interest in what Anthony had to say was greatly stirred and she spurred her husband on.

'Well, what did you say?' Sarah's voice was loaded with both anxiety and excitement.

'It wasn't so much what I said, but what Sean said. He made it clear to me that he would not mind if we were to return home. Well, I've been thinking. I've taken all things into account ... how you feel, what I myself have come to accept, and of course, events of seventeen years ago. So Sarah, I need to ask you a question, and I need an honest answer.'

'Anthony, would I give you any other?'

Taking a hold of Sarah's hands, Anthony stressed the importance for such in saying searchingly, 'Then tell me. Do you believe we will be in danger, if returning?'

Sarah was sincere in her reply. 'Honest and truthfully, I don't know. But I'd like to think that too many years have past for anyone to be able to drag us into anything. Events today overshadow those of yesterday.'

Anthony accepted that Sarah had indeed been honest. Though she had not been able to reassure him totally, she had said the next best thing. So with a good heart and with a heavy burden largely lifted from his mind, he revealed his proposal to her.

'What would you say, if I was to suggest that we wait until summer, then bail out of here ... to Donegal.' Anthony saw Sarah's eyes light up. 'We could rent a house until I find some land to build on,' he added, a little excited. 'We have enough money put by. Sean could complete his education there ... in Dublin or Cork City perhaps. There are universities there too. Your folks could come to visit, to stay for as long as they wished.'

Sarah gave a huge sigh of relief and Anthony heard her say sincerely, 'I'd say you've made me so happy this night. I love you, Anthony Brennan. Truly I do.'

Sarah moved closer to Anthony. He took her into his arms. In that moment they both felt as they had when reunited that day, some sixteen years before.

Chapter Sixty-One

Out of love for his mother and father and wishing to see them happy at heart, Sean had readily agreed to what his father had proposed, knowing his mother was on top of the world at the prospect of returning to Ireland. And for Sean, the thought of returning to his homeland, of which he had learnt so much from his mother's lips, good and not so good, left him pleasantly excited. The thought of leaving London and all its demands did not depress him much. But breaking the news to his best friend, proved to be the hardest thing for Sean to do.

Seeing Drew Malpass close to tears as they sat at the foot of that great oak, the very tree to which they had laid claim with carved initials many years earlier, left Sean suddenly so aware of the intensity of their sense of belonging to each other, born out of the happy childhood together. They had shared each and every day of their innocent youth for as far back as they could both remember. They had darted to and from each other's houses, had shared the same seat at primary school, and treasured, long summer evenings in the wood, itself a school of learning like no other, wherein they had both laughed and cried, and nearly died, and broken each other's heart. They had fought the same street wars with neighbouring gangs, had chased the same girls, and had experienced the same thrills and disappointments which life had thrown at them thus far.

'When will you be going exactly?' Drew sniffed, regaining his composure a little.

'August,' Sean replied quietly. 'What will you do with yourself, Drew?'

Drew wore a forlorn expression. 'God knows. I just might go off and join the bleeding army after all.' And it was with an even greater sense of despair that he added, 'Oh, I don't know. Something will turn up.'

'Listen. We can still keep in touch. You can even come to Ireland for your holidays. We'll have great fun.' Sean's forced enthusiasm did little to lift Drew's depression and this was evident in his voice still. 'Who knows what will happen, eh Sean? Life's full of surprises.'

As darkness fell Sean and Drew both walked out of the wood without another word said, each knowing that they would never again together set foot in their Eden.

Sean did not see Drew for days after and finding his seat empty at the picture house on Friday night, he thought he had better call at the Malpass flat. Doing so, Sean was informed by an anxious mother, that Drew had packed a bag the day before and had gone, simply saying he was going off to find himself a job. What and where? No one knew. Privately, Sean knew why Drew had up and left. To say goodbye in August would have been too painful for both of them. Knowing it was unlikely that Drew would show himself before he left England, Sean was left wondering when and where, he might see his best friend again. For Sean doubted not, that he and Drew would be reunited some day.

Letters received from Ireland in answer to their own individual letters informing loved ones of their proposed return, had Sarah and Anthony greatly more excited over their plans. Sarah's parents were 'over the moon with joy' and promised to visit them once settled in Donegal, while Anthony's mother and Christy were thrilled also at the prospect of their return. Meantime Christy agreed to help find Anthony a suitable house to rent in Buncrana, but stressed in his letter of reply, that Anthony need not look for land on which to build a house, as there was 'land a plenty' on the homestead to do just that, and no shortage of helping hands when it came to 'laying the bricks and mortar'.

Though somewhat nervous of finally meeting his extended family, Sean eagerly counted down the days. The return to Ireland had been pencilled in for a fortnight's time - the fifteenth of August, the feast day of our Blessed Lady. His mother considered this a good omen. Sean had faith in his mother's belief.

With almost each day that came to pass, Anthony was moved to assure Sarah that Sean would cope well with the transition and would 'handle himself' in any difficult situation. Sarah was a little anxious at the prospect of her son being given a rough ride over his English accent and was served cold comfort somewhat in bed one night, with Anthony saying, 'We should be more concerned if we were returning to Belfast.'

Happy at heart just to be returning to Irish soil, Sarah was content knowing she and her son would at least see her family in Donegal, of which she held fond memories. She concluded that the occasional weekend spent together amid such peaceful surroundings, would do her mother and ailing father the power of good. For Sarah, it would be heaven sent to be one big happy family once again. Sarah too, was counting down the days.

Anthony was also impatient to return home. He had grown tired and weary of London life, the constant hustle and bustle, the endless lines of traffic, the choking smog and fumes, and work and more work. While the Londoners were fair and friendly people, he knew he could never be one of them. Despite the daily slog, life in London had in many ways been good to him. Through providing ample opportunity to work, and damn hard at that, he had been able to put money behind him which, when added to that he had saved from the days at Edenderry Abbey, was enough to build a simple but comfortable house back home. At last, he would indeed try his luck at starting up his own furniture production workshop in Buncrana, which was itself slowly growing in size and populace. Many more people were reported to be moving into the town from the rural community, and families, as if in keeping with tradition, were forever on the increase. Houses would have to be built and furnished. Anthony was confident he could provide good quality furniture at a competitive price. There was a roaring trade to be had, he was sure. As for his son's future, Anthony was satisfied knowing Sean had showed a willingness to complete his education in Ireland and that he was considering pursuing a professional career. Sarah meanwhile, was also pleased that her son was willing to return home without any protest or concern. Once there, she too would be open to new opportunities. For the first time in a long time, both she and Anthony were happy at heart.

Painful as it was to do so, the handful of very good friends made locally over the years were all personally informed by Anthony and Sarah of their plan to return to Ireland in the summer. Frances, Jack Kilty, Donegal Danny and his good wife, Maureen, though sad to learn of the Brennans' imminent departure, were happy that the family was happy in their decision and all the friends offered to help in the move in whatever way they could. For Anthony and Sarah those same friends would remain friends for a lifetime.

Sean Mor felt gravely ill. This time he feared it was for the worst. It felt as though the disease riddling his muscles and bones was eating away at him from inside with a vengeance. Each day that God blessed him was a welcomed bonus, but he was not fooling himself. Sean Mor accepted the fact that his time was short.

Feeling himself go downhill rapidly at the close of June, Sean Mor prayed God would spare him long enough to see his eldest grandchild once again. If so, he would die a happy man. Leaving nothing to chance, he had given his permission to others to take measures to minimise the risk of a further attempt on his life by the UVF, and so slept a little easier in his bed at night knowing some of the boys stood vigilant on the street corner.

Rosie and her daughters, Caithlin and Bridget, seeing a worrying change in the man, also longed for August to come soon. They were quietly preparing themselves for their father's passing and only hoped that Sarah would see her father before the end, as she had been closest to him as a child. They knew it would be terribly hard on her if she did not see him while he lived, if only to say goodbye. They knew also that for Sean Mor not to see his one and only grandson before the final hour, would be so cruel, and would leave the husband, father and grandfather, dying with a broken heart.

Fearing his dear friend and comrade's time was running out fast, Barratt was beginning to make plans in his head as to the most honourable way of seeing Sean Mor through the gates of Milltown, where he'd be laid to rest alongside comrades of old in the Republican Plot. Barratt's main concern was that the RUC would try to disrupt the funeral of a committed foe. As for a firing party to give a final salute? There was just about enough revolvers left in the hands of the Belfast Brigade to do just that. With reports from QM's across the North now received, the military standing of the IRA in the North, in terms of weapons and the number of men in the field at his disposal, painted a depressing picture indeed. Together with the six handguns and one Lee Enfield rifle held by the brigade in Belfast, Barratt personally had in his charge the prized Thompson machinegun and two fully loaded drums. The Thompson had been finally retrieved from the derelict house in Ardoyne, where it had lain undiscovered for months in a cavity wall. The RUC had searched the old house and many others, both derelict and occupied in the days after the shooting of Black, but the gun had slipped their searching eyes and hands. Now, after many hours of greasing and cleaning, the Thompson was once again a lethal weapon, stored safely in the loft of a sympathiser's house further along the Falls.

Even more depressing for the leading IRA man was to know that ammunition was in dire supply. Every bullet had been counted and he was in a quandary as to whether or not the few rounds could be spared for the volley at Sean Mor's graveside.

When meeting with his brigade in recent days, Barratt had stressed once again for every bullet to be collected in and made ready. He'd forewarned that the day the unionists would force their hand in smashing the civil rights movement, would not be long in coming, and had again forecast that such an action would culminate in the Catholic people of the ghettos turning to the IRA for help. Knowing what he did, the sorry state of the brigades, Barratt hoped that such a day would not come to pass too soon. Barratt had also warned, that for the IRA to be seen to be raising fresh supplies of arms, would not only serve the unionists with the excuse to set about smashing - what was in their eyes - the IRA/NICRA conspiracy, but would also trigger a massive purge against northern republicans by the leadership down south. They would seek to remove the potential of a strong opposition to those changes proposed at the forthcoming ard fheis. And so, Barratt's hands were tied meantime. Until the time was right for a legitimate split to come about in January, the arming of the new IRA to be could not happen.

With large-scale street protests organised by the NICRA and the annual Orange Order parades scheduled for the summer months, and the newly elected Unionist Prime Minister at Stormont promising tougher measures to withstand any 'subversive conspiracy', Barratt was a very restless and concerned man as tension across the province intensified. A slogan appearing overnight on a gable end along the Falls, served an ominous warning of things to come. It read: IT'S GOING TO BE A LONG HOT SUMMER!

Sean celebrated his seventeenth birthday happy in the belief that Drew was safe. After weeks of unnerving silence, Drew's mother had received a postcard, postmarked Brighton, from her son days earlier. Drew claimed to be holding down a good job with good pay and to have found himself comfortable lodgings in the seaside town. He had forwarded best regards to Sean on his 17th and promised to meet up with him someday soon. Although Drew had been vague in telling his mother what exactly it was he was doing, where he was living, Sean knew that if Drew were indeed working, it would be doing something he enjoyed. He assumed Drew's discretion as to his exact whereabouts was down to him shacking up with some bird, the thought of which left Sean a little envious. He himself was yet to seal his first date. His father's promise though, to fix him up with a 'fine country girl' on their return to Ireland, left Sean nervous. He held a rather narrow-minded perception of countrywomen generally, that of big, abrasive types with fiery tempers. Drew had always bragged that he would be the first of the two of them to lay a girl and Sean was resigned to the truth of this, knowing Drew would take full advantage of his newfound freedom.

Yet to succeed in chatting up any girl, Sean lay restless in his bed that sticky July night wondering with whom and in what circumstances he would lose his virginity. With only weeks left before he sailed to Ireland, he pondered to think what the first girl's name would be. He saw her face, beautifully created in his own mind's eye, and she was worlds' apart in comparison to those he had previously conjured up in his head. She would be his dream girl meantime.

Sean Mor could not bear up to the pain any longer and was forced to take to his bed once again, knowing this time he would die in it.

Paying visits twice daily to No72 during the remainder of July, the family doctor tried in vain to persuade his patient to be admitted to hospital. But Sean Mor knew where and among whom he preferred to spend his last hour, when his time came. Knowing it was not far away, he continued to quietly pray each day and night that came to pass, that God would give him the strength to at least see August out. He knew that if he could not make it across the border to see his only grandson, then Sarah, come what may, would come to him, with Sean, and this he did not want. The tension in Belfast was explosive and August threatened to be a violent month with both Orange Order parades and civil rights marches set to clash head-on.

Rosie slept a little during the day and sat up with her husband all night, every night. The doting couple would drink tea into the wee small hours and talk about the 'Good old days', few and far between though they had been. Caithlin and Bridget took it in turns every other night to sit up with mother in keeping vigil over father when he at last succumbed to the drugs.

The three granddaughters found it all so exciting coming to visit their grandfather, to sit on the edge of the big bed, the sick bed, in which Sean Mor would grit his teeth and force a smile in telling his 'little princesses' a story or two, most often about Belfast characters of old, who had made everyone laugh in their day, even during those more difficult times.

Barratt slipped in and out of No72 on occasion also, but could never stay long in one place. He and Sean Mor did not talk politics. They had respectfully agreed to disagree on the best way forward. Instead, Barratt and Sean Mor discussed the successes and failures of their favourite Gaelic football team, but it was very difficult for Barratt to sit and watch helplessly as the big man wasted away in front of his very eyes.

Come August, Barratt did not trouble Sean Mor with any more talk of their team's dismal performance on the field as it was obvious to Barratt that Sean Mor was not always aware of the presence of those around him.

The incessant pain often left Sean Mor delirious, and on occasion, completely numbed by ever increasing dosages of pain killing drugs. To see Sean Mor suffer so, and to see him lost in a trance-like state was so hard for all who stayed close by his side to accept. Seeing a man who was once so incredibly fit and active become a mere shadow of his former self, was beginning to break all their hearts, while knowing at the same time that a daughter, a sister, was only days away from arriving back in Ireland. But would she make it in time? That was the question they all asked of themselves, but were obliged to do little else. The man dying had made each of them promise in recent days when momentarily raising himself above the pain, not to call Sarah home before her time.

For Rosie, on her last legs due to the want of sleep, all that had been promised her husband was to be broken on being told by the visiting doctor on the twelfth day of August that there was 'no hope' for the man, to whom she had been married for forty years, and that he had only days to live. Stunned into silence while her two youngest wept inconsolably in the scullery downstairs, Rosie knew she had to have Sarah home. The hard, cruel reality of what had just been told left her fearful that with the loss of her man she may well also lose a daughter. She knew Sarah would never forgive her if not informing her of what was imminent.

As a heavily burdened wife and mother gave instruction to a reliable neighbour to send word to her daughter in England to come home as quickly as possible, the streets of Derry City, less than seventy miles west of Belfast, erupted in bloody violence. The political crisis unfolding that day would change the course of the whole island's history, the pattern of life for its people so dramatically, and so painfully for many, many years to come.

Sean watched aghast the latest television pictures of angry youth, their faces masked against the dense, acrid clouds of CS gas, bombard the Northern Ireland Police with bricks and petrol bombs on the streets of Derry - or Londonderry, as referred to by the British media. Dishevelled RUC men and B Specials, some engulfed by fire, were being forced to retreat by the sheer volume of missiles raining down upon them from the rooftops of grim multi-story flats and from behind improvised street barricades comprising overturned cars and burning buses. The ashen-faced, red-eyed reporter at the scene, taking shelter behind a low wall, his voice gripped by near hysteria, proclaimed under the riotous din, that the 'Battle of the Bogside' was raging.

Struggling with the lock snibs of the larger suitcase, Anthony and Sarah were left dumbstruck as they knelt on the living-room floor by what they witnessed also. While Sarah feared that the violence would soon spread to Belfast, where as yet she did not know her father lay close to death, Anthony could not help but think that the latest outburst of street violence was a dark omen for them not to return to Ireland. But he knew that there was no turning back and he received some welcomed comfort knowing that the family had no plans to set foot north of the border.

A loud knock on the front door just then, had Sarah investigating. Receiving into her hand the telegram sent from Belfast calling her home urgently, Anthony was facing the worst scenario imaginable. His wife was now making ready to travel to Belfast and Sean was stating his willingness to accompany his mother on the same journey.

Anthony's frustration over this sudden turn of events at the eleventh hour, just as they had been making final preparations to travel to Donegal via ferry to Dublin and to the town house that Christy had secured for them, boiled over, on realising the horrendous situation unfolding before his very eyes. Sarah was demanding he contact the ferry port to book her and Sean onto the next sailing to Belfast, making it clear, without even saying it, that he could go his own way if he wanted.

'For Christ sake Sarah, just think for a moment what you're doing! Going to Belfast at this moment in time is sheer madness.' Anthony soon discovered his plea to be to no avail. Standing to face Anthony in the middle of the living-room, itself turning into a battlefield of sorts, while Sean, seated on the settee close by looked on nervously, Sarah said firmly, 'I never thought I'd hear it implied by you, Anthony Brennan, that to want to see a loved one ... one's own father, before he dies, was an act of madness. *How dare you*!'

'I didn't mean it like ...'

'I know what you meant!' Sarah snapped. 'But I don't give a damn about the troubles right now. I'm going home to where I am expected ... to where I should rightfully be. Do you understand me?'

Grabbing Sarah's wrist in anger, Anthony said forcibly, 'No, I don't understand. What about the safety of our son?'

'Sean's old enough to make up his own mind.' Sarah retorted, trying hard, but in vain, to prise herself free. Anthony felt the blood surge to his head and he was lost for words on hearing Sarah, her eyes glinting with defiance, add with contempt, 'If he wishes to see his own grandfather before he dies, I'm not going to stand in his way. *Are you?*'

In blind rage over his authority being challenged so in front of his son and with that deep-rooted anxiety over past events suddenly raising its ugly head, Anthony raised an open hand to forcibly bring it across Sarah's daring face. A voice, crying out from across the room, jolted him to take stock of the ugliness of the moment.

'No! Don't do it Dad!'

A child once not so very long ago, now a young man, had cried a plea from the heart. Trembling, Sean came to stand between his warring parents.

Turning to their son, a witness to their own frustration, hopes and fears, and seeing his young face white with fear, both parents let go of their own concerns. Feeling Anthony release his grip on her, Sarah pulled

Sean close. Holding her son ever so tightly she sobbed aloud upon his shoulder, out of pity for him.

Weighed down by an enormous sense of guilt, Anthony saw his son's tearful eyes search his for an explanation and did not hesitate to speak his heart, through a few simple words.

'I'm sorry.'

Anthony felt his burden of guilt lift a little on seeing Sean force a smile. Anthony knew and accepted that the onus was now on him to hold the family together in face of the dark shadow cast over them all through the renewed out-spilling of violence back in Ireland.

'If we are to go anywhere ... we will go together, as one. We will leave for Belfast first thing in the morning.'

With a tortured look chiselled upon her face, Sarah turned to Anthony and as on the day he had taken his leave from her on Belfast dock, held out a hand to him. He took Sarah's hand in his, and joining his wife and son, they held each other close. In that moment of blissful peace, each prayed silently that God would keep them safe in the days ahead.

Rosie and the girls remained close by the side of a heavily sedated Sean Mor that night. A steady stream of visitors called to the house to offer comfort and practical help, and to join in the Rosary, which was offered in hourly cycles. Those who prayed beseeched the Blessed Lady to act in all her mercy in sparing the final hour until all the dying man's family was reunited. No one gathered, doubted that Sean Mor was entering the final hours of his life on earth.

Father Crossan and Doctor Gill, seeking to lend moral support also, had joined the family around the sick bed. In between the prayers, muted conversation was of the day's headlined events in Derry, from where latest reports told of the riots escalating and gaining in intensity. There was rumour abound of many people killed and injured. Rosie McParland offered up her decade of the Rosary for those dead and dying.

Very few people in Belfast slept that night, knowing it was only a matter of hours before their own city erupted in ugly violence. Vigilantes were out in force in all Catholic ghettos. The night air crackled with unholy potential for death and destruction.

Barratt paced the streets along the Falls throughout the night, checking regularly on those parts of the area most prone to loyalist mob attack. Nowhere was more vulnerable than his own tiny parish; the Clonard was encircled on three points of the map by the loyalist Shankill, which, from where he observed, was also a hive of activity. Sinister movements by large groups of men, some dressed in black militia-type uniform, were detectable in the not-too-far distance amid the shadows cast by the unnatural glare of the streetlights. He had already mobilised his men across the city on the first reports coming through of the violence in Derry's Bogside, where the Catholic people struggled to hold off the might of the Unionist Government who had thrown down the gauntlet in seeking to smash the civil rights campaign. The sixty or so IRA men at his disposal, with less than a dozen low velocity weapons shared out between them, had been dispersed between those areas most prone to loyalist attack - the Lower Falls, Ardoyne, New Lodge, and the Short Strand, in the east of the city. The IRA men stood on stand-by. Their orders meantime, required them not to go into action unless faced with the overwhelming prospect of their areas being overrun by loyalists. Barratt knew it was critically important for the short-term benefit of the new IRA, that come what may the unionists must be recorded in the journals of history to be written, as being the ones who turned to the gun first, so that any IRA response would be legitimised in the eyes of the world. It was this reasoning which Barratt had been able to sell easily to his men across the North in the past few days.

Now, from the televised news reports on the 'Battle of the Bogside' earlier that day, the RUC and B Specials had undoubtedly been made to appear the antagonists. And not a shot had yet been fired by the IRA.

After a long and tiresome drive north to Liverpool, Anthony, Sarah and Sean wearily climbed the steep stairwell from the hull of the ferry, where the family car, its boot loaded, stood parked in line alongside those heavy trucks bound for Belfast harbour. At such short notice they had only been able to book themselves onto the following day's night sailing and were due to arrive in Belfast just after eight the next morning, the fourteenth of August, a day ahead of their earlier scheduled return to Ireland.

Sarah had sent a reply telegram ahead informing family that she was on her way home. The Brennans had packed all that they had wanted and needed to take with them. Jack Kilty had agreed to settle the business of selling off their furniture and forwarding the money raised.

Goodbyes had been said earlier in the day. Jack Kilty and Donegal Danny had called to the home at midday, with Anthony letting them know of developments. Sarah and Sean had called briefly on Frances the night before to inform her of their early departure. Both women, who had befriended each other in times of great need, had shed many tears. Their friendship had been so special and would remain so for all time. They'd parted company with the promise to each other to keep in touch. Sarah left Frances both her parents' address and that of the house in Donegal to where they were eventually destined. Frances promised to post on Sean's exam results and to let Drew know where he could contact Sean. A reuniting someday had not been ruled out. Sean had kissed his 'second Mum' goodbye.

Anthony had sent a short letter to his mother and Christy, to let them know of the change of circumstances. He assured them that he would be in Donegal within a few days of arriving in Belfast.

As the night ferry set sail, Sean lay in his bunk dreaming of happier times to come. Anthony and Sarah lay wide-awake in theirs in the adjoining cabin. Sarah prayed quietly that her father would live long enough for his eldest daughter to tell him how much she loved him.

Anthony prayed their time in Belfast would be short and swift and that the violence, still ravaging Derry, would pass them by.

Chapter Sixty-Two

Joe McNab stood waiting on the quay at the very same spot where he had bid farewell to Anthony seventeen years earlier. Bringing the car to a quiet halt beside his old friend, Anthony saw that McNab, now much greyer and heavier, wore the same worried frown as he had that day when stepping into the maternity ward, to tell him of Sean Mor's arrest. Anthony's first thoughts were that they were too late. Winding down the driver's side window, Anthony reached out a hand to boldly shake McNab's. With McNab stooping to push his head into the opening in the door, the local man's accent sounded much sharper to Anthony's ear, than that of Sarah's.

'It's great to see you, Anthony. Welcome back.'

McNab gestured to Sarah, anxious for news, and eased her mind a little. 'Sarah, your father is sticking it out like the fighter he is. But there's not a moment to lose.' Looking over Anthony's shoulder at the tall, well-built, fair-haired young man sitting on the car's back seat eyeing him with interest in turn, McNab quipped, in his none subtle, though harmless way, 'You must be the Sean fellah. The last time I saw you, you were in your nappies!'

Sean laughed at this and took an instant liking to the odd-looking fellow badgering him. McNab addressed Anthony on a more serious note.

'Remember Anthony, when you left it was all go here? Well, not much has changed. The city is hiving with B Specials. There's been non-stop rioting in Derry these past two days and nights and they're bracing themselves for some of the same here at anytime. So listen ...' The Brennan family did so attentively '... I'm parked up over yonder.' McNab gestured over his shoulder with a thumb. 'Follow me out and keep close. We're gonna drive straight to Leger Street, all right?' Their lives were in McNab's hands. McNab proceeded to give instruction. 'Sarah, your Aunt Bella's old house is ready for youse. That's where you'll be staying in between time, know what I mean like?' She nodded. 'C'mon. We'd better be going.'

For Anthony, it was as if he had never left the cursed place. He followed McNab's old car, still in pristine condition, out of the docks and across the city centre, which apart from the rush of early morning workers as in any industrial town and city, presented a more sinister face. Convoys of armoured military vehicles were ominously parked in side streets adjacent to the bottom of the Falls Road, which they soon approached. Dozens of heavily armed B Specials seemingly impatient for something to happen lurked at the rear of their vehicles.

Apart from the ugly grey concrete blocks of newly erected flats at the mouth of the lower Falls, the main road which ran through it and the maze of crisscrossing side streets on both sides of it, had not changed one iota. And just as on that day when McNab had driven him back to Leger Street from the City Hospital, Anthony was acutely aware of the potential for blood spilling which threatened to explode on every street corner.

In Sean's observant eyes, it was a war zone to which he had returned. Suddenly, with his fears raised, the Ireland he now saw was a far cry from the picturesque, tranquil setting rooted in his mind's eye when a child back in Clapham Common.

As the car swung into Leger Street, Sarah looked over her shoulder and with a reassuring smile, said to Sean, 'Everything is going to be okay.' No one heard Anthony whisper, 'I hope so.'

Sarah was stepping out of the car before it had pulled up proper to the kerb and was dashing in through the front door of her family home. She quickly climbed the stairs to that room wherein she knew her father lay. Entering the dimly lit front bedroom, which smelt of decay and lingering death, Sarah's gaze fell onto her father's pitiful, tortured face and she sighed with relief on seeing his large brown eyes, though heavily glazed, open slowly. In her eyes, her father was barely recognisable. His sickly, yellow skin seemed to be thinly painted over his skeleton, his once wavy and sandy hair was now lank and grey. Movement both sides of the bed caught Sarah's attention and she threw her arms open in greeting as her mother and sisters, the long years appearing to have been very hard on each one of them, came surging towards her. Embracing, they held each other tightly, silently. It felt so good to be together again, albeit under such circumstances.

After a few moments the four women quietly flocked around the sick bed once more to resume the vigil. Sarah bent low over her father to whisper softly into his ear, 'Da, it's Sarah. I'm here with you. I'm home!' A comforting hand upon her shoulder had Sarah looking up to see Sean standing behind her, looking down at his grandfather with tear-filled eyes. Anthony stood a little further back, looking on solemnly. Sarah turned to her father again, and said a little louder, 'Your grandson Sean is here. Anthony too. The whole family is with you now.'

All in the room saw the dying man's right hand rise slowly from off the bed and reach out, which Sean instinctively took in his. Managing to smile defiantly in the face of his suffering, Sean Mor's lips seemed to tremble and all heard him say in a faint whisper, 'God bless you, Sean.'

Sean Mor drifted into a deep sleep. His wife insisted that all gathered join her in offering up a Rosary in thanks to God and his Holy

Mother for reuniting the family. All knelt around the deathbed to pray. For Sean it was a moment in time he was sure he would never forget.

By the time darkness fell Sean was having difficulty remembering the names of all the people - family, friends and formal peers, to whom he'd been introduced as they called to the house to ask about his grandfather. Knowing himself that the man must be suffering terribly, Sean understood why one woman visitor said to another, when leaving the house together, 'It would be an act of mercy if God were to take Sean Mor before the night is through.'

Long after dark the immediate family were left to attend to the one dying. Sean Mor was to be washed and turned to prevent the breakdown of skin. Sarah was keen to do her duty and helping her mother and sisters with the task received the shock of her life on drawing back the bed covers to discover both her father's legs appear like long, black pokers. Forced to withdraw to one side, Sarah wept silently. Sarah's mother comforted her in one corner of the room as she fought to regain her composure, while Sarah's sisters, hardened to the gory scene, proceeded to wash their heavily sedated father with gentle, caring hands.

    Rosie took her eldest daughter in her arms and whispered in her ear with a resilient voice.

    'Your father paid a heavy price for the years of internment, Sarah. Many a stronger man would not have taken the beatings he took. That is why his body is in such a terrible state ... that's why he's suffering such an agonising death. But we must not be bitter. I know it's hard not to be, but we must pray for those who did this to him. And most of all, we must pray for your father, for life is sacred and God given.'

    Sarah knew what her mother inferred. They knew that the man they both cherished and loved had, if not by his doing, then through ordering others, the blood of many on his hands. Though understanding the price to be paid by republicans, Sarah understood also that others, those devout to the faith, such as her mother, took a different view. So she respected her mother's position, though did not always agree with it. Not wanting to add to her mother's pain, Sarah simply returned to the task in hand, very bitter of heart toward those who had treated her father so brutally, when defenceless and at their mercy.

Retreating downstairs to the quietness of the front room, Anthony received a run down of events occurring locally over the past seventeen years from McNab. His old friend kept him company long after Sean had fallen into a deep sleep on the nearby sofa.

    Amid familiar surroundings, with little in the house indeed the room wherein Sarah and Anthony had often courted, changed, Anthony heard in graphic, nauseating detail, how Craig and Black had died, how people had celebrated over the news, and grieved so on the double murder of their women neighbours, shot dead right outside the front door of the house in which they sat. Although Anthony suspected rightly who the killer's intended target had been on that occasion, McNab never once mentioned Sean Mor's name in any dubious circumstances. Anthony was left wondering was this purely out of concern and respect for the man or fear? Even though the same man lay close to death.

Both McNab and Anthony shared some of their own life experiences since parting company all those years ago. Anthony spoke of the loss of his father and his good friend, Mick Onion, which McNab was particularly sad to hear, having first met the elder and Anthony's friend and neighbour at the time of the Brennan family's double tragedy back in 1949. By comparison, McNab appeared to have continued to live a fairly ordinary life, content it seemed to remain a bachelor. The long years apart had left both men a little wary of the other, insomuch that there was a certain degree of non-disclosure. Anthony was reluctant to talk of his brief encounter with Finn Spiceland, his worry at the height of IRA activity in England. McNab kept quiet about those hair-raising moments when ferrying IRA men, their guns and explosives, back and forth during the days of the border campaign; all that was expected of a trusted sympathiser.

Conversation gradually turned to events more recent, with McNab once again warning of grave times to come. But neither one of the men could have foreseen what was about to unfold in Belfast that very night.

In light of what the Derry Brigade OC requested with urgency via the messenger dispatched from the besieged city, Barratt was under incredible pressure to order the Belfast Brigade into action. He faced such a dilemma with the Derry man pleading with him to alleviate the pressure on the Bogsiders – struggling to hold off repeated RUC and B Special attempts to invade the Bogside - by stretching the forces of the state thinly on the ground by instigating widespread civil riots across nationalist Belfast. The scenario proposed was exacerbated by the Derry man's fears that the RUC and B Specials, if successful in breaching the barricades encircling the Bogside, would set out to massacre those resisting. The B Specials particularly, were baying for blood, having taken a real hammering the past forty-eight hours. Not wishing to go down in folklore as the one who had aided and abetted such an atrocity against his own people by doing nothing, Barratt gave the nod to Bonar to get things moving. As Bonar set out from the safe house in Beechmount, and the messenger returning to Derry with the good news, a breathless Cassidy met up with the three men on the front doorstep of the house. 'It's started, Frankie ... over in Ardoyne. The Orangemen lured some of the local men to the church there, by sending in one of their own screaming that it was under attack. When the lads approached the bastards opened up with machineguns from the church grounds. At least three have been shot. They're rioting like fuck over there now!' Just as the last word left Cassidy's parched mouth, a car, with its horn tooting incessantly, came roaring up the Falls Road at great speed and screeched to a sudden halt on the nearby corner. Carmichael, his face very white, alighted from the passenger side and came charging toward the group of men shouting at the top of his voice, 'Divis Street is under attack! Our people are fleeing for their lives!' Barratt turned to the Derry youth to say dryly, 'It sounds as if the Orangemen here are about to save the day for us all. Be on your way lad, and be careful.'

Bonar had new orders to execute, while Barratt raced to the waiting car along with Carmichael. Once on board, Barratt ordered D'Arcy, the driver, to first drive up the Falls. Barratt had something to collect. As they did so, Barratt and Carmichael shouted from the open windows of the vehicle to spread the news of the loyalist attack on the lower Falls to the many young men standing idly on street corners. The IRA men urged some of the youths, but not all, to go to the aid of the people in Divis, while those remaining behind were warned to be on the lookout for an attack at any moment on Clonard, another vulnerable area of the Falls.

Once personally collecting the Thompson and loaded magazine drums from another safe house in the heart of the Falls, Barratt had D'Arcy put his boot down. The car sped back along the Falls towards Divis Street from where plumes of thick black smoke rising above the rooftops was almost lost against a deep-blue summer night sky. An orange glow from the rising flames as Catholic homes were petrol bombed by the advancing mob of loyalists and B Special gradually illuminated the skyline over the lower Falls. As D'Arcy pulled the car up to the kerb a few streets back from Divis Street, the car vibrated violently as an ear-shattering prolonged burst of heavy gunfire raked the whole area up ahead. Looking straight in front the three IRA men could see the illuminated lines of red-hot lead cut across the night's sky from the direction of the Shankill and explode in tiny bursts of flame against the grey cement walls of the high rise flats in the new Divis complex, to their right.

'Fucking hell, Frankie. The poor bastards in them flats don't stand a chance. The walls are paper-thin.'

Neither Barratt nor Carmichael doubted D'Arcy. He, his wife and three weans had been moved into one of the concrete monstrosities when their old slum had at long last been bulldozed to make way for homes in the sky. Barratt gave his snatched analysis of the situation to those not really knowing what to do now.

'Lads, this is turning fucking nasty. Let's get down there quick and give the bastards a taste of their own medicine.'

Carmichael, and D'Arcy who was very worried for the safety of his family, followed Barratt as he ran slouched from the car with the loaded Thompson tucked under an arm toward the corner of Divis Street a little further along the Falls, now eerily deserted as sporadic bursts of gunfire continued to ring out. The shooting sounded even more intense as it echoed around the maze of side streets and back alleys and rattled the rooftops of the remaining condemned slums. The roof slates cracking under the intense heat as houses burned out of control at the far end of Divis Street, sounded like a fusillade of rifle shots. Barratt calculated that the B Specials would be quick to claim that they'd returned fire, when fired on first by IRA gunmen operating in the Falls. So he was greatly more determined to give the B Specials something of real substance to mouth about.

Taking his life into his hands during a lull in the shooting to steal a glance along the street on fire, Barratt saw that both sides of it, as far as halfway down from the Shankill Road end, was beyond saving. With that side of his face exposed to intense heat, Barratt was forced to quickly pull his head back in, but had estimated that an RUC Shorland armoured car, its mounted Browning machinegun known to fire eleven heavy calibre rounds per second and sitting in the middle of the road toward the far end of the burning street, was within range. Barratt prepared to step out to fire a concentrated burst of gunfire in the general direction of the armoured car in the hope of repulsing any continued loyalist advance into the Falls. Just then, consumed by the strangest of feelings, Barratt was compelled to look over his shoulder. Barratt could just pick out from among the smoky shadows cast, what he thought to be a priest, sheltering in the doorway of a derelict shop on the opposite corner, across the Falls Road. The vague figure with an indistinguishable chalk-white face, was heard to say without opening his mouth, 'There has been the death of innocents tonight. So put away your gun.'

He's right, thought Frankie. We'll be playing right into their hands if we open up. Barratt weighed up the situation for a moment longer. Turning to D'Arcy, to see the lad's face drained of blood, his feeble frame shake like a leaf while he stared straight across the road as if transfixed by something extraordinary, Barratt heard himself say firmly, without prior thought, 'Get back to your family, D'Arcy. See if they're safe and well.' Not dropping his gaze, D'Arcy simply nodded. Staying low, he sprinted across the main road and disappeared into the high-rise flats set further back.

Turning his attention toward the shop doorway again to investigate whom the mystery man was, Barratt was left perplexed. He simply could not understand it. The doorway was empty. No one was to be seen along the length of the Falls, apart from Carmichael moving closer to his side. Barratt was moved to ask, 'Where did he go?'

'Who?' Carmichael asked.

'Whoever it was in that doorway over there.'

'I saw no one, Frankie. No one but D'Arcy has moved.'

'Perhaps whoever it was, went into the shop itself, eh, Carmichael?'

'I doubt it, Frankie. That shop's been bricked-up for many a year.' Barratt felt a chill sweep over him on hearing this. He could not understand to where the man had disappeared. It was as if he'd vanished into thin air.

'C'mon Carmichael. Let's head back up the Falls.'

Barratt and Carmichael dashed back to the borrowed car. On quickly completing a three-point turn, the car sped on towards Clonard, where unknown to the two men, a full-scale attack by loyalists and B Specials on the pocket of a dozen or so back streets, was wreaking carnage and despair, and gaining ground.

All the way to Clonard, Barratt remained unsettled by the odd experience back along the lower Falls. If he saw the night through safely, he was determined to find out who the mystery man had been.

Anthony and McNab's lighter conversation had been abruptly interrupted by a commotion rising just beyond the front room window and which had them both moving into the long hallway and toward the front door to investigate. McNab protectively held Anthony back with an open hand as he pulled the front door open to look out. Standing just behind Barratt, Anthony could hear heavy feet running along the pavement and raised, though incoherent voices as more than one man was shouting at the same time. The voices were angry and panic-stricken in tone and people coughed violently, as if choking. In the streets beyond, others screamed and dogs barked wildly. Suddenly, Anthony felt his eyes sting violently. An acrid taste filled his mouth. Just then, one very angry man running along the street announced with more than a hint of irony permeating his words, 'The Clonard's being burnt to the ground, and the bastards are firing CS Gas - *at us*!'

Tears streaming his face and heaving as if about to vomit, McNab stepped quickly back into the hallway and slammed the front door out. Catching his breath, he turned to Anthony, struggling to catch his, and with urgency, croaked, 'Get up the stairs quick. Make sure all the windows are shut tight. If Sean Mor gets a dose of gas, it will surely kill him.'

Nauseated, his eyes burning in their sockets and with a shortness of breath, Anthony took to the stairs with great difficulty. Entering the dying man's bedroom feeling like death himself, he found the women already experiencing common traits of being gassed. Sarah had been quick though to shut the smaller of the double windows, which had been ventilating the room all day, but which a moment ago had allowed a haze of CS gas carried on a cool evening breeze, to pollute the room. Thankfully her mother had been just as quick to draw the bed's top sheet over her husband's mouth and nose and had prevented him falling foul of the gas, though all four women had evidently been badly affected. All coughed and spluttered violently into handkerchiefs as they resumed their positions around the bed, content at least that the man dying had been spared the same. Sean Mor's short rasps of breath still came, but much fainter. Steadying himself against the dressing table and feeling as though someone's hands were tightening around his throat, Anthony spoke with great difficulty.

'There's something serious ... going on. They're ... firing gas ... into the area.'

It was Sarah, leaning over her father, who called out to Anthony from across the room, 'Anthony, we need a priest quickly. Father is slipping fast. Where's McNab?'

'Downstairs.'

'Tell him to go quickly and fetch Father Crossan.'

'I'll go with him.'

'No! Stay close to Sean.'

Hearing Sean's name mentioned had Anthony panicking. He suddenly realised that Sean had been left sleeping in the front room, its top window opened earlier to let the build-up of heat escape. Anthony was out of the room and down the stairs a lot quicker than he had ascended them. He felt his heart thump harder on seeing McNab kneeling over Sean, who was propped up against the wall at the foot of the stairs.

'It's okay! It's okay!' McNab assured, both father and son.

Reaching the bottom of the stairs and crouching down beside his son, whose eyes were red raw and streaming with tears, and who gasped for breath, Anthony was confused on seeing McNab produce a vinegar soaked handkerchief and place it fully over Sean's nose and mouth.

'Vinegar's the boy. It'll soon put him right,' McNab predicted confidently. Sure enough, much to Anthony's surprise, but more so his relief, Sean soon came around. The smell of vinegar wafting along the hallway and up the stairs of the house was a welcome change for all in comparison to what they'd inhaled minutes earlier.

'Are you all right, Sean?' Anthony shook with anger. Afraid of vomiting if opening his mouth to talk, Sean just nodded.

Sarah cried from the top of the stairs, 'My God, what's happened?' Turning to see his wife standing there fraught with worry, Anthony didn't know whether to curse her or comfort her.

'I'm okay ... Mum. I think ... I was gassed. But I'm ... okay now.' Sean's words of gentle reassurance took the heat out of the moment. Anthony's icy stare from the bottom of the stairs cut through Sarah like a knife. But their moment alone together would have to wait. Another's need took precedence now.

'McNab. Father Crossan. Go bring him here, quick!' ordered Sarah. Rising to his feet to leave at once, McNab handed the vinegar soaked cloth to Anthony and sought to assure the father, concerned only for his son in that moment. 'The lad's going to be okay, Anthony. Don't worry.' McNab was gone in a flash, pulling the front door of No72 tightly shut behind him.

Turning sharply off the Falls Road into a side street, the car's headlights picked out Father Crossan amid the mayhem. Barratt's sinking morale with the streets of Clonard ablaze also, its people in flight with whatever few possessions they'd barely had time to grab, received a huge boost on seeing the priest fight back. Still in his soutane, Father Crossan was throwing whatever purposefully came to hand toward the advancing mob of loyalists, already a third of the way down the street and hurling petrol bombs through the windows of terraces on both sides as they came. The dozen or so men of the street attempting desperately to defend their homes alongside the priest, whose church stood under threat in the very next street, were no match for the hundred or so loyalists facing them.

'Stop the car or we'll be roasted alive!' Barratt screamed. Carmichael slammed on the brakes. The car came to an abrupt halt fifty yards behind the straggly line of men defending. Barratt knew exactly what his next move was to be if saving the rest of the street, the local church, the Falls Road itself, from being burnt to the ground.

'When I step out Carmichael, keep your hand on the car horn.' That said, Barratt stepped out of the car with the Thompson and the driver did as he had been told. The dozen or so men to the front of the car turned their heads to investigate the blaring horn. Seeing Barratt standing stride-legged in the middle of the street with a gun pointing directly at them and knowing what was coming next, the men, including the priest, threw themselves flat onto their bellies. With the line of fire open to him, Barratt opened up. The IRA man levelled the barrel of the gun at knee height as he raked the street with lead, not wanting to cause a bloodbath that would evoke a full-scale backlash from Protestants. In the glow of the two dozen houses which burnt fiercely, Barratt saw the shadowy figures of the attacking mob - two hundred yards ahead - scatter in blind panic as the rattle of the Thompson rocked the street and the bones of friend and foe. Six or more loyalists, with blasted kneecaps and shattered shinbones, fell to the ground and writhed in agony.

Barratt had emptied half a drum in one short burst and now fired the occasional single shot into the air to keep the retreating mob at bay. Dragging their squealing wounded behind them, the loyalists soon disappeared into the night, back into the relative safety of the Shankill.

A loud cheer struck up behind Barratt and what seemed like a hundred men suddenly appeared from nowhere and advanced up the street past him with renewed confidence to drive off any loyalist stragglers and to set about fire-fighting, if only to save the rest of the street. A few men slapped Barratt on the back and praised his good deed done.

'God bless you, Frankie.' 'We'll not forget you, Frankie.' Then there was another acknowledgement of sorts, softly spoken.

'I hope God will understand your actions tonight, my son.' Turning to investigate, Barratt found himself face-to-face with Father Crossan, who threw him a half smile.

'I hope so too, Father.' Barratt replied, tucking the smoking gun under his coat.

'Father Crossan! Father Crossan!' McNab called out, spying the priest from a distance. Fearing more bad news, Barratt and the priest waited for McNab to approach. Surely the situation could not get any worse. Half choked, his eyes ablaze from the effects of the gas, McNab urged, 'Come quick, Father. It's Sean Mor. He's breathing his last.'

All three men left the battle scene together and were headed in the same direction. Barratt handed the prized gun to Carmichael and ordered him to stand on and give cover to the men of the street, busy saving those homes still standing intact. Reaching the Falls Road, black with more folk turning out to defend their area, the priest, the IRA man, and the Good Samaritan, ran the remainder of the way to No72 Leger Street.

Sarah had needed Anthony to be by her side when re-entering her parents' bedroom. She knew that she would be fatherless by the time she left it. Seeing her pain, so intense, so potentially destructive, Anthony had run up the stairs to be by Sarah's side, and Sean, by theirs and his grandfather's. They had all assembled around the man's sick bed when the almighty crescendo of gunfire in the neighbouring street, that in which Aunt Bella had once lived, had shook the house. Sean Mor had heard it too. They all saw him look at each one of them in turn now with sunken and glazed eyes, from left to right. First to Caithlin, then Bridget, Anthony, Sean, Sarah, and finally to his wife Rosie, who was seated on the edge of the bed by his right shoulder. With a vague hint of a smile upon his pitiful face, Sean Mor was heard to say to his wife, in a quiet, almost youthful voice, 'Place your arms around me, love. Hold me close.'

With tears gathering in her eyes, his devoted wife did just that. Mustering the last of his greatly diminished strength, Sean Mor was speaking again. 'I hear it has started, Rosie. There'll be no turning back this time.' The woman nodded. Still looking his wife in the eye, his own becoming ever more lifeless, Sean Mor said, 'If I had my life to live over, I'd do it all again. But remember, you were always my first love. Thank you for standing by me.' His wife smiled at him and held him tightly. Sean Mor winked his right eye. 'You're a great girl.' The man died then, his head resting upon his wife's shoulder.

To the horror of the heart-wrenched silent, Sean Mor's body, within seconds of breathing his final breath, turned almost black in colour. So horrific did his corpse appear, all present truly realised just how much the man had silently suffered and endured over the years, and all in the cause of seeking to see his country free, and which, through his last words, he had been proud to do.

Rosie led the prayers bravely. The weeping widow began: 'Sweet Jesus have Mercy on his soul.'

Barratt, McNab, and Father Crossan, realising from the prayers being recited on quietly entering No72 that Sean Mor had just passed away, slipped discreetly into the wake room.

McNab, and Barratt, smelling strongly of cordite, knelt at the back of the room out of respect for their old friend and comrade, while Father Crossan proceeded to bless the dead.

Sarah, standing close by, thanked God through silent prayer for at last giving her father peace.

Chapter Sixty-Three

The RUC and B Specials lost the fight to control the Bogside. By mid-morning of the following day, 15th August, British troops marched onto the streets of Derry to forge the uneasy peace. They were received with open arms by the defenders of 'the Bog' at Free Derry Corner. With their appearance, the bedraggled and demoralised RUC and B Specials, thoroughly exhausted by three solid days and nights of intensive rioting, during which they'd been bombarded from a great height with bricks, bottles, lumps of cast iron grating, petrol bombs, and even old television sets, were ordered by embarrassed, disgruntled Northern Ireland ministers to withdraw to barracks. Westminster politicians now interfered in the state's internal affairs, which suddenly were no longer so.

The Irish and British newspapers were full of headline stories detailing the overnight violence that had threatened to result in an international incident with the Irish Government, at the height of the rioting, indicating by public address that they could not stand aside while northern Catholics were under sectarian attack.

The British Government had defused such a development by deploying troops onto the streets of the city and by promising to examine with fairness the grievances of nationalists, whose anger had exploded with such fury and so dramatically in the face of the international community.

While the Derry clashes had lit the fuse to major political upheaval not only at Stormont but also within the British Government, the overlord of the troubled state, and with the injustices of Northern Ireland exposed to world scrutiny, it was the powder keg of sectarian violence exploding in Belfast on the fourteenth night that marked a turning point in Ireland's history, insomuch that never again would an oppressed minority lie down under the jackboot of state oppression.

The newspaper headlines gave only a snapshot of the hatred and fury that had been unleashed in Belfast. It was reported that at least six people had been killed and hundreds wounded. Tens of millions of pounds worth of damage had been caused to industrial and commercial shops and factories, and hundreds of homes had been fire bombed, sending as many

Catholic and a smaller number of Protestant families fleeing into their own community heartlands from flash-points along the so-called peace-line and more isolated areas.

The *Irish News* reported that the nationalist Falls, Ardoyne, the New Lodge, and Short Strand had been under siege from orchestrated attacks by loyalists mobs, blatantly supervised and led by B Specials and, on occasion, regular serving policemen.

On the streets of those same besieged areas it was known that only for the heroics of ordinary men folk facing up to such firepower in defending their homes and parish churches, and the women and elder children gathering in back alleys and cleared sculleries to prepare the Molotov cocktails, vinegar soaked improvised gas masks, and to render first aid, whole Catholic ghettos would have been razed and the casualty list doubtless longer.

As dawn broke over the province at war with itself, a much welcomed lull from the overnight bedlam enabled the warring sides to grab a moment's rest; those interested parties to calculate the cost of human suffering and material loss. Many parts of Derry and Belfast appeared like those French towns and cities that had found themselves exposed along the front-line during the Great War. All were left wondering how long the uneasy peace would hold, for none doubted something had begun which was far from over.

Leaving the McParlands and Brennans to mourn amid the chaos, Barratt took to the near deserted streets of the Falls to assess the aftermath of the night's developments. Making his way first by foot across the Falls Road and into Clonard, to where both sides had faced up to each other hours earlier, he acknowledged the handful of battle-weary vigilantes who still stood lookout on a street corner and was relieved to find the McParlands' old aunt's house still standing unscathed. But seeing a dozen or more homes on both sides of upper Maxwell Street and three neighbouring streets running horizontal to it at its far end, including his own humble abode, completely gutted, Barratt felt choked. The streets where he had once played as a child and courted the girls were gone. Burnt out shells of houses, his family home, wherein his mother had slaved in rearing him and the others while father was away in Scotland looking for work, and neighbours homes, where he'd had many a laugh and a hearty feed and sometimes slept during those nights on the run, stood as black blots on the landscape. The smell of charred timber, and soot, hung thick in the air.

Making his way with a heavy heart back onto the Falls and down along it toward Divis, Barratt felt his temper boil. On the gable end of that street which had been beyond saving the previous night, a slogan scrawled in white paint paid him and his comrades alive and dead, a gross insult. It read: I.R.A. = I RAN AWAY!

Looking about him for the culprits responsible, Barratt spied a gang of smirking youths lingering on a nearby street corner, turn their backs to him and lay claim to their handiwork in so doing. As he set out to reproach them, the shout of his name caught his attention. Turning to investigate, Barratt saw that it was Carmichael and Bonar who sought his attention. Throwing the sniggering youths a chilling glare, which went unnoticed, Barratt sensed correctly the urgency in the manner of the two brigade staff officers.

Keen to break the latest news, Bonar, waving a rolled up newspaper, shouted out to Barratt as he approached. 'Frankie. The British Government has just ordered its troops into Derry.' In that moment Barratt thought to himself, Now the fight is truly on.

Meeting up with the two younger men on the corner, Barratt received a full report on overnight events from Bonar, who had been in the thick of it. Bonar was downhearted as he spoke.

'There's a lot of ill feeling towards us, Frankie. I've lost count of the number of people who have demanded to know where the IRA was last night? Why there is no guns?' Bonar caught his breath before continuing, his voice trembling with emotion. 'I got caught up in Ardoyne. I've never seen anything like it. I was running from street corner to street corner like someone demented, firing one shot here, another there, to give the impression the area was well defended. When I'd emptied my revolver, the lads were shouting across the street at each other to pass out the guns, to fool the Specials into thinking there was more to come, and it worked. The bastards fled for their lives. All we had left between us was some eegit with a catapult firing ball bearings. But fair play to him! Later on, to keep morale high, we sang *Faith Of Our Fathers* from behind the barricades. And do you know ... the Specials never showed again. But we'd already taken a hammering, so had the New Lodge, Unity, and Short Strand.'

'And no doubt we're in for more of the same tonight,' added Carmichael gloomily.

Barratt was left greatly depressed by what he'd heard. He thought for a moment before responding with forced optimism, barely rising above his despondency.

'Listen up. Carmichael, I want you to call together all those coordinating the vigilantes across the city, Sinn Fein members and sympathisers. Tell them that so-called republicans in the Free State have sold us out ... that we stand alone. They must understand that it is crucial we stand together and prepare for the worst to come. Tell them the IRA in the North are desperate for men and weapons, that we need help. But that we will do everything possible to defend our areas, and this we must do.' With an even greater sense of urgency Barratt turned his attention to Bonar. 'I want you to leave for Derry within the hour. Meet up with our men there. They may know where we can lay our hands on some gear down south. There may just be some Free Staters willing to help us now.' Both subordinates acknowledged that they had received their commands. Handing Barratt the early morning paper, its print barely dry, Bonar informed his senior rank of the tragedy locally.

'Frankie, first reports in the paper give only a snippet of information on events. But it was bedlam here last night. We've got a youngster in the flats behind us with his brains blown out.' Barratt winced on hearing this. There was more gory detail to come. 'The fuckers riddled the place without a second thought. The poor lad died in his bed. Entire streets have been burned out, and I hear there's not much left of Clonard. We've opened the schools to accommodate the homeless. We're doing all we can with what little we've got.'

'Good man, Bonar,' Barratt said, keen to give credit where due. 'See it continues in your absence.'

'Will do, Frankie.'

Barratt flash read the newspaper's pages. It was indeed all doom and gloom - death, injury and destruction on a massive scale. The editor believed civil war loomed. Looking about him then at the carnage of the past twelve hours and having listened to the reports from Bonar, Barratt's feelings was that civil war had already come to town.

Carmichael suggested that they move from the corner. With the odd single shot heard in the past hour, it was believed that snipers were at large in the Shankill. Quick of step the three IRA men moved into the Divis complex, with Barratt proposing they call on D'Arcy. He wanted to have a private word with the young man over a development that had occurred the previous night, not-too-far away. Climbing the concrete stairwell littered with debris and stinking of stale urine and reaching the fifth floor of the main block, Barratt inquired of Carmichael as to the whereabouts of the Thompson. Carmichael had left it wrapped in an old blanket in the boot of the borrowed car parked up safely in a side street close to Casement Park in the heart of the Falls.

'Collect the car later and pick me up outside the Coat of Arms at eight without fail,' Barratt ordered. 'We've got an important run on. Sean Mor died last night. His corpse will be returned to the house at around eight-thirty. We will escort it back across the city. I wouldn't be surprised if those Orange bastards tried to intercept the hearse before it gets back into the Falls. Then we need to sit down and make plans for the man's funeral. He'll be seen off with full honours ... given the final farewell a true republican deserves.'

Bonar and Carmichael were of a younger generation, but nevertheless felt as though they had incurred a major loss on learning of Sean Mor's passing - and this coming on top of everything else at such a time.

Entering D'Arcy's flat was like entering a darkened bunker in the sky. Returning home safely the night before to find his wife and children cowering petrified beneath the big bed and bullet holes the size of dinner plates in the walls of every room, D'Arcy had proceeded quickly to throw mattresses and wardrobes against those windows on the most exposed side of the building. The family had crawled on their hands and knees to and from the bathroom throughout the night in fear of being caught in another burst of gunfire on the flats, and even now, moved about the cramped space cautiously.

Gesturing to D'Arcy to follow him into the kitchen, situated on the less exposed side of the flat, Barratt left Bonar and Carmichael to reassure D'Arcy's wife, who was at her wits end, while the three weans still lay huddled in an uneasy sleep beneath their parents' bed in the adjoining room.

'Close the door behind you, lad,' Barratt instructed, leaning his bulk against the kitchen sink. Though in his own home, D'Arcy did as he was told. With his back to the door, D'Arcy felt extremely nervous. He knew the reason for Barratt's visit. Barratt's face was deadly serious as he spoke, his voice likewise.

'Last night, D'Arcy, you heard what I did on the street corner. Who was that man?'

D'Arcy hesitated; his face turned a deathly white as it had the previous night.

'C'mon. Out with it sonny! I haven't got all fucking day!'

Looking Barratt straight in the face across the kitchen table, D'Arcy spoke with a shaky voice. 'It was m'Da. I saw him as clear as day.'

Barratt thought long and hard for a moment before responding matter-of-fact. 'Your oul da's been dead eleven years, son.'

D'Arcy shuffled uncomfortably, his eyes filling up. 'I know. But that's who it was. On the lives of my children.' Silence prevailed for a moment longer. Both men stared each other out. Barratt moved toward the kitchen door and placed a comforting hand on D'Arcy's shoulder.

'Have peace of mind lad, knowing your old man is watching over you all. Stay with your wife and kiddies tonight.' Barratt moved to leave the room. D'Arcy grabbed his left arm. 'Thanks Frankie.' Barratt smiled and nodded. He took his leave then. There was much to do.

Exiting the multi-storey, Bonar and Carmichael went their separate ways to undertake their orders, leaving Barratt to walk the short distance back onto the Falls with a mission of his own to complete.

The five denim-clad youths still stood admiring their brush strokes from the opposite side of the street when Barratt rounded the corner and approached them, cracking his fingers as he went. The youths eyed him contemptuously and slandered the man with mouthed whispers. Barratt read their lips and coming to stand inches from them, could not contain his fury any longer. Gesturing over his shoulder with a thumb, Barratt inquired coolly, 'Which one of you pieces of scitter is responsible for this?' All five youths erupted in a fit of giggling. Barratt's eyes fell on the tallest, gangly two, who were identical, bar their hair colour and sensed he had seen their pug-nosed, mischievous faces, somewhere before. 'Don't I know you two?'

'Yeh probably knew our Da, Fergal McHugh, even better,' snarled the ginger-haired one, standing cockily with his thumbs hooked in his trouser pockets. 'He was a true IRA man. Not like you, yeh cowardly wee cunt!'

Barratt felt his blood run cold and lunged forward to viciously head-butt the youth full in the face and felt the other's nose break on impact. As the youth fell onto his back out cold, his thumbs still in his pockets, Barratt grabbed his stunned, mousy-haired twin by the throat, while the other three louts ran off. Barratt dragged the struggling, petrified youth across the street. Grabbing a fistful of the twin's hair and forcing an arm far up his back, he proceeded to rub his face forcibly, from left to right, across the coarse brickwork painted white, until his nose was red raw and bleeding profusely. Still forcing the youth's face against the gable end, Barratt served warning. 'If I catch you or your fucking brother, defacing another wall, anywhere, I'll break your arms and legs. Do you hear me?' The fear-stricken youth screamed: 'I hear yeh! I hear yeh!' Barratt swung the lad around and kneed him hard in the balls, before releasing his grip. The blood splattered youth slid down the gable end clutching his crotch and collapsed in an agonising heap at Barratt's feet.

'A better man than your fucking da, you and I, died along this road last night. I'll kill any bastard that brings disgrace on his name!' Looking down his nose, Barratt fumed again: 'So you, yeh wee gobshite, be warned!' Fixing his attire before continuing up the Falls, Barratt had meant every word.

Chapter Sixty-Four

The Catholic firm of undertakers in the centre of the city had not been so busy for many a year and the body of a well-known Belfast republican was only one of several due to be returned to the Falls later that night, all victims of the latest troubles in some way or other. Carmichael had been instructed not to let any other vehicle pull in between his car and the hearse in front, and Barratt, the loaded Thompson hidden beneath the overcoat covering his lap, was the front seat passenger in the escort vehicle as Sean Mor's corpse journeyed the four miles across the city.

On arriving safely in Leger Street, Barratt and two other appointed IRA men carried the long, solid oak coffin into No72. Once the coffin lid was removed they placed the Irish Tricolour over the corpse, so that only Sean Mor's face was left exposed and it bore all the hallmarks of his long suffering.

Although Sean Mor had not been a member of the IRA at the time of his death, at Barratt's behest the widow had given her permission willingly for her late husband to be honoured with a traditional republican-style funeral. The corpse would lie in state for a further two days and two nights. On the third day, the coffin was to be carried shoulder high the mile or so along the Falls Road to the Republican Plot in Milltown Cemetery, where a graveside oration and final salute would be given before the coffin was lowered into the ground alongside comrades of old.

Sarah had already prepared Anthony and Sean for the military trappings on the return of her father's body to the house, saying simply that it was 'republican tradition'.

As news of Sean Mor's death spread throughout the Falls and among republican circles across Belfast - its people braced for another night's violence - a stream of mourners had quickly formed a queue the length of Leger street as the bereaved family gathered at the front door to receive the corpse home. Folk from all over the city sought to pay final homage to a well-liked, much-respected man, who for some had been a great GAA man first and foremost.

Remaining in the background somewhat as the wake house became crammed, Anthony and Sean observed with muted interest the build-up of people, young and old, who had come to bid farewell to and pray for the deceased.

The coffin had been placed under the window in the sitting-room, where the emerald green brush velvet curtains served as an appropriate backdrop. Rosie, Sarah, Caithlin and Bridget, were seated close by the coffin and they received each mourner with a subdued handshake. An army of neighbours, women with sleeves rolled up, offered everyone over the age the choice of a cigarette and a tot of whiskey. The children among the throng were excited at the prospect of receiving free sweets - caramel toffees being the favourite choice of most. Sitting on an upright wooden chair placed against the opposite wall and between his father, newfound cousins, distant aunts and uncles, Sean was certain that he saw more than one child rejoin the queue throughout the evening, so to get their greedy hands on another toffee, piled high in a large glass bowl on a nearby sideboard.

Anthony was also quietly concerned that the military overtones of the funeral would somehow catch the imagination of his son, who had been obviously riled earlier in the day when hearing first-hand accounts of the previous night's street-battles from those locals calling to the house just after dawn to pay sympathy to the relatives of the deceased.

The fact also that Sean had experienced being gassed, albeit a brief exposure, had left him bitter with his words for the supposed forces of law and order. Sensitive to all the mouthing, the posturing, which signalled only one message, Anthony was greatly more determined to get out of Belfast with his family as soon as the funeral was over. He feared the longer they stayed, the greater the danger would be that they would be dragged into the ugliness of what was developing on the streets. However, an opportune moment to talk to Sarah was yet to present itself.

Anthony's concern for Sean was not unwarranted. Sean had been inspired later in the day, when hearing details of the heroics of the local men and women who had fought bravely, desperately, to save their homes, though be it in vain most often. Now, Sean was impressed by how ordinary folk could turn out in such vast numbers in consideration for another family, only hours after they themselves had experienced such trauma.

Conscious that he was an observer of something profoundly Irish, Sean held a burning desire to be a greater part of it all. For the first time in his life, he felt as though he truly belonged to those he found himself among and whom, on second thoughts, he considered to be not so ordinary at all.

With plans made for Sean Mor's funeral, Barratt was reassured by Carmichael that all else was in hand on seeing the men of the Falls mobilised and well prepared with stockpiles of petrol bombs lined up at the ready behind those barricades sealing off streets prone to further attack. The Falls was now a no-go area to the RUC and B Specials, who had the blood of those murdered the previous night dripping from their hands. Never again would they safely walk the Falls Road or be accepted by its people. Above the Coat of Arms, serving as a nerve centre, Barratt and Carmichael met up with Cassidy, Doyle and McElwee, the brigade staff officers who had overseen the defence of the Catholic areas across Belfast in Bonar and D'Arcy's absence, and received a comprehensive update on developments. Once sitting themselves down among the stacked crates empty of beer bottles that now contributed to the armaments of the area, Carmichael delivered his report with an optimistic voice.

'All the local defence leaders are behind us ... Sinn Fein too. Word is on the street that the IRA in the North seeks arms and volunteers. Every area is doing all it can to strengthen its defences and to accommodate the refugees. Rumour has it, that the British Army is already in Belfast, but no one doubts that the Specials will attack again tonight. But I tell you Frankie, they'll get one hell of a hot reception. I don't think there's an empty milk bottle going spare between here and Ardoyne. Folk around have even siphoned the petrol tanks of their cars to fill the empties. If we can't shoot the bastards, we'll burn them alive.'

All nodded in agreement. Barratt spoke now.

'Whether troops are to be deployed or not, it's paramount that we don't concede any more ground. We've got our dead to bury in the next few days. I don't want hysteria and panic to break out among our people if they think the Orangemen are going to overrun the areas. We must fight tooth and nail to hold them back.' Barratt paused for a moment to consider the importance of what he was about to say. 'If British soldiers are not deployed tonight, they will be within forty-eight hours. This will give us a little breathing space. But believe me, that is when the fight will truly begin. The Free State Army will not cross the border now. I never believed for one moment that the ragged-arsed bunch of toy soldiers would, for they haven't the stomach for it. We can only hope that some among them will at least give us the means to do our own fighting. But we must look further afield for help. Once Sean Mor is buried, I'll go south to see what the Jackeens in Dublin have to say for themselves. I wonder if they're still so keen on going down the political path at any expense.'

Bonar interjected. 'Do you think that's wise, Frankie? They might make an example of you.'

'For what? *Trying to defend our people*! If by chance they do, I want every single one of the bastards wiped out. Understood?'

'No fear, Frankie! We'll save the first bullets for them!' Cassidy declared, his anger up.

'Good!' Barratt affirmed. 'Now, let's hold our heads high and get back onto the streets. We've got no reason to run and hide.'

Sensitive to the build-up of cigarette smoke forming a thick cloud above the heads of the living and the dead in that crammed small back room, Sean, when his father's back was turned, slipped out of the room and negotiated his way past those folk who lined the hallway even after midnight to pay their respects. He stepped out into the night to breathe in deeply the much welcomed fresh air, but was immediately conscious of the smell of petrol and burnt timber which clung to every breeze, and an atmosphere which crackled with tension. Glancing down the street where very little went on, then up it, where, halfway, the queue of mourners tailed off, Sean's irritated eyes came to focus on a tall, slim girl, with long, dark flowing hair, who had exited the house immediately above No72. The pretty girl stood alone while looking blankly into the gutter. Sean overheard a woman mourner nearby turn to another and say, 'She's done that every night since her mother and her friend were shot. Poor soul.' Sean recalled the incident. It had been on the news and reported in the papers back in England. *CHURCHGOERS SLAIN!* had been the headline of one. He felt an urge to approach the girl to share in her grief, and to share a little of his own also in so doing. The girl did not notice as Sean stepped closer to her. Only when he quietly said, 'Hello', did she flinch and turn to face him. Under the neon glare of a streetlight, the full beauty of her face captivated Sean. So innocent, so poor of malice was it, her eyes, soft and gentle, but sad. Sean's voice trembled. 'I'm sorry. My name is Sean. Sean Brennan.'

'You're English,' said the girl, as if telling him something awful. Sean was quick to put matters straight. 'I was born here. My parents had to leave when I was very young.' She smiled a little on revealing some history. 'I know who you are. You're Sean Mor's grandson. I remember my mother telling me about you when I was young.' Sean was all-ears. 'Do you know,' continued the girl, gesturing to No72 with her head, 'when babies, you and I used to sit in our prams right under your grandparents' front window, while your mother and my mother stood nattering on the doorstep.' Tears welled in the girl's eyes. 'I was sorry to hear of your mother's death,' Sean said, mournfully. The girl nodded, acknowledging his kind thoughts, then said likewise, 'I was sad to hear about your grandad. He was very good to me ... and my brothers and sisters.' The girl was sharing a little more local history then. 'He had us all learning the Irish. He was great craic. We will miss him terribly.' Sean could not take his eyes off the girl. She's gorgeous, he thought, enjoying her company, even though the conversation was as sad as it was. 'I haven't been in to see him,' confessed the girl, sadly. 'I'm afraid to after my mother's death. She didn't look very nice. The fall into the gutter there, left her face all bruised.' A torturous moment's silence ensued before the girl said, a little more upbeat, 'I'd prefer to remember your grandfather as the happy sort he was, always cracking wee jokes and singing us rebel songs, and dancing too. No one could dance a jig like him.'

'The Orangemen are attacking Clonard!'

The shouted warning just then, from the top of the street, had the few men among the gathered mourners racing to the front line, the women scurrying back to their posts, and the girl turning to face Sean, her voice terror-stricken as painful memories stirred.

'Quick, go inside out of harm's way.'

She was making her way back into her own house when Sean called out to her amid the panic. 'Can I see you tomorrow?'

The girl stopped and turned on the doorstep to look at him slightly bewildered, then said coyly, 'Come around if you like. I won't be going anywhere.'

'And your name, what is it?' Sean begged, as if his life depended on knowing it.

'Roisin Carlin.' She was gone in a flash then, leaving his heart thumping, his mind racing. Sean felt as though he had just inherited all the riches of the world and tripping back indoors, wondered how love at first sight truly felt.

News of the renewed attack on Clonard quickly spread around the wake house by frenzied whisper. Learning of the latest development, a concerned Anthony looked about him searchingly and caught sight of Sean entering the room, his cheeks aglow. Anthony waited until his son was sat beside him again before quietly demanding to know where he had been.

'I just went to the front door for some fresh air.'

'Listen good, son. I don't want you venturing outside without my permission. Do you hear?' Accepting the reasons why his father worried so, Sean gave a nod, knowing nothing would stop him, bar being killed himself that night, from calling on Roisin that following morning.

As reports filtered through to the bereaved family throughout the night, telling of the blood and gore fighting raging in nearby streets and the loyalists failed attempts to breach the barricades around the Falls, Sean was not distracted by any of it, and in the small hours, dozed off where he sat, thinking only of the girl next door, Roisin Carlin, his dream girl incarnate.

Chapter Sixty-Five

With death, injury and destruction sweeping Belfast, and with civil disorder spreading across the province, a despairing British Government deployed hundreds more British troops onto the streets of Belfast late in the evening of 15th August, but too late to prevent the orgy of violence which had ensued.

Standing on the doorstep of No72, which was bathed in early morning sunshine, Sean, his father standing behind him, curiously looked on as a platoon of British soldiers marched four abreast in steel helmets and with rifles shouldered up Leger Street toward the Falls Road, where a small crowd of women and men, up all night, stood on the corner with grim, unwelcoming faces.

'My father would not have wanted to see this day,' Sarah sighed, joining her husband and son on the doorstep, having heard the stomp of marching feet pass by her family home.

Stepping onto the pavement from No70 as the soldiers wheeled right onto the Falls, Roisin Carlin caught Sean's keen eye. He instinctively called out to her. 'Roisin!' She turned and smiled. Anthony and Sarah looked at each other puzzled. Roisin approached. Sean turned to his mother. 'Guess who? *Roisin Carlin*, my pram mate, remember?' Sarah smiled, and squeezing between Sean and Anthony, stepped out onto the pavement to embrace the girl. Happy at heart, Sean turned to his father to ease his confusion.

'We met last night, Dad. Roisin's the girl from next door.'

Anthony smiled and gestured with his head for Sean to join his mother and the girl. Moving toward his mother and Roisin, Sean heard his mother call out to his father, 'Roisin has some old photographs to show Sean ... when they were babies.'

Anthony nodded and looked on as Sean and Roisin went into the neighbouring house. Sarah joined Anthony on the doorstep again and said with a stamp of approval, 'It will do Sean good to get out of the house for a while. There's too much pain and despondency surrounding him just now. He'll be okay, don't worry.' Anthony considered guiding Sarah into the front room to have that much needed talk, but seeing her dither on her feet through exhaustion, instead urged her to catch up on her sleep.

Anthony saw his wife safely to the spare bedroom upstairs and slipped off her shoes as she lay herself on top of the bed. On descending the stairs a few minutes later, Anthony could not believe his eyes on seeing Felix Gresham push himself in his wheelchair along the hallway. Anthony extended a hand and said quietly, 'Felix, it's great to see you again.'

'And you too, Anthony,' whispered Felix, gripping his hand. You haven't changed one bit.'

While it may have been only half the man he had known physically once upon a time, Anthony did not doubt, given the firm handshake, that Felix had the strength of two men in what remained of his fleshy bulk. Anthony noted that there was no sign of Bernadette, but a young, fit-looking lad of about twenty, had come to stand close by.

'Bernadette couldn't make it. This is young Patsy, my apprentice barman. He takes me everywhere when he's not pulling pints.' Anthony acknowledged the amiable-faced lad with a nod. The lad nodded back.

'I've come to pay my respects to Missus Mc and her family,' Felix informed. 'Sarah was a welcomed visitor to the bar long before you arrived in town, Anthony. She would call every Easter and Christmas with gifts from the girls at the mill for the local orphanage.'

Anthony gestured to the sitting-room door slightly ajar, behind which Mrs Mc and two of her daughters still kept the death vigil. 'I'll wait in the front room, Felix. There's much to talk over.'

Felix winked an eye, before wheeling himself into the wake room.

Sitting in a front room not unlike that in his grandmother's house next door, Sean was well pleased with the black and white photographs of himself, smiling and pulling funny faces in his pram in the street outside, taken by Roisin's father all those years ago. Appearing in the photos alongside him, Roisin hadn't looked too bad as a baby either, in his opinion. And looking at her now as the sunlight streaming through the front window caught her rich black hair and brilliantly sparkling blue eyes, there was no doubting her beauty. Roisin gently brushed against Sean on leaning forward to turn the pages of the photo album. Sean felt his body tingle with excitement. The girl smelt so sweet, so fresh, her milky-white skin, so soft and warm. Only for the sad occasion that overshadowed their meeting, Sean would not have hesitated in that moment to take Roisin into his arms to kiss her full on her cherry-red lips. And he sensed she wanted him too.

Sitting side-by-side on the big comfy sofa they chatted and sometimes laughed in sharing their life stories.

Roisin's is much more interesting by comparison, thought Sean, listening intently, not taking his eyes off her for a moment as she told a story, a true story, about life as a young girl growing up on the Falls. Sean was surprised to learn that very little had changed since his own mother's childhood days in the city, and could only ponder what life would have held in store for him, had he been reared in it himself.

Left alone together in the front room of No72, Anthony and Felix were keen to resume their friendship of old, although each man carried some unease over how he was now perceived by the other. Felix wondered if Anthony had ever learnt the truth about his role in helping the IRA, and the real story behind his car accident? Thus, why Bernadette had not accompanied him to the McParland home. While Felix held no malice over past events, accepting his fate as the risk he had taken, his wife was still very, very bitter over it all. She had made this known again to Felix in no uncertain terms earlier that morning, when he had informed her of his destination. But such was his sense of loyalty to the deceased, for whom he'd had the highest respect, both as a republican and a just man, Felix was prepared to live with his wife's silence for the next few days as a consequence of his determination to pay his last respects to a former comrade.

Knowing Sean Mor had assured Anthony that *he*, Felix, had not betrayed their friendship by misusing what Anthony had disclosed to him about his life at Edenderry Abbey, Felix felt it only appropriate to tell Anthony himself, that this was indeed true. But Felix would tell Anthony only that which would put to rest finally any remaining doubts he may still hold, but no more. Although Sean Mor had assured him all those years ago, that what had happened in Liverpool had been accepted by the leadership as being simply an accident, that he had not been under any suspicion of double-crossing the movement, Felix knew the golden rule of secrecy still held precedence within the IRA, and that with Sean Mor gone, his own standing, if ever suspected of revealing army business, would mean nothing in the minds of those who had succeeded the deceased.

As though still in the company of the dead, Felix spoke secretively to Anthony, sitting opposite, in Sean Mor's old armchair.

'Anthony, I want you to know two things straight away.' Anthony braced himself to hear some hard facts. 'Firstly, I had no hand in events of seventeen years ago. Secondly, my days of being involved in anything other than the brewery trade, are long since over.' A pause. 'And although the day is not yet ours, I want us to be the best of friends again. Will you shake my hand on it?'

Sensing that Felix had said all that he could say on events that day and that he had been truthful with his words, Anthony reached out and shook the hand of Felix firmly. With that handshake, suspicions of old and new were let go by both men and a friendship, much like that of old, rekindled.

Both men sat long into the afternoon talking of the past years and, unlike the reunion with McNab, Anthony went on to share all the major happenings in his life. Felix though, staying true to the oath to which he had sworn allegiance all those years ago, and not least in consideration for his own life, skipped one or two chapters of his life story.

Greatly refreshed by the few hours' sleep she had managed to steal, Sarah joined her husband and former comrade in the front room on descending the stairs and was delighted to see an old friendship renewed. With Anthony excusing himself momentarily and leaving his wife and Felix alone together, Felix extended his sympathy to Sarah over the loss of her father. Grateful for the kind words, Sarah reminded Felix of their commitment as former republican activists, once in the thick of things taking place in their day.

'I've told Anthony nothing of your past involvement, Felix. And that's how it will remain.'

Felix sought to assure Sarah that nothing of any real substance had ever been or would ever be disclosed by him about his own involvement in the IRA. 'That's the way it should be, Sarah.'

Never discovering to that day, just as her father had not, the real facts as to why Colonel Cartwell had been killed, and having always accepted her father's explanation over events that July, Sarah did not feel the urge to question Felix directly, and so, as far as she was concerned, there was nothing left to say on the events of yesteryear.

Anthony's return to the front room had the conversation turning to events overnight and the danger looming in face of the latest attacks on the area. It was on Felix innocently inquiring as to the whereabouts of their son that Anthony and Sarah realised that a whole morning had come and gone since they'd left Sean alone with Roisin. Sarah thought it time for Sean to return and went to call next door, but was to discover Sean standing alongside Roisin on the pavement outside No72, where once they had sat in their prams as babies. Now though, they stood looking sadly at the very spot where Roisin's mother had fallen dead on being shot. Roisin pointed to where her mother's blood still stained the grey paving stone. No amount of scrubbing had shifted it. Each night since that dreadful moment, Roisin revealed that she had come to stand in silent prayer where her mother's life had trickled away into the gutter. The brutality of it all sent a shudder of fear through Sean, only too pleased to find his own mother by his side. Sarah joined them both in a quiet prayer for the two women so cruelly snatched from their loved ones.

The only man alive who fully knew of the sinister circumstances surrounding Colonel Cartwell's death, the mercenary thinking and scheming which had lain behind it, but which he had kept secret all these years out of consideration for others - Sean Mor and his family - observed from a safe distance with sleepy eyes, British troops take up position along the peace-line, which for the past two days and nights had become the battleground for Catholics and Protestants to wage civil war on each other. With the army of occupation reinforcing the line of division with their barbed wire and battlefield tanks, Barratt considered it safe enough to get some much-needed rest. His eyelids were so heavy from not having slept a wink those past three days and nights, he knew that feeling the way he did, he would be no good to anyone, particularly with so much still to oversee, not least Sean Mor's funeral in two days time. Staggering away from the street corner to get his head down in a sympathiser's house nearby, Barratt wondered what the reaction of the foreign soldiers would be on seeing the IRA parade one of its dead under their very noses. He was heartened in that moment on witnessing at close hand, how the local people would react if the troops interfered on the day. To the applause of a good many others, one woman lifted her foot and kicked the tea and sandwich laden tray out of a neighbour's hand as she went to feed and water the enemy, masquerading as saviours. To Barratt's thinking, it was another ominous sign of worse times to come.

Under a bright August sun, British soldiers sweated profusely in their khaki tunics and could only stand idly by and look on with indifference from side streets as five thousand or more mourners escorted the tricolour draped coffin, flanked on both sides by four men dressed smartly in black military-style attire, as it was carried shoulder high on its final journey along the Falls Road to Milltown Cemetery. The lone piper to the front of the leading hearse played a farewell lament to an Irish soldier.

Rosie, Sarah, Caithlin and Bridget, their heads respectfully covered with black lace scarves, walked in step a short distance behind the coffin. Each carried a fresh flower wreath of green, white and yellow arrangement, bearing a personal message from them to a loving and sadly missed husband and father, never to be forgotten. In a solid, proud line the breadth of the road followed other family members spanning three generations, among them, an excited Sean and his nervous father, taking up their respective places. Behind them, walking twelve abreast and three lines deep came the representatives of all the Sinn Fein Cummans from each of the thirty-two counties, who each bore a wreath with sympathy card attached. Among the thick black mass of mourners following, IRA men and women, young and old, from all over the country, mingled inconspicuously. But in Barratt's observant eyes the absence of those former colleagues of the deceased, those Free Staters making up the Army Council, was not only a disgrace, but an ominous signal too. Despite the latter concern, Barratt was determined to leave the Army Council with a lot to answer to when meeting with their number the following day.

The GAA had been more considerate. One of their number proudly carried Sean Mor's old hurley stick and games shirt, worn in his younger days.

It took an hour for all the staying mourners to file into the cemetery and to each find a spot among the thousands of gravestones. Quietly assembled, they patiently awaited the final oration, to be read from the makeshift platform overlooking the open grave and coffin within the Republican Plot.

Barratt, who feared not to bare his face to the world in publicly proclaiming his republicanism and his association with the dead, for it was already well-known among certain circles, prepared himself to deliver a final, fitting tribute to his old friend and comrade. Barratt spoke with a fiery passion.

'Today, we gather as one to bid final farewell to a truly great man. Ever since his first days of youth, Sean McParland - Sean Mor - as we knew him best, dedicated his life to the long struggle for Irish freedom. Just as Pearse, Connolly and Sean McDermott before him made the ultimate sacrifice, Sean Mor too, was prepared to offer his life to that same cause for which thousands of Irishmen and women have died unselfishly. And while Sean did not die with a gun in his hand, believe me, he is yet another victim of British and unionist injustice ...

'A veteran of many campaigns, Sean spent long years imprisoned without trial and endless days and nights on the run, separated from his devoted wife Rosie and his daughters. I remember, when interned with Sean in Crumlin Road Jail, Sean would always wear a smile, sing a song and crack a joke to keep morale high. And in the evening, after lights out, would have us all on our knees in our cells as he gave out the Rosary in Gaelic from behind his cell door. In the eyes of the screws, he was everything they feared, and no doubt, secretly admired. Sean Mor was the one they would drag out frequently to beat to a pulp ... to hose down in attempting to pacify the rest of us. But he never gave into them and set a fine example to us all. But not one of us can ever hope to live up to his stature ...

'Knowing only a little of how he suffered over recent months, though he never once complained, and having seen how a once fine athletic man, fit of mind and body, could be reduced to mere skin and bone, broken and blackened from the beatings meted out mercilessly in prison cells, there is no doubt in my mind who is responsible for driving our dear friend, good neighbour and comrade, into an early grave ...

'And so, let those who turned their back on him, who informed on him, who refused to stand by him in the fight, hang their heads in shame for all time. And I say to you young men and women gathered here today, the struggle for Irish freedom is entering a new, but final phase. We have the unionists on the run, and we will drive the British Army from our shores too, for let us not forget its past atrocities against our people. They are the bastard sons of yesteryears Black and Tans ...

'All that remains for me to say, is this: join the fight, for it is no one else's but yours! God bless you Sean Mor, and rest peacefully in the knowledge that our day will surely come!'

The crowd broke into spontaneous applause, and as the orator slipped away from the makeshift platform, three men dressed in smart black leather jackets, and berets, suddenly appeared from out of the crowd, falling silent and tense now. The firing party quickly lined up beside the coffin resting on wooden trestles, and on shouted commands in Gaelic by one of their number on the edge of the crowd, raised their shiny black revolvers skyward and fired three rapid volleys of single shots into the air. The IRA men then disappeared into the crowd, cheering and clapping louder now, their faces so excited by the fine military spectacle.

After a few moments a solemn calm descended on the crowd again as two of the original guard of honour stepped forward and preceded to fold neatly, in sequence, the Irish Tricolour which had covered the coffin, and which one of the men presented to the dead man's widow before saluting the whole family. The hurley and games shirt belonging to the deceased was then placed on top of the coffin lid by the GAA official. They were to be buried with the dead. It had been judged to be the appropriate thing to do as no other could fill the man's place within the association or on the field.

Rosie considered it a fitting tribute to a man who devoted so much effort to promoting Gaelic culture, especially among the youth.

Young Sean felt so proud to be one of that family with whom he stood and looked on with an anger stirring in the pit of his stomach as his grandfather's coffin, complete with tribute, was lowered into the ground by formidable looking men in civilian clothes, one of whom was the man who had spoken so well of his grandfather moments earlier. An ageing, distinguished-looking man played the last post nearby, while Father Crossan offered final prayers over the resting place. With the crowd dispersing silently, leaving the bereaved and wreath-bearers to pay final homage to the deceased by carefully laying their wreaths on the grave, Barratt sought to pay a little personal comfort to that family left heartbroken. Moving slowly along the line of sobbing women by the graveside, he shook each of their hands, and in return, received their warm, sincere thanks.

Sean felt his body tremble with both excitement and fear combined as the orator, the IRA man, came finally to stand in front of him, his hand extended in saying coolly, 'You must be young Sean.' Sean nodded immediately. 'Your grandfather spoke of you often. Y'know, he lived as long as he did, so he would see you again.' Sean smiled, not sure whether it was the right thing to do. 'That's a fine name you have there, son, carry it well, do you hear?' So very conscious of the thick fingered hand cupping his much smaller hand, Sean could only wonder how many people the man had killed, and instinctively, reassuringly replied, 'I will, Sir.'

With a discreet nod, Barratt acknowledged Anthony, coming to stand protectively by his son. 'You've nothing to worry about Mister Brennan,' said Barratt simply, but tellingly. 'Everything will be okay.' Anthony felt greatly relieved on hearing this for he quickly deciphered the real message. And so did Sean, knowing what he did. He too, felt so relieved.

Long after the bulk of mourners had dispersed, no one among the remaining family and close friends gathered around the grave of Sean Mor, paid any particular attention to the few people standing here and there among the surrounding gravestones. It was not uncommon for relatives or friends of the many buried in the cemetery to stop and say a prayer at the grave of a loved one before carrying on home. But one man used this common feature of life in graveyards as cover to fulfil his ulterior motive for being in that particular cemetery, on that particular day. The short, stocky man with the steely-hard face, who had assumed command of the Belfast UVF in the aftermath of Silver Wallace's capture, pretended to pray at the graveside of some stranger, when in fact he made a mental note of the two dozen or so faces assembled within the Republican Plot, some of whom he recognised easily, Barratt especially, as he now topped the UVF's assassination list. But Samuel 'Sammy' Vickers was surprised to see the face of another, the wheelchair-bound man whom he knew to be the publican of a bar close to the city centre. He observed closely, though discreetly, the friendly handshakes between Barratt and Gresham, and with that handshake, Vickers, having seen enough, murmured to himself, 'You've just signed your death warrant, Mister Gresham.'

On the short journey back to Clonard in his father's car and sitting on the back seat beside his grandmother, who clutched the tricolour on her lap, Sean observed another funeral take up the far side of the road as it too weaved its way agonisingly to Milltown. It was the first of three scheduled for the afternoon ahead - victims of the violence of the past two days and nights, and more such funerals were expected along the road over the next few days.

No one spoke throughout the journey home. There was too much pain, despair and death surrounding all for anyone to dare say an inappropriate word.

Once arriving back in Leger Street, Sean followed his peers back into the house that bore an atmosphere of irreplaceable loss. His Aunts Caithlin and Bridget, their husbands and children, and distant family and a handful of their closest friends, including McNab, arrived at the house within minutes of each other soon after. Tea and sandwiches had been made ready by those women folk still helping out and all assembled in the back room to console each other through recalling better days shared with the man now gone forever.

Sean had a burning desire to be alone for a while and so retreated to the front room. Despite all that he had experienced the past four days leaving his head spinning, thoughts of the girl next door still predominated. And how he longed to be in her company once again. What troubled him now was that his father would soon want to go south, to Donegal. Sean's feelings for Roisin were so strong he could not even contemplate leaving her. Suddenly, the prospect of leaving Belfast seemed threatening, so unrealistic to him.

With only the immediate family left together in No72 and with time passing on, Caithlin and Bridget returned to their own family homes. They had husbands and children of their own to attend to once more, after nearly a solid week away from their humble abodes.

Taking his place at the dining table, back in its usual place in the centre of the living-room, Sean heard his mother suggest to his grandmother, sitting at the opposite end of the table, that they keep her company through staying the night.

'Ma, why don't you and I sleep in the back room tonight? Anthony and Sean can sleep down here on the bed-settee. Isn't that right, Anthony?'

Sitting across the table from Sean, Anthony, while eager to get out of Belfast as quickly as possible despite Barratt's reassuring words in the cemetery, did not wish to appear unsympathetic.

'Sarah's right. You'll sleep a little better in the back room.'

Her thoughts with someone no longer by her side, Rosie said with a distant voice, 'Even when Sean was not with me at night physically, I felt safe and comforted knowing that he was with me in thought. He will always be in my thoughts now, day and night. No! I'll sleep in our own marriage bed, for in what other bed would I sleep? Goodnight to you all.' They all bid the widow goodnight in turn, and heard her climb the stairs wearily, and alone. The Brennans were tired and longed for a good night's rest, but Anthony thought it an appropriate moment to draw Sarah and Sean's attention back to the original schedule.

'In a day or so we'll continue on to Donegal as planned,' he said. 'The house there will be ready for us and there'll be much to be going on with.'

Sarah's reply came quick and sharp. 'I'll not be going anywhere for a while yet. I'm not leaving my mother, not in these troubled times.'

Sean looked intensely at his parents without interrupting, though if opportunity presented itself to air his own view, he knew where he would be arguing to stay.

Left deeply concerned by what he'd just heard, Anthony tried to reason with Sarah, without raising his voice. 'We can't stay in Belfast, Sarah. It's just too dangerous!'

Sarah was not budging and was resolute in what she had to say. 'Listen, Anthony. We've just buried my father. The loyalists are trying to burn my mother and her neighbours out of their homes. You've heard all the stories. Now, do you really expect me to leave my mother at such a time? Would you do it to your mother?' What could he say? Anthony could not even suggest they take Sarah's mother with them. He knew that the widow would never leave her home, her husband's side, even in death. Anthony spoke with a voice that held both his wife and son's full attention.

'For however long we are to remain in Belfast, I want us all to be very, very careful. But most of all, I want us to be together as one. I never want this city or anyone in it, to come between us ever again.'

For Sean, a prayer had been answered.

A prayer was to be answered for another man a little further along the Falls Road later that night. At first wary of the sudden and unexpected appearance of the IRA's Adjutant General in the Coat of Arms, Barratt was soon at ease on the Dubliner speaking to him in the privacy of the upstairs meeting room, to where they mutually withdrew as a precaution against the risk of being eavesdropped by an RUC tout.

'I came north this morning alone, to see and observe,' the Dubliner said, looking Barratt straight in the eye through a haze of cigarette smoke. The Dubliner was a self-confessed chain smoker. Sitting on an upturned empty beer crate, Barratt listened intently as his senior rank delivered his analysis of the crisis in the North.

'With my own eyes and ears, I've seen and learnt of the fight for survival these past seventy-two hours, here in Belfast and in the Bogside. And I want you to know, I stand with you all the way.'

Barratt did not hesitate to ask, 'How am I to know that you have not come to deceive me ... to force your hand?'

His integrity as an individual in his own right and his commitment to the republican cause renowned throughout the movement, the Dubliner respected Barratt's gall. He knew Barratt's concerns were for the Catholic people of the ghettos in face of overwhelming odds if the loyalists were to launch an all-out, full-scale attack.

Leaning forward in the ladder-back chair and removing the cigarette from his mouth, the Dubliner said with a purpose, 'I too heard your graveside oration today. Your words prompted me to decide finally as to where my loyalty will lie from this day forth. So I say to you once more, I stand with you.' The Dubliner offered his hand to rubberstamp as true what he had just said. Barratt, pausing to search the man's heart through looking him in the eye long and hard, finally took the Dubliner's hand in his and shook it firmly.

With that handshake, the destiny of both men was sealed.

Chapter Sixty-Six

I think I'm in love, thought Sean, as he adoringly eyed Roisin by his side as they lazily strolled along in the Falls Park on the magnificently sunny Sunday afternoon. The sweet scent rising from the splendid array of brightly coloured flowers in full bloom nearby, intermingling with the warm, fresh smell of Roisin's tanning skin, her shiny soft hair so alive under the blazing sun, and her long, slim body moving invitingly under the light summer dress she wore so easily, left his passions aroused, his imagination fired. She had been on his mind day and night ever since that first moment they'd met. And presently, Sean spent his days at his Granny McParland's in the hope of meeting with Roisin, and most often he did. With Mr Carlin shuffling aimlessly between the Coat of Arms and the corner bookie and squandering his meagre state handout in the process, and with her elder brothers and sisters having gradually drifted away from home, Roisin, the youngest of nine children, was tied to the house in looking after her father, who had turned to the drink in the aftermath of her mother's murder.

Sean had been a regular caller at No70 in the days immediately following his grandfather's death and Mr Carlin did not seem to mind his daughter spending so much time with the grandson of the late Sean Mor, of whom he always spoke fondly, whether drunk or sober. Sean had been happy to sit in with Roisin each night and watch television and to listen to rock music on the radio in the front room; Roisin was a fireside girl, just as her mother had been. That Sunday was the first day she had ventured away from the house in a long time and she felt like a goddess kissed by the sun.

Sitting close beside Roisin at the foot of one of the tall oak trees in a quiet corner of the park, Sean could not wait a moment longer to tell her the news he carried. Turning to look into her sparkling eyes, his body tingling with excitement, Sean spoke nervously in revealing shyly a snippet of what was on his mind and in his heart.

'Roisin, there's a chance I will be staying in Belfast. My mother doesn't want to leave her family. I hope she never does.'

'Why not, Sean?' Roisin inquired gently, edging him on. Sean paused for a moment, and with his eyes transfixed unto hers, served a revelation. 'I don't want to leave you.' Sean felt his heart leap on seeing Roisin's angel face beam with delight, those sparkling eyes dance with joy. She served him a look then that captured his heart and stoked his sense of wonder. Her words, spoken softly, broke down the last barrier to his feelings being exposed. 'I don't want you to ever leave.' Sean leaned forward so very slowly and gently resting a hand upon the side of Roisin's face, placed his lips against hers to begin a long and passionate kiss. He felt Roisin's hot, inviting mouth draw him closer, his broad muscular chest gently crush her pert, firm breasts. A warm, silky-smooth hand was upon the nape of his neck and feather-light fingers teasingly stroked his flesh. Sean was in Heaven.

Neither one of them would ever forget their first kiss amid the battle scars of recent days - all a million miles away in that moment for the two blossoming young lovers.

Anthony too had been quick to notice Sarah taking root again amid familiar surroundings and among familiar faces, and not least Sean's increasing liaisons with the girl next door, which Sarah appeared to be at ease with. Recognising the spoils to their original plans and hopes for the future, Anthony knew he had to speak to Sarah quickly, but alone, to get her mind focused once again on goals set earlier. He knew he had to win Sarah over to stand a chance of getting Sean to leave the girl, the city, to which he clearly held a strong sense of attachment.

That Sunday evening, with Sean still out with Roisin, Anthony sat in contemplative mood in Aunt Bella's old house to where the family had returned the night before and patiently awaited Sarah's return from her mother's. He braced himself in the fireside chair on hearing a key turn in the front door and Sarah's step along the hallway. Sweating slightly under her summer dress, Sarah had just stepped into the front room when Anthony spoke out, calm and collect. 'Sarah, we need to talk.' Exhausted, Sarah sounded somewhat irate as she threw herself onto the parlour sofa. 'Over what, Anthony?'

'You know what. Our future!' Anthony affirmed. 'I think you've no intention of leaving Belfast.' Sarah had been waiting for this moment with much uncertainty as to its outcome.

'What if I were to say, I haven't, Anthony? What would you think of me?'

Out of a sense of desperation, Anthony was moved to open his heart. 'I'm frightened we may lose everything, Sarah, if we stay here too long.'

Sarah felt his anguish and was herself left facing a hard, painful reality. 'For Christ sake, Sarah. We have soldiers with guns on every street corner. You can see the mood of the people change toward them. One of these days there's going to be an eruption of violence as yet unseen, and with so many guns around there can only be one outcome. I don't want any of us to be caught up in it. You and I were lucky to have come through it all once before, but perhaps we won't be so lucky next time.'

Sarah eyed Anthony sympathetically. She was torn between two worlds, that of her rekindled concern and sense of responsibility toward her widowed mother, and that with Anthony, and where he wanted them all to be, in a much safer place yes, but yet another strange corner.

Anthony forced Sarah into a corner then by pleading, 'Let's get out of here Sarah, before it's too late.' Sarah knew deep down in her heart that his fears were real and genuine ones. There was only one reply she could give him.

'Okay. We will go. But just let us stay until the end of next month. It would be terribly hard on my mother if we were to go right now.' Though reluctantly, Anthony agreed, fearing they may be stretching whatever luck they had to the limits by staying even a day more.

'And what of Sean, Sarah? You know how attached he is to that girl.'

'Leave it to me,' Sarah said. 'I know it will be hard on him. He has settled down so well and is very fond of Roisin. But I will make him aware of the dangers here if we stay, our concerns for him. He will listen to me and see sense. I'll talk with him soon, don't worry.'

Anthony sighed with relief and proceeded to inform Sarah of his plans meantime. 'I'll need to go down south for a few days to see that everything is ready for our arrival. Perhaps, while I'm away, you can talk with Sean ... prepare him for the move.'

With an air of resignation, Sarah said, 'I'll see to it.'

Knowing Sarah's predicament, Anthony added, 'Everything's okay. It's not as if we will be a million miles away. Your mother can come and stay with us as often as she likes.' Anthony stood and crossed the room to where Sarah sat, to place a comforting arm around her shoulders. 'It's for the best we do this, Sarah, believe me.'

Though her heart was breaking at the prospect of leaving her mother, whom she knew would never leave the family home, nor her father's grave unattended for more than a day, Sarah knew that what she'd just heard, to be true. And it was so terribly hard to accept.

Hand-in-hand and with a spring in their step, Sean and Roisin made their way home along the Falls as dusk fell. With eyes only for each other they were oblivious to the patrolling soldiers looking on enviously and the gang of noisy, denim-clad youths on the street corner they approached. 'G'wan yeh girl ya,' Leo McHugh heckled as the young couple walked by. 'Give him a good ride when you get him home!' The twin brother, Vincent, and their friends, all laughed and jeered, forcing Sean to turn to face them.

'Leave it, Sean. They're all gobshites!' Roisin's plea fell on deaf ears.

Sean's fists were clenched by his side on demanding with an unmistakable south London accent, 'Which one of you is looking for a slap then, eh?' The English accent was received with a deadly silence. The look upon the bitter faces of all seven local youths unnerved Sean. Roisin was fearful of what might happen next.

The ringleader, Leo McHugh, the ginger-haired twin who sported a badly scraped nose, was quick to jump to conclusions and prepared to move in for the kill.

'Fucking hell, Carlin. Your mother will be turning in her grave knowing you're going out with a bastard of an English soldier!'

Suddenly losing all sense of fear, Roisin barged forward to stand protectively between Sean and the twin. Drawing on his little known but much practised Irish Gaelic, passed on by mother at the fireside down through the years, Sean surprised them all, including Roisin, by saying in a tongue foreign to all their ears, 'I'm Sean McParland. Belfast born and bred, and proud of it!'

The seven boys and one girl looked at Sean greatly puzzled. Only Roisin had a faint idea what he was speaking and seeing the twins and their hangers-on baffled, burst into a fit of laughter that distracted them all momentarily.

'What the fuck's going on?' demanded Leo McHugh, losing his patience with the girl. Roisin sniffed and said mockingly, 'You're an idiot, McHugh. He's speaking Irish! And pity the one who lays a finger on him,' she warned, and boldly announced to the open-mouthed louts, 'This is Sean Brennan. Sean Mor's grandson. He was born here, just like you and I.' Moving forward to jab a finger into Leo McHugh's weedy chest, Roisin snarled, 'Now what was it you were saying, loudmouth?' Roisin saw the others step back out of respect, out of fear.

Looking over Roisin's shoulder, Sean saw the twin's face turn pale and heard his voice tremble. 'Ah, sorry Roisin, I hadn't a fucking clue who yer man was. I ... I'm sorry what I said, about yer ma like.'

'And so you bloody well should be!' Roisin spat. 'Now pish off, all of youse, before I get the boys to sort youse out.' No one doubted her. The gang of seven turned about and hurried off down the Falls. Turning to face Sean again, Roisin, her countenance so divine, quipped, 'Good craic, eh Sean?' And added with confidence, 'Your name is good. Don't let anyone around here trouble you. D'you hear?'

Sean nodded.

'C'mon, let's get back. M'Da will be wanting his supper.'

Walking alongside Roisin, Sean felt as though he were ten feet tall.

Returning home to find her father out for the count on top of his bed after another day's heavy drinking, and once ensuring that he was lying safely on his side, Roisin's thoughts were racing. She knew exactly what she wanted to do now to seal that memorable, golden day in her heart for all time.

Slipping quietly into the front room to surprise Sean - stretched out on the sofa eagerly awaiting his girl - Roisin leaned over the wide arm of the sofa to plant a wet kiss upon Sean's forehead, then came to stand over him in the near darkness. Looking down teasingly, she slowly and sensually rolled her summer frock up and over her naked and slim tanned thighs, tiny waist, firm pert breasts, and head, and tossed it without a care into one corner.

His heart thumping, his blood surging through his veins, Sean feasted his eyes over Roisin's shapely, firm nakedness, and it was all and much more than he imagined it to be.

Stepping out of her shoes, Roisin came to lie on top of Sean and felt him hard and trembling a little beneath her. Letting her hair fall forward over his face, she brushed her hot wet lips over his right ear to say softly, 'I want you, Sean.'

They kissed passionately, and with Roisin helping Sean to strip naked between reluctant pauses, they made love slowly, tenderly.

Sitting astride Sean, Roisin was forced to purse her lips tightly, not wanting to alert father in the room directly above them as Sean brought her to a powerful climax. Sean, climaxing too then with a girl for the very first time, sucked hard on Roisin's swollen right nipple to mute his own ecstatic groans.

They lay silent now, only the rasps of erratic breathing breaking the stillness of the night. Holding each other tightly, they vowed quietly unto themselves, never to let the other go. Never, ever.

Chapter Sixty-Seven

Sitting alongside his mother halfway up Black Mountain that following Monday morning and scanning the industrial skyline of Belfast, which basked in brilliant sunshine, Sean listened intently as his mother recalled childhood memories.

'You know, son, I used to picnic here with my father on long summer days,' Sarah said dreamily. 'Buttercup summers he used to call them. And my mother would lead us girls up here during the blitz. We could see the searchlights and flares pick out German bombers sweeping in low over Belfast Lough to drop their bombs on Queen's Island.' Sarah pointed to the towering twin yellow cranes standing tall in the Harland and Wolff Shipyard over in the east of the city. 'One old fella would cheer each time a bomb hit the shipyard; he said it was only the Orangemen who were getting it ... for they ruled the docks. But most often it was ordinary folks on both sides of the divide who bore the brunt. Whole rows of terraces were flattened ... young and old killed in their beds. Mother lived at her wits end in fear of the Germans targeting the Crumlin Road Jail ... mistaking it for a munitions factory. Y'see, your grandfather was interned at the time.' Sarah sighed heavily. 'Yes, Belfast had its fair share of that war too, and another one is surely coming.'

Sean turned to face his mother, sensing he was about to hear a truth that was going to be so very hard to bear. His mother's face confirmed his suspicions, her words tore at his heart, leaving him reeling in hurt and shock.

'Sean, we must leave Belfast soon. There's terrible times ahead for this city, its people.' The mother saw her son saddened by this revelation, and knew the added importance of what she had yet to say. 'Your father and I are gravely worried for your safety. We must leave. Believe me son.'

Sean did not doubt that his mother read the signs well, knew what was to come. But the thought of leaving Roisin, the girl he had fallen in love with, was unbearable. He was not able to speak due to the lump rising in his throat. His mother sought to soothe his pain. 'I know, son. I know. I've been through the pain of it all myself. Believe me. But it's for the best.'

'When do we go, Mum?' asked Sean.

'At the end of next month, son,' confirmed Sarah. 'That's why your father has gone to Donegal today, to see that all will be ready for our arrival.'

Sean could not bring himself to even begin to think how he would tell Roisin this news. Down-hearted, he picked out the Falls Road from among the jigsaw of main roads and back streets below, and thought, I'll be back again some day, Roisin. I just hope you'll be here for me.

Each lost in their own troubled thoughts, mother and son set out on the long walk back to the city, where talk was of violent days to come.

It was the first full-scale brigade meeting since Barratt and Bonar's return from south of the border. Once gathered together in the safe house in Beechmount, Barratt, in buoyant mood, knowing what he did, called the meeting to order. Bonar, Cassidy, Carmichael, D'Arcy, McElwee and Doyle, were all on the edge of their seats in anticipation of what news Barratt carried, and they were not to be disappointed.

Barratt's four-day mission down south had indeed been fruitful and he reported to the brigade that 'key figures' at leadership level, in the wake of the Belfast and Derry street-battles, had resumed a more militant posture. Barratt confirmed that a 'source' close to the Chief of Staff was pressing him to lend full support to the northern brigades in their hour of need and a major rethink as to the sole pursuit of a political agenda at such a time. Such had the conscience of the Adjutant General been pricked in the aftermath of coming north to assess the crisis for himself, Barratt, without mentioning anybody's name, elaborated with zest.

'Our *comrades* in the Free State are in a quandary presently. They know of the resentment felt by many here in the North over their failure to rally to our aid. A sizeable number among them are coming back over to our way of thinking. Efforts are being made right at this very moment to secure fresh supplies of weapons. We even have one or two men in high places pulling a few strings too. For now though, we will have to make do with the few but invaluable weapons that Bonar managed to round-up from the border counties.' It was with words designed to stimulate new hope and vision among all assembled, that Barratt brought his brief to a close. 'We must make ready. There is a lot of angry youth out there who want to wreck the establishment. We need to channel that anger positively, to best effect. Bonar, I want you to launch a major recruitment drive. Cassidy, call together the Sinn Feiners. We need to build a strong political base in the community by way of advice and emergency centres, and we need to make arrangements to police our own streets, to be seen to be proactive in providing for our people. We also need women to be to the forefront of it all, to campaign and raise public awareness, and in time, there will be guns and explosives to be moved into place. They can do it under the noses of the Brits before they get too familiar with who's who and what's what.' There was a consensus of agreement among the brigade on the latter point. Barratt added. 'Our people are beginning to see the Brits in their true colours, that they're B Specials in khaki at the end of the day. I will meet with community leaders - priests, student reps, and our so-called nationalist politicians. I'll let them know in time that the fight for social justice is about to take on a new dimension, that they are not to stand in our way.' It was at this juncture, that Barratt considered it appropriate to draw the attention of the brigade to the danger lurking at the back door, that to which he had been warned against by the Adjutant General. 'Now to matters more immediate.' All others listened with increased interest. 'You need to know, that while there is the promise of support from among some down south, there remains those who are determined to push through a purely political agenda. As part of their strategy, they will seek to stir opposition against those of us who are militarists. So we all need to be extremely cautious, for the budding politicos in the Free State made contact in recent weeks with so-called republican elements in the North and have instructed them to infiltrate and seize positions of influence within those movements spearheading the street protests, and, where possible, to counter any attempt by us to capitalise on present developments. But I stress, we must not be drawn into conflict with such elements. We must await with patience the forthcoming ard fheis. This will be the platform on which the cause of our strategy will be fought and won.'

Everyone had heard Barratt loud and clear and doubted not that the republican movement was about to go through a major upheaval of its own, one which would see a parting of the ways, and which could well prove bloody.

It was Bonar who took the floor then, to warn of another threat.

'Any day now, Silver Wallace will be going up for sentencing. We can expect a backlash from the UVF. So our people must be vigilant. A small haul of guns will be arriving here tonight from the Free State and are to be quickly dispersed to all flashpoint areas. They're to be used in the event of further loyalist attacks.'

There was an immediate buzz of excitement in the room at the prospect of at last coming into ownership of much-needed guns and ammunition. Bonar was quick to issue another directive.

'I want someone up at the Court House in the morning to make a note of those in support of Wallace. We need to know who the new UVF key-players are.'

Carmichael winked an eye.

The rest of the meeting was consumed by agreeing plans for the receiving and distribution of weapons, for securing area defences, and how best to rally people power through political activity and organisation at street level.

With the brigade identifying a number of specific tasks to undertake immediately, Barratt prepared to set out for Counties Down, Tyrone, Armagh, Fermanagh and Derry, to share the news he carried. Before doing so, he left his men in even higher spirits.
    'Don't fear lads. Soon enough there will be fresh slogans appearing on the gable ends, which will be a truer reflection of our efforts. And momentous those efforts will be in bringing this bastard state to its knees!'

Sean stayed away from Roisin's house that evening and the next day and, lounging about his great aunt's old house, cooked his brains in thinking how best to break the news to Roisin, and how, if at all, he would cope with leaving her.

In the late afternoon of the following day, 27th August, news broke of Silver Wallace being sentenced to life imprisonment for the double murder of the two Falls Road women. Following the televised news report detailing the three day trial and Wallace's defiance on being taken down, shouting, 'God Save the Queen and Ulster!' Sean knew that Roisin would be expecting him that night without fail. She would be in need of comforting in the wake of all the painful publicity arising from the UVF man's trial.
    Deciding it best not to tell her of the plans made at such a sensitive time, knowing her torturous emotions over her mother's murder would have resurfaced, Sean cautiously called on Roisin that night and not surprisingly, discovered her alone and in tears. Her father, as expected, was seeking escapism down the pub. Roisin fell into Sean's arms on the doorstep of No70 and revealed with mixed emotions her joy that Wallace would never again walk the streets, and her fear that the killer's associates would return some night to wreak revenge for their man's jailing.
    'I feel safe when you're around, Sean,' Roisin declared tearfully. 'I wish we could be together always.'
    It was the last thing Sean wanted to hear. He held Roisin tightly in his arms and bore a heavy, heavy burden, silently.

Anthony set out on the return trip to Belfast the next day, happy in the knowledge that mother, Christy, and Colleen were all fine. Ann-Marie was expecting her second child at anytime and was full of life despite her weighty bulk and aching back. The working of the land went well with his brother and sister making a good team. Christy had kept to his word and had built that extra bedroom onto the house.
    The house that Christy had secured for rent in Buncrana was ideal. It had an adjoining large shed that Anthony considered ideal for setting up his furniture-making workshop. The few business people in town with whom he had spoken had shown an interest in his proposal to provide handmade furniture to local retailers to sell on.

Passing unhindered through the many British Army roadblocks thrown up around Belfast to arrive safely back in the Falls, Anthony's excitement over what awaited his family once returning south was cast into shadow on becoming sensitive to Sean's depressed state.

With Sarah dashing off to the local shops to buy essential groceries as speculation of impending riots was rife, Anthony was left alone with Sean in the front room of the house in Maxwell Street and sought to reach out a helping hand to his son, whom he knew to be hurting badly over the prospect of leaving Belfast, and the girl Roisin.

'Sean, I hope you're not mad at me,' Anthony said sincerely. 'It's only that your mother and I don't want any harm to come to you. Things here are going from bad to worse by the day.'

'I'm not mad at you,' Sean replied. 'It's others I'm mad at. Look out of the window and what do you see? British soldiers pointing guns in the faces of the people.' Sean looked his father straight in the eye from across the room to say with ease, 'I even know of your own troubles, Dad. Mum told me.' Anthony was moved to sit upright in his armchair on hearing this. 'I know it all,' continued Sean, determined now to get it all off his chest. 'The killing of Cartwell, the policemen, the IRA men, how you feared you might be caught up in it all; my grandfather urging you to leave this city ... and *me*, only a day old. We're all victims, Dad, and the suffering goes on.'

Reeling from the truth of it all, Anthony was struggling to find words that would serve as an appropriate response. Sean continued with his revelation. 'Even though I've spent my childhood in England, I've come here with my eyes wide open. I heard the gunfire too that first night, choked on the gas, and read the papers the next day to learn how a father scraped his young son's brains off a bedroom wall with a spoon. And do you know, something? I don't know what's going to be the hardest for me to do: to leave Roisin or to walk away from what's going on here.' Sean sensed his father's raised concern and quickly moved to allay anxieties stewing. 'Don't worry, I'm not about to rush out and grab a gun. But I'd be lying to you if not admitting that I felt like doing just that a little earlier. Whenever you're ready, I will be ready to leave Belfast with you.'

Still on the rebound from his son's frankness, his honesty, Anthony could only bring himself to say quietly, 'Good lad.'

With Sean wearily climbing the stairs to bed early that night, Anthony approached Sarah - busy loading the larder with essentials - over the matter of Sean knowing what he did, and was again left open-mouthed over Sarah's revelation that Sean had known what he knew for a long time. Sarah went on to admit that she had told Sean the facts herself and readily identified the reason why. Explaining to Anthony why she had then wanted their son to know the facts, helped Anthony to see reason - why it had been so important to reveal the truth to a child, their son, to prevent him carrying, possibly for a lifetime, an anxiety, a doubt, as to whether his mother and father were decent people. Realising suddenly, that what truly mattered was for his son to know such truth, Anthony felt as though his own anxiety over the events of the 4th July 1952, had at last been exorcised. But having heard Sean confess that he had contemplated picking up a gun to avenge *their* falling victim to the misery stemming from Ireland's troubled past, and the injustices he had become attuned to since arriving in Belfast, Anthony was extremely anxious to get his son out of the trouble-stricken city before there was an event which had Sean deciding to confront all the injustices - past and present.

Anthony begged Sarah to consider leaving Belfast before the week's end. Forced to take stock of Anthony's fears due to the brutal fact that they were of real substance, Sarah promised Anthony she would. Anthony quietly thanked God for showing his wife the way ahead.

Barratt returned to Belfast from the border counties later that night much perturbed. To have discovered that the Chief of Staff had since sent a 'delegation' to each of the border brigades in order to pressurise them to support - at the forthcoming ard fheis - the abandoning of the armed struggle in favour of pursuing a political agenda only, he knew that he had a fight of a more urgent cause, well and truly on his hands. Knowing that all bar the Armagh brigade had caved in to the southerner's gentle arm twisting, insomuch that they had not given a resounding No! to his proposals, Barratt judged the capitulation to indicate that it could well be left solely to the IRA in Belfast and the newfound ally in Dublin to see achieved the ultimate goal of Irish republicans. However, Barratt feared that there could first be the spilling of much republican blood as a consequence of so-called anti-militant republicans using their guns in eliminating those republicans who advocated the use of force to remove the British from Ireland; a paradox of the extreme kind to Barratt's thinking. Barratt's pessimism was due to the Adjutant General's forewarning that his fellow Dubliners would not hesitate to use those guns held in reserve to eliminate any source that defiantly stood between they, and the achievement of their goals. It was in consideration of this fact that the sympathetic Dubliner preferred to keep his true loyalty largely under wraps. But come the ard fheis, if the politicos were seemingly about to have their way, the Adjutant General had vowed to Barratt that through using the considerable influence his rank afforded, he would call on those delegates attending the ard fhies, which normally determined the republican movement's political and militarist policy, to vote with their feet in full view of the general public. Whether joining him or not at an adjoining venue, he would then set about upholding republican tradition, that of abstensionism and armed struggle in seeking the destruction of the Protestant Parliament in the occupied North, British disengagement from Ireland, and the restoration of power to the rightful inheritors of the first

Dail Eireann - those keeping true the ideals of Irish Republicanism in its purest form.

Considering the Dubliner's plan to be the best way forward, Barratt was resigned to awaiting the ard fheis in January. Then any split and subsequent formation of a new Provisional Army and Sinn Fein would be formal and merited in the history books, given the occasion on which it would undoubtedly take place.

Chapter Sixty-Eight

Anthony and Sarah were left greatly more assured of their own and Sean's safety on finding vigilantes posted on every street corner along the Falls following the sentencing of Wallace, the fear being, the UVF would launch a revenge attack on the area. The whole community was on its guard despite a heavy presence of British troops on the ground. The people's initial relief at having the soldiers around was beginning to wane. Local people were growing more incensed each day at the soldiers' intimidating presence, their guns now pointing at them as the British Army took over the policing role of the RUC, who remained as lepers in the eyes of the locals for crimes committed on the 15th night.

With only two days remaining before their departure south, Anthony, growing increasingly impatient to get out of the city on becoming more attuned to the open and hostile attitude of the locals towards the British Army, and Sarah, keeping to her word, began to pack those few suitcases they had brought with them from London. Meanwhile Sean, having not breathed a word to Roisin yet as to what was to come, made his mind up to tell her the facts that very night. He was dreading doing so, for he had declared his love for her in the height of passion. Ever since that first night, they had made love at every opportunity once Roisin's father's back was turned.

Sean had thought long and hard over the past few days especially about the relationship and events unfolding, and had decided to do his utmost to convince Roisin that they could keep the relationship alive. Hopefully by winning his parents' approval, Sean intended to visit Belfast as often as he could, and to invite Roisin to Donegal for holidays. While he suspected that she would not leave her father alone in such a sorry state, Sean was determined to keep their love strong until circumstances allowed them to be together again.

When meeting with Felix at Sean Mor's wake, Anthony had agreed to visit the Gresham Bar for a drink before departing Belfast, so with time short and with suitcases packed for the forthcoming Sunday, the last day of the month, Anthony was set to keep the promise made. Alone in that upstairs bedroom where Sean had been conceived, Anthony checked his smart attire in the long, upstanding bedroom mirror. He laughed quietly to himself on recalling those happier times spent with Felix and Bernadette, and concluded it best to finally drown those darker memories of Belfast life through having a good drink with old friends. Anthony did not intend to stay out too late and had arranged for McNab to drop him off and pick him up. First though, he would walk Sarah and Sean to Leger Street, from where McNab was to collect him in half an hour. Intent on spending as much of her remaining time in Belfast with her mother, Sarah prepared to make her nightly visit, and Sean, not surprisingly, would spend his evening with Roisin.

The Falls Road vigilantes were out in force again that night and only icy looks of indifference were exchanged between the local men and the British Army foot patrols. Walking protectively alongside Sean and Sarah, Anthony noted that the nights were on the turn again. The light faded fast and a cold nip penetrated his light summery jacket.

Finally reaching No70 Leger Street, Anthony turned to Sean and with gentle authority, said, 'I'll see you back at the house at eleven. Okay?'

'Okay,' Sean confirmed. 'Have a good night yourself.'

Anthony smiled and winked at Sean before his son disappeared into the Carlin home. Anthony followed Sarah into her mother's and checked his wristwatch. McNab was due to pick him up in ten minutes. On entering the living-room Sarah's mother motioned Anthony and Sarah to sit, before sitting herself down in Sean Mor's old armchair opposite the settee. Once they were all seated comfortably, the widow spoke, quietly, but with an air of conviction and mild authority.

'I'm glad to have a chance to speak with you alone,' she said. 'I want you both to know I'm relieved you're leaving Belfast soon. To know Sean will be safely away from this place is a great worry off my mind.' The woman looked to a framed photograph of her late husband upon the mantle-piece. 'Y'know, I miss my Sean terribly. But I'm glad he is where he is today. For I know, if he were alive, he'd be in the thick of it all again.' Turning in her chair to focus her full attention on her daughter, sad of face, the heartbroken mother said, 'So Sarah, don't worry about me, love. I'll not be shedding any more tears for your father. I know his suffering is over ... that he's in a better place today, God rest him.' Sarah choked back tears. 'I'll be okay here; Caithlin and Bridget are only a few streets away and I've got good neighbours too, and a few bob coming in from the rent on the shop. So I'll want for nothing. There's money put by if anything happens to me, and you girls and the grandchildren will be seen all right. So all's fine.'

'Ack Ma ...'

'No, it's best to talk about it,' stressed Sarah's mother. 'No one knows the hour or day, so it's been said, and that's that.' Looking Anthony in the eye, the mother-in-law spoke with sincerity. 'All I want to say to you, Anthony, is this: Sarah's father and I always thought the world of you. You've been good to our Sarah, and you've both got a lovely son. Do what's right for yourselves and the boy.' Anthony smiled warmly. The woman sighed, 'I've had my life and a happy one at that, despite all the heartache. And if I were to meet Sean Mor tomorrow, I would still fall for him. He was a good man and I loved him. And I know he loved me, truly.'

Sarah silently wept where she sat. Anthony was on his feet and crossed the room and stooped to kiss his mother-in-law on the cheek. Taking Anthony's head in her hands, the woman whispered, close to his ear, 'God bless you, son.'

A car horn signalled McNab's arrival. Anthony smiled at Mrs McParland then turned to Sarah, wiping away her tears with her hanky. 'I'll see you later, love,' Anthony said, and planted a quick kiss on Sarah's lips.

'Don't stay out too long, Anthony, and be careful.'

Pausing by the door leading into the hallway, Anthony turned, and with a smile, said, 'Don't worry, I'll be okay. See you later.' Anthony gave both women a little wave before leaving the room and on hearing the front door close out, Sarah asked God to keep her man safe.

A mother and daughter were left alone together to talk of fears and hopes for the future.

'You're quiet tonight, Sean. What's up?' Roisin asked, snuggling up to Sean on the sofa. Though he wanted to, Sean could not bring himself to tell Roisin at that moment what was truly on his mind, and so gave the excuse that he was a little tired, hoping he would muster enough courage to reveal all before the night was through. With Roisin's father out at the pub and with the night young, Roisin, taking Sean's excuse as being genuine, wasted no time in seducing him right there on the sofa.

Though his head was loaded with confused words, Sean was captivated by the beauty of Roisin's nakedness and so excited by her raw energy. He was a slave to her demands when making love. It was impossible to rebuff her advances and soon they were both naked and entwined on the floor.

Although it was all new faces standing at the bar and occupying the snugs, Anthony felt at home in his old seat in that snug close by the front door of the Gresham Bar. The otherwise familiar surroundings proved to be a warm comfort to the returning patron, as did his choice of company. Felix, relaxed in his wheelchair parked at the opening to the snug, and Bernadette, her face bearing the hallmarks of the strenuous years of coming to terms with her husband's disability for life, her once jet black ringlets prematurely greying, talked of better times shared. Felix was his usual bubbly self, while Bernadette seemed a little tense this side of the bar, thought Anthony, noting that the woman constantly looked toward the bar, to her left, behind which two young apprentice barmen were kept busy with the steady custom from the forty or so patrons in that Friday night.

Downing the last of his first pint, Felix boisterously shouted across the bar, 'Keep the black stuff coming lads!' Turning to Anthony, seated on his left, Felix said with resignation, 'Not so long ago, you'd have seen both sections of the community in here. Now only those from up the Falls and the Short Strand come in for a drink. No sir, the city will never be the same again.' Bernadette shuffled in her seat and sighed, 'I'd better leave you two to it. It seems the boys need a pull out behind the bar.'

With Bernadette returning to her familiar role, Felix went on to share with Anthony some of the darker times experienced by himself and his wife in the weeks, months and the first few years after his 'accident' in Liverpool. It was a nightmare story of endless hours spent in hospital receiving aftercare; sleepless nights shared due to pain and discomfort, mood swings and bouts of deep depression; and the lack of will to go on living as a cripple for the rest of one's life.

'Let me tell you something, Anthony,' Felix said in a considered whisper, 'Only for that woman of mine, I would have gassed myself a long time ago. She's been my saviour, my best friend.' On hearing this, Anthony was left in no doubt as to the hell his old friend had been through. Felix drank a large mouthful of stout from one of the two fresh pints brought to the table. 'She worked like a Trojan to get me this fit, so able mentally. And all that on top of keeping this place going.' Licking the froth from his top lip Felix continued. 'These days I only do a wee bit to keep myself occupied. Bernadette attends to it all, and the two boys do a fine job. D'you know, the one who just brought the drinks, young Patsy, he's a university graduate. But because he's a Catholic, he can't get the job he really wants. No, nothing has changed here, Anthony, though all is about to.' Anthony was suddenly reminded of a conversation that had taken place with the same man and in the very same barroom some sixteen years previously, and felt a little uneasy. 'But my days of fighting a war are over.' Hearing this, Anthony relaxed a little. 'But I'll tell you this,' Felix added, collecting his pint in hand, 'If I were my old self today, I'd be out there dragging this state down, by whatever means. Enough is enough!'

Anthony knew exactly to what Felix inferred and while the North's troubles were something he did not wish to get caught up in, he was nevertheless interested to know how a former IRA man viewed the present situation.

'What do you think will happen next?'

Speaking so not to be overheard, Felix gave his analysis.

'The Catholic people will turn against the British Army once realising whose side they're really on, while the army will be used to suppress them. Stormont will fall, the B Specials will most probably be disbanded, but the British Government will rule directly with a rod of iron, for they're not about to pull out of Ireland in a hurry. Yes, it's only about to start my old mate, and Heaven help us all when it does.'

Anthony thought for a moment before saying, 'I'm doing the right thing then, getting Sarah and Sean out.'

'I'll be sorry to see you go, Anthony, but I can't blame you. You're doing the best thing all right. Good luck to you.'

The same apprentice brought another two pints of stout to the table, a drink from one of the patrons at the bar who remembered Anthony's face from old. Vaguely recalling the face of the other patron, Anthony nodded in acknowledgement.

Felix raised his glass and offered a toast, 'Here's to you, Anthony. All the best for the future.' Anthony raised his glass in turn and acknowledged the toast.

At that moment, just beyond the main door of the bar, a dark coloured saloon car hijacked on the Shankill Road twenty minutes earlier by two masked and armed men, pulled up suddenly to the kerb. The front seat passenger, Sammy Vickers, his steely-hard face masked by a balaclava, jumped out and dashed under cover of dark to the open doorway of the pub. On reaching the smoked glass door leading to the barroom, he paused to retrieve a double-barrel sawn-off shotgun from inside his combat jacket, and laughed quietly in saying under his breath, 'Any fucking second now, youse Fenian bastards!'

Before putting the pint glass to his lips, Anthony looked toward the front door of the bar and recalled to mind that occasion when he had first laid eyes on his Sarah. So pretty, so radiant she had been. He saw only her face in front of him now, as it had been on that very same night. The presence of the gunman in the barroom, standing only a few feet away, was to Anthony but a blur on the edge of the blissful image.

Calmly entering the busy barroom unnoticed, the gunman could barely believe his luck. It was his key target, Felix Gresham, in the ominous company of another republican identified in the graveyard, on whom his eyes came to focus. The gunman made his move quickly. Following Anthony's gaze out of curiosity, Felix turned his head to the right while looking over the top of his pint glass and saw the shotgun, held at waist height, pointed straight at him, the whites of the gunman's eyes narrow in the slits of his mask. Knowing he was a sitting target, Felix quietly begged God to have mercy on his soul. But it was Anthony who died first, and instantly. A powerful shotgun blast ripped into his chest, violently throwing his lifeless body across the seat of the snug. A drinking glass crashed to the floor – and there was pandemonium.

Felix Gresham, whom the UVF man calculated to have no chance of making a charge at him, was next to die, his head blasted at close range.

As those other patrons and the two apprentices in the barroom scrambled over each other to take cover behind upturned tables and chairs, and as Bernadette Gresham stood rigid with total shock and horror behind the bar on seeing her husband murdered, the gunman made good his escape in the waiting car which sped off towards the Shankill Road.

Sean and Roisin, dressing themselves in the front room of No70, and Sarah, making her mother a cup of tea in the back scullery of the house next door, all heard the hellish scream in the not-too-far distance.

'*Christ*, who was that?' Roisin begged, moving to the window to look outside. Sean shrugged his shoulders and braced himself to tell her what was on his mind.

Next door, Sarah heard her mother say aloud from the living-room, 'Jesus have Mercy,' and was forced to put down the heavy teapot on the scullery table as a cold, cold chill swept over her in that instant. All a tremble, Sarah was gripped by a sense of fear never before experienced, and moved slowly, sluggishly into the living-room where her mother, sat by the fireside, looked up to see her daughter appear as if she had seen a ghost.

'What is it, Sarah?'

Staring her mother straight in the face, Sarah replied, 'Something terrible has happened. I know it.'

Sarah instinctively ran out of the house to investigate the scream, closely followed by her mother. Outside the front door a young girl stood sobbing on the footpath as six British soldiers went racing up the street toward the Falls Road, where a crowd was gathering on the corner. Sarah went to the distraught teenager's side and demanded, 'What's wrong? What's happened?'

Sniffing back tears and at last catching her breath, the girl spluttered out, 'I ... I heard it come o-o-over the soldier's walkie-talkie. There's been a-a fatal shooting at the Gre-Gresham Bar. My boyfriend went there tonight with his pals...'

Sarah felt herself go numb from head to toe. She looked up to the black starless night sky and screamed, '*ANTHONY*!'

Chapter Sixty-Nine

The RUC had confirmed an Anthony Brennan dead at the scene of the Gresham Bar shooting. Joe McNab accompanied a distraught Sean to the City Hospital mortuary in the early hours. Sean had come to stand by the body of his father who lay covered on a trolley and, gritting his teeth, had immediately identified his father when the white plastic sheet was rolled back. To see his father's face unmarked served Sean a little peace amid the horror. Indeed, his father appeared to be merely asleep. With Sean's back turned, the sullen-faced morgue official soberly whispered to McNab,

'It's a good job he doesn't have to identify the other fella. One side of his head was completely blown off.'

A line of tragic faces passed before a despairing grief-stricken mother and son over those following three days and nights as Anthony's corpse was waked in the very same room where Sean Mor had been only several weeks before. Anthony's devastated mother, sisters and brother, and his Uncle Peader had together travelled across the border for the wake and funeral and were all housed and attended to by family and friends of the bereaved McParlands. Telegraphed messages of deepest sympathy were received at the house on the last day of the wake from Donegal Danny and Jack Kilty.

It had been mutually agreed between Sarah and Anthony's mother, that Anthony be buried locally, in Milltown Cemetery. For Sarah, there was no corner of the world to where she could run to escape the horror experienced, and considered it only wise to bear her pain in the company of family and friends. Being able to visit Anthony's grave each day, would also be a comfort for her.

Never having had the opportunity to tell Roisin that night what had been planned, Sean knew he would never have to, for Belfast was to be his home also.

My father's killer has me committed to staying in Belfast to see justice done, Sean thought, as he proceeded with his Uncle Christy, Great Uncle Peader, and McNab, to lower his father's coffin into its grave on a windswept September day in Belfast's Milltown Cemetery. Nearby, among the embittered hundreds silently gathered, Roisin stood and painfully observed the heart-wrenching scene and prayed that God would give Sean the strength to carry on, as He had her, through her own tragic loss.

As the last of the mourners shuffled off home with a stiff wind against their backs, and as McNab escorted Sean's sobbing mother, grandmother and his father's family and friends to the fleet of waiting cars, Sean remained at the graveside. After a few minutes he asked Roisin to wait for him as he approached the group of four men standing a short distance away, over by the Republican Plot. Sean boldly stepped up to Frank Barratt. Shadowing Barratt, Bonar, D'Arcy and Carmichael each simply acknowledged Sean with a nod. Shaking Barratt's hand firmly, Sean spoke with a confident voice. 'Mister Barratt, I want to join the IRA.'

Barratt and company looked at Sean intensely. Barratt knew exactly what was going through Sean's mind, what was in his heart, so had no reason to ask him *why*, but sought to throw cold water on his designs out of concern for the lad's safety, and his mother's concern for him.

'Son, there is no personal reward or crusade to be had from being in the IRA. The risk of many, many years imprisoned, of being killed, is very high.'

'I accept that. I am not afraid.' Sean said, with determination. Barratt tried a little harder. 'You must be patient, and take orders. You will undertake no action without sanction from a senior rank. Do you understand what I am saying?'

'I understand,' Sean replied, keen to prove he listened and obeyed, though put Barratt on the spot when saying with added determination, 'You told me not so long ago, standing at this very spot, that I bore a good name, and to carry it well. Is my name good enough to be accepted by you?' Barratt knew he had lost the means of persuasion, and that he could give only one answer.

'It is that, lad.' Quietly admiring the youth's nerve, Barratt said, 'If you are still determined to see this through, meet with me at midday in two days time at the Coat of Arms.' Shaking Barratt's hand again, Sean simply said, 'Thank you.'

Returning to Roisin, who had witnessed the meeting from a short distance, Sean heard the concern in her voice. 'Sean, those were some of the boys you were talking to. They're in the thick of it all. Stay well clear!'

'Don't worry, Roisin. I was only thanking them for coming,' Sean lied. 'Come on, let's get back.'

Travelling on toward Leger Street in the rear of a waiting car with Roisin at his side, just as she had been solidly the past three days and nights, Sean felt so much better knowing he would see justice done unto those who had murdered his father, and who had left his mother heartbroken and his own life in ruin.

Before leaving for Donegal that next day, Anthony's mother made a point of throwing her arms around Sarah and Sean on the doorstep of No72, to kiss and hug them close in letting them know that they still had another family who would care for them always. A tragedy-bruised mother shared what was in her heart with another grief-stricken mother over recent events. With a strong belief in her faith, Anthony's mother sought to give strength to her widowed daughter-in-law. 'Sarah, I never thought I would live to see three young sons and a husband lowered into the ground. Life is so short, at times so cruel. But never let go of your faith. Keep strong, for Sean's sake.' The grandmother turned to her grandson. 'You're a fine lad, Sean, the double of your father. Take good care of your mother. Just as your father would have done.'

Sean smiled through the heartbreak. More hugs and kisses were exchanged between all before Christy drove the hire car away slowly from the street, knowing full well now the tragic truth of his younger brother's warning five short years earlier. Swinging the car onto the Falls Road and noting the British soldiers lurking nervously on street corners, the unpredictable movement of denim-clad youths gathering, Christy held no intention of setting foot across the border ever again.

Home for Sarah and Sean was to be Aunt Bella's old house. While McNab took Anthony's car away to be sold on the day following the funeral, and as an exhausted Sean lay in a deep sleep in the back bedroom, Sarah, fighting off the sleep, spent the rest of that day bagging Anthony's belongings, except those few sentimental things she would keep for all time - his tool bag and work tools, and the cuff-links which she had bought him to celebrate their last wedding anniversary. Sarah sobbed her heart out knowing that in a few months time they would have celebrated eighteen years of marriage. More agony was heaped upon her already shattered world by recalling her mother's fateful words only hours before they were proven to be so tragically true. Through the action of the UVF, all that had been planned, the new life she had been preparing to share with Anthony in Donegal, had been cruelly denied. And what was devouring Sarah's very soul was the thought that if she had gone south a day or two after her father's funeral, Anthony would still be alive. Sarah knew she would have to live with this knowledge for the rest of her life. She prayed, as Anthony's mother had said she must, that she would keep her faith and stay strong - if only for Sean's sake.

Two days later and keeping to the appointed time, Sean arrived at the designated meeting place as instructed. Entering a near deserted barroom, Sean was met by D'Arcy, who led him through a low door behind the bar counter and up a narrow stairwell to the cramped stock room above, wherein he was warmly received by Barratt, rising out of his chair from behind a tricolour-draped table.
'Welcome Sean.' Sean shook Barratt's hand firmly. Barratt got proceedings underway immediately.
'Before becoming a volunteer in the Irish Republican Army, you will need to raise your right hand and swear the oath, while placing the other on the tricolour. Is this to your acceptance?'
'Yes,' said Sean.
Barratt continued. 'We are about to follow a custom of old. But having said that, what we are about to do is not to be taken lightly or undermined in any way.'
Sean straightened himself, placed the palm of his left hand on the white of the Irish Tricolour, and raising his right hand, said firmly, 'I'm ready.'
After half an hour of following formalities, Barratt informed Sean that he was now a 'soldier', expected to do what a soldier does, which firstly, was to obey orders. Sean left the public house in the company of D'Arcy, who, on Barratt's order, was to break the new recruit in gently.
Feeling as though he had achieved something great, Sean was enthusiastically anticipating what lay ahead of him as an IRA volunteer. Barratt though, was not taking any chances. Suspecting it to be Sean's intention to get his hands on a gun as quickly as possible to wreak revenge

on the Shankill, he assigned D'Arcy, the youngest of the brigade officers, to 'mind' Sean through the first three months at least, before placing him with one of the increasing number of IRA units forming along the Falls. The UVF's attack on the Gresham Bar had seen the IRA's ranks swell in number. And while Barratt was gutted over the double killing, he had instructed Bonar to capitalise on the people's anger by drawing in additional recruits. Despite this turnaround of sorts, Barratt was a worried man as he walked the streets of the Falls in making his way to another meeting in Beechmount, where Bonar would brief him on efforts made to date to identify the UVF men involved in the shooting. Assessing the mood of the people on the street, Barratt sensed there existed great expectations of him and his men. The same people were seeking swift retribution on those responsible for the Gresham Bar attack. For Barratt, as with learning the name of the UVF gunman, those guns due from down south could not come soon enough.

Sean was being careful in what he said to the new people in his life. He hadn't said anything when being sworn-in to lead Barratt to suspect that he was simply out to avenge his father's murder nor would he, he decided, reveal his true motives for joining the IRA to D'Arcy. He feared the IRA would still reject him if they knew just how much he wanted to get his hands on a gun, then at those who had shot his father. Sean accepted that he would have to be patient as Barratt stressed, and live in hope that he would learn soon enough the identity of those men who had carried out the attack. If so doing, Sean was determined, come what may, to make it very difficult for Barratt to refuse him the opportunity, the right, to play a full and active role in seeing the UVF men dead.

Sean had taken a liking to D'Arcy immediately when meeting with him for the first time. As D'Arcy took him on a guided tour of the Falls to show him the lay of the land, to point out the boundary which marked home ground and enemy territory, to introduce him to the local battalion OC, who would in turn inform only those who needed to know of Sean's newfound status in the community, Sean felt at ease in the other's company and hoped that a good friendship would be born out of their being thrown together.

Conscious of appearing as an outsider in the eyes of many others, Sean knew he would have to work extra hard in order to be accepted, to win the trust and respect of those men about him, for whom the English accent would be reason enough to be wary, regardless of his family connection. Only by achieving this, he knew, would he stand a chance of being accepted for being his own man.

Sean consciously displayed to D'Arcy that he was listening intently to what he was being told, that he was keen to learn everything there was to know, and sensed D'Arcy was happy enough to be doing what he was doing.

In the company of D'Arcy the night had passed quickly for Sean, and with it being quite late, he decided to give Roisin a miss, and so went straight home. Juking his head around his mother's bedroom door to find her asleep, Sean carried on to his own bed eager for dawn to break and another day out with D'Arcy on visits to other IRA heartlands across the city. Sean did not doubt his mother would at some point discover that he had joined the IRA, but was confident that when or indeed if she approached him over this, that once revealing his motives for so doing, she would understand. But for the moment he was keeping true to the oath and was breathing not a word to anyone as to his involvement in the IRA. His only fear was what Roisin would say and do if discovering his role. Sean knew she would be very concerned for him, and most probably angry too. Determined that she would never know, Sean fell asleep wondering what excuse he could best give for not arriving on her doorstep that night.

Roisin lay awake in her bed asking that very question. She wondered too what the reason was for Sean to have been in the Coat of Arms earlier, at the same time as Frank Barratt. Sitting up one corner of the barroom from the minute it had opened its doors that morning, her father had seen Sean come and go through the bar each time, just ahead of Barratt, and had slobbered about it at the kitchen table when popping home briefly for his dinner in the early evening. Roisin had heard every one of her father's disgruntled words over Sean being 'mixed up with the boys', and with her suspicions aroused, would challenge Sean over it all when next seeing him. Roisin was determined that this would be the very next day.

Chapter Seventy

Leaving with McNab that following morning to visit the graves of her late husband and father, Sarah left Sean alone at the breakfast table to read the kind letter of sympathy and Mass card received from Frances Malpass. Sean noted her words of sincere sorrow over his father's death and was pleased to learn that the woman and his best friend Drew - still living and working on the coast - were both well. The seven enclosed O' Level exam results, all achieved with distinction by Sean, were of no significance to him now.

A loud knock on the front door had Sean checking his wristwatch. D'Arcy was not due for another half hour. Sean moved towards the door wondering who called so early. Remembering his mother's words of warning not to open the door without first checking, Sean called out, 'Who's there?' He was not entirely surprised to hear Roisin reply. Opening the front door, Roisin breezed in, stern-faced. Sean closed out the door and followed Roisin into the front room, tentatively. Roisin stood in the middle of the floor with hands on hips, barely able to keep her mouth shut for a moment longer. Her eyes narrowed on Sean as he came to stand in front of her.

'Is your mother in?'

'No.'

'Good. We need to talk seriously, Sean.'

'What is it?'

'What were you doing in the Coat of Arms yesterday?'

'Who told you that?'

'Who the bloody hell do you think? My Da of course! Sure there's a rumour going about that he's moved in there permanently!'

No one was laughing.

'I went in for a drink.'

'You don't drink, Sean Brennan.'

'When you lose a father, anything is possible.'

A brittle silence.

Sean realised the error he had just made and wanted the ground to open up and swallow him.

'Don't lie to me, Sean. And don't you get using your father's name so cheaply. Why were you there?'

Sean felt his face flush and he shuffled uneasily on his feet. Roisin would not relent.

'Frankie Barratt was there too, wasn't he?' Roisin fired. 'You're caught up with the boys, aren't you?' Sean was lost for words. Roisin's face signalled that she demanded an answer. Sean fumbled, 'I'd prefer to say nothing, Roisin.' Roisin hurt him hard with her tongue. 'Is that right? Well, let me tell you this, Sean Brennan. My heart is already broken over the loss of my mother. I don't want to be involved with someone who is going to tear my soul apart too. You've a choice, Sean. It's either the IRA or me. And if you love me, like you say you do, you lie to me again, God help me, I'll kill you!' Roisin pushed past Sean as she fled the room and the house, slamming the front door out behind her, and leaving Sean to think long and hard.

Shoulder to shoulder, Sean walked boldly alongside D'Arcy across the city and in turn to Unity Flats and Ardoyne. It had been the New Lodge and the even smaller enclave of Short Strand on which the two IRA men had then called, before finally returning to the Falls later that evening.

With the tour of north and east Belfast proving to have been a moving experience for Sean, his mind had been left full of the disturbing images of the poverty witnessed, though his spirits had been heartened by the steadfast comradeship and steely determination of the earthy people he had met. If any doubt had still existed in his mind as to his decision earlier in the day to end the relationship with Roisin in order to pursue vengeance for his father's death, Sean knew it would have evaporated on taking stock of what he had seen and heard on his travels that day. He was convinced he had made the right decision to join the IRA, and seeing with his own eyes the reasons why the nationalist people were a risen people, an angry people, Sean considered it a privilege to be bearing arms in the advance of their cause.

Knowing it would be very hard to have to walk away from Roisin, Sean was prepared to, knowing it would be even harder on him to turn his back on his native city and his people in their hour of need.

Inviting D'Arcy in for a late night cup of tea, and with his mother evidently still at his gran's, Sean picked D'Arcy's brains for more information on the causes of the latest conflict and the key figures, political and otherwise who were central to it all.

Comparing the youth's hunger for knowledge to that of his own when he had first joined the republican movement, D'Arcy gladly fed the latest recruit all that there was to be told at the kitchen table, bar the more delicate details as to the IRA's short-term strategy. But he felt comfortable enough with Sean, Sean Mor's grandson, to elaborate on those major developments taking shape within the movement and shared by Barratt the previous day, which was to leave Sean with a sound insight into the wider situation he currently found himself in.

D'Arcy went into detail when talking about the movement's organisation present day, militarily and politically, the opposing arguments prevailing within the movement as to its future direction and the anticipated outcome from the Sinn Fein ard fheis in January, when, according to a confident D'Arcy, a new, more militant IRA would officially emerge. D'Arcy stressed how frustrating it was meantime for northern volunteers to remain accountable to the present 'geriatric' leadership in Dublin, though D'Arcy assured Sean a change would not be long in coming.

'I hope not, D'Arcy. I want to pick up a gun and fight soon,' Sean declared.

'And kill?' D'Arcy tested.

'Yes! Definitely!' Sean replied without hesitation.

'I understand your urgency,' sympathised D'Arcy. 'But you must remain patient and disciplined, remember?'

Sean nodded.

'Anyway,' continued D'Arcy, 'before you can fire a gun you must know how to use one. We'll have to send you across the border for a long weekend to get trained up.'

'And if you learn the identity of my father's murderers, you'll let me know?'

Admiring the youth's determination, D'Arcy simply said, 'We'll see.'

'I must be allowed to get even, D'Arcy. I just must!'

Sympathetic to Sean's plea, D'Arcy replied, 'I'll see what I can do if that day comes. But I can't promise.'

Sean smiled broadly and offered a hand to D'Arcy and felt a genuine comradeship born out of their handshake.

Returning home from her mother's, Sarah recognised D'Arcy for who and what he was when she met him on the doorstep. The IRA man bid Sarah goodnight, which she acknowledged with a friendly smile. Finding Sean about to climb the stairs to bed, Sarah called to him along the hallway. 'Can bed wait a while, Sean?'

Sean turned and faced his mother, knowing that she must have seen D'Arcy, a prominent face at his father's funeral, take his leave. Sarah stepped up close to Sean and spoke softly, meaningfully.

'Sean, I would never stand in your way if your heart is set on doing something,' she revealed. 'It's your life. I know how you're feeling about your father. All I will say is this, be careful, whatever you do.'

Knowing exactly what his mother implied, Sean gently embraced her.

'I love you, Mum.'

'And I love you too, Sean,' replied a quietly despairing mother.

Barratt sat up late in the safe house in Beechmount pondering how his men could kill the man they had discovered to have succeeded Wallace, and to have carried out the Gresham Bar attack. His identity had been learnt, not on the streets of Belfast, but on a wing in the Crumlin Road Jail, where a convicted republican prisoner had by chance overheard two loyalist screws conversing on the pub shooting, and one Samuel Vickers had been named as 'the trigger man'. The same two screws were known by republican prisoners to be close to the UVF, and who treated the loyalist prisoners favourably. It was common knowledge that Wallace wanted for nothing and was treated like a VIP by the vast majority of the POs, who were all Protestant. Word had been passed to Bonar by the republican prisoner via a sympathiser on a jail visit. Barratt had come up with several ideas as to how his men could get to Vickers, a butcher by trade, and who managed his own butcher shop on the Shankill Road. He considered the more simplistic scheme as being the most likely to succeed in terms of killing Vickers and his men escaping the Protestant heartland in one piece.

Barratt's dilemma presently was that if the boys succeeded in eliminating their target, the resources were not at hand to fend off any mass loyalist revenge attacks on Catholic areas. Stockpiles of new weapons promised from down south had been due to arrive in Belfast at the end of August, but because of a 'technical hitch' the drop was not expected now until after Christmas. The IRA man was caught between giving the order to his men to go after Vickers immediately or to wait until the means to defend was at hand, but at the risk of Vickers fleeing the country to escape the wrath of the IRA. Barratt decided to sleep on it and lay himself down on the makeshift bed, always at the ready in that safe house.

Meeting with Bonar at the Coat of Arms early that following morning, Barratt laid down his plans for the remainder of the year and Bonar was expected to follow orders to the letter. Speaking in a hushed, conspiratorial voice over his pint, Barratt translated his late night scheming into a clear and definite course of action.

'We will not hit Vickers just yet. We'll wait until we have the means to defend 'cause it's more than likely that the UVF will retaliate. There's no way we can be caught cold again. The people would lynch us.'

'Too true!' Bonar seconded.

'When we get our hardware, we'll need to get the lads across the border quickly to be trained up. Ninety percent of them have never held a gun never mind fire one. Then, we'll go after Vickers and give the loyalists the biggest shock of their lives.'

'Too fucking right, Frankie! The fuckers have a lot to answer for.'

'We must sit out the rest of the year patiently and meanwhile prepare the new volunteers as best we can,' added Barratt. 'I want them to know what they're going to be fighting and dying for. Only after the ard fheis can we fully play our hand. Then it'll be all guns blazing.'

Bonar injected a concerned thought. 'The only thing that bothers me, Frankie, is that the longer we leave Vickers alone, the greater the risk that the bastard will see another Gresham Bar carried out.' Barratt had thought this through the night before, but had his mind made up. There was no way he was going to risk an even greater massacre by ordering Vickers killed at that time. 'I hear what you say, Bonar. But believe me, I know what I'm doing. The waiting game will be the hardest bit. Let's just hope the bastard lies low for a while. But don't fear, we'll get the fucker, without doubt.'

For Barratt, the 'hardware' could not come soon enough.

Chapter Seventy-One

Bitter violent clashes that October between besieged Catholics cocooned in Unity Flats on the edge of the Shankill and the loyalist mob attempting to put them to flight in retaliation for the disbanding of the B Specials, placed added pressure on the Belfast IRA to respond. Consequently, Frank Barratt was at his wits end at not being able to turn out his men with the necessary gear to effectively defend the ghettos. The local Catholic people remained cynical toward the republican excuse, genuine though it was, at not being able to show a hand of force.

With an uneasy calm descending over that part of the city at the end of two consecutive days and nights of pitched street-battles, Barratt, his patience waning over his Chief of Staff's failure to immediately sanction full-scale IRA action to counter the loyalist threat, made contact with his ally in Dublin. Once sharing insight to his plan of action with the Adjutant General, who was quick to endorse it, Barratt executed step one of the plan by requesting that an urgent Army Council meeting be convened. In collusion with the Adjutant General, it was Barratt's plan to put the Chief of Staff on the spot by demanding he place 'all' resources at the disposal of the Belfast and Derry Brigades in view of the mounting attacks on Catholics in the North. It was the militarist's intention to force a vote of no confidence in the Chief of Staff, by daring those other moderates at leadership level to go down in history as having been the ones to have abandoned the nationalist people in the North.

The Chief of Staff had received Barratt's message and word was sent to Belfast within hours that a special meeting of the Army Council would convene the very next day. Barratt was content with this, knowing that the split he so desired would finally come about and be made official at the ard fheis in January. Then, it was anticipated, the newly formed IRA would be free to secure arms and quickly.

Eager to play his part in changing the face of Irish republicanism and the fight for national self-determination so dramatically, Barratt spent the evening alone, by choice, in the back bedroom of a safe house to prepare himself mentally and physically for the day ahead, which he suspected would be the most testing of his life.

Though somewhat concerned for Sean over his break-up with Roisin and for what he was involved in, but of which she was proud, Sarah looked forward to the New Year with a little renewed hope. She had been lucky enough to land herself a part-time job as a Product Inspector in a part of the old flax mill which had managed to keep going over the years, while the rest of the building now housed the newly arrived British Army regiment to the area. Several of Sarah's old friends still worked at the mill also.

Sean was delighted for his mother, knowing it would do her good to get a break from the house, and indeed granny's, where lately the women had sat and wallowed in augmented grief. Subsequently, he only called to his gran's occasionally, but was not fooling himself. Sean knew deep down that he did not wish to see Roisin. To lay eyes on her, he knew, would only cause him added pain. Blanking her out of his mind was so very hard to do. He lay awake most nights tossing and turning, knowing Roisin lay alone only a few streets away. But he accepted that she had meant what she had said and he wasn't prepared to give up the path he'd set out on, even though at times it had been so frustrating, with yet only another

IRA educational class to attend. However news shared by an excited D'Arcy one October night, changed all that. Calling to Sean's home and beckoning him into the front room, D'Arcy rubbed his hands in glee. 'Barratt's just back from Dublin. The split is definitely on. Barratt and the second-in-command walked out of an important leadership meeting, declaring their intention to set-up their own Army Council, to form a new army.

Sean only hoped that with the coming of the new IRA, so too would some action. His hopes were further raised on hearing D'Arcy continue, 'You're to make yerself ready. You'll be off across the border at anytime. It'll be guns you'll be learning about then, Sean.'

Never had Sean imagined that he would see the hills of Donegal in such circumstances. Dressed in khaki and army issue boots, a heavy rucksack on his back weighing him down, and carrying a US Army issue M1 Carbine, complete with fully loaded magazine, he and nine other rookies made slow but steady progress over the hard mountainous terrain towards their improvised training camp, five hundred feet above sea level. A sea of mist and fine rain cut them off from that other world below. The ten were made up of eight volunteers from the 1st Battalion Belfast Brigade IRA, who were all local to the Falls Road. The other two, were Donegal men, farm labourers under normal circumstances, but who for the next seven days would turn the eight young, pale-faced youths into fighting men, prepared to kill and die for their country. The eight volunteers were split into two units of four, with one of the two Northwestern Brigade staff taking responsibility for training up each group in the techniques of guerrilla warfare: methods of road ambush, the preparation of firing positions, the laying of landmines, the mixing of home-made explosives and the making of bombs for deployment in beer kegs. Also, the maintenance and firing of weapons and the construction of secure field dumps were all covered and were to be adopted where possible for use in the urban setting. Sean was among the first batch of fifty volunteers from the 1st Battalion to be sent south of the border that bitter cold month of December, a week before Christmas. More volunteers from all over the North were receiving similar training at remote camps dotted across the twenty-six counties. Whenever possible, many other volunteers in the North, by way of the few weapons available, were undergoing training in their own areas by experienced hands, most often in the back kitchens of sympathisers houses.

By now, Sean had been accepted by the vast majority of his comrades in the 1st Batt' as one of their own, more so due to his own persona rather than who he was - Sean Mor's grandson. Although others recognised that Sean came from good republican stock, consideration had been given also to the fact that despite being raised in England and among the English, his commitment to the cause of Irish freedom was genuine. Consequently, this left many in admiration and one or two jealous. One such person from the latter camp was among the seven with whom Sean had travelled south. To Sean's thinking, it was unfortunate that he and his budding adversary had been placed in the same unit.

While Sean held good rapport with six of the Belfast lads in tow, he had known from day one that in Scullion's book, his face didn't fit. Each of the eight were in their late teens or early twenties, but Scullion had an 'old head' on his shoulders, but really knew 'fuck all' in the expressed opinion of Paddy 'Toby' Tober. On a few occasions Scullion had been heard mouthing off about the 'Englishman within' by several of the other lads more friendly and accepting of Sean, and they had warned Scullion to 'button it'.

Sean had grown increasingly sensitive to Scullion's snide remarks and dirty looks but had ignored them all in the hope that through time, Scullion would let his vendetta drop, but he never had, despite the warnings. But now, Sean was ready and waiting for Scullion to open his mouth the wrong way once more, for he was determined to shut it for good. In recent months an anger had stirred within Sean over his father's murder, an anger which he had let simmer so to save it for when he got back to the North, where he knew events - continuing loyalist attacks, increasing RUC and British Army harassment of the Catholic people on the streets and in their homes, would come to a head. After much consideration though, Sean had concluded before setting out for Belfast, that if Scullion got on the wrong side of him again, he would physically take him apart.

By the end of the second day an explosive tension existed between the two. Scullion vented his frustration at Sean over the unrelenting pace the unit leaders were setting for the volunteers, and in such atrocious weather conditions, while Sean, apart from Scullion's harangue, was enjoying every minute of life on the hilltop. The two huge Donegal men had deliberated over the same hostile atmosphere and keen to prevent it from completely overshadowing the remaining five days at camp, were agreed as to how it could be best resolved. On the morning of the third day, with a damp mist rolling off the hillside as the IRA volunteers scrambled out of their warm sleeping bags and field tents, the two local men, going by the names of Malachy and Liam, called Sean and Scullion together and instructed the others to form a wide circle around them. Malachy laid down the law to the sleepy-eyed duo, wondering what it was all about.

'Listen up, you two. I want men to leave this hill with one common aim and purpose. So whatever anger and hate you have for each other, this is the time and place to offload it. Otherwise, me and yer man here will have to be taken on, for we're determined to beat it out of you if need be!' Both Sean and Scullion eyed the two older men with concern and knew instantly that they would not stand a chance against them. Turning then to eyeball each other, it was Sean whose patience snapped first.

'Come on, spit it out!' Sean snarled at Scullion. 'What's your fucking difficulty with me?' Sean saw Scullion's pale face turn even paler. Everyone looked on with expectation. Scullion knew he could not be seen to back down and squared up to Sean, his face inches away from his.

'I just don't feel comfortable with you around, Brennan,' he seethed. 'That bastard English accent of yours makes me sick, and you, thinking you know it fucking ...' Before Scullion could spit out the last word, Sean head-butted Scullion full in the face. Scullion was sent reeling backwards, but quickly gathering his bearings, lashed out with a swinging right fist and caught Sean on the side of the head as he closed in. Sean was sent crashing to the hard, frosted ground. Scullion was quick to follow in viciously with the boot. Sean felt the full force of Scullion's bulky weight crash into his ribs as he struggled to get up.

'C'mon Sean. Get up t'fuck!' Fra McErlane urged from the sidelines, willing his man on. Sean's mind was in turmoil with Scullion following in with more crippling kicks to his gut. The one down was badly winded, his head was spinning and everything was a blur except the soaring pain. Fearing for his life, Sean, down on all fours, mustered all his sapped strength and energy to catch hold of his attacker's right boot wading in, and simultaneously lifted and pushed with all his might to send Scullion falling onto his back. Sean had raised himself onto his feet and pushed forward to jump and land astride Scullion's chest. He proceeded to methodically cudgel Scullion's face with both fists, while hissing from behind clenched teeth, 'Fuck you, Scullion. I'll fucking kill you!'

All looking on for a moment longer winced on seeing each forced blow connect with Scullion's vulnerable head, which quickly turned to a bloody, swollen mess. The Donegal men had seen enough. They both dragged Sean from Scullion.

'Okay! Okay! For fuck sake! We don't want a death on our hands,' pleaded Malachy, effortlessly throwing Sean to one side.

Liam checked on a motionless Scullion. 'He's out cold,' he announced with little surprise. Malachy was laying down the law again to everyone. 'Now listen up you lot. No more fucking squabbling! There'll be plenty of fighting to do when you go back over the border. This is finished with. D'yeh hear?' No one spoke. 'Now get these two cleaned up. We're weapons training in half an hour and I want you all to have your wits about yeh. So move it!'

Toby and Fra helped carry Sean into one of the two large tents where they proceeded to strap up his cracked ribs and apply a wet cloth to a swollen lip. Toby coaxed Sean back onto his feet with praises aplenty. 'Good man yerself, Sean. You soon shut Scullion's mouth ... fucking shite-ass that he is.'

'Too fucking right!' Fra affirmed.

His head thumping, his chest aching with every breath, Sean was only concerned about one thing - how he would look at the end of the week. He had planned to call on his father's home place across Lough Swilly before setting out for Belfast, where war loomed.

That evening, in a remote farmhouse set amid the lowlands of County Down, men drawn from each of the six counties in the North, and from Dublin City, came together to formally appoint themselves the Army Council of the Provisional Republican Movement and to prepare a strategy for an imminent military offensive in the occupied North. Barratt, Adjutant General elect, addressed the other eleven men sitting around the well-scrubbed kitchen table, with an optimistic voice.

'Comrades. Tonight we set forth plans that will see the longest war ever to be waged against the British. We know, that despite our intention to bring Northern Ireland to its knees, and if need be, English cities to a standstill, the British will not go tomorrow, next week, next year or in five years and more. Let us not think any different. But go they will!'

Someone was heard to say, 'God's speed to them.'

Barratt proceeded. 'As I stand here, the means to wage an intensive military campaign are being moved into position throughout the North, while many of our volunteers are undergoing training in the hills of Donegal. The clock is ticking away. I propose that whatever we decide here tonight, as to whom or what constitutes a legitimate target for IRA volunteers, armed action should commence as soon as possible to carry the struggle forward.' A circle of heads nodded in approval. Barratt was upbeat. 'But before we move on, let me update you on the state of play between those who decided to go the political road and ourselves. I received a communiqué this morning from the former Chief of Staff, which states that he and his comrades, while steadfast in pursuing their political agenda, have mobilised active service units of their own to engage loyalist paramilitaries and the RUC/British Army where appropriate, and that his men will be willing to cooperate with us on the ground.' There were expressions of surprise around the table. 'While I personally welcome this, I suspect others do not want to lose out completely on the support of the people. I am convinced however, that in time, given our overwhelming strength and rising support, the expedient politicos will disappear off the scene entirely. Meantime, I suggest we keep them in check, for at the end of the day, there can only be one IRA.'

There were murmurs of support from among those gathered. The twelve men, old hands and rising figureheads, were to sit into the small hours in formulating the Provisional Movement's tier of leadership, north and south of the border, and the military and political agenda for the next twelve months. The North, with its own Northern Command, which would determine operations there, was to be the battlefield on which bloody violent guerrilla warfare was to be launched within weeks, while political strategists would be active on both sides of the border. Apart from using minimum force, if necessary, in the pursuit of raising funds in the South to finance the war in the North, no direct military action was to be employed south of the border by IRA personnel. It was felt, and agreed by all, that the key aim was to wage war first and foremost against the British, and once driving them out of the North, attention would then turn to 'sorting out' the Free State, where the newly formed Provisional leadership did not wish to open up a second front, just yet.

The former Adjutant General was unchallenged in seeking the rank of Chief of Staff. It was then unanimously agreed that GHQ should remain Dublin based for numerous reasons, not least logistically, but most importantly, to serve as a reminder to friend and foe alike, that the conflict in the North was not a purely northern affair, nor only a concern to the people there. It was agreed also, without any dissent, that the Chief of Staff should lead the walk out at the forthcoming ard fheis. This action, it was hoped, would officially signal the split. It was envisaged that greater numbers of southern republicans would then crossover to the 'traditionalists', who would uphold the abstensionist policy and advocate the pursuit of self-determination for the Irish people through armed struggle, as a right.

Content in mind, Barratt returned to Belfast just before dawn with a blueprint in his head for sheer carnage soon to follow.

With their training complete and a train to catch back to the war zone, the Belfast eight, dressed in their civilian garb and carrying only their rucksacks on their backs, piled into a battered old van and set out on the road north. Nursing their wounds, Sean and Scullion had made up that morning, with Scullion offering Sean a hand and murmuring an apology for the hassle caused. The Donegal men had indeed succeeded in their mission in more ways than one.

Sean had talked Liam, the Donegal man driving, into taking a slight detour from the main road to Derry, so to be dropped off at the crossroads a half mile or so from his father's home place. After a thirty minute bumpy and agonising ride along pot-holed back roads, Sean alighted at the spot requested and was allocated an hour to make his call and then return to be collected. Meantime, the others were to kill time in a pub in the local market town.

Sean could not comprehend the beauty and peacefulness engulfing him, the magnitude of it all distracting his mind from his own physical discomfort. The rain had eased and the wind had dropped and the sun shone magnificently for the first time in seven days. Now, as the winter sun faded on the Atlantic skyline away to his right and with a cool sea breeze stirring, Sean, noting the weather-beaten signpost to his left, set out along the narrow tarmac road stretching out directly ahead of him like a silver-plated highway cutting through a wild bog. The same road would lead him to where his father had been born and bred.

A little further on, Sean was left feeling self-conscious under the silent glare of a dozen or so ruddy-faced school children. The boys and girls stood as if made of stone and peered over the school wall as the lone, odd-looking, long-haired figure, clad in well-worn denim, heavy boots and combat jacket passed along the road. Realising it must be the same school his father had attended as a child, Sean laughed quietly on imagining how his father would have reacted if seeing, in his day, what those same children saw now. Sean knew he would not look out-of-place in some battlefield front line. Further on, having climbed the hill in the road, Sean sensed he was not far from the old home place. A cluster of mainly thatched cottages stood to one side of the road. Sean was pleased to see an old man persevere in riding a black bicycle up hill toward him.

'Excuse me, mister. Could you tell me where I can find the Brennan home?'

The man, about ninety years old to Sean's thinking, his face scorched by the salty sea air and his piercing blue watery eyes dancing with devilment in his Celtic head, topped by a well-worn black beret, brought the bike to a screeching halt by Sean's side and weighed him up with a curious face. Studying the old man's leathery face and rickety frame in turn, Sean realised the full truth of his late father's tales of hard times on the land. The old man's soft, almost saintly voice was ill matched against the story his face told. 'You'd be a Brennan, for sure! You're the deadspit of old Dan Brennan, God rest him.'

'I'm his grandson, Sean Brennan.' said Sean, with a sense of pride.

'I knew it. So you'd be Anthony's boy?'

Sean nodded and he saw the man's face fall sad, his watery eyes become more watery, and heard his voice shake with emotion.

'Your father was a good man. As a boy he often lent me a hand with the harvest. He knew what hard work was. He didn't deserve to die the way he did. May God curse the bastard who murdered him.' The old man wiped away a tear with the back of his hand, then half turned in his saddle to point a withered finger back along the road. 'The house with the new slate roof, just in off the road, that's your father's home place.' Turning to Sean again, old Mick Onion added with a pitiful voice, 'And God knows, it's had more than its fair share of grief.'

Sean thanked the old man and bid him good day before setting off again to cover the short distance ahead. Feeling he belonged, an affinity with all that surrounded him, the very ground he walked upon, Sean approached the white walled cottage which, with its slate roof, stood out from among six thatched houses scattered about it, and felt his emotions stir. Knocking on the brightly red painted half door, Sean saw the harried grey face of his Granny Brennan come alive on opening the door to him. The delighted grandmother threw her arms around her grandson to hug him close. Though this proved physically very painful for him, Sean braved a smile.

Sean knew he would savour that hour spent in his father's home place for the rest of his life. The happy, smiling faces of all the family flocking round him, their warmth and friendliness amid such humble surroundings, even the simple little things about it all and experienced: the smell of burning turfs in an open fire, the pure goodness of the freshly baked home-made bread he ate, the creamy cows milk he drank. But it was the sheer beauty and homeliness of Toome, the peace that came with it, which was engraved vividly on his mind for eternity.

Settling down alongside Toby on the Belfast-bound train and trying to be as inconspicuous as his other comrades scattered throughout the carriages, Sean reflected on the previous six days as the train pulled out from Derry. He knew he was returning to Belfast a different man from when he'd left. Now, he was knowledgeable and skilled in the use of firearms and explosives. On his return to the Falls he would be expected to go out and kill and maim. He was ready to do so. His anger over his father's loss, having discovered what a good and decent man he had truly been, where he had come from, what he had been through, and fully realising just what had been denied his father, them all, as a consequence of a loyalist murder squad, left Sean craving revenge.

Chapter Seventy-Two

Slipping back into the Falls under cover of darkness the eight volunteers scurried down side streets and back alleys, on toward their prearranged rendezvous with the rest of their company. The night's meeting, to be addressed by the battalion OC, was to be held in a local youth club in Clonard at eight-thirty.

    Sean and his comrades arrived in a sweat at the inhospitable, dimly lit hall a few minutes late. Two dozen other volunteers and staff officers, including seven members of Cumann na mBan - the women's wing of the IRA, had already assembled at ease in five lines of four in the middle of the open floor and all turned to eye, some condemningly, others amused, the eight bedraggled campers sweeping in.

    'Get them fucking bags off your backs and get fell in!'

    The snarling company OC, standing up at the front, was known to be shit-hot on timekeeping. Sean and the others, once dropping their kit just inside the hall's doorway, joined the parade double quick and behind the last line-up, formed two lines of four. Sean stood on the outside edge of the back line. With some frenzied movement on a makeshift platform up at the front, the company OC shouted the command in Gaelic for all to stand to attention, and all did. The sound of stomping feet echoed around the cold concrete shell. The 1st Battalion OC, Patrick Spillane, a twenty-six year old former Christian Brothers' pupil, took centrestage and addressed his subordinates with a calm, articulate voice, which demanded everyone's attention.

'Listen carefully. Further to agreement reached by those committed to the armed struggle, you are now members of the newly formed Provisional Irish Republican Army. Full-scale military operations will soon commence against the RUC and Brits and those collaborating with the enemy. Also, all industrial, commercial and government buildings across the North are to be regarded as legitimate targets. We are to wage war on both, while strengthening our defences against further loyalist attack. It is not a campaign of sectarian murder we pursue, but the right to wage armed struggle to bring Stormont down and to free our country of British interference. You are expected to obey orders from staff officers without question. You are volunteers. Do not expect financial reward or pats on the back for heroism. There's no stardom to be had within the republican movement, only plenty of sacrifice to give. If you are captured red-handed or arrested as a suspect, say nothing. And if it comes to it, take your punishment on the chin. You're not to recognise the British courts. And remember, if imprisoned, you will be a political prisoner of war. Resist all efforts to criminalise you. Finally, beware, all informers will be executed!' The battalion OC nodded to the company OC at his side, then left the platform and the hall by way of a side door, shadowed by two other young men who had been waiting in the wings.

O'Connor, the small, wiry company OC, a notorious hard man who was feared by all, called the parade to dismiss and ordered his volunteers to slip home in small groups at intervals.

Sean was keen to be among the first out. He felt tired, sore and hungry, but was called back by O'Connor. As his OC came marching towards him, Sean saw that the twenty year old lived on his nerves as his hands trembled uncontrollably on lighting a cigarette. Exhaling cigarette smoke through his nose, O'Connor spoke with much secrecy.

'Sean, yer man D'Arcy wants you to meet with him at the Coat of Arms at ten, tonight.' O'Connor toked long and hard on the plain cigarette before continuing, the smoke escaping with his words. 'Another thing: it was fucking mayhem here when you lot were away. The Brits tore the place apart searching for gear, and a few of the lads were caught carrying ... poor bastards.' O'Connor took another drag. 'The Brits paid a visit to your ma and granny's place. But everyone's okay. The cunts just ripped up a few floorboards.' Sean felt his anger boil; his first thoughts were for his mother and was anxious to see her. But O'Connor had more to say. 'Now that you're trained up, Sean, I want you to spend the next couple of weeks getting those others into shape, okay?' His mind preoccupied with concerned thoughts for his mother, Sean simply nodded. 'Don't worry,' O'Connor grinned. 'When the action starts, you'll be in there!' Sean thought, No doubt about it! 'One more thing,' said O'Connor, 'I've heard good reports about you from brigade, so I want you as my adjutant. The lads here have a lot of respect for you. As for the girls, watch out for yerself, they're seven randy bitches!' O'Connor laughed at his own attempt at a little humour but failed to impress Sean, who thought it inappropriate that he, the OC, should be talking of his comrades in such a derogatory manner. However, given what he knew about O'Connor, he thought it best to let the matter drop, this time. Pleased though with his new rank, Sean checked his wristwatch to signal to O'Connor that he wanted to be on his way. O'Connor got the message, but had one more issue to raise with his new staff officer.

'What happened to Scullion, Sean? He looks as if he's been in a scrap with a bear.' Sean gave O'Connor the facts. 'He was mouthing, so I slapped him around a little. It's all over and done with.' O'Connor deliberated for a moment. 'Good. He'd better keep his fucking gob shut from now on ... what with you being the adjutant and all, eh Sean?' Hardening to the cynical Belfast humour with each day, Sean just smiled and nodded in jest.

Slipping away into the night, turning unbearably cold, Sean ached all over and made for home, eager to see that his mother was okay. Entering the house by the front door and quickly moving through to the sitting-room, Sean discovered his mother standing on a stool hanging a picture of the Sacred Heart above the hearth. Hearing someone enter, Sarah turned to face Sean and smiled broadly through her anguish, which he sensed.

'Are you okay, Mum?'

Sarah stepped down heavily off the stool. Fighting back tears, she held out her arms to him just as she had when he had been a child. Slipping the rucksack off his back, Sean went and embraced his mother gently in his arms and heard her sob into his chest.

'I heard about the raid, Mum. Did they hurt you or Nan?'

Sarah drew back to look up at her soldier son and shook her head from side to side, then sniffed, 'No, we're both fine. They just threw a few things around. It just brought old memories back to me, that's all.'

Although he had not said specifically to where in Donegal he had been destined when leaving the week previous, Sarah had a fair idea what Sean had been doing the past seven days, and not wanting to question him over his involvement in the movement, was just glad to see him home safe.

'Get changed, son, and I'll go make us both something to eat.'

'That'll be great,' said Sean, glad to be home.

Over supper, Sarah listened with a keen interest as Sean told of his last minute visit to his father's home place. Sarah was pleased to learn all there were well. Anne-Marie had had her second child, another little boy, safely. There had been concern that the shock over Anthony's murder would have caused his sister complications. Sarah agreed that Sean's idea of a visit there in the summer would do them both good and suggested August as the best month to go, in between her father and Anthony's first anniversary.

Pleased to see his mother's spirit uplifted a little over the proposed break, Sean, checking his watch again, informed his mother that he had 'somewhere to go' and that he would be back as soon as possible.

'Mind yourself, son,' urged Sarah as Sean took his leave. On hearing the front door close out behind him, Sarah sat in the fireside chair and painfully wept. Though she had worn a brave face for Sean, talk of Donegal, of Anthony and his family, brought back fond memories of those honeymoon days when she and Anthony had been head over heels in love. Sarah searched her heart and mind for an answer in asking herself if she could truly set foot in Donegal ever again, knowing that but for her, they could all have been living happily there that very day. Grieving so sorely and agonising over her sense of guilt, Sarah was determined to suffer in silence. She could not bear to expose her real distress to Sean as she did not want to add additional pain to that which she knew he already bore over his father's violent death.

D'Arcy awaited Sean outside the Coat of Arms. And once meeting up with him, led him up the Falls Road away from the pub.

'It's too noisy in there,' said D'Arcy, tossing his head back. 'We can talk as we dander.'

His cracked ribs creasing him, Sean just nodded. With all the walking he had done over the past week, the soles of his feet burned too, but he was prepared to push himself a bit more, sensing D'Arcy had something of major importance to share with him. The Falls Road buzzed with Christmas spirit as they walked, though vigilantes remained in force on street corners despite British Army foot patrols lurking in the poorly lit side streets. Most of the streetlights had been bricked by rioters as a deterrent against loyalist snipers firing into the area from the Shankill. Now, the coloured fairy lights decorating those Christmas trees placed in the front windows of houses all along the Falls, added a surreal backdrop for those heavily-armed soldiers as they walked the beat along hostile streets. The same darkened side streets came as welcomed cover to local IRA units, as it allowed the volunteers to shift their newly received gear more safely from dump to dump.

D'Arcy put an anxious Sean in the picture by sharing the latest piece of information passed to him earlier in the day by Bonar, the brigade Chief of Staff.

'Don't breathe a word of what I'm about to say, to anyone. Okay?'
'Okay.'
'We know who murdered your father!'

As if suddenly struck by some crippling disability from the waist down, Sean stalled and grabbed hold of D'Arcy's arm.

'I must get the bastard, D'Arcy. Whoever he is.'

D'Arcy held up an open hand. 'Take it easy, Sean. I've already had a word with Barratt and told him what you needed to do. He was a bit concerned because of your age and for your mother if you got nabbed, or killed!'

'I'm an IRA volunteer for fuck sake, not a boy scout!' Sean snapped.

'I know! I know!' said D'Arcy. 'Barratt has just got your welfare at heart. But I told him how you felt ... assured him you could handle it. He said it would be okay, if we did the business together. And we will.'

Ecstatic now, Sean felt his discomfort and pain disappear in a flash.

'That's great news, D'Arcy. When do we make our move?'

Beckoning Sean to walk on, D'Arcy went into detail as to who the target was, his whereabouts and routine, and the problems they faced in getting to him. Both volunteers walked on for miles, bouncing ideas off each other as to how they could get in close for the kill. Eventually it was Sean who came up with an idea that D'Arcy considered brilliant. All they had to agree was when to make their move.

In view of the impending ard fheis in Dublin, Barratt had instructed D'Arcy to do nothing until after its outcome, with the intention of exploiting Vickers' assassination to win popular support for the Provisionals throughout nationalist Belfast. Sharing this with Sean, D'Arcy suggested the 14th January, three days after the ard fheis, if everything required was in place. A Wednesday it would be, just before half-day closing. Sean readily agreed. D'Arcy was to take care of arrangements. All Sean had to do was meet him at the Coat of Arms at ten in the morning on the day.

Reaching the top of the White Rock Road, some three miles from where they'd set out, both men, their conspiracy agreed, turned and headed for home again, with Sean, near exhausted, but content knowing that he would soon be serving justice onto the man who had cruelly stolen his father from him. The thought of taking another's life did not trouble him in the slightest. For Sean, the 14th could not come quick enough.

Sean parted company with D'Arcy a few streets away from his own and hurried home to get to his bed. Turning into Maxwell Street just after midnight, Sean found himself suddenly looking down the muzzle of a Self Loading Rifle, brandished by a nervous-eyed British soldier, his face blackened.

'Up against the fackin' wall, Paddy, and spread 'em!' That said, Sean felt a grappling hand on his shoulder pull him forcibly up the street, to be thrown against the gable end. He instinctively threw up his outstretched hands toward the wall to prevent his face from being smashed against it. His feet were kicked wide apart and a stranger's hand frenziedly ran up and down the length of his body, along his arms, legs, and crotch as he stood spread-eagled with his feet four or five feet away from the wall. In this forced position his fingertips bore his whole body weight, some fifteen stones of solid muscle. Soon, his arms felt as though they were about to snap and his chest felt as though it were about to explode. He gritted his teeth and bore the pain.

'Turn around you Irish bastard and give us your name and address!'

It was the same cockney soldier who barked at him. Doing as he was told, Sean grimaced under his discomfort and turned to see four soldiers close in around him. The whites of their eyes shifted erratically in the dark as they weighed him up and continually checked the street up and down. The smaller one of the four was doing all the mouthing.

'I said give us ya fackin' name and address, *Paddy*!' Sean was tempted to give this soldier one with the head just as he had done Scullion, but knew he would be slaughtered.

'Sean Brennan, 38 Maxwell Street.'

The soldiers froze on hearing the south London accent.

'Come again, chum,' insisted the mouthy one.

'Sean Brennan, 38 Maxwell Street.'

'Gor blimey! He's a fackin' limey!' The patrol leader confirmed, wrongly.

'What's your fackin' game mate?' A second soldier was not so sure.

Sean was a little amused by their confusion. 'I'm not English. I was born here. I left when I was very young and returned recently.'

Big mouth was cynical. 'You mean to tell me, you left the Smoke to come back here. You need your fackin' head examined, mate!' Another sniped from out of the dark: 'Well, at least it confirms he's a Paddy!' Sean remained silent. 'Yeah, too fackin' true! Go on then. Faghh off home,' big mouth cruelly sneered. 'Go and crawl into your stinking flea pit, you fackin' Irish cant!'

Sean eased himself through the four soldiers, who oozed contempt for him, and crossed over the road to the front door of his house. Only when trying to put his key in the lock did he realise how upset he was. His hand trembled uncontrollably. Turning to look back down the street, Sean saw the last British soldier disappear out of sight onto the Falls Road. '*Bastards*!' he seethed, his hatred for the soldiers boiling over.

Entering the still house cast in darkness, in which no thought or symbol of Christmas existed, Sean quietly climbed the stairs. His ribs hurting again, he struggled to slip off his shoes in the back bedroom but on doing so, he gently lay his weary body down on top of the bed and fell asleep within seconds.

Hearing Sean come in safely, only now could Sarah close her burning eyes in trying to escape the torturous thoughts over Anthony, which plagued her mind.

Chapter Seventy-Three

Christmas had brought little or no joy to the McParland and Brennan families. Empty spaces around the dinner table on Christmas Day made the loss of loved ones all the more difficult to accept.

Rarely venturing outdoors, Sean had been a good companion to his mother, who found a little comfort through knowing that the tragedy had at least strengthened their own love for, and loyalty to, each other.

By the first day of the New Year, Sean's eagerness to avenge the hurt done unto his mother, he, and many others, could not be contained much longer. He was pacified only by the detail of the plan in his head, which, if so executed, would see Sammy Vickers meet a bloody and violent end.

On the morning of the 14th Sean, much rested and fit, set out from Maxwell Street under an ominous sky in time to meet with D'Arcy. On rounding the corner at the bottom of Maxwell Street, Sean was both surprised and concerned to see an ashen-faced Roisin dodge the Falls Road traffic with little consideration for her own safety and approach him as if on a mission. He had not seen her for some months and as she came closer to him, could not believe his eyes. Gone were her stunning good looks, her long curling hair and the petite figure. Tired and drawn, her hair limp and greasy, Roisin came to stand in front of Sean, shocked by what he saw.

'We need to talk, Sean,' Roisin's voice shook with emotion. 'I've so much to tell you. Can we go somewhere quiet?'

Conscious that he was due to meet with D'Arcy in five minutes, Sean felt so awkward at having to tell Roisin that he had to be somewhere else, fast, but promised to call on her later that day. He saw the disappointment in her face and heard her retort, 'If you can spare the time!' Roisin turned heel and stomped off. Sean stood and looked on with increased concern as Roisin, seemingly holding a death wish, darted recklessly between the oncoming traffic. A red double-decker bus, city centre bound, was forced to screech to a halt. Rubber burned and pistons hissed in protest. Quick to slide open his driver's side window, the irate bus driver turned a few heads, all but that of the fleeing culprit. 'You stupid wee bitch! If I get a houl of ye!'

Sean's concern for Roisin turned to anger in that moment. 'Girls! A pain in the arse!' Seeing one particular girl disappear into Leger Street, Sean looked straight ahead and spied D'Arcy standing impatiently by the Coat of Arms, three streets away. Sean walked on with haste.

On reaching the public house, D'Arcy gestured to Sean to join him in the car parked in the nearby side street in which a third man, unknown to Sean, sat behind the driving wheel. With Sean sliding into the back seat, D'Arcy, the front seat passenger, half turned in his seat to speak.

'Everything is ready, Sean. We go to Ardoyne now. It will be easier to get onto the Shankill from there.' Nodding toward the driver, D'Arcy added, 'This is our driver for the day. He's sound.' Turning to the driver, D'Arcy gave the command. 'We go.'

Cutting through the city centre to avoid the joint army and RUC checkpoints on the so-called peace-line separating the Falls from the Shankill, they arrived in old Ardoyne after ten minutes. D'Arcy and Sean scurried into an untidy mid-terrace situated down one of the ghetto's many back streets. Meantime the car stolen overnight on the outskirts of the city and disguised with false plates was to be parked at a safer location, as troop presence in the area was heavy.

Once inside the cramped, untidy safe house, both men quickly changed out of their own clothing and each donned a postman's uniform, stolen from a nearby depot the previous day. The outfits were not stolen to measure and Sean's cap was a little too big for his head.

'All the better for you,' D'Arcy quipped, his own uniform a little tight for him. 'It'll cover up those good looks of yours.' Sean managed a smile, though his thoughts were caught between concern for Roisin and matters in hand.

Knowing of Sean's past relationship with Roisin and seeing the shenanigans earlier that morning, D'Arcy sought to sharpen Sean's focus on what lay ahead.

'Sean, clear your head of all thoughts other than for what we're about to do.'

D'Arcy reached behind the back of a tattered settee and produced the old Thompson. Taking a moment to scrutinise the gun, he then handed it to Sean as if presenting him with a trophy.

'D'yeh know, Sean,' D'Arcy said with an air of suspense, 'this is the very gun we used to shoot a B Special not so long ago. Your grandfather's old foe, a right evil bastard he was. Use it proudly.'

Sean gladly received the gun into his hands. He was thinking of only one person now, the UVF man, Samuel Vickers, his father's killer.

They spent the following half-hour in the sympathiser's house by drinking tea and eating toast and had taken it in turn to read the morning newspaper which was full of speculation as to what the Provisional IRA's next move would be in the wake of the split, as publicly witnessed at the recent ard fheis in Dublin.

With only a few minutes remaining before they were picked-up again, both IRA men made ready for the road. Sean slid the Thompson into the deep postbag hanging from his left shoulder, then, looking into the cracked mirror above the hearth, straightened his postman's cap. D'Arcy checked the loaded chamber of the .38 Smith and Wesson he carried, before tucking it into the waistband of his post office trousers.

Three raps on the front room windowpane was the signal that their pick-up had returned. D'Arcy turned to Sean. 'Just as we planned it, d'yeh hear?' Sean nodded. 'And don't forget. Whatever happens, don't get opening yer gob. That English accent of yours could get us hung.'

'I know, I know. My lips are sealed,' Sean assured.

'Right, let's move it!' D'Arcy ordered, and they made for the car.

As the car progressed out of the side street, where only the resident mongrels made an appearance so early, the driver, a local man, casually informed his passengers that Vickers was indeed in his shop on the Shankill. D'Arcy had arranged for a local Cumman na mBan volunteer to bus it up the Shankill to Ardoyne earlier that morning. With a bus stop literally on the butcher's front doorstep, the inconspicuous volunteer, purposefully sitting on the lower deck of the bus, had clocked the target busy behind his counter.

The stolen car sneaked out of Ardoyne under the noses of a mobile British Army patrol cruising by and within minutes was headed for the Protestant heartland via that road where Black had been cut down five years earlier by the very same gun nestling in Sean's lap.

To Sean's observant eye, the Shankill, bar its various tacky wall murals celebrating the Battle of the Boyne, appeared just like the Falls Road on any other week day; its ordinary folk going about a normal routine. In that instant, Sean found it incredibly hard to accept that both peoples were so bitterly divided. Suddenly the car was pulling up in a side street. D'Arcy nudged Sean in the ribs, 'Are you set?'

Surprised to be at the target zone so soon, Sean nodded. He proceeded to follow D'Arcy out of the car and was moved to slide the cap he wore back a little from his forehead. Joining D'Arcy on the pavement, they walked side-by-side without a second glance from any of the early morning shoppers. The two IRA men soon made an appearance on the Shankill Road itself, where, to their right, and three doors down from the corner fruit shop, the butcher's shop stood. It was five minutes to closing time. With his mind strictly set on fulfilling his part of the mission, Sean boldly stepped into the butcher shop a few paces ahead of D'Arcy, who was to cover his rear. On easily placing the steely-hard face behind the meat counter to a name, Sean was reaching into the postbag. Vickers was busily engaged in light conversation with the woman customer, whose four year old daughter stood impatient by her side. Sean had his mind set on a kill as he raised the gun to his shoulder. Nothing, no one, would stop him now. With Vickers turning to serve his next customer, and realising he wasn't, the UVF man made a sudden and desperate dash into the adjoining storage room. Sean was about to squeeze the trigger when he found his aim falling on the terrified faces of the woman and child, and hesitated. With both civilians directly in his line of fire, Vickers was out of sight.

From behind Sean, D'Arcy screamed at the petrified woman and child, 'Get t'fuck out of the way!'

Turning a deathly grey, the woman stepped back into a corner, dragging her wide-eyed daughter with her. Sean seized the moment and hotly pursued Vickers into the storage room. Entering the room cautiously Sean caught a glimpse of Vickers beyond the swaying hanging joints of meat and dead fowl. Vickers tried so hard to slide the heavy bolts on the back door. Sean stood and from a distance of thirty feet he could clearly see a look of sheer terror fixed upon the UVF man's face on realising his number was up. Putting the gun's stock to his right shoulder, its barrel in line with Vickers thick chest, Sean squeezed and held back the trigger. He felt his ears explode and his body vibrate violently, and saw dead meat, gristle and bone disintegrate in front of him as he emptied the entire magazine of its fifty rounds. After a few seconds of screaming hell, the gun fell silent. Looking on for just a moment, Sean saw Vickers' bullet riddled body lying slumped against the back door, his bloody face contorted in a peculiar sort of way. The white tiled walls of the storage room streamed with both animal and human blood, smashed bone and brain tissue. Only the hind legs of dead animals remained hanging from the meat hooks above Sean's head. Unmoved by the gory sight and happy to see Vickers clearly dead, Sean turned and headed briskly for the shop's front doorway from where D'Arcy, revolver in hand, checked the road up and down. Throwing the woman and child a sideways glance, Sean saw the child urinate where she stood clinging to her sobbing mother for sheer life. The disturbing sight had Sean rooted to the ground. He felt a lump rise in his throat, the bliss experienced a moment ago sink in dark depths of guilt.

'C'mon. Move it!' D'Arcy sounded almost hysterical. With his mind focused again, Sean, sliding the gun into the postbag, followed D'Arcy out of the shop, and keeping his head down as instructed, followed D'Arcy at a run to the waiting car. Once onboard, the car raced from the scene at top speed.

Arriving back in Ardoyne within a few short minutes and with the getaway car pulling up sharply in one of the many side streets, Sean, as told, left the Thompson alongside D'Arcy's revolver on the rear seat, and quickly followed D'Arcy through the maze of back alleys. The driver was to get rid of the gear and the car. Entering a house by its rear door soon after, Sean found himself back in that room from where he had set out to kill a man less than half an hour earlier.

'Get out of them clothes fast,' D'Arcy ordered, pulling off his. It was the first words spoken since the shooting; the three IRA men had all concentrated on the road ahead, expecting an army patrol to jump out in front of them at any moment. But so far so good, thought Sean.

Stripping to their underclothes, both volunteers took it in turns at the scullery sink to have a scrub up. Once back in their own clothes, D'Arcy threw the two uniforms onto that blanket which had covered the Thompson, and making a bundle, left the lot up one corner. He assured Sean over it. 'Yer man will burn this lot later. C'mon, let's be off.'

Keeping to the overall plan, D'Arcy and Sean quickly made their way out of Ardoyne on foot. Cutting through a residential area they soon reached the city centre from where the lower Falls could be reached within a few minutes.

Safely back on their home ground, it was clear to both IRA men that news of the shooting of Vickers had broken along the Falls. There was an air of excited chat among folk on street corners the length of the main road.

'Morale will be sky high, Sean, thanks to you,' D'Arcy predicted confidently. With a wink of an eye, he added, 'Let's grab a jar.'

Both men continued casually on their way as an army mobile patrol, on the look out for suspicious characters, cruised by.

D'Arcy anonymously telephoned the local BBC television studio from the privacy of the back room in the Coat of Arms to claim responsibility on behalf of the Provisional IRA for the 'execution of leading loyalist paramilitary, Sammy Vickers,' whom D'Arcy posthumously denounced as 'responsible for the sectarian murder of innocent Catholics in the Gresham Bar attack.'

On the stroke of six, the packed barroom in the Coat of Arms fell silent as the main evening news theme tune blasted out from the black and white television placed on a high shelf behind the bar. Sitting quietly up one corner, Sean and D'Arcy watched and listened intently as their deed of the day made headline news. With the serious-faced newscaster confirming the dead man's identity, the whole bar erupted in cheers and clapping. The odd shout of 'Up the Provos!' rang out above it all. Turning to face each other, D'Arcy and Sean raised their beer glasses and without needing to say a word, toasted each other's work that day.

On each finishing their pint, D'Arcy and Sean made a move. D'Arcy headed home to grab a bite to eat, with the intention of calling on Barratt a little later to give a run down of events. Sean, agreeing to meet up with D'Arcy that following morning, set out to keep a promise.

On making his way to Roisin's, Sean was glad to see plenty of local men out on the street. Serious trouble was now expected. Knowing the loyalists would be baying for Fenian blood, Sean felt content in the knowledge that if the loyalists tried to rush the area, they would receive a rude awakening.

Reaching Roisin's front door, Sean was left feeling a little nervous not knowing what to expect. It was a completely different looking Roisin who opened the door to him, one who had suddenly recaptured those stunning good looks which had first stolen his heart. In Sean's admiring eyes, so lovely, so desirable was she now.

'Come in, Sean,' said Roisin, and smiled a little. Sean brushed past her somewhat sheepishly and proceeded to the front room, once their secret love nest. Coming to face Sean there, Roisin spoke softly, though hesitantly, in sharing a long held and not so long held secret with him.

'I miscarried your child twenty-one days ago. Christmas Eve it was.' Sean suddenly felt ill. 'Sean, I was very low in myself following our break up. I'm so sorry.'

Sean had been stunned into silence and was empty of all emotion.

Not knowing exactly what Sean was feeling, for his face told her nothing, Sarah added, 'My father's gone. He left a note last week saying he was away to England, to look for work.' Roisin let a little nervous laugh slip, then added deadpan, 'That's a laugh, eh? A hard day's work would kill him.'

Sean saw tears well in Roisin's eyes and heard her mumble, 'He left when I told him I'd miscarried your child. He was so drunk he had never noticed my distress. Hearing his eighteen year old, unmarried daughter, had been pregnant, was the last straw for him. He'll be so ashamed to ever come back and face me.' Roisin burst into tears.

Taking stock, realising the enormity of it all, Sean took Roisin in his arms. Feeling her body so warm against his, smelling the freshness of her hair, he said soothingly, 'It's okay Roisin. I'll stand by you.' Holding Roisin closer still, Sean added with a passion, 'I love you.'

Roisin lifted her head off Sean's chest and looked him in the eye. 'I love you too, Sean,' she sniffed. 'I want us to be together, no matter what.'

Sean was so relieved. For if Roisin truly wanted him, she would have to accept the way of life he had chosen, and which he was determined to pursue at all cost.

Chapter Seventy-Four

Sean's silent ways around the house in the days immediately following Vickers' death was evidence enough for Sarah to conclude that her son had had a hand in the killing of the UVF man. Sarah suspected that Sean was struggling to come to terms with the fact that he had aided and abetted the taking of someone's life, bringing home cruelly to him even more so perhaps, the reality that his own father had been violently killed. For Sarah though, slowly coming to terms with this reality, there was no remorse felt for the man who had ruined her life totally. To her thinking, justice had been rightly served on Samuel Vickers, and she held no anxiety over her son's involvement in his death. As a former republican activist, she knew only too well the harsh reality of a volunteer's life, the burden on one's conscience when life and limb was left exposed to the consequences of one's actions when executing orders. The fact that it had been a war she and her comrades had fought then, as did the volunteers presently, would, she was confident, in time prove to be her son's salvation, just as it had been for her all those years ago, even when it had been innocents who had unfortunately suffered. And so, knowing the life her son pursued, the pains to come with it for them both, Sarah was nonetheless content with his decision, having made the same one herself some twenty years earlier. She too had joined up, unknown to her mother and father at the time. And like then, how could she now say or do anything, even if she wanted to, to stop Sean, just as her folk could not have stopped her fighting for the cause.

Though conscious of the very real danger posed to Sean each and every day, Sarah, so very proud of her son, sought to quell his restless mind at the breakfast table that following Saturday morning.

'Sean, they're burying Vickers today, so be careful, won't you?'

'I will Mum,' Sean replied, preparing to leave the house.

'All I can say is, I hope he rots in Hell!' Sarah affirmed. 'As for the brave one who went after him, may God bless him and keep him safe.'

Sean felt heartened on hearing this. He knew immediately what his mother was attempting to achieve, but his real pain over Roisin's revelation days earlier, had not been eased in any way. He could not bring himself to share with anyone his sense of loss over the miscarriage coming so soon after the death of his father. It was Roisin's wish also, that no one else know. Out of consideration for her feelings, her standing in the community, Sean was prepared to grieve in silence, alongside Roisin.

Slipping on his three-quarter length combat jacket, Sean forced a smile out of consideration for his mother, realising her concern for him, even though he felt no remorse over the killing of Vickers. 'Don't worry. I'm okay. I'll look after myself.' Sean leaned forward to kiss his mother gently on one cheek, then added tellingly, 'We're all that little bit safer with Vickers gone from our streets.' Sarah nodded and smiled a little in turn. She was pleased by her soldier son's awakening.

Sean was on his way then, keen to keep to plans set for the day. He was due to meet with O'Connor for there was much to do. Real concern existed within the brigade that loyalists, once they had buried their dead, would attempt reprisal attacks on nationalists and republicans across the city. All IRA personnel were to be mobilised and made ready for action, and nowhere was such an attack anticipated more than on the Falls. The UVF, acknowledging Vickers as their commander in Belfast had, only the night before, vowed to exact heavy retaliation on the Falls, condemning the area as a 'haven for IRA murdering scum'.

Once ordering a mug of tea for himself and Sean, O'Connor, sitting hunched over the small window table in Arthur's Café, wasted no time in giving Sean a run down on developments since they had last met. As restless as ever, O'Connor talked quietly out of the corner of his mouth as a precaution against being overheard by the other customers. His stale breath stank of nicotine as he spoke.

'It's all fucking go this morning, Sean. We were landed with another load of gear late last night. We need to get it shifted fast. We'll go and get Fra and a couple of the girls to give us a hand. Two or three runs should do it.'

Sitting opposite, Sean inquired with a whisper, 'Where's the gear now?' Lighting up another cigarette, O'Connor replied, 'We were forced to dump it in a derelict house just around the corner. There were too many Brits on the ground to get it to a safe house a few streets back. But this morning will be okay. The Brits will all be on the peace-line for Vickers' funeral.' Sean was thankful to hear this, as volunteers were being caught almost daily when on operation. O'Connor proceeded to inform Sean of another overnight development. 'Spillane came to see me last night. Guess what?' Sean didn't have a clue. 'The Official IRA went to Barratt to tell him that their people want to cooperate with us where possible, on operations ... the defence of the area. Well, it seems Barratt agreed, and now we have to double check with brigade before we do a move. *Can you imagine it*? If it had been me, I'da told the stickies to fuck off! As they say in the movies, This town ain't big enough for the both of us. If I had my way, I'd exterminate the whole fucking lot of them ... the yellow bastards!'

The conversation dried up with Greasy Arthur bringing two mugs of steaming hot tea to the table.

'Good man Arthur,' said O'Connor, slipping Arthur a handful of coppers. With the café owner's back turned, O'Connor beckoned Sean closer with a nod. 'Did yeh see the grease down the front of the oul fucker's apron. He'll scrape it off in a minute to do the morning fry-ups!'

Sean had to laugh at O'Connor's sharp observation, and was glad he had already breakfasted.

In between mouthfuls of tea, the company OC and his adjutant debated the plan of action for the day. Once rallying numbers and moving the gear to the appropriate safe house, they would mobilise the remainder of the company and place at the ready at strategic locations in and around Clonard enough weapons and ammunition for use in the event of any surprise loyalist attack.

Monitoring the progress of an army foot patrol along the Falls from the direction of Leger Street, it was O'Connor who first spied Barratt come walking inconspicuously along the road from the opposite direction. On seeing Barratt casually stroll past the Brits, who didn't look at him twice, O'Connor mused, 'If only they knew who yer man was, one of them may just be tempted to put a bullet in his back.'

Sean studied the nervous antics of the four boy soldiers as they past by the café window, each one of them not much older than he. O'Connor remarked mockingly and loud enough for all indoors to hear,

'Look at the fucking state of them. They're shitting their pants. They know the honeymoon is over.'

Quickly gathering together Paddy Tober and Fra MacErlean, plus two Cumann na mBan volunteers, O'Connor and Sean, confident the immediate area behind the Coat of Arms was clear of Brit patrols, led the others to the derelict house midway up a side street by way of a back alley. On filing into the ruined kitchen of the century old mid-terrace and standing back as O'Connor, down on his knees, yanked free a number of rotting floorboards to reveal the hidden arsenal wrapped in polythene, Sean was amazed at the array of brand new high velocity rifles, automatic pistols and machineguns now at their disposal. O'Connor retrieved an ex-US Army, Vietnam combat-tested Armalite Rifle from out of the hole and ripped off its protective covering. He handed the 'widow-maker' to Sean and said with a grin, 'Here, stick this up yer coat, Sean. It's got your name on it.'

Barratt was made welcome by Sarah once he assured her Sean was okay, for the expression on her face when opening the front door to him had left him clear in mind what she was thinking. Sitting comfortably in the privacy of Sarah's living-room, Barratt sought to learn the wishes of a former comrade, whose son's destiny they could both greatly determine.
    'Sarah, you know why I'm here. What you say goes.'
    Glad to know the man cared for her, Sarah managed a smile. 'I know of Sean's involvement, Frank; what he has done, not that he told me of course, just intuition on my part. I know well the risk presented to him and what I may also be letting myself in for. But all I want is whatever Sean wants. And I'm sure he wants more than just revenge.'
    Barratt did not doubt this any longer.
    'I will stand by him, Frank, all the way. I can hardly do anything else or expect another mother's son to fight the war. All I ask, Frank, is that whatever he is to do, that it's justified.'
    Barratt had heard every word clearly and was inspired by the woman's commitment still to their common cause. He took his leave once assuring Sarah that her wish would be respected to the letter.
    With a Rosary in her hands, Sarah was left alone to pray where she sat, for her one and only son's safekeeping.

The first run had gone smoothly, with the two girl volunteers each carrying a rifle under their long winter coats, while O'Connor and Sean, their newly prized weapons somewhat more bulky under their own shorter coats, each paired off with one of the girls to give the impression of courting couples out for an early morning stroll. With Fra MacErlane scouting thirty yards ahead and Toby taking up the rear, they had briskly cut across a half dozen busy back streets and on toward the safe house where the weapons were left wrapped tightly in old blankets beneath the floorboards of a young married couple's front sitting-room. To Sean's thinking, the couple didn't seem to worry in the slightest over the lethal load they harboured and for which, if caught in possession of, they would each receive twenty years in jail.

As sharp-eyed as ever, it was O'Connor who came up with the idea of transporting the remainder of the cache from the derelict house through the use of the young couple's pram, standing empty in the hallway. On requesting the loan of the pram from the attractive young mother, Sean was left speechless when seeing O'Connor being handed the rousing infant and hearing the mother casually say, 'Sure, no problem. Here, take the baby for the walk while you're at it.' With Sean and the others unable to stop themselves laughing aloud at the sight of a petrified O'Connor left holding the baby, his arms outstretched as if handed a bomb about to go off, a gravely embarrassed and agitated O'Connor wasted no time in taking control of the situation in hand. He was soon delegating responsibilities to others, not least were the child was concerned.

With O'Connor and Sean leaving the others to complete the final run with the aid of the pram, and the baby, both men set out for the Coat of Arms, where O'Connor was due to meet with his company QM to agree the locations in Clonard for weapons to be left ready for use, now that the funeral of the UVF man was underway. Lighting up his last cigarette to calm his nerves as they walked, O'Connor, much stressed over his ordeal just, mustered enough enthusiasm to share a little black humour.

'At least the others have a good decoy if stopped by the Brits, eh?'

Sean smiled but could not help but wonder what would become of the child, if the others were indeed caught red-handed.

Turning onto the Falls Road, heaving with early morning shoppers buying in bulk in anticipation of a long, violent weekend, Sean caught sight of Barratt on the opposite side walking back along the Falls. Spying him in turn, Barratt smiled broadly and gave a discreet salute. Sean recognised it for what it was - an acknowledgement of a good job done. His morale high, Sean simply nodded, but thoughts over Roisin's revelation still lay heavy on his mind and he wondered if, and when, he would get chance that day to at least see her again.

It had taken O'Connor, Sean attentive at his side, all of half an hour to confer with his QM in a corner of the Coat of Arms and for the UVF to bury their man with full military honours in a graveyard on the outskirts of Belfast. Now, with the IRA actively implementing a defensive strategy across the city, the UVF's units on the Shankill prepared to initiate the plan of attack on the Falls in revenge for Vickers.

With Sean agreeing to meet up again with O'Connor in a few hours time, once they had both been home to get fed, he instead headed straight to Roisin's house. Sean's yearning to spend time alone with Roisin had left him feeling impatient and frustrated during that last half hour with O'Connor and company, but had bided his time under the circumstances. With Roisin opening the front door to him and smiling warmly, her long flowing hair falling gently onto her shoulders just as it should, and finding her dressed only in a flimsy dressing gown, Sean boldly stepped into the hallway of the house and closed the door out gently behind him with the heel of his shoe. He lifted Roisin into his arms and carried her effortlessly up the stairs and into the front bedroom, where he lay her down gently on top of the double bed. Roisin did not speak, but simply untied the belt knot and pulled her dressing gown open to reveal her full nakedness. Roisin let Sean know what she wanted without speaking a word. Feasting his eyes on what was his, and his alone, Sean pulled off his clothes and shoes. Once naked, he lay himself down on top of Roisin's heaving body and found her so hot and wet. They made love in ways new to them, using the freedom of the big bed imaginatively. As a bitter cold January wind gripped the streets without, the sweat poured from the young lovers as they pushed their energetic bodies to new limits once, twice and a third time.

Just after two in the afternoon, a UVF inspired attack was launched on those houses still occupied in Kashmir Road, at the exposed end of Clonard. Seventy loyalists from the Shankill appeared from out of nowhere to charge across the peace-line armed with bricks, bottles and petrol bombs, which they blindly tossed over the heads of British soldiers, a straggled line of defence suddenly caught unawares. The endless coils of barbed wire dragged across roads served as no protection to those inhabitants on the far side of the dividing line who were suddenly caught in a hail of deadly missiles. Women out walking and the few children playing along the footpaths ran screaming for cover as the road became a battlefield once again. The ineffective numbers of soldiers deployed were first and foremost concerned for their own safety. They swiftly took shelter in the rear of armoured cars idly parked on waste ground - the scars of earlier such attacks.

Running out to defend their homes, the men of the Kashmir Road ran straight into the trap set by the UVF. A sniper, armed with a Sterling sub-machine gun and crudely positioned in the upstairs room of an abandoned corner shop in the Protestant Sugarfield Street, directly opposite, opened fire through a broken window and sprayed bullets at those Catholic men caught out in the open. Five men fell to the ground wounded, some seriously. The gunman reloaded and continued to fire short, sporadic bursts down the road to pin down civilians and soldiers alike, while those wounded writhed in agony and helpless on the ground, their life blood draining from them into the gutter.

Sean had awoken to a beautiful singing voice, that of his Granny McParland in the upstairs room of the house next door, who sang an old Irish air truly beautifully.

'Where Lagan streams sing lullabies, there blows a lily fair ...'

With Roisin's head nestled against his chest, the perfect bliss of the moment was shattered by a sudden burst of gunfire that seemed never ending. And when eventually it did, the screams of women and children and the barking of frightened dogs in distant streets left Sean's heart pounding in his chest. He sprang upright in the bed and checked his wristwatch in the half-light. Roisin had been startled by the sudden movement beside her and sat up in the bed. Not hearing the shooting, she inquired, bleary-eyed, 'What is it?' A second, shorter burst of gunfire supplied the answer. Sean leapt out of bed and was pulling on his clothes hurriedly. He should have met up with O'Connor twenty minutes earlier. Roisin felt her blood drain on realising what was unfolding. As Sean prepared to take his leave, she pleaded, 'Please be careful, Sean.' Hearing her heartfelt plea, Sean paused by the bedroom door then returned to the bedside. Looking far into Roisin's eyes, he sought to reassure her. 'I'll be back as soon as I can.' He bent forward to kiss her softly on the lips. 'I love you.'

He was gone then, leaving the house by the back door, conscious of the fact that his gran sang no more. A different sound filled his ears as he ran the back entry toward the Falls Road - the sound of raw violence raging in the streets beyond.

Barratt and D'Arcy, chatting with some local men on the corner of O'Neill Street and Clonard Street, about a quarter of a mile from the Kashmir Road when the first shots rang out, were quick to approach O'Connor, standing on the Falls Road impatiently checking his watch. Barratt demanded he supply them with firearms immediately. Within minutes, Barratt and D'Arcy were led to a backyard of an end terrace close by. A fully loaded Thompson MK1A1 machinegun complete with a thirty round box magazine and a fully loaded Browning automatic pistol were retrieved from a coal shed by O'Connor.

Barratt took charge of the Thompson, D'Arcy, the pistol, then headed back toward the source of the gunfire, leaving O'Connor cursing Sean Brennan for not having shown. Hurrying back towards the Falls to oversee his volunteers into action, O'Connor was already conjuring up in his head methods of violence to exact on his adjutant for not meeting with him at that prearranged spot, on time.

Guns openly carried through the streets to the relief of most, to the horror of a few, Barratt and D'Arcy were briefed by an elderly resident of Clonard on the location from where the loyalist gunman was sniping. Standing on the corner of Clonard Gardens and Kashmir Road, out of the line of fire, a gaunt, silver-haired sympathiser spoke in a panic to the two IRA gunmen.

'The bastard is firing from the upstairs window of the derelict shop on the faraway corner,' informed the ex-serviceman. 'Those soldiers must see him, but they're not lifting a finger to stop it. Our lads are lying dying out there.' Just then, another burst of gunfire raked the Kashmir. The continued shooting added urgency to Barratt and D'Arcy's next move. Barratt made his mind up quickly.

'Don't worry, Barney, we'll sort it. Just make sure everyone sits still for the next few minutes.' Barratt beckoned D'Arcy to follow him. Moving back along Clonard Gardens, then turning first left, both men dashed along that narrow back entry running parallel to the houses on one side of the Kashmir Road - including the McHughs. The back entry led them to the rear of the abandoned houses that miraculously still stood on the corner of Kashmir Road and Bombay Street. It was Barratt's intention to somehow get into the upstairs front room of that corner house which directly faced the derelict shop.

D'Arcy was surprised at Barratt's speed of foot and the ease with which he shoulder-charged open the back entry door to that house which would hopefully allow them to repel the attack on their area. Quickly following Barratt through the abandoned property, both men climbed the bare timber staircase that creaked in protest under their feet. Reaching the landing the house echoed thunderously to another prolonged burst of gunfire from across the road.

Moving carefully into the unkempt, musty smelling front bedroom, Barratt darted across the room to take up position on one side of the sash window - D'Arcy to the other. Barratt gripped tightly the gun in his hands and was ready to open fire once spying his target. He gingerly peered through the threadbare net curtain. The few seconds of eerie silence that followed seemed an eternity for both IRA men. Then, catching sight of a shadowy figure at the window opposite, Barratt moved in a flash. Stepping back from the window to raise the Thompson to his right shoulder, he fired a concentrated burst of gunfire through the window and across the road just as the UVF gunman had opened fire again. Barratt saw his line of fire blast away what remained of the window opposite, and a darkly clad figure suddenly disappear from sight.

'*Yes*! Got the bastard!' Barratt proclaimed excitedly.

'Good on yeh, Frank! Now let's get t'fuck out of here!' D'Arcy urged, and made for the stairs.

Both men were exiting from the rear of the house quicker than they had entered. They knew the Brits would be more eager to get to the gunmen operating from the Catholic side of the peace-line. Stepping out of the backyard into the back entry, D'Arcy paused to slip the Browning into his trouser waistband. Forced to a halt three feet behind, Barratt heard the single shot ring out and saw D'Arcy's head disintegrate simultaneously in a misty red haze in front of him, his body fall in a heap. Turning to his left instinctively, knowing the shot had come from an adjoining derelict house

Barratt heard a second shot and felt the searing red-hot lead tear through his chest and exit through his back. Gasping for breath, his mouth filling with blood, the Thompson slid from Barratt's hands as he stumbled backwards to fall onto the flat of his back, critically wounded.

The two infantrymen, one a first class marksman, the other a radio operator, lying on the flat of their bellies in the covert observation post concealed in the roof space of the abandoned house two doors below that from which Barratt had shot and killed the UVF man, shook hands in glee over their handiwork. Wallowing in self-glory the two soldiers failed to spy from their peepholes the two identical youths drag away the second gunman felled, and retrieve his gun.

Witnessing events just from the back bedroom of their house, the McHugh twins risked their lives to drag Barratt, barely breathing, by his arms through the other IRA man's spilled brains and into the adjoining back entry, out of sight of the hidden soldiers. But on identifying the wounded man as the same man who had ridiculed them in the street months earlier, the twins eagerness to make a name for themselves by going to the aid of an IRA man and to have saved a weapon from capture, took on an ugly twist. Each twin did not have to utter a word to know what the other was thinking. Their minds thought alike, identically on occasion. They checked to see if anyone looked on. No one did. They signalled their readiness to each other with a simple nod. Looking down on a semiconscious Barratt as though he were vermin, Leo McHugh hissed, 'Fuck you, yeh bastard!' and proceeded to stomp a hobnail boot repeatedly upon Barratt's face until it was unrecognisable and too sickening to look at. Vincent McHugh was to strike the final blow. Gripping the barrel of the Thompson with both hands, he brought its hardwood butt crashing down against Barratt's holed chest.

'That's it, for fuck sake. We'll be drenched in blood!' Leo McHugh warned. 'C'mon! Leave the cunt where he is. We'll tell everyone we tried to save him. And shove that gun under your coat.' Vincent McHugh did as he was told on this occasion. Both twins ran off down the back entry and on toward the Falls, where they would lie their hearts out to the whole world.

Hearing the burst of machinegun fire, the pause, then the two single shots as he walked back onto the Falls Road, now almost deserted, O'Connor had a gut feeling something tragic had just happened to Barratt and D'Arcy. However his mind was distracted on seeing Sean stand on the street corner up ahead, appearing lost and confused.

Sean knew he was in for a bollocking from O'Connor, especially in light of events ongoing around them. Bracing himself as O'Connor closed in, his face working with fury, both Sean and O'Connor's attention was drawn to a car which raced up the Falls to pull up to the kerb beside them. They both froze where they stood, expecting a blazing gun to be poked out of a window at any moment. But both men breathed easy on seeing a familiar, though tense face, at the rear passenger window.

'O'Connor, have you seen Barratt?' Spillane shouted. 'It's urgent!'

Reaching Sean's side, O'Connor stooped to the car window to answer. 'Barratt's on an operation; there's a sniper firing into the area. People have been shot.'

'Fuck it!' Spillane spat. The battalion OC's face grew longer. After a moment's deliberation, he said, 'Get youse into the car. There's something major on.'

O'Connor didn't argue and gestured to Sean to get into the front passenger seat. As Sean moved to do so, O'Connor, out of earshot of Spillane, said threateningly, 'I'll sort you out later, Brennan.'

The car, driven by a man Sean only knew by sight, burned rubber doing a 'U' turn. As the car raced down the Falls Road, Sean could hardly believe what Spillane excitedly revealed.

'We've only landed ourselves a Brit in civvies. The stupid wee fucker walked right up to two volunteers on a street corner in Divis and asked for directions to Clonard. They wasted no time getting him off the street. And sure enough, on searching him, found his I.D. He's a fucking Green Jacket! Whoever the fuck they are.'

'Where is he now?' O'Connor itched to get his hands on the Brit.

'Up fucking shite street!' the driver cracked, but no one laughed.

'Just fucking concentrate on your driving, you,' Spillane snarled, and turned to O'Connor again. 'We've got him in a safe house in Divis. God knows what the cunt was up to.'

'Was he carrying?' O'Connor probed. Spillane sighed, 'That's the odd thing about it, he wasn't.' Spillane's last words provided food for thought for all.

The car pulled up outside a mid-terrace in Divis Street. Spillane ordered the driver to remain at the wheel in case of needing to make a quick move. Spillane then led O'Connor and Sean into the safe house, up the stairs and into the small back bedroom. In the sword of daylight cutting through the gap in the curtains, Sean could make out the pathetic hooded figure of a young man sitting on a ladder-back chair in the middle of the otherwise spartan room, his hands lashed together behind him. The two volunteers stood guard behind the prisoner. Sean could not help but wonder what was going through the soldier's head, knowing, as he must, that it was unlikely he would get out of his sorry predicament alive.

'Well, has the wee shite said anything of interest while I've been away?' Spillane inquired aloud.

'Not a word,' replied one of the two volunteers looming over the prisoner, who sat with his covered head lowered to his chest.

'Is that fucking right?' Spillane snarled, producing a revolver from his trouser waistband. He cocked the weapon close to the soldier's right ear. Sean saw the soldier's legs begin to tremble.

'The cunt will shite himself if we're not careful,' O'Connor cruelly remarked, and all laughed, bar Sean, uneasy with the other's sick sense of humour.

Spillane uncocked the gun and tucked it back in his trousers. He clicked his fingers and demanded from the other volunteer: 'The I.D., give it to me.'

Receiving the soldier's I.D. in hand, Spillane passed the passport-sized handbook to O'Connor. He in turn examined the official-looking document closely, before handing it to Sean, whose heart sank on flicking open the military-issue handbook, bearing a regimental insignia on its front cover. It was what was printed on the inside leaf that left Sean numb from head to toe. It read: Rifleman Drew Malpass. Royal Green Jackets Regiment. Serial number G7210093. D.O.B. 30.3.1950.

Sean silently read the last line twice over and held a little hope. The Drew he knew had been born on the thirtieth of March, yes, but in the same year as he, 1952. Praying to himself that Drew had not bluffed his way into the British Army by forging his birth certificate, Sean handed back the I.D. to Spillane without making any comment, but felt his hope diminish on weighing up the prisoner's build, his approximate height if standing.

Recalling to mind the circumstances of Drew's sudden disappearance, the subsequent mystery as to what had become of him, Sean's fears that he may well be standing over his best friend - trapped in a lion's den - were heightened greatly in realising there was more evidence to suggest that it was indeed Drew, as opposed to two numbers on a piece of paper which stated it wasn't. But which, if proving to be forged, also confirmed that Drew shouldn't even be in the British Army, never mind the clutches of the IRA.

Given the fact that this supposed soldier had been intending to visit Clonard of all places, Sean knew it was too coincidental to be for any other reason than to call on him. Drew would have known his address, for his mother wrote occasionally still to Frances in London. And Drew would have, given his determined mind, ignored all warning signals to the contrary if deciding to seek him out for a surprise visit. Sean also knew why the prisoner had not given any information. He knew that Drew would want to protect him. The dilemma facing Sean at that moment was, could he protect Drew?

The question put to Spillane by O'Connor at that moment had Sean's mind in even greater turmoil. 'What we gonna do with the bastard?'

The driver of the car, poking his head around the bedroom door, made Spillane's mind up for him.

'Word has just come down the Falls. Barratt and D'Arcy have been shot dead by the Brits.'

A numbed silence filled the room. All the IRA men stood stony-faced. The prisoner's fate was well and truly sealed.

Spillane broke the silence. 'Paulo, bring that toolbox up from the car. I'll get this cunt to talk all right.' That said, Spillane pulled the hood off the prisoner's head. Sean's worst fear was realised.

Seeing Drew's grossly disfigured face and knowing what was coming next - a slow, agonising death at the hands of men now baying for revenge, pure and simple, Sean, convinced that there was no other way out of it, made his move very quickly. Rushing Spillane, Sean seized the gun from his trouser belt, while pushing the man against a far wall. With all others in the room recoiling in fear for their own safety and Paulo disappearing from the door in a flash, Sean turned to face Drew. Cocking the gun, he pressed the tip of its barrel against the centre of Drew's chest.

'May God forgive me.'

Sean squeezed the trigger and killed Drew instantly with a bullet clean through the heart.

Not daring to move, the other four IRA men continued to look on in sheer horror, not believing their eyes.

Sean fell to his knees at Drew's feet and placed the smoking barrel of the revolver inside his mouth. He closed his eyes and visualised his mother and father happily together. A second shot rang out. The revolver dropped to the floor. Sean's lifeless body slumped forward and what remained of his head came to rest against Drew's blood-soaked chest.

In death, the blood of two best friends flowed as one, just as it had when in the prime of their youth.

Epilogue

IRA MURDER BOY SOLDIER! screamed one leading British newspaper on the Ministry of Defence in London revealing that Drew Malpass, in his absence, had been 'ejected' from the armed forces six months earlier, when discovered as being under age at the point of sign-up; this fact had been unearthed by investigating Military Police pursuing Malpass for his serious assault on a senior rank.

The newspaper also revealed the *childhood friendship* between the *victim and executioner* and condemned Sean Brennan as a *twentieth century Judas*.

Greatly perplexed and worried by the dramatic revelations, coming as they did on top of the incredulous but unyielding accounts of the bizarre, bloody events the previous day, Bonar had been eager to combat, in his analysis, such black propaganda. So he wasted no time in releasing a statement on behalf of the Belfast Brigade to a local newspaper, together with Malpass's military papers. The statement read: *Volunteer Sean Brennan was killed on active service while assisting the capture of Private Malpass in west Belfast. Private Malpass was found in possession of documents that confirmed his status as a serving British soldier and was consequently interrogated and executed by the IRA.*

O'Connor, Spillane and others had been sworn to secrecy over the Divis shooting, with Bonar threatening death if word got out. All were informally reprimanded by the brigade OC for having 'made a bollocks' of the squaddie's imprisonment, but were allowed to retain their rank. The last thing Bonar had wanted to do was stoke-up further doubts or suspicions in the minds of others, not least the new IRA leadership in Dublin.

Calling on Sarah Brennan had been no less a worry for Bonar.

Lifting herself periodically above the agony of tragically losing a son also, and knowing the full story surrounding Sean's death, Sarah took heart knowing her son had indeed died for a worthy cause: Love, Loyalty and Friendship. And so she knew and accepted too, the reason why he had taken his own life. Sarah was confident that Sean had done what he thought to be right. Holding dear to this belief would keep her sane. She was determined to turn a blind eye, a deaf ear, to whatever else people said or printed in time to come.

Having the English newspaper's report as to the childhood friendship confirmed by the proud, grieving mother, Bonar assured Sarah that it was not an issue of concern for the IRA. That said, permission had been sought and granted for a full military-style funeral and burial for Sean Brennan.

Sean was buried with full military honours alongside Frank Barratt and Gervaise D'Arcy in the Republican Plot at Milltown Cemetery. The killing of Brennan 'in the struggle to capture Malpass' and the 'gunning down' of his comrades as they had bravely defended the area; the 'mutilation of Barratt's corpse by those British soldiers first on the scene', left many among the thousands of mourners dispersing a bleak, windswept cemetery, queuing up to join the Provisionals, among them, the McHugh twins, much praised now along the Falls. But Bonar, knowing what he did, where the bones of their father lay, and nauseated at the thought of his good friend and comrade Frank Barratt breathing his last in their shadow, ordered O'Connor to give the twins the 'thumbs down', with the added warning to stay well clear of republicans and places frequented by republicans.

Left alone together by the graveside to mourn their loved one, Sarah offered up a prayer for the repose of the soul of her soldier son and that of his best friend Drew, and beseeched our Blessed Lady to give peace of mind to that other mother, whose son, that same best friend, was being laid to rest that very hour in a churchyard across the water. Standing by Sarah Brennan's side, a broken-hearted Roisin painfully recalled her lover's last kiss, his final words, never to be forgotten.

Standing at a discreet distance and looking on sorrowfully, Bonar, suddenly propelled to the top of the IRA infrastructure through Barratt's violent death, found a little, though valued comfort in knowing now where the loyalty of the younger of the three deceased IRA men had truly lain that bloody afternoon. Privately, Bonar admired Sean Brennan, and knew that his death and that of the British squaddie had been needless, a sheer waste of young life. The defunct military papers carried by Malpass had sealed both their fates. Bonar was left asking himself why the English lad had still been carrying the I.D. on his person in Belfast of all places, but held no doubts why he had come to be in the city. Consequently, Bonar considered the old saying, 'Good friendships die hard', as cruelly ironic.

Meanwhile, back along the Falls Road, a rebel youth, carrying out his very first order as a raw recruit, busily completed with paintbrush and tin in hand, the latest slogan to appear on a prominent gable end. In bold artistic red letters, it read:

LET THERE BE PEACE WITH JUSTICE IN OUR TIME!

Other published writing by the author

A Man Of No Property © **2000** *(A short story taken from the author's evolving project titled: 'Testimony', involving the Irish Writers' & Artists' Collective)*

Under Napoleon's Nose © **1999** *(A poem taken from the author's personal collection of poems and short stories titled: 'This Orange Is Lovely And Sweet')*

To read these and other published writings by Irish authors please visit:

www.irishpulp.com